PITTSBURGH BUSINESS TIMES

PITTSBURGH BUSINESS DIRECTORY

PITTSBURGH BUSINESS TIMES

PITTSBURGH BUSINESS DIRECTORY

JEFFREY P. LEVINE

Pittsburgh Business Times
2313 E. Carson St., Ste. 200
Pittsburgh, PA 15203
(412) 481-6397

Publisher:	Alan Robertson
Author:	Jeffrey P. Levine
Author's Assistant:	Daniel Z. Kirk
Art Director:	Jim Snively
Production Manager:	Richard Cerilli
Production Assistant:	Glenn McGee
Cover Designer:	Debbie Zuzindlak
Proofreader:	Brenda A. Furiga

ISBN: 0-9650280-1-1
ISSN: 1093-457X

Are you looking for a job?
Look no further.

The Employment Paper is loaded with career information, job listings, and helpful hints for Pittsburgh's job seekers. Best of all it's **<u>FREE!</u>**
The Employment Paper can be picked up at 600 convenient locations that include, Giant Eagle's, Pharmor's, Wal Mart's and libraries.
Call **481-JOBS (5627)** for a location nearest you.

Contents

Introduction

Welcome to the second edition of the Pittsburgh Business Directory!

The Pittsburgh Business Directory is a must for anyone desiring concise, factual information on Pittsburgh's business community. Whether you are generating new business or sales leads, identifying employers, researching the competition, relocating to the area, designing fund-raising programs or seeking investment ideas, this book will keep you informed on the corporate marketplace and save you countless hours of research.

While there are a multitude of nationwide and statewide business directories providing varying amounts of information on companies, few are city-specific. The vast majority of these costly, complex and cumbersome publications, covering enormous geographic areas, contain abbreviated profiles in a phone book-style format. But since the release of the first edition of the Pittsburgh Business Directory in January 1996, there has been a new product on the market! The Pittsburgh Business Directory is an affordable, portable directory with a local orientation containing detailed profiles on more than 1,300 industrial, financial and service companies.

The businesses profiled in the Pittsburgh Business Directory are either headquartered in the Pittsburgh seven-county metropolitan area, encompassing Allegheny, Armstrong, Beaver, Butler, Fayette, Washington and Westmoreland counties in Pennsylvania, or are affiliates, divisions or subsidiaries with major operations in this region. The directory's focus is on businesses with 35 or more employees—public, private, nonprofit, subsidiary and others (including cooperative, employee-owned, foreign and mutual businesses)—with few government-related entities.

The Pittsburgh Business Directory is a bible for doing business in the Pittsburgh seven-county metropolitan area:

For the **Job Seeker**, the Pittsburgh Business Directory supplies crucial information for identifying and contacting potential employers (including a human resources contact when available), and provides comprehensive company descriptions to prepare you for the job interview.

For the **Sales Representative**, the Pittsburgh Business Directory contains hundreds of sales leads, giving background information on potential clients and always keeping you one step ahead of the competition.

For the **Marketing Manager**, the Pittsburgh Business Directory provides a broad base of information to identify product and service compatibilities.

For the **Investor**, the Pittsburgh Business Directory offers valuable information on 73 publicly traded companies headquartered in the Pittsburgh seven-county metropolitan area, from start-ups to America's industrial giants.

For the **Nonprofit Organization**, the Pittsburgh Business Directory helps in evaluating the philanthropic potential of major companies. The biographies of prominent business executives are ideal for identifying individuals to serve on boards and committees.

The Pittsburgh Business Directory is also a valuable resource for a wide range of other users, from librarians to economic developers, and diverse businesses, from outplacement firms to providers of corporate premium/incentive services.

User's Guide

The Pittsburgh Business Directory is divided into three easy-to-use segments:

73 Public Company Profiles

The Public Company Profiles segment begins with rankings of all 73 public companies by total assets, employees and revenues. This is followed by alphabetically arranged profiles of these companies providing a detailed look into the makeup of the corporations, including descriptive overviews, officer and subsidiary lists, financial information and much more. Also included are biographies of each company's top executive, creating an invaluable who's who of Pittsburgh's business leaders. See page 19 for additional information.

1,239 Private, Nonprofit, Subsidiary and Other Company Profiles

This segment contains profiles of private, nonprofit, subsidiary and other companies (including cooperative, employee-owned, foreign and mutual businesses), alphabetically arranged (when applicable, under the name of their local parent or holding company). It provides comprehensive information that would be difficult to obtain elsewhere. See page 197 for additional information.

Indexes

The Indexes segment contains a wealth of information for easy reference to the material detailed within the book and is comprised of seven categories: Alphabetical Index, County Index, Executive Biography Index, Geographic Index, Officer Index, Standard Industrial Classification (SIC) Code Index and ZIP Code Index.

Refer to the Abbreviations Guide on page 14 and the Special Designations Symbol Guide on page 17 for additional information.

What's New in the Second Edition

In this edition of the Pittsburgh Business Directory, we have expanded the amount of corporate information provided, increasing the number of businesses profiled from 1,079 to 1,312. Approximately 325 of the profiles are new to this edition of the directory.

The Public Company segment has increased from 69 companies to 73. We have added the names of each company's purchasing contact, auditor and general counsel, as well as their web site address, when available. In addition, we have expanded the financial review table from two years of information to four years.

The Private, Nonprofit, Subsidiary and Other Company segment has increased from 1,010 companies to 1,239. We have added the names of each company's purchasing contact and web site address, when available, and have lengthened many of their descriptions.

The Indexes segment has added three additional indexes, a County Index, an Executive Biography Index and a Geographic Index. These three new indexes should help to make the retrieval of information more efficient.

Sources

Information in the Pittsburgh Business Directory was obtained through surveys, telephone interviews, annual reports, 10-Ks, proxy statements, prospectuses, press releases, news clippings, public documents and agencies, and the Pittsburgh Business Times' Book of Lists.

Every effort has been made to ensure the reliability of the data. Due to the time lapse between initial research and publication, some companies may have undergone changes as a result of mergers, acquisitions, reorganizations or relocations. In addition, some significant businesses and/or data were not included because information was not obtainable from the companies. Therefore, the author and publisher cannot guarantee the complete accuracy of the information provided.

Companies have not paid any fees to be included in the Pittsburgh Business Directory. Their inclusion does not warrant the author's or the publisher's endorsement of any aspect of the companies' operations.

About the Author's Other Business Directories

Jeffrey P. Levine, the author of the Pittsburgh Business Directory, has written similar books on other major U.S. cities. His titles include Doing Business in New York City and Doing Business in Chicago, both published by Dow Jones-Irwin, now known as Irwin Professional Publishing; Doing Business in Boston, published by the Boston Business Journal; Ingram's Business Directory of Kansas City (also available on CD-ROM), published by Ingram Media L.L.C.; and soon to be released, Doing Business in Central Pennsylvania, published by Journal Publications Inc.

Here's what's been said about his directories:

"The best all-around guide (for New York City): Doing Business in New York City."

—Thomas Easton, The Baltimore Sun

"The book is a time- and money-saver for the traveler who is not familiar with the Big Apple."

—Memphis Business Journal

"Libraries desiring an inexpensive directory of this sort should purchase this book."

—Booklist

"Mr. Levine is on to a good thing here...Both books are the first definitive directories of businesses in these cities. Both represent major research efforts...The book is exceptionally informative and easy to use."

—Hispanic Business

"If you're looking for a job in business, this is the book for you."

—Chicago Enterprise

"An excellent resource for prospecting new business, job hunting and doing business here, and a great gift for job hunters."

—Today's Chicago Woman

"This is a thick book and the most useful book you could possibly have...I think every office can use it...I know it sounds like an ad, but this is an unusual book."

—Terry Savage, Money Talks WBBM-TV2 CBS Chicago

For information on these directories, write to: Jeffrey P. Levine, 10531 Cedar Lake Rd., Ste. 512, Minnetonka, MN 55305. Please send your comments and/or suggestions for future editions of this publication to the same address. To order additional copies of the Pittsburgh Business Directory or for information on bulk purchases, contact the Pittsburgh Business Times' Circulation Department at (412) 481-6397.

Acknowledgements

I would like to express my special thanks and appreciation to Dan Kirk for his hundreds of hours of work on this project, doing everything from writing, editing and proofreading copy, to making countless phone calls and managing the database.

Also, my thanks to Alan Robertson, the publisher of the Pittsburgh Business Times, for his foresight and commitment to making this second edition of the Pittsburgh Business Directory a reality; Richard Cerilli, for his production and marketing assistance, sense of humor and friendship; and Jim Snively, for his computer expertise and manuscript preparation work.

And of course, I would like to thank the hundreds of people at all of Pittsburgh's major companies for their cooperation in providing the information that made this directory possible.

Lastly, my thanks to my parents, Byron and Shirley, for their love and ongoing support.

I wish you the best of luck and prosperity doing business in Pittsburgh!

Jeffrey P. Levine
Author
June 1997

Abbreviations Guide

Staff Positions

ADM	Administration
AST	Assistant
AVP	Assistant Vice President
C-CEO	Co-Chief Executive Officer
C-CH	Co-Chairperson of the Board
C-COO	Co-Chief Operating Officer
C-DIR	Co-Director
C-FND	Co-Founder
C-OWN	Co-Owner
C-P	Co-President
CACO	Chief Accounting Officer
CAO	Chief Administrative Officer
CEO	Chief Executive Officer
CFO	Chief Financial Officer
CH	Chairperson of the Board
CIO	Chief Information Officer
CLK	Clerk
CLO	Chief Legal Officer
CON	Controller
COO	Chief Operating Officer
CTO	Chief Technical Officer
DEV	Development
DIR	Director
EDIR	Executive Director
ENG	Engineering
EVP	Executive Vice President
FIN	Finance
FND	Founder
FVP	First Vice President
GC	General Counsel
GMGR	General Manager
GPTR	General Partner
GVP	Group Vice President
INTL	International
MDIR	Managing Director
MEM	Member
MER	Merchandise
MFG	Manufacturing
MGR	Manager
MGT	Management
MIS	Management Information Systems
MKT	Marketing
MPTR	Managing Partner
NATL	National
OPR	Operations
OWN	Owner
P	President
PDEV	Product Development
PTR	Partner
R&D	Research and Development
RES	Research
SAL	Sales
SEC	Secretary
SEVP	Senior Executive Vice President

SVP	Senior Vice President
TRS	Treasurer
TRU	Trustee
VCH	Vice Chairperson of the Board
VP	Vice President

Miscellaneous

ASE	American Stock Exchange
Assn.	Association
Assoc.	Associates
Ave.	Avenue
Aves.	Avenues
Bldg.	Building
Blvd.	Boulevard
Bros.	Brothers
Cir.	Circle
Co.	Company
Comm.	Committee
Corp.	Corporation
Corps.	Corporations
Cos.	Companies
Ct.	Court
Dr.	Drive
Drs.	Drives
E.	East
FDA	U.S. Food and Drug Administration
Fl.	Floor
Hwy.	Highway
Inc.	Incorporated
L.P.	Limited Partnership
LAN	Local Area Network
Ltd.	Limited
N.	North
N/A	Not Available
NASDAQ	National Assn. of Securities Dealers Automated Quotations
NSCap	NASDAQ Small Cap Issue
NYSE	New York Stock Exchange
OEM	Original Equipment Manufacturer
OTC	Non-NASDAQ Over-the-Counter Security
Plz.	Plaza
Pwy.	Parkway
Rd.	Road
Rte.	Route
S.	South
Sq.	Square
St.	Street
Ste.	Suite
Sts.	Streets
Ter.	Terrace
Tfy.	Trafficway
U	University
VAR	Value Added Reseller
W.	West
WAN	Wide Area Network

Pittsburgh Business Directory Ordering Information

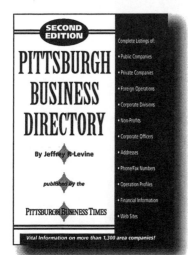

SECOND EDITION

PITTSBURGH BUSINESS DIRECTORY

By Jeffrey R. Levine

published by the

PITTSBURGH BUSINESS TIMES

Complete Listings of:
- Public Companies
- Private Companies
- Foreign Operations
- Corporate Divisions
- Non-Profits
- Corporate Officers
- Addresses
- Phone/Fax Numbers
- Operation Profiles
- Financial Information
- Web Sites

Vital Information on more than 1,300 area companies!

The Ultimate Sales & Marketing Tool For Pittsburgh Is Back! "Buy The Book" Call: (412) 481-6397

Fax Your Order Now (412) 481-9956

To order by mail, photocopy this coupon, complete and return to:

Pittsburgh Business Times

2313 East Carson Street

Suite 200

Pittsburgh, PA 15203

Book(s) will be shipped immediately upon receipt of payment.

Order Now: Immediate Delivery

☐ **YES,** please expedite my order for the second edition of the PBD at $54.95* each. (Includes shipping & Handling)

Name _____

Company _____

Address_____

City, State, Zip _____

Daytime Phone _____

☐ Check or Money Order Enclosed (Payable to Pittsburgh Business Times)

☐ Bill Me

☐ VISA ☐ MasterCard ☐ American Express

Credit Card No. _____

Exp. Date Signature _____

*Quantity discounts available for orders of 4 or more. Please call for pricing.

Special Designations Symbol Guide

Companies that appear on some of the nation's well-known business lists and/or are included as components of the Dow Jones Averages have been indicated with the designated symbols listed below. Only companies with corporate headquarters in the Pittsburgh seven-county metropolitan area have been identified.

DJIA   Component of Dow Jones Industrial Average

DJUA   Component of Dow Jones Utilities Average

ENR_{100} *Engineering News-Record*: The Top 100 Construction Managers (6/10/96)

ENR_{400} *Engineering News-Record*: The Top 400 Contractors (5/26/97)

ENR_{500} *Engineering News-Record*: The Top 500 Design Firms (4/14/97)

FB_{200} *Forbes*: The 200 Best Small Cos. in America (11/4/96)

FB_{500} *Forbes*: The Forbes 500s (4/21/97)

$FB\text{-}P_{500}$ *Forbes*: The 500 Largest Private Cos. in the U.S. (12/2/96)

FT_{100} *Fortune*: America's 100 Fastest-Growing Cos. (10/14/96)

FT_{500} *Fortune*: The Fortune 500 (4/28/97)

$FT\text{-}G_{500}$ *Fortune*: The Global 500 (8/5/96)

FW_{100} *Financial World*: 100 Hottest Small Cos. (10/21/96)

INC_{500} *Inc.*: The Inc. 500 Fastest-Growing Private Cos. in America (10/22/96)

IW_{1000} *Industry Week*: The Industry Week 1000-World's Largest Manufacturing Cos. (5/20/96)

Are you looking for a job?
Look no further.

The Employment Paper is loaded with career information, job listings, and helpful hints for Pittsburgh's job seekers. Best of all it's **FREE!**
The Employment Paper can be picked up at 600 convenient locations that include, Giant Eagle's, Pharmor's, Wal Mart's and libraries.
Call **481-JOBS (5627)** for a location nearest you.

73 Public Company Profiles

This segment contains detailed information on 73 publicly traded companies that have their corporate headquarters located within the Pittsburgh seven-county metropolitan area, encompassing Allegheny, Armstrong, Beaver, Butler, Fayette, Washington and Westmoreland counties in Pennsylvania. Each company is listed on a stock exchange; closed-end funds have been excluded.

In the first part of this segment, the companies are ranked by total assets, employees and revenues. Following the rankings, profiles of the companies are arranged alphabetically. Each profile includes a detailed description of the company; a listing of officers; up to four years of financial data; a list of affiliates, divisions and/or subsidiaries; and supplemental data such as primary SIC code, total employees, year established, state of incorporation, stock symbol, number of stockholders, common shares outstanding and special designations (i.e., Fortune 500). Also included is a biographical sketch of the company's CEO.

Minor discrepancies may occur due to the way companies report their information. For instance, the year a company was established may vary as a result of reincorporations, mergers or name changes, making it difficult to determine the actual date of corporate origin. Similarly, the number of employees may represent full-time equivalents; the number of stockholders reported may be based on street name registrants. The percentage of ownership of affiliates, divisions and/or subsidiaries appears only when reported by the parent company. In addition, in cases where the exact birth date of the CEO was not available, this information was extrapolated from the age listed in the company's proxy statement. Lastly, the CEO's periods of employment and titles were indicated only when provided by the company.

The revenues indicated for industrial companies include sales, other operating revenues and income; for financial firms, income from all sources is included; for banks and bank holding companies, interest income and other revenues have been combined; and for insurance companies, both premium receipts and investment income have been included.

As of our press deadline, initial public stock offerings were pending for several companies, including JLK Direct Distribution Inc. and Spring Hill Savings Bank FSB. In addition, merger, acquisition and/or spin-off deals were pending or in process for several companies, including DQE, Inc., SMT Health Services Inc., and Westinghouse Electric Corp.

Total Assets Ranking

Total Assets ($000)	Company	Total Employees	Total Revenue ($000)	Fiscal Year End
73,260,000	PNC Bank Corp.	25,500	6,333,000	12/31/96
42,596,000	Mellon Bank Corp.	24,700	4,762,000	12/31/96
21,307,000	Westinghouse Electric Corp.	50,000	8,449,000	12/31/96
13,449,900	Aluminum Co. of America	76,800	13,128,400	12/31/96
8,623,691	Heinz Co., H. J.	43,300	9,112,265	5/1/96
6,580,000	USX-U.S. Steel Group	20,433	6,547,000	12/31/96
6,441,400	PPG Industries, Inc.	31,300	7,218,100	12/31/96
6,000,605	Consolidated Natural Gas Co.	6,426	3,794,309	12/31/96
4,638,992	DQE, Inc.	3,810	1,225,195	12/31/96
2,606,400	Allegheny Teledyne Inc.	24,000	3,815,600	12/31/96
2,096,299	Equitable Resources, Inc.	2,109	1,861,799	12/31/96
1,867,800	Armco Inc.	6,000	1,724,000	12/31/96
919,242	Parkvale Financial Corp.	280	69,175	6/30/96
883,761	Interstate Hotels Co.	22,000	190,385	12/31/96
799,491	Kennametal Inc.	7,300	1,079,963	6/30/96
779,355	General Nutrition Cos., Inc.	10,906	990,845	2/1/97
771,928	J&L Specialty Steel, Inc.	1,346	628,022	12/31/96
755,358	Southwest National Corp.	385	58,076	12/31/96
692,009	Mylan Laboratories Inc.	1,733	392,860	3/31/96
634,048	GA Financial, Inc.	220	43,810	12/31/96
518,934	Associated Group, Inc., The	300	20,035	12/31/96
424,362	FORE Systems, Inc.	1,400	235,189	3/31/96
412,858	Century Financial Corp.	209	33,280	12/31/96
407,682	Mine Safety Appliances Co.	4,200	506,855	12/31/96
397,251	Calgon Carbon Corp.	1,297	290,196	12/31/96
363,236	Westinghouse Air Brake Co.	3,043	453,512	12/31/96
331,416	IBT Bancorp, Inc.	170	24,166	12/31/96
320,105	Cable Design Technologies Corp.	2,500	357,352	7/31/96
317,874	Fidelity Bancorp, Inc.	120	21,718	9/30/96
315,314	International Technology Corp.	2,400	400,042	3/29/96
304,802	NSD Bancorp, Inc.	150	22,841	12/31/96
278,111	Commercial National Financial Corp.	111	21,204	12/31/96
259,622	WVS Financial Corp.	60	18,700	6/30/96
234,044	MotivePower Industries, Inc.	2,102	291,407	12/31/96
228,724	Allegheny Valley Bancorp, Inc.	85	16,750	12/31/96
225,409	Dravo Corp.	781	158,133	12/31/96
212,870	Carbide/Graphite Group, Inc., The	1,280	259,394	7/31/96
199,885	Pitt-Des Moines, Inc.	2,006	468,274	12/31/96

Total Assets Ranking

Total Assets ($000)	Company	Total Employees	Total Revenue ($000)	Fiscal Year End
196,947	Laurel Capital Group, Inc.	51	15,412	6/30/96
195,713	Slippery Rock Financial Corp.	102	14,590	12/31/96
195,330	Pittsburgh Home Financial Corp.	58	13,302	9/30/96
188,170	Ampco-Pittsburgh Corp.	1,225	162,403	12/31/96
181,769	Iron and Glass Bancorp, Inc.	75	13,577	12/31/96
155,544	Black Box Corp.	600	193,427	3/31/96
153,412	Matthews International Corp.	1,400	171,978	9/30/96
143,947	Respironics, Inc.	1,217	125,766	6/30/96
131,169	Tuscarora Inc.	2,000	182,590	8/31/96
126,082	Baker Corp., Michael	3,720	418,388	12/31/96
123,398	Foster Co., L. B.	526	243,071	12/31/96
117,814	First Carnegie Deposit	21	8,984	3/31/96
114,640	Prestige Bancorp, Inc.	38	7,045	12/31/96
110,438	American Eagle Outfitters, Inc.	5,441	326,404	2/1/97
101,412	Education Management Corp.	2,223	147,863	6/30/96
99,523	North Pittsburgh Systems, Inc.	336	59,933	12/31/96
88,364	Astrotech International Corp.	1,051	122,190	9/30/96
86,912	Sylvan Inc.	900	79,111	12/29/96
81,857	Robroy Industries, Inc.	1,000	122,461	6/30/96
77,509	Mastech Corp.	2,049	123,400	12/31/96
52,924	National Record Mart, Inc.	1,324	99,084	3/30/96
47,950	Sulcus Computer Corp.	467	52,145	12/31/96
44,169	II-VI Inc.	554	37,940	6/30/96
43,431	ANSYS, Inc.	230	47,066	12/31/96
42,098	Universal Stainless & Alloy Products, Inc.	208	60,258	12/31/96
39,498	SMT Health Services Inc.	123	19,212	12/31/96
39,218	Industrial Scientific Corp.	211	36,648	1/25/97
34,626	Tollgrade Communications, Inc.	184	37,490	12/31/96
28,489	Carnegie Group, Inc.	252	28,409	12/31/96
15,391	Ansoft Corp.	150	8,695	4/30/96
11,199	Noxso Corp.	20	188	6/30/96
8,908	Action Industries, Inc.	6	30,212	6/30/96
6,165	PDG Environmental, Inc.	216	16,183	1/31/97
3,459	Computer Research, Inc.	54	7,462	8/31/96
1,998	Wilson Bros.	87	5,715	12/31/96

Total Employees Ranking

Total Employees	Company	Total Assets ($000)	Total Revenue ($000)	Fiscal Year End
76,800	Aluminum Co. of America	13,449,900	13,128,400	12/31/96
50,000	Westinghouse Electric Corp.	21,307,000	8,449,000	12/31/96
43,300	Heinz Co., H. J.	8,623,691	9,112,265	5/1/96
31,300	PPG Industries, Inc.	6,441,400	7,218,100	12/31/96
25,500	PNC Bank Corp.	73,260,000	6,333,000	12/31/96
24,700	Mellon Bank Corp.	42,596,000	4,762,000	12/31/96
24,000	Allegheny Teledyne Inc.	2,606,400	3,815,600	12/31/96
22,000	Interstate Hotels Co.	883,761	190,385	12/31/96
20,433	USX-U.S. Steel Group	6,580,000	6,547,000	12/31/96
10,906	General Nutrition Cos., Inc.	779,355	990,845	2/1/97
7,300	Kennametal Inc.	799,491	1,079,963	6/30/96
6,426	Consolidated Natural Gas Co.	6,000,605	3,794,309	12/31/96
6,000	Armco Inc.	1,867,800	1,724,000	12/31/96
5,441	American Eagle Outfitters, Inc.	110,438	326,404	2/1/97
4,200	Mine Safety Appliances Co.	407,682	506,855	12/31/96
3,810	DQE, Inc.	4,638,992	1,225,195	12/31/96
3,720	Baker Corp., Michael	126,082	418,388	12/31/96
3,043	Westinghouse Air Brake Co.	363,236	453,512	12/31/96
2,500	Cable Design Technologies Corp.	320,105	357,352	7/31/96
2,400	International Technology Corp.	315,314	400,042	3/29/96
2,223	Education Management Corp.	101,412	147,863	6/30/96
2,109	Equitable Resources, Inc.	2,096,299	1,861,799	12/31/96
2,102	MotivePower Industries, Inc.	234,044	291,407	12/31/96
2,049	Mastech Corp.	77,509	123,400	12/31/96
2,006	Pitt-Des Moines, Inc.	199,885	468,274	12/31/96
2,000	Tuscarora Inc.	131,169	182,590	8/31/96
1,733	Mylan Laboratories Inc.	692,009	392,860	3/31/96
1,400	FORE Systems, Inc.	424,362	235,189	3/31/96
1,400	Matthews International Corp.	153,412	171,978	9/30/96
1,346	J&L Specialty Steel, Inc.	771,928	628,022	12/31/96
1,324	National Record Mart, Inc.	52,924	99,084	3/30/96
1,297	Calgon Carbon Corp.	397,251	290,196	12/31/96
1,280	Carbide/Graphite Group, Inc., The	212,870	259,394	7/31/96
1,225	Ampco-Pittsburgh Corp.	188,170	162,403	12/31/96
1,217	Respironics, Inc.	143,947	125,766	6/30/96
1,051	Astrotech International Corp.	88,364	122,190	9/30/96
1,000	Robroy Industries, Inc.	81,857	122,461	6/30/96
900	Sylvan Inc.	86,912	79,111	12/29/96

Total Employees Ranking

Total Employees	Company	Total Assets ($000)	Total Revenue ($000)	Fiscal Year End
781	Dravo Corp.	225,409	158,133	12/31/96
600	Black Box Corp.	155,544	193,427	3/31/96
554	II-VI Inc.	44,169	37,940	6/30/96
526	Foster Co., L. B.	123,398	243,071	12/31/96
467	Sulcus Computer Corp.	47,950	52,145	12/31/96
385	Southwest National Corp.	755,358	58,076	12/31/96
336	North Pittsburgh Systems, Inc.	99,523	59,933	12/31/96
300	Associated Group, Inc., The	518,934	20,035	12/31/96
280	Parkvale Financial Corp.	919,242	69,175	6/30/96
252	Carnegie Group, Inc.	28,489	28,409	12/31/96
230	ANSYS, Inc.	43,431	47,066	12/31/96
220	GA Financial, Inc.	634,048	43,810	12/31/96
216	PDG Environmental, Inc.	6,165	16,183	1/31/97
211	Industrial Scientific Corp.	39,218	36,648	1/25/97
209	Century Financial Corp.	412,858	33,280	12/31/96
208	Universal Stainless & Alloy Products, Inc.	42,098	60,258	12/31/96
184	Tollgrade Communications, Inc.	34,626	37,490	12/31/96
170	IBT Bancorp, Inc.	331,416	24,166	12/31/96
150	Ansoft Corp.	15,391	8,695	4/30/96
150	NSD Bancorp, Inc.	304,802	22,841	12/31/96
123	SMT Health Services Inc.	39,498	19,212	12/31/96
120	Fidelity Bancorp, Inc.	317,874	21,718	9/30/96
111	Commercial National Financial Corp.	278,111	21,204	12/31/96
102	Slippery Rock Financial Corp.	195,713	14,590	12/31/96
87	Wilson Bros.	1,998	5,715	12/31/96
85	Allegheny Valley Bancorp, Inc.	228,724	16,750	12/31/96
75	Iron and Glass Bancorp, Inc.	181,769	13,577	12/31/96
60	WVS Financial Corp.	259,622	18,700	6/30/96
58	Pittsburgh Home Financial Corp.	195,330	13,302	9/30/96
54	Computer Research, Inc.	3,459	7,462	8/31/96
51	Laurel Capital Group, Inc.	196,947	15,412	6/30/96
38	Prestige Bancorp, Inc.	114,640	7,045	12/31/96
21	First Carnegie Deposit	117,814	8,984	3/31/96
20	Noxso Corp.	11,199	188	6/30/96
6	Action Industries, Inc.	8,908	30,212	6/30/96

Total Revenues Ranking

Total Revenue ($000)	Company	Total Employees	Total Assets ($000)	Fiscal Year End
13,128,400	Aluminum Co. of America	76,800	13,449,900	12/31/96
9,112,265	Heinz Co., H. J.	43,300	8,623,691	5/1/96
8,449,000	Westinghouse Electric Corp.	50,000	21,307,000	12/31/96
7,218,100	PPG Industries, Inc.	31,300	6,441,400	12/31/96
6,547,000	USX-U.S. Steel Group	20,433	6,580,000	12/31/96
6,333,000	PNC Bank Corp.	25,500	73,260,000	12/31/96
4,762,000	Mellon Bank Corp.	24,700	42,596,000	12/31/96
3,815,600	Allegheny Teledyne Inc.	24,000	2,606,400	12/31/96
3,794,309	Consolidated Natural Gas Co.	6,426	6,000,605	12/31/96
1,861,799	Equitable Resources, Inc.	2,109	2,096,299	12/31/96
1,724,000	Armco Inc.	6,000	1,867,800	12/31/96
1,225,195	DQE, Inc.	3,810	4,638,992	12/31/96
1,079,963	Kennametal Inc.	7,300	799,491	6/30/96
990,845	General Nutrition Cos., Inc.	10,906	779,355	2/1/97
628,022	J&L Specialty Steel, Inc.	1,346	771,928	12/31/96
506,855	Mine Safety Appliances Co.	4,200	407,682	12/31/96
468,274	Pitt-Des Moines, Inc.	2,006	199,885	12/31/96
453,512	Westinghouse Air Brake Co.	3,043	363,236	12/31/96
418,388	Baker Corp., Michael	3,720	126,082	12/31/96
400,042	International Technology Corp.	2,400	315,314	3/29/96
392,860	Mylan Laboratories Inc.	1,733	692,009	3/31/96
357,352	Cable Design Technologies Corp.	2,500	320,105	7/31/96
326,404	American Eagle Outfitters, Inc.	5,441	110,438	2/1/97
291,407	MotivePower Industries, Inc.	2,102	234,044	12/31/96
290,196	Calgon Carbon Corp.	1,297	397,251	12/31/96
259,394	Carbide/Graphite Group, Inc., The	1,280	212,870	7/31/96
243,071	Foster Co., L. B.	526	123,398	12/31/96
235,189	FORE Systems, Inc.	1,400	424,362	3/31/96
193,427	Black Box Corp.	600	155,544	3/31/96
190,385	Interstate Hotels Co.	22,000	883,761	12/31/96
182,590	Tuscarora Inc.	2,000	131,169	8/31/96
171,978	Matthews International Corp.	1,400	153,412	9/30/96
162,403	Ampco-Pittsburgh Corp.	1,225	188,170	12/31/96
158,133	Dravo Corp.	781	225,409	12/31/96
147,863	Education Management Corp.	2,223	101,412	6/30/96
125,766	Respironics, Inc.	1,217	143,947	6/30/96
123,400	Mastech Corp.	2,049	77,509	12/31/96
122,461	Robroy Industries, Inc.	1,000	81,857	6/30/96

Total Revenues Ranking

Total Revenue ($000)	Company	Total Employees	Total Assets ($000)	Fiscal Year End
122,190	Astrotech International Corp.	1,051	88,364	9/30/96
99,084	National Record Mart, Inc.	1,324	52,924	3/30/96
79,111	Sylvan Inc.	900	86,912	12/29/96
69,175	Parkvale Financial Corp.	280	919,242	6/30/96
60,258	Universal Stainless & Alloy Products, Inc.	208	42,098	12/31/96
59,933	North Pittsburgh Systems, Inc.	336	99,523	12/31/96
58,076	Southwest National Corp.	385	755,358	12/31/96
52,145	Sulcus Computer Corp.	467	47,950	12/31/96
47,066	ANSYS, Inc.	230	43,431	12/31/96
43,810	GA Financial, Inc.	220	634,048	12/31/96
37,940	II-VI Inc.	554	44,169	6/30/96
37,490	Tollgrade Communications, Inc.	184	34,626	12/31/96
36,648	Industrial Scientific Corp.	211	39,218	1/25/97
33,280	Century Financial Corp.	209	412,858	12/31/96
30,212	Action Industries, Inc.	6	8,908	6/30/96
28,409	Carnegie Group, Inc.	252	28,489	12/31/96
24,166	IBT Bancorp, Inc.	170	331,416	12/31/96
22,841	NSD Bancorp, Inc.	150	304,802	12/31/96
21,718	Fidelity Bancorp, Inc.	120	317,874	9/30/96
21,204	Commercial National Financial Corp.	111	278,111	12/31/96
20,035	Associated Group, Inc., The	300	518,934	12/31/96
19,212	SMT Health Services Inc.	123	39,498	12/31/96
18,700	WVS Financial Corp.	60	259,622	6/30/96
16,750	Allegheny Valley Bancorp, Inc.	85	228,724	12/31/96
16,183	PDG Environmental, Inc.	216	6,165	1/31/97
15,412	Laurel Capital Group, Inc.	51	196,947	6/30/96
14,590	Slippery Rock Financial Corp.	102	195,713	12/31/96
13,577	Iron and Glass Bancorp, Inc.	75	181,769	12/31/96
13,302	Pittsburgh Home Financial Corp.	58	195,330	9/30/96
8,984	First Carnegie Deposit	21	117,814	3/31/96
8,695	Ansoft Corp.	150	15,391	4/30/96
7,462	Computer Research, Inc.	54	3,459	8/31/96
7,045	Prestige Bancorp, Inc.	38	114,640	12/31/96
5,715	Wilson Bros.	87	1,998	12/31/96
188	Noxso Corp.	20	11,199	6/30/96

Action Industries, Inc.

A

460 Nixon Rd.
Cheswick, PA 15024
County: Allegheny

Phone: (412) 274-8104
Fax: (412) 274-0925

Action Industries has undergone significant change in connection with a major restructuring effort. In October 1996, the Company entered into an agreement to sell its inventory and related intellectual property associated with its Replenishment (Powerhouse) business and Promotional business. The Powerhouse-related assets were sold on October 18, 1996. The Promotional-related assets were sold on February 12, 1997, pursuant to a foreclosure sale by Foothill Capital Corp., the Company's secured lender. The assets sold represented substantially all of the operating assets employed in the Company's business. Trade accounts receivable were retained, as were non-operating notes and other receivables from prior sales of its headquarters' facility and certain business units. The Company also retained its substantial income tax net operating loss carryforward. On April 9, 1997, the Company announced that it had signed a letter of intent to acquire General Vision Services, Inc. (GVSI), a direct and third-party provider of retail vision services primarily in the New York City metropolitan area, as well as elsewhere in New York and surrounding states, and in Florida. GVSI operates from 104 locations, including 23 company-owned locations, and believes that it has the largest client base of labor unions and insurance carriers among the optical companies operating in its geographic area. In addition, GVSI provides retail hearing and dental management services, which it expects to expand. The merger is subject to a number of conditions, including approval by the shareholders of both the Company and GVSI, and was expected to take 120 days or more to complete.

Recent Events: On October 21, 1996, the ASE halted trading in the Company's common stock. The ASE has determined to delist the Company's common stock, but has granted a brief period for the Company to effect an acquisition to satisfy the criteria for ASE listing. The proposed merger with General Vision Services, Inc. may or may not result in the Company qualifying for ASE listing.

Officers: Joel M. Berez *CH*
T. Ronald Casper *P & CEO*

Human Resources: Kenneth L. Campbell *SVP-FIN & CFO*
Auditor: Ernst & Young LLP, Pittsburgh, PA

Total Employees	6	**Regional Employees**	6
Year Established	1917	**Incorporated**	PA
Stock Symbol	ACZ	**Annual Meeting**	December
Stock Exchange	ASE	**SIC Code**	9999
Stockholders			2,700
Shares Outstanding			5,539,458

Fiscal Year End	Total Revenues ($000)	Net Income/(Loss) ($000)	Total Assets ($000)
[1]6/30/96	30,212	(12,899)	8,908
6/24/95	45,088	(3,715)	39,546
6/25/94	60,049	125	39,363
6/26/93	76,684	(14,380)	56,873

[1]*Changed fiscal year end from the last Saturday in June to June 30.*

Executive Biography: T. Ronald Casper

Birth Date: 11/25/43   **Birthplace:** Philadelphia, PA
Spouse: Bonnie   **Children:** 3

Education:
Lehigh U, B.A. 1965.

Career History:
Mellon Bank Corp., various positions for 22 years including EVP; Cornerstone Capital Advisors, Ltd., C-FND, MDIR 1988-present; Action Industries, Inc., P & CEO 1995-present.

Directorships/Memberships/Activities:
Innovative Systems, Inc., DIR.

Allegheny Teledyne Inc.

Six PPG Place, Ste. 1000
Pittsburgh, PA 15222
County: Allegheny

Phone: (412) 394-2800
Fax: (412) 394-3033

Type of Business: Group of technology-based manufacturing businesses serving worldwide customers with specialty metals for consumer, industrial and aerospace applications; commercial and government-related aerospace and electronics products; and industrial and consumer products.

Allegheny Teledyne is a group of technology-based manufacturing businesses with significant concentration in specialty metals, complemented by aerospace and electronics, industrial and consumer products. The Company operates in four business segments—specialty metals, aerospace and electronics, industrial and consumer—which accounted for 54.3%, 26.2%, 11.9% and 7.6%, respectively, of the Company's fiscal 1996 revenues. The specialty metals segment produces a wide array of stainless steels; high performance nickel-based superalloys; titanium; thin-rolled and coated metals; tool steels; and high purity metals such as zirconium, hafnium and niobium and their alloys. The product forms include sheet, strip, foil and plate; ingot, billet, bar, rod and wire; tube and shapes; castings; and forgings. Zirconium chemicals as byproducts of manufacturing are used to make fibers for fiber optics, paper and paint treating, fertilizers and drying agents for antiperspirants. The aerospace and electronics segment produces unmanned aer-

A

ial vehicles and targets; small gas turbine engines; sensors and analyzers; hybrid microcircuits; electromechanical and solid state relays; commercial encryption systems; a variety of electronic components, including devices for the microwave industry, amplifiers, converters and flexible printed circuit interconnections; piston engines for small private aircraft; commercial airline avionics, including telemetering equipment and software that sense and transmit data from remote sources to "black box" recording devices; and a wide range of engineering services. The industrial segment produces super-hard tungsten carbide cutting tools and inserts; tungsten, tungsten carbide and molybdenum powders and their sintered products; nitrogen gas springs and pressure systems; metal stamping dies and plastic compression molds; valves, pumps and boosters; transportable forklift-type material handlers; and heavy equipment used in mining, construction and quarry work. The consumer segment produces pulsating water shower heads; oral health devices, including sonic and automatic toothbrushes and oral irrigators; residential water filtration devices and systems; heating and water treatment systems, water flow control valves and electronic control systems for swimming pools; commercial and industrial water heaters; and metal, plastic and laminate collapsible tubes for packaging varied consumer products. In fiscal 1996, foreign sales accounted for 17% of its revenues. The Company was formed on August 15, 1996, by the combination of Allegheny Ludlum Corp. (ALC) and Teledyne, Inc. (TI), which became wholly owned subsidiaries of the Company. In the combination, ALC shareholders received one share of the Company's common stock for each of their ALC common shares. TI stockholders received 1.925 shares of the Company's common stock for each of their TI common shares.

Special Designations: FB_{500} FT_{500}

Officers: Richard P. Simmons *CH, P & CEO*
Robert P. Bozzone *VCH*
Arthur H. Aronson *EVP & Segment Executive-Specialty Metals*
James L. Murdy *EVP-FIN & ADM, & CFO*
Hudson B. Drake *VP & Segment Executive-Aerospace & Electronics*
Robert S. Park *VP & TRS*
Gary L. Riley *VP & Segment Executive-Consumer & Industrial*
Gary R. Stechmesser *VP-Corporate Communications &*
Investor Relations
John D. Walton *VP, GC & SEC*
Dale G. Reid *CON*

Auditor: Ernst & Young LLP, Pittsburgh, PA
Affiliates/Divisions/Subsidiaries:

Allegheny Ludlum
Pittsburgh, PA

Allvac
Monroe, NC

Casting Service

La Porte, IN

Portland Forge
Portland, IN

Rodney Metals
New Bedford, MA

Teledyne Advanced Materials
Huntsville, AL

Teledyne Brown Engineering
Huntsville, AL

Teledyne Continental Motors
Mobile, AL

Teledyne Controls
Los Angeles, CA

Teledyne Economic Development
Los Angeles, CA

Teledyne Electronic Technologies
Los Angeles, CA

Teledyne Fluid Systems
Brecksville, OH

Teledyne Laars
Moorpark, CA

Teledyne Packaging
Chester, PA

Teledyne Ryan Aeronautical
San Diego, CA

Teledyne Specialty Equipment
Canal Winchester, OH

Teledyne Water Pik
Fort Collins, CO

Wah Chang
Albany, OR

Total Employees......................24,000   **Regional Employees** 5,400

A

Year Established 1938	**Incorporated** ....DE
Stock Symbol ....ALT	**Annual Meeting** ....May
Stock Exchange ....NYSE	**SIC Code** 3312

Stockholders 9,342
Shares Outstanding 174,693,558

Fiscal Year End	Total Revenues ($000)	Net Income/(Loss) ($000)	Total Assets ($000)
12/31/96	3,815,600	213,000	2,606,400
12/31/95	4,048,100	273,900	2,628,900
12/31/94	3,457,300	9,800	2,479,400
12/31/93	3,562,000	(45,700)	2,535,100

Executive Biography: Richard P. Simmons

Birth Date: 1931
Education:
MIT, B.S. 1953.

Career History:
Allegheny Ludlum Corp., CEO -1990, CH -1996; Allegheny Teledyne Inc., CH 1996-present, P & CEO 1997-present.

Directorships/Memberships/Activities:
Consolidated Natural Gas Co., DIR; PNC Bank Corp., DIR.

Allegheny Valley Bancorp, Inc.

5137 Butler St.
Pittsburgh, PA 15201
County: Allegheny

Phone: (412) 781-0318
Fax: (412) 781-2024

Type of Business: Bank holding company.

Allegheny Valley Bancorp is a bank holding company for the Allegheny Valley Bank of Pittsburgh (Bank). The Bank offers a wide variety of banking-related services, including direct deposit of social security and other federal recurring payments, mortgage loans, personal and installment loans, business loans, leasing-- auto, machinery and equipment, home improvement loans, auto loans, student loans, personal lines of credit, money orders, safe deposit boxes, cashier's checks, traveler's checks, wire transfers, U.S. savings bonds, bank by mail, Christmas clubs, Visa debit cards and after-hour depository. Its depository products include checking accounts, passbook savings, statement savings, NOW accounts, Super NOW accounts, money market accounts, certificates of deposit and IRAs. In addition to the Company's corporate headquarters and the Bank's main office, which are both located at the above address, it operates six branch banking facilities located in Monroeville, and in the Blawnox, downtown, Greentree and Shaler areas and on Penn Ave. in Pittsburgh, PA. In addition, there is a drive-through banking facility located at 1100 Mt. Royal Blvd. in the Shaler area of Pittsburgh.

The Company's subsidiary, A. V. Financial Services, Inc., provides leasing-related services.

Officers: David O. Tritsch *P & CEO*
Richard C. Gehringer *EVP & COO*
John L. Brooks *VP*
Ralph A. Goldbach *VP*
Dorothy A. Pawlak *VP*
Raymond J. Andres *AVP*
Margaret E. Grzandziel *AVP & Branch Coordinator*
Michael J. Loftis *AVP*
Carole A. Piriano *AVP*
Patrick Zollner *CON & EDP OPR Officer*
Lisa R. Bobrowsky *Cashier & OPR Officer*
Katherine Hayes *AST Cashier*
Tammy Rocco *AST Cashier*
Bernice Gutowski-Budd *Internal Auditor*
Carol Hoffmann *AST-SEC*

Human Resources: Mary Lou Ries *AVP & Security Officer*
Purchasing Director: Susan M. DeLuca *VP & SEC*
Auditor: S. R. Snodgrass, A.C., Wexford, PA
Affiliates/Divisions/Subsidiaries:

Allegheny Valley Bank of Pittsburgh 100%
Commercial bank.

A. V. Financial Services, Inc. 100%
Provider of leasing-related services.

Total Employees............................85	**Regional Employees**....................85
Year Established 1900	**Incorporated**.................................PA
Stock Symbol..........................AVLY	**Annual Meeting**......................April
Stock Exchange ....OTC	**SIC Code**...................................6712
Stockholders 330	
Shares Outstanding 1,129,842	

Fiscal Year End	Total Revenues ($000)	Net Income/(Loss) ($000)	Total Assets ($000)
12/31/96	16,750	3,408	228,724
12/31/95	15,511	3,265	225,502
12/31/94	13,783	2,917	200,238
12/31/93	13,713	2,689	203,819

Executive Biography: David O. Tritsch

Birth Date: 3/25/43   **Birthplace:** Pittsburgh, PA
Spouse: Rosalie   **Children:** 1

Career History:
Allegheny Valley Bancorp, Inc., P & CEO 1996-present.

Aluminum Co. of America

A

Alcoa Bldg., 425 Sixth Ave.
Pittsburgh, PA 15219
County: Allegheny
Phone: (412) 553-4545
Fax: (412) 553-4498

Type of Business: Integrated producer of aluminum products.

Aluminum Co. of America (Alcoa) claims to be the world's largest integrated aluminum company and the world's largest alumina producer, with close proximity of bauxite mines to its refineries in Australia, Jamaica and Suriname, and high-quality bauxite in Brazil. Alumina, a white powdery material, is an intermediate step in the production of aluminum from bauxite and is a valuable chemical on its own. The Company produces and markets primary aluminum and semi-fabricated and finished aluminum products used in and on beverage containers, airplanes and automobiles, commercial and residential buildings, chemicals, and a wide array of consumer and industrial applications. These products are sold directly to industrial customers and other end users or through independent distributors in the U.S., South America, Europe and the Far East. In 1996, approximately 26% of the Company's revenues were derived from packaging (beverage can sheet, plastic and aluminum enclosures, foil products and packaging machinery), 20% from transportation (automotive components), 16% from distribution and other (sheet, plate and extrusions to distributors), 15% from alumina and chemicals, 12% from building and construction (siding), and 11% from aluminum ingot. The Company's integrated operations consist of three segments. The Alumina and Chemicals segment includes the production and sale of bauxite, alumina, alumina-based chemicals used principally in industrial applications, and transportation services for bauxite and alumina. The Aluminum Processing segment comprises the production and sale of molten metal, ingot and aluminum products that are flat-rolled, engineered or finished. Also included in this segment are power, transportation and other services. The Nonaluminum Products segment includes the production and sale of electrical, plastic and composite materials products, manufacturing and packaging equipment, gold, magnesium products, and aluminum and titanium forgings. The Company is organized into 21 independently-managed business units, with 178 operating locations in 28 countries, serving a broad range of markets in developing and industrialized economies. Close to one-half of its consolidated sales are derived from non-U.S. markets. Pittsburgh region operations are located in Baltimore, MD; Barberton, Cleveland, Lima, North Royalton, Northwood, Sidney and Wapakoneta, OH; and Lebanon, Leetsdale and New Kensington, PA. The Company's research activities are principally conducted at the Alcoa Technical Center, located near Pittsburgh, though several subsidiaries and divisions conduct their own research and development, as do many plants. In 1996, expenditures for research and development totaled $166 million.

Recent Events: The Company will be relocating during the summer of 1998 to a new corporate headquarters facility at 201 Isabella St. in Pittsburgh, PA 15212.

Special Designations: DJIA FB$_{500}$ FT$_{500}$ FT-G$_{500}$ IW$_{1000}$

Officers: Paul H. O'Neill *CH & CEO*
Alain J. P. Belda *P & COO*
Peter R. Bridenbaugh *EVP-Automotive*
Richard L. Fischer *EVP & CH's Counsel*
Richard B. Kelson *EVP & CFO*
G. Keith Turnbull *EVP-Alcoa Business System*
Earnest J. Edwards *SVP & CON*
George E. Bergeron *VP; P-Rigid Packaging Division*
Ronald A. Glah *VP; P-Alcoa Closure Systems INTL*
L. Patrick Hassey *VP; P-Aerospace/Commercial Rolled Products*
Patricia L. Higgins *VP; CIO*
Frank L. Lederman *VP; CTO*
L. Richard Milner *VP; Corporate DEV*
Joseph C. Muscari *VP; Audit*
Joseph C. Pellegrino *VP; Pension Fund Investments & Analysis*
G. John Pizzey *VP; P-Alcoa Primary Metals*
Robert F. Slagle *VP; P-Alcoa World Alumina*
Roger A. G. Vines *VP; MDIR-Alcoa of Australia Ltd.*
Robert G. Wennemer *VP; TRS*
Russell C. Wisor *VP; Government Affairs*
Denis A. Demblowski *SEC & Senior Counsel*
Cynthia E. Holloway *AST-TRS*
Rudolph P. Huber *AST-TRS*
Bruce W. Robinson *AST-TRS*
Janet F. Duderstadt *AST-SEC & Counsel*
Kathy L. Lang *AST-SEC & MGR-EHS & Communications/Recognition*
Barbara S. Jeremiah *AST-GC*
William G. Nichols *AST-CON*

Human Resources: Ronald R. Hoffman *EVP-Human Resources*
& Communications

Auditor: Coopers & Lybrand L.L.P., Pittsburgh, PA

Affiliates/Divisions/Subsidiaries:

Aerospace/Commercial Rolled Products
Davenport, IA
Producer of general purpose & specialty aluminum sheet & plate for aerospace, automotive, printing & other industries.

Alcoa Asia Ltd.
Tokyo, Japan
Provider of sales & marketing services, business development & management in the Asian region.

Alcoa Automotive Structures-Europe
Munich, Germany
Designer & manufacturer of aluminum components & assemblies for

automotive body structures.

Alcoa Automotive Structures-North America and Asia
Detroit, MI
Designer & manufacturer of aluminum components & assemblies for automotive body structures.

Alcoa Bauxite and Alumina
Pittsburgh, PA
Miner of bauxite & refiner of alumina.

Alcoa Building Products
Sidney, OH
Producer of coated-aluminum, vinyl-extruded & injection-molded building products.

Alcoa Closure Systems International
Indianapolis, IN
Producer of plastic & aluminum closures, plastic bottles, & services & supplies for packaging markets.

Alcoa Engineered Products
Charlotte, NC
Producer of aluminum extrusions & tube, & aluminum wire, rod & bar.

Alcoa Foil Products
Lebanon, PA
Producer of aluminum sheet, foil & laminated materials.

Alcoa Forged Products
Cleveland, OH
Producer of aluminum forged & cast structural parts.

Alcoa Fujikura Ltd.
Brentwood, TN
Producer of automotive electrical/electronic systems, electronic components & specialty fiber-optic products.

Alcoa Industrial Chemicals
Charlotte, NC
Producer of alumina & other inorganic chemical products.

Alcoa Italia S.p.A.
Milan, Italy
Provider of aluminum smelting & sheet, plate & extrusions.

Alcoa Nederland Holding B.V.
Drunen, The Netherlands
Producer of aluminum coil sheet, extrusions & other fabricated products.

Alcoa of Australia Ltd.
Melbourne, Australia
Miner of bauxite & gold, refiner of alumina & alumina chemicals, & aluminum smelting.

Alcoa Packaging Equipment
Englewood, CO
Producer of engineered packaging equipment.

Alcoa Primary Metals
Knoxville, TN
Producer of primary aluminum products.

Alcoa Rigid Packaging
Knoxville, TN
Producer of aluminum sheet for beverage & food cans, & recycling.

Alcoa World Alumina
Pittsburgh, PA
Strategic, commercial & operational leadership of Company's global bauxite & alumina activities.

Latin America and Alcoa Aluminio S.A.
Sao Paulo, Brazil
Miner of bauxite, refiner of alumina, smelter of aluminum, producer of packaging components & aluminum truck bodies, & retailer of home building products.

Northwest Alloys, Inc.
Addy, WA
Producer of magnesium.

Total Employees......................76,800	**Regional Employees** 1,545
Year Established 1888	**Incorporated**..................................PA
Stock Symbol.................................AA	**Annual Meeting** ....May
Stock Exchange ....NYSE	**SIC Code**....................................3334
Stockholders 88,300	
Shares Outstanding 172,803,703	

Fiscal Year End	Total Revenues ($000)	Net Income/(Loss) ($000)	Total Assets ($000)
12/31/96	13,128,400	514,900	13,449,900
12/31/95	12,654,900	790,500	13,643,400

12/31/94	10,391,500	375,200	12,353,200	
12/31/93	9,148,900	4,800	11,596,900	**A**

Executive Biography: Paul H. O'Neill

Birth Date: 12/4/35   **Birthplace:** St. Louis, MO

Education:
Fresno State College, B.A.-Economics 1960; Indiana U, M.A.-Public
Administration 1966.

Career History:
Morrison-Knudsen, Inc. (Anchorage, AK), ENG; U.S. Veterans Administration,
Computer Systems Analyst 1961-66; U.S. Office of Management & Budget, vari-
ous positions 1967-74, Deputy DIR 1974-77; International Paper Co., VP-
Planning 1977-81, SVP-Planning & FIN 1981-83, SVP-Paperboard & Packaging
1983-85, P 1985-87; Aluminum Co. of America, CH & CEO 1987-present.

Directorships/Memberships/Activities:
Council for Excellence, DIR; Gerald R. Ford Foundation, DIR; Institute for
International Economics, DIR; Lucent Technologies Inc., DIR; Manpower
Demonstration Research Corp., DIR; The RAND Corp., CH; Allegheny
Conference on Community Development, MEM; Allegheny Policy Council for
Youth and Workforce Development, MEM; Business Council, MEM; Business
Roundtable, MEM-Policy Comm.; The Conference Board, MEM; Institute for
Research on the Economics of Taxation, MEM; Management Executives Society,
MEM; National Academy of Social Insurance, MEM; U of Virginia, MEM-White
Burkett Miller Center of Public Affairs; American Enterprise Institute, TRU.

American Eagle Outfitters, Inc.

150 Thorn Hill Dr.
P.O. Box 788
Warrendale, PA 15086
County: Allegheny

Phone: (412) 776-4857
Fax: (412) 776-6160
Internet Address: www.@ae-outfitters.com

Type of Business: Operator of a retail chain specializing in men's and women's
apparel, footwear and accessories.

American Eagle Outfitters is a specialty retailer of casual fashion merchandise.
The Company targets men and women, aged 16 to 34, and sells its own brand of
fashion apparel, blended with an assortment of quality basics such as denim and
khakis. A key component of the Company's merchandise strategy focuses on
developing and maintaining the strength of its private label brands of apparel,
footwear and accessories—American Eagle Outfitters™, AE™ and AE Supply™.
In fiscal 1996, private label merchandise accounted for approximately 98% of the
dollar value of merchandise purchased by the Company. Its private label strategy enables it to offer merchandise that management believes differentiates the
Company from many of its competitors. It also allows the Company to better con-

trol merchandise quality and to maximize cost savings, resulting in improved initial markup on the merchandise. The Company employs an in-house design team to interpret fashion trends for its customer and to design private label merchandise accordingly. The merchandising group determines the Company's merchandise needs for the upcoming season and the in-house design team creates styles to fill those needs. The merchandise designs are then manufactured to its specifications by outside vendors. The Company has a program to test-market various styles and colors of an item in selected stores, before finalizing the details of merchandise production and introducing the item chain-wide. The Company believes that it is important to frequently update its merchandise with new colors, patterns and fabrics. As of May 1, 1997, the Company operated a chain of 312 American Eagle Outfitter retail stores in 40 states. These stores are principally in the Midwest, Northeast and Southeast and are located in regional, enclosed shopping malls. The Company planned to open at least 20 new stores during fiscal 1997. In fiscal 1996, the Company derived approximately 47% of its net sales from womenswear, 36% from menswear, and 17% from outdoorwear, accessories and footwear. On April 13, 1994, the Company completed its initial public stock offering.

Officers: Jay L. Schottenstein *CH & CEO*
George Kolber *VCH & COO*
Saul Schottenstein *VCH*
Roger S. Markfield *P & Chief Merchandising Officer*
Joseph E. Kerin *EVP & DIR-Store OPR*
Laura A. Weil *EVP & CFO*
Steven Baum *VP & DIR-Design*
Dale E. Clifton *VP, CON & CACO*
Michael J. Fostyk *VP-Distribution*
Howard Landon *VP-Production & Sourcing*
Michael J. Leedy *VP-MKT*
William M. Matsko *VP-Real Estate*
William P. Tait *VP, SEC & TRS*

Human Resources: Michael E. Bergdahl *VP-Human Resources*
Auditor: Ernst & Young LLP, Pittsburgh, PA
General Counsel: Porter, Wright, Morris & Arthur, Columbus, OH

Total Employees........................5,441		**Regional Employees** 750	
Year Established 1903		**Incorporated** ....OH	
Stock Symbol ....AEOS		**Annual Meeting** ....May	
Stock Exchange................NASDAQ		**SIC Code**....................................5621	
Stockholders..110			
Shares Outstanding 9,917,950			

Fiscal Year End	Total Revenues ($000)	Net Income/(Loss) ($000)	Total Assets ($000)
2/1/97	326,404	5,925	110,438
¹2/3/96	226,569	7,142	95,363
7/29/95	296,563	6,765	134,484
7/30/94	199,688	12,198	82,863

¹On 1/3/96, the Company elected to change its fiscal year from a 52/53-week year that ends on the

Saturday nearest to July 31 to a 52/53-week year that ends on the Saturday nearest to January 31, effective for the transition period ended on 2/3/96. The transition period refers to the 27-week period from 7/30/95 to 2/3/96.

A

Executive Biography: Jay L. Schottenstein

Birth Date: 1954

Career History:
Valley Fair Corp.; Schottenstein Stores Corp., VCH 1986-92, CH & CEO 1992-present; Value City Department Stores, Inc., CEO 1991-present, CH 1992-present; American Eagle Outfitters, Inc., VP-predecessors of company 1980-92, CH & CEO 1992-present.

Directorships/Memberships/Activities:
Schottenstein Stores Corp., DIR.

Ampco-Pittsburgh Corp.

USX Tower, 600 Grant St., Ste. 4600
Pittsburgh, PA 15219
County: Allegheny

Phone: (412) 456-4400
Fax: (412) 456-4404

Type of Business: Manufacturer and marketer of engineered equipment.

Ampco-Pittsburgh operates several businesses which manufacture engineered equipment. Aerofin Corp. in Lynchburg, VA, claims to manufacture the industry's most extensive line of heat exchange coils for such installations as nuclear and conventional power plants, pulp and paper mills, and municipal waste treatment centers. It also provides coils for use in heating, ventilating and air conditioning systems. Buffalo Air Handling Co. in Amherst, VA, is a producer of large standard and custom air handling systems. These systems control indoor air quality for such buildings as hospitals, manufacturing plants, universities and high-rise office structures. Buffalo Pumps, Inc. in North Tonawanda, NY, is a producer of centrifugal pumps for commercial and marine applications serving the power generation, refrigeration, lube oil and marine defense markets. New Castle Industries, Inc. (NCII), through its Feed Screws Division in New Castle, PA, and Bimex operation in Wales, WI, offers an integrated product line of extrusion and injection feed screws and bimetallic barrels for the plastics processing industry. NCII also engineers, builds and retrofits extrusion processing machinery and manufactures hard chrome chill rolls for the paper, glass, film and plastics industries. It recently secured a patent for its ContraBend® chill roll, permitting plastic sheets to be processed perfectly flat. Union Electric Steel Corp. (UESC), the Company's largest business, is a manufacturer of forged hardened steel rolls for the ferrous and nonferrous material finishing industries. Its rolls are sold principally to steel and aluminum producers, which supply strip and sheet products to the automotive, appliance, aircraft, packaging and construction markets worldwide. UESC has its headquarters in Carnegie, PA, also the site of the largest of its three finishing plants. Other finishing plants are in Valparaiso, IN, and Tessenderlo, Belgium. Melting, forging and some machining operations are located in Burgettstown, PA, and an electroslag remelt facility is in Erie, PA. UESC claims that in addition to being the market leader in North America and a significant producer of forged hardened steel rolls in Western Europe, it has continued to increase its participation in global markets. In 1996, substantial shipments were made to India, Indonesia, Japan, the Philippines, South Korea and Taiwan.

Officers: Louis Berkman *CH*
Robert A. Paul *P & CEO*
Ernest G. Siddons *EVP & COO*
Robert J. Reilly *VP-FIN & TRS*
Rose Hoover *SEC*

Human Resources: Robert F. Schultz *VP-Industrial Relations & Senior Counsel*
Auditor: Price Waterhouse LLP, Pittsburgh, PA
Affiliates/Divisions/Subsidiaries:

Aerofin Corp. 100%
Lynchburg, VA
Manufacturer of finned tube heat exchange coils.

Buffalo Air Handling Co. 100%
Amherst, VA
Manufacturer of large standard & custom air handling systems.

Buffalo Pumps, Inc. 100%
North Tonawanda, NY
Manufacturer of centrifugal pumps.

New Castle Industries, Inc. 100%
New Castle, PA
Manufacturer of feed screws, barrels & chill rolls.

Union Electric Steel Corp. 100%
Carnegie, PA
Manufacturer of forged hardened steel rolls.
Union Electric Steel, N.V. 100%
Tessenderlo, Belgium

Total Employees	1,225	**Regional Employees**	500
Year Established	1887	**Incorporated**	PA
Stock Symbol	AP	**Annual Meeting**	April
Stock Exchange	NYSE	**SIC Code**	3547
Stockholders			1,418
Shares Outstanding			9,577,621

Fiscal Year End	Total Revenues ($000)	Net Income/(Loss) ($000)	Total Assets ($000)
12/31/96	162,403	12,390	188,170
12/31/95	143,785	9,050	171,424
12/31/94	113,836	8,051	151,912
12/31/93	108,846	(4,516)	138,494

Executive Biography: Robert A. Paul

Birth Date: 10/28/37   **Birthplace:** New York, NY

Education:
Cornell U, B.A. 1959; Harvard U, J.D. 1962; Harvard U, M.B.A. 1964.

Career History:
Ampco-Pittsburgh Corp., Plant MGR 1964-66, AVP 1966-69, VP-Corporate DEV 1969-70, VP-FIN 1970-72, EVP & TRS 1972-79, COO 1979-94, P 1979-present, CEO 1994-present; The Louis Berkman Co., VP 1969-94, EVP 1994-present; Romar Trading Co., GPTR.

Directorships/Memberships/Activities:
The Louis Berkman Co., DIR; National City Bank of Pennsylvania, DIR; National City Corp., DIR; U of Pittsburgh Medical Center, DIR; American Bar Assn., MEM; Duquesne Club, MEM; Massachusetts Bar Assn., MEM; Oakland Country Club, MEM; Pittsburgh Athletic Assn., MEM; Williams Country Club, MEM; Louis and Sandra Berkman Foundation, VP & TRU; Cornell U, TRU; Fair Oaks Foundation, P & TRU; Jewish Healthcare Foundation, TRS & TRU.

Ansoft Corp.

Four Station Sq., Ste. 660
Pittsburgh, PA 15219
County: Allegheny

Phone: (412) 261-3200
Fax: (412) 471-9427
Internet Address: www.ansoft.com

Type of Business: Developer, marketer and supporter of electronic design automation software.

   Ansoft develops, markets and supports electronic design automation (EDA) software, based upon electromagnetic principles, for the design of high performance electrical devices and systems, such as cellular phones, satellite communications, circuit boards, motors and ABS braking systems. The Company believes that its proprietary products enable design engineers to develop smaller systems with higher performance and greater yields than can be developed with traditional EDA tools, and result in reduced time-to-market, lower risk of failure and elimination of costly and time-consuming product redesign. The Company's products are generally marketed under the Maxwell® name. Its electromechanical software analyzes the electrical performance of product designs to increase yields and is applied in the design of sensors, solenoids, motors and transformers for the automotive and consumer electronics industries. Its signal integrity (SI) software analyzes the degradation in signal integrity that results from the higher clock speeds and smaller physical dimensions of micron and deep-submicron integrated circuits and computer interconnects for the computer and semiconductor industries. In addition, the Company's SI software analyzes electromagnetic radiation from electronic systems, including radio frequency integrated circuits, antenna and radar systems, and is used in the communications, aerospace and defense industries. The Company's products are available on Unix workstations from Digital Electronics, Hewlett-Packard, IBM, Silicon Graphics and Sun Microsystems and Intel-based PCs running Microsoft Windows/Window NT®. The Company has a significant installed base with more than 500 customers, including AT&T, General Motors, Hitachi, Lucky-Goldstar, Mitsubishi, Motorola, Raytheon, Texas Instruments and TRW. In fiscal 1997, export sales, principally to Asia, accounted for 40% of its revenue. On April 3, 1996, the Company completed its initial public stock offering.

Officers: Zoltan J. Cendes, Ph.D. *CH & Chief RES Scientist*
Nicholas Csendes *P & CEO*
Padmanabhan Premkumar *VP-MKT*
Tony Ryan *CON*

Auditor: KPMG Peat Marwick LLP, Pittsburgh, PA
General Counsel: Buchanan Ingersoll P.C., Pittsburgh, PA

Total Employees............................150	**Regional Employees** 60
Year Established 1984	**Incorporated** ....DE
Stock Symbol ....ANST	**Annual Meeting** ....September
Stock Exchange................NASDAQ	**SIC Code**....................................7372
Stockholders...118	
Shares Outstanding 7,690,859	

Fiscal Year End	Total Revenues ($000)	Net Income/(Loss) ($000)	Total Assets ($000)
4/30/96	8,695	1,300	15,391
4/30/95	6,154	(305)	1,792
4/30/94	5,121	(140)	1,417
4/30/93	3,471	(967)	950

Executive Biography: Nicholas Csendes

Birth Date: 1944

Career History:
American Banner Resources, Inc., officer 1985-present; IT Network, Inc., FND; Southwest Gas Systems, Inc., officer 1989-94; Ansoft Corp., C-FND, P & CEO 1992-present.

ANSYS, Inc.

Southpointe, 275 Technology Dr.
Canonsburg, PA 15317
County: Washington

Phone: (412) 746-3304
Fax: (412) 514-9494
Internet Address: www.ansys.com

Type of Business: Supplier of analysis and engineering software for optimizing the design of new products.

ANSYS develops, markets and supports software solutions for design analysis and optimization. Using the Company's software products, engineers can construct computer models of structures, compounds, components or systems to simulate performance conditions and physical responses to varying levels of stress, pressure, temperature and velocity. This helps reduce the time and expense of physical prototyping and testing. The Company's product family features open, flexible architecture that permits easy integration into its customers' enterprise-wide engineering systems and facilitates effective implementation of process-centric engineering. Since its founding as Swanson Analysis Solutions, Inc., the Company claims that it has become a technology leader in the market for computer-aided engineering (CAE) analysis software. The Company has long-standing relationships with customers in many industries, including automotive, aerospace and electronics. Its product line ranges from ANSYS/Multiphysics, a sophisticated multi-disciplinary CAE tool for engineering analysts, to AutoFEA™, a computer-aided design integrated design optimization product for design engineers. The Company's product family features a unified database, a wide range of analysis functionality, a consistent, easy-to-use graphical user interface, support for multiple hardware platforms and operating systems (including Windows 95, Windows NT and Unix), effective user customization tools and integration with leading CAD systems. The Company markets its products principally through its global network of 36 independent regional ANSYS Support Distributors, who have 70 offices in 28 countries. The Company's products have an estimated installed base of 36,000 seats at commercial sites and approximately 69,000 seats at university sites worldwide. Its products are utilized by organizations ranging in size from small consulting firms to the world's largest industrial companies. In 1996, international sales accounted for approximately 50% of the Company's revenue. On June 20, 1996, the Company completed its initial public stock offering.

Officers: Peter J. Smith *CH, P & CEO*
Paul A. Chilensky *VP-Customer Service*
Mark C. Imgrund *VP-Corporate Quality*
Paul A. Johnson *VP-PDEV*
Richard C. Miller *VP & GMGR-DesignSpace*
Scott D. Owens *VP-MKT*
John M. Sherbin II *VP-FIN & ADM, & CFO*
James C. Tung *VP-INTL SAL*

Leonard Zera *VP-North American SAL*
John A. Swanson, Ph.D. *Chief Technologist*
David Conover *MGR-PDEV*
Joseph S. Solecki, Ph.D. *Corporate Fellow*
Shah M. Yunus, Ph.D. *Corporate Fellow*

Auditor: Coopers & Lybrand L.L.P., Pittsburgh, PA
General Counsel: Buchanan Ingersoll P.C., Pittsburgh, PA

Affiliates/Divisions/Subsidiaries:

ANSYS Operating Corp. 100%

ASN Systems Ltd. 100%

SAS IP, Inc. 100%

Total Employees............................230
Year Established 1970
Stock Symbol ....ANSS
Stock Exchange................NASDAQ
Stockholders 2,652
Shares Outstanding 16,183,744

Incorporated ....DE
Annual Meeting ....May
SIC Code....................................7372

Fiscal Year End	Total Revenues ($000)	Net Income/(Loss) ($000)	Total Assets ($000)
12/31/96	47,066	1,304	43,431
12/31/95	39,616	(1,580)	42,921
¹12/31/94	26,254	(1,789)	44,669

¹*Period from 3/14/94 through 12/31/94. On 3/14/94, the Company acquired substantially all of the assets of Swanson Analysis Systems, Inc., its predecessor corporation.*

Executive Biography: Peter J. Smith

Birth Date: 1945

Education:
Northeastern U, B.S.-Electrical Engineering; U of Notre Dame, M.B.A.

Career History:
Digital Equipment Corp., various positions including VP-European OPR 1991-94; ANSYS, Inc., P & CEO 1994-present, CH 1995-present.

Armco Inc.

A

One Oxford Centre, 301 Grant St.
Pittsburgh, PA 15219
County: Allegheny

Phone: (412) 255-9800
Fax: (412) 255-9805
Internet Address: www.armco.com

Type of Business: Producer of specialty flat-rolled steels, electrical and galvanized steels.

Armco claims to be the second-largest (based on sales revenues) domestic producer of stainless steels and the largest domestic producer of electrical steels. The Company operates in two primary business segments. Its Specialty Flat-Rolled Steels segment produces and finishes flat-rolled stainless, electrical and galvanized steels at manufacturing operations located in Butler, PA, and Coshocton, Dover, Mansfield and Zanesville, OH. The Butler and Mansfield Operations produce both semi-finished and finished stainless and electrical steels in sheet and hot band form. The Coshocton Operations finish stainless steel in strip and sheet form and the Zanesville Operations finish stainless and electrical strip and sheet. The Dover Operations is a dedicated galvanizing facility. This segment also includes the results of European trading companies that buy and sell steel and manufactured steel products. In 1996, approximately 44% of this segment's sales were to the automotive market, 28% to industrial and electrical equipment markets, 16% to other markets and 12% to service centers. The Company's Fabricated Products segment consists of two businesses. Douglas Dynamics, L.L.C. (DDL) claims to be the largest North American manufacturer of snowplows for four-wheel drive pick-up trucks and utility vehicles. DDL, which is headquartered in Milwaukee, WI, and has manufacturing plants in Rockland, ME, Johnson City, TN, and Milwaukee, WI, sells its snowplows and ice control products under the names Western Products and Fisher Engineering through independent distributors in the United States and Canada. The Sawhill Tubular Division manufactures a wide range of steel pipe and tubular products for use in the construction, industrial and plumbing markets at plants in Warren, OH, and Sharon and Wheatland, PA. The Company has recently divested numerous businesses and investments to focus on producing specialty flat-rolled steels.

Special Designations: IW$_{1000}$

Officers: James F. Will *CH, P & CEO*
Jerry W. Albright *VP & CFO*
James L. Bertsch *VP & TRS*
John B. Corey *VP; P-Douglas Dynamics, LLC*
John N. Davis *VP & CON*
David A. Higbee *VP; P-Sawhill Tubular*
Gary R. Hildreth *VP, GC & SEC*
Gary L. McDaniel *VP-OPR*
M. Dennis McGlone *VP-Commercial*

Pat J. Meneely *VP-Information & Organizational Effectiveness*
Daniel E. Smigielski *VP-Purchasing & Traffic*
Human Resources: Michael Couch
Auditor: Deloitte & Touche LLP, Pittsburgh, PA
Affiliates/Divisions/Subsidiaries:

Douglas Dynamics, L.L.C. 100%
Milwaukee, WI
Manufacturer of snowplows & ice control products.

Sawhill Tubular Division 100%
Warren, OH; Sharon & Wheatland, PA
Manufacturer of standard pipe & tubular products.

Total Employees......................6,000		**Regional Employees**.............2,600	
Year Established.....................1899		**Incorporated**.............................OH	
Stock Symbol.............................AS		**Annual Meeting**.....................April	
Stock Exchange.....................NYSE		**SIC Code**...................................3312	
Stockholders...22,641			
Shares Outstanding..................................106,457,166			

Fiscal Year End	Total Revenues ($000)	Net Income/(Loss) ($000)	Total Assets ($000)
12/31/96	1,724,000	32,500	1,867,800
12/31/95	1,559,900	29,800	1,896,600
12/31/94	1,437,600	77,700	1,934,900
12/31/93	1,664,000	(641,800)	1,904,700

Executive Biography: James F. Will

Birth Date: 10/12/38 **Birthplace:** Pittsburgh, PA
Spouse: Mary Ellen **Children:** 2

Education:
St. Vincent College; Penn State U, B.S.-Electrical Engineering; Duquesne U, M.B.A.

Career History:
United States Steel Corp., various positions 1961-72; Miami Industries, 1972-74; Kaiser Steel Corp., various positions 1974-81, P & COO 1981-82; Cyclops Industries, Inc., EVP-Steel OPR 1982-84, EVP & P-Industrial Group 1984-86, COO 1986-88, P 1986-92, CEO 1989-92; Armco Inc., COO, P & CEO 1994-present, CH 1996-present.

Directorships/Memberships/Activities:
Allegheny Corp., DIR; Boy Scouts of America, CH-Greater Pittsburgh Council; Catholic Charities-Diocese of Pittsburgh, P; Pittsburgh Opera, C-CH; The Specialty Steel Industry of North America, CH; United Way of Allegheny County, DIR; Penn's Southwest Assn., MEM; National Flag Foundation, TRU.

Associated Group, Inc., The

200 Gateway Towers
Pittsburgh, PA 15222
County: Allegheny

Phone: (412) 281-1907
Fax: (412) 281-1914
Internet Address: www.agrp.com

Type of Business: Provider of wireless communication services, radio broadcaster and operator of an art gallery.

The Associated Group is primarily engaged in the ownership and operation of, and also owns interests in, a variety of wireless communications-related businesses. The Company operates principally in three segments: wireless communication services in major cities across the United States and Southeastern Mexico, radio broadcasting in Ohio and retail art in New York, NY. Microwave Services, Inc. (MSI), a wholly owned subsidiary, was formed to pursue the provision of digital voice, high speed data and video services over a broadband wireless radio network. Through a joint venture, MSI manages or holds licenses to provide broadband digital wireless services in 31 U.S. markets, with licenses for an additional 44 markets pending. Associated RT, Inc., another wholly owned subsidiary, is developing and seeking to commercialize systems and related services for locating cellular telephones and other wireless transmitters, through its TruePosition™ Wireless Location System. TruePosition is an overlay system designed to enable mobile wireless service providers to determine the location of any cellular or personal communication services telephone. Associated Communications of Mexico, Inc., another wholly owned subsidiary, has investments in a provider of cellular telephone services in Southeastern Mexico. The Company's predominantly communications-oriented businesses and assets include a portfolio of marketable equity securities, which includes equity securities of Tele-Communications, Inc., a developer and operator of cable television systems; an indirect equity interest in a provider of personal communications services; an indirect equity interest in a Mexican corporation which operates specialized mobile radio systems in Mexico; owner and operator of five radio broadcasting stations, WRKY-FM and WSTV-AM in Steubenville, OH, WOMP-AM/FM in Bellaire, OH, and WLYR-FM (formerly WCEZ-FM) in Delaware, OH; owner and operator of a digital wireless communications network in the Los Angeles, CA, market; and owner and operator of Associated American Artists, an art gallery that sells original prints, drawings, oil paintings, sculptures and related works of art.

Officers: Myles P. Berkman *CH, P, CEO & TRS*
David J. Berkman *EVP*
Lillian R. Berkman *VP*
Monroe E. Berkman *VP*
John K. Dion *VP*
Kent R. Sander *VP*
Scott G. Bruce *GC & SEC*

Keith C. Hartman *CON & AST-SEC*

Auditor: Ernst & Young LLP, Pittsburgh, PA

General Counsel: Skadden, Arps, Slate, Meagher & Flom LLP, New York, NY
Fleischman and Walsh, L.L.P., Washington, D.C.

Affiliates/Divisions/Subsidiaries:

Associated American Artists 100%
New York, NY
Marketer of original prints, drawings, oil paintings, sculptures &
related art.

Associated Communications of Los Angeles 100%
Los Angeles, CA
Operator of digital wireless communications network.

Associated Communications of Mexico, Inc. 100%
Pittsburgh, PA
Owner of partnership interest in Grupo Holdings, L.L.C.

Grupo Holdings, L.L.C. 61.6%

Grupo Portatel, S.A. de C.V. 30.2%

Portatel del Sureste, S.A. de C.V.
Provider of cellular telephone services in Southeastern Mexico.

Associated PCN Holding Co. 100%
Pittsburgh, PA
Owner of partnership interest in Associated PCN Co.

Associated PCN Co. 75%
Pittsburgh, PA
General partnership holding 4.42% interest in Omnipoint
Communications, Inc.

Associated RT, Inc. 100%
Philadelphia, PA
Developer of systems & related services for locating cellular tele
phones & other wireless transmitters.

Teletrac, Inc. 12.7%
Provider of location services primarily for vehicle & fleet manage
ment.

Associated SMR, Inc. 100%
Pittsburgh, PA

A

Corporacion Mobilcom, S.A. de C.V. 14%
Operator of specialized mobile radio systems in Mexico.

Microwave Services, Inc. 100%
Provider of digital termination services.

Associated Communications, L.L.C. 55%
Alexandria, VA
Manager of digital termination services networks.

TCI Satellite Entertainment, Inc. 5.8%

Tele-Communications, Inc. 5.6%
Developer & operator of cable television systems.

WLYR-FM 100%
Delaware, OH
Owner & operator of radio station.

WOMP-AM/FM 100%
Bellaire, OH
Owner & operator of radio stations.

WRKY-FM 100%
Steubenville, OH
Owner & operator of radio station.

WSTV-AM 100%
Steubenville, OH
Owner & operator of radio station.

Total Employees............................300		**Regional Employees** 14	
Year Established 1979		**Incorporated** ....DE	
Stock Symbol..........AGRPA AGRPB		**Annual Meeting** ....June	
Stock Exchange................NASDAQ		**SIC Code**....................................4812	
Stockholders ....Class A 495 Class B 457			
Shares Outstanding ....Class A 9,382,962 Class B 9,398,410			

Fiscal Year End	Total Revenues ($000)	Net Income/(Loss) ($000)	Total Assets ($000)
12/31/96	20,035	(17,196)	518,934
12/31/95	4,272	(13,213)	574,471
12/31/94	4,664	(9,436)	478,555
12/31/93	6,075	(1,088)	653,282

Executive Biography: Myles P. Berkman
Birth Date: 1937

Career History:

Rust Craft Cable Communications, Inc., P 1968-72; Control Systems Research, Inc., FND, CH & CEO 1973-76; Consultant to Control Systems Research, Inc., 1976-78; Associated Communications Corp., P & COO & TRS 1979-94; The Associated Group, Inc., CH & P & CEO & TRS 1994-present.

Directorships/Memberships/Activities:
Cellular Telecommunications Industry Assn., DIR; Mobile Satellite Corp., DIR; Telocator, DIR.

Astrotech International Corp.

Convention Towers Bldg., 960 Penn Ave., Ste. 800
Pittsburgh, PA 15222
County: Allegheny

Phone: (412) 391-1896
Fax: (412) 391-3347

Type of Business: Provider of engineering, design, fabrication, maintenance services and construction of steel structures for a variety of industries.

Astrotech International provides engineering, design, fabrication, maintenance services and construction of steel structures for a variety of industries, including refining, petrochemical, water storage, pulp and paper, mining, alcohol, agriculture, wastewater treatment, power generation and process systems. The Company's broad range of products include large aboveground storage tanks (ASTs) and related parts and constituent products, pressure vessels, bins, silos, stacks and liners, scrubbers and shop built tanks (both underground and aboveground). It also provides non-destructive testing and inspection services for large ASTs, pressure vessels and piping, and offers mobile storage tank leasing services. Approximately 70% of the Company's revenues are derived from the petroleum and petrochemical industries. In response to increasingly stringent safety standards and heightened environmental and product waste concerns, ASTs must be continually inspected and maintained, and periodically require repair and upgrading. Through its various subsidiaries, the Company maintains offices in close proximity to the operating facilities of existing and potential customers so that its regional and area personnel can maintain frequent personal contact with the individuals who make purchase decisions regarding ASTs. HMT Inc. (HI) maintains offices in Cerritos, San Francisco and Santa Fe Springs, CA; Baton Rouge, LA; Beaumont, Corpus Christi, Houston and Midland, TX; and Seattle, WA. HMT Construction Services, Inc., a subsidiary of HI, serves the eastern region of the United States and maintains offices in Ann Arbor, MI; Mooresville, NC; and Kelton, PA. HI's Australian subsidiary, Australasian HMT Pty., Ltd., maintains its operations in Australia and along with HMT Singapore, PTE., LTD., services the Pacific Rim; while HI's United Kingdom subsidiary, HMT Rubbaglas Ltd., markets HI's products in Europe, Africa and the Middle East. HMT Canada Ltd. services the Canadian market. Brown-Minneapolis Tank & Fabricating Co., acquired on March 1, 1994, maintains strategically located offices and fabrication facilities in Birmingham, AL; Port Allen, LA; Eagan, MN; Houston, TX; and Orem, UT. Graver Holding Co. and its wholly owned subsidiary, Graver Tank & Manufacturing Co., Inc., acquired on March 28, 1996, designs, manufactures and erects storage tanks and pressure vessels for the petroleum and process industries. It also offers nickel-clad installations for the power generation and air pollution industries, providing fabrication and erection of scrubbers, chimneys and stack liners.

Special Designations: FT_{100}

Officers: S. Kent Rockwell *CH, CEO & CFO*
                T. Richard Mathews *P & COO*
                Raymond T. Royko *VP, SEC & GC*
                Edward C. Sherry, Jr. *VP-Corporate Relations*
                Helen Vardy Gricks *TRS & CACO*

Auditor: Coopers & Lybrand L.L.P., Pittsburgh, PA

Affiliates/Divisions/Subsidiaries:

Brown-Minneapolis Tank & Fabricating Co. 100%
Eagan, MN
Designer, fabricator & erector of ASTs.

Graver Holding Co. 100%
Pasadena, TX

Graver Tank & Manufacturing Co., Inc. 100%
Pasadena, TX
Designer, manufacturer & erector of storage tanks & pressure vessels, & provider of nickel-clad installations for the power generation & air pollution industries.

HMT Inc. 100%
Houston, TX
Provider of proprietary products & maintenance & construction services for ASTs.

Australasian HMT Pty., Ltd. 100%
Edgecliff, N.S. Wales, Australia

HMT Canada Ltd. 100%
Calgary, Alberta, Canada

HMT Construction Services, Inc. 100%
Kelton, PA

HMT Inspection & Engineering Systems Division 100%

Houston, TX

HMT Rubbaglas Ltd. 100%
London, England
Designer, manufacturer & installer of equipment for ASTs in
.....Europe, Africa & the Middle East.

HMT Sentry Systems, Inc. 100%
Tomball, TX

HMT Singapore, PTE., LTD. 100%
Singapore

HMT Thermal Systems, Inc. 100%
Tomball, TX
Manufacturer of portable vapor thermal oxidation units & other
products.

HMT Tonkawa Tank Co., Inc. 100%
Tonkawa, OK
Provider of maintenance & construction services for ASTs.

Texoma Tank Co., Inc. 100%
Houston, TX
Lessor of mobile storage tanks.

Total Employees........................1,051   **Regional Employees** 9
Year Established 1973   **Incorporated** ....DE
Stock Symbol..............................AIX   **Annual Meeting**.........................May
Stock Exchange..........................ASE   **SIC Code**....................................7600
Stockholders 9,000
Shares Outstanding 9,934,920

Fiscal Year End	Total Revenues ($000)	Net Income/(Loss) ($000)	Total Assets ($000)
9/30/96	122,190	4,010	88,364
9/30/95	100,203	2,731	66,551
9/30/94	68,726	3,881	64,906
9/30/93	39,549	1,151	34,012

Executive Biography: S. Kent Rockwell

Birth Date: 9/11/44
Children: 2
Education:
Lafayette College, Economics; U of Pennsylvania, M.B.A.

Career History:
Rockwell International Corp., VP-Strategic Planning, P-Energy Products Group
1976-79; McEvoy Oil Field Equipment Services (Houston, TX), CH 1979-81;

Tallahassee Associates, GPTR; Special Metals Corp., CH & CEO 1986-87; Astrotech International Corp., CEO 1987-present, P 1988-95, CH 1989-present; Appalachian Timber Services, Inc., CH; Rockwell Venture Capital, Inc., CH & P.

Directorships/Memberships/Activities:
American Gas Assn., DIR; American Waterworks Assn., DIR; Gas Appliance Manufacturing Assn., DIR; S. T. Research, Inc., DIR; Aircraft Owners and Pilots Assn., MEM; American Petroleum Institute, MEM; Duquesne Club, MEM; Rolling Rock Club, MEM; Forbes Health System, TRU; Institute of Gas Technology, TRU; Institute of International Education, TRU; Lafayette College, TRU; Waynesburg College, TRU.

Baker Corp., Michael

Airport Office Park, 420 Rouser Rd., Bldg. 3
Coraopolis, PA 15108
County: Allegheny

Phone: (412) 269-6300
Fax: (412) 269-6097
Internet Address: www.mbakercorp.com

Type of Business: Provider of engineering, construction, and operations and technical services worldwide.

Michael Baker, through its operating subsidiaries and joint ventures, provides engineering, construction, and operations and technical services worldwide. The Company is organized into five market-focused business units. The Buildings unit provides architecture, engineering, planning, construction management and consulting, design-build and general construction services. The Civil unit provides engineering, planning, design and program management, geographic information systems, photogrammetric mapping, water/wastewater systems development, water resources management, military facilities planning and program management, military base operations support, fiber-optic cable engineering and design-build-operate services. The Energy unit provides facility operations and maintenance, operations analysis, equipment maintenance and overhaul, training programs, pipeline development and design, technical consulting and personnel, engineering and construction management, and design-build-operate oil and gas facilities services. The Environmental unit provides site characterization, remediation design and construction management, air quality management, process safety management, human health/ecological risk assessment, occupational health and safety compliance, environmental regulation compliance, audits and permitting, groundwater/wastewater treatment and facility design-build-operate services. The Transportation unit provides planning, design, construction, construction management and inspection, program management for surface and air transportation, and design-build-operate services. According to the annual listings published by Engineering News Record magazine, the Company ranked 40th among U.S. design firms, 15th among transportation design firms, 41st among international design firms, 89th among environmental firms and 165th among U.S. construction contractors. The rankings were based on revenues. The Company operates offices throughout the U.S. and around the world. Approximately 88% of its 1996 total contract revenues were derived from work performed within the U.S. The Company is publicly-owned, but management and employees hold a significant stake through an Employee Stock Ownership Plan.

Special Designations: ENR$_{400}$ ENR$_{500}$

Officers: Richard L. Shaw *CH*
Charles I. Homan *P & CEO*
Glenn S. Burns *EVP-Buildings*
Donald P. Fusilli, Jr. *EVP-Energy*
John C. Hayward, Ph.D. *EVP-Transportation*
Philip A. Shucet *EVP-Environmental*
J. Robert White *EVP, CFO & TRS*
Edward L. Wiley *EVP-Civil*
H. James McKnight *VP, GC & SEC*
Ronald J. Patten *VP-Information Technology*
Craig O. Stuver *CON & AST-TRS*

Human Resources: Kimberly W. Foltz *VP-Human Resources*
Auditor: Price Waterhouse LLP, Pittsburgh, PA
General Counsel: Reed Smith Shaw & McClay, Pittsburgh, PA

Affiliates/Divisions/Subsidiaries:

Baker and Associates 100%
Coraopolis, PA
Provider of architectural & engineering services.

Baker Engineering, Inc. 100%
Chicago, IL
Provider of consulting engineering & planning services.

Baker Engineering NY, Inc. 100%
New York, NY
Provider of consulting engineering & planning services.

Baker Environmental, Inc. 100%
Coraopolis, PA
Provider of environmental engineering services.

Baker Heavy & Highway, Inc. 100%
Coraopolis, PA
Provider of infrastructure construction & construction management services.

Baker Mellon Stuart Construction, Inc. 100%
Coraopolis, PA

B

Provider of building construction & construction management services.

Baker OTS, Inc. 100%
London, England
Provider of personnel procurement & operations support.

Baker Support Services, Inc. 100%
Dallas, TX
Provider of operations & maintenance services.

Baker/MO Services, Inc. 100%
Houston, TX
Provider of operations & maintenance services.

Mellon Stuart Construction International, Inc. 100%
Coraopolis, PA

Michael Baker de Mexico, S.A. de C.V. 100%
Mexico City, Mexico

Michael Baker Jr., Inc. 100%
Beaver, PA
Provider of consulting engineering & planning services.

Total Employees........................3,720	**Regional Employees**................1,200
Year Established 1940	**Incorporated**...................................PA
Stock Symbol.............................BKR	**Annual Meeting**........................May
Stock Exchange.........................ASE	**SIC Code**......................................8711
Stockholders...1,566 Series B 706		
Shares Outstanding...............................7,057,981 Series B 1,346,435		

Fiscal Year End	Total Revenues ($000)	Net Income/(Loss) ($000)	Total Assets ($000)
12/31/96	418,388	4,180	126,082
12/31/95	354,728	2,900	117,376
12/31/94	437,193	(7,945)	134,794
12/31/93	434,791	(15,128)	145,805

Executive Biography: Charles I. Homan

Birth Date: 1943　　　　**Birthplace:** Ridgeville, WV
Spouse: Nancy　　　　　**Children:** 3

Education:
West Virginia U, B.S.-Civil Engineering 1965; Harvard U, Advanced Management Program 1990.

Career History:
Michael Baker Corp., various positions 1965-83, P-Michael Baker Jr., Inc. 1983-94, SVP 1988-89, EVP 1990-94, P & CEO 1994-present.

Directorships/Memberships/Activities:
Boy Scouts of America, DIR-Greater Pittsburgh Council; Century Financial
Corp., DIR; Greater Pittsburgh Chamber of Commerce, DIR; Passavant
Memorial Homes, DIR; River City Brass Band, DIR; Geneva College, MEM-
Advisory Board; Robert Morris College, TRU; Pennsylvania Society of
Professional Engineers, Beaver County Chapter-Engineer of the Year 1991;
American Society of Civil Engineers, Pittsburgh Engineer of the Year 1992;
Pennsylvania Society of Professional Engineers, State Engineer of the Year 1994.

Black Box Corp.

1000 Park Dr.
Lawrence, PA 15055
County: Washington

Phone: (412) 746-5500
Fax: (412) 746-0746
Internet Address: www.blackbox.com

Type of Business: Direct marketer and technical service provider of computer
communications and networking equipment and solutions.

Black Box is a worldwide direct marketer and technical service provider of
computer communications and networking equipment and solutions. In fiscal
1997, the Company mailed 8.1 million catalogs and direct marketing pieces in 11
languages to targeted customers, including MIS and business professionals, purchasing agents and resellers, who make computer systems design decisions. Its
catalogs offer businesses in 77 countries access to more than 7,000 Black Box® private label computer communications and networking products, including PC
communications and accessories, cables and connectors, tools and racks, testers
and equipment protection, video and mass storage, switches, printer devices,
converters, line drivers, modems, CSUs and DSUs, muxes and LANs. The
Company intends to continue to broaden its existing product lines by offering
line extensions and new technologies. In addition, the Company has manufacturing and engineering capabilities to customize products for specialized customer applications. In fiscal 1997, it manufactured products representing approximately 18% of its total revenues. The Company has built a proprietary mailing
list containing approximately 1.3 million names representing nearly 650,000 buying sites. The Company complements its catalog mailings with approximately 80
technical support professionals, located in 14 countries, who are available 24
hours per day by phone. The Company sells to businesses of all sizes around the
world, including the majority of the Fortune 500 companies in the U.S. It operates
subsidiaries in 13 countries and has joint venture and distributor arrangements in
65 other countries. In fiscal 1997, 47% of the Company's revenues were generated outside of North America.

Officers: Jeffery M. Boetticher *CH, P & CEO*
Frederick C. Young *SVP, COO, CFO, TRS & SEC*
Human Resources: Richard Mandia, Ph.D.

Auditor: Arthur Anderson LLP, Pittsburgh, PA
General Counsel: Buchanan Ingersoll P.C., Pittsburgh, PA

B

Affiliates/Divisions/Subsidiaries:

Black Box Canada Corp. 100%
Ontario, Canada

Black Box Catalog Australia Pty., Ltd. 100%
Croydon, Australia

Black Box Catalogue, Ltd. 100%
Reading, England

Black Box Communicaciones, S.A. 50%
Madrid, Spain

Black Box Communication SANV 100%
Zaventem, Belgium

Black Box Datacom, B.V. 100%
Utrecht, The Netherlands

Black Box de Mexico, S.A. de C.V. 100%
Mexico City, Mexico

Black Box Deutschland GmbH 100%
Munich, Germany

Black Box do Brazil Industria e Comercio Ltda. 70%
Sao Paulo, Brazil

Black Box France, S.A. 100%
Rungis, France

Black Box Italia, SpA 100%
Vimodrone, Italy

Black Box Japan Kabushiki Kaisha 100%
Tokyo, Japan

Black Box-PA 100%
Lawrence, PA

Datacom Black Box Services AG 100%
Altendorf, Switzerland

Total Employees............................600		**Regional Employees** 400	
Year Established 1976		**Incorporated** ....DE	

Stock Symbol ....BBOX	Annual Meeting...................August
Stock Exchange................NASDAQ	SIC Code.....................................3577

Stockholders 163

Shares Outstanding 16,349,569

Fiscal Year End	Total Revenues ($000)	Net Income/(Loss) ($000)	Total Assets ($000)
3/31/96	193,427	18,278	155,544
4/2/95	164,766	14,515	152,132
4/3/94	142,004	13,370	150,722
3/28/93	125,063	6,634	153,736

Executive Biography: Jeffery M. Boetticher

Birth Date: 1951

Career History:
Black Box Corp., various executive positions with Black Box Corp. of Pennsylvania 1987-91, P & CEO-Black Box Corp. of Pennsylvania 1991-94, P & CEO 1994-present, CH 1995-present.

Directorships/Memberships/Activities:
CME Information Services, Inc., DIR; Holden Corp., DIR; Pittsburgh High Technology Council, DIR.

Cable Design Technologies Corp.

Foster Plaza 7, 661 Andersen Dr.
Pittsburgh, PA 15220
County: Allegheny

Phone: (412) 937-2300
Fax: (412) 937-9690
Internet Address: www.cdtc.com

Type of Business: Designer and manufacturer of electronic data transmission cables.

Cable Design Technologies is a designer and manufacturer of electronic data transmission cables and connectors made of copper, fiber optics and copper/fiber-optic composites for network structured wiring sytems; automation, sound and safety; computer interconnect; and communications applications. The network structured wiring group encompasses the cables, connectors, racks, panels, outlets and interconnecting hardware to complete the end-to-end network system requirements of LANs and WANs. Automation, sound and safety encompasses three distinct applications for data and signal transmission cables. Automation applications include climate control and sophisticated security and signal systems involving motion detection, electronic card and video surveillance technologies. Sound includes voice activation, evacuation and other similar systems. Safety cable refers to certain attributes of data transmission cable that improve the safety and performance of such cable under hazardous conditions, particularly in buildings for advanced fire alarm and safety systems. Computer interconnect

C

refers to a family of data transmission cables used to internally connect components of computers, telecommunication switching and related electronic equipment, and to externally connect large and small computers to a variety of peripheral devices. Through the February 2, 1996 acquisition of Northern Telecom Ltd.'s
structured wiring and communications cable businesses (now known as
NORDX/CDT), the Company entered the market for outside communications,
switchboard and equipment cable. The Company also manufactures products for
a variety of other electronic wire and cable applications and markets, including
broadcast, CATV, microwave antenna, medical electronics, electronic testing
equipment, automotive electronics, robotics, electronically controlled factory
equipment, copiers, home entertainment and appliances. In addition, a division
of the Company manufactures precision molds used in the tire manufacturing
industry. The Company markets its products directly to OEMs, regional Bell operating companies and established distributors. In fiscal 1996, the Company
derived approximately 52% of its sales from network structured wiring products,
19% from automation, sound and safety products, 14% from communica-
tions/multimedia products and 5% from computer interconnect products.
During this same period, international sales accounted for 24% of its revenue. On
November 24, 1993, the Company completed its initial public stock offering.

Officers: Bryan C. Cressey *CH*
Paul M. Olson *P & CEO*
Normand R. Bourque *EVP; P-NORDX/CDT*
Michael A. Dudley *EVP; P-CDT INTL*
George C. Graeber *EVP; P-Montrose/CDT*
David R. Harden *SVP; P-West Penn/CDT*
Kenneth O. Hale *VP, CFO & SEC*

Auditor: Arthur Andersen LLP, Pittsburgh, PA
Affiliates/Divisions/Subsidiaries:

Admiral/CDT 100%
Wadsworth, OH
Manufacturer of precision molds for tire producers.

Anglo/CDT 100%
Leeds, England
Distributor of LAN system products & broadcast cable.

CDT International 100%
Leeds, England

Cekan/CDT 100%
Gjern, Denmark
Manufacturer of telecommunications connectors.

Dearborn/CDT 100%
Wheeling, IL
Manufacturer of electronic wire & cable for aerospace & wireless communications.

Manhattan/CDT 100%
Manchester, CT
Supplier of electronic & industrial wire/cable for automation & robotics.

Mohawk/CDT 100%
Leominster, MA
Manufacturer of network cable (copper/fiber) for LANs, WANs & multimedia.

Montrose/CDT 100%
Auburn, MA
Manufacturer of OEM specialty electronic cable for computer interconnect.

NEK/CDT 100%
Kinna, Sweden
Manufacturer of electronic computer, broadcast & network cables.

NORDX/CDT 100%
Saint Laurent, Quebec, Canada
Manufacturer of LAN & network structured wiring systems products.

Phalo/CDT 100%
Manchester, CT
Manufacturer of specialty electronic cable for LANs.

Raydex/CDT 100%
Lancashire, England
Manufacturer of electronic and high-performance wire and cable products.

West Penn/CDT 100%
Washington, PA
Manufacturer of electronic wire for sound, signal, security & automation.

X-Mark/CDT 100%
Washington, PA
Manufacturer of specialized metal enclosures & wiring panels.

C

Total Employees	2,500
Year Established	1985
Stock Symbol	CDT
Stock Exchange	NYSE
Stockholders	118
Shares Outstanding	18,191,710

Regional Employees	115
Incorporated	DE
Annual Meeting	December
SIC Code	3357

Fiscal Year End	Total Revenues ($000)	Net Income/(Loss) ($000)	Total Assets ($000)
7/31/96	357,352	15,285	320,105
7/31/95	188,941	14,713	118,976
7/31/94	145,389	6,140	102,719
7/31/93	126,650	6,026	83,749

Executive Biography: Paul M. Olson

Birth Date: 10/30/33   **Birthplace:** Duluth, MN

Education:
Hobart College, B.A.-Economics.

Career History:
U.S. Army, 1954-56; General Cable, 1960-63; General Electric Co., 1963-67; Phalo Corp. (Shrewsbury, MA), DIR-SAL & MKT 1967-72, P 1972-84; Cable Design Technologies Corp., P 1985-present, CEO 1993-present.

Directorships/Memberships/Activities:
Assn. of Publicly Traded Cos., MEM; Building Industry Consulting Services International, MEM; Electronic Industries Assn., MEM; National Assn. of Electrical Representatives, MEM; National Electrical Manufacturers Assn., MEM; Wire Assn. International, MEM; Who's Who International Business; Charles Scott Distinguished Career Award.

Calgon Carbon Corp.

400 Calgon Carbon Dr.
P.O. Box 717, Pittsburgh, PA 15230
Pittsburgh, PA 15205
County: Allegheny

Phone: (412) 787-6700
Fax: (412) 787-4511
Internet Address: www.calgoncarbon.com

Type of Business: Producer, designer and marketer of products and services specifically developed for the purification, separation and concentration of liquids and gases.

Calgon Carbon is engaged in the manufacture and marketing of products and services employed for separation, concentration or purification of liquids and gases. The Company's activities consist of four integrally related areas. The activated carbons area produces and markets a broad range of untreated, impregnated or acid-washed carbons, in either powdered, granular, pellet or cloth form. The services area provides carbon reactivation, handling and transportation, and on-site purification, separation and concentration services. The systems area designs, assembles and markets systems that employ activated carbon, advanced oxidation, ion exchange or chromatographic separation technology for purification, separation and concentration. The charcoal area produces and markets charcoal to consumer markets. The Company sells its activated carbon products, systems and services to three primary markets. The industrial process market consists of customers who use the Company's products either for purification, separation or concentration of their products in the manufacturing process or direct incorporation into their product. The industrial process market includes four significant submarkets consisting of the food market, the OEM market, the chemical and pharmaceutical market, and a group of other submarkets. The environmental market consists of customers who use the Company's products to control air and water pollutants. The environmental market has two submarkets, the industrial market and the municipal market. The consumer market consists of sales of charcoal for outdoor barbecue grilling. The charcoal is primarily sold through distributors principally in Germany. In 1996, the Company derived approximately 47% of its net sales from the industrial process market, 46% from the environmental market and 7% from the consumer market. Also in 1996, its products and services were purchased by approximately 4,000 active customers. The Company owns nine production facilities, two of which are located in Pittsburgh, PA; and one each in Blue Lake, CA; Catlettsburg, KY; Pearlington, MS; Feluy, Belgium; Grays, England; Bodenfelde and Brilon-Wald (closed in 1995), Germany. It leases four production facilities in Tucson, AZ; Lakeland, FL; Markham, Ontario, Canada; and Houghton Le Spring, England. On June 9, 1987, the Company completed its initial public stock offering.

Officers: Thomas A. McConomy *CH*
Colin Bailey *P & CEO*
Joseph A. Fischette *SVP, GC & SEC*
R. Scott Keefer *SVP & CFO*
John M. MacCrum *SVP*
Robert T. Van Haute *SVP*
Jonathan H. Maurer *VP*
Robert P. O'Brien *VP*
Dennis J. Sulick *VP*
Marshall J. Morris *TRS*
Clarence J. Kenney *CON*

Human Resources: Robert W. Courson
Auditor: Price Waterhouse LLP, Pittsburgh, PA
Affiliates/Divisions/Subsidiaries:

Advanced Separation Technologies Inc. 100%

Calgon Carbon Canada, Inc. 100%
Toronto, Ontario, Canada

C

Calgon Carbon Export Inc. 100%

Calgon Carbon Investments Inc. 100%

Calgon Far East Co., Ltd. 50%
Tokyo, Japan
Joint venture operator of reactivation facility in Japan.

Charcoal Cloth (International) Ltd. 100%

Charcoal Cloth Ltd. 100%

Chemviron Carbon GmbH 100%
Frankfurt, Germany

Chemviron Carbon Ltd. 100%

Solarchem Environmental Systems Inc. 100%

Vara International Division 100%
Vero Beach, FL

Total Employees.........................1,297   **Regional Employees** 350
Year Established 1942   **Incorporated** ....DE
Stock Symbol.............................CCC   **Annual Meeting**......................April
Stock Exchange ....NYSE   **SIC Code**....................................2819
Stockholders 984
Shares Outstanding 39,674,660

Fiscal Year End	Total Revenues ($000)	Net Income/(Loss) ($000)	Total Assets ($000)
12/31/96	290,196	21,638	397,251
12/31/95	291,898	21,345	338,001
12/31/94	274,244	(8,609)	343,484
12/31/93	269,424	19,153	337,329

Executive Biography: Colin Bailey

Birth Date: 1947   **Birthplace:** Bury, England
Education:
John Dalton College (Manchester, England), Chemical Engineering.

Career History:
Calgon Carbon Corp., various positions 1971-83, MDIR-Chemviron Carbon Ltd.
1983-85, VP 1985-87, SVP 1987-91, responsible for Vara International Divison
1991-92, COO 1992-, EVP 1992-94, P & CEO 1994-present.

Directorships/Memberships/Activities:
Pittsburgh Public Theater, DIR; World Affairs Council of Pittsburgh, DIR; Robert
Morris College, TRU.

Carbide/Graphite Group, Inc., The

One Gateway Center, 19th Fl.
Pittsburgh, PA 15222
County: Allegheny

Phone: (412) 562-3700
Fax: (412) 562-3739
Internet Address: www.cggi.com

Type of Business: Manufacturer of graphite electrode products and calcium carbide products.

The Carbide/Graphite Group's operations consist of two segments: graphite electrode products and calcium carbide products. The graphite electrode products segment manufactures and markets graphite electrodes and related raw materials and products. Graphite electrodes are used to conduct electrical current to melt scrap steel in electric arc steel furnaces, the process by which scrap is reprocessed into finished steel. This segment also manufactures needle coke, the principal raw material used in the manufacture of graphite electrodes. The Company claims that it is the only manufacturer of graphite electrodes that produces its own requirements of needle coke. In addition, it sells needle coke to other manufacturers of graphite products. The Company's annual capacity for graphite electrode production is approximately 110 million pounds and 130,000 tons for needle coke. The calcium carbide products segment manufactures and markets calcium carbide and its direct derivatives, primarily acetylene, for use in the manufacture of specialty chemicals, as a fuel in metal cutting and welding, and for iron and steel desulfurization. This segment also manufactures electrically calcined anthracite coal used in the aluminum industry. The Company's annual capacity for calcium carbide production is approximately 200,000 tons. The Company's graphite electrode production facilities are located in Niagara Falls, NY and St. Marys, PA; needle coke in Seadrift, TX; and calcium carbide in Calvert City and Louisville, KY. In fiscal 1996, sales of graphite electrode products and calcium carbide products accounted for 66.5% and 33.5%, respectively, of the Company's revenues. On September 19, 1995, the Company completed its initial public stock offering.

Officers: Walter B. Fowler *CH, P & CEO*
Ara Hacetoglu *VP & GMGR-Carbide Products*
Michael F. Supon *VP & GMGR-Electrode Products*
Stephen D. Weaver *VP-FIN & CFO*
Roger Mulvihill *SEC*
Jeffrey T. Jones *CON*

Human Resources: Walter E. Damian *VP-Human Resources*
Auditor: Coopers & Lybrand L.L.P., Pittsburgh, PA

Total Employees	1,280	Regional Employees	30
Year Established	1899	Incorporated	DE
Stock Symbol	CGGI	Annual Meeting	December
Stock Exchange	NASDAQ	SIC Code	3624
Stockholders			94
Shares Outstanding			8,355,522

Fiscal Year End	Total Revenues ($000)	Net Income/(Loss) ($000)	Total Assets ($000)
7/31/96	259,394	12,142	212,870
7/31/95	241,456	28,708	214,409
7/31/94	207,536	(60)	192,434
7/31/93	193,918	5,477	171,870

Executive Biography: Walter B. Fowler

Birth Date: 1954

Spouse: Mary   **Children:** 2

Education:
Washington and Jefferson College, B.A.-Economics; U of Pittsburgh, M.B.A.-Finance.

Career History:
The Carbide/Graphite Group, Inc., VP-FIN & CFO & TRS & AST-SEC 1988-91, VP & GMGR-Graphite Specialties 1991-95, VP & GMGR-Graphite Electrode Products 1995, P-Electrodes & Graphite Specialty Products 1995-97, CH & P & CEO 1997-present.

Carnegie Group, Inc.

Five PPG Place
Pittsburgh, PA 15222
County: Allegheny

Phone: (412) 642-6900
Fax: (412) 642-6906
Internet Address: www.cgi.com

Type of Business: Provider of client/server software development services.

   Carnegie Group provides client/server software development services that integrate advanced user-centered, intelligent software technologies with clients' existing computing infrastructures to automate and enhance complex business processes. The Company performs business and technical consulting, custom software development and systems integration services to improve clients' productivity and market position in two business areas: customer interaction and logistics, planning and scheduling. Within these areas, the Company targets its services to clients in the financial services, government, manufacturing and telecommunications industries. The Company's expertise encompasses a wide range of advanced software technologies, including knowledge-based systems, object-oriented technology, advanced graphical user interfaces, constraint-directed search and distributed computing. The Company captures certain aspects of its business area experience and advanced technology expertise in a portfolio of reusable software templates that can be used as building blocks to create software solutions quickly and effectively. In addition, the Company employs an iterative or "spiral" approach to software design that begins with the construction of a prototype and continues through testing of successive versions of the software against project requirements. This iterative design approach facilitates rapid software development, encourages client feedback and leads to greater congruence with client needs and expectations. Since inception, the Company has emphasized relationships with leading corporations in its targeted industries. These relationships have provided the Company with opportunities for growth through the provision of additional services to existing clients and through references to other businesses within the Company's targeted industries. Its clients include BellSouth Telecommunications, Caterpillar, First USA Bank, Highmark Blue Cross Blue Shield, Philips Medical Systems, U.S. Army, United States Transportation Command and US WEST Communications. The Company maintains regional offices in Oakland, CA; Denver, CO; Atlanta, GA; Fairview Heights, IL; and Arlington, VA. On November 29, 1995, the Company completed its initial public stock offering.

Officers: Raj Reddy *CH*
Dennis Yablonsky *P & CEO*
John W. Manzetti *EVP, CFO, TRS & SEC*
Bruce D. Russell, Ph.D. *EVP & COO*

Human Resources: Heather Perinis
Auditor: Price Waterhouse LLP, Pittsburgh, PA
General Counsel: Morgan, Lewis & Bockius, LLP, Pittsburgh, PA

Affiliates/Divisions/Subsidiaries:

Carnegie Federal Systems Corp. 100%

Carnegie Group Investments, Inc. 100%

Carnegie Investment Services, Inc. 100%

Carnegie Services, Inc. 100%

Total Employees............................252	**Regional Employees** 188
Year Established 1983	**Incorporated** ....DE
Stock Symbol ....CGIX	**Annual Meeting** ....May
Stock Exchange................NASDAQ	**SIC Code** 7373
Stockholders 4,100	
Shares Outstanding 6,283,091	

Fiscal Year End	Total Revenues ($000)	Net Income/(Loss) ($000)	Total Assets ($000)
12/31/96	28,409	3,360	28,489
12/31/95	25,650	4,676	24,989
12/31/94	17,875	1,439	8,943
12/31/93	12,817	(2,021)	6,025

Executive Biography: Dennis Yablonsky
Birth Date: 1953

Education:
U of Cincinnati, B.S.-Industrial Management.

Career History:
Cincom Systems (Cincinnati, OH), P & COO; Carnegie Group, Inc., P & CEO 1987-present.

Directorships/Memberships/Activities:
Greater Pittsburgh Chamber of Commerce, DIR; Pittsburgh High Technology Council, DIR; Software Engineering Institute, DIR; St. Bernard's School, DIR.

Century Financial Corp.

One Century Place
Rochester, PA 15074
County: Beaver

Phone: (412) 774-1872
Fax: (412) 728-8431
Internet Address: www.centbank.com

Type of Business: Bank holding company.

Century Financial is a bank holding company engaged principally in commercial banking activities through its banking subsidiary, Century National Bank and Trust Co. (Bank). The Bank offers full-service commercial and consumer banking and trust services. Its services include accepting time, demand and savings deposits, including NOW accounts, regular savings accounts, money market accounts, certificates of deposit and club accounts. Its services also include commercial transactions either directly or through regional industrial development corporations, making construction and mortgage loans, and the renting of safe deposit facilities. Additional services include making residential mortgage loans, revolving credit loans with overdraft protection and small business loans. The Bank's business loans include seasonal credit collateral loans and term loans. Trust services provided by the Bank include services as executor and trustee under will and deeds, as guardian and custodian and as trustee and agent for pension, profit sharing and other employee benefit trusts, as well as various investment, pension and estate planning services. Trust services also include service as transfer agent and registrar of stock and bond issues and escrow agent. The Bank provides services to its customers through 13 full-service offices which include drive-in facilities. Its banking offices are located in Aliquippa, Ambridge, Baden, Beaver, Beaver Falls (2), Cranberry Township, Freedom, Midland, Monaca (2), New Brighton and Rochester (at the above address). Twelve of the offices are located in Beaver County, PA, the Bank's primary market area, and one branch is located in Butler County, PA.

Officers: Del E. Goedeker *CH*
Thomas K. Reed *VCH*
Joseph N. Tosh II *P & CEO; P & CEO-Century National Bank and Trust Co.*

Donald A. Benziger *SVP & CFO; SVP & CFO-Century National Bank and Trust Co.*

Edwin C. Schaffnit *SVP & Senior Lending Officer-Century National Bank and Trust Co.*

C. David Becker *VP-MKT-Century National Bank and Trust Co.*

Colleen O. Butterfield *VP-Electronic Banking SAL/Service-Century National Bank and Trust Co.*

Wayne A. Grinnik *VP-Lending-Century National Bank and Trust Co.*

Charles D. Price, Jr. *VP-Branch ADM-Century National Bank and Trust Co.*

Allen R. Spring *VP & Trust Officer-Century National Bank and Trust Co.*

Mary A. Flint *AVP-Loan Processing & Compliance-Century National Bank and Trust Co.*

Sam R. Fuller *AVP-Collections-Century National Bank and Trust Co.*

Twila K. Green *AVP, Training DIR & SAL Coordinator-Century National Bank and Trust Co.*

Ronald A. Pompeani *AVP & Business DEV Officer-Century National Bank and Trust Co.*

Michael R. Tarnovich *AVP & MGR-Data Processing-Century National Bank and Trust Co.*

Human Resources: Mary E. Welch *VP-Human Resources*
Auditor: S. R. Snodgrass, A.C., Wexford, PA
Affiliates/Divisions/Subsidiaries:

Century National Bank and Trust Co. 100%
Commercial bank.

Total Employees............................209	**Regional Employees** 209	
Year Established 1872	**Incorporated**..................................PA	
Stock Symbol ....CYFN	**Annual Meeting**.......................April	
Stock Exchange................NASDAQ	**SIC Code**.....................................6712	
Stockholders 980		
Shares Outstanding 3,370,806		

Fiscal Year End	Total Revenues ($000)	Net Income/(Loss) ($000)	Total Assets ($000)
12/31/96	33,280	4,906	412,858
12/31/95	30,259	4,268	376,989
12/31/94	26,041	3,681	331,780
12/31/93	24,661	3,347	317,936

Executive Biography: Joseph N. Tosh II

Birth Date: 4/14/42   **Birthplace:** Beaver, PA
Spouse: Karen   **Children:** 2

Education:
Bowling Green State U, B.S.-Business Administration 1964; Duquesne U, M.B.A. 1967; Rutgers U, Banking 1980.

Career History:
Freedom National Bank, AVP 1967-73; Century National Bank and Trust Co.,
VP-ADM 1973-85, EVP 1985-87, P & CEO 1988-present; Century Financial Corp.,
P & CEO 1988-present.

Directorships/Memberships/Activities:
Federal Home Loan Bank of Pittsburgh, DIR; Beaver County Foundation, MEM;
Beaver Municipal Authority, MEM; Beaver School District Education
Foundation, MEM; Beaver Valley Chamber of Commerce, MEM; Credit Bureau
of Beaver County, MEM; Pennsylvania Bankers Assn., MEM-Governing
Council; Pennsylvania Bankers Assn., MEM-PAC; Salvation Army, MEM-
Rochester, PA Unit; United Way of Beaver County, MEM.

Commercial National Financial Corp.

900 Ligonier St.
P.O. Box 429
Latrobe, PA 15650
County: Westmoreland

Phone: (412) 539-3501
Fax: (412) 539-0816

Type of Business: Bank holding company.

   Commercial National Financial is a bank holding company. Its subsidiary bank,
Commercial National Bank of Westmoreland County (Bank), offers the full range
of banking services normally associated with the general commercial banking
business. These services include demand, savings and time deposits, as well as
loan programs which encompass commercial loans, mortgage loans, personal
credit lines, home equity credit lines and consumer installment loans. In addition,
the Bank offers Visa and Mastercard credit card programs, and since mid-1994,
asset management and trust services. In 1996, it implemented a comprehensive
electronic home-banking system. This product, known as the Maxcess Account,
provides customers with the option of paying bills through personal computer,
screenphone, touchtone phone and even rotary phone. The Bank's facilities are
located in Greensburg, Hempfield Township, Latrobe (2), Ligonier, Murrysville,
Unity Township (2) and West Newton, all of which are in Westmoreland County,
PA.

Officers: Louis A. Steiner *CH & CEO*
        Gregg E. Hunter *VCH & CFO*
        Louis T. Steiner *VCH*
        Edwin P. Cover *P & COO*

Human Resources: Donna L. Belluchie
Auditor: Jarrett Stokes & Kelly, Allison Park, PA
General Counsel: McDonald Moore Mason & Snyder, Latrobe, PA

Affiliates/Divisions/Subsidiaries:

Commercial National Bank of Westmoreland County 100%
Latrobe, PA
Nationally chartered bank.

Total Employees 111	**Regional Employees** 111
Year Established 1934	**Incorporated** ....PA
Stock Symbol ....CNAF	**Annual Meeting** ....April
Stock Exchange ....NASDAQ	**SIC Code** 6712

Stockholders 625
Shares Outstanding 1,800,000

Fiscal Year End	Total Revenues ($000)	Net Income/(Loss) ($000)	Total Assets ($000)
12/31/96	21,204	3,756	278,111
12/31/95	20,335	3,693	266,176
12/31/94	18,399	3,485	251,142
12/31/93	18,258	3,754	243,527

Executive Biography: Louis A. Steiner

Birth Date: 1/29/31
Children: 3

Education:
Dickinson College.

Career History:
U.S. Navy; Latrobe Foundry Machine and Supply Co., various positions including VP, P -present; Commercial National Bank of Westmoreland County, P 1977-89, CH & CEO 1977-present; Commercial National Financial Corp., CH & CEO 1977-present.

Directorships/Memberships/Activities:
Boy Scouts of America, DIR-Westmoreland-Fayette Council; Eastern Westmoreland Development Corp., CH; Latrobe Area Hospital, DIR; Latrobe United Methodist Church, DIR; Ligonier Valley YMCA, DIR; U of Pittsburgh at Greensburg, DIR; Ligonier Writers Guild, MEM; Pennsylvania Bankers Assn., MEM-Regional Governing Council; Southwestern Pennsylvania Regional Planning Commission, MEM-Transportation Plan Policy Comm.; Boy Scouts of America, Silver Beaver Award 1972; Latrobe Area Chamber of Commerce, Community Service Award 1992.

Computer Research, Inc.

Cherrington Corporate Center, Bldg. 200
Coraopolis, PA 15108
County: Allegheny

Phone: (412) 262-4430
Fax: (412) 262-5254
Internet Address: www.crix.com

Type of Business: Provider of data processing, accounting and recordkeeping services.

Computer Research is a data processing service company providing accounting services to securities firms, banks and other financial institutions. The principal data processing service offered by the Company is its computerized "Accounting and Recordkeeping System", a fully integrated subsystem of software modules which, when operated on the Company's electronic computing equipment, offers a comprehensive automated system for serving financial institutions with brokerage accounting, institutional safekeeping, capital markets and portfolio accounting. The system provides such firms with on-line retrieval, reports and records on a day-to-day basis utilizing data supplied by the client. The Company is equipped to service both stock and bond brokerage clients, including brokerage subsidiaries and capital markets divisions of banks. This service is utilized by approximately 55 financial institutions throughout the country. The Company is also engaged, on a limited basis, in the selling of communications equipment, micro- and mini-computer equipment, software and equipment maintenance services to the clients of its data processing accounting service. In addition to the Company's principal office and eastern data center located at the above address, it maintains a western data center in Denver, CO, and a service and sales support office in New York City.

Officers: James L. Schultz *P & TRS*
David J. Vagnoni *EVP*
Richard D. Iriye *VP-Systems-Western Data Center*
William R. McNamee *VP-Systems-Eastern Data Center*
Frank H. Moser, Jr. *VP-Computer Applications*
David B. Rockacy *VP-Technical Support*
William Lerner *SEC*

Auditor: Grant Thornton LLP, Cleveland, OH

Affiliates/Divisions/Subsidiaries:

Western Data Center 100%
Denver, CO
Provider of data processing services.

Total Employees	54	**Regional Employees**	29
Year Established	1960	**Incorporated**	PA
Stock Symbol	CRIX	**Annual Meeting**	January
Stock Exchange	OTC	**SIC Code**	5045
Stockholders			990

Shares Outstanding 4,037,255

Fiscal Year End	Total Revenues ($000)	Net Income/(Loss) ($000)	Total Assets ($000)
8/31/96	7,462	1,028	3,459
8/31/95	6,204	398	2,087
8/31/94	5,494	5	1,660
8/31/93	5,083	(273)	1,582

Executive Biography: James L. Schultz

Birth Date: 8/6/36 **Birthplace:** Jefferson Borough, PA
Spouse: Helen
Education:
U of Pittsburgh.

Career History:
U. S. Steel Corp. (Homestead, PA), Programmer 1959-63; Computer Research, Inc., Programmer, VP 1963-75, P & TRS 1975-present.

Directorships/Memberships/Activities:
Cortland Trust, TRU.

Consolidated Natural Gas Co.

CNG Tower, 625 Liberty Ave.
Pittsburgh, PA 15222
County: Allegheny

Phone: (412) 227-1000
Fax: (412) 227-1020
Internet Address: www.cng.com

Type of Business: Public utility holding company.

   Consolidated Natural Gas is a public utility holding company. It is engaged solely in the business of owning and holding all of the outstanding equity securities of 15 directly owned subsidiary companies. The subsidiary companies are involved in the exploration, production, purchasing, gathering, transmission, storage, distribution and marketing of natural gas and related by-product operations. The Company's principal gas distribution subsidiaries are: The East Ohio Gas Co. in Cleveland, OH, serving nearly 1.2 million customers in Ohio; The Peoples Natural Gas Co. in Pittsburgh, PA, serving 337,000 customers in western Pennsylvania; Virginia Natural Gas, Inc. in Norfolk, VA, serving 209,000 customers in southeastern Virginia; and Hope Gas, Inc. in Clarksburg, WV, serving 114,000 customers in West Virginia. CNG Transmission Corp. (CTC) in Clarksburg, WV, operates a regional interstate gas pipeline system with its principal pipeline and storage facilities located in New York, Ohio, Pennsylvania and West Virginia. CTC offers gas transportation, storage and related services to its affiliates, as well as to utilities and end users in the Northeast, Mid-Atlantic and Midwest regions of the country. Exploration and production operations are conducted by CNG Producing Co. in New Orleans, LA, which explores for and produces gas and oil in the Gulf of Mexico, the Appalachian region, the Southwest, the West and in Canada. CNG Energy Services Corp. in Pittsburgh, PA, arranges gas sales, transportation, storage and other services for large customers; markets electricity and other fuels throughout North America; and owns and operates electric power plants. CNG International Corp. in Reston, VA, and Syndey, Australia, was formed to own and operate natural gas and electric businesses involving generation, transportation and distribution. The Company's total gross investment in property, plant and equipment was $8.3 billion on December 31, 1996. The largest portion of this investment (60%) is in facilities located in the Appalachian area. Another significant portion (25%) is located in the Gulf of Mexico.

Special Designations: DJUA FB$_{500}$ FT$_{500}$

Officers: George A. Davidson, Jr. *CH & CEO*
David M. Westfall *SVP & CFO*
Stephen E. Williams *SVP & GC*
Stephen R. McGreevy *VP-Accounting & Financial Control*
Laura J. McKeown *SEC*
Thomas F. Garbe *CON*
Ronald L. Adams *P-CNG Transmission Corp.*
Jerry L. Causey *P-Virginia Natural Gas, Inc.*
William A. Fox *P-The Peoples Natural Gas Co. & Hope Gas, Inc.*
Tom D. Newland *P-The East Ohio Gas Co.*
Joseph H. Petrowski *P-CNG Energy Services Corp.*
H. Patrick Riley *P-CNG Producing Co.*
James S. Thomson *P-CNG International Corp.*

Human Resources: Joseph S. Usaj *VP-Human Resources & ADM*
Auditor: Price Waterhouse LLP, Pittsburgh, PA
Affiliates/Divisions/Subsidiaries:

CNG Energy Services Corp. 100%
Pittsburgh, PA
Marketer of energy.

CNG International Corp. 100%
Reston, VA, & Sydney, Australia
Engaged in energy-related activities outside of U.S.

CNG Producing Co. 100%
New Orleans, LA
Explorer & producer of energy.

CNG Transmission Corp. 100%
Clarksburg, WV
Operator of interstate gas transmission pipeline.

The East Ohio Gas Co. 100%
Cleveland, OH
Gas distribution utility.

Hope Gas, Inc. 100%
Clarksburg, WV
Gas distribution utility.

The Peoples Natural Gas Co. 100%
Pittsburgh, PA
Gas distribution utility.

Virginia Natural Gas, Inc. 100%
Norfolk, VA
Gas distribution utility.

Total Employees........................6,426	**Regional Employees** 1,273	
Year Established 1942	**Incorporated** ....DE	
Stock Symbol............................CNG	**Annual Meeting** ....May	
Stock Exchange ....NYSE	**SIC Code**....................................4923	
Stockholders 35,816		
Shares Outstanding 94,940,555		

Fiscal Year End	Total Revenues ($000)	Net Income/(Loss) ($000)	Total Assets ($000)
12/31/96	3,794,309	298,273	6,000,605
12/31/95	3,307,325	21,344	5,418,293
12/31/94	3,036,028	183,171	5,518,673
12/31/93	3,184,085	205,916	5,437,188

Executive Biography: George A. Davidson, Jr.

Birth Date: 7/28/38   **Birthplace:** Pittsburgh, PA

Education:
U of Pittsburgh, B.S.-Petroleum Engineering 1960.

Career History:
Federal Power Commission, 1961-66; Consolidated Natural Gas Service Co., Inc. (subsidiary of Consolidated Natural Gas Co.), Senior Rate ENG 1966-74, MGR 1974-75, AVP-Rates & Certificates Department 1975-81, VP-System Gas OPR 1981-84, P-CNG Transmission Corp. 1984-85; Consolidated Natural Gas Co., VCH 1985-87, COO 1987, CH & CEO 1987-present.

Directorships/Memberships/Activities:
Civic Light Opera of Pittsburgh, CH Emeritus; B. F. Goodrich Co., DIR; The Pittsburgh Cultural Trust, CH; PNC Bank Corp., DIR; United Way of Allegheny County, DIR; Allegheny Conference on Community Development, MEM-Executive Comm.; National Petroleum Council, MEM; The Pittsburgh Foundation, MEM-Distribution Comm.; U.S. Environmental Protection Agency, MEM-Clean Air Act Advisory Comm.; U of Pittsburgh, MEM-Properties & Facilities Comm.; U of Pittsburgh, MEM-Board of Visitors for School of ENG;

Carnegie Institute, TRU; U of Pittsburgh, TRU; Financial World, Bronze Award-CEO of the Year 1992.

D

DQE, Inc.

Cherrington Corporate Center, 500 Cherrington Pwy., Ste. 100
Coraopolis, PA 15108
County: Allegheny
Phone: (412) 262-4700
Fax: (412) 393-6448
Internet Address: www.dqe.com

Type of Business: Energy services holding company.

DQE is an energy services holding company. Its subsidiaries are Duquesne Light Co. (DLC), Duquesne Enterprises (DE), Montauk, DQE Energy Services (DES) and DQEnergy PARTNERS (DP). DLC, the Company's largest subsidiary, is an electric utility engaged in the production, transmission, distribution and sale of electric energy. It provides electric service to customers in Allegheny County, including the City of Pittsburgh, and Beaver and Westmoreland Counties, PA. This represents a service territory of approximately 800 square miles. In addition to serving more than 580,000 direct customers, DLC sells electricity to other utilities beyond its service territory. DE was formed in 1989 to make strategic investments beneficial to the Company's core energy business. These investments, which enhance the Company's capabilities as an energy provider, increase asset utilization and act as a hedge against changing business conditions, include: Allegheny Development Corp., a subsidiary that provides all energy services for the Pittsburgh International Airport; EnSite L.P., a joint venture with ITRON Inc., to provide wireless monitoring and control services in the region; Exide Electronics Group, Inc., an integrated provider of non-interruptible power quality products, systems and services, both domestic and international; H Power Corp., a fuel cell development company; and Property Ventures, Ltd., a subsidiary that owns and develops real estate in southwestern Pennsylvania. Montauk was formed in 1990 and is a financial services company that makes long-term investments and provides financing for the Company's other market-driven businesses and their customers. DES was formed in 1995 and is a diversified energy services company offering a wide range of energy solutions for industrial, utility and consumer markets worldwide. Its initiatives include energy facility development and operation, domestic and international independent power production, and the production and supply of innovative fuels. DP was formed in 1996 to align the Company with strategic partners to capitalize on opportunities in the dynamic energy services industry. These alliances enhance the utilization and value of the Company's strategic investments and capabilities while establishing the Company as a total energy provider.

Recent Events: On April 7, 1997, Allegheny Power System, Inc. (APSI), which is headquartered in Hagerstown, MD, and listed on the NYSE, and the Company announced that they had signed a definitive agreement to merge in a tax-free, stock-for-stock transaction. The merger, which was unanimously approved by both companies' boards of directors will create a diversified energy company with 2 million customers in five states and generating capacity of more than 11,000 megawatts of electricity. The combined company will be called Allegheny Energy. Under the terms of the transaction, the Company's shareholders will receive 1.12 shares of APSI common stock for each share of the Company's common stock. The companies are hopeful that the required approvals can be obtained within 12 to 18 months.

Special Designations: FB_{500}

Officers: David D. Marshall *P & CEO*
Gary L. Schwass *EVP & CFO*
James D. Mitchell *VP*
Victor A. Roque *VP & GC*
Jack E. Saxer, Jr. *VP*
Donald J. Clayton *TRS*
Diane S. Eismont *SEC*
Joan S. Senchyshyn *AST-SEC*
Morgan K. O'Brien *CON*
Deborrah E. Beck *AST-CON*

Auditor: Deloitte & Touche LLP, Pittsburgh, PA

Affiliates/Divisions/Subsidiaries:

DQE Energy Services
Provider of energy solutions.

DQEnergy PARTNERS
Developer of strategic alliances.

Duquesne Enterprises
Investor in strategic businesses.

Allegheny Development Corp.
Provider of energy services.

EnSite L.P.
Provider of wireless monitoring & control services.

Exide Electronics Group, Inc.
Provider of non-interruptible power quality products, systems & services.

H Power Corp.
Fuel cell developer.

Property Ventures, Ltd.
Owner & developer of real estate.

Duquesne Light Co.
Electric utility.

Montauk
Provider of capital.

Total Employees........................3,810	**Regional Employees** 3,500
Year Established 1880	**Incorporated**..................................PA
Stock Symbol ....DQE	**Annual Meeting**........................April
Stock Exchange ....NYSE	**SIC Code** 4911
Stockholders 76,005
Shares Outstanding 77,281,441

Fiscal Year End	Total Revenues ($000)	Net Income/(Loss) ($000)	Total Assets ($000)
12/31/96	1,225,195	179,138	4,638,992
12/31/95	1,220,162	170,563	4,458,843
12/31/94	1,223,910	156,816	4,427,005
12/31/93	1,183,180	143,982	4,550,378

Executive Biography: David D. Marshall

Birth Date: 1952

Education:
Colby College, B.A.-Economics & Mathematics; Dartmouth College, M.B.A.

Career History:
Charles River Associates (Boston, MA); Resource Planning Associates (Washington, D.C.); Central Vermont Public Service Corp.; DQE, Inc., various positions 1985-89, VP 1989-95, EVP 1995-96, Interim P & CEO 1996-97, P & CEO 1997-present.

Directorships/Memberships/Activities:
Southwestern Pennsylvania Industrial Resource Center, DIR; United Way of Allegheny County, DIR; Penn's Southwest Assn., VP & SEC & TRU.

Dravo Corp.

One Oliver Plaza, Ste. 3600
Pittsburgh, PA 15222
County: Allegheny

Phone: (412) 566-3000
Fax: (412) 566-3116

Type of Business: Producer of lime.

Dravo is primarily a lime company operating principally in the United States. Its operations are carried on by a wholly owned subsidiary, Dravo Lime Co. (DLC). DLC's activities include the production of lime for utility, metallurgical, pulp and paper, municipal, construction, and miscellaneous chemical and industrial applications, as well as the development and marketing of related environmental technologies, products and services. DLC, which claims to be one of the nation's largest lime producers, owns and operates three integrated lime production facilities, with an annual quicklime production capacity of more than 3,300,000 tons. The Longview plant in Saginaw, AL, is an integrated facility that produces high calcium quicklime, and bulk and bagged hydrated lime from owned limestone reserves. The plant also produces dolomitic quicklime from limestone purchased from a nearby dolomitic stone quarry. Due to its material handling and storage capabilities and its ability to produce high calcium and dolomitic lime, the Longview plant is able to custom blend quicklime to its customers' chemical specifications. Also located at this facility is an aggregates processing plant that annually produces between 500,000 to 1,000,000 tons of aggregates for purchase by Martin Marietta Materials, Inc. The Black River plant in Butler, KY, is an integrated facility that produces Thiosorbic® quicklime, high calcium pebble and pulverized quicklime, and bulk and bagged hydrated lime. In excess of 60% of the plant's output is committed under long-term contracts to utility customers. The Maysville plant in Maysville, KY, produces Thiosorbic quicklime, which has a product chemistry ideally suited for removing sulfur dioxide from power plant stack gases. All of the plants output is committed under long-term contracts with utility companies in the Ohio Valley region. DLC's products are distributed through quicklime distribution terminals in Ft. Lauderdale, Sanford and Tampa, FL; Brunswick, GA; Porterfield, OH; and Aliquippa, Donora and Monaca, PA. In Baton Rouge, LA, DLC owns and operates a lime hydration and bagging facility from which quicklime, and bulk and bagged hydrated lime products are distributed. All of DLC's reserves are located on properties physically accessible for purposes of mining and processing limestone into lime.

Officers: Arthur E. Byrnes *CH*
Carl A. Gilbert *P & CEO*
Ernest F. Ladd III *EVP & CFO*
Marshall S. Johnson *VP-OPR & ENG*
John R. Major *VP-ADM*
James J. Puhala *VP, GC & SEC*
Richard E. Redlinger *VP-Corporate DEV & TRS*
Donald H. Stowe, Jr. *VP-SAL & Technology*
Larry J. Walker *VP & CON*

Auditor: KPMG Peat Marwick LLP, Pittsburgh, PA

Affiliates/Divisions/Subsidiaries:

Dravo Basic Materials Co., Inc. 100%

Dravo Natural Resources Co. 50%

Dravo Equipment Co. 100%

Dravo Lime Co. 100%

Dravo Natural Resources Co. 50%

Princeton Ridge, Inc. 100%

Total Employees 781		**Regional Employees** 80	
Year Established 1891		**Incorporated** ....PA	
Stock Symbol ....DRV		**Annual Meeting** ....April	
Stock Exchange ....NYSE		**SIC Code** 1400	
Stockholders 2,741			
Shares Outstanding 14,771,620			

Fiscal Year End	Total Revenues ($000)	Net Income/(Loss) ($000)	Total Assets ($000)
12/31/96	158,133	14,128	225,409
12/31/95	146,067	10,981	213,261
12/31/94	278,052	(10,557)	307,329
12/31/93	277,590	(177)	272,072

Executive Biography: Carl A. Gilbert

Birth Date: 1/9/42 **Birthplace:** Pittsburgh, PA

Spouse: Mary Ann **Children:** 4

Education:

U of Pittsburgh, B.S.-Mechanical Engineering 1970; U of Pittsburgh, M.S.-Industrial Engineering 1976.

Career History:

Dravo Lime Co., various positions 1973-80, VP-OPR & ENG 1980-83, P 1983-present; Dravo Corp., SVP -1994, COO 1994-95, P 1994-present, CEO 1995-present.

Directorships/Memberships/Activities:

The Assn. for the Development of Inland Navigation on America's Ohio Valley (Pittsburgh, PA), DIR; National Lime Assn., P & DIR; Assn. of Iron and Steel Engineers, MEM; Engineers Society of Western Pennsylvania, MEM; Liberty Mutual Insurance Co., MEM-Pittsburgh Advisory Board; Pennsylvania Economy League, Inc., MEM-Western Division Board of Governors; Society of Mining Engineers of AIME, MEM.

Education Management Corp.

300 Sixth Ave.
Pittsburgh, PA 15222
County: Allegheny

Phone: (412) 562-0900
Fax: (412) 562-0934
Internet Address: www.edumgt.com

Type of Business: Provider of proprietary post-secondary educational programs offering degree and non-degree programs.

Education Management claims that it is among the largest providers of proprietary post-secondary education in the United States based on student enrollments and revenues. The Company's schools have graduated more than 100,000 students. Through its operating units, the Art Institutes (AI), the New York Restaurant School (NYRS), the National Center for Paralegal Training (NCPT) and the National Center for Professional Development (NCPD), the Company offers associate's and bachelor's degree programs and non-degree programs in the areas of design, media arts, culinary arts, fashion and paralegal studies. Its main operating unit, AI, consists of 13 schools in 12 cities throughout the country. AI programs are designed to provide the knowledge and skills necessary for entry-level employment in various fields, including computer animation, multimedia, advertising design, culinary arts, graphic, interior and industrial design, video production and commercial photography. Those programs typically are completed in 18 to 27 months and culminate in an associate's degree. While five AIs currently offer bachelor's degree programs, the Company expects to introduce additional bachelor's degree programs at schools in states in which applicable regulations permit proprietary post-secondary institutions, such as AI, to offer such programs. The Company also offers a culinary arts curriculum at seven AIs. In addition, in August 1996, it acquired NYRS, a culinary arts and restaurant management school in New York, City, which offers an associate's degree program and certificate programs. The Company offers paralegal training at NCPT in Atlanta, GA, which offers certificate programs that are generally completed in four to nine months. NCPD maintains consulting relationships with eight colleges and universities to assist in the development, marketing and delivery of paralegal, nurse legal consultant and financial planner test preparation programs for recent college graduates and working adults. The Company intends to open or acquire additional schools and to expand its educational programs. For the spring quarter of fiscal 1997, enrollment at the Company's schools totaled 15,100, representing students from all 50 states and approximately 85 countries worldwide. On October 31, 1996, the Company completed its initial public stock offering.

Officers: Robert B. Knutson *CH & CEO*
Miryam L. Drucker *VCH*
Patrick T. DeCoursey *EVP*
Robert T. McDowell *SVP, CFO & TRS*
Human Resources: Robert A. Cypher

Auditor: Arthur Andersen LLP, Pittsburgh, PA

Affiliates/Divisions/Subsidiaries:

The Art Institutes International, Inc. 100%

The National Center for Paralegal Training, Inc. 100%
Atlanta, GA

The National Center for Professional Development 100%

The New York Restaurant School 100%
New York, NY

Total Employees...........................2,223	**Regional Employees** 361
Year Established 1962	**Incorporated**..................................PA
Stock Symbol...........................EDMC	**Annual Meeting**..................October
Stock Exchange................NASDAQ	**SIC Code**......................................8299
Stockholders 3,500		
Shares Outstanding 14,382,342		

Fiscal Year End	Total Revenues ($000)	Net Income/(Loss) ($000)	Total Assets ($000)
6/30/96	147,863	5,920	101,412
6/30/95	131,227	1,513	102,303
6/30/94	122,549	(1,702)	78,527
6/30/93	117,234	(1,174)	85,091

Executive Biography: Robert B. Knutson

Birth Date: 1934
Spouse: Miryam
Education:
U of Michigan, B.A. Economics 1956.

Career History:
U. S. Air Force, Pilot 1957-62; Morgan Guaranty Trust Co. of New York, various positions including lending officer & VP 1962-69; Drexel Harriman Ripley, VP-Corporate Acquisitions 1969-70; Education Management Corp., P 1971-86, CH & CEO 1986-present.

Directorships/Memberships/Activities:
Western Pennsylvania Conservancy, DIR.

Equitable Resources, Inc.

420 Blvd. of the Allies
Pittsburgh, PA 15219
County: Allegheny

Phone: (412) 261-3000
Fax: (412) 553-5914
Internet Address: www.eri2000.com

Type of Business: Developer, producer and marketer of natural gas, oil and related products and services.

Equitable Resources, through its subsidiaries, is engaged primarily in the exploration, development, production, purchase, transmission, storage, distribution and marketing of natural gas and electricity; extraction of natural gas liquids; exploration, development, production and sale of oil; contract drilling; cogeneration development; water efficiency and program development; central facility plant operations; and performance contracting for commercial, industrial and institutional customers and various government facilities. The Company's three business segments consist of supply and logistics, utilities and services. The supply and logistics segment's activities include the exploration and production of natural gas and oil, trading of natural gas and electricity, extraction and sale of natural gas liquids, underground storage and intrastate transportation. Exploration and production functions are conducted by Equitable Resources Energy Co. (EREC) through its divisions and Equitable Resources (Canada) Ltd. EREC's exploration and production activities are primarily in the Appalachian area where it explores for, develops, produces and sells natural gas and oil, extracts and markets natural gas liquids, and performs contract drilling and well maintenance services. EREC also owns an interest in two natural gas liquids plants in Texas. In Louisiana, Louisiana Intrastate Gas Co. L.L.C. provides intrastate transportation of gas and extracts and markets natural gas liquids; and Equitable Storage Co. L.L.C. provides underground gas storage services. The supply and logistics segment's operations also include nationwide natural gas marketing, supply, peak shaving and transportation arrangements, and electricity marketing conducted by Equitable Power Services Co. The utilities segment's activities comprise distribution operations by Equitable Gas Co. (EGC), the Company's state-regulated local distribution company, and transmission operations conducted by three FERC-regulated gas pipelines: Equitrans, L.P., Kentucky West Virginia Gas Co., L.L.C. and Nora Transmission Co. The territory served by EGC encompasses prinicipally the City of Pittsburgh and surrounding municipalities in southwestern Pennsylvania, a few municipalities in northern West Virginia and field line sales in eastern Kentucky. The services segment was created in 1996 and functions in a non-regulated environment. Its activities include natural gas brokering, resource management, energy consulting and engineering services such as energy use analysis, customized energy systems, financing, facility management, and energy procurement and management.

Officers: Frederick H. Abrew *P & CEO*
A. Mark Abramovic *SVP & CFO*

E

R. Gerald Bennett *SVP*
John C. Gongas, Jr. *SVP*
Edward J. Meyer *SVP*
Gregory R. Spencer *SVP & CAO*
Craig G. Goodman *VP-Regulatory Affairs & Public Policy*
Audrey C. Moeller *VP & SEC*
Johanna G. O'Loughlin *VP & GC*
Richard D. Spencer *VP-Planning & CIO*
Jeffrey C. Swoveland *VP-FIN & TRS*
Philip P. Conti *AST-TRS-FIN*
Elliot M. Gill *AST-SEC*
Janice A. Haas *AST-SEC*

Human Resources: Sylvia Griffin
Purchasing Director: Harold King
Auditor: Ernst & Young LLP, Pittsburgh, PA
Affiliates/Divisions/Subsidiaries:

Equitable Gas Co. 100%
Public utility engaged in the purchase, distribution, marketing &
transportation of natural gas.

Equitable Power Services Co. 100%
Provider of supply & logistics services.

Equitable Resources (Canada) Ltd. 100%
Explorer & producer of gas & oil.

Equitable Resources Energy Co. 100%
Explorer & producer of gas & oil.

Equitable Storage Co. L.L.C. 100%
Erath, LA
Provider of underground gas storage services.

Equitrans, L.P. 100%
Pittsburgh, PA
Gas pipeline.

ERI Services, Inc. 100%
Pittsburgh, PA
Provider of customized energy solutions.

Kentucky West Virginia Gas Co., L.L.C. 100%
Prestonsburg, KY
Gas pipeline.

Louisiana Intrastate Gas Co. L.L.C. 100%
Pineville, LA
Provider of intrastate transportation of gas & extracts.

Nora Transmission Co. 100%
Gas pipeline.

Three Rivers Pipeline Corp. 100%

Total Employees..........................2,109		**Regional Employees** 1,100	
Year Established 1888		**Incorporated**..................................PA	
Stock Symbol..............................EQT		**Annual Meeting**.........................May	
Stock Exchange ....NYSE		**SIC Code** 1311	

Stockholders 7,735
Shares Outstanding 35,519,102

Fiscal Year End	Total Revenues ($000)	Net Income/(Loss) ($000)	Total Assets ($000)
12/31/96	1,861,799	59,379	2,096,299
12/31/95	1,425,990	1,548	1,963,313
12/31/94	1,397,280	60,729	2,019,122
12/31/93	1,094,794	73,455	1,946,907

Executive Biography: Frederick H. Abrew

Birth Date: 9/19/37
Spouse: Betty   **Children:** 3

Education:
Manhattan College, B.S.-Civil Engineering.

Career History:
Equitable Resources, Inc., Operating MGR 1980-81, VP-OPR 1981-84, VP-Utility
OPR 1984-, P-Equitable Gas Co. 1986-88, VP-Utility Services 1987-88, EVP-
Utility Services 1988-91, EVP 1991-93, COO 1992-94, P 1993-present, CEO 1995-
present.

Directorships/Memberships/Activities:
American Gas Assn., DIR; Corporate Campaign Comm., CH; Greater Pittsburgh
Chamber of Commerce, DIR; River City Brass Band, DIR; Salvation Army of
Western Pennsylvania, DIR; Institute of Gas Technology Board of Trustees,
MEM; National Petroleum Council, MEM; National Society of Professional
Engineers, MEM; Pennsylvania Gas Assn., MEM; Pennsylvania Society of
Professional Engineers, MEM; Pittsburgh Society of Professional Engineers,
MEM; Pittsburgh Symphony Society, MEM-Development Comm.; West Virginia
Oil and Natural Gas Assn., MEM; Carlow Coll., TRU.

Fidelity Bancorp, Inc.

F

1009 Perry Hwy.
Pittsburgh, PA 15237
County: Allegheny

Phone: (412) 367-3300
Fax: (412) 364-6504
Internet Address: www.fidelitybk.com

Type of Business: Bank holding company.

Fidelity Bancorp was organized to operate principally as a holding company for its wholly owned subsidiary, Fidelity Bank PaSB (Bank). The Bank is a Pennsylvania-chartered stock savings bank conducting business through eight offices located in Allegheny and Butler Counties in Pennsylvania. The Bank's principal business consists of attracting deposits from the general public and investing such deposits primarily in single-family (one-to-four family) residential loans, mortgage-backed securities and, to a lesser extent, commercial real estate loans in the Bank's primary market area. In recent years, the Bank has been an active originator of home equity and consumer loans and, to a limited extent, has originated loans to small businesses in its immediate market area. Deposits in the Bank are insured by the Savings Assn. Insurance Fund of the Federal Deposit Insurance Corp. In addition to the Bank's main office and corporate headquarters located at the above address, it operates branch offices in Allison Park, Pittsburgh (Bloomfield, Brighton Road, Mt. Lebanon (2) and Northway) and Zelienople, PA.

Officers: William L. Windisch *P & CEO*
Michael A. Mooney *VP*
Richard G. Spencer *VP, CFO & TRS*
Sandra L. Graham *SEC*
Lisa L. Griffith *AST-TRS*

Human Resources: Lisa M. Cline *VP-Human Resources & Administrative Services, & AST-SEC*

Auditor: KPMG Peat Marwick LLP, Pittsburgh, PA

Affiliates/Divisions/Subsidiaries:

Fidelity Bank PaSB 100%

Total Employees............................120
Year Established 1927
Stock Symbol.............................FSBI
Stock Exchange................NASDAQ
Stockholders 650
Shares Outstanding 1,380,977

Regional Employees 120
Incorporated..................................PA
Annual Meeting................February
SIC Code......................................6712

Fiscal Year End	Total Revenues ($000)	Net Income/(Loss) ($000)	Total Assets ($000)
9/30/96	21,718	1,317	317,874
9/30/95	19,651	1,515	281,810
9/30/94	18,279	2,372	273,564
9/30/93	19,892	2,194	267,205

Executive Biography: William L. Windisch

Birth Date: 11/11/32   **Birthplace:** Pittsburgh, PA
Spouse: Margaret   **Children:** 4

Career History:
Fidelity Savings Bank, various positions 1955-present including P & CEO;
Fidelity Bancorp, Inc., P & CEO -present.

Directorships/Memberships/Activities:
North Boroughs Rotary Club, MEM; Pittsburgh Sierra Club, MEM.

First Carnegie Deposit

242 E. Main St.
Carnegie, PA 15106
County: Allegheny

Phone: (412) 276-2424
Fax: (412) 276-2424

Type of Business: Federally chartered mutual savings bank.

First Carnegie Deposit is a federally chartered mutual savings bank which conducts business from its main office at the above address, and two branch offices, one each in McKees Rocks and Washington, PA. The Bank conducts a non-traditional savings institution business, attracting deposit accounts from the general public and using these deposits, together with other funds, primarily to invest in mortgage-backed and other investment securities, Small Business Administration and other federal agency guaranteed real estate and commercial loans, and to originate and purchase one- to four-family mortgage loans. The Bank is primarily a purchaser of loans and mortgage backed securities, not an originator of loans. Deposits at the Bank are insured up to the legal maximum by the Savings Assn. Insurance Fund as administered by the Federal Deposit Insurance Corp. The Bank was formerly known as First Federal Savings and Loan Assn. of Carnegie. On April 4, 1997, the Bank completed its initial public stock offering. Skibo Bancshares, M. H. C., which is also located at the above address, owns approximately 55% of the Bank's common stock.

Officers: John C. Burne *CH*
               Walter G. Kelly *P & CEO*
               Alexander J. Senules *VP & SEC*
               Carol A. Gilbert *COO, CFO & TRS*

Auditor: KPMG Peat Marwick LLP, Pittsburgh, PA
Affiliates/Divisions/Subsidiaries:

First Carnegie Deposit 100%

Carnegie Federal Funding Corp., Inc. 100%
Issuer & servicer of CMO's.

F

Fedcar, Inc. 100%
Collector of insurance commissions.

Total Employees............................21	**Regional Employees** 21		
Year Established 1924	**Incorporated**..................................PA		
Stock Symbol ....SKBO	**Annual Meeting**.......................July		
Stock Exchange....................NSCap	**SIC Code**..................................6035		
Stockholders 605			
Shares Outstanding 2,300,000			

Fiscal Year End	Total Revenues ($000)	Net Income/(Loss) ($000)	Total Assets ($000)
3/31/96	8,984	1,047	117,814
3/31/95	8,028	1,056	120,309
3/31/94	8,013	1,314	119,535
3/31/93	9,048	1,684	118,026

Executive Biography: Walter G. Kelly

Birth Date: 2/1/46   **Birthplace:** Pittsburgh, PA
Spouse: Bobbie   **Children:** 3

Education:
Duquesne U, B.A.-Economics & Political Science; Carnegie Mellon U, Masters-Management.

Career History:
First Federal Savings and Loan Assn. of Carnegie, various positions 1976-81, CEO 1981-present, P 1993-present; Skibo Bancshares, M. H. C., P & CEO 1997-present.

Directorships/Memberships/Activities:
Chartier Valley Industrial Development Authority, CH.

FORE Systems, Inc.

174 Thorn Hill Rd.
Warrendale, PA 15086
County: Allegheny

Phone: (412) 772-6600
Fax: (412) 772-6500
Internet Address: www.fore.com

Type of Business: Designer, developer, manufacturer and marketer of networking products based on Asynchronous Transfer Mode technology.

FORE Systems designs, develops, manufactures and markets high-performance networking products based on Asynchronous Transfer Mode (ATM) technology. ATM is a communications technology that provides a dramatic increase in network speed and capacity—or bandwidth—compared to conventional network technologies. ATM improves the performance of network applications and also enables new applications that integrate video, audio and data communications. The Company believes that it currently offers the most comprehensive ATM product line available, including ForeRunner® ATM switches and adapter cards, PowerHub® LAN switches for ATM connectivity, CellPath™ WAN multiplexing products for WAN access, ForeThought™ inter-networking software and ForeView® network management software. The Company's networking products enable customers to connect computers to form clusters, workgroups and LANs, to build backbones for enterprise-wide networks and to provide transparent, end-to-end LAN and WAN connectivity. Its networking products are designed to be both flexible and scalable, allowing customers to increase the capacity and extend the utility of their existing networks or to install a new ATM-based network. In response to evolving market needs, the Company has made, and may continue to make, acquisitions that add products and technologies and enhance its ability to offer customers a smooth migration path to ATM. As of March 31, 1997, the Company had delivered networking solutions to more than 4,000 customers, including Fortune 500 companies, telecommunications service providers, government agencies, research institutions and universities. Its products are sold to end users via a direct sales force, independent distributors and third-party channel distributors. As of March 31, 1997, the Company had over 100 independent distributors in the United States and 65 countries around the world. International sales accounted for approximately 37% of its revenue in fiscal 1997. During that same period, the Company invested approximately 13% of its revenue into research and development. On May 23, 1994, the Company completed its initial public stock offering.

Special Designations: FB_{200}

Officers: Eric C. Cooper, Ph.D. *CH & CEO*
Onat Menzilcioglu *P*
Thomas J. Gill *COO & CFO*
Francois J. Bitz *VP-ENG*
Michael I. Green *VP-Worldwide SAL*
Ron McKenzie *VP-MKT*
Robert D. Sansom *VP-ENG & SEC*

Human Resources: Tom Armour *VP-Human Resources*
John Lawton *DIR-Human Resources*

Auditor: Price Waterhouse LLP, Pittsburgh, PA
General Counsel: Morgan, Lewis & Bockius LLP, Pittsburgh, PA

Total Employees	1,400	**Regional Employees**	830
Year Established	1990	**Incorporated**	DE
Stock Symbol	FORE	**Annual Meeting**	July
Stock Exchange	NASDAQ	**SIC Code**	3577
Stockholders			764
Shares Outstanding			89,248,403

Fiscal Year End	Total Revenues ($000)	Net Income/(Loss) ($000)	Total Assets ($000)
3/31/96	235,189	9,737	424,362
3/31/95	106,188	12,860	131,482
3/31/94	39,340	3,678	59,026
3/31/93	12,527	(1,367)	14,794

Executive Biography: Eric C. Cooper, Ph.D.

Birth Date: 1/10/59   **Birthplace:** Brooklyn, NY
Spouse: Naomi   **Children:** 4

Education:
Harvard U, B.A.-Math 1980; U of California (Berkeley, CA), Ph.D.-Computer Science 1985.

Career History:
Carnegie Mellon U, MEM-Computer Science Faculty 1985-90; FORE Systems, Inc., C-FND, P 1990-94, CH & CEO 1990-present.

Directorships/Memberships/Activities:
Pittsburgh High Technology Council, DIR.

Foster Co., L. B.

415 Holiday Dr.
Pittsburgh, PA 15220
County: Allegheny

Phone: (412) 928-3400
Fax: (412) 928-7891
Internet Address: www.lbfoster.com

Type of Business: Manufacturer, fabricator and distributor of rail and track accessories, construction and highway products, and tubular products.

L. B. Foster is engaged in the manufacture, fabrication and distribution of rail and trackwork, piling, pile driving equipment, highway products and tubular products. The Company classifies its activities into three business segments. The rail products segment provides a full line of new and used rail, trackwork and accessories to railroads, mines and industry. It also designs and produces insulated rail joints, power rail, track fasteners, catenary systems, coverboards and special accessories for mass transit and other rail systems. The construction products segment sells and rents steel sheet piling and H-bearing pile for foundation and earth retention requirements, and pile driving equipment and accessories for driving piling. It also supplies bridge decking, expansion joints, overhead sign structures and other products for highway construction and repair. The tubular products segment supplies pipe and pipe coatings for pipelines and utilities. It also manufactures spiralweld pipe for water transmission lines, foundation piling, slurry lines and many other applications. In addition, this segment produces pipe-related products for special markets, including water wells and irrigation.

The Company generally markets its products directly in all major industrial areas of the United States through a national sales force. It maintains 10 sales offices and 14 plants or warehouses nationwide. In 1996, the Company derived 46% of its sales from rail products, 32% from construction products and 22% from tubular products. During that same period, approximately 7% of the Company's sales were from exports.

Officers: James W. Wilcock *CH*
Lee B. Foster II *P & CEO*
Dean A. Frenz *SVP-Rail Products*
Stan L. Hasselbusch *SVP-Construction & Tubular Products*
Roger F. Nejes *SVP-FIN & ADM, & CFO*
Henry M. Ortwein, Jr. *GVP-Rail MFG Products*
Anthony G. Cipicchio *VP-OPR*
William S. Cook, Jr. *VP-Strategic Planning & Acquisitions*
Paul V. Dean *VP-Piling Products*
Samuel K. Fisher *VP-Relay Rail*
David L. Minor *VP & TRS*
John L. Rice *VP-Rail Distribution*
Robert W. Sigle *VP-Tubular Products*
David L. Voltz *VP, GC & SEC*
Donald F. Vukmanic *VP & CON*

Human Resources: Linda M. Terpenning *VP-Human Resources*
Auditor: Ernst & Young LLP, Pittsburgh, PA
Affiliates/Divisions/Subsidiaries:

Allegheny Rail Products Division
Producer of insulated rail joints for railroads & industry.

Fabricated Products Division
Supplier of rail & transit-related products.

Fosterweld Division
Producer of coated, lined & fabricated water transmission pipelines.

Midwest Steel Division
Pomeroy, OH
Producer of specialty trackwork for mining & industrial markets.

Transit Products Division
Supplier of products for mass transit systems.

Total Employees............................526			
Year Established.........................1902	**Incorporated**..................................DE		
Stock Symbol..........................FSTRA	**Annual Meeting**........................May		
Stock Exchange................NASDAQ	**SIC Code**.....................................5051		
Stockholders...1,249			
Shares Outstanding..10,162,738			

Fiscal Year End	Total Revenues ($000)	Net Income/(Loss) ($000)	Total Assets ($000)
12/31/96	243,071	3,858	123,398
12/31/95	264,985	4,824	124,423
12/31/94	234,262	5,440	122,585
12/31/93	212,291	1,569	108,137

Executive Biography: Lee B. Foster II

Birth Date: 3/47
Children: 2

Education:
Cornell U; U of Pittsburgh, M.S.-Anthropology; U of Pittsburgh, M.A.-English 1972.

Career History:
L. B. Foster Co., various positions 1974-80, MGR-Latin American District 1980-85, MGR-INTL Division 1986-87, MGR-Houston District 1987, VP-Tubular Products 1987-89, EVP-OPR 1989-90, P & CEO 1990-present; Foster Industries, Inc., AST-SEC 1989-present.

Directorships/Memberships/Activities:
Boy Scouts of America, DIR; The Carnegie, DIR; Combined Health Appeal, DIR; Fostin Capital Corp., DIR; Health Education Center, DIR; Jewish Healthcare Foundation, DIR; Planned Parenthood, DIR.

GA Financial, Inc.

4750 Clairton Blvd.
Pittsburgh, PA 15236
County: Allegheny

Phone: (412) 882-9946
Fax: (412) 882-8580
Internet Address: www.gaf.com

Type of Business: Savings and loan holding company.

GA Financial is a unitary savings and loan holding company for Great American Federal Savings and Loan Assn. (Association). On March 25, 1996, the Association completed its conversion from a federally chartered mutual savings and loan association to a stock form of ownership, while simultaneously, the Company issued 8,900,000 shares of common stock, utilizing a portion of the net proceeds to acquire all of the outstanding stock of the Association. Currently, other than investing in various securities, the Company does not directly transact any material business other than through the Association. The Association's principal business is to operate a customer-oriented savings and loan association. It attracts retail deposits from the general public and invests those funds mostly in fixed-rate one- to four-family owner-occupied mortgage loans, consumer loans, and investment, mortgage-backed and mortgage-related securities. To a lesser extent, the Association invests in construction and development loans, multi-family loans and commercial real estate loans. Its revenues are derived mostly from interest on mortgage loans, and interest and dividends on investment, mortgage-backed and mortgage-related securities and, to a much lesser extent, short-term investments and other fees and service charges. The Association's sources of funds include retail deposits, principal and interest repayments on loans, mort-gage-related securities and investments, Federal Home Loan Bank of Pittsburgh advances, and sales of loans and investments. The Association's primary market area is the areas surrounding its branch offices while its lending activities include areas throughout Allegheny, Beaver, Butler, Washington and Westmoreland Counties, PA. In addition to its principal office located at the above address, the Association operates branch offices in Clairton, Elizabeth, Forest Hills, Homestead, McKeesport, Munhall, North Huntingdon, Pittsburgh and White Oak, PA. It also operates three branch offices located in Wal-Mart stores in Belle Vernon, North Fayette Township and West Mifflin, PA.

Officers: John M. Kish *CH & CEO*
John G. Micenko *P; P & CEO-Great American Federal Savings and Loan Assn.*
Raymond G. Suchta *CFO & TRS; VP & CFO-Great American Federal Savings and Loan Assn.*
Wayne A. Callen *VP-Data Processing-Great American Federal Savings and Loan Assn.*
Aaron T. Flaitz, Jr. *VP & AST-SEC-Great American Federal Savings and Loan Assn.*
Andrew R. Getsy *VP & TRS-Great American Federal Savings and Loan Assn.*
Eugene G. Hreha *VP-MKT-Great American Federal Savings and Loan Assn.*
Norman A. Litterini *VP-Lending-Great American Federal Savings and Loan Assn.*
Judith A. Stoeckle *VP & Systems Coordinator-Great American Federal Savings and Loan Assn.*

Human Resources: Lawrence A. Michael *SEC; VP & SEC-Great American Federal Savings and Loan Assn.*

Auditor: Coopers & Lybrand L.L.P., Pittsburgh, PA

Affiliates/Divisions/Subsidiaries:

Great American Federal Savings and Loan Assn. 100%
Federally chartered savings & loan association.

Great American Financial Services, Inc. 100%
Inactive.

Total Employees............................220	**Regional Employees** 220
Year Established 1914	**Incorporated** ....DE
Stock Symbol.............................GAF	**Annual Meeting**.......................April
Stock Exchange..........................ASE	**SIC Code**.....................................6035
Stockholders 1,905	
Shares Outstanding 8,455,000	

Fiscal Year End	Total Revenues ($000)	Net Income/(Loss) ($000)	Total Assets ($000)
12/31/96	43,810	5,602	634,048
12/31/95	33,255	2,820	521,398
12/31/94	31,905	3,260	467,655
12/31/93	36,715	5,312	486,278

Executive Biography: John M. Kish

Birth Date: 1946 **Birthplace:** Pittsburgh, PA
Spouse: Jeane **Children:** 4

Education:
Westminster College, B.A. 1967; Duquesne U, J.D. 1972.

Career History:
Kish, Kish & Yarsky, PTR; GA Financial, Inc., CH 1990-present, CEO -present.

General Nutrition Cos., Inc.

300 Sixth Ave.
Pittsburgh, PA 15222
County: Allegheny

Phone: (412) 288-4600
Fax: (412) 288-2074

Type of Business: Retailer of vitamin and mineral supplements, sports nutrition products and herbs, and provider of personal care and other health-related products.

General Nutrition, collectively with its subsidiaries, claims to be the only nationwide specialty retailer of vitamin and mineral supplements, sports nutrition products and herbs, and a leading provider of personal care and other health-related products. The Company's marketing emphasizes high-margin, value-added vitamin and mineral supplements, sports nutrition products and herbs sold under its proprietary brands and other nationally recognized third-party brand names. The Company operates in three distinct business segments: retail, franchising and manufacturing. Domestically, the Company's products are sold through 2,809 General Nutrition Centers and GNC Live Well stores, of which 1,760 are owned and operated by the Company and 1,049 are franchised. It also generates retail revenue from 73 stores operating under various names, including Amphora™, Natures Food Centres® and Nature's Fresh™. Internationally, the Company operates 20 Health and Diet Centres and nine General Nutrition Centres in the United Kingdom, 10 General Nutrition Centres in Canada and holds a controlling interest in one store in New Zealand. In addition, there are 125 operating franchise stores in 15 different countries. The Company has actively been engaged in opening new stores as well as acquisitions of existing locations. It expects to continue its store expansion program for both Company-owned and franchised locations. In franchising, as of February 1, 1997, there were 218 domestic and one international franchises awarded that had not yet opened and development agreements to open 41 and 373 franchise stores in domestic and international markets, respectively. The Company claims that its main manufacturing plant, located in Greenville, SC, is one of the largest vitamin and mineral supplement manufacturing facilities in the United States. The Company's three distribution centers are located in Phoenix, AZ; Atlanta, GA; and Pittsburgh, PA.

Officers: Jerry D. Horn *CH*
William E. Watts *P & CEO*
Louis Mancini *P-General Nutrition Corp.*
Edwin J. Kozlowski *EVP & CFO*
John A. DiCecco *SVP-Logistics/MFG-General Nutrition, Inc.*
David R. Heilman *VP-Strategic Planning & Corporate DEV*
Curtis J. Larrimer *VP & CON*
James M. Sander *VP-Law, CLO & SEC*
J. Kenneth Fox *TRS*
Gregory T. Horn *Chief MKT Officer; SVP-General Nutrition Corp.*

Auditor: Deloitte & Touche LLP, Pittsburgh, PA
Affiliates/Divisions/Subsidiaries:

General Nutrition Corp. 100%

General Nutrition, Inc. 100%

General Nutrition Investment Co. 100%

GNC (U.K.) Holding Co. 100%

Total Employees......................10,906
Year Established.........................1935   **Incorporated**................................DE
Stock Symbol............................GNCI   **Annual Meeting**........................June
Stock Exchange................NASDAQ   **SIC Code**....................................5499
Stockholders...16,000+
Shares Outstanding..80,252,080

Fiscal Year End	Total Revenues ($000)	Net Income/(Loss) ($000)	Total Assets ($000)
2/1/97	990,845	3,935	779,355
2/3/96	845,952	69,146	682,851
2/4/95	672,945	37,194	626,571
2/5/94	546,253	23,469	466,726

Executive Biography: William E. Watts

Birth Date: 1952

Education:
State U of New York (Buffalo), B.A.-Social Science 1974.

Career History:
General Nutrition, Inc., DIR-Retail OPR, VP-Retail OPR 1984-85, SVP-Retailing 1985-88, SVP 1988, P 1988-present, CEO 1990-present; General Nutrition Cos., Inc., P & CEO 1991-present.

Directorships/Memberships/Activities:
Allegheny Club, MEM; Duquesne Club, MEM; National Retail Federation, MEM; Pittsburgh Club, MEM; Rivers Club, MEM; Sewickley Heights Golf Club, MEM; Westminster College, TRU.

Heinz Co., H. J.

USX Tower, 600 Grant St.
P.O. Box 57, Pittsburgh, PA 15230
Pittsburgh, PA 15219
County: Allegheny

Phone: (412) 456-5700
Fax: (412) 456-6128
Internet Address: www.hjheinz.com

Type of Business: Manufacturer and marketer of processed food products.

H. J. Heinz is a global provider of processed food products and nutritional services. The Company offers more than 4,000 products to consumers in over 200 countries and territories. Its products include ketchup and sauces/condiments, pet food, tuna and other seafood products, baby food, frozen potato products, soup (canned and frozen), lower-calorie products (frozen entrees, frozen desserts, frozen breakfasts, dairy and other products), beans, full calorie frozen dinners and entrees, pasta, coated products, bakery products, chicken, vegetables (frozen and canned), edible oils, margarine/shortening, vinegar, pickles, juices and other processed food products. The Company operates principally in one segment— processed food products—which represents more than 90% of consolidated sales. It also operates and franchises weight control classes and operates other related programs and activities. While many of the Company's products are marketed under the Heinz trademark, other important trademarks include Star-Kist for tuna products, 9-Lives for cat foods, Kibbles N' Bits and Ken-L-Ration for dog foods, Ore-Ida for frozen potato products, Budget Gourmet for frozen entrees and dinners, Earth's Best for baby food, Rosetto and Domani for frozen pasta products, and Bagel Bites for pizza snack products. Weight Watchers is used in numerous countries in conjunction with owned and franchised weight control classes, programs, related activities and certain food products. Each week, more than one million people attend Weight Watchers meetings. The Company operates 42 food processing plants in the United States and its possessions, as well as 62 food processing plants in foreign countries. It also leases two can-making factories in the United States. The Company's products are sold through its own sales force and through independent brokers and agents to chain, wholesale, cooperative and independent grocery accounts, to pharmacies, to food service distributors and to institutions, including hotels, restaurants and certain government agencies. In fiscal 1995, the Company invested $1.2 billion in acquisitions which included the purchase of Quaker Oats' North American Pet Foods division. In fiscal 1996, international sales accounted for 43% of the Company's revenue.

Recent Events: On March 14, 1997, the Company announced its largest ever reorganization plan designed to strengthen the Company's six core businesses and improve its profitability and global growth. Brand-building, increasing media spending by 30% over two years, overseas expansion, efficient consumer response, value-added manufacturing, price-based costing and working capital savings are important elements of the plan to make the Company one of the three preeminent branded food companies in the world. As part of the plan, the Company will close or sell at least 25 plants throughout the world while investing heavily to upgrade and build plants to add capacity in fast-growing markets. Excluding the sale of plants and businesses, the global workforce will be reduced by approximately 2,500.

Special Designations: FB_{500} FT_{500} IW_{1000}

Officers: Anthony J. F. O'Reilly, Ph.D. *CH & CEO*
Joseph J. Bogdanovich *VCH*
William R. Johnson *P & COO*
Luigi Ribolla *EVP; P-Heinz Europe*
William C. Springer *EVP-The Americas*
David R. Williams *EVP*
Lawrence J. McCabe *SVP & GC*
Paul F. Renne *SVP-FIN, TRS & CFO*
George C. Greer *VP-Organization DEV & ADM*
Walter G. Schmid *VP*
D. Edward I. Smyth *VP-Corporate Affairs*
John Cranshaw *Area VP-Pacific Rim*
Ed McMenamin *CON*
Benjamin E. Thomas, Jr. *SEC & Associate GC*

Human Resources: Gary D. Matson
Auditor: Coopers & Lybrand L.L.P., Pittsburgh, PA
Affiliates/Divisions/Subsidiaries:

AIAL (Arimpex S.r.l. Industrie Alimentari)
Commessaggio, Italy

Alimentos Heinz C.A.
Caracas, Venezuela
Producer of baby food, bouillon, drink mixes, ketchup, sauces, soups & vinegar.

Cairo Food Industries SAE
Cairo, Egypt
Producer of ketchup & tomato paste.

COPAIS Food & Beverage Co. S.A.
Athens, Greece

Producer of fruit concentrates, fruit dices, fruit halves, tomato paste & tomato products.

Crestar Food Products, Inc.
Brentwood, TN
Producer of pre-made pizza, pizza components & pizza crusts.

Custom Foods Ltd.
Dundalk, Ireland

Dega S.r.l.
Mori, Italy

Fattoria Scaldasole S.p.A.
Monguzzo, Italy
Processor of organic yogurts, milks & juices.

H. J. Heinz Central Eastern Europe
Pittsburgh, PA

> H. J. Heinz Co. CIS
> Moscow, Russia
> Producer of baby food & infant formula.

> Heinz Kecskemeti Konzervgyar RT
> Kecskemet, Hungary
> Producer of baby food & juices.

> Heinz Polska Sp
> Warsaw, Poland

> PMV/Zabreh
> Zabreh, Czech Republic
> Producer of formulas & dairy products.

H. J. Heinz Co. (Ireland) Ltd.
Dublin, Ireland
Marketer in Republic & North of Ireland.

H. J. Heinz Co., Ltd.
Hayes, Middlesex, England
Producer of baby food, baked beans, ketchup, pasta & soups.

H. J. Heinz Co. of Canada Ltd.
North York, Ontario, Canada
Producer of baby food & juices, cat & dog food, mustard, vinegar & other food products.

Heinz Bakery Products
Mississauga, Ontario, Canada
Producer of breads & rolls, cakes, cookies, muffins, puff pastry &
other food products.

Omstead Foods Ltd.
Wheatley, Ontario, Canada
Producer of breaded & battered cheese, fish, onion rings & other
food products.

Shady Maple Farm Ltd.
LaGuadeloupe, Quebec, Canada
Producer of maple syrup.

H. J. Heinz Northern Europe
Hayes, Middlesex, England

Ets. Paul Paulet S.A.
Douarnenez, France
Producer of canned fish, salads & seafoods.

H. J. Heinz B.V.
Elst, Gelderland, The Netherlands

H. J. Heinz Branch Belgium
Brussels, Belgium

H. J. Heinz GmbH
Cologne, Germany

H. J. Heinz S.A.R.L.
Paris, France

IDAL (Industrias de Alimentacao, Lda.) Fish Division
Lisbon, Portugal

Indian Ocean Tuna Ltd.
Victoria, Mahe, Seychelles

Pioneer Food Cannery Ltd.
Tema, Ghana

H. J. Heinz Pacific Rim

H. J. Heinz Australia Ltd.
Doveton, Victoria, Australia
Producer of baby food, pickles, salad dressings, spaghetti & other
food products.

Heinz Japan Ltd.
Tokyo, Japan
Producer of canned & retort curries, ketchup, pet food, soups & other food products.

Heinz Win Chance Ltd.
Bangkok, Thailand
Producer of baby cereal, chili sauce, ketchup & oyster sauce.

Heinz-UFE Ltd.
Guangzhou, People's Republic of China
Producer of cereals for infants & children, & extruded snacks.

Seoul-Heinz Ltd.
Seoul, South Korea
Producer of chocolate, ketchup, margarine, mayonnaise & shortening.

Wattie's Ltd.
Auckland, New Zealand
Producer of animal feeds, baby food, canned goods & other food products.

H. J. Heinz Southern Africa
Johannesburg, South Africa

Chegutu Canners (Pvt) Ltd.
Chegutu, Zimbabwe
Producer of canned beans, soups & vegetables, & ketchup.

H. J. Heinz (Botswana) (Proprietary) Ltd.
Gaborone, Botswana
Producer of soap & refiner of vegetable oils.

Heinz Frozen Foods (Pty) Ltd.
Klerksdorp, South Africa

Heinz South Africa (Pty) Ltd.
Johannesburg, South Africa

Kgalagadi Soap Industries (Pty) Ltd.
Gaborone, Botswana
Producer of dish washing liquid, & laundry & toilet soap.

Olivine Industries (Private) Ltd.
Harare, Zimbabwe
Producer of baker's fat, candles, glycerine, protein meals, soaps & other food products.

Refined Oil Products (Pty) Ltd.
Gaborone, Botswana
Refiner of vegetable oils.

Heinz Iberica, S.A.
Madrid, Spain
Producer of anchovies, canned vegetables, mayonnaise, sauces &
other food products.

Heinz India Private Ltd.
Bombay, India
Producer of infant feeding products, medicated powders & nutrition-
al drinks.

Heinz U.S.A.
Pittsburgh, PA
Producer of baby food & juices, condiments, gravy, ketchup & other
food products.

IDAL (Industrias de Alimentacao, Lda.)
Lisbon, Portugal
Producer of chili sauce, ketchup, pizza sauce, tomato paste & other
food products.

Mareblu S.r.l.
Milan, Italy

Ore-Ida Foods, Inc.
Bosie, ID
Producer of cheese products, frozen baked goods, potato products &
other food products.

PLADA S.p.A. (Plasmon Dietetici Alimentari S.p.A.)
Milan, Italy
Producer of infant formulas, isotonic drinks, low-calorie drinks &
other food products.

Star-Kist Foods, Inc.
Newport, KY
Producer of canned cat & dog food, canned tuna, fish meal & other
food products.

Star-Kist Caribe, Inc.
Mayaguez, Puerto Rico
Producer of canned fish.

H

Star-Kist Samoa, Inc.
Pago Pago, American Samoa
Producer of canned tuna, fish meal & pet food.

Weight Watchers Gourmet Food Co.
Hamden, CT
Producer of various dietary & weight control food products.

Weight Watchers International, Inc.
Woodbury, NY
Provider of weight control services & products.

Cardio-Fitness Corp.
New York, NY
Provider of fitness & health programs.

The Fitness Institute
Willowdale, Ontario, Canada
Provider of fitness, sports programs & services.

Total Employees......................43,300	
Year Established 1869	**Incorporated**................................PA
Stock Symbol...........................HNZ	**Annual Meeting** ....September
Stock Exchange ....NYSE	**SIC Code**....................................2032
Stockholders 62,496	
Shares Outstanding 368,592,384	

Fiscal Year End	Total Revenues ($000)	Net Income/(Loss) ($000)	Total Assets ($000)
5/1/96	9,112,265	659,319	8,623,691
¹5/3/95	8,086,794	591,025	8,247,188
4/27/94	7,046,738	602,944	6,381,146
4/28/93	7,103,374	396,313	6,821,321

¹*Fiscal year ended 5/3/95 includes 53 weeks.*

Executive Biography: Anthony J. F. O'Reilly, Ph.D.

Birth Date: 5/7/36   **Birthplace:** Dublin, Ireland
Spouse: Chryss   **Children:** 6

Education:
Belvedere College (Dublin, Ireland); U College Dublin; Incorporated Law
Society of Ireland; U of Bradford (England), Ph.D.-Agricultural Marketing 1980.

Career History:
Irish Dairy Board, CEO 1962-66; Irish Sugar Co. (Dublin, Ireland), MDIR 1966-
69; Erin Foods Ltd. (Dublin, Ireland), MDIR 1966-69; H. J. Heinz Co., MDIR-H. J.
Heinz Co., Ltd. (England) 1969-71, SVP-North America & Pacific 1971-72, COO
1972-, EVP 1972-73, P 1973-96, CEO 1979-present, CH 1987-present.

Directorships/Memberships/Activities:
The American Ireland Fund, CH; Duquesne Club, DIR; Fitzwilton Plc (Dublin,

Ireland), CH; Independent Newspapers Plc (Dublin, Ireland), CH; Matheson
Ormsby Prentice (Dublin, Ireland), CH; Waterford Wedgwood Plc, CH; Fox
Chapel Golf Club, MEM; Grocery Manufacturers of America, Inc., MEM-
Executive Comm.; Kildare Street and University Club (Dublin, Ireland), MEM;
The Links (New York), MEM; Lyford Cay Club (Nassau), MEM; Pittsburgh Golf
Club, MEM; Rockefeller U, MEM; Rolling Rock Club (Ligonier, PA), MEM; St.
Stephen's Green (Dublin, Ireland), MEM; Turf Club, Co., MEM; South African
Free Election Fund, C-CH; Dr. of Laws, Wheeling College 1974; Dr. of Business
Studies, Rollins College 1978; Dr. of Laws, Trinity College 1978; Dr. of Civil Law
Honoris Causa, Indiana State U 1980; Medal of the American-Irish Historical
Society 1982; Dr. of Laws, Allegheny College 1983; Dr. of Business ADM, Boston
College 1985; Irish Management Institute, Life Fellow 1987; Order of Australia,
Honorary Officer 1988; Dr. of Laws, De Paul U 1988; Dr. of Economic Science,
The National U of Ireland 1989; Dr. of Economic Science, The Queen's U of
Belfast 1989; Dr. of Laws, Carnegie Mellon U 1990; Dr. of the U, U of Bradford
1992; Dr. of Laws, U of Leicester 1992; Dr. of Business ADM, Westminster
College 1993.

IBT Bancorp, Inc.

309 Main St.
Irwin, PA 15642
County: Westmoreland

Phone: (412) 863-3100
Fax: (412) 863-3069

Type of Business: Bank holding company.

IBT Bancorp is a bank holding company for its wholly owned subsidiary, Irwin
Bank and Trust Co. (Bank). The Bank provides a variety of banking-related products and services to individuals and corporate customers located in Allegheny
and Westmoreland Counties, PA. Its lending products include mortgage loans,
home improvement loans, home equity loans, installment loans, PHEAA and
PLUS education loans, auto loans and commercial loans. Its savings products
include passbook savings, statement savings, checking accounts, NOW accounts,
money market accounts, certificates of deposit, IRAs and Christmas clubs. The
Bank also offers traveler's checks, safe deposit box rentals, stock purchases and
sales, stock transfers and re-registration, treasury bill purchases and sales, trust
services, collection service, U.S. savings bonds and its own IBT MasterCard, VISA
and VISA Gold credit cards. The Bank operates six branch facilities in addition to
its main office and corporate headquarters located at the above address. The
branches are in Irwin, Monroeville (2), Penn Township, Pitcairn and White Oak.
It also maintains a loan center in Irwin, PA.

Officers: Richard L. Ryan *CH*
J. Curt Gardner *P & CEO*
Charles G. Urtin *EVP, SEC & TRS*

Human Resources: Tracy A. Austin *AVP-Human Resources-Irwin Bank and
Trust Co.*

Auditor: Edwards Leap & Sauer, Pittsburgh, PA
Affiliates/Divisions/Subsidiaries:

Irwin Bank and Trust Co. 100%
Commercial bank.

Total Employees............................170	**Regional Employees** 170
Year Established 1922	**Incorporated**..................................PA
Stock Symbol ....IBTB	**Annual Meeting**.......................April
Stock Exchange ....OTC	**SIC Code**.....................................6712
Stockholders 494	
Shares Outstanding 960,000	

Fiscal Year End	Total Revenues ($000)	Net Income/(Loss) ($000)	Total Assets ($000)
12/31/96	24,166	4,458	331,416
12/31/95	22,270	3,751	299,435
12/31/94	18,701	3,081	272,818
12/31/93	17,628	2,675	255,261

Executive Biography: J. Curt Gardner

Birth Date: 1938
Spouse: Patty   **Children:** 2

Career History:
Irwin Bank and Trust Co., P & CEO -present; IBT Bancorp, Inc., P & CEO -present.

II-VI Inc.

375 Saxonburg Blvd.
Saxonburg, PA 16056
County: Butler

Phone: (412) 352-4455
Fax: (412) 352-4980
Internet Address: www.optics.org/ii-vi/

Type of Business: Designer, manufacturer and marketer of optical and electro-optical components, devices and materials for precision use in infrared, near-infrared, visible-light and x-ray/gamma-ray instruments and applications.

II-VI designs, manufactures and markets optical and electro-optical components, devices and materials for precision use in infrared, near-infrared, visible-light and x-ray/gamma-ray instruments and applications. The Company is a materials-based enterprise. Its infrared components and materials primarily are made from compounds composed of elements from Groups II and VI of the Periodic Table of Elements (II-VI Compounds). II-VI Compounds, a class of non-hygroscopic (do not absorb water) materials, are leading infrared transmitting materials. The Company's infrared products are used in high-power carbon dioxide (CO_2) lasers for industrial processing, and for commercial and military sensing systems. The CO_2 laser emits infrared energy at a wavelength which is optimal for many industrial processes such as the cutting, welding, drilling and heat treating of various materials, including steel and other metals or alloys, plastics, wood, paper, cardboard, ceramics and numerous composites. This wavelength is also desirable for certain types of medical surgery and for various surveillance and sensing systems that must penetrate adverse atmospheric conditions. Its near-infrared and visible-light products are used in industrial, scientific and medical instruments, and solid-state yttrium aluminum garnet lasers. Frequency-doubling and single-crystal substrate materials produced by the Company are utilized as building blocks in the emerging blue-light laser market segment. In addition, it is developing and marketing solid-state x-ray and gamma-ray products for the nuclear radiation detection industry. The majority of the Company's revenues are attributable to the sale of optical parts and components for the laser processing industry. The Company's products are sold to over 3,000 customers throughout the world, with foreign sales accounting for approximately 43% to 47% of its revenues in each of the last three fiscal years. The Company's principal international markets are Germany and Japan. On October 2, 1987, the Company completed its initial public stock offering.

Special Designations: FW_{100}

Officers: Carl J. Johnson, Ph.D. *CH & CEO*
Francis J. Kramer   *P & COO*
Herman E. Reedy *VP & GMGR-Quality & ENG*
James Martinelli *TRS & CFO*

Human Resources: Marlene Acre
Auditor: Deloitte & Touche LLP, Pittsburgh, PA
General Counsel: Sherrard, German & Kelly, P.C., Pittsburgh, PA

Affiliates/Divisions/Subsidiaries:

eV Division 100%
Developer of radiation detection products.

II-VI Delaware, Inc. 100%

II-VI Japan Inc. 100%
Japan

II-VI Optics (Suzhou) Co. Ltd. 100%
People's Republic of China

II-VI Singapore Pte., Ltd. 100%
Singapore
Fabricator & coater of infrared optics.

II-VI U.K. Ltd. 100%
United Kingdom

II-VI Worldwide, Inc. 100%
Barbados

VLOC Inc. 100%
Manufacturer of near-infrared & visible-light products.

Total Employees............................554	**Regional Employees** 285
Year Established 1971	**Incorporated**..................................PA
Stock Symbol IIVI	**Annual Meeting** ....November
Stock Exchange.................NASDAQ	**SIC Code**.....................................3827
Stockholders 700	
Shares Outstanding 6,331,738	

Fiscal Year End	Total Revenues ($000)	Net Income/(Loss) ($000)	Total Assets ($000)
6/30/96	37,940	4,371	44,169
6/30/95	27,760	2,518	24,367
6/30/94	18,681	1,135	17,570
6/30/93	17,169	75	17,265

Executive Biography: Carl J. Johnson, Ph.D.

Birth Date: 1942

Education:
Purdue U, B.S.-Electrical Engineering; MIT, M.S.-Electrical Engineering; U of Illinois, Ph.D.-Electrical Engineering 1969.

Career History:
Bell Telephone Laboratories, MEM-Technical Staff 1964-66; Essex International, Inc., DIR-R&D 1966-71; II-VI Inc., C-FND, P 1971-85, CH & CEO 1985-present.

Directorships/Memberships/Activities:
Ben Franklin Technology Center of Western Pennsylvania, CH; Xymox Technology, Inc., DIR; American Assn. for Crystal Growth, MEM; American Optical Society, MEM; Institute of Electrical and Electronic Engineers, Inc., MEM; Materials Research Society, MEM.

Industrial Scientific Corp.

1001 Oakdale Rd.
Oakdale, PA 15071
County: Allegheny

Phone: (412) 788-4353
Fax: (412) 788-8353
Internet Address: www.indsci.com

Type of Business: Designer, manufacturer, marketer and servicer of gas monitoring instruments, systems and other related products.

Industrial Scientific designs, manufactures, markets and services instruments and other technical products for detecting, measuring and monitoring a wide variety of gases, including toxic and combustible gases and oxygen, to preserve life and property. The Company's products are used by individuals for safety and industrial hygiene purposes in many different industries, often in confined spaces posing risks of asphyxiation, poisoning and explosion. Each portable or permanently installed instrument detects, measures and monitors gases singly or in combination, including oxygen, carbon monoxide, hydrogen sulfide, chlorine, nitrogen dioxide, sulfur dioxide and flammable hydrocarbons such as methane (natural gas), hexane and propane. The Company also manufactures and markets various accessories such as sampling pumps, external warning devices and battery chargers. Its portable instruments range from single-gas to four-gas monitors, while its permanently installed systems can monitor literally hundreds of specific locations. In addition, the Company sells replacement sensors, other replacement parts and a full line of accessories for its gas monitoring instruments, including sampling pumps and probes (for remote monitoring prior to entry), battery chargers, carrying cases, calibration kits and gases, and external alarm devices. Principal markets for its gas monitoring instruments include oil refineries, oil drilling operations including offshore rigs, utilities including telephone and electric companies, mining, government regulatory agencies such as EPA, OSHA and MSHA, food processors, natural gas transmission companies, fire and police departments, insurance companies, hazardous materials handlers, wastewater treatment facilities and breweries. Sales of gas monitoring instruments, accessories, replacement parts and service accounted for 97% of the Company's revenues in fiscal 1996. The Company also manufactures and markets air filtration and monitoring products which filter compressed air and monitor carbon monoxide levels; conveyor belt fire detection systems for unmanned areas in coal mines; water deluge systems triggered by heat sensors; and carbon monitoring systems for enclosed areas such as coal preparation storage areas, parking garages and motor pools. International sales accounted for approximately 20% of its revenues in fiscal 1996. On July 8, 1993, the Company completed its initial public stock offering.

Officers: Kenton E. McElhattan *CH*
Kent D. McElhattan *P & CEO*
James P. Hart *VP-FIN & CFO*
Garth F. Miller *VP-SAL & Service*

Jeffrey B. Morgan *VP-MFG*
Annie Q. Wang, Ph.D. *VP-Science & Technology*
Human Resources: Patricia L. Gerney *SEC*
Auditor: Coopers & Lybrand L.L.P., Pittsburgh, PA
General Counsel: Buchanan Ingersoll P.C., Pittsburgh, PA

Affiliates/Divisions/Subsidiaries:

Industrial Scientific Arabia, Ltd. 49%
Kingdom of Saudi Arabia

Industrial Scientific Devices, Inc. 100%
St. Thomas, U.S. Virgin Islands
Foreign sales corporation.

Industrial Scientific of Delaware, Inc. 100%
Wilmington, DE
Investment holding corporation.

Industrial Scientific Pty. 100%
Australia

Total Employees 211	**Regional Employees** 188	
Year Established 1984	**Incorporated** PA	
Stock Symbol ISCX	**Annual Meeting** June	
Stock Exchange NASDAQ	**SIC Code** 3829	
Stockholders 1,455		
Shares Outstanding 3,375,087		

Fiscal Year End	Total Revenues ($000)	Net Income/(Loss) ($000)	Total Assets ($000)
1/25/97	36,648	3,725	39,218
1/27/96	34,133	4,067	35,479
1/28/95	31,421	4,227	32,213
1/29/94	30,891	4,449	28,897

Executive Biography: Kent D. McElhattan

Birth Date: 1/17/49   **Birthplace:** Franklin, PA
Spouse: Martha   **Children:** 3

Education:
Washington & Jefferson College; Davis & Elkins College, B.A. 1970.

Career History:
National Mine Service Co., various positions 1970-81, VP & GMGR-Industrial Safety Division 1981-85; Industrial Scientific Corp., P & CEO 1985-present.

Directorships/Memberships/Activities:
American Industrial Hygiene Assn., MEM; American Society of Mining Engineers, MEM; American Society of Safety Engineers, MEM; Duquesne Club, MEM; Duquesne U, MEM-Ethics Advisory Board.

International Technology Corp.

2790 Mosside Blvd.
Monroeville, PA 15146
County: Allegheny

Phone: (412) 372-7701
Fax: (412) 373-7135
Internet Address: www.itcorporation.com

Type of Business: Provider of a broad range of environmental management services.

   International Technology provides a wide range of environmental management services and technologies, including the assessment, decontamination and remediation of situations involving hazardous materials, and pollution prevention and minimization. The major part of the Company's business is the management of complex hazardous waste remediation projects involving the assessment, planning and execution of the decontamination and restoration of property, plant and equipment that have been contaminated by hazardous substances. These projects include the cleanup of land disposal sites where hazardous or toxic substances have been disposed and pose a threat to the surrounding environment; rivers, streams and groundwater contaminated by chemical substances; and buildings, production facilities and storage sites contaminated with hazardous chemical and/or radioactive materials. These projects require considerable strategic environmental management, technical engineering and analytical effort to determine the substances involved, the extent of the contamination, the appropriate alternatives for containing or removing the contamination, and the selection of the technologies for treatment, including transportable treatment equipment, to perform the cleanup of the site as well as strong project management and construction and remediation skills to execute the ultimate remediation projects in the field. The Company is involved in all areas of the United States and performs selected projects internationally in the assessment or cleanup phases of site remedial action projects. In addition, the Company performs a variety of consulting services for clients to help them comply with environmental and/or health and safety regulations. It also provides assistance to these clients in developing corporate policies and procedures in areas such as pollution prevention and waste minimization that integrate environmental regulations into their business decisions. In fiscal 1996, 65% of the Company's revenues were derived from federal governmental agencies, primarily the U.S. Department of Defense and the U.S. Department of Energy. The Company operates 44 offices, including project offices, located across the United States.

Recent Events: On June 27, 1997, the Company relocated its corporate headquarters from Torrance, CA, to Monroeville, PA.

Special Designations: ENR$_{400}$ ENR$_{500}$

Officers: Daniel A. D'Aniello *CH*
 Anthony J. DeLuca *P & Acting CEO*
 Franklin E. Coffman *SVP-Department of Energy Programs & Business DEV*

James R. Mahoney *SVP-Consulting & Ventures Group, Corporate DEV & Strategy*
Raymond J. Pompe *SVP-ENG & Construction Group*
James G. Kirk *VP, GC & SEC*
Philip H. Ockelmann *VP-FIN & TRS*
Harry J. Soose *VP & CON*
David E. Troxell *VP-Quality*
James M. Redwine *Senior Corporate Counsel & AST-SEC*
Edward Salcedo, Jr. *DIR-Government Contract Compliance & Accounting, & AST-SEC*

Human Resources: Ann C. Harris *VP-Human Resources*
Purchasing Director: Frank C. Rice *VP-Risk MGT & Corporate Procurement*
Auditor: Ernst & Young LLP, Los Angeles, CA
General Counsel: Gibson, Dunn & Crutcher LLP, Los Angeles, CA

Affiliates/Divisions/Subsidiaries:

Brownfields Services Corp.

Chi Mei Environmental

Gradient Corp.

IT Corp. of New York

IT Corp. of North Carolina

IT Hanford, Inc.

PHR Environmental Consultants, Inc.

Quanterra, Inc.

Servicios Ecologicos Especializados S.A. de C.V.

Universal Professional Insurance Co.

Zentox Corp.

Total Employees	2,400	**Regional Employees**	546
Year Established	1926	**Incorporated**	DE
Stock Symbol	ITX	**Annual Meeting**	November
Stock Exchange	NYSE	**SIC Code**	9511
Stockholders			2,128
Shares Outstanding			36,602,401

Fiscal Year End	Total Revenues ($000)	Net Income/(Loss) ($000)	Total Assets ($000)
[1]3/29/96	400,042	546	315,314
3/31/95	423,972	(14,283)	362,152
3/31/94	392,803	(1,106)	359,203
3/31/93	410,539	309	369,178

[1]*Changed fiscal year in 1996 to consist of four 13-week fiscal quarters with the fourth quarter ending on the last Friday of March.*

Executive Biography: Anthony J. DeLuca

Birth Date: 1947

Education:
U of New Haven, B.S.-Accounting.

Career History:
Ernst & Young LLP (Los Angeles, CA), Accountant 1970-83, PTR 1983-90; International Technology Corp., SVP & CFO 1990-96; P & Acting CEO 1996-present.

Directorships/Memberships/Activities:
American Institute of Certified Public Accountants, MEM; California Society of Certified Public Accountants, MEM.

Interstate Hotels Co.

Foster Plaza 10, 680 Andersen Dr.
Pittsburgh, PA 15220
County: Allegheny

Phone: (412) 937-0600
Fax: (412) 937-8055
Internet Address: www.ihc-hotels.com

Type of Business: Owner, manager and lessor of hotels and provider of related services.

Interstate Hotels was named for the fifth consecutive year by Hotel Business and Hotel & Motel Management as the largest independent hotel management company in the United States based on number of properties, number of rooms and total revenues produced for owners. As of March 1, 1997, the Company owned, managed, leased or performed related services for 212 hotels with a total of 43,158 rooms in the United States, Canada, the Caribbean, Israel, Panama, Russia and Thailand, with the largest concentration of hotels in the states of California and Florida. It owned or had a majority equity interest in 28 of these properties with 7,986 rooms (Owned Hotels), all of which are geographically diverse upscale or luxury properties operating under various brand names. The Owned Hotels operate under the Embassy Suites®, Hilton™, Holiday Inn®, Marriott®, Radisson™ and Westin™ trade names principally in major metropolitan markets such as Atlanta, Boston, Chicago, Denver, Fort Lauderdale, Houston, Los Angeles, Miami, Philadelphia, Phoenix and Washington, D.C. The Company claims to be the largest franchisee of upscale hotels in the Marriott system, owning, managing or providing services to 39 hotels totaling 13,539 rooms, bearing the Marriott flag. It also operates in the mid-scale, upper economy and budget segments of the lodging industry and claims to be the largest franchisee and independent manager in the Hampton Inn® system, providing services to 40 hotels totaling 4,754 rooms, bearing the Hampton Inn flag. In 1996, 83% of the Company's management fee revenues were derived from upscale or luxury hotels and resorts. The Owned Hotels produced superior operating results, achieving an average occupancy rate of 74.6%, an average daily room rate of $94.29 and room revenue per available room of $70.36. The Company maintains regional offices in Scottsdale, AZ, and Orlando, FL. On June 20, 1996, the Company completed its initial public stock offering.

Officers: Milton Fine *CH*
W. Thomas Parrington, Jr. *P & CEO*
Robert L. Froman *EVP-DEV*
Thomas D. Reese *EVP-OPR*
J. William Richardson *EVP-FIN & ADM, & CFO*
Henry L. Ciaffone *SVP & TRS*
Marvin I. Droz *SVP & GC*
Kevin P. Kilkeary *SVP; P & COO-Crossroads Hospitality Co.*
Jay A. Litt *SVP-OPR/Staff Support*
Patricia L. Cole *VP-Compensation, Training & Benefits*
Colin Dunkley *VP-Architecture & Construction*
Timothy Q. Hudak *VP & AST-GC*
Norman C. Hull *VP-Continental Design & Supplies*
Andrew D. Katz *VP-Asset MGT*
Robert J. McKinley *VP-DEV SAL & MKT*
Gregory R. Smith *VP & CON*
John L. Sonnier *VP-DEV & Acquisitions*
Donald L. Stanczak *VP-Food & Beverage*
Randall Sumner *VP-Architecture & Construction-Western Region*
Charles R. Tomb *VP-DEV & Acquisitions*
Gregory W. Ade *Regional VP*
Robert D. Cowan *Regional VP*
Robert C. Holland *Regional VP*
Jay C. Wold *Regional VP*

Human Resources: David P. Rowe *VP-Human Resources*
Auditor: Coopers & Lybrand L.L.P., Pittsburgh, PA
General Counsel: Jones, Day, Reavis & Pogue, New York, NY

Affiliates/Divisions/Subsidiaries:

Crossroads Hospitality Co.

Total Employees	22,000	**Regional Employees**	1,100
Year Established	1961	**Incorporated**	PA
Stock Symbol	IHC	**Annual Meeting**	May

Stock Exchange ....NYSE   **SIC Code** 7011
Stockholders 5,000
Shares Outstanding 35,324,968

Fiscal Year End	Total Revenues ($000)	Net Income/(Loss) ($000)	Total Assets ($000)
12/31/96	190,385	(1,616)	883,761
12/31/95	45,018	15,839	61,401
12/31/94	36,726	12,389	30,741
12/31/93	25,564	6,910	24,436

Executive Biography: W. Thomas Parrington, Jr.

Birth Date: 1945   **Birthplace:** New York, NY
Spouse: Mary Lee   **Children:** 3

Education:
Georgetown U, B.A. & B.S. 1966.

Career History:
Arthur Andersen & Co. (Washington, D.C.); Marriott International, Inc.
(Washington, D.C.), Group CON; Ramada Inns, Inc. (Phoenix, AZ), VP;
Westmount International Hotels (Scottsdale, AZ), SVP; Interstate Hotels Co.,
various positions 1981-94 including CFO, P 1994-present, CEO 1996-present.

Directorships/Memberships/Activities:
American Hotel Foundation, DIR.

Iron and Glass Bancorp, Inc.

1114 E. Carson St.
Pittsburgh, PA 15203
County: Allegheny

Phone: (412) 488-5200
Fax: (412) 488-5224

Type of Business: Bank holding company.

   Iron and Glass Bancorp is a holding company for the Iron and Glass Bank
(Bank). The Bank is a state-chartered bank and a member of the Federal Reserve
Bank of Cleveland. The Bank grants commercial and industrial loans, commercial
and residential mortgages, and consumer loans to customers located within the
greater Pittsburgh metropolitan area. It also selectively purchases and funds residential loans originated outside of its principal lending area provided such loans
meet the Bank's credit policy guidelines. The Bank operates five branch facilities
in addition to its main office and corporate headquarters located at the above
address. The branches are in Scott Township and West Mifflin, and the
Brentwood, Castle Shannon and South Park areas of Pittsburgh, all in
Pennsylvania.

Officers: Daniel A. Goetz *CH*
            Michael J. Hagan *P & CEO*

Karen Joyce *EVP & Senior Loan Officer*
James R. Rendulic *SVP, Senior Financial Officer & SEC*
Amy Carroll *VP & Technology Officer*
Donald LaJevic *VP-Retail Services*
Russell Peck *VP-OPR*
Peter Zerega *VP-Commercial Loans*

Human Resources: Mary Catherine Rossi *VP-Human Resources*
Auditor: S. R. Snodgrass, A.C., Wexford, PA
Affiliates/Divisions/Subsidiaries:

Iron and Glass Bank 100%
Pittsburgh, PA
Commercial bank.

Total Employees	75	**Regional Employees**	75
Year Established	1871	**Incorporated**	PA
Stock Symbol	IRGB	**Annual Meeting**	July
Stock Exchange	OTC	**SIC Code**	6712
Stockholders			333
Shares Outstanding			600,000

Fiscal Year End	Total Revenues ($000)	Net Income/(Loss) ($000)	Total Assets ($000)
12/31/96	13,577	1,806	181,769
12/31/95	12,053	1,401	166,823
12/31/94	10,019	578	143,876
12/31/93	10,453	1,724	146,249

Executive Biography: Michael J. Hagan

Birth Date: 6/24/46   **Birthplace:** Niagara Falls, NY
Spouse: Angela   **Children:** 3

Education:
U of Notre Dame, B.B.A. 1968; U of Pittsburgh, M.B.A. 1971.

Career History:
Commercial Bank & Trust Co., CON 1971-75; Keystone Bank, TRS 1975-80; U of Pittsburgh, AST-TRS 1980-89; North Side Deposit Bank, CFO 1989-93; Pittsburgh Steelers Sports, Inc., CON 1993-96; Iron and Glass Bancorp, Inc., P & CEO 1996-present.

J&L Specialty Steel, Inc.

One PPG Place
P.O. Box 3373
Pittsburgh, PA 15230
County: Allegheny

Phone: (412) 338-1600
Fax: (412) 338-1746

Type of Business: Manufacturer of flat-rolled stainless steel.

J&L Specialty Steel is a manufacturer of both austenitic and ferritic flat-rolled stainless steels. The Company manufactures various grades of stainless steel in the form of cold-rolled stainless steel sheet and strip, hot-rolled stainless steel sheet and strip, and continuous mill plate, as well as semi-finished stainless steel slabs and coils. Its stainless steel is used in a wide variety of industrial, commercial and consumer products, including pressure vessels, chemical and refinery equipment, environmental control equipment, cargo containers, sinks, transportation equipment, beer kegs, fast food equipment, automated bank teller machines, automobile trim, exhaust systems, and kitchen appliances and utensils. The Company produces a large portion of its stainless steel in response to specific customer orders rather than for inventory. The products manufactured for inventory are usually in standard grades and sizes. Approximately 50% of the Company's products are sold to steel service centers. The remainder of its products are sold to stainless steel converters, manufacturers of finished industrial and consumer products, and exporters. In 1996, approximately 4% of its shipments were exported, primarily to Canada, Mexico and South America. The Company operates three manufacturing plants. Its Midland, PA, plant is both a melting and finishing facility, and its Detroit, MI, and Louisville, OH, plants are finishing facilities. For 1996, the Company's utilization of its production capacity was approximately 80%. The Company maintains regional sales offices in Fullerton, CA; Atlanta, GA; Bloomingdale, IL; and Pittsburgh, PA. Additional sales representatives are also located in Detroit, MI; Boston, MA; Houston, TX; and Milwaukee, WI. Based on statistics, the Company believes it is the third largest manufacturer of stainless steel sheet and strip products in the United States and the second largest United States producer of austenitic cold-rolled stainless steel, which is the largest part of the domestic stainless steel market. On December 15, 1993, the Company completed its initial public stock offering. Usinor Sacilor, a French corporation, owns 53.6% of the Company's outstanding common stock.

Officers: Philippe Choppin de Janvry *CH*
Claude F. Kronk *VCH & CEO*
Eugene A. Salvadore *P & COO*
Geoffrey S. Gibson *VP-Commercial*
Paul J. Grandy *VP-ENG*
Michael F. McGuire *VP-Technology*
Kirk F. Vincent *VP-FIN & Law*
John A. Wallace *VP-OPR*

Human Resources: Daryl K. Fox *VP-Human Resources*

Purchasing Director: Gerald L. Kosko *VP-Purchasing & Traffic*

Auditor: Arthur Andersen LLP, Pittsburgh, PA

Affiliates/Divisions/Subsidiaries:

> Detroit Plant 100%
> Detroit, MI
> Finisher of stainless steel.

> Louisville Plant 100%
> Louisville, OH
> Finisher of stainless steel.

> Midland Plant 100%
> Midland, PA
> Producer of stainless steel sheet, strip & plate products.

Total Employees......................1,346	**Regional Employees**..................683
Year Established......................1986	**Incorporated**................................PA
Stock Symbol..................................JL	**Annual Meeting**.......................June
Stock Exchange......................NYSE	**SIC Code**....................................3312
Stockholders..230
Shares Outstanding...38,670,000

Fiscal Year End	Total Revenues ($000)	Net Income/(Loss) ($000)	Total Assets ($000)
12/31/96	628,022	24,265	771,928
12/31/95	867,022	84,402	753,818
12/31/94	711,660	53,575	674,361
12/31/93	648,192	18,784	626,038

Executive Biography: Claude F. Kronk

Birth Date: 1932   **Birthplace:** West Jefferson, OH

Education:

Ohio Wesleyan U, B.A.

Career History:

Jones and Laughlin Steel Corp., SAL Trainee 1957, various SAL positions -1965, Philadelphia District SAL MGR 1965, various positions including Product MGR, MKT MGR, GMGR & VP -1984, P-Specialty Steels Division 1984; LTV Steel Co., P-Specialty Steels Division 1984-86; J&L Specialty Products Corp., P & CEO 1986-90; Ugine ACG (acquired J&L Specialty Products Corp.), P & CEO 1990-93; J&L Specialty Steel, Inc., P 1993-95, CEO 1993-present, VCH 1995-present.

Directorships/Memberships/Activities:

Cold Metal Products, Inc., DIR; Triumph Group, Inc., DIR.

Kennametal Inc.

State Rte. 981 S.
P.O. Box 231
Latrobe, PA 15650
County: Westmoreland

Phone: (412) 539-5000
Fax: (412) 539-4710
Internet Address: www.kennametal.com

Type of Business: Manufacturer and supplier of tooling, specializing in powder metallurgy.

Kennametal markets, manufactures and distributes a broad range of tools, industrial supplies and accessories for the metalworking, mining and highway construction industries. The Company claims that it is one of the world's leading producers and suppliers of cutting tools and wear-resistant parts made of cemented carbides and other hard materials. While many of the Company's products are similar in composition, sales are classified into three markets: metalworking, industrial supply, and mining and construction. The Company supplies a full line of products and services for the metalworking industry. It provides cutting tools, tool holding and work holding devices, accessories and advanced technical application support for all metal cutting operations, including turning, milling and drilling. The Company markets a broad line of industrial supplies to the metalworking industry, including products it manufactures and a wide array of items made by others. Industrial supply products generally include anything used in the machining process, such as metal cutting inserts, drills, taps, abrasives and other supplies, such as precision-measuring devices, fixtures and accessories. The Company claims that it is the world's leading producer of mining and highway construction tools. Mining tools include drums, blocks, bits, compacts and accessories. Construction tools include blocks, bits, grader blades and snowplow blades. The Company also manufactures proprietary metallurgical powders for use in its products and produces a variety of powders for specialized markets. The Company's products are sold through a direct sales force, full-service supply programs and mail-order catalogs. Its principal international operations are conducted in Canada and western Europe. In fiscal 1996, international sales accounted for 38% of its revenues.

Recent Events: On April 28, 1997, the Company announced that its Board of Directors approved a proposal to sell, through an initial public offering, up to 20% of common stock by its newly formed subsidiary, JLK Direct Distribution Inc. (JDDI). Following the offering, the Company will own approximately 80% of the outstanding common stock of JDDI and will retain a majority of both the economic and voting interests of JDDI. The Company also announced the filing of a registration statement with the Securities and Exchange Commission covering this offering. JDDI will market the full Kennametal line of metal cutting

K

products, a broad range of metalworking tooling and related products, including a full line of cutting tools, carbide and other metalworking inserts, abrasives, drills, machine tool accessories and other industrial supplies.

Officers: William R. Newlin *CH*
Robert L. McGeehan *P & CEO*
James W. Heaton *SVP & DIR-Customer Satisfaction*
David B. Arnold *VP & CTO*
James R. Breisinger *VP & CON*
David T. Cofer *VP, SEC & GC*
Derwin R. Gilbreath *VP & DIR-Global Manufacturing*
Richard C. Hendricks *VP & DIR-Corporate Business DEV*
H. Patrick Mahanes, Jr. *VP & COO*
Richard V. Minns *VP & DIR-Metalworking SAL-North America*
James E. Morrison *VP & TRS*
Richard J. Orwig *VP, CFO & CAO*
Michael W. Ruprich *VP & DIR-Global MKT & SAL; P-J&L America Inc.*
P. Mark Schiller *VP & DIR-Kennametal Distribution Services*
Lawrence L. Shrum *VP & DIR-Global MIS*
Kevin G. Nowe *AST-SEC & AST-GC*
Richard P. Gibson *AST-TRS & DIR-Taxes*

Human Resources: Timothy D. Hudson *VP & DIR-Human Resources*
Auditor: Arthur Anderson LLP, Pittsburgh, PA
General Counsel: Buchanan Ingersoll P.C., Pittsburgh, PA

Affiliates/Divisions/Subsidiaries:

Adaptive Technologies Corp. 100%
Troy, MI

Birla Kennametal Ltd. 40%
India

Circle Machine Co. 100%
Monrovia, CA

Drillco Hertel Ltd. 50%
India

J&L America Inc. 100%
Livonia, MI

Kennametal Australia Pty. Ltd. 100%
Australia

Kennametal Ca.Me.S., S.p.A. 51%
Italy

Kennametal (China) Ltd. 100%
People's Republic of China

Kennametal de Mexico, S.A. de C.V. 100%
Mexico

Kennametal Foreign Sales Corp. 100%
Barbados

Kennametal Hardpoint Inc. 90%

Kennametal Hardpoint H.K. Ltd.
Hong Kong

Kennametal Hardpoint (Taiwan) Ltd.
Taiwan

Kennametal Hertel AG 95%
Fuerth, Germany

Kenci, S.A. 20%
Spain

Kennametal GTS GmbH. Korea
South Korea

Kennametal Hertel Belgium S.A.
Belgium

Kennametal Hertel France S.A.
France

Matériels de Precision ET de Production S.A. 100%
France

Kennametal Hertel G. Beisteiner GmbH 26%
Austria

Kennametal Hertel GmbH
Germany

Kennametal Hertel Nederland B.V.
The Netherlands

Kennametal Hertel S.p.A. 40%
Italy

K

Nederlandse Hardmetaal Fabrieken B.V.
The Netherlands

Wilke Carbide B.V. 50%
The Netherlands

Kennametal Hertel Co., Ltd. 48%
Thailand

Kennametal Hertel (Malaysia) SDN. BHD. 100%
Malaysia

Kennametal Hertel (Singapore) Pte. Ltd. 100%
Singapore

Kennametal Hertel UK 100%
England

Kennametal Ltd. 100%
Canada

Kennametal (Shanghai) Ltd. 100%
People's Republic of China

Kennametal South Africa (PTY) Ltd. 100%
South Africa

Kennametal/Becker-Warkop Ltd. 84%
Poland

Kobe Kennametal K.K. 51%
Japan

PIGMA-Kennametal Joint Venture 49%
Russia

Shanxi-Kennametal Mining Cutting Systems Manufacturing
Co. Ltd. 70%
People's Republic of China

Xuzhou-Kennametal Mining Cutting Systems Manufacturing
Co. Ltd. 70%
People's Republic of China

Total Employees	7,300	**Regional Employees**	700
Year Established	1938	**Incorporated**	PA
Stock Symbol	KMT	**Annual Meeting**	October
Stock Exchange	NYSE	**SIC Code**	3545

Stockholders 2,863
Shares Outstanding 26,747,827

Fiscal Year End	Total Revenues ($000)	Net Income/(Loss) ($000)	Total Assets ($000)
6/30/96	1,079,963	69,732	799,491
6/30/95	983,873	68,294	781,609
6/30/94	802,513	(4,088)	697,532
6/30/93	598,496	20,094	448,263

Executive Biography: Robert L. McGeehan

Birth Date: 11/10/36   **Birthplace:** Midland, PA
Spouse: Carol   **Children:** 4

Education:
Chaffey College (Ontario, CA); Bradley U (Peoria, IL).

Career History:
Kaiser Steel Corp.; Kennametal Inc., various positions 1973-84, VP 1984-89, GMGR-Machining Systems Division 1985-88, DIR-Metalworking Systems Division 1988-89, P 1989-present, CEO 1991-present.

Laurel Capital Group, Inc.

2724 Harts Run Rd.
Allison Park, PA 15101
County: Allegheny

Phone: (412) 487-7400
Fax: (412) 487-1259

Type of Business: Bank holding company.

Laurel Capital Group is a bank holding company for Laurel Savings Bank (Bank), a state-chartered savings bank. The Bank is primarily engaged in attracting deposits from the general public and using these funds to originate permanent first mortgage loans on single-family residential properties. It also originates multi-family residential loans, construction loans, commercial real estate loans and consumer loans. The Bank's revenue is primarily derived from interest income on its loan portfolio. The Bank's principal expenses are interest on deposits, salaries, provision for loan losses, and other general and administrative expenses. The primary sources of funds for the Bank's lending activities are its deposits, and amortization and prepayments of outstanding loans. Deposits with the Bank are insured to the maximum extent provided by law through the Savings Assn. Insurance Fund administered by the Federal Deposit Insurance Corp. Substantially all of the Bank's deposits are received from residents of its principal market area consisting of Allegheny and Butler Counties, PA, and most of its loans are secured by properties located in this same region. The Bank's business is conducted through its corporate office, located at the above address, and five branch offices located in Glenshaw, Pittsburgh (2), Russellton and Saxonburg, PA.

Officers: Richard J. Cessar *CH*
Edwin R. Maus *P & CEO*
John A. Howard, Jr. *SVP, CFO, TRS & SEC*
Richard P. Bruckman *VP & CON-Laurel Savings Bank*
Bernard W. Prazer *VP-Lending-Laurel Savings Bank*
Nancy Krulac Faust *AST-VP-Audit & Compliance-Laurel Savings Bank*
William T. Puz *AST-VP-Credit & Collections-Laurel Savings Bank*

Auditor: KPMG Peat Markwick LLP, Pittsburgh, PA

Affiliates/Divisions/Subsidiaries:

Laurel Savings Bank 100%
Allison Park, PA
Savings bank.

Laurel Financial Services Corp. 100%
Inactive.

Total Employees............................51	**Regional Employees** 51
Year Established 1887	**Incorporated**..................................PA
Stock Symbol ....LARL	**Annual Meeting** ....November
Stock Exchange....................NSCap	**SIC Code**...................................6712
Stockholders 522	
Shares Outstanding 1,514,285	

Fiscal Year End	Total Revenues ($000)	Net Income/(Loss) ($000)	Total Assets ($000)
6/30/96	15,412	2,665	196,947
6/30/95	14,316	2,543	188,916
6/30/94	13,632	2,844	177,729
6/30/93	14,993	2,340	175,931

Executive Biography: Edwin R. Maus

Birth Date: 12/10/41   **Birthplace:** Pittsburgh, PA
Spouse: Lorraine   **Children:** 3

Education:
U of Pittsburgh.

Career History:
U.S. Air Force; Columbia Savings and Loan Assn.; Concord Liberty Savings and Loan Assn., VP-OPR 1964-86; Laurel Savings Bank, VP-OPR 1987-89, P & CEO 1989-present; Laurel Capital Group, Inc., P & CEO 1992-present.

Mastech Corp.

1004 McKee Rd.
Oakdale, PA 15071
County: Allegheny

Phone: (412) 787-2100
Fax: (412) 787-7450
Internet Address: www.mastech.com

Type of Business: Provider of information technology services to large organizations.

Mastech is a worldwide provider of information technology services to large organizations. The Company provides its clients with a single source for a broad range of applications solutions and services, including client/server design and development, conversion/migration services, Year 2000 services, Enterprise Resource Planning package implementation services and maintenance outsourcing. These services are provided in a variety of computing environments and use leading technologies, including client/server architectures, object-oriented programming, distributed databases and the latest networking and communications technologies. To enhance its services, the Company has formed business alliances with software companies such as Baan, Oracle and Viasoft. In addition, the Company has developed its own proprietary methodologies and tools, known as SmartAPPS, that provide a complete solution set for each of its services. During 1996, the Company provided information technology services to over 350 clients worldwide in a diverse range of industries. These clients include AT&T, Citibank, EDS, IBM, Intel, Oracle and Wal-Mart. Historically, the Company has primarily provided information technology services on a time-and-materials basis to support client-managed projects. The Company plans to generate an increasing portion of its revenues from Company-managed projects, international markets, offshore software development projects and fixed-price engagements. The Company is now replicating its business model in key international markets to meet the large and growing demand for information technology services overseas and to serve its client base of large multinational corporations that need support on a global basis. The Company maintains offices in San Mateo, CA; Falls Church, VA; Sydney, Australia; Mississuaga, Ontario, Canada; Bucknell, Berkshire, England; Tokyo, Japan; and Singapore. It plans to add additional offices in South Africa, the Middle East and Continental Europe. Through its Mascot Systems Pvt., Ltd. subsidiary, the Company is investing in an extensive offshore software development infrastructure in India, including four state-of-the-art software development centers. On December 17, 1996, the Company completed its initial public stock offering.

Special Designations: INC$_{500}$

Officers: Sunil Wadhwani *C-CH & CEO*
Ashok Trivedi *C-CH & P*
John Brendel *VP-Legal Affairs*
Ajmal Noorani *VP-INTL OPR*

M

Sushma Rajagopalan *VP-Global Recruiting*
Steven Shangold *VP-SAL*
Denny Stocker *VP-SAL*
Michael Zugay *VP-FIN*
Don Hamed *DIR-MIS*
Maggie Oberst *DIR-Corporate Communications*

Human Resources: Murali Balasubamanyam *VP-Human Resources*
Auditor: Arthur Andersen LLP, Pittsburgh, PA
General Counsel: Buchanan Ingersoll P.C., Pittsburgh, PA

Affiliates/Divisions/Subsidiaries:

Mascot Systems Pvt., Ltd. 100%
India
Offshore developer of software.

Scott Systems Pvt., Ltd. 100%
India

Total Employees.........................2,049   **Regional Employees** 250
Year Established 1986   **Incorporated**.................................PA
Stock Symbol...........................MAST   **Annual Meeting**.......................June
Stock Exchange................NASDAQ   **SIC Code**.....................................7371
Stockholders 5,000
Shares Outstanding 21,654,600

Fiscal Year End	Total Revenues ($000)	Net Income/(Loss) ($000)	Total Assets ($000)
12/31/96	123,400	8,692	77,509
12/31/95	103,676	18,396	25,754
12/31/94	70,050	11,444	22,847
12/31/93	38,709	2,724	12,461

Executive Biography: Sunil Wadhwani

Birth Date: 1953

Education:
Indian Institute of Technology, B.S.-Mechanical Engineering; Carnegie-Mellon
U, M.S.-Industrial Administration.

Career History:
Management Consultant -1981; Uro-Valve, Inc., P 1981-86; Mastech Corp., various positions 1986-96 including VP & SEC & TRS, CH 1986-96, C-CH & CEO
1996-present.

Matthews International Corp.

Two NorthShore Center
Pittsburgh, PA 15212
County: Allegheny
Phone: (412) 442-8200
Fax: (412) 442-8290

Type of Business: Designer, manufacturer and marketer of custom-made products used to identify people, places, products and events.

Matthews International is a designer, manufacturer and marketer of custom-made identification products. The Company's products and operations are comprised of three business segments: Bronze, Graphic Systems and Marking Products. The Bronze segment, which is the Company's largest business segment, is a manufacturer and marketer of cast bronze memorial products used primarily in cemeteries. The segment also manufactures and markets cast bronze and aluminum architectural products used to identify or commemorate people, places and events. Memorial products, which comprise the majority of the segment's sales, include flush bronze memorials, flower vases, crypt letters, cremation urns, niche units and cemetery features, along with other related products. The Graphic Systems segment manufactures and provides a line of custom identification-related products and services used by the corrugated packaging industry and the flexible packaging industry. The segment's principal products are printing plates used by packaging manufacturers to print corrugated boxes and flexible packaging with graphics that provide information such as product identification, logos, bar codes and other packaging detail specified by the manufacturer. The segment also provides electronic pre-press and art design services to manufacturers of corrugated and flexible packaging, and end users of such packaging. The Marking Products segment designs, manufactures and distributes a range of equipment and consumables used by customers to mark or identify various consumer and industrial products, components and packaging containers. The segment employs contact printing, indenting and ink-jet printing to meet customer needs, sometimes using a combination of these marking methods. These identification methods apply product information required to facilitate inventory and quality control, regulatory compliance and brand name communication. In fiscal 1996, the Company derived approximately 19% of its revenue from foreign markets. The Company operates manufacturing and marketing facilities in the United States, Canada, Australia and Sweden, as well as sales and distribution facilities in France and the United Kingdom. On July 20, 1994, the Company completed its initial public stock offering.

Officers: David M. Kelly *CH, P & CEO*
Geoffrey D. Barefoot *P-Graphic Systems Division*
David J. DeCarlo *P-Bronze Division*
Edward J. Boyle *VP-Accounting & FIN, & SEC*
Steven F. Nicola *CON*

Human Resources: Richard C. Johnson *VP-Corporate DEV & Human Resources*

Auditor: Coopers & Lybrand L.L.P., Pittsburgh, PA
Affiliates/Divisions/Subsidiaries:

Applied Technology Developments, Ltd. 49%
United Kingdom
Manufacturer of impulse ink-jet printing equipment.

Industrial Equipment and Engineering Co., Inc. 100%
Orlando, FL
Manufacturer of cremation equipment & related cremation products.

Matthews Bronze Pty. Ltd. 100%
Melbourne, Australia
Bronze division.

Matthews Canada Ltd. 100%
Milton, Ontario, Canada
Bronze & marking products division.

Matthews Industries 100%
Pittsburgh, PA

Matthews International (Arkansas) Corp. 100%
Searcy, AR
Bronze division.

Matthews International (Australia) Pty. Ltd. 100%
Melbourne, Australia
Marking products division.

Matthews International Trading Co., Ltd. 100%
U.S. Virgin Islands

Matthews Properties Pty. Ltd. 100%
Melbourne, Australia

Matthews Swedot AB 100%
Gothenburg, Sweden
Marking products division.

Matthews Swedot France S.A.R.L. 100%
Pontoise, France
Marking products division.

Tukaiz Litho, Inc. 50%
Franklin Park, IL
Provider of pre-press services.

Venetian Investment Corp. 100%
Wilmington, DE

Total Employees.........................1,400
Year Established 1850   **Incorporated**................................PA
Stock Symbol ....MATW   **Annual Meeting**................February
Stock Exchange...............NASDAQ   **SIC Code** 3366
Stockholders...Class A 453 Class B 364
Shares Outstanding.................Class A 6,148,784 Class B 2,581,977

Fiscal Year End	Total Revenues ($000)	Net Income/(Loss) ($000)	Total Assets ($000)
9/30/96	171,978	20,258	153,412
9/30/95	166,748	15,451	138,206
9/30/94	158,700	14,028	120,683
9/30/93	151,094	(881)	110,569

Executive Biography: David M. Kelly

Birth Date: 1943

Education:
Boston College, B.S.-Physics 1964; Yale U, M.S.-Molecular Biophysics 1966;
Harvard U, M.B.A. 1968.

Career History:
Carrier Corp. (division of United Technologies Corp.), with exception of four-year affiliation with Arthur Andersen Consulting, spent 22 years with Carrier Corp., including MKT VP-Asia Pacific, P-Japanese OPR, VP-MFG, P-North American OPR, SVP-Residential & Light Commercial Businesses; Matthews International Corp., P & CEO 1995-present., CH 1996-present.

Directorships/Memberships/Activities:
Jas. H. Matthews & Co. Educational and Charitable Trust, CH; Mestek, Inc., DIR; United Way of Allegheny County, DIR.

Mellon Bank Corp.

One Mellon Bank Center, 500 Grant St.
Pittsburgh, PA 15258
County: Allegheny

Phone: (412) 234-5000
Fax: (412) 236-1662
Internet Address: www.mellon.com

Type of Business: Multibank holding company.

   Mellon Bank is a multibank holding company which provides a comprehensive range of financial products and services in domestic and selected international markets. The Company's banking subsidiaries are located in Delaware, Maryland, Massachusetts, New Jersey and Pennsylvania. Other subsidiaries are located in key business centers throughout the United States and abroad. As of

M

December 31, 1996, the Company claimed to be the 22nd-largest bank holding company in the United States in terms of assets, with balance sheet assets of nearly $43 billion and assets under management or administration of more than $1.1 trillion. The Company's banking subsidiaries operate 1,104 domestic retail banking locations, including 420 retail offices. For analytical purposes, management has focused the Company into four core business sectors. The Consumer Investment Services sector provides a broad array of personal trust services, investment services and retail mutual funds to consumers. The Consumer Banking Services sector includes consumer lending and deposit products, business banking, branch banking, credit card, mortgage loan origination and servicing, and jumbo residential mortgage lending. The consumer lending, branch banking and small business banking services are primarily offered through the Company's retail banking network which is comprised of 347 retail branch offices, 72 supermarket facilities, 684 ATM's, eight loan sales offices and a telephone banking center. This network is primarily located in the Central Atlantic region of the United States. The Corporate/Institutional Investment Services sector serves institutional markets (including employee benefit plans) by providing institutional asset and institutional mutual fund management and administration, institutional trust and custody, securities lending, foreign exchange, cash management, stock transfer and corporate trust. The Corporate/Institutional Banking Services sector includes large corporate and middle market lending, asset-based lending, lease financing, commercial real estate lending, insurance premium financing, securities underwriting and trading, and international banking. On August 24, 1994, Mellon Bank, N.A. acquired The Dreyfus Corp. (TDC) as an operating subsidiary. TDC is one of the nation's largest mutual fund companies and manages or administers over $85 billion in more than 150 mutual funds.

Special Designations: FB_{500} FT_{500}

Officers: Frank V. Cahouet *CH, P & CEO*
John T. Chesko *VCH & Chief Risk Officer*
Christopher M. Condron *VCH; P & CEO-The Dreyfus Corp.*
Steven G. Elliott *VCH & CFO*
Jeffery L. Leininger *VCH-Specialized Commercial Banking*
David R. Lovejoy *VCH-Financial Markets & Corporate DEV*
Martin G. McGuinn *VCH-Retail Financial Services*
Keith P. Russell *VCH-West Coast*
W. Keith Smith *VCH-Mellon Trust; CH & CEO-The Boston Co., Inc.*
Jamie B. Stewart, Jr. *VCH-Wholesale Banking & Cash MGT*
Frederick K. Beard *EVP; CH, P & CEO-Mellon Bank (MD) N.A.*
Paul S. Beideman *EVP-Retail Financial Services*
Richard B. Berner *EVP & Chief Economist*
Paul H. Dimmick *EVP-Capital Markets*
Kenneth R. Dubuque *EVP-INTL Trust & Investment*
Richard L. Holl *EVP-Real Estate Credit Recovery*
Paul Holmes *EVP-Mortgage Banking*
Lawrence S. Kash *EVP-Investment Services; VCH Distribution-The Dreyfus Corp.*

Daniel M. Kilcullen *EVP-Global Securities Services*
Allan C. Kirkman *EVP-Real Estate FIN*
Martin J. Lippert *EVP-Information MGT & RES*
J. David Officer *EVP-Mellon Private Asset MGT*
Robert M. Parkinson *EVP & Chief Auditor*
Peter Rzasnicki *EVP-Global Trust & Services*
William J. Stallkamp *EVP; CH & CEO-Mellon PSFS*
Robert W. Stasik *EVP-Global Cash MGT*
Sherman White *EVP-Credit Recovery*
Allan P. Woods *SVP-Mellon Information Services*

Human Resources: D. Michael Roark *EVP-Human Resources*
Auditor: KPMG Peat Marwick LLP, Pittsburgh, PA
Affiliates/Divisions/Subsidiaries:

Access Capital Strategies
Cambridge, MA, & Milwaukee, WI
Provider of economically targeted investments.

AFCO Credit Corp.
New York, NY
Financer of insurance premiums with offices in the United States &
Canada.

The Boston Co. Advisors, Inc.
Boston, MA
Provider of custody & administrative services to registered invest-
ment companies.

The Boston Co. Asset Management, Inc.
Greenbrae & Palo Alto, CA; & Boston, MA
Provider of institutional investment management services.

The Boston Co., Inc.
Boston, MA, & Pittsburgh, PA
Provider of institutional trust & custody, institutional asset manage-
ment & private asset management services.

Boston Safe Deposit and Trust Co.
Boston, MA
Provider of trust & custody administration, private asset manage-
ment & jumbo mortgage lending.

CCF-Mellon Partners
Pittsburgh, PA
Marketer of investment advisory & discretionary money manage-
ment services; joint venture with Credit Commercial de France.

ChaseMellon Shareholders Services

New York, NY
Provider of securities processing & custody services.

The Dreyfus Corp.
New York, NY
Manager & administrator of mutual funds.

Dreyfus Investment Services Corp.
Pittsburgh, PA
Provider of securities brokerage services.

Dreyfus Management, Inc.
New York, NY
Provider of investment management services for institutions.

Dreyfus Retirement Services
Provider of investment products to defined contribution plans nationwide.

Dreyfus Service Corp.
New York, NY
Provider of advertising, marketing & servicing to all Dreyfus funds.

Dreyfus Trust Co.
Uniondale, NY
Provider of investment management services to institutional market-
place.

Franklin Portfolio Assoc. Trust
Boston, MA
Provider of investment management services for employee benefit
funds & institutional clients.

Mellon Bank Canada
Toronto, Ontario, Canada
Provider of banking services to corporate market throughout Canada.

Mellon Bank Community Development Corp.
Pittsburgh, PA
Developer of affordable housing & minority-owned businesses.

Mellon Bank (DE) N.A.
Wilmington, DE
Provider of banking services to consumer & commercial markets in
Delaware & nationwide cardholder processing services.

Mellon Bank, F.S.B.
Paramus, NJ
Provider of banking services to consumer & commercial markets.

Mellon Bank (MD) N.A.
Rockville, MD
Provider of banking services to consumer & commercial markets in Maryland.

Mellon Bank, N.A.
Pittsburgh, PA
Provider of banking services comprising six regions.

> Mellon Bank—Central Region
> State College, PA
> Provider of banking services in central Pennsylvania.

> Mellon Bank—Commonwealth Region
> Harrisburg, PA
> Provider of banking services in south central Pennsylvania.

> Mellon Bank—Northeastern Region
> Wilkes-Barre, PA
> Provider of banking services in northeastern Pennsylvania.

> Mellon Bank—Northern Region
> Erie, PA
> Provider of banking services in northwestern Pennsylvania.

> Mellon Bank—Western Region
> Pittsburgh, PA
> Provider of banking services in western Pennsylvania.

> Mellon PSFS
> Philadephia, PA
> Provider of banking services to consumer & commercial markets in Philadelphia region.

Mellon Bond Assoc.
Pittsburgh, PA
Provider of structured management for bond portfolios of national institutional clients.

Mellon Business Credit
Marketer of commercial finance products & banking services to corporations.

M

Mellon Capital Management Corp.
San Francisco, CA
Provider of portfolio & investment management services.

Mellon Equity Assoc.
Pittsburgh, PA
Provider of equity management services to pension & public fund markets.

Mellon Leasing Corp.
San Francisco, CA; Chicago, IL; & Pittsburgh, PA
Marketer of leasing & lease-related services to corporations throughout the United States.

Mellon Mortgage Co.
Houston, TX
Originator, purchaser & servicer of mortgage loans.

Mellon Securities Transfer Services
Encino, CA; Hartford, CT; Ridgefield, NJ; & Pittsburgh, PA
Provider of securities transfer & shareholder services.

The Network Services Division
Pittsburgh, PA
Provider of electronic fund transfer services to financial institutions & corporations.

Pareto Partners
New York, NY, & London, England
Provider of investment management services for employee benefit funds.

Premier Unit Trust Administration
Brentwood, Essex, England
Servicer of unit trusts in the United Kingdom.

The R-M Trust Co.
Canada
Provider of stock transfer & indenture trustee services to Canadian clients; joint venture with Gentra, Inc. of Toronto.

Total Employees	24,700	**Regional Employees**	9,920
Year Established	1869	**Incorporated**	PA
Stock Symbol	MEL	**Annual Meeting**	April
Stock Exchange	NYSE	**SIC Code**	6712
Stockholders			23,856
Shares Outstanding			129,397,642

Fiscal Year End	Total Revenues ($000)	Net Income/(Loss) ($000)	Total Assets ($000)
12/31/96	4,762,000	733,000	42,596,000
12/31/95	4,514,000	691,000	40,646,000
12/31/94	3,957,000	433,000	38,644,000
12/31/93	3,622,000	460,000	37,052,000

Executive Biography: Frank V. Cahouet

Birth Date: 5/25/32   **Birthplace:** Cohasset, MA

Education:
Harvard College, B.A. 1954; U of Pennsylvania, M.B.A. 1959.

Career History:
Security Pacific National Bank, various positions 1960-84 including VCH & CFO; Crocker National Corp., CH & P & CEO 1984-86; Federal National Mortgage Assn., P & COO 1986-87; Mellon Bank Corp., CH & CEO 1987-present, P 1990-present; Mellon Bank, N.A., CH & CEO 1987-present, P 1990-present.

Directorships/Memberships/Activities:
Allegheny General Hospital, DIR; Allegheny Teledyne Inc., DIR; Avery Dennison Corp., DIR; The Bankers Roundtable, P & DIR; Boy Scouts of America, DIR-Greater Pittsburgh Council; Greater Pittsburgh Chamber of Commerce, DIR; Penn's Southwest Assn., VCH; Pittsburgh Regional Alliance, CH; Saint-Gobain Corp., DIR; U.S.-Japan Business Council, Inc., DIR; World Affairs Council, DIR; Allegheny Conference on Community Development, MEM; Carnegie Mellon U, TRU; Historical Society of Western Pennsylvania, TRU; U of Pittsburgh, TRU.

Mine Safety Appliances Co.

RIDC Industrial Park, 121 Gamma Dr.
P.O. Box 426, Pittsburgh, PA 15230
Pittsburgh, PA 15238
County: Allegheny

Phone: (412) 967-3000
Fax: (412) 967-3326
Internet Address: www.msanet.com

Type of Business: Manufacturer and marketer of safety and health equipment.

Mine Safety Appliances manufactures and markets products designed to protect the safety and health of workers throughout the world. The Company's principal products include respiratory protective equipment that is air-purifying, air-supplied and self-contained in design. It also produces instruments that monitor and analyze workplace environments and control industrial processes; personal protective products including head, eye and face, body and hearing protectors; mine safety equipment and monitoring instruments such as mine lighting, rock-dusting equipment, fire-fighting foam and foam application equipment; and

M

health-related products including emergency care items and hospital instruments. Many of these products are sold under the registered trademark MSA and have applications for workers in a variety of industries, including manufacturing, fire service, power generation, telecommunications, mining, chemicals, petroleum, construction, pulp and paper processing, transportation, government, automotive, aerospace, asbestos abatement and hazardous materials cleanup. The Company's safety and health products account for more than 90% of its revenues, operating profits and assets. Other activities which do not fall within the safety and health equipment segment of the Company's business include the manufacturing and marketing of boron-based and other specialty chemicals. While the Company's principal U.S. manufacturing and research operations are located in the Pittsburgh metropolitan area, other U.S. manufacturing and research facilities are located in Englewood and Lyons, CO; Sparks, MD; Lawrence, MA; Jacksonville, NC; Dayton, OH; and Esmond, RI. Manufacturing facilities of international affiliates of the Company are located in major cities in Australia, Brazil, Canada, France, Germany, Italy, Japan, Mexico, Peru, Scotland, Spain and Sweden.

Officers: John T. Ryan III *CH & CEO*
　　　　　Thomas B. Hotopp *P*
　　　　　Werner E. Christen *VP*
　　　　　Donald H. Cuozzo *VP & SEC*
　　　　　James E. Herald *VP-FIN*
　　　　　George R. McGee *VP & GMGR-Instrument Division*
　　　　　George W. Steggles *VP*
　　　　　Dennis L. Zeitler *TRS*
　　　　　Joseph M. Barendt, Ph.D. *GMGR-Callery Chemical Division*
　　　　　William M. Lambert *GMGR-Safety Products Division*

Human Resources: Benedict V. DeMaria *DIR-Human Resources*
Auditor: Price Waterhouse LLP, Pittsburgh, PA
Affiliates/Divisions/Subsidiaries:

　　　　　AB Tegma
　　　　　Malmo, Sweden

　　　　　Aritron Instrument A.G.
　　　　　Forch, Switzerland

　　　　　Auergesellschaft GmbH
　　　　　Berlin, Germany

　　　　　Baseline Industries, Inc.
　　　　　Lyons, CO

　　　　　Better Breathing, Inc.
　　　　　Lawrence, MA

　　　　　Boart MSA (Pty.) Ltd.
　　　　　Johannesburg, South Africa

Callery Chemical
Callery, PA

Hazco Canada, Inc.
Toronto, Ontario, Canada

HAZCO Services, Inc.
Dayton, OH

MSA (Aust.) Pty. Ltd.
Sydney, Australia

MSA (Britain) Ltd.
Glascow, Scotland

MSA Canada
Toronto, Ontario, Canada

MSA de Argentina S.A.
Buenos Aires, Argentina

MSA de Chile Ltda.
Santiago, Chile

MSA de France
Paris, France

MSA de Mexico, S.A. de C.V.
Mexico City, Mexico

MSA del Peru S.A.
Lima, Peru

MSA do Brasil Ltda.
Sao Paulo, Brazil

MSA Espanola, S.A.
Barcelona, Spain

MSA Europe
Berlin, Germany

MSA Export Ltd.
Barbados

MSA (India) Ltd.
Calcutta, India

M

MSA Italiana S.p.A.
Milan, Italy

MSA Japan Ltd.
Tokyo, Japan

MSA Middle East
Abu Dhabi, United Arab Emirates

MSA Nederland, B.V.
Hoorn, The Netherlands

MSA S.E. Asia Pte. Ltd.
Singapore

MSA Switzerland Ltd.
Berne, Switzerland

MSA Zimbabwe (Pvt.) Ltd.
Harare, Zimbabwe

MSA-Auer Polska Sp. z o.o.
Warsaw, Poland

MSA-Auer Safety Technology
Budapest, Hungary

Rose Manufacturing Co.
Englewood, CO

Sibertech
Novosibirsk, Russia

Wuxi-MSA Safety Equipment Co., Ltd.
Wuxi, Peoples Republic of China

Total Employees	4,200	**Regional Employees**	1,500
Year Established	1914	**Incorporated**	PA
Stock Symbol	MNES	**Annual Meeting**	April
Stock Exchange	NASDAQ	**SIC Code**	3842
Stockholders			410
Shares Outstanding			5,195,022

Fiscal Year End	Total Revenues ($000)	Net Income/(Loss) ($000)	Total Assets ($000)
12/31/96	506,855	23,061	407,682
12/31/95	491,859	18,912	406,600
12/31/94	465,070	15,329	417,051
12/31/93	435,105	10,555	407,884

Executive Biography: John T. Ryan III

Birth Date: 8/6/43 **Birthplace:** Pittsburgh, PA
Spouse: Catharine **Children:** 3

Education:
U of Notre Dame, B.A. 1965; Harvard U, M.B.A. 1969.

Career History:
U.S. Army; Mine Safety Appliances Co., various positions 1969-74, International Division 1974-86, EVP 1986-90, P 1990-96, CH & CEO 1991-present.

Directorships/Memberships/Activities:
Federal Reserve Bank of Cleveland, DIR-Pittsburgh Branch; Regional Industrial Development Corp. of Southwestern Pennsylvania, DIR; Allegheny Conference on Community Development, MEM-Executive Comm.; Council on Foreign Relations, MEM; U of Notre Dame, MEM-Advisory Council of the College of Business Administration; Penn's Southwest Assn., TRU.

MotivePower Industries, Inc.

1200 Reedsdale St.
Pittsburgh, PA 15233
County: Allegheny

Phone: (412) 237-2250
Fax: (412) 231-2698

Type of Business: Manufacturer and distributor of engineered locomotive components; provider of locomotive fleet maintenance, overhauls and remanufacturing; and manufacturer of switcher and commuter locomotives.

MotivePower and its subsidiaries, formerly known as MK Rail Corp., design, manufacture and distribute engineered locomotive components and parts; provide locomotive fleet maintenance, remanufacturing and overhauls; and manufacture environmentally friendly switcher, commuter and mid-range, DC traction, diesel-electric and liquefied natural gas locomotives up to 4,000 horsepower. The Company operates principally through two business units, the Components Group and the Locomotive Group. The Components Group manufactures and distributes primarily aftermarket, or replacement components and parts for freight and passenger railroads, including every Class I Railroad in North America, metropolitan transit and commuter rail authorities, OEMs and other customers internationally. The Company provides most aftermarket components for locomotives manufactured by the Electro-Motive Division of General

M

Motors Corp. and certain components for locomotives made by the GE Transportation Systems unit of General Electric Co. The Company believes that it is the leading independent supplier in North America of aftermarket locomotive components such as traction motors, alternators, turbochargers, cooling systems and overhauled diesel engines. The Locomotive Group provides fleet maintenance, overhauling and remanufacturing, and manufacturing of environmentally friendly switcher, commuter and mid-range, DC traction, diesel-electric and liquefied natural gas locomotives up to 4,000 horsepower. The Company's fleet maintenance business unit provides locomotive maintenance under long-term contracts. These contracts generally cover normal, expected maintenance costs but also allow the Company to bill additional amounts to cover extraordinary maintenance. The Company was formed in April 1993 by Morrison Knudsen Corp. (MKC), which later sold 35% of the Company's common stock in an initial public stock offering in April 1994. In October 1996, MKC distributed all of its remaining ownership stake in the Company to MKC's creditors as part of MKC's bankruptcy settlement.

Officers: John C. Pope *CH*
Michael A. Wolf *P & CEO*
William F. Fabrizio *SVP & CFO*
Jeannette Fisher-Garber *VP, GC & SEC*
William D. Grab *VP & CON*
Thomas P. Lyons *VP & TRS*
Timothy R. Wesley *VP-Investor & Public Relations*

Human Resources: Scott E. Wahlstrom *VP-Human Resources & ADM*
Auditor: Deloitte & Touche LLP, Pittsburgh, PA
General Counsel: Doepken Keevican & Weiss, Pittsburgh, PA

Affiliates/Divisions/Subsidiaries:

Boise Locomotive Co. 100%
Boise, ID
Provider of locomotive remanufacturing, overhauling & manufacturing.

Clark Industries, Inc. 100%
Gilman, IL
Manufacturer of cylinder heads, pistons and liner assemblies for locomotive engines.

Engine Systems Co., Inc. 100%
Latham, NY
Remanufacturer of turbochargers for locomotive, industrial & marine engines.

MK Rail Systems of Argentina, S.A. 19%

Motor Coils Manufacturing Co. 100%
Braddock, PA

Remanufacturer of locomotive traction motors & manufacturer of rotating electrical components.

MPI de Mexico S.A. de C.V. 100%
Acambaro, Mexico City & San Luis Potosi, Mexico
Provider of locomotive fleet maintenance services.

Power Parts Co. 100%
Elk Grove Village, IL
Distributor of more than 7,000 parts for locomotives.

Touchstone Co. 100%
Jackson, TN
Manufacturer, remanufacturer & distributor of locomotive radiators, oil coolers, brake adjusters & other industrial heat exchangers.

Trenes de Buenos Aires S.A. 19%

Total Employees.........................2,102		**Regional Employees** 450	
Year Established 1993		**Incorporated** ....DE	
Stock Symbol..........................MOPO		**Annual Meeting** ....June	
Stock Exchange...............NASDAQ		**SIC Code** 3743	
Stockholders 983			
Shares Outstanding 17,562,793			

Fiscal Year End	Total Revenues ($000)	Net Income/(Loss) ($000)	Total Assets ($000)
12/31/96	291,407	11,509	234,044
12/31/95	263,718	(40,414)	280,948
12/31/94	368,537	(42,793)	311,297
12/31/93	218,160	3,632	181,930

Executive Biography: Michael A. Wolf

Birth Date: 1943   **Birthplace:** Dayton, OH
Spouse: Pam   **Children:** 2

Education:
U of Dayton, B.S.-Industrial Management 1966; U of Dayton, M.B.A. 1971; U of Pennsylvania, International Finance Program 1987; Harvard U, Advanced Management Program 1988.

Career History:
U.S. Marine Corps; International Harvester Co.; Combustion Engineering Inc.; Firestone/Bridgestone, Inc., various positions 1972-88 including EVP; Case Corp., EVP & GMGR 1988-92; Hobart Bros., Co., P & COO 1992-94; Pandrol Jackson, Inc., P & CEO 1994-96; MotivePower Industries, Inc., P & CEO 1996-present.

Directorships/Memberships/Activities:
Roadmaster Assn., MEM.

Mylan Laboratories Inc.

M

1030 Century Bldg., 130 Seventh St.
Pittsburgh, PA 15222
County: Allegheny

Phone: (412) 232-0100
Fax: (412) 232-0123
Internet Address: www.mylan.com

Type of Business: Developer, manufacturer and distributor of pharmaceutical products for resale.

Mylan Laboratories and its subsidiaries are engaged in the development, licensing, manufacturing and marketing of numerous generic and proprietary finished pharmaceutical and wound care products. These products include solid oral dosage forms, as well as suspensions, liquids, injectables and transdermals, many of which are packaged in specialized systems. Mylan Pharmaceuticals Inc. produces a range of generic pharmaceutical products including analgesic, antiangina, antianxiety, antibiotic, antidepressant, antidiabetic, antidiarrheal, antigout, antihypertensive, antihypolipidemic, anti-inflammatory, antineoplastic, antipsychotic, anxiolytic, beta blocker, bronchial dilator, calcium channel blocker, diuretic, hypnotic agent, H2 antagonist, muscle relaxant and uricosuric products. Mylan Inc. operates pharmaceutical manufacturing plants located in Caguas and Cidra, Puerto Rico. Bertek, Inc. is a manufacturer of transdermal drug delivery systems technology, with coating, laminating, extrusion and labeling operations. In addition, it provides components, using internally developed technology, for transdermal patches marketed by other companies. Dow Hickam Pharmaceuticals, Inc. is a branded pharmaceutical company. It manufactures and markets specialty pharmaceutical products and medical devices used principally as wound and burn care treatments through its nationwide sales force. Somerset Pharmaceuticals, Inc., pursuant to a license agreement with a Hungarian pharmaceutical company, has exclusive marketing rights to the product Eldepryl® in the United States and certain other countries. Eldepryl is a drug used to treat Parkinson's disease. UDL Laboratories, Inc., acquired during fiscal 1996, is a supplier of unit dose generic pharmaceuticals to the institutional and long-term care markets. A majority of the Company's products are sold to food and drug store chains, and to pharmaceutical distributors and wholesalers, who market to retailers, managed care entities, hospitals and government agencies. Certain other products are marketed to institutional accounts who in turn obtain the products from pharmaceutical distributors and wholesalers. The Company has entered into strategic alliances with several branded pharmaceutical companies. These alliances, through distribution and licensing agreements, provide the Company with additional products, broadening its product line. In fiscal 1996, research and development expenses totaled approximately $39 million.

Officers: Milan Puskar *CH, P & CEO*
Dana G. Barnett *EVP*
Roderick P. Jackson *SVP*
C. B. Todd *SVP*

Louis J. DeBone *VP-OPR*
Roger L. Foster *VP & GC*
John P. O'Donnell, Ph.D. *VP-RES & Quality Control*
Patricia Sunseri *VP-Investor & Public Relations*
Robert W. Smiley *SEC*

Human Resources: Robert Myers *DIR-Human Resources*
Auditor: Deloitte & Touche LLP, Pittsburgh, PA
Affiliates/Divisions/Subsidiaries:

American Triumvirate Insurance Co. 100%
Burlington, VT
Insurance company.

Bertek, Inc. 100%
St. Albans, VT
Manufacturer of transdermal drug delivery systems.

Dow Hickam Pharmaceuticals, Inc. 100%
Sugar Land, TX
Manufacturer & marketer of wound & burn care products.

Mylan Holding Inc. 100%
Pittsburgh, PA
Cash management company.

Mylan Inc. 100%
Caguas, Puerto Rico
Manufacturer of pharmaceuticals.

Mylan Pharmaceuticals Inc. 100%
Morgantown, WV
Manufacturer of generic & proprietary pharmaceuticals.

Somerset Pharmaceuticals, Inc. 50%
Tampa, FL
Researcher, developer & marketer of pharmaceutical products.

UDL Laboratories, Inc. 100%
Rockford, IL
Supplier of unit dose generic pharmaceuticals.

Total Employees	1,733	**Regional Employees**	8
Year Established	1961	**Incorporated**	PA
Stock Symbol	MYL	**Annual Meeting**	July
Stock Exchange	NYSE	**SIC Code**	2834
Stockholders			106,022
Shares Outstanding			121,733,916

Fiscal Year End	Total Revenues ($000)	Net Income/(Loss) ($000)	Total Assets ($000)
3/31/96	392,860	102,325	692,009
3/31/95	396,120	120,869	546,201
3/31/94	251,773	73,067	403,325
3/31/93	211,964	70,621	351,105

Executive Biography: Milan Puskar

Birth Date: 9/8/34   **Birthplace:** Vintondale, PA
Children: 1

Education:
Youngstown State U, B.S.-Engineering 1960.

Career History:
U.S. Army, 1954-57; Mylan Laboratories Inc., C-FND, various positions including SEC, TRS & EVP 1961-72; ICN Pharmaceuticals Inc., VP & GMGR-Cincinnati Division 1972-75; Elan Corp. (Dublin, Ireland), PTR 1975-76; Mylan Laboratories Inc., P 1976-present, VCH 1980-93, CH & CEO 1993-present; West Virginia U, Adjunct AST Professor-School of Pharmacy 1979-present.

Directorships/Memberships/Activities:
Duquesne U, DIR; VivoRx, Inc., DIR.

National Record Mart, Inc.

507 Forest Ave., P.O. Box 2003
Carnegie, PA 15106
County: Allegheny

Phone: (412) 276-6200
Fax: (412) 276-6201

Type of Business: Specialty retailer of prerecorded music and entertainment products.

   National Record Mart is a specialty retailer of home entertainment products, including compact discs, prerecorded audio cassettes, videos and related accessories. The Company claims that it is the seventh-largest specialty retailer of prerecorded music in the country as measured by the number of stores. The Company has developed five distinct store concepts, each of which targets a different customer base. National Record Mart or NRM Music focuses on the 12-28 year-old demographic group and is located primarily in enclosed shopping malls. Waves Music is designed to appeal to the adult consumer with locations in upscale retail centers. Music Oasis, a larger, value-price oriented store featuring a broad music selection for the heavy music user, is typically located in strip centers or freestanding locations as a destination store. Vibes Music is a college-based concept with an eclectic product mix geared to appeal to students situated on campus. Waves Music and Gifts is a new concept that is positioned to capitalize on the dense seasonal population of families on summer vacation at resorts along the Atlantic coast. The Company's stores sell a broad array of CDs and cassettes in all major music categories, including rock, pop, alternative, country, easy listening, classical, jazz, religious, new age, rhythm and blues, children's, educational, show tunes and movie soundtracks, and world music. The stores offer from 6,000 to 35,000 titles, with an average of 15,000 titles per location. The stores also sell prerecorded videocassettes, including instructional, exercise, children's, sports, music and movies. In addition, the stores carry a variety of accessories such as blank video and audio cassette tapes, maintenance and cleaning products, home and portable storage cases, sheet music, posters, T-shirts, magazines, books and other items. To increase customer traffic, the Company offers tickets in most of its stores located in certain markets, including Chicago, IL; Louisville, KY; Cincinnati, Cleveland, Columbus, Dayton and Youngstown, OH; Pittsburgh, PA; and Madison and Milwaukee, WI. Its ticket outlets provide customers with access to tickets offered by Ticketmaster as well as tickets to other local concerts and sporting events. As of March 29, 1997, the Company operated 148 stores located primarily in the eastern part of the United States. On August 4, 1993, the Company completed its initial public stock offering.

Officers: William A. Teitelbaum *CH & CEO*
    Larry Mundorf *P & COO*
    Theresa Carlise *SVP, CFO & TRS*
    George Balicky *VP-MKT*
    Lynda J. Huffman *SEC & Audit MGR*

Human Resources: Charles Costello *DIR-Human Resources*
Purchasing Director: John Grandoni *DIR-Purchasing*
Auditor: Ernst & Young LLP, Pittsburgh, PA
General Counsel: Reed Smith Shaw & McClay, Pittsburgh, PA
Affiliates/Divisions/Subsidiaries:

   National Record Mart Investments, Inc. 100%

Total Employees............................1,324		**Regional Employees** 500
Year Established 1937		**Incorporated** ....DE
Stock Symbol............................NRMI		**Annual Meeting** ....September
Stock Exchange................NASDAQ		**SIC Code**......................................5735
Stockholders 1,096			
Shares Outstanding 4,844,624			

Fiscal Year End	Total Revenues ($000)	Net Income/(Loss) ($000)	Total Assets ($000)
¹3/30/96	99,084	(3,884)	52,924
3/25/95	95,697	712	53,824
3/26/94	80,628	2,490	45,809
3/27/93	72,720	2,275	32,644

¹*Fiscal year ended 3/30/96 includes 53 weeks.*

Executive Biography: William A. Teitelbaum

Birth Date: 8/5/50	**Birthplace:** New York, NY
Spouse: Michelle	**Children:** 2

Education:
State U of New York (Albany, NY), B.S. 1972; New York U, M.B.A. 1974.

N

Career History:
L. F. Rothschild Unterberg & Towbin, Associate-Corporate FIN 1976-79; Bear Stearns & Co., PTR 1980-85; Remsen Partners, Ltd., CH 1985-present; National Record Mart, Inc., VP & TRS 1986-91, P 1991-1997, CH 1986-present, CEO 1991-present.

Directorships/Memberships/Activities:
Vista Properties, Inc., DIR.

North Pittsburgh Systems, Inc.

4008 Gibsonia Rd.
Gibsonia, PA 15044
County: Allegheny

Phone: (412) 443-9600
Fax: (412) 443-9663
Internet Address: www.nauticom.net

Type of Business: Provider of telecommunications equipment and services.

North Pittsburgh Systems is a holding company operating through its four subsidiaries. The Company, through North Pittsburgh Telephone Co. (NPTC) and Penn Telecom, Inc. (PTI), is primarily engaged in providing telecommunications equipment and services to its customers generally located in Western Pennsylvania. NPTC furnishes wireline telecommunication services in all or parts of Allegheny, Armstrong, Butler and Westmoreland Counties, PA. As of January 31, 1997, NPTC served approximately 61,500 customers through nine digital fiber-linked central offices (eight exchanges) in its franchised area. Telephone service by NPTC to locations outside of its franchised telephone service territory, but within the Local Access Transport Area (identified in this case as the 412 Numbering Plan Area), is furnished through switched and special access connections with Bell Atlantic-Pennsylvania, Inc., other independent telephone companies and, in some instances, interexchange carriers, competitive access providers or resellers. NPTC also provides facilities for special circuits (alarms, data transmission, etc.), mobile telephone and other services and receives revenues from the sale of advertising space in telephone directories. In addition, NPTC has investments in three cellular limited partnerships which serve markets in the Pittsburgh metropolitan area, and Clarion and Lawrence Counties. The principal business activities of PTI consist of the sale, rental and servicing of telecommunication equipment to end users, the resale of bulk-billed message toll services and high-capacity intercity facilities. Management Consulting Solutions, Inc. (MCSI) and Pinnatech, Inc. (PI) were formed in 1995. MCSI provides consulting and computer outsourcing services to health care and other industries. PI provides Internet access services in Western Pennsylvania.

Officers: Charles E. Thomas, Sr.   *CH*
                 Gerald A. Gorman   *P*

N. William Barthlow *VP & AST-SEC*
Harry R. Brown *VP*
Allen P. Kimble *VP, SEC & TRS*
Kevin J. Albaugh *AVP*
Frank A. Macefe *AVP*
Flo E. Allison *AST-SEC*
Dorothy J. Spithaler *AST-SEC & Shareholder Services*
Kathleen F. Newcomer *AST-TRS*

Auditor: KPMG Peat Marwick LLP, Pittsburgh, PA
Affiliates/Divisions/Subsidiaries:

Management Consulting Solutions, Inc. 100%
Cranberry Township, PA
Provider of consulting & computer outsourcing services.

North Pittsburgh Telephone Co. 100%
Gibsonia, PA
Telephone public utility.

Penn Telecom, Inc. 100%
Cranberry Township, PA
Provider of telecommunications equipment & services.

Pinnatech, Inc. 100%
Gibsonia, PA
Provider of Internet access services.

Total Employees............336		**Regional Employees** 336	
Year Established 1906		**Incorporated**...................................PA	
Stock Symbol............NPSI		**Annual Meeting**.....................May	
Stock Exchange.........NASDAQ		**SIC Code**.....................................4813	
Stockholders 3,146			
Shares Outstanding 15,040,000			

Fiscal Year End	Total Revenues ($000)	Net Income/(Loss) ($000)	Total Assets ($000)
12/31/96	59,933	11,730	99,523
12/31/95	52,757	10,687	96,156
12/31/94	49,188	9,904	91,578
12/31/93	44,241	9,165	89,771

Executive Biography: Gerald A. Gorman
Birth Date: 1929
Spouse: Flo   **Children:** 2

Education:
Penn State U, B.S.

Career History:
Deloitte & Touche LLP, Accountant; North Pittsburgh Telephone Co., CON
1966-68, TRS 1968-79, SEC 1968-93, VP-FIN 1972-92, AST-GMGR 1986-92, EVP

1992-93, GMGR 1992-present, P 1993-present; North Pittsburgh Systems, Inc., TRS 1968-79, SEC 1968-93, VP-FIN 1985-92, AST-GMGR 1986-92, EVP 1992-94, P 1994-present.

Noxso Corp.

2414 Lytle Rd., Ste. 300
Bethel Park, PA 15102
County: Allegheny

Phone: (412) 854-1200
Fax: (412) 854-5729
Internet Address: www.noxso.com

Type of Business: Developer, tester and marketer of a process capable of removing certain emissions from the flue gas generated by the burning of coal.

NOXSO is a development stage company engaged in developing, testing and marketing a process (NOXSO Process) to remove a high percentage of those pollutants which cause acid rain and ground level ozone from flue gas generated by burning fossil fuel. The Company has developed a patented process to control the nitrogen and sulfur oxides that would otherwise result from burning high sulfur coal to make electricity. The NOXSO Process does not produce any waste generated by cleaning the flue gas. Laboratory and pilot demonstrations of the NOXSO Process have been conducted by the Company aided by substantial funds and support provided by W. R. Grace & Co. (Grace), the United States Department of Energy and the Ohio Coal Development Office. In these demonstrations, between 70% and 95% of the nitrogen oxide emissions and in excess of 95% of the sulfur oxide emissions were simultaneously removed. The NOXSO Process employs a reusable sorbent material to adsorb the sulfur oxides and nitrogen oxides from the polluted flue gas. The sorbent is licensed to and manufactured by Grace. The Grace license is nonexclusive. The Company has entered into an exclusive license agreement with FLS miljo a/s (FLS), a Danish corporation engaged in the construction and design of utility power plants, to permit FLS to market and construct plants which utilize the NOXSO Process in Europe, Indonesia, Russia, Taiwan, Thailand and Turkey. The principal focus of the Company in the near term is to complete the construction of a full-scale commercial demonstration of the NOXSO Process, planned for operation in Alcoa Generating Corps.' Warrick Generating Station in Newburgh, IN. Its long-term goal is to derive revenue from licensing the NOXSO Process to engineering firms which specialize in construction of pollution control systems and from royalties on the sale by the suppliers of sorbent to users of the NOXSO Process. The Company also intends to use its engineering expertise to develop other technologies, processes, substances and facilities to assist others to comply with environmental laws and regulations, and to perform research and development projects for others. In 1980, the Company completed its initial public stock offering.

Recent Events: On June 4 1997, the Company announced that it would consent to the jurisdiction of the Bankruptcy Court for the Eastern District of Tennessee pursuant to the involuntary petition in bankruptcy which was filed by Olin Corp. and two other creditors on 2/6/97; and that it would convert the bankruptcy proceeding to a Chapter 11 reorganization.

Officers: Edwin J. Kilpela *P & CEO*
John L. Haslbeck *VP & TRS*
Robert M. Long *SEC*

Human Resources: Rita Bolli *MKT MGR*
Auditor: Arthur Anderson LLP, Pittsburgh, PA
General Counsel: Doepken Keevican & Weiss, P.C., Pittsburgh, PA

Affiliates/Divisions/Subsidiaries:

PROJEX, Inc. 70%
Provider of construction management services.

Total Employees............................20	**Regional Employees** 20
Year Established 1979	**Incorporated** ....VA
Stock Symbol..........................NOXO	**Annual Meeting** ....May
Stock Exchange ....OTC	**SIC Code**....................................8731
Stockholders 830	
Shares Outstanding...9,656,611	

Fiscal Year End	Total Revenues ($000)	Net Income/(Loss) ($000)	Total Assets ($000)
¹6/30/96	188	(394)	11,199
¹6/30/95	888	(1,761)	3,424
¹6/30/94	1,194	(1,932)	3,690
¹6/30/93	1,930	(2,292)	4,964

¹*Revenues consist of project cost reimbursements, government grants and interest income.*

Executive Biography: Edwin J. Kilpela

Birth Date: 5/2/46   **Birthplace:** Pittsburgh, PA
Children: 2

Education:
Carnegie Mellon U, Engineer; U of Pittsburgh, M.B.A.

Career History:
Westinghouse Electric Corp., various positions for 28 years including GMGR-Commercial Environmental Business; NOXSO Corp., P & CEO 1997-present.

Directorships/Memberships/Activities:
PDG Environmental, Inc., DIR.

NSD Bancorp, Inc.

N

5004 McKnight Rd.
Pittsburgh, PA 15237
County: Allegheny

Phone: (412) 231-6900
Fax: (412) 359-2673
Internet Address: www.northsidebank.com

Type of Business: Bank holding company.

NSD Bancorp is a single-bank holding company which acquired NorthSide Bank (Bank) as its wholly owned subsidiary on August 2, 1993. The Company derives substantially all of its income from the banking and bank-related services provided by the Bank. The state-chartered Bank is a full-service bank offering retail banking services, such as demand, savings and time deposits, money market accounts, secured and unsecured loans, mortgage loans, safe deposit boxes, holiday club accounts, wire transfers, money orders and traveler's checks. Services to commercial customers are also offered, including real estate mortgage loans, lines of credit, inventory and accounts receivable financing, and equipment leasing. The Bank's deposits are derived from more than 50,000 individual and commercial accounts. Its service area includes the northern portion of Allegheny County and southern Butler County, PA. In addition to the Bank's main office located at 100 Federal St. in downtown Pittsburgh, it operates nine additional branch offices located in Allison Park (2), Cranberry Township and Pittsburgh (6).

Officers: Lawrence R. Gaus *CH*
Lloyd G. Gibson *P & CEO*
Edward A. Balmer *VP*
James P. Radick *TRS*

Human Resources: Gloria J. Bush *SEC; Human Resource Department MGR*
NorthSide Bank

Auditor: Coopers & Lybrand L.L.P., Pittsburgh, PA

Affiliates/Divisions/Subsidiaries:

NorthSide Bank 100%
State-chartered bank.

100 Federal Street, Inc. 100%

Total Employees	150	**Regional Employees**	150
Year Established	1934	**Incorporated**	PA
Stock Symbol	NSDB	**Annual Meeting**	April
Stock Exchange	NASDAQ	**SIC Code**	6712
Stockholders			439
Shares Outstanding			1,631,845

Fiscal Year End	Total Revenues ($000)	Net Income/(Loss) ($000)	Total Assets ($000)
12/31/96	22,841	3,689	304,802
12/31/95	21,148	3,673	258,732
12/31/94	17,987	2,811	242,009
12/31/93	17,504	2,634	228,449

Executive Biography: Lloyd G. Gibson

Birth Date: 9/2/55 **Birthplace:** Pittsburgh, PA
Spouse: Regina Ann **Children:** 2

Education:
U of Pittsburgh, B.S.; U of Pittsburgh, M.A.; U of Pennsylvania, M.B.A.1980.

Career History:
Mellon Bank, 1980-89; The Dollar Savings and Trust Co. (Youngstown, OH), VP 1989-91; The Miners and Mechanics Savings and Trust Co. (Steubenville, OH), P & CEO 1991-93; NorthSide Bank, P & CEO 1993-present; NSD Bancorp, Inc., P & CEO 1993-present.

Directorships/Memberships/Activities:
The Allegheny Club, MEM; Pennsylvania Bankers Assn., MEM-Executive Comm.; Wildwood Golf Club, MEM; Pittsburgh History & Landmarks, TRU.

Parkvale Financial Corp.

4220 William Penn Hwy.
Monroeville, PA 15146
County: Allegheny

Phone: (412) 373-7200
Fax: (412) 373-1570
Internet Address: www.parkvale.com

Type of Business: Bank holding company.

Parkvale Financial is a unitary savings and loan holding company. Its subsidiary, Parkvale Savings Bank (Bank), is a state-chartered permanent reserve fund stock savings bank. The Bank conducts business in the greater Pittsburgh metropolitan area through its main office located at the above address and 29 branch offices in Allegheny, Beaver, Butler and Westmoreland Counties, PA. As of June 30, 1996, the Bank stated that it was the fifth-largest financial institution headquartered in the Pittsburgh metropolitan area, based on assets. The primary business of the Bank consists of attracting deposits from the general public in the communities that it serves and investing such deposits, together with other funds, in residential real estate loans, mortgage-backed securities, consumer loans, commercial loans and investment securities. The Bank focuses on providing a range of consumer and commercial services to individuals, partnerships and corporations. It also offers various types of deposit and checking accounts, including commercial checking accounts and automated teller machines. The Bank derives its income primarily from interest charged on loans and interest on

P

investments, and, to a lesser extent, fees and service charges. Its principal expenses are interest on deposits and borrowings, and operating expenses. Funds for lending activities are provided primarily by deposits, loan repayments, Federal Home Loan Bank advances and other borrowings, and earnings provided by operations. To supplement the demand for loans in its primary market area at acceptable yields and to achieve geographic asset diversification, the Bank purchases adjustable rate residential loans subject to its normal underwriting standards. In addition, the Bank operates loan production offices through its subsidiary, Parkvale Mortgage Corp., with offices in Raleigh, NC; Columbus, OH; and Fairfax, VA.

Officers: Robert D. Pfischner *CH*
Robert J. McCarthy, Jr. *P & CEO*
Steven A. Friedman *SVP-Audit & Compliance*
Bruce C. Gilleylen *SVP & Chief Lending Officer*
Timothy G. Rubritz *SVP, TRS & CFO*
Nancy E. Kelly *VP-Branch Coordination*
Charles M. Murslack *VP-Data Processing*
Thomas R. Ondek *VP-Savings*
Robert A. Stephens *VP-Mortgage Lending*
Erna A. Golota *SEC*
Joseph C. DeFazio *AST-TRS*
Mirta L. Engel *AST-CON*

Human Resources: Gail A. Bieri *VP-Human Resources & MKT*
Auditor: Ernst & Young LLP, Pittsburgh, PA
General Counsel: Elias Matz Tiernan & Herrick, Washington, D.C.

Affiliates/Divisions/Subsidiaries:

Parkvale Savings Bank 100%

P. V. Financial Service Inc. 100%
Service corporation.

Parkvale Mortgage Corp. 100%
Fairfax, VA
Lender in Washington, D.C., Raleigh, N.C. & Columbus, OH, areas.

Renaissance Corp. 100%
Provider of collateral evaluations on consumer loans.

Total Employees	280	**Regional Employees**	275
Year Established	1943	**Incorporated**	PA
Stock Symbol	PVSA	**Annual Meeting**	October
Stock Exchange	NASDAQ	**SIC Code**	6712
Stockholders			520
Shares Outstanding			3,233,478

Fiscal Year End	Total Revenues ($000)	Net Income/(Loss) ($000)	Total Assets ($000)
6/30/96	69,175	9,618	919,242
6/30/95	63,050	8,071	896,422
6/30/94	61,724	7,228	873,786
6/30/93	69,216	6,791	886,074

Executive Biography: Robert J. McCarthy, Jr.

Birth Date: 4/22/43   **Birthplace:** Washington, D.C.
Spouse: Jean Marie   **Children:** 3

Education:
U of Maryland, B.S.-Accounting & Finance 1967; George Washington U, M.B.A. 1976.

Career History:
Ernst & Ernst (Baltimore, MD), Accountant; Metropolitan Federal Savings Bank (Bethesda, MD), P & CEO; Parkvale Savings Bank, P & CEO 1984-present; Parkvale Financial Corp., P & CEO 1987-present.

Directorships/Memberships/Activities:
Federal Home Loan Bank of Pittsburgh, VCH & DIR; PACB Foundation, CH; PACB Services, Inc., CH.

PDG Environmental, Inc.

300 Oxford Dr.
Monroeville, PA 15146
County: Allegheny

Phone: (412) 856-2200
Fax: (412) 856-6914
Internet Address: www.pdge.com

Type of Business: Provider of asbestos abatement services to the public and private sectors.

PDG Environmental is a holding company which, through its wholly owned operating subsidiaries, is engaged primarily in providing asbestos abatement services to the public and private sectors. Through its operating subsidiaries, the Company has expertise in all types of asbestos abatement, including removal and disposal, enclosure (constructing structures around asbestos-containing area) and encapsulation (spraying asbestos-containing materials with an approved sealant). Asbestos abatement is principally performed in commercial buildings, government and institutional buildings, schools and industrial facilities. The Company's operating subsidiaries provide asbestos abatement services on a project contract basis. Individual projects are competitively bid, although most contracts with private owners are ultimately negotiated. The majority of contracts undertaken are on a fixed price basis. The length of the contracts are typically less than one year; however, larger projects may require two or three years to complete. The Company closely monitors contracts by assigning responsibility for each contract

P

to a project manager who coordinates the project until its completion. The asbestos abatement process is performed by a qualified labor force in accordance with regulatory requirements, contract specifications and the Company's written operating procedures manual which describes worker safety and protection procedures, air monitoring protocols and abatement methods. The Company's asbestos abatement operations have been generally concentrated in the northeastern, mid-Atlantic, southeastern and southwestern portions of the United States. The majority of its national marketing efforts are performed by members of senior management located in its headquarters facility at the above address. Regional marketing and project operations are also conducted through branch offices located in Fort Lauderdale, FL; Atlanta, GA; New York, NY; Export and Hazleton, PA; Rock Hill, SC; and Houston, TX. In fiscal 1997, approximately 72% of its operating subsidiaries' revenues were derived from private sector clients, 23% from government contracts and 5% from schools.

Officers: John C. Regan *CH & CEO*
   Todd Fortier *CFO*
Human Resources: Dulcia Maire *SEC*
Auditor: Ernst & Young LLP, Pittsburgh, PA
Affiliates/Divisions/Subsidiaries:

   Enviro-Tech Abatement Services 100%

   PDG, Inc. 100%

   Project Development Group, Inc. 100%

Total Employees.............................216		**Regional Employees** 50	
Year Established 1984		**Incorporated** ....DE	
Stock Symbol ....PDGE		**Annual Meeting**.........................July	
Stock Exchange ....OTC		**SIC Code**.....................................1799	
Stockholders 2,203			
Shares Outstanding 5,923,868			

Fiscal Year End	Total Revenues ($000)	Net Income/(Loss) ($000)	Total Assets ($000)
1/31/97	16,183	(486)	6,165
¹1/31/96	16,215	(2,451)	7,564
¹1/31/95	17,659	473	9,690
¹1/31/94	16,310	(1,445)	7,904

¹*Restated to reflect the treatment of PDG Remediation, Inc. as a discontinued operation.*

Executive Biography: John C. Regan
Birth Date: 1944

Education:
Carnegie Mellon U, B.S.-Civil Engineering 1965; Carnegie Mellon U, M.S.-Civil Engineering 1966; U of Pittsburgh, M.B.A. 1971.

Career History:
Project Development Group, Inc. (subsidiary of Company), FND, CH & P 1984-present; PDG Environmental, Inc., CH & CEO 1990-present.

Directorships/Memberships/Activities:
Associated Soil and Foundation Engineers, DIR; Pennsylvania Asbestos Council, DIR; Allegheny County Advisory Board on Asbestos Issues, MEM.

Pitt-Des Moines, Inc.

3400 Grand Ave.
Pittsburgh, PA 15225
County: Allegheny

Phone: (412) 331-3000
Fax: (412) 331-7403
Internet Address: www.pdm.com

Type of Business: Provider of engineering and construction services, and processor and distributor of steel products.

Pitt-Des Moines is a diversified engineering and construction company that also processes and distributes a broad range of carbon steel products. The Company is comprised of three business segments. The Engineered Construction segment is organized into two divisions, PDM Water and PDM Engineered Construction. This segment designs, fabricates and erects many types of facilities and structures, including elevated- and flat-bottom water storage tanks for water service and fire protection requirements, and treatment tanks for the purification, filtration and softening of water; oil and chemical storage tanks used for storing crude oil, petroleum, gasoline and other petroleum derivatives and chemicals; and high speed wind tunnels, altitude test chambers, hydrospace test facilities, and high vacuum and thermal test facilities for use in connection with energy, aerospace and defense research. This segment also fabricates and erects various vessels used in the processing of a variety of oil and chemical products; and miscellaneous plate work, including penstocks and breechings, stacks and stack liners, scrubbers, absorbers, flow conductors and heat exchangers for utilities and private industry. In addition, this segment designs and builds supercritical fluid extraction facilities for the food processing industry and anaerobic digestors for the wastewater treatment industry. The Steel Construction segment fabricates and erects structural steel for commercial, institutional and public sector buildings for government agencies, private developers and general contractors; and fabricates structural steel for new bridges, and fabricates and erects structural steel for bridge rehabilitation for government agencies and general contractors. The Steel Service Centers segment operates seven steel service centers and three culvert facilities located in the West and Midwest regions of the United States. This segment processes and distributes to the end users a general line of carbon steel products, including plates, sheets, structural shapes, bars, tubes, pipe and other miscellaneous metal products. This segment also manufactures and markets to the end users corrugated metal culvert pipe and accessories. The Steel

P

Service Centers' primary markets include steel fabricators, OEMs and the mining, logging, agricultural and road construction industries. In 1996, approximately 41% of the Company's revenues were derived from the Engineered Construction segment, 34% from the Steel Service Centers segment and 25% from the Steel Construction segment.

Special Designations: ENR_{400}

Officers: William R. Jackson *CH Emeritus*
Phillip O. Elbert *CH*
William W. McKee *P & CEO*
Richard A. Byers *VP-FIN & TRS*
Marvin L. Fry *CON*
Thomas R. Lloyd *GC & SEC*
Richard F. Gisler *AST-SEC*

Human Resources: Carolyn J. Price
Auditor: Ernst & Young LLP, Pittsburgh, PA
General Counsel: Buchanan Ingersoll P.C., Pittsburgh, PA

Affiliates/Divisions/Subsidiaries:

Candraft Detailing, Inc. 100%
Port Coquitlam, British Columbia, Canada

General Steel Corp. 90%
Vancouver, WA

HyCon, Inc. 81%
Harpersville, AL

Oregon Culvert Co., Inc. 81%
Tualatin, OR

PDM Bridge Division 100%
Eau Claire & Wasau, WI

PDM International Ltd. 100%
The Woodlands, TX

PDM Latin America Ltd. 100%
The Woodlands, TX

PDM Strocal, Inc. 100%
Stockton, CA

Stockton Culvert 100%
Stockton, CA

Total Employees.........................2,006   **Regional Employees** 150
Year Established 1892   **Incorporated**..................................PA

Stock Symbol...........................PDM
Stock Exchange........................ASE
Stockholders 435
Shares Outstanding 3,483,001

Annual Meeting ....May
SIC Code.....................................3443

Fiscal Year End	Total Revenues ($000)	Net Income/(Loss) ($000)	Total Assets ($000)
12/31/96	468,274	12,551	199,885
12/31/95	461,274	13,019	201,136
12/31/94	408,061	12,060	214,201
12/31/93	323,707	1,038	177,803

Executive Biography: William W. McKee

Birth Date: 1939

Education:
Georgia Tech, B.S.-Civil Engineering 1960; Graduate studies in Industrial Psychology & Organizational Development.

Career History:
Bethlehem Steel Corp., various positions 1960-63 including MGT Trainee, Foreman, Field ENG, AST-Shop Superintendent; Allied Structural Steel Corp., various positions 1963-67 including AST-Chief ENG, Plant MGR, VP-OPR; Herrick Corp. (Hayward, CA), various positions 1967-73 including MGR-MFG, VP & GMGR, P 1973-79; Hogan Manufacturing, P 1980-; McKee and Associates, Consultant 1983-; Elbert and McKee Co., PTR 1984-; Chicago Steel Corp., SEC 1986-87; Pitt-Des Moines, Inc., EVP-PDM Structural Group 1987-, P-PDM Plate Group 1987-, P & CEO 1990-present.

Directorships/Memberships/Activities:
American Institute of Steel Construction, DIR; Boy Scouts of America, DIR-Greater Pittsburgh Council; Harley Owners Group, MEM.

Pittsburgh Home Financial Corp.

438 Wood St.
Pittsburgh, PA 15222
County: Allegheny

Phone: (412) 281-0780
Fax: (412) 281-3750

Type of Business: Bank holding company.

Pittsburgh Home Financial is a unitary bank holding company and the sole stockholder of Pittsburgh Home Savings Bank (Bank). The Company was organized for the purpose of acquiring all of the capital stock of the Bank in connection with the reorganization of the Bank to the stock holding company form, which was completed on April 1, 1996. The Bank is a state-chartered savings bank. It conducts business through its corporate office, located at the above address, and six branch offices located in Butler and Pittsburgh (Bloomfield,

Dormont, Mt. Lebanon, Mt. Oliver and Oakland), PA. The Bank is a community-oriented financial institution engaged primarily in the business of attracting deposits from the general public and using such funds, together with other borrowings, to invest primarily in real estate loans, investment securities and mortgage-backed securities. The Bank's deposits are insured by the Federal Deposit Insurance Corp. under the Savings Assn. Insurance Fund.

Officers: J. Ardie Dillen *CH, P & CEO; P & CEO-Pittsburgh Home Savings Bank*
Michael J. Kirk *SVP & CFO; SVP-Pittsburgh Home Savings Bank*
Jess B. Mellor *SEC; SEC-Pittsburgh Home Savings Bank*

Auditor: Ernst & Young LLP, Pittsburgh, PA
General Counsel: Ruffenach and Lochner, Pittsburgh, PA

Affiliates/Divisions/Subsidiaries:

Pittsburgh Home Savings Bank 100%
Savings bank.

Total Employees............................58	**Regional Employees** 58
Year Established 1942	**Incorporated**.................................PA
Stock Symbol ....PHFC	**Annual Meeting** ....January
Stock Exchange...............NASDAQ	**SIC Code**....................................6712
Stockholders 607
Shares Outstanding 2,134,840

Fiscal Year End	Total Revenues ($000)	Net Income/(Loss) ($000)	Total Assets ($000)
9/30/96	13,302	772	195,330
9/30/95	10,330	705	157,570
9/30/94	8,394	351	130,646
9/30/93	9,788	925	135,403

Executive Biography: J. Ardie Dillen

Birth Date: 1958   **Birthplace:** Altoona, PA
Spouse: Cynthia   **Children:** 3

Education:
Carnegie Mellon U, 1980.

Career History:
Main Hurdman (Pittsburgh, PA), Auditor 1980-86; Pittsburgh Home Savings Bank, SVP-FIN & ADM 1986-92, P & CEO 1992-present; Pittsburgh Home Financial Corp., CH & P & CEO -present.

Directorships/Memberships/Activities:
Pennsylvania Assn. of Community Bankers, DIR; Rotary Club of Pittsburgh, DIR.

PNC Bank Corp.

One PNC Plaza, 249 Fifth Ave.
Pittsburgh, PA 15222
County: Allegheny

Phone: (412) 762-2000
Fax: (412) 762-7074
Internet Address: www.pncbank.com

Type of Business: Bank holding company.

PNC Bank is a bank holding company. Since 1983, the Company has diversified its geographical presence and product capabilities through strategic bank and nonbank acquisitions and the formation of various nonbanking subsidiaries. The Company is one of the largest financial services enterprises in the United States and operates five lines of business. Each line of business focuses on specific customer segments and offers financial products and services in its primary geographic locations in Delaware, Kentucky, New Jersey, Ohio and Pennsylvania, and nationally through retail distribution networks and alternative delivery channels. The Consumer Banking line of business provides lending, deposit, personal trust, brokerage, investment management, credit card, auto leasing and financial advisory services to individuals and small businesses. Its services are provided on a national basis through online banking, telephone access and ATMs, as well as a network of community banking offices in eight geographic markets, serving 3.3 million households and 135,000 small businesses. The Corporate Banking line of business includes Middle Market, which serves customers with annual sales of $5 million to $250 million and those in certain specialized industries; Large Corporate, which serves customers with annual sales of more than $250 million; and Equity Management, which makes venture capital investments. The Mortgage Banking line of business includes the acquisition, origination, securitization and servicing of residential mortgages, as well as the retention of selected loans in the portfolio. The Asset Management line of business includes Investment Management and Mutual Fund Processing. Investment Management provides liquidity, fixed income and equity advisory services to institutional, family wealth and retail clients. It also performs wholesale marketing activities for Compass Capital Funds, the Company's proprietary mutual funds. Mutual Fund Processing provides accounting, administration, transfer and custody services to financial institutions and integrated banking services to the brokerage community. With $109 billion in assets under management, the Company claims to be the nation's second largest bank manager of mutual funds and the 21st-largest investment manager. The Real Estate Banking line of business serves national, regional and local real estate developers, owners, property managers and mortgage bankers by providing credit and other financial services, including mortgage securitization, private debt placement and treasury management services. In 1996, the Company derived approximately 57% of its revenues from Consumer Banking, 20% from Corporate Banking, 10% from Mortgage Banking, 8% from Asset Management and 5% from Real Estate Banking. While the Company manages five lines of business, its corporate legal structure currently consists of 10 subsidiary banks and over 140 active nonbank subsidiaries.

Special Designations: FB$_{500}$ FT$_{500}$

Officers: Thomas H. O'Brien *CH & CEO*
James E. Rohr *P*
Walter E. Gregg, Jr. *SEVP*
Susan B. Bohn *EVP-Corporate DEV & Communications*
Richard C. Caldwell *EVP-Asset MGT*
Frederick J. Gronbacher *EVP-Consumer Banking*
Ralph S. Michael III *EVP-Corporate Banking*
Bruce E. Robbins *EVP-Real Estate Banking*
Robert L. Haunschild *SVP & CFO*
William J. Johns *SVP & CACO*
Thomas E. Paisley III *SVP & CH-Corporate Credit Policy Comm.*
Helen P. Pudlin *SVP & GC*
Timothy G. Shack *SVP-Technology & Processing Services*
Peter K. Classen *P & CEO-PNC Bank, N.A., Northeast PA*
John C. Haller *P & CEO-PNC Bank, Ohio, N.A.*
Michael N. Harreld *P & CEO-PNC Bank, Kentucky, Inc.*
Sy Holzer *P & CEO-PNC Bank, N.A., Pittsburgh*
Calvert A. Morgan, Jr. *CH, P & CEO-PNC Bank, Delaware*
Saiyid T. Naqvi *P & CEO-PNC Mortgage Corp. of America*
Charles C. Pearson, Jr. *P & CEO-PNC Bank, N.A., Central PA*
Richard L. Smoot *P & CEO-PNC Bank, N.A., Philadelphia/ Southern New Jersey*
David E. Zuern *P & CEO-PNC Bank, N.A., Northwest PA*

Human Resources: William E. Rosner *SVP-Corporate Human Resources*
Auditor: Ernst & Young LLP, Pittsburgh, PA
Affiliates/Divisions/Subsidiaries:

BlackRock Financial Management, Inc.
New York, NY
Provider of fixed income investment management services.

CastleInternational Asset Management Ltd.
Edinburgh, Scotland
Provider of international equity management services.

Compass Capital Group, Inc.
New York, NY
Provider of mutual fund sales.

PFPC Inc.
Wilmington, DE
Provider of mutual fund, administration, accounting & shareholder services.

PFPC International Ltd.
Dublin, Ireland
Provider of mutual fund administration, accounting & shareholder services.

PNC Asset Management Group, Inc.
Philadelphia, PA
Provider of investment services.

PNC Bank, Delaware
Wilmington, DE

PNC Bank, FSB
Naples, Tampa & Vero Beach, FL
Provider of trust services.

PNC Bank, Indiana, Inc.

PNC Bank, Kentucky, Inc.
Louisville, KY

PNC Bank, N.A.
Pittsburgh, PA

PNC Bank, New England
Boston, MA

PNC Bank, Ohio, N.A.
Cincinnati, OH

PNC Brokerage Corp.
Pittsburgh, PA
Provider of brokerage services & underwriter of securities.

PNC Capital Markets, Inc.
Pittsburgh, PA

PNC Equity Advisors Co.
Philadelphia, PA
Provider of growth equity investment management services.

PNC Equity Management Corp.
Pittsburgh, PA
Provider of direct investment services.

PNC Institutional Investment Service
Philadelphia, PA

Provider of investment research for financial institutions.

PNC Institutional Management Corp.
Wilmington, DE
Provider of institutional liquidity management services.

PNC Leasing Corp.
Pittsburgh, PA
Provider of leasing services.

PNC Leasing Corp., Kentucky
Louisville, KY
Provider of leasing services.

PNC Mortgage Bank, N.A.
Pittsburgh, PA
Provider of mortgage services.

PNC Mortgage Co.
Louisville, KY
Provider of mortgage services.

PNC Mortgage Corp. of America
Vernon Hills, IL
Provider of mortgage services.

PNC Mortgage Securities Corp.
Vernon Hills, IL
Provider of mortgage services.

PNC National Bank
Wilmington, DE
Provider of credit card services.

PNC National Bank of Delaware
Wilmington, DE

PNC Trust Co. of New York
New York, NY
Provider of securities clearing services.

Provident Capital Management, Inc.
Philadelphia, PA
Provider of value & international institutional investment management services.

Total Employees......................25,500   **Regional Employees** 7,600
Year Established 1818   **Incorporated**...................................PA

Stock Symbol..............................PNC
Stock Exchange.......................NYSE
Stockholders 65,642
Shares Outstanding 322,038,350

Annual Meeting.......................April
SIC Code....................................6712

Fiscal Year End	Total Revenues ($000)	Net Income/(Loss) ($000)	Total Assets ($000)
12/31/96	6,333,000	992,000	73,260,000
12/31/95	6,109,000	408,000	73,404,000
12/31/94	5,763,000	884,000	77,461,000
12/31/93	5,159,000	899,000	76,012,000

Executive Biography: Thomas H. O'Brien

Birth Date: 1937   **Birthplace:** Pittsburgh, PA

Education:
U of Notre Dame, B.S.-Commerce 1958; Harvard U, M.B.A. 1962.

Career History:
Pittsburgh National Bank, various positions 1962-67, VP 1967-73, SVP 1973-80, EVP 1980-83, VCH 1983-, CH & CEO; PNC Bank Corp., VCH 1983-88, P 1985-, CEO 1985-present, CH 1988-present.

Directorships/Memberships/Activities:
Allegheny Conference on Community Development, CH; Bell Atlantic Corp., DIR; The Carnegie, DIR; Children's Hospital of Pittsburgh, DIR; Hilb, Rogal & Hamilton Co., DIR; Pittsburgh Opera, C-CH; U of Pittsburgh, DIR; U of Pittsburgh, CH-Board of Visitors-Graduate School of Business; United Way of Southwestern Pennsylvania, DIR; The Bankers Roundtable, MEM.

PPG Industries, Inc.

One PPG Place
Pittsburgh, PA 15272
County: Allegheny

Phone: (412) 434-3131
Fax: (412) 434-2545
Internet Address: www.ppg.com

Type of Business: Manufacturer and supplier of coatings, glass and chemicals.

PPG Industries is a diversified global manufacturer and supplier of protective and decorative coatings, flat glass, fabricated glass products, continuous-strand fiber glass products, and industrial and specialty chemicals. The Company is comprised of three basic business segments—coatings, glass and chemicals. The coatings segment supplies protective and decorative finishes for automotive original equipment, appliances, industrial equipment and packaging; factory-finished aluminum extrusions and coils for architectural uses; and other industrial and consumer products. In addition to the supply of finishes to the automotive original equipment market, this segment supplies automotive refinishes to the aftermarket. The Company's automotive original and industrial coatings are for-mulated specifically for the customer's needs and application methods. This seg-ment also manufactures adhesives and sealants for the automotive industry and metal pretreatments for automotive and industrial applications. The architectur-al finishes portion of this segment consists primarily of coatings used by painting and maintenance contractors, and by consumers for decoration and maintenance. The glass segment's major markets are automotive original equipment, automo-tive replacement, residential and commercial construction, aircraft transparen-cies, the furniture, marine and electronics industries, and other markets. The chemicals segment is a major producer of chlor-alkali and specialty chemicals. The primary chlor-alkali products are chlorine, caustic soda, vinyl chloride monomer, chlorinated solvents and chlorinated benzenes. The primary specialty chemical products are Transitions® lenses; optical monomers; precipitated silicas for the tire, shoe and battery separator businesses; surfactants for food emulsifi-cation, sugar processing and personal care products; and phosgene derivatives for the pharmaceutical, agricultural and fuel additives businesses. The Company operates 74 major manufacturing facilities in Australia, Canada, China, France, Germany, Ireland, Italy, Mexico, the Netherlands, Portugal, Spain, Taiwan, the United Kingdom and the United States. In 1996, the Company's research and development costs, including depreciation of research facilities, totaled $255 mil-lion.

Special Designations: FB_{500} FT_{500} IW_{1000}

Officers: Jerry E. Dempsey *CH*
Raymond W. LeBoeuf *P & CEO*
Frank A. Archinaco *EVP*
E. Kears Pollock *EVP*
Charles E. Bunch *SVP-Strategic Planning & Corporate Services*
James C. Diggs *SVP & GC*
William H. Hernandez *SVP-FIN*
Gary W. Weber *SVP-Science & Technology*
Donald W. Bogus *VP-Industrial Coatings*
L. Blaine Boswell *VP-Public Affairs*
Rae R. Burton *VP-Chlor-Alkali & Derivatives*
David C. Cannon, Jr. *VP-Environment, Health & Safety*
James W. Craig *VP-Coatings Europe; P-PPG Europe*
Thomas A. Craig *VP-Automotive Refinishes*
Stanley C. DeGreve *VP-Fiber Glass Europe*
Garry A. Goudy *VP-Automotive Replacement Glass*
Gerald W. Gruber *VP-Coatings R&D & Technology Services*
Ernest A. Hahn *VP-Automotive Glass*
Richard B. Leggett *VP-Flat Glass*
H. Kennedy Linge *VP, Associate GC & SEC*
Barry J. McGee *VP-Glass Technology & Manufacturing Services*
Margaret H. McGrath *VP-Coatings Canada; P-PPG Canada*
Maurice V. Peconi *VP-Architectural Coatings*
David W. Smith *VP-Information Technology*

Kevin F. Sullivan *VP-Fiber Glass*
Thomas M. Von Lehman *VP-Specialty Chemicals*
Arend W. D. Vos *VP-Coatings Asia/Pacific; P -PPG Asia/Pacific*
David R. Wallis *VP-Corporate DEV*
Roderick I. A. Watters *VP-Automotive Coatings Europe*
Richard Zahren *VP-Automotive Coatings*
John Maaghul *P-PPG South America*

Human Resources: Russell L. Crane *SVP-Human Resources & ADM*
Purchasing Director: Michael A. Ludlow *VP-Purchasing & Distribution*
Auditor: Deloitte & Touche LLP, Pittsburgh, PA

Total Employees......................31,300   **Regional Employees** 3,060
Year Established 1883   **Incorporated**...................................PA
Stock Symbol ....PPG   **Annual Meeting**.......................April
Stock Exchange ....NYSE   **SIC Code** 2851
Stockholders 33,232
Shares Outstanding 182,470,438

Fiscal Year End	Total Revenues ($000)	Net Income/(Loss) ($000)	Total Assets ($000)
12/31/96	7,218,100	744,000	6,441,400
12/31/95	7,057,700	767,600	6,194,300
12/31/94	6,331,200	514,600	5,893,900
12/31/93	5,753,900	22,200	5,651,500

Executive Biography: Raymond W. LeBoeuf

Birth Date: 12/30/46   **Birthplace:** Chicago, IL
Spouse: Loralee   **Children:** 2

Education:
Northwestern U; U of Illinois, M.B.A.

Career History:
Ford Motor Co.; PPG Industries, Inc., TRS 1980-, CON 1984-, VP-Purchasing 1986-, VP-FIN & CFO 1988-, VP-Coatings 1994-, EVP 1994-95, COO 1995-, P 1995-present, CEO 1997-present.

Directorships/Memberships/Activities:
Chemical Manufacturers Assn., DIR; Extra Mile Education Foundation, DIR; Magee-Womens Hospital, DIR; Robert Morris College, TRU.

Prestige Bancorp, Inc.

P

710 Old Clairton Rd.
Pittsburgh, PA 15236
County: Allegheny

Phone: (412) 655-1190
Fax: (412) 655-1772
Internet Address: www.prestigebank.com

Type of Business: Bank holding company.

Prestige Bancorp is a unitary savings and loan holding company. It was formed in March 1996 in connection with the conversion of Prestige Bank, A Federal Savings Bank (Bank) from a mutual-chartered savings association to a stock-chartered savings association. Upon completion of the conversion on June 27, 1996, the Company commenced operations as the holding company for the Bank, then existing as a stock-chartered federal savings association. The Bank's lending operations follow the traditional pattern of a savings association by primarily emphasizing the origination of one- to four-family residential loans for portfolio retention and to a substantially lesser degree, the origination of commercial real estate loans, construction loans on residential properties and consumer loans, including home equity or home improvement loans, automobile loans, student loans, credit card loans and cash collateral personal loans. Its loan portfolio contains no loans to foreign governments, foreign enterprises or foreign operations of domestic companies. The Bank's deposit services include passbook savings accounts, money market savings accounts, NOW accounts, non-interest bearing checking accounts and certificates of deposit with a minimum maturity of six months and a maximum maturity of five years. It does not utilize the services of deposit brokers. The Bank's deposits are insured by the Savings Assn. Insurance Fund of the the Federal Deposit Insurance Corp. to the maximum permitted by law. The Bank conducts business from its corporate and main offices located at the above address and from two full-service branch offices located in Bethel Park and in the Mt. Oliver area of Pittsburgh, PA.

Officers: John A. Stiver *CH*
Robert S. Zyla *P*
Patricia A. White *SEC & TRS*
James M. Hein *CON*

Auditor: Arthur Andersen LLP, Pittsburgh, PA
General Counsel: Tucker Arensberg, P.C., Pittsburgh, PA

Affiliates/Divisions/Subsidiaries:

Prestige Bank, A Federal Savings Bank 100%
Federally chartered savings bank.

Total Employees 38	**Regional Employees** 38
Year Established 1935	**Incorporated** ....PA
Stock Symbol ....PRBC	**Annual Meeting** ....April
Stock Exchange ....NASDAQ	**SIC Code** 6712
Stockholders 668
Shares Outstanding 963,023

Fiscal Year End	Total Revenues ($000)	Net Income/(Loss) ($000)	Total Assets ($000)
12/31/96	7,045	146	114,640
12/31/95	5,941	161	91,841
12/31/94	5,608	548	87,745
12/31/93	5,720	685	82,522

Executive Biography: Robert S. Zyla

Birth Date: 1947

Career History:

Prestige Bank, A Federal Savings Bank, various positions 1967-89, P 1989-present, CEO & TRS 1995-present; Prestige Bancorp, Inc., P 1996-present.

Respironics, Inc.

1501 Ardmore Blvd.
Pittsburgh, PA 15221
County: Allegheny

Phone: (412) 731-2100
Fax: (412) 473-5010
Internet Address: www.respironics.com

Type of Business: Designer, developer, manufacturer and marketer of cardio-pulmonary aid products.

Respironics designs, develops, manufactures and markets medical devices used for the treatment of patients suffering from respiratory disorders. The Company's products are used principally in the home and hospitals, as well as emergency medical settings and alternative care facilities. Its primary product lines are continuous positive airway pressure devices and bi-level positive airway pressure devices for the treatment of obstructive sleep apnea, a serious disorder characterized by the repeated cessation of breathing during sleep; bi-level non-invasive ventilatory support devices; patient mask products; and single-use resuscitation products. In fiscal 1996, 67% of the Company's sales consisted of obstructive sleep apnea products and related accessories and replacement parts; 27%, non-invasive ventilatory support products and related accessories and replacement parts; 17%, patient mask products (including some masks which are components of obstructive sleep apnea products, non-invasive ventilatory support products and resuscitation products and which are also included in the sales figures for those product groups); and 2%, resuscitation products. The Company's sales are comprised of 68% equipment and 32% consumable and single-use products. The Company markets its products to a network of more than 2,500 home care and hospital dealers. These customers in turn resell and rent its products to end users. In fiscal 1996, international sales accounted for approximately 24% of its revenue. While Canada and Europe are the Company's primary foreign markets, South America, Latin America, Australia and the Far East are becoming more significant. The Company's manufacturing operations are located in the United States, Hong Kong and the People's Republic of China. In June 1988, the Company completed its initial public stock offering.

Special Designations: FB_{200} FW_{100}

R

Officers: Gerald E. McGinnis *CH*
Dennis S. Meteny *P & CEO*
Daniel J. Bevevino *VP & CFO*
Robert D. Crouch *VP-SAL & MKT*
Robert M. Oates *VP-ENG*
Ronald J. Zdrojkowski, Ph.D. *VP-R&D*
Dorita A. Pishko *SEC*
James C. Woll *TRS*
Steven P. Fulton *GC*

Human Resources: William Decker *DIR-Human Resources*
Auditor: Ernst & Young LLP, Pittsburgh, PA
Affiliates/Divisions/Subsidiaries:

Respironics (HK) Ltd. 100%
Hong Kong

Respironics Medical Products (Shenzen) Ltd. 100%
People's Republic of China

RIC Investments, Inc. 100%
Delaware

Total Employees..........................1,217	**Regional Employees** 390	
Year Established 1976	**Incorporated** ....DE	
Stock Symbol ....RESP	**Annual Meeting** ....November	
Stock Exchange................NASDAQ	**SIC Code**.....................................3841	
Stockholders 1,400		
Shares Outstanding 19,312,535		

Fiscal Year End	Total Revenues ($000)	Net Income/(Loss) ($000)	Total Assets ($000)
6/30/96	125,766	15,339	143,947
6/30/95	99,450	11,677	78,039
6/30/94	78,171	4,741	58,917
6/30/93	69,286	7,379	54,331

Executive Biography: Dennis S. Meteny

Birth Date: 1953

Education:
Penn State U, 1975; U of Pittsburgh, M.B.A. 1988.

Career History:
Ernst & Young, Accountant 1975-84; Respironics, Inc., VP 1984-92, GMGR & CFO 1988-92, EVP & COO 1992-94, P & CEO 1994-present.

Directorships/Memberships/Activities:
Pittsburgh Children's Museum, DIR; School-to-Work Opportunities, CH-Business Consortium; American Institute of Certified Public Accountants, MEM;

Pennsylvania Institute of Certified Public Accountants, MEM; Pittsburgh High Technology Council, MEM; U of Pittsburgh, MEM-Health Policy Institute Advisory Council; North Allegheny School District, active in youth athletic programs.

Robroy Industries, Inc.

River Rd.
Verona, PA 15147
County: Allegheny

Phone: (412) 828-2100
Fax: (412) 828-3952

Type of Business: Manufacturer and marketer of conduit, enclosure, oil field and computer packaging products.

Robroy Industries is a multinational manufacturer of various products related principally to the electrical industry. The Company recently completed a restructuring which resulted in the formation of four independent operating divisions with distinct product groups consisting of conduit products, enclosure products, oil field products and computer packaging products. The Company is best known in the electrical industry for its Plasti-Bond line of corrosion-resistant steel conduit products. It also manufactures a line of galvanized elbows, couplings and nipples. The Conduit Division is headquartered in Gilmer, TX, with an additional manufacturing facility in Avinger, TX. The Company offers a broad line of enclosure products under the trade names of Stahlin (fiberglass) and Electromate (steel, stainless steel and aluminum). The Enclosureuse Division is headquartered in Belding, MI, with additional plants in Jacksonville, FL, and Fremont, IN. The Company's primary oil field product, Duoline®, is steel down-hole tubing which is lined with either PVC or fiberglass to resist corrosion from salt water or carbon dioxide in secondary oil recovery applications. Oil field product operations are conducted by Rice Engineering Corp., which is headquartered in Midland, TX, with its manufacturing facility in Odessa, TX. The Company's Trimm Technologies produces computer packaging products consisting of enclosures for computers and computer peripherals such as disk drives. These are sold to OEMs, value-added resellers and systems integrators. Its manufacturing plants are located in Las Vegas, NV, and Nottingham, England.

Officers: Peter McIlroy II *CH, P & CEO*
Louis J. Kirchner *EVP & CFO*
Michael T. Deane *VP-ADM & CON*
Loy B. Goodheart *P-Rice Engineering Corp.*
Michael Mackenzie *P-Trimm Technologies, Inc.*
David A. Marshall *P-Conduit Division*
Lawrence M. McKenna *P-Enclosure Division*

Auditor: Deloitte & Touche LLP, Pittsburgh, PA
General Counsel: Cohen & Grigsby, P.C., Pittsburgh, PA

R

Affiliates/Divisions/Subsidiaries:

Conduit Division 100%
Avinger & Gilmer, TX

Enclosure Division 100%
Jacksonville, FL; Fremont, IN; & Belding, MI

Rice Engineering Corp. 100%
Odessa, TX

Rice Operating Co. 100%
Hobbs, NM

Trimm Technologies, Inc. 100%
Las Vegas, NV

Trimm Technologies Ltd. 100%
Nottingham, England

Total Employees..........................1,000		**Regional Employees** 25	
Year Established 1905		**Incorporated**....................................PA	
Stock Symbol ....RROYA		**Annual Meeting**...................October	
Stock Exchange ....OTC		**SIC Code**......................................3089	

Stockholders..Class A..218; Class B ..100
Shares Outstanding.................Class A 1,999,944; Class B 1,302,862

Fiscal Year End	Total Revenues ($000)	Net Income/(Loss) ($000)	Total Assets ($000)
6/30/96	122,461	4,726	81,857
6/30/95	109,311	2,316	75,021
6/30/94	103,109	6,457	72,497
6/30/93	92,917	6,309	68,630

Executive Biography: Peter McIlroy II

Birth Date: 4/13/43   **Birthplace:** Birmingham, MI
Children: 2

Education:
Hamilton College, A.B. 1965; Harvard U, Program for Management Development 1972.

Career History:
Robroy Industries, Inc., CH & P & CEO -present.

Directorships/Memberships/Activities:
Riverview Children's Center (Verona, PA), DIR; Electrical Manufacturers Club, SEC; Fox Chapel Golf Club, MEM; Fox Chapel Presbyterian Church, MEM; National Electrical Manufacturers Assn., MEM-Board of Governors & VCH.

Slippery Rock Financial Corp.

100 S. Main St.
Slippery Rock, PA 16057
County: Butler

Phone: (412) 794-2210
Fax: (412) 794-2259

Type of Business: Bank holding company.

Slippery Rock Financial is a one-bank holding company for The First National Bank of Slippery Rock (Bank). The Company's primary business is the holding of all of the outstanding common shares of the Bank. The Bank is a nationally chartered full-service financial institution. Its products and services include various time and demand deposits, and the origination of secured and unsecured commercial, consumer and mortgage loans. The Bank also has a full-service trust department. Its deposits are insured by the Federal Deposit Insurance Corp. In addition to the Bank's main office located at the above address and a drive-through facility also located in Slippery Rock, it operates branch offices in Grove City, Harrisville, Portersville and Prospect, PA, as well as an operations center located in Slippery Rock Township, PA.

Officers: Grady W. Cooper *CH*
John W. Conway *VCH*
William C. Sonntag *P & CEO-The First National Bank of Slippery Rock*
Dale R. Wimer *EVP-The First National Bank of Slippery Rock*
Mark A. Volponi *CON-The First National Bank of Slippery Rock*

Human Resources: Eleanor L. Cress *VP-Branch ADM-The First National Bank of Slippery Rock*

Purchasing Director: Doris R. Blackwood *SEC-The First National Bank of Slippery Rock*

Auditor: S. R. Snodgrass, A.C., Wexford, PA

Affiliates/Divisions/Subsidiaries:

The First National Bank of Slippery Rock 100%

Total Employees............................102
Year Established 1897
Stock Symbol............................SRCK
Stock Exchange ....OTC
Stockholders 532
Shares Outstanding 1,378,124

Incorporated..................................PA
Annual Meeting......................April
SIC Code....................................6712

Fiscal Year End	Total Revenues ($000)	Net Income/(Loss) ($000)	Total Assets ($000)
12/31/96	14,590	2,670	195,713
12/31/95	13,388	2,499	162,011
12/31/94	11,851	2,266	147,374
12/31/93	11,158	2,209	141,268

Executive Biography: William C. Sonntag

Birth Date: 12/6/48   **Birthplace:** New Castle, PA

Education:
Slippery Rock U, B.A.-Economics 1970; Youngstown State U; Rutgers U, Banking 1981.

Career History:
U.S. Army, 1970-73; Mahoning National Bank (Youngstown, OH), various positions including MGT Trainee & Branch MGR 1973-76; The First National Bank of Slippery Rock, P & CEO -present; Slippery Rock Financial Corp., P & CEO - present.

Directorships/Memberships/Activities:
Butler Memorial Hospital, DIR & TRS; Slippery Rock U Foundation, DIR & SEC; American Bankers Assn., MEM; Pennsylvania Assn. of Community Bankers, MEM; Pennsylvania Bankers Assn., MEM; Robert Morris Assoc., MEM; Slippery Rock American Legion Post 393, MEM; Slippery Rock Development Assn., MEM; Slippery Rock U, MEM-Alumni Assn.

SMT Health Services Inc.

10521 Perry Hwy.
Wexford, PA 15090
County: Allegheny

Phone: (412) 933-3300
Fax: (412) 933-3311
Internet Address: www.smthealth.com

Type of Business: Provider of medical diagnostic imaging services to hospitals, physicians and patients.

   SMT Health Services is primarily engaged in the business of operating mobile magnetic resonance imaging (MRI) units. The Company, through its subsidiaries, operates 19 mobile MRI units, which service health care providers located in Kentucky, North Carolina, Ohio, Pennsylvania, South Carolina, Virginia and West Virginia. The MRI equipment is transported in specially designed vans that are driven to the health care provider's facility where the imaging occurs. The Company typically charges fees on a fee-per-scan basis. All of the Company's mobile MRI equipment is financed through capital leases and the Company expects that it will continue to finance all of its equipment. Generally, the Company orders its equipment from the manufacturer while simultaneously contracting with health care providers for its use, thereby reducing the Company's risk. Many health care providers do not own MRI equipment because of insufficient patient volume to justify the costs associated with the acquisition and operation of such equipment. Depending upon type, features and options selected, the MRI equipment costs between $1.6 million and $2.2 million. Among the reasons for healh care providers to use the Company's equipment is the elimination of the need to recruit and employ qualified technicians, avoidance of the risk of technological obsolescence of the equipment, provision of short-term mobile services allow the customer to learn the technology, establishment of a patient base before an in-house unit is installed, provision of additional coverage when patient demand exceeds in-house capacity, lack of a suitable interior location, reduction of risks of medical malpractice suits by utilizing state-of-the-art medical technology, and related services and changes in third-party reimbursement systems. A significant marketing resource for the Company has been existing customer referrals. Additionally, the Company is the preferred vendor of services for Amerinet, which is a nonprofit consortium of approximately 3,000 hospitals and other health care providers nationwide. On March 4, 1992, the Company completed its initial public stock offering.

Recent Events: On June 24, 1997, the Company announced that it had entered into a definitive agreement with Three Rivers Acquisition Corp. (TRAC), an affiliate of Apollo Management, L.P., whereby TRAC would acquire all the outstanding shares of the Company's common stock.

Officers: Jeff D. Bergman *CH, P & CEO*
Daniel Dickman *EVP, COO & SEC*
David W. Spindler *SVP-Clinical OPR & MKT*

Human Resources: David A. Zynn *CFO, TRS & AST-SEC*
Auditor: KPMG Peat Marwick LLP, Pittsburgh, PA
General Counsel: Buchanan Ingersoll P.C., Pittsburgh, PA

Total Employees............................123		**Regional Employees** 35	
Year Established 1987		**Incorporated** ....DE	
Stock Symbol ....SHED		**Annual Meeting** ....May	
Stock Exchange................NASDAQ		**SIC Code**......................................8071	
Stockholders 1,550			
Shares Outstanding 5,685,080			

Fiscal Year End	Total Revenues ($000)	Net Income/(Loss) ($000)	Total Assets ($000)
12/31/96	19,212	2,411	39,498
12/31/95	15,158	1,373	23,348
12/31/94	13,282	410	20,623
12/31/93	11,906	(2,311)	18,392

Executive Biography: Jeff D. Bergman

Birth Date: 1954   **Birthplace:** Pittsburgh, PA
Spouse: Beth Anne   **Children:** 3

Education:
Robert Morris College, B.S.-Business Administration 1977.

Career History:
BOC-AIRCO, MKT Representative-Corporate Steel Division 1979-82; Mobile Diagnostech, Inc., Developer & MGR 1983-87; Shared Medical Technologies, Inc., P & CEO 1987-; Shared MRI-4, Inc., P & CEO 1990-; SMT Health Services Inc., CH & P & CEO 1991-present.

Directorships/Memberships/Activities:
National Football League, Official.

Southwest National Corp.

111 S. Main St.
P.O. Box 760
Greensburg, PA 15601
County: Westmoreland

Phone: (412) 834-2310
Fax: (412) 832-6044

Type of Business: Bank holding company.

Southwest National is a bank holding company owning all of the outstanding common stock of the Southwest National Bank of Pennsylvania (Bank). The Company is engaged principally in commercial banking activities through its banking subsidiary. The Bank is a national banking association. Through 16 locations in Allegheny and Westmoreland Counties, PA, the Bank engages in full-service commercial banking, retail banking and trust activities, serving a primary market area within a 35-mile radius of its headquarter's office. Deposit services include savings accounts, NOW accounts, money market accounts, certificates of deposit, individual retirement accounts and checking accounts. Lending services include commercial loans to businesses and governmental units, construction financing, real estate and mortgage loans, as well as installment, home improvement, home equity and personal credit lines, credit card, automobile and other consumer loans. Its loan portfolio contains no loans to foreign governments, foreign enterprises or foreign operations of domestic companies. In addition to depository and lending services, the Bank provides various other services, including night-deposit facilities, safe deposit boxes, collection services and a wide range of trust and financial management services. These management services include administration of estates, trust and agency accounts, employee benefit services, and other personal and fiduciary services. The Bank's branch offices are located in Brackenridge, Delmont, Derry, Export, Greensburg (4), Latrobe, Murrysville, Natrona Heights, New Alexandria, New Stanton, Tarentum and Youngwood.

Officers: David S. Dahlmann *P & CEO*
David M. Hanna *VP*
Donald A. Lawry *SEC & TRS*

Human Resources: C. Kim Michael *SVP-Southwest National Bank of Pennsylvania*
Auditor: KPMG Peat Marwick LLP, Pittsburgh, PA
General Counsel: Tucker Arensberg, P.C., Pittsburgh, PA

Affiliates/Divisions/Subsidiaries:

Southwest National Bank of Pennsylvania 100%
Greensburg, PA
Commercial bank.

Total Employees............................385
Year Established 1900
Stock Symbol...........................SWPA
Stock Exchange...............NASDAQ
Stockholders 1,280
Shares Outstanding 3,122,382

Regional Employees 385
Incorporated..................................PA
Annual Meeting......................April
SIC Code.....................................6712

Fiscal Year End	Total Revenues ($000)	Net Income/(Loss) ($000)	Total Assets ($000)
12/31/96	58,076	9,610	755,358
12/31/95	56,470	9,038	710,816
12/31/94	52,557	8,606	685,283
12/31/93	52,502	8,102	702,794

Executive Biography: David S. Dahlmann

Birth Date: 9/25/49
Spouse: Kathy

Birthplace: Greensburg, PA
Children: 2

Education:
Indiana U of Pennsylvania, B.A.-Economics 1971; Indiana U of Pennsylvania, M.B.A. 1983.

Career History:
Southwest National Bank of Pennsylvania, various positions since 1971 including EVP & COO, P & CEO -present; Southwest National Corp., P 1990-present, CEO 1991-present.

Directorships/Memberships/Activities:
Caregivers of Southwestern Pennsylvania, DIR; Chamber of Commerce Service Corp., DIR; Federal Reserve Bank of Cleveland, DIR; Westmoreland County Museum of American Art, DIR; Westmoreland Health System, DIR; Westmoreland Hospital Foundation, DIR; Westmoreland Symphony Orchestra, DIR; Westmoreland Trust, DIR; Boy Scouts of America, MEM-Advisory Board-Westmoreland-Fayette Council; U of Pittsburgh at Greensburg, TRU; Westmoreland County Community College Foundation, TRU.

Sulcus Computer Corp.

Sulcus Centre, 41 N. Main St.
Greensburg, PA 15601
County: Westmoreland

Phone: (412) 836-2000
Fax: (412) 836-1440
Internet Address: www.sulcus.com

Type of Business: Developer, manufacturer, marketer and installer of micro-computer systems.

Sulcus Computer develops, manufactures, markets and installs microcomputer systems designed to automate the creation, handling, storage and retrieval of

information and documents. The Company offers turnkey systems consisting of
hardware, software, supplies, training, maintenance and support to the hospitality and real estate industries and to a lesser extent, the legal profession. The
Company's systems include a network of hardware, software and cabling as well
as stand-alone systems for which the hardware and software are not separately
sold. Its systems have been installed in more than 6,000 hotels, restaurants, property management firms, title insurance companies, real estate loan and closing
offices, law firms, country clubs, resorts, cruise lines, casinos and others on six
continents. Its customers include such names as Applebee's, Canadian Pacific
Hotels, Chi-Chi's, CitiCorp, El Torito, Embassy Suites, Holiday Inn Worldwide,
Houlihan's, Marriott Hotels & Resorts, Nikko Hotels, Sheraton Hotels, Spago,
UCLA, the Department of the Army and Westin Hotels. The Company markets
its systems through more than 80 locations in over 20 countries. These include
locations maintained by the Company as sales offices and locations of distributors.

Officers: Robert D. Gries *Acting CH*
Leon D. Harris *CEO*
William F. Mclay *SVP & COO*
John W. Ryba *SVP & Chief Legal Officer*
H. Richard Howie *CFO, Principal Accounting Officer & TRS*
Margaret Santone *SEC*
Barry Logan *P-Restaurant Division-Sulcus Hospitality Group*
Bernhard Mantel *VP-OPR-Sulcus Hospitality Group EMEA, AG*
Jappe Kjaer *P-Sulcus Scandinavia, A.S.*

Human Resources: Toni Tesauro
Auditor: Crowe, Chizek and Co. LLP, Columbus, OH
Affiliates/Divisions/Subsidiaries:

Lodgistix, Inc.
Delaware
Integrator of property management systems.

Lodgistix UK
Sales & support office.

NRG Management Systems, Inc.
Pennsylvania
Developer & marketer of energy & room management software to the
hotel & motel industry.

NRG Management Systems (U.K.)
Sales & support office.

Radix Systems, Inc.
Conshohocken, PA
Provider of field engineering & support services, including site analy-
sis, cabling & Novell® training.

Squirrel Cos., Inc.
Georgia
Developer & marketer of touch-screen software systems to the hospitality industry.

Squirrel Systems of Canada, Ltd.
Vancouver, British Columbia, Canada
Manufacturer & marketer of Squirrel products.

Squirrel (U.K.) Ltd.
Sales & support office.

Sulcus (Australia) Pty. Ltd.
Australia
Sales office.

Sulcus Hospitality Group (Belgium)
Belgium
Customer support office.

Sulcus Hospitality Group EMEA, AG
Switzerland
Marketer & supporter of full-range of Company's property management & point-of-sale systems.

Sulcus Hospitality Ltd.
Hong Kong
Sales office.

Sulcus Hospitality (U.K.) Ltd.
Sales & support office.

Sulcus (Malaysia) Sdn Bhd
Malaysia
Sales & support office.

Sulcus Scandinavia, A.S.
Norway
Sales & support office.

Sulcus Singapore, Pte. Ltd.
Singapore
Sales office.

Total Employees............................467
Year Established 1979
Stock Symbol ....SUL

Regional Employees 45
Incorporated..................................PA
Annual Meeting....................August

Stock Exchange .... ASE   SIC Code 3571

Stockholders 4,732

Shares Outstanding 16,752,032

Fiscal Year End	Total Revenues ($000)	Net Income/(Loss) ($000)	Total Assets ($000)
12/31/96	52,145	1,395	47,950
12/31/95	45,984	(1,369)	47,327
12/31/94	43,143	(11,668)	47,869
12/31/93	49,283	(3,050)	58,716

Executive Biography: Leon D. Harris

Birth Date: 1939

Career History:
Commodore Computer Corp., P -1983; Olympia U.S.A., P & CEO; Olivetti Office USA, P & CEO 1985-93; Physalia Corp., OWN & P 1993-present; Sulcus Computer Corp., CEO 1997-present.

Sylvan Inc.

828 S. Pike Rd.
Sarver, PA 16055
County: Butler

Phone: (412) 295-3910
Fax: (412) 295-4111

Type of Business: Producer and marketer of fresh mushrooms, mushroom spawn and spawn-related products.

Sylvan is a worldwide producer of mushroom spawn (the equivalent of seed for mushrooms) and a major distributor of other products for use by commercial mushroom growers. The Company is also a producer of fresh mushrooms for sale to retailers, distributors and processors of mushroom products in the U.S. In addition to spawn-related products, it has distribution rights for products manufactured by others, such as mushroom crop nutritional supplements and pest control agents. The Company distributes its spawn products primarily in North America, Europe, Australia and South America, and is expanding to markets in Asia. The Company claims to hold the leading market share in most of the countries where it sells spawn. The Company operates U.S. spawn production facilities in Dayton, NV, and Kittanning, PA, and a mushroom farm in Quincy, FL. It has international spawn plants in Windsor, Australia; Yaxley, Peterborough, England; Langeais, France; Dunaharaszti, Hungary; and Horst, The Netherlands. The Company's production experience and research capabilities lend themselves to a variety of microbial production applications. In 1996, the Company's research and development expenditures totaled $2 million.

Officers: Dennis C. Zensen *CH, P & CEO*
William P. Mooney *CFO*
Fred Y. Bennitt *SEC & TRS*

Monir K. Elzalaki *P-Sylvan America, Inc.*
Richard F. Lazzarini, Jr. *P-Quincy Corp.*
Michael A. Walton *MDIR-Sylvan Europe*

Auditor: Arthur Andersen LLP, Pittsburgh, PA

Affiliates/Divisions/Subsidiaries:

Quincy Corp.
Quincy, FL
Producer & marketer of mushrooms.

Somycel S.A.
Langeais, France
Producer & marketer of mushroom spawn.

Sylvan America, Inc.
Kittanning, PA
Producer & distributor of mushroom spawn & various spawn-related products.

Sylvan America, Inc.
Dayton, NV
Producer & distributor of mushroom spawn & various spawn-related products.

Sylvan Foods Netherlands B.V.
The Netherlands

Sylvan Horst B.V. 75%
Horst, The Netherlands
Producer of mushroom spawn.

Sylvan Pilz AG
Gossau, Switzerland
Distributor of mushroom spawn & researcher of fungi.

Sylvan Spawn Laboratory Hungary Ltd.
Dunaharaszti, Hungary
Producer & distributor of mushroom spawn.

White Queen Ltd. 55%
Yaxley, Peterborough, England
Producer of mushroom spawn.

Total Employees	900	**Regional Employees**	62
Year Established	1937	**Incorporated**	NV
Stock Symbol	SYLN	**Annual Meeting**	May
Stock Exchange	NASDAQ	**SIC Code**	182

Stockholders 3,000
Shares Outstanding 6,392,200

Fiscal Year End	Total Revenues ($000)	Net Income/(Loss) ($000)	Total Assets ($000)
12/29/96	79,111	7,819	86,912
12/31/95	75,751	6,477	81,784
1/1/95	69,839	6,357	74,492
1/2/94	105,346	(8,714)	73,978

Executive Biography: Dennis C. Zensen

Birth Date: 1938

Career History:
Ralston Purina Co., various positions 1968-80 including DIR-Northwest OPR & Division VP-Venture MGT Group; Quincy Corp. (subsidiary of Sylvan Inc.), C-FND, P & CEO 1982-91; Sylvan Inc., P & CEO 1989-present, CH 1990-present.

Tollgrade Communications, Inc.

493 Nixon Rd.
Cheswick, PA 15024
County: Allegheny

Phone: (412) 274-2156
Fax: (412) 274-8014
Internet Address: www.tollgrade.com

Type of Business: Designer, engineer, marketer and supporter of proprietary electronic equipment for use by telephone companies to use their existing line test systems to remotely diagnose problems in lines containing both copper and fiber optics.

Tollgrade Communications designs, engineers, markets and supports proprietary products that enable telephone companies to use their existing line test systems to remotely diagnose problems in "plain old telephone service" (POTS) lines containing both copper and fiber optics. POTS lines comprise the vast majority of lines in service today throughout the world. In addition to traditional voice service, POTS includes lines for popular devices such as computer modems and fax machines. POTS excludes the more complex lines, such as data communications service lines, commonly referred to as "special services." POTS line test systems, located at telephone companies' central offices, diagnose problems in the "local loop", which is the portion of the telephone network that connects end users to a telephone company's central office, and is comprised primarily of copper wireline. The ability to remotely test reduces the time needed to identify and resolve problems and eliminates or reduces the cost of dispatching a technician to the problem site. Most POTS line test systems were designed for use over copper wireline only, so that the introduction of fiber-optic technology into the local loop renders it inaccessible to these test systems. The Company's metallic channel unit (MCU®) product line solves this problem by extending test system access through the fiber-optic portion into the copper portion of the local loop. Other MCU technology is also used with home and business alarm systems. As with home service line testing, home alarm systems must be monitored from the alarm company's headquarters along a hybrid copper and fiber-optic line. The Company's alarm-related MCU products are used to facilitate the transport of analog alarm signals from subscriber homes to alarm company monitoring stations across the hybrid telephone network. These units plug into equipment at both central office and remote locations. In 1996, MCU products accounted for more than 93% of the Company's sales. During this same period, the seven regional Bell operating companies accounted for 86% of total sales. On December 14, 1995, the Company completed its initial public stock offering.

Officers: R. Craig Allison *CH*
Rocco L. Flaminio *VCH & CTO*
Christian L. Allison *CEO*
Robert Cornelia *EVP-OPR*
Herman Flaminio *SVP-MKT & Strategic Products*
Mark C. Frey *SVP-ENG*
Frederick J. Kiko *SVP-Design ENG*
Geoffrey Lea *VP-SAL*
G. Wayne Lloyd *VP-North American SAL*
Gregory Nulty *VP-MKT*
Samuel C. Knoch *CFO & TRS*
Sara M. Antol *Chief Counsel & SEC*
Bradley N. Dinger *CON*
Ruth Dilts *DIR-Communications*
Kristee Williams *DIR-Quality Assurance*

Human Resources: Joseph Giannetti *VP-Human Resources, Safety & Security*
Purchasing Director: Matthew J. Rosgone *VP-Purchasing*
Auditor: Coopers & Lybrand L.L.P., Pittsburgh, PA
General Counsel: Reed Smith Shaw & McClay, Pittsburgh, PA

Total Employees............................184
Year Established 1986   **Incorporated**.................................PA
Stock Symbol ....TLGD   **Annual Meeting**......................April
Stock Exchange...............NASDAQ   **SIC Code** 3661
Stockholders 475
Shares Outstanding 5,662,896

Fiscal Year End	Total Revenues ($000)	Net Income/(Loss) ($000)	Total Assets ($000)
12/31/96	37,490	5,597	34,626
12/31/95	22,310	2,522	25,728
12/31/94	14,723	2,145	7,151
12/31/93	10,089	601	3,590

Executive Biography: Christian L. Allison
Birth Date: 1961

T

Career History:
Mangus/Catanzano and Skaare Public Relations and Advertising, Account Executive; Ketchum Communications, Inc., Senior Account Executive; Tollgrade Communications, Inc., DIR-Communications 1988-, COO 1990-93, SEC 1992-96, TRS 1992-, P 1993-95, CEO 1995-present.

Tuscarora Inc.

800 Fifth Ave.
New Brighton, PA 15066
County: Beaver

Phone: (412) 843-8200
Fax: (412) 843-4402
Internet Address: www.tuscarora.com

Type of Business: Designer and manfacturer of interior protective packaging and material handling solutions.

Tuscarora designs and manufactures interior protective packaging and material handling solutions for a broad range of manufactured products. The Company also supplies customers with molded foam plastic and thermoformed components for industrial and consumer product applications. In addition, it integrates multiple materials, such as corrugated paperboard, molded and/or diecut foam plastics, thermoformed plastics and wood to meet each customer's specific end use requirements. The Company claims that it is one of the world's largest manufacturers of custom-molded products made from expanded foam plastic materials. The Company manufactures three types of products: custom-molded products, integrated materials products and rigid plastic products. The Company's custom-molded products include packaging and material handling products, and thermal insulation products and components. The packaging products are primarily foam plastic shapes which are used to protect a wide range of finished consumer and industrial goods during shipment. The material handling products are also primarily unique foam plastic shapes which serve many of the same purposes and functions as the packaging products, but are designed primarily for use in intraplant or interplant movement of components rather than for shipment of finished goods. The thermal insulation products are foam plastic shapes used primarily in the manufacture of refrigeration equipment such as home and commercial refrigerators, freezers, air conditioners and water coolers. Like most of the Company's custom-molded products, integrated materials products are produced for interior packaging and material handling applications to protect goods during shipment and handling. The rigid plastic products are also custom-made for material handling applications and component parts. The Company serves nearly 3,000 customers located in the United States, Canada, Mexico and the United Kingdom from 34 manufacturing locations, including four in the United Kingdom and one in Mexico. Among its customers are manufacturers in the high technology, consumer electronics, major appliance and automotive industries.

Officers: John P. O'Leary, Jr. *CH, P & CEO*
James H. Brakebill *VP-MFG*
Del E. Goedeker *VP-Corporate DEV*
Brian C. Mullins *VP & TRS*
David C. O'Leary *VP-SAL & MKT*
Harold F. Reed, Jr. *SEC*

Human Resources: Irene F. McAllister *Human Resource MGR*
Auditor: Ernst & Young LLP, Pittsburgh, PA
General Counsel: Reed, Luce, Tosh, McGregor & Wolford, Beaver, PA
Reed, Smith, Shaw & McClay, Pittsburgh, PA

Total Employees........................2,000	**Regional Employees** 150
Year Established 1962	**Incorporated**..................................PA
Stock Symbol............................TUSC	**Annual Meeting** ....December
Stock Exchange................NASDAQ	**SIC Code** 3086
Stockholders 824	
Shares Outstanding 6,285,817	

Fiscal Year End	Total Revenues ($000)	Net Income/(Loss) ($000)	Total Assets ($000)
8/31/96	182,590	9,653	131,169
8/31/95	163,300	8,980	117,721
8/31/94	120,085	5,703	94,225
8/31/93	101,075	4,270	79,769

Executive Biography: John P. O'Leary, Jr.

Birth Date: 1947

Education:
Gettysburg College, B.A.-Economics; U of Pennsylvania, M.B.A.

Career History:
Tuscarora, Inc., various positions for 27 years including P-Western Region Division -1990, VP 1983-1990, P & CEO 1990-present, CH 1994-present.

Directorships/Memberships/Activities:
Beaver County Corp. for Economic Development, DIR; Beaver County Educational Trust, DIR; First Western Bancorp, DIR; Foam Polystyrene Alliance, CH-Executive Comm.; Gateway Rehabilitation Center, DIR; McGuire Memorial Home, DIR; Matthews International Corp., DIR; Gettysburg College, TRU.

Universal Stainless & Alloy Products, Inc.

U

600 Mayer St.
Bridgeville, PA 15017
County: Allegheny

Phone: (412) 257-7600
Fax: (412) 257-7640

Type of Business: Manufacturer and marketer of semi-finished and precision cold-rolled steel products.

Universal Stainless & Alloy Products manufactures and markets semi-finished and precision cold-rolled products, including stainless steel, tool steel and certain other alloyed steels. While the Company operates in a manner characteristic of a mini-mill, emphasizing a low operating cost structure, efficient use of production and management personnel and flexible production capabilities, its extensive range of manufacturing equipment allows it to achieve product breadth and quality similar to that of a large, integrated specialty steel producer. The Company's products are manufactured in a wide variety of grades, widths and gauges in response to customer specifications. It is capable of fabricating semi-finished specialty steel products that include both long products (ingots, blooms, billets and bars), which are used by customers to produce bar, rod and wire, and flat-rolled products (slabs and plates), which are used by customers to produce fine-gauge plate, sheet and strip products. It also produces customized shapes that are cold rolled from purchased coiled strip, flat bar or extruded bar. The Company's products are sold to rerollers, forgers, service centers and OEMs. Its products are then finished by its customers and marketed for use primarily in the heavy equipment manufacturing, power generation and aerospace industries. In addition, the Company provides conversion services on materials supplied by customers that lack certain of its production facilities or that are subject to their own capacity constraints. The Company's Bridgeville Facility consists of approximately 600,000 square feet of floor space on approximately 50 acres; its Titusville Facility consists of more than 10 acres and comprises seven separate buildings, including two principal buildings of approximately 265,000 square feet in total area. The Company was incorporated in June 1994 and is the successor by merger to a company of the same name which was incorporated in January 1994 for the principal purpose of acquiring substantially all of the idled equipment and related assets located at the Bridgeville, PA, production facility of Armco Inc. On December 22, 1994, the Company completed its initial public stock offering.

Officers: Clarence M. McAninch *P & CEO*
Bradford C. Bowman *COO*
Daniel J. DeCola, Sr. *VP-OPR*
Richard M. Ubinger *CFO & TRS*
Paul A. McGrath *SEC, GC & DIR-Employee Relations*
Anthony J. Biondi *DIR-Purchasing & Production Planning*
Keith A. Engleka *DIR-Technology*
Christoper S. Reynolds *GMGR-PRP Division*

Purchasing Director: Anthony J. Biondi *DIR-Purchasing & Production Planning*
Auditor: Price Waterhouse LLP, Pittsburgh, PA
Affiliates/Divisions/Subsidiaries:

> PRP Division 100%
> Titusville, PA
> Producer of precision shapes & provider of vacuum-arc remelting.

Total Employees............................208		**Regional Employees** 153	
Year Established 1994		**Incorporated** ....DE	
Stock Symbol ....USAP		**Annual Meeting** ....May	
Stock Exchange................NASDAQ		**SIC Code**.....................................3312	
Stockholders 237			
Shares Outstanding 6,283,734			

Fiscal Year End	Total Revenues ($000)	Net Income/(Loss) ($000)	Total Assets ($000)
12/31/96	60,258	4,793	42,098
12/31/95	46,992	2,723	32,437
¹12/31/94	5,743	(2,476)	14,757

¹*August 15, 1994 is deemed to be the inception date of the Company.*

Executive Biography: Clarence M. McAninch

Birth Date: 4/21/35 | **Birthplace:** Freeport, PA
Spouse: Kay | **Children:** 3

Education:
U of Pittsburgh, 1960.

Career History:
Reese Steel & Metal Supply Co., EVP 1986-90; Cyclops Steel Manufacturing, VP-SAL 1990-92; Armco Inc., VP-SAL & MKT-Stainless & Alloy Products Division 1992-94; Universal Stainless & Alloy Products, Inc., P & CEO 1994-present.

USX-U.S. Steel Group

USX Tower, 600 Grant St.
Pittsburgh, PA 15219
County: Allegheny

Phone: (412) 433-1121
Fax: (412) 433-6847
Internet Address: www.usx.com

Type of Business: Producer and marketer of steel mill products, coke and taconite pellets.

USX-U.S. Steel Group, a business unit of USX Corp. (refer to the USX Corp. profile for additional information), includes U.S. Steel (USS), which is primarily engaged in the production and sale of steel mill products, coke and taconite pellets. USS claims to be the largest integrated steel producer in the United States. Beginning in the early 1980s, USS responded to competition resulting from excess steel industry capacity by eliminating less efficient facilities, modernizing those that remain and entering into joint ventures, all with the objective of focusing production on higher value-added products. These products include bake hardenable steels and coated sheets for the automobile and appliance industries, laminated sheets for the manufacture of motors and electrical equipment, improved tin mill products for the container industry and oil country tubular goods. Since 1982, the number of USS raw steel production facilities has been reduced from ten to three, consisting of Gary Works in Indiana, Mon Valley Works in Pennsylvania and Fairfield Works in Alabama. In 1996, these plants produced 11.4 million tons of raw steel which the Company states comprised approximately 11% of the domestic steel market. The Company is also involved in the management of mineral resources, domestic coal mining, engineering and consulting services, and technology licensing. Its other businesses include real estate development and management, and leasing and financing activities. The Company's U.S. Steel Mining Co., LLC subsidiary has domestic coal properties with demonstrated bituminous coal reserves of approximately 860 million net tons. The reserves are located in Alabama, Illinois, Indiana, Pennsylvania, Virginia and West Virginia. Approximately 80% of the reserves are owned and the rest are leased. The Company also controls domestic iron ore properties having demonstrated iron ore reserves in grades subject to beneficiation processes in commercial use by USS of approximately 716 million tons. USS's iron ore operations at Mt. Iron, MN, produced 15.1 million net tons of taconite pellets in 1996. The Company's Resource Management administers the remaining mineral lands and timber lands of USS and is responsible for the lease or sale of these lands and their associated resources, which encompass approximately 300,000 acres of surface rights and 1.5 million acres of mineral rights in 16 states. USX Engineers and Consultants, Inc. sells technical services worldwide to the steel, mining, chemical and related industries. Together with its subsidiary companies, it provides engineering and consulting services for facility expansions and modernizations, operating improvement projects, integrated computer systems, coal and lubrication testing, and environmental projects.

Special Designations: FB_{500} FT_{500} $FT\text{-}G_{500}$ IW_{1000}

Officers: Paul J. Wilhelm *P*
Roy G. Dorrance *EVP-Sheet Products*
Charles C. Gedeon *EVP-Raw Materials & Diversified Businesses*
Charles G. Carson III *VP-Environmental Affairs*
John J. Connelly *VP-INTL Business; P-United States Steel International, Inc.*
Edward F. Guna *VP-Accounting & FIN*
Bruce A. Haines *VP-Technology & MGT Services*
J. Paul Kadlic *VP-SAL*
Donald M. Laws *GC*
Leonard H. Chuderewicz *P-USS/Kobe Steel Co.*
John D. Ewing *P-USS-POSCO Industries*
Albert E. Ferrara, Jr. *P-USX Realty Development*
John H. Goodish *P-USX Engineers and Consultants, Inc.*
Gretchen R. Haggerty *P-USX Credit*
George T. Weber, Jr. *P-U.S. Steel Mining Co., LLC*

Human Resources: Thomas W. Sterling *VP-Employee Relations*

Auditor: Price Waterhouse LLP, Pittsburgh, PA
Affiliates/Divisions/Subsidiaries:

Double Eagle Steel Coating Co. 50%
Dearborn, MI
Operator of electrogalvanizing facility; joint venture with Rouge Steel Co.

PRO-TEC Coating Co. 50%
Leipsic, OH
Owner & operator of hot dip galvanizing line; joint venture with Kobe Steel Ltd.

RMI Titanium Co. 27%
Niles, OH
Producer of titanium metal products.

Transtar, Inc. 46%
Provider of transportation services.

U.S. Steel Mining Co., LLC 100%
Pittsburgh, PA
Miner of coal.

United States Steel International, Inc. 100%
Pittsburgh, PA

USS/Kobe Steel Co. 50%
Lorain, OH
Owner & operator of former U.S. Steel Lorain, OH Works; joint venture with Kobe Steel Ltd.

USS-POSCO Industries 50%
Pittsburgh, PA
Owner & operator of former U.S. Steel Pittsburgh, PA Plant; joint venture with Pohang Iron & Steel Co., Ltd.

USX Credit 100%
Pittsburgh, PA
Provider of real estate & equipment loans.

USX Engineers and Consultants, Inc. 100%
Pittsburgh, PA
Provider of engineering & consulting services.

USX Realty Development 100%
Pittsburgh, PA
Developer of real estate & manager of property.

Worthington Specialty Processing 50%
Jackson, MI
Operator of steel processing facility; joint venture with Worthington
Industries, Inc.

Total Employees......................20,433	**Regional Employees** 5,931	
Year Established 1901	**Incorporated** ....DE	
Stock Symbol X	**Annual Meeting**.......................April	
Stock Exchange ....NYSE	**SIC Code**....................................3312	
Stockholders 70,479		
Shares Outstanding 84,984,069		

Fiscal Year End	Total Revenues ($000)	Net Income/(Loss) ($000)	Total Assets ($000)
12/31/96	6,547,000	273,000	6,580,000
12/31/95	6,475,000	301,000	6,521,000
12/31/94	6,077,000	201,000	6,480,000
12/31/93	5,797,000	(238,000)	6,629,000

Executive Biography: Paul J. Wilhelm

Birth Date: 1932   **Birthplace:** Pittsburgh, PA

Education:
Carnegie Mellon U, B.S.-Mechanical Engineering 1964.

Career History:
U.S. Steel, various positions at National Plant in McKeesport, PA 1964-75, AST-
Superintendent-Seamless Pipe Mill 1975-80, Superintendent-Texas Works 1980-
81, MGR Pipe Mill-Fairfield Works 1981-86, GMGR-Fairfield Works 1986-87,
GMGR-Tubular Products in Pittsburgh 1987-92; U.S. Steel Group, VP-
Technology & MGT Services 1992-94, VP-OPR 1994, P 1994-present; USS/Kobe
Steel Co., P 1993-.

Directorships/Memberships/Activities:
Boy Scouts of America, DIR-Greater Pittsburgh Council; Japan-American
Society of Pennsylvania, DIR; USX Corp., DIR; American Iron and Steel
Institute, MEM; Assn. of Iron and Steel Engineers, MEM; Carnegie Mellon U,
TRU.

Westinghouse Air Brake Co.

1001 Air Brake Ave.
Wilmerding, PA 15148
County: Allegheny
Phone: (412) 825-1000
Fax: (412) 825-1019

Type of Business: Manufacturer of railroad value-added equipment and related safety and efficiency products for locomotives, freight cars and passenger transit vehicles.

Westinghouse Air Brake, also known as WABCO, claims to be North America's largest manufacturer of value-added equipment for locomotives, railway freight cars and passenger transit vehicles. The Company's products, which are sold to both the original equipment market and aftermarket, are intended to enhance safety, improve productivity and reduce maintenance costs for its customers. The Company's product segments consist of the following—electronics, freight, transit, locomotive, friction and other. The electronics segment produces high quality, hardened electronics for the rail industry in the form of on-board systems and braking for locomotives and freight cars. The freight segment consists primarily of brake control valves, draft gears, hand brakes, slack adjusters and articulated car connectors. The transit segment's principal products include a variety of electronic brake equipment, couplers, door controls, pneumatic control equipment, air compressors, air conditioning equipment, tread brakes and disc brakes. Substantially all of the Company's transit products are engineeered to customer specifications. The locomotive segment produces pneumatic braking equipment and compressors. The compressors and control equipment supply the air needed to run an entire train's braking system. The friction segment produces products that are sold as original equipment and as aftermarket brake shoe replacements primarily to its freight, transit and locomotive markets. The Company's other operations consist primarily of the manufacture and sale of industrial rubber products and iron foundry products, and metal finishing. In 1996, approximately 53% of the Company's net sales were generated from the aftermarket sale of replacement parts, repair services and upgrade work purchased by end users of rail vehicles such as railroads, transit authorities, utilities and leasing companies. The remaining 47% of its net sales were derived from sales made directly to OEMs of locomotives, freight cars and passenger transit vehicles. In 1996, international sales (excluding Canada) accounted for approximately 9% of the Company's total net sales. On June 16, 1995, the Company completed its initial public stock offering.

Officers: William E. Kassling   *CH, P, CEO & GMGR-Freight Products OPR*
Emilio A. Fernandez   *EVP-Integrated Railway Products Group*
Howard J. Bromberg   *VP & GMGR-Locomotive & Molded Products*
Robert J. Brooks   *VP & CFO*
Alvaro Garcia-Tunon   *VP-Corporate Planning & Investor Relations*
David M. Kerr   *VP & GMGR-Vapor Corp.*
Timothy J. Logan   *VP-INTL*
John M. Meister   *VP & GMGR-Passenger Transit*

George A. Socher *VP & CON*
Mark C. Van Cleave *VP & GMGR-Cardwell Westinghouse*

Human Resources: Kevin P. Conner *VP-Employee Relations*
Auditor: Arthur Andersen LLP, Pittsburgh, PA
General Counsel: Reed Smith Shaw and McClay, Pittsburgh, PA

Affiliates/Divisions/Subsidiaries:

Benn Iron Foundry
Wallaceburg, Ontario, Canada

Cardwell Westinghouse Co.
Chicago, IL

Futuris Industrial Products
Melbourne & Sydney, Australia

Pioneer Friction Products
Calcutta, India

Pulse Electronics
Rockville, MD

Railroad Friction Products Corp.
Laurinburg, NC, & Wissenbourg, France

Stone Safety Service Corp.
Hackensack, NJ

Thermo Sealed Castings
Burlington, Ontario, Canada

Thermo Sealed Machining
Burlington, Ontario, Canada

Universal Railway Devices Co.
Chicago, IL

Vapor Corp.
Niles, IL, & Montreal, Quebec, Canada

Vapor United Kingdom
East Sussex, England

WABCO Locomotive Products
Wilmerding, PA

WABCO Passenger Transit
Spartanburg, SC

WABCO Rubber Products
Ball Ground, GA, & Greensburg, PA

Westinghouse Railway (Canada) Ltd.
Stoney Creek, Ontario, Canada

Total Employees..........................3,043
Year Established 1869
Stock Symbol............................WAB
Stock Exchange ....NYSE
Stockholders 244
Shares Outstanding 37,488,733

Regional Employees 500
Incorporated ....DE
Annual Meeting.......................April
SIC Code.......................................3743

Fiscal Year End	Total Revenues ($000)	Net Income/(Loss) ($000)	Total Assets ($000)
12/31/96	453,512	32,725	363,236
12/31/95	424,959	33,725	263,407
12/31/94	347,469	36,841	187,728
12/31/93	285,274	28,101	175,625

Executive Biography: William E. Kassling

Birth Date: 1944

Career History:
American Standard Inc., Head-Business Planning 1978-80, Head-Building
Specialties Group 1980-84, Head-Railway Products Group 1984-90;
Westinghouse Air Brake Co., CH & P & CEO 1990-present.

Directorships/Memberships/Activities:
Commercial Intertech, Inc., DIR; Dravo Corp., DIR; Scientific Atlanta, Inc., DIR.

Westinghouse Electric Corp.

Westinghouse Bldg., 11 Stanwix St.
Pittsburgh, PA 15222
County: Allegheny

Phone: (412) 642-6000
Fax: (412) 642-4985
Internet Address: www.westinghouse.com

Type of Business: Diversified corporation operating in the principal business
areas of television and radio broadcasting, cable program-
ming, chemical and nuclear materials management, transport temperature control and power generation systems.

Westinghouse Electric is a global corporation operating in the principal business areas of television and radio broadcasting, cable programming, chemical and
nuclear materials management, transport temperature control and power generation systems. The Company operates its media businesses through the
Westinghouse/CBS Group, which combines the operations of CBS Inc., Group W

Broadcasting and, beginning on December 31, 1996, Infinity Broadcasting Corp.
The Westinghouse/CBS Group provides a variety of communications services
consisting primarily of commercial broadcasting, program production and distribution. It operates the CBS Television Network, a programming provider for
approximately 200 affiliates, and sells advertising time to radio, television and
cable advertisers through national and local sales organizations. It also owns and
operates 14 television broadcasting stations and 79 radio stations. In addition, it
provides programming and distribution services to the cable television industry.
CBS Cable (formerly known as Group W Satellite Communications) provides
sports programming; the marketing and advertising for two country music entertainment networks; and operates a 24-hour, Spanish-language news service. The
Company's Industries & Technology Group consists of five segments—Power
Generation, Energy Systems, Process Control, Thermo King and Government and
Environmental Services. The Power Generation segment designs, develops, manufactures and services nuclear and fossil-fueled power generation systems. The
Energy Systems segment performs this work for nuclear plants and is a leading
supplier of reload nuclear fuel to the global electric utility market. The Process
Control segment provides distributed control, communications, data acquisition
and information systems to nuclear and fossil-fuel electric utilities and to other
industries. The Company states that approximately 40% of the world's operating
commercial nuclear power plants incorporate its technology. The Thermo King
segment designs, manufactures and distributes transport temperature control
equipment, including units and their associated service parts, for trucks, trailers,
seagoing containers, buses and rail cars. These products provide air conditioning
for people and preserve not only food, but pharmaceuticals, flowers, cosmetics,
electronic gear and many other temperature-sensitive goods and products by
heating and cooling as necessary. The Government and Environmental Services
segment includes the management and operation of several government-owned
facilities for the U.S. Department of Energy and the U.S. Army, and support for
the U.S. naval nuclear reactors program.

Recent Events: On November 13, 1996, the Company announced that its Board
of Directors had approved, subject to certain conditions, a plan
to separate the Company's industries and technology businesses from its media businesses. This separation is expected to be
effected by way of a tax-free dividend to shareholders, forming
a publicly-traded company to be called Westinghouse Electric
Co. (WEC). The plan also provides that Thermo King Corp.,
the Company's transport temperature control company, will
conduct a public offering of up to 20% of its common stock and
will become a majority-owned subsidiary of WEC. If the separation is completed, shares of WEC common stock will be distributed on a pro rata basis to the shareholders of record of the
Company's common stock as of a date to be determined. As
currently contemplated, after the separation, the Company will
be renamed "CBS Corp." (to be headquartered in New York,
NY) and will consist primarily of the businesses in the
Westinghouse/CBS Group and WEC will consist primarily of
Industries & Technology Group.

Special Designations: FB$_{500}$ FT$_{500}$ FT-G$_{500}$ IW$_{1000}$

Officers: Michael H. Jordan *CH & CEO*
Gary M. Clark *VCH & P*
Ernest H. Drew *CEO-Industries & Technology*
Fredric G. Reynolds *EVP & CFO*
John D. Bergen *SVP-Corporate Relations*
Louis J. Briskman *SVP & GC-Law & Environmental Affairs*
J. Philip Adams *VP & General Tax Counsel*
Lawrence D. Bridge *VP-Investor Relations*
James A. DePalma *VP-Audit & Control*
Richard J. Hadala *VP*
John F. Hay *VP-Government Affairs*
Claudia E. Morf *VP & TRS*
Samuel R. Pitts *VP-Law, Environmental Affairs & Insurance*
Carol V. Savage *VP & CACO*
Angeline C. Straka *VP, SEC & Associate GC*
Mel Karmazin *CH & CEO-CBS Radio*
Charles W. Pryor, Jr. *P-Energy Systems*
James F. Watson *P-Thermo King Corp.*
Randy H. Zwirn *P-Power Generation*

Human Resources: David Zemelman *SVP-Human Resources*
Joseph J. Colosimo *SVP-Human Resources-Industries & Technology Group*

Auditor: KPMG Peat Marwick LLP, Pittsburgh, PA

Affiliates/Divisions/Subsidiaries:

Infinity Broadcasting Corp. 100%

Safe Sites of Colorado L.L.C. 65%

Thermo King Corp. 100%

West Valley Nuclear Service Co. 100%

Westinghouse Canada, Inc. 100%

Westinghouse CBS Holding Co., Inc. 100%

　　CBS Inc. 100%

Westinghouse Holdings Corp. 100%

　　Westinghouse de Puerto Rico, Inc. 100%

　　Westinghouse Electric S.A. 100%

　　Westinghouse International Technology Corp. 100%

Westinghouse World Investment Corp. 100%

Westinghouse Foreign Sales Corp. 100%

Westinghouse Industry Products International Co. 100%

Westinghouse Savannah River Co., Inc. 100%

Total Employees......................50,000
Year Established 1886
Stock Symbol ....WX
Stock Exchange......................NYSE
Stockholders 125,376
Shares Outstanding 608,654,292

Regional Employees 7,300
Incorporated................................PA
Annual Meeting.......................April
SIC Code.....................................3629

Fiscal Year End	Total Revenues ($000)	Net Income/(Loss) ($000)	Total Assets ($000)
12/31/96	8,449,000	30,000	21,307,000
12/31/95	5,599,000	15,000	18,614,000
12/31/94	5,210,000	77,000	11,838,000
12/31/93	5,158,000	(326,000)	14,521,000

Executive Biography: Michael H. Jordan

Birth Date: 1937
Spouse: Kathryn

Birthplace: Kansas City, MO
Children: 2

Education:
Yale U, B.S.-Chemical Engineering 1957; Princeton U, M.S.-Chemical
Engineering 1959.

Career History:
U.S. Navy, 1960-64; McKinsey and Co., Consultant 1964-74; PepsiCo, Inc., various positions 1974-91, CH-PepsiCo International Foods and Beverages Division
1991-92; Clayton, Dubilier & Rice, Inc., PTR 1992-93; Westinghouse Electric
Corp., CH & CEO 1993-present.

Directorships/Memberships/Activities:
Aetna Life and Casualty Co., DIR; Dell Computer Corp., DIR; Melville Corp.,
DIR; Rhone-Poulenc Rorer Inc., DIR; United Negro College Fund, Inc., DIR;
President's Export Council, MEM.

Wilson Bros.

902 S. Main St.
P.O. Box 307
Point Marion, PA 15474
County: Fayette

Phone: (412) 725-5231
Fax: (412) 725-1016

Type of Business: Supplier of mugs for the advertising specialty market.

Wilson Brothers is a holding company. Through its subsidiary, Houze Glass Corp. (HGC), the Company is engaged in the specialty decoration of glass and ceramic items. HGC's core business consists principally of the decoration of mugs which are sold to advertising specialty distributors. HGC uses a "magic" process which is a thermal chromatic process whereby ceramic pigment is activated by either high or low temperatures. This allows for a visual change in the product to reveal an advertisement or artistic effect. Clients for HGC's ceramic mugs include pharmaceutical companies that utilize the "magic" process to demonstrate a change which occurs when a particular medication is prescribed as well as businesses desiring to advertise a particular product or perhaps a change in their company (i.e., name or logo). Its sales are made through sales representatives and are generally for advertising specialties, premiums, souvenirs and the retail trade. HGC maintains a nationwide distribution network through over 13,800 distributors offering its products. The custom-decorated ceramic mug product line accounts for approximately 85% of HGC's overall business. Additionally, it is decorating beverage coolers, plastic items and sublimated mugs. The Company is looking to expand HGC's decorative products to include custom-imprinted ceramic steins, shot glasses and travel mugs.

Recent Events: On September 14, 1993, the Company's common stock was delisted from the Pacific Stock Exchange for failure to comply with minimum listing criteria. Since that time, its common stock has been traded over the counter through National Quotation Bureau's "pink sheets". Since December 12, 1993, the "pink sheets" have listed no bid for the Company's common stock.

Officers: John Sanford *P, CFO, TRS & SEC*

Auditor: Arthur Andersen LLP, Roseland, NJ

Affiliates/Divisions/Subsidiaries:

Houze Glass Corp. 100%
Point Marion, PA

Total Employees............................87	**Regional Employees** 87	
Year Established 1898	**Incorporated** IL	
Stock Symbol ....None	**SIC Code** 3231	
Stock Exchange ....OTC		
Stockholders 3,027		
Shares Outstanding 3,321,039		

Fiscal Year End	Total Revenues ($000)	Net Income/(Loss) ($000)	Total Assets ($000)
12/31/96	5,715	(58)	1,998
12/31/95	5,041	(602)	2,095
12/31/94	5,495	(749)	2,655
12/31/93	7,021	(5,329)	3,104

Executive Biography: John Sanford

Birth Date: 1965

Education:
U of North Carolina, M.B.A. 1993

Career History:
Fortress Marine Construction, P 1990-91; Carr Securities Corp., Equity Trader 1993-present; Wilson Bros., VP 1994-96, CFO & TRS 1994-present, SEC 1995-present, P 1996-present.

WVS Financial Corp.

9001 Perry Hwy.
Pittsburgh, PA 15237
County: Allegheny

Phone: (412) 364-1911

Type of Business: Bank holding company.

WVS Financial was organized in July 1993 as a state-chartered unitary bank holding company and acquired the common stock of West View Savings Bank (Bank) in November 1993. The Bank's principal source of funds for use in lending and for other general business purposes has traditionally come from deposits. It also derives funds from amortization and prepayment of outstanding loans and mortgage-backed securities and from maturing investment securities. The Bank's deposit products include regular savings accounts, demand accounts, NOW accounts, money market deposit accounts, certificates of deposit ranging in terms from 30 days to 10 years and IRA certificates. Historically, the Bank's lending activities have been concentrated in single-family residential loans secured by properties located in its primary market area of northern Allegheny County, southern Butler County and eastern Beaver County, PA. The Bank has increased its emphasis in recent years in construction lending, primarily for residential properties, and on the origination of home equity loans, all in its primary market area. On occasion, the Bank has also purchased whole loans and loan participations secured by properties located outside of its primary market area but predominantly in Pennsylvania. The Bank believes that all of its mortgage loans are secured by properties located in Pennsylvania. Moreover, substantially all of the Bank's nonmortgage loan portfolio consists of loans made to residents and businesses located in its primary market area. The Bank's business is conducted through its corporate office, located at the above address, and five branch offices located in Cranberry Township (2), Pittsburgh (2) and Wexford, PA. It also operates a loan production office in Wexford, PA.

Officers: James S. McKain, Jr. *CH*
Robert C. Sinewe *P & CEO*
Margaret VonDerau *SVP & SEC*
David J. Bursic *VP, TRS & CFO*
Edward M. Wielgus *VP & Chief Lending Officer*

Auditor: S. R. Snodgrass, A. C., Wexford, PA

General Counsel: Bruggeman & Linn, Pittsburgh, PA

Affiliates/Divisions/Subsidiaries:

West View Savings Bank 100%
Pittsburgh, PA
Savings bank.

Total Employees...............................60
Year Established.........................1908
Stock Symbol..........................WVFC
Stock Exchange................NASDAQ
Stockholders 1,023
Shares Outstanding 1,736,960

Regional Employees 60
Incorporated..................................PA
Annual Meeting..................October
SIC Code......................................6712

Fiscal Year End	Total Revenues ($000)	Net Income/(Loss) ($000)	Total Assets ($000)
6/30/96	18,700	3,577	259,622
6/30/95	15,919	1,790	227,368
6/30/94	14,930	2,235	221,315
6/30/93	16,324	1,876	210,633

Executive Biography: Robert C. Sinewe

Birth Date: 1942

Career History:

West View Savings Bank, P & CEO 1984-present; WVS Financial Corp., P & CEO 1993-present.

1,239 Private, Nonprofit, Subsidiary and Other Company Profiles

This segment contains profiles of 1,239 private, nonprofit, subsidiary and other companies (including cooperative, employee-owned, foreign and mutual businesses) operating in the Pittsburgh seven-county metropolitan area, encompassing Allegheny, Armstrong, Beaver, Butler, Fayette, Washington and Westmoreland counties in Pennsylvania. To be included in this segment, the companies had to have at least 35 employees based on their direct reporting. A handful of businesses employing 30-34 persons were included when a comprehensive survey was provided. Due to the sheer number of companies that reside in the region, it is impossible to list them all. We have made every effort to include a representative cross section of industries operating within the area.

The majority of companies profiled in this segment are private businesses headquartered in the Pittsburgh seven-county metropolitan area. However, we have included additional companies that play an integral role in the local economy yet are headquartered elsewhere. The companies profiled represent a diverse assortment of enterprises including branch offices, factory locations, affiliates, divisions and subsidiaries. The foreign companies are multinational conglomerates with operations in the region. The affiliate, division and subsidiary companies also have significant operations in the area, yet their parent companies are located elsewhere, some private, some foreign and others public.

In this segment, each profile includes a description of the company, a listing of officers and a primary SIC code. The profiles also include a human resources contact, a purchasing contact, employee counts, revenues and year of establishment, when available. The companies are arranged alphabetically (when applicable, listed under the name of the local parent or holding company).

Minor discrepancies may occur due to the way companies provide their information. For instance, some businesses may report revenues based on gross billings (i.e., advertising agencies) or gross sales (i.e., real estate firms) and some employee counts may represent full-time equivalents. Similarly, the year a company was established may vary as a result of reincorporations, mergers or name changes, making it difficult to determine the actual date of corporate origin. Lastly, some companies did not always provide complete information. As a result, profiles may list total employees, Pittsburgh metropolitan area employees, or both; and some businesses chose not to indicate a revenue figure.

#1 Cochran, Inc.

4200 William Penn Hwy.
Monroeville, PA 15146
County: Allegheny

Phone: (412) 373-3333
Fax: (412) 373-9231

Automotive dealer selling new and used cars and trucks. The Company also offers service and parts and performs body repairs. It operates out of two Pittsburgh area locations with nine vehicle franchises. The facility located at the above address carries Cadillac, GMC Truck, Infiniti, Isuzu, Oldsmobile, Pontiac, Saturn and Suzuki vehicles. A Robinson Township facility, located at 5200 Campbells Run Rd. in Pittsburgh, PA, carries Buick, GMC Truck, Isuzu, Pontiac and Saturn vehicles.

Officers: Robert E. Cochran *CH, P & CEO*
Margaret E. Cochran *EVP*
Barbara Cochran Manley *VP & TRS*
Carol Cochran Tsudis *VP & SEC*

Human Resources: Sue Gross

Total Employees	400	**Regional Employees**	400
Year Established	1965	**SIC Code**	5511
Annual Revenues ($000)	215,000		

84 Lumber Co.

Rte. 519
P.O. Box 8484
Eighty Four, PA 15330
County: Washington

Phone: (412) 223-8400
Fax: (412) 225-2530
Internet Address: www.84lumber.com

Owner and operator of retail home building and improvement centers. The Company claims to be the largest privately owned retail building materials enterprise in the United States. It operates 396 stores in 30 states from coast to coast, with 63 located in Pennsylvania. The Company's stores offer a full line of building supplies and hardware products to both do-it-yourself consumers and professional contractors.

Special Designations: FB-P$_{500}$

Officers: Joseph A. Hardy, Sr. *OWN & CH*
Maggie Hardy Magerko *P & COO*
Denny Brua *EVP-OPR*

Purchasing: Bill Myrick *VP-Purchasing*

Total Employees..............4,500	**Regional Employees** 750
Year Established..............1956	**SIC Code**..............2439
Annual Revenues ($000) 1,500,000	

A&L, Inc.

R.D. 3, Rte. 51 S.
P.O. Box 320-A
Belle Vernon, PA 15012
County: Fayette

Phone: (412) 929-2125
Fax: (412) 929-9480

Provider of general contracting services with an emphasis in heavy/highway construction and industrial construction. The Company performs work for the Pennsylvania Department of Transportation, the Pennsylvania Turnpike Commission and other local, state and federal agencies.

Officers: Louis D. Ruscitto *P*

Human Resources: Michelle T. Herron *SEC & TRS*

Total Employees..............225	**Regional Employees** 225
Year Established..............1984	**SIC Code**..............1622
Annual Revenues ($000) 40,000	

AAA West Penn/West Virginia

AAA Motor Sq. Garden, 5900 Baum Blvd.
Pittsburgh, PA 15206
County: Allegheny

Phone: (412) 363-5100
Fax: (412) 362-6981

Travel agency and nonprofit automobile association offering a full range of member benefits, discounts and services. The Association's travel services include worldwide air, cruise and rail tickets; hotel and rental car reservations; and tours. In addition, it offers insurance products; travel-related publications such as TourBooks and maps; individually tailored routings; traveler's checks; credit cards; and a wide variety of vehicle-related and emergency services. The regional operation serves more than 980,000 people through 51 branch offices in Western Pennsylvania, South Central Ohio and West Virginia. It is one of 99 independent members of the American Automobile Assn., a federation of clubs with national headquarters in Heathrow, FL. With over 1,080 offices throughout the United States and Canada, the federation has a total of more than 39 million members.

Officers: Richard S. Hamilton *P & CEO*
Robert C. Irwin *SVP*

John D. Haver *VP-Public Affairs*
Raymond M. Komichak *VP & Legal Counsel*
James Lehman *VP-Travel*
James J. McGrath *VP-ADM*
W. Jeffrey Nelson *VP & CFO*
Bruce Taylor *VP-Insurance*
Portia Ulinski *VP-Information Services*

Human Resources: Allison Lee-Mann *VP-Human Resources*

Total Employees	810	**Regional Employees**	581
Year Established	1902	**SIC Code**	8699
Annual Revenues ($000)	300,000		

ABARTA, Inc.

1000 RIDC Plaza, Ste. 404
Pittsburgh, PA 15238
County: Allegheny

Phone: (412) 963-6226
Fax: (412) 963-1782

Diversified holding company engaged in the soft drink bottling and publishing businesses and oil and gas development, through its wholly owned subsidiaries. The Company's soft drink bottling businesses include Buffalo Coca-Cola Bottling Co. in Tonawanda, NY; Cleveland Coca-Cola Bottling Co. in Cleveland, OH; Coatesville Coca-Cola Bottling Co. in Coatesville, PA; and Coca-Cola Bottling Co. of Lehigh Valley in Bethlehem, PA. Its other subsidiaries include ABARTA Metro Publishing Co. in Miami, FL; ABARTA Oil & Gas Co., Inc. located at the above address; South Jersey Publishing Co. in Pleasantville, NJ; and Refreshment Products, Inc., a beverage distributor located at the R. J. Casey Industrial Park in Pittsburgh, PA. Summit Supply Co., also located at the above address, provides the Company with a wide variety of support services.

Officers: James A. Taylor *CH*
John F. Bitzer III *P & CEO*
Joseph E. Ford *VP-Corporate Services*
Charles R. Hanlon *VP & CFO*

Total Employees	1,200	**Regional Employees**	70
Year Established	1972	**SIC Code**	6719
Annual Revenues ($000)	177,000		

ABB Daimler-Benz Transportation (North America) Inc.

1501 Lebanon Church Rd.
Pittsburgh, PA 15236
County: Allegheny

Phone: (412) 655-5700
Fax: (412) 655-5860
Internet Address: www.adtranz.com

Provider of transportation products, systems and services to transit authorities worldwide. The Company, also known as Adtranz North America, designs and manufactures complete vehicles for automated guideway transit, light rail, metro, commuter and high-speed intercity rail systems. Some of the world's busiest cities rely on the Company to provide state-of-the-art rail vehicles and subsystems, including hundreds of millions of commuters each day in San Francisco, CA; Boston, MA; New York, NY; Philadelphia, PA; Sao Paulo, Argentina; Toronto, Ontario, Canada; Hong Kong; and Taipei, Taiwan. In addition, the Company supplies electric propulsion and automatic train control systems for transit applications. Its total rail systems capabilities encompass design to development, engineering to construction, production to delivery, and long-term service and support. The Company has designed 20 automated transit systems, including 16 in operation and four under construction. These automated transit systems provide a vital link between terminals for airport passengers worldwide. In city centers, its automated transit systems link offices, retail shops and hotels. The Company, which is headquartered in Berlin, Germany, is a 50/50 joint venture between ABB Asea Brown Boveri Ltd., which is headquartered in Zurich, Switzerland, and Daimler-Benz AG, which is headquartered in Berlin, Germany, and listed on the Frankfurt and New York Stock Exchanges. The Company's North American headquarters are located at the above address along with a manufacturing facility. Two other plants are located in Pittsburg, CA, and Elmira Heights, NY. Other field sites locations include Denver, CO; Tampa, FL; Atlanta, GA; Las Vegas, NV; Newark, NJ; Frankfurt, Germany; Rome, Italy; and Singapore.

Officers: Raymond T. Betler *P & CEO*
Anthony C. Domabyl *EVP-MFG*
Edward A. Gordon *EVP-MKT*
Anthony F. Jost *EVP-ENG & Quality*
Manfred R. Kaiser *EVP-Financial Support*

Human Resources: Paul I. Overby *EVP-Corporate Services*

Purchasing: Frank Donini *DIR-Supply MGT*

Total Employees........................1,350   **Regional Employees** 890
Year Established 1887   **SIC Code**....................................3799

ABB Extrel

575 Epsilon Dr.
Pittsburgh, PA 15238
County: Allegheny

Phone: (412) 963-7530
Fax: (412) 963-6578

A

Developer and manufacturer of scientific instruments that analyze the chemical composition of gases. The Company's mass spectrometers instantly determine the chemical composition of gases and vapors. These products are used by utilities and by chemical, biotechnology and steel industries for process control. The Company is a division of ABB Process Analytics, Inc., based in Lewisburg, WV, which is a subsidiary of ABB Asea Brown Boveri Ltd., headquartered in Zurich, Switzerland.

Officers: Gregory Cessna *P*

Total Employees............................70	**Regional Employees** 65
Year Established 1964	**SIC Code** 3826

ABB Power T&D Co., Inc.

125 Theobold Ave.
Greensburg, PA 15601
County: Westmoreland

Phone: (412) 838-5200
Fax: (412) 838-5299

Manufacturer and marketer of high voltage power circuit breakers and circuit switchers, and optical sensors and systems for metering, relaying and protection of systems for the electric utility industry. The Company also markets air switches and offers parts and service. The Company is headquartered in Raleigh, NC, and is a subsidiary of ABB Inc. (AI), which is headquartered in Norwalk, CT. AI is a subsidiary of ABB Asea Brown Boveri Ltd., which is headquartered in Zurich, Switzerland. Located at the above address is the Company's Power Circuit Breaker Division.

Officers: Nicholas J. Stroud *EVP-High Voltage Switchgear*

Human Resources: Philip Woods

Purchasing: Elise Woolfort

Total Employees........................5,800	**Regional Employees** 200
Year Established 1988	**SIC Code** 3613
Annual Revenues ($000) 1,100,000	

ABBY Health Care, Inc.

R.D. 1, Edison St.
Box 619-S
Uniontown, PA 15401
County: Fayette

Phone: (412) 439-8330
Fax: (412) 439-8806

Provider of a variety of state-licensed and Medicare-certified home care services to homebound patients. The Company's services include skilled nursing care, occupational therapy, medical social work services, nutritional services, physical therapy, speech therapy, intravenous therapy, terminal care and other home health aide services. It provides care to patients in Allegheny, Cambria, Fayette, Greene, Somerset, Washington and Westmoreland counties in Pennsylvania. The Company operates branch offices in Belle Vernon, Carmichaels and Somerset, PA. An affiliated company, Beverlee Ann, Inc., doing business as Abby Helping Hands, serves clients in Youngwood, PA.

Officers: Beverly Fazio *P*
Karen Merryman *DIR-Clinical Services*

Human Resources: Raymond Royesky *DIR-Human Resources*

Purchasing: Constance E. Slampak *DIR-FIN*

Total Employees	100	Regional Employees	88
Year Established	1984	SIC Code	8082
Annual Revenues ($000)	6,000		

ABC Travel, Inc.

2690 Stroschein Rd.
Monroeville, PA 15146
County: Allegheny

Phone: (412) 373-3838
Fax: (412) 373-3600
Internet Address: www.eztravelnet.com/abctvl

Full-service travel agency serving commercial and leisure travelers. The Company maintains profiles for its corporate travelers including records of frequent flyer numbers as well as seat, hotel, car size and provider preferences. It also offers city-wide ticket delivery. ABC Travel of Greensburg, Inc. is an affiliate of the agency.

Officers: Thomas L. Marmins *P*

Human Resources: Ronny Webb Martine

Total Employees	36	Regional Employees	36
Year Established	1978	SIC Code	4724
Annual Revenues ($000)	12,000		

ABCO, Inc.

15 Forbes Rd.
P.O. Box E
Trafford, PA 15085
County: Westmoreland

Phone: (412) 374-8060
Fax: (412) 374-8064

Manufacturer and distributor of more than 500 specialty maintenance chemicals. The Company's sales representatives call on accounts throughout the mid-Atlantic section of the United States, selling to businesses, institutions and municipalities.

Officers: Allan Apter *P (Human Resources)*
Donna Dipadova *VP-FIN*
Charlotte Tlumac *SEC & TRS*
Joe Sycz *SAL MGR*

Purchasing: Lily Kretchek *VP-MFG*

Total Employees...............................30	**Regional Employees** 7
Year Established 1950	**SIC Code**......................................2819
Annual Revenues ($000)...5,000+	

ABF Freight System, Inc.

770 Beechnut Dr.
Pittsburgh, PA 15205
County: Allegheny

Phone: (412) 928-8270
Fax: (412) 928-9805
Internet Address: www.abfs.com

Regular-route common carrier concentrating on the long-haul transportation of general commodities freight, involving primarily less-than-truckload shipments. General commodities include all freight except hazardous waste, dangerous explosives, commodities of exceptionally high value, commodities in bulk and those requiring special equipment. General commodities transported by the Company include, among other things, food, textiles, apparel, furniture, appliances, chemicals, nonbulk petroleum products, rubber, plastics, metal and metal products, wood, glass, automotive parts, machinery and miscellaneous manufactured products. The Company, which is headquartered in Fort Smith, AR, is a subsidiary of Arkansas Best Corp., which is also headquartered in Fort Smith, AR, and listed on the NASDAQ. The Company serves all 50 states in the U.S., Puerto Rico and nine provinces across Canada. Its international operation offers service to 301 ports in 161 countries. The Company operates additional Pittsburgh-area branch facilities in Butler, PA, at 133 Hindman Lane; and in Greensburg, PA, at 100 Jamison Ave. All of these facilities report to the Company's regional office in Dayton, OH.

Officers: Dave Stubblefield *P*
John Dake *VP-Transportation*
Wes Kemp *VP-OPR*
Walt Willard *VP-SAL*
Roy Slagle *TRS*
Bud Elliott *Branch MGR-Greensburg*
Steve Riha *Branch MGR-Pittsburgh*
Joan Taylor *Terminal MGR-Butler*

Human Resources: John Greer

Purchasing: Rick Nolte

Total Employees 14,000	**Regional Employees** 80
Year Established 1935	**SIC Code** 4213
Annual Revenues ($000) 1,300,000	

Abraxas Group, Inc.

One Gateway Center, 5th Fl.
Pittsburgh, PA 15222
County: Allegheny

Phone: (412) 208-4000
Fax: (412) 208-4001

Nonprofit provider of comprehensive service programs for the treatment and rehabilitation of delinquent and dependent juveniles. The Organization began as a pilot project of the Governor's Council on Drug and Alcohol Abuse in Pennsylvania to serve as an alternative to incarceration for young offenders. It provides a continuum of services, including screening and assessment; campus and community-based intensive residential treatment; a nontraditional boot camp; residential special needs programs for sex offenders, adolescent females, drug sellers, youth with emotional and behavioral disorders, and youth with mental health problems; halfway house services; and educational management service in public institutions and transitional care residences. Abraxas Community Treatment services, an integral part of the treatment continuum, include a broad range of nonresidential, coeducational services consisting of intensive continuing care, family preservation/crisis intervention/stabilization, day treatment, intensive case management, wrap-around services, community service/restitution programs, detention advocacy programs, and specialized programs for sex offenders and adolescent females. The Organization's philosophy is to provide a replication of the healthy family, with the structure and support to empower individuals to overcome their disadvantages and grow toward stable, productive lives. It operates programs and provides services at 16 sites located throughout the District of Columbia, Delaware, Ohio and Pennsylvania. The Organization serves nearly 1,400 young people every day from a national referral base, with 436 residential treatment beds and 942 community treatment slots. It also operates six schools.

Officers: Arlene Lissner *P & CEO*
Tom Jenkins *VP-OPR*
Richard Kelly *VP-Business DEV*
Kenneth F. Pompi, Ph.D. *VP-RES & Information MGT*
Jack A. Metcalf *SEC, TRS & CFO*

A

Human Resources: Joanne Bruscemi *VP-Human Resources*

Purchasing: Gary Filbert

Total Employees............................714	**Regional Employees** 143
Year Established 1973	**SIC Code**.....................................8399

Acacia Financial Center of Pittsburgh, The

The Acacia Bldg., Parkway Center
Pittsburgh, PA 15220
County: Allegheny

Phone: (412) 922-4360
Fax: (412) 921-3990

Provider of a variety of financial services consisting of insurance, securities and business services to individual and corporate clients. The Company's products and services include asset allocation, corporate employee benefit analysis, disability income insurance through intercompany marketing arrangements, discount brokerage, estate planning, executive compensation planning, financial planning, fixed annuities, key person and credit, line indemnification, life insurance, money market funds, mutual funds, portfolio design, private money management, qualified retirement plans, retirement planning, stocks and bonds, strategic business planning, variable annuities, and business continuation and business transfer alternatives. The Acacia Financial Center of Pittsburgh, serving a client base of over 10,000 in the Tri-State area, is a regional office of The Acacia Group (TAG), which is headquartered in Washington, D.C. TAG markets the products of its subsidiaries, which consist of Acacia Federal Savings Bank, Acacia Mutual Life Insurance Co., Acacia National Life Insurance Co., The Advisors Group, Inc., Calvert Group, Ltd. and Enterprise Resources, Inc.

Officers: Charles T. Nason *P & CEO*
Richard B. Worth *MDIR-The Acacia Financial Center of Pittsburgh*

Human Resources: Margy Beerman *(Purchasing)*

Total Employees............................382	**Regional Employees** 65
Year Established 1869	**SIC Code**.....................................6300

Accutrex Products, Inc.

112 Southpointe Blvd.
Canonsburg, PA 15317
County: Washington

Phone: (412) 746-4300
Fax: (412) 746-0711

Manufacturer of custom shims, gaskets, sheet metal fabrications, metal stampings and precision machined parts. The Company, which is ISO 9002 certified, offers laser and waterjet cutting as well as painting and powder coating services. The Company's Gasket Division is located at the West Point Industrial Park in Washington, PA, and its Precision Parts Division is located in Lancaster, SC.

Officers: Martin P. Beichner, Jr. *P & CEO*
Samuel R. Bruckner *VP*
Thomas J. Wild *CON*
Lauren W. Naumoff *MKT MGR*

Human Resources: Leslie Welsh

Purchasing: Bob Tomayko

Total Employees............................160	**Regional Employees** 125
Year Established 1980	**SIC Code**......................................3469
Annual Revenues ($000) 15,000	

Ace Wire Spring & Form Co., Inc.

1105 Thompson Ave.
McKees Rocks, PA 15136
County: Allegheny

Phone: (412) 331-3353
Fax: (412) 331-1602
Internet Address: www.industry.net/acewire.com

Manufacturer of precision custom springs and wire forms. The Company also produces its patented SuperClip, which securely holds up to 100 sheets of paper. The SuperClip is currently available at KMart, Office Depot, Penn-Daniels, Target, Thrift Drug and other retail stores.

Officers: Richard Froehlich *C-OWN & P*
Linda Froehlich *C-OWN, SEC & TRS*

Purchasing: Denise Vidmar

Total Employees..............................50	**Regional Employees** 50
Year Established 1939	**SIC Code**......................................3495
Annual Revenues ($000) 5,500	

Acme Building Services Co.

104 W. North Ave.
Pittsburgh, PA 15212
County: Allegheny

Phone: (412) 231-1017
Fax: (412) 231-1019

Provider of commercial cleaning and building maintenance services. The Company serves clients throughout the Tri-State area.

Officers: Steve R. Gaber, Sr. *CH*
Steve Gaber, Jr. *P*
William Wappler *VP*

Total Employees............................162
Year Established 1953   **SIC Code**......................................7349
Annual Revenues ($000)...2,000+

Acme Stamping & Wire Forming Co.

201-229 Corliss St.
Pittsburgh, PA 15242
County: Allegheny

Phone: (412) 771-5720
Fax: (412) 771-6812

Contract job shop engaged in the integrated manufacturing of metal parts with engineering, development and construction capabilities. The Company fabricates metal components from raw materials like coiled, sheet, bar and wire metals, both ferrous and nonferrous. Its power presses range from five-ton to 200-ton capacity. It also performs various subassembly operations, including riveting and mechanical assembly as well as electric resistance, spot, butt and projection welding. All work is done to customers' specifications, with parts designed and built in the Company's Tool and Die Shop. The Company serves the automotive, defense, electric, electronic, personal safety equipment and appliance industries.

Officers: Donald L. Moody *P*

Purchasing: Doug Speer

Total Employees.............................30   **Regional Employees** 30
Year Established 1921   **SIC Code**......................................3469
Annual Revenues ($000) 3,000

Acordia of Pennsylvania, Inc.

The Gulf Tower, 707 Grant St., Ste. 700
Pittsburgh, PA 15219
County: Allegheny

Phone: (412) 765-3510
Fax: (412) 765-1164

Provider of property and casualty insurance brokerage (commercial and personal lines), workers' compensation programs, employee benefits programs, managed health care integration, consulting and loss control services. The Company targets mid-market and upscale mid-market firms with between 100 and 4,000 employees, or with annual revenues of $5 million to $500 million. It is a subsidiary of Acordia, Inc., which is headquartered in Indianapolis, IN, and listed on the NYSE. The local branch office is known as Acordia of Pittsburgh. Its affiliates are Acordia of Central Pennsylvania in Mechanicsburg, Acordia of Eastern Pennsylvania in Bala Cynwyd and Acordia of Western Pennsylvania in Erie. The local branch office primarily serves clients in Southwestern and Central Pennsylvania. The Pennsylvania offices report to Acordia Northeast, Inc., in Morristown, NJ.

Officers: Mark F. Susco *COO*
John B. Kelley *SVP*
J. Ronald Lenart *SVP*
Louis F. Locante *SVP*
Craig T. Wisotzki *SVP*

Human Resources: Rose Donohue *(Purchasing)*

Total Employees......................6,910	**Regional Employees** 55
Year Established 1979	**SIC Code** 6411
Annual Revenues ($000)......................10,000 (Pittsburgh)	

Action Supply Products, Inc.

1065 Montour W. Industrial Park
P.O. Box 200
Imperial, PA 15126
County: Allegheny

Phone: (412) 695-2721
Fax: (412) 695-2730

Master wholesale stocking distributor of spill control products, safety supplies, wiping materials, protective clothing, rainwear, boots, gloves, containment products and building maintenance supplies. The Company has an active inside and outside sales staff to act as consultants and problem solvers. In addition, it offers 24-hour emergency delivery service. The Company serves clients in the Tri-State area.

Officers: Lynn Fink *CEO (Human Resources)*
Don Fink *P*
Gary Fink *GMGR*
Chris Beauregard *OPR-MGR*

Purchasing: Sandy Ireson

Total Employees	30	**Regional Employees**	30
Year Established	1983	**SIC Code**	5087
Annual Revenues ($000)	7,000		

Action Transit Enterprises, Inc.

330 Poplar St.
Pittsburgh, PA 15223
County: Allegheny

Phone: (412) 781-7906
Fax: (412) 781-8230

Provider of a variety of transportation-related services. The Company transports school children on trips and provides routing for many school districts and camps. It also operates vans, vehicles for the handicapped, and people movers, and motor coaches that are available for travel all over the United States. In addition, the Company leases triaxle trucks to contractors and builders.

Officers: Claire Klein *P (Human Resources)*
Richard G. Decker *VP-FIN*
Seymour Klein *SEC & TRS*

Purchasing: Alan H. Klein *VP-OPR*

Total Employees	200	**Regional Employees**	200
Year Established	1976	**SIC Code**	4151

Adams Manufacturing Corp.

109 West Park Rd.
P.O. Box 1
Portersville, PA 16051
County: Butler

Phone: (412) 368-8837
Fax: (412) 368-9311

Manufacturer of suction cups, hooks, hangers, stakes, fasteners and protectors. The Company claims to be the world's largest manufacturer of suction cups. It also produces a wide variety of indoor and outdoor Christmas decorating accessories, including hooks, hangers, suction cups and tree stands. The Company sells its products in bulk or in quantities packaged for the retail market.

Officers: William E. Adams *OWN, CH & CEO*
William O'Hara *P & COO*
John A. Fischer *VP-SAL & MKT*
Stephen Sabo *CON*
John Heim *Plant MGR*

Human Resources: Marcy Slaughenhoupt *DIR-Human Resources*

Purchasing: Dianna Sroka

Total Employees ....100+	**Regional Employees** ....100+
Year Established 1981	**SIC Code** 3089

ADC/ITS Corp.

375 Valley Brook Rd.
McMurray, PA 15317
County: Washington

Phone: (412) 941-1500
Fax: (412) 941-4603

Manufacturer of television transmission equipment. The Company is comprised of the Broadcast Systems division, the Microwave Systems division and the Filter Technology division, as well as a subsidiary, ITS Service Co. (ISC). The two primary lines of equipment manufactured by the Company are broadcast and microwave transmitters. Broadcast transmitters cover the VHF and UHF television channel range. The microwave transmitter line used for instructional television and premium entertainment program delivery directly to homes is known as "wireless cable." The Filter Technology division designs and manufactures filters for the Broadcast Systems and Microwave Systems divisions, while ISC performs transmission system installation and field support services worldwide. The Filter Technology division and ISC are both located at the above address. The Broadcast Systems division is located in Lawrence, PA; and the Microwave Systems division is located in McMurray, PA. The Company, formerly known as Information Transmission Systems Corp., is a subsidiary of ADC Telecommunications, Inc., which is headquartered in Minnetonka, MN, and listed on the NASDAQ.

Officers: Jeffrey M. Lynn *P*

Human Resources: David J. Baker *DIR-Human Resources*

Purchasing: Frank Gaspar

Regional Employees 350	
Year Established 1982	**SIC Code** 3663
Annual Revenues ($000) ....40,000+	

Adelphoi, Inc.

352 Main St.
Latrobe, PA 15650
County: Westmoreland

Phone: (412) 537-3052
Fax: (412) 539-7060

A

Nonprofit agency providing programs aimed at addressing human needs through support services, property management, fund-raising, leadership development and new enterprise. The Agency provides these services to the following organizations and programs: Adelphoi Village, Human Resources Education Consortium, Human Services Center, Latrobe Community Children's Center, Latrobe Union Mission, Planned Giving, Redstone Highlands and Westmoreland Community Housing Development Organization. It also operates the Human Services Center at 1011 Old Salem Rd. and the Fourth Street Square at 105 W. Fourth St., both located in Greensburg, PA.

Officers: James Bendel *EDIR*

Human Resources: Wallace Perkins

Total Employees............................60	**Regional Employees** 60	
Year Established 1989	**SIC Code**.....................................8741	
Annual Revenues ($000) 2,500		

Adience, Inc.

27 Noblestown Rd.
Carnegie, PA 15106
County: Allegheny

Phone: (412) 276-1750
Fax: (412) 276-7823

Manufacturer and installer of specialty refractory products for the steelmaking industry, doing business as BMI-France. Over the past year, the Company claims that it has provided refractory products and services to every integrated steel producer in the United States and Canada. The Company also manufactures specialty refractory products for use in the production of aluminum and glass and is one of the few rebuilders of coke ovens in the United States. Its extensive product line includes fireclay and high alumina brick and shapes, gunites, shotcretes, plastic and ramming mixes, conventional and low cement castables, mortars, maintenance coatings and blast furnace casthouse products, with total turn-key installation capabilities coast to coast. The Company operates sales facilities in Birmingham, AL; Phoenix, AZ; Canon City, CO; Chicago, IL; Louisville, KY; Baltimore, MD; Detroit, MI; St. Louis, MO; Buffalo and Long Island City, NY; Cincinnati and Cleveland, OH; Philadelphia, Pittsburgh and Snow Shoe, PA; Salt Lake City, UT; and Sault Ste. Marie and Smithville, Ontario, Canada. Its manufacturing plants are in Canon City, CO; Crown Point, IN; South

Webster, OH; Altoona and Snow Shoe, PA; and Smithville, Ontario, Canada. Research and laboratory facilities are located in South Webster, OH, and Snow Shoe, PA. The Company is a subsidiary of The Alpine Group, Inc., which is headquartered in New York, NY, and listed on the NYSE.

Officers: Stephen M. Johnson *P*
Gary J. Hoyson *VP-Commercial OPR*
Gary D. Snook *VP-OPR*
Richard W. Yennerell *VP-FIN*
David A. Knowlton *DIR-R&D*
C. Ted Arther *P-Furnco Construction*
Willard Bellows *P-Findlay Refractories*

Human Resources: Frank A. Miller *VP-Human Resources*

Purchasing: Ronald V. Kilgore *VP-Quality & Purchasing*

Total Employees	800	**Regional Employees**	150
Year Established	1985	**SIC Code**	3255
Annual Revenues ($000)	115,000		

ADP-GSI Logistics and Distribution

1380 Old Freeport Rd.
Pittsburgh, PA 15238
County: Allegheny

Phone: (412) 963-6770
Fax: (412) 963-6779
Internet Address: www.adpgsild.com

Provider of business software solutions and consulting services. The Company's software product, TOLAS, is utilized for distribution, logistics and financial management applications. In addition, the Company is a strategic business partner of Baan Co. (BC), a provider of Enterprise Resource Planning systems. This multi-faceted partnership involves the Company as a reseller, implementer and co-developer of BC's applications with emphasis on distribution-intensive industries in make-to-stock, make-to-order and assemble-to-order environments. The Company operates sales and service branch offices in Huntington Beach, CA; Marlborough, MA; and Tarrytown, NY; as well as in Brussels, Belgium; Camberley, England; Grenoble and Paris, France; and Barcelona, Spain. It serves more than 450 customers representing 1,500 individual sites. The Company is a division of Automatic Data Processing, Inc., which is headquartered in Roseland, NJ, and listed on the NYSE.

Officers: Philippe Beaurain *P*
Ron Book *VP-Customer Satisfaction*
Jeff Dubell *VP-SAL*
Liz Welsh *VP-ADM*
Tom George *CON*

Human Resources: Pati Roberson

Total Employees............................280	**Regional Employees** 125
Year Established 1971	**SIC Code**.....................................7372
Annual Revenues ($000) 35,000	

Advanced Manufacturing Technologies, Inc.

9001 Corporate Cir.
Export, PA 15632
County: Westmoreland

Phone: (412) 327-3001
Fax: (412) 327-3040

Electronics contract manufacturer serving an array of clients with approximately 80% located within a 100-mile radius of the Pittsburgh metropolitan area. The Company's major services include through-hole, semi-automated printed circuit board assembly; electromechanical assembly, cables, harnesses, enclosures and control panels; Humiseal conformal coating; functional testing; full range procurement (Windows '95 based materials requirement plan software) including fabricated assemblies; customer inventory management; and bill of material/revision control.

Officers: Buck T. Helfferich *C-OWN & P*
Thomas J. Scanio *C-OWN & VP*

Total Employees..............................30	**Regional Employees** 30
Year Established 1990	**SIC Code**.....................................3679

Advanced Metallurgy, Inc.

Murry Corporate Park, 1003 Corporate Dr.
Export, PA 15632
County: Westmoreland

Phone: (412) 733-8332
Fax: (412) 733-2880

Manufacturer of electrical contacts and brazed assemblies for a wide range of industrial customers. The Company operates plants in Cedar Knolls, NJ; Delmont, Lancaster and McKeesport, PA; and Luquillo, Puerto Rico. It is a subsidiary of Technitrol, Inc., which is headquartered in Trevose, PA, and listed on the NYSE.

Officers: James J. Rafferty, Jr. *P & CEO*
Dario Perez *VP & GMGR*
Donald Creaves *DIR-FIN*
Thomas A. Frederick *General SAL & MKT MGR*
Joseph C. Carothers *SAL MGR*

Purchasing: Raymond J. Matsey *Materials MGR*

Total Employees............................600   **Regional Employees** 300
Year Established 1969   **SIC Code**.......................................3643
Annual Revenues ($000)..50,000+

Advanced Systems Engineering, Inc.

The Landmarks Bldg., One Station Sq.
Pittsburgh, PA 15219
County: Allegheny

Phone: (412) 471-1900
Fax: (412) 471-2557
Internet Address: www.aseinc.com

Provider of management consulting services helping organizations to identify and achieve their business goals. The Firm's team of business analysts, trainers, process control experts and software engineers enable clients to determine their target business; the best way for them to conduct that business; the capabilities they need; the best way to organize, measure and manage themselves; and their needed training and development. Its practice areas include project management, human resources development and training, and Web-enabled software applications for government and industry. The Firm operates a sales office in Hudson, OH.

Officers: Arthur R. Crivella *P*
Robert C. Plunkett *COO*
Ernest C. Emery, Jr. *VP*
Wayne J. West *VP*

Total Employees.............................45   **Regional Employees** 43
Year Established 1986   **SIC Code**.......................................8742

Advanced Technology Systems, Inc.

3000 Tech Center Dr.
Monroeville, PA 15146
County: Allegheny

Phone: (412) 829-2208
Fax: (412) 829-2415

Consulting engineering and scientific research firm providing a full range of technical and management services, including air quality management, environmental management, geotechnical engineering and construction management to clients in the public and private sectors. The Company's services include testing, analysis, modeling, permitting, engineering control design, pollution prevention strategy development and implementation, and analytical methods research and development. Its staff is comprised of meteorology experts, architects, geologists, chemists and civil, electrical, chemical, mechanical, mining, metallurgical, environmental and safety engineers.

Officers: Robert O. Agbede *P & CEO*
James Veri *SVP*
Michael O. Bodinsky *VP & CFO*
Robinson Khosah, Ph.D. *VP*

Human Resources: Jan Elliott *Human Resources MGR (Purchasing)*

Total Employees	60	**Regional Employees**	57
Year Established	1987	**SIC Code**	8711

Advanced Telecomm of Pittsburgh

105 Broughton Rd.
Bethel Park, PA 15102
County: Allegheny

Phone: (412) 831-1300
Fax: (412) 831-1323
Internet Address: www.atiteam.com

Retail provider of an array of telecommunications products and services, including interconnect (business telephone systems and voice mail), cellular telephones and other wireless services, long distance service, digital satellite television, Internet access and other network services. The Company, doing business as ATI Communications, operates additional facilities in the Washington, D.C./Baltimore, MD, metropolitan area (16); and in Harrisburg, New Castle and Pittsburgh (6), PA. It also operates approximately 25 kiosks at various retail locations. The Company is a subsidiary of Applied Cellular Technology, Inc., which is headquartered in Nixa, MO, and listed on the NASDAQ.

Officers: Vincent A. Lo Castro *CEO*
Scott R. Silverman *P*
Mark D. Jackson *VP & TRS*
Bruce Reale *VP*

Human Resources: Rose Anne Lackovic

Purchasing: Barbara Corbin

Total Employees	400	**Regional Employees**	160
Year Established	1984	**SIC Code**	5999
Annual Revenues ($000)	30,000+		

Advantage Health Harmarville Rehabilitation Corp.

Guys Run Rd.
P.O. Box 11460
Pittsburgh, PA 15238
County: Allegheny

Phone: (412) 828-1300
Fax: (412) 828-0748

Owner and operator of the 202-bed HEALTHSOUTH Harmarville Rehabilitation Hospital (Hospital), which is also located at the above address, and seven comprehensive outpatient centers. The Hospital provides inpatient, outpatient and transitional physical rehabilitation for adolescents and adults in the region. Its outpatient facilities consist of Butler-Harmarville Outpatient Rehabilitation Center in Cranberry Township, PA; Connellsville Outpatient Rehabilitation Center in Connellsville, PA; Latrobe Area Hospital-Harmarville Outpatient Rehabilitation Center in Latrobe, PA; Ohio Valley General Hospital-Harmarville Outpatient Rehabilitation Center in Moon Township, PA; Outpatient Rehabilitation Center at Harmarville in Pittsburgh, PA; Washington Outpatient Rehabilitation Center in Washington, PA; and The Western Pennsylvania Hospital-Harmarville Outpatient Rehabilitation Center in Pittsburgh, PA. The Company is a subsidiary of HEALTHSOUTH Corp., which is headquartered in Birmingham, AL, and listed on the NYSE.

Officers: Frank Delisi III *CEO*
Ken Anthony *DIR-Business DEV*
Richard Bonfiglio, M.D. *Medical DIR*
Jim Steinkirchner *CON*

Human Resources: Jerry Maier *DIR-Human Resources*

Total Employees............................500	**Regional Employees** 500
Year Established 1913	**SIC Code**.....................................8093

Advest, Inc.

One Oxford Centre, 301 Grant St., Ste. 3300
Pittsburgh, PA 15219
County: Allegheny

Phone: (412) 391-6500
Fax: (412) 391-3274

Full-service broker-dealer and investment banking firm. The Company is headquartered in Hartford, CT, and operates more than 90 branch offices throughout the United States. It is a subsidiary of The Advest Group, Inc., which is also headquartered in Hartford, CT, and listed on the NYSE.

Officers: Garry L. Hogan *SVP & Branch MGR*

Total Employees..........................1,900
Year Established 1898

Regional Employees 31
SIC Code......................................6211

AEA Technology Engineering Services, Inc.

241 Curry Hollow Rd.
Pittsburgh, PA 15236
County: Allegheny

Phone: (412) 655-1200
Fax: (412) 655-4093

Provider of engineering analysis services to power industry and general industry clients. The Company's capabilities include American Society of Mechanical Engineers Code design, as well as stress, thermal and vibration analysis. It also performs specialized services, including time-of-flight nondestructive ultrasonic examinations, rotor bore and retaining ring nondestructive examinations for power plants. In addition, the Company provides sponge-abrasive decontamination services for nuclear and government projects. It operates a regional office located in Huntersville, NC. The Company is a subsidiary of AEA Technology Plc, which is headquartered in England, and listed on the London Stock Exchange.

Officers: Thomas E. Sliva *P & CEO*
Van B. Walker *EVP*
Manu Badlani *VP-ENG*
Michael Kopec *VP-FIN*

Total Employees..............................60
Year Established 1991
Annual Revenues ($000) 10,000

Regional Employees 30
SIC Code......................................8711

Aerotech, Inc.

101 Zeta Dr.
Pittsburgh, PA 15238
County: Allegheny

Phone: (412) 963-7470
Fax: (412) 963-7459
Internet Address: www.aerotech.industry.net

Manufacturer of precision motion control systems and components primarily for applications in the electronic, semiconductor and automotive industry. The Company's products include motion controllers ranging from single-axis microstepping indexers to 16-axis synchronized machine automation controllers; microstepping, DC servo and brushless motors and drives; linear motors;

precision linear and rotary positioning stages, including air bearing stages and linear motor-based stages; linear motor-based gantry systems; and patented laser interferometer systems. The Company maintains sales offices in Aptos and Huntington Beach, CA; Farmington, CT; Tampa, FL; Chicago, IL; Ferndale, MI; Raleigh, NC; Lisbon, OH; West Chester, PA; Waco, TX; and New Richmond, WI. Its subsidiaries include Aerotech GmbH in Germany and Aerotech Ltd. in England.

Officers: Stephen J. Botos *P & CEO*
Emery Hornok *EVP*
David F. Kincel *VP-ADM & Quality Control*

Human Resources: Karen Taylor

Purchasing: Joseph Garofalo

Total Employees..........................234	**Regional Employees** 205	
Year Established 1970	**SIC Code**......................................3625	
Annual Revenues ($000) 25,000		

Affiliated Computer Services, Inc.

One Marquis Plaza, 5315 Campbells Run Rd.
Pittsburgh, PA 15205
County: Allegheny

Phone: (412) 788-3800
Fax: (412) 788-3507

Commercial outsourcing company providing a comprehensive range of technology solutions, including data center operations, transaction processing, client/server computing, network services, data warehousing, electronic and micrographic imaging, and professional services. The Company, which is headquartered in Dallas, TX, is listed on the NYSE, with 80 offices worldwide. The local facility oversees its northeastern U.S. operations and includes a major data center.

Officers: Thomas Solomon *SVP*

Human Resources: Janet Caryll *MGR*

Total Employees........................8,000	**Regional Employees** 200	
Year Established 1984	**SIC Code**......................................7374	
Annual Revenues ($000) 396,000		

Affordable Interior Systems, Inc.

McClure Industrial Park, 4903 Old William Penn Hwy.
Monroeville, PA 15146
County: Allegheny

A

Phone: (412) 733-1555
Fax: (412) 733-2255
Internet Address: www.aisystems.com

Remanufacturer of Knoll/Westinghouse office panel systems and related components. The Company also distributes various new components ranging from desks and seating to filing systems and accessories. The Company markets its products through a variety of nationwide channels, including dealers and installers. In addition, the Company provides CAD design, space planning, product design, specifications and installation services.

Officers: Richard D. Sharp *P & CEO*

Purchasing: Michele Sharp

Total Employees............................48	**Regional Employees** 48
Year Established 1986	**SIC Code**.....................................5021
Annual Revenues ($000)...5,000+	

Afftrex, Ltd.

600 State St., Ste. 201
Clairton, PA 15025
County: Allegheny

Phone: (412) 233-8780
Fax: (412) 233-8111

Provider of project management, engineering, and technical and administrative support services for decontamination and decommissioning projects dealing with radioactive, hazardous and mixed wastes. The Company's primary line of business is radiological decontamination of U.S. Department of Energy (DOE) and commercial nuclear facilities. Its other business segments include environmental remediation, including full turnkey decontamination and decommissioning operations, site characterization, procedure preparation and operations planning; health physics and technical services, including risk analysis, health and safety plans, sampling and analysis, source leak testing, instrument calibration, DOP testing, site investigations and nuclear/hazardous laundry services; training, including DOE-approved curricula for Radiological Control Technician and Radiological Worker II certification, Hazwoper training, including OSHA forty hour, eight hour supervisor, eight hour refresher, asbestos worker and lead training; and general contracting/construction, including construction management, excavations, demolition and renovations. The Company operates regional offices in Blackfoot, ID, and Harriman, TN, with project offices in Idaho Falls, ID, Argonne, IL, and West Mifflin, PA.

Officers: William H. Button *CH*
Douglas J. Button *P & CEO*
Robert J. Pastor *SVP*
Stephen A. Carpenter *VP*
Peter Collopy *VP*
S. Thomas Curry *VP*
Charles F. Eason, Jr. *VP & SEC*
W. Douglas Homer *VP*
Stephen T. Simcic *TRS*

Human Resources: Thomas G. Jones *Human Resources MGR*

Total Employees............................210   **Regional Employees** 75
Year Established 1981   **SIC Code**....................................8744
Annual Revenues ($000) 12,000

AGR International, Inc.

615 Whitestown Rd.
P.O. Box 149, Butler, PA 16003
Butler, PA 16001
County: Butler

Phone: (412) 482-2163
Fax: (412) 482-2767

Manufacturer and exporter of inspection systems for the packaging industry. The Company's products include automated on-line inspection systems, automated sampling inspection systems, process control information systems and laboratory test instruments. Its factory technologies include container handling, leak detection, optical inspection and measurement, part positioning, pressure testing, production monitoring software, thickness measurement and volume differential measurement. In addition, the Company offers feasibility studies, site evaluation, production line drawings, project definition, system design, software development, system integration, product documentation and product training. Its inspection systems are sold to manufacturers in 76 countries.

Officers: Henry M. Dimmick, Sr. *CH & CEO*
David A. Rugaber *P*

Human Resources: Dwight R. Byers

Total Employees............................220   **Regional Employees** 220
Year Established 1957   **SIC Code**....................................3829

Air Ground Xpress, Inc.

438 Matchette Rd.
P.O. Box 438
Clinton, PA 15026
County: Allegheny

Phone: (412) 695-1110
Fax: (412) 695-1116

A

   Provider of ground transportation services to air courier businesses, including Emery, TWA and USAirways, specializing in the expedited shipment of time sensitive freight. The Company offers local pickup and delivery throughout the Tri-State area as well as linehaul services nationwide. It carries all types of products, from raw fish to helicopters. The Company's fleet consists of approximately 150 vehicles. It operates satellite terminals in Altoona and Clarion, PA.

Officers: Phillip Fall *OWN & P*
   Michael Snyder *GMGR*
   John Gormley *Terminal MGR*
   Ron Sayer *MKT DIR*
   Terry Waxler *Supervisor-Heavyweight Division*

Human Resources: Richard Rubesne *VP*

Purchasing: Richard Patterson *CON*

Total Employees	153	**Regional Employees**	86
Year Established	1981	**SIC Code**	4215
Annual Revenues ($000)	8,200		

Air Products and Chemicals, Inc.

Freeport Rd., Rte. 28
P.O. Box 565
Creighton, PA 15030
County: Allegheny

Phone: (412) 226-1513
Fax: (412) 226-1648
Internet Address: www.airproducts.com

   Producer of industrial gases, including argon, hydrogen, nitrogen and oxygen, primarily for regional customers such as steel mills, hospitals and food manufacturers. The Company, which is headquartered in Allentown, PA, is listed on the NYSE.

Officers: Jessie Park *Plant MGR*
   Randy Sobotka *Facilities MGR*
   Steve Chubon *MGR-Cylinder Products*
   Mike Pohlman *MGR-Liquid Bulk Products*
   Brian Zimik *MGR-Retail & Distribution Products*

Human Resources: Mike Jones *Human Resources MGR*

Total Employees......................13,300	**Regional Employees** 91
Year Established 1949	**SIC Code**....................................2813
Annual Revenues ($000) 4,008,000		

Air & Waste Management Assn.

One Gateway Center, 3rd Fl.
Pittsburgh, PA 15222
County: Allegheny

Phone: (412) 232-3444
Fax: (412) 232-3450
Internet Address: www.awma.org

Nonprofit scientific, technical and educational association with more than 17,000 individual members in 60 countries. The Association serves its members and the public by promoting environmental responsibility, by providing leadership in global environmental management and by producing opportunities for technical exchange worldwide. The Association's members represent all disciplines that have an interest in environmental science, technology and policy. Through specialty conferences and symposia, technical exhibits, continuing education courses and workshops, it fosters the exchange of technical information on a wide variety of environmental topics and encourages the development of new environmental technology. The Association operates branch offices in Washington, D.C., and Ottawa, Ontario, Canada.

Officers: Dick Baldwin *P*
John Thorner *EDIR*
Steve Stasko *Deputy EDIR*

Human Resources: Jim Dougherty *MGR-Human Resources (Purchasing)*

Total Employees...........................43	**Regional Employees** 42
Year Established 1907	**SIC Code**....................................8621
Annual Revenues ($000) 7,000		

Algor, Inc.

150 Beta Dr.
Pittsburgh, PA 15238
County: Allegheny

Phone: (412) 967-2700
Fax: (412) 967-2781
Internet Address: www.algor.com

Manufacturer of engineering design, analysis and simulation software. The Company offers a comprehensive selection of software, training tools, educational seminars and services to more than 16,000 engineers in over 60 countries. Its major product lines include a range of design and finite element analysis (FEA) software. FEA is a process by which engineers create a computer model of a proposed design or structure, then test it to determine how it will sustain under real work conditions. The ability to perform FEA on a computer reduces the need for costly prototypes and laboratory testing. The Company's analysis capabilities include linear and nonlinear stress, vibration, natural frequency (modal), heat transfer, electrostatic and fluid flow analysis. In 1997, the Company pioneered "virtual engineering" software, which enables mechanical engineers to see everything graphically on the computer screen that was once confined to numbers. The Algor Publishing Division, which is also located at the above address, provides technical training through books, videos and CD-ROM-based multimedia.

Officers: Michael L. Bussler *P*
Virginia A. Goebel *VP & COO*

Total Employees............................60	**Regional Employees** 60
Year Established 1977	**SIC Code**....................................7372
Annual Revenues ($000) 10,200	

Allan Steel Co., J.

829 Beaver Ave.
P.O. Box 99397
Pittsburgh, PA 15233
County: Allegheny

Phone: (412) 321-3111
Fax: (412) 321-8833

Operator of a full-line carbon steel service center, providing wholesale angles, bars, channels, beams, floor plate, plate, sheet and coil. The Company receives, stores and ships the products from its facilities at the above address and from sites on Neville Island in Pittsburgh, PA, and Masury and Martins Ferry, OH. The latter facilities handle coil plus sheet, plate and strip slit from coil. The Pittsburgh-area facilities provide burning, sawing and shearing operations as required by various customers. In addition, it has a scrap division, JAS Scrap Management in Pittsburgh, PA, which stores and sells scrap purchased on the open market and/or generated internally from the Company's own processing operations. The Company's subsidiary, J. Allan Steel Products Co. in Pittsburgh, PA, is a wholesale distributor and operates divisions in Martins Ferry (coil processing) and Masury (wholesale distributor), OH. It was initially formed for the carbon plate market but has since expanded to market hot- and cold-rolled coil, coated coil, product slit from coil and some structurals associated with those markets.

Officers: Joseph A. Gnazzo *P & CEO*
Michael W. Bitcko *VP*
John M. Matig *VP*

Human Resources: Richard L. Ross *VP & CFO*

Purchasing: Marilyn J. Rogalla

Total Employees	142	Regional Employees	128
Year Established	1976	SIC Code	5051
Annual Revenues ($000)			56,250

Allegheny Bindery Corp.

3700 Bigelow Blvd.
Pittsburgh, PA 15213
County: Allegheny

Phone: (412) 681-9050
Fax: (412) 681-9058

Trade bindery providing bookbinding services primarily for printers throughout the Tri-State area.

Officers: Edward R. Gumm *P*
Harris I. Price *SEC & TRS*

Total Employees	70	Regional Employees	70
Year Established	1960	SIC Code	2789
Annual Revenues ($000)			2-4,000

Allegheny Cemetery

4734 Butler St.
Pittsburgh, PA 15201
County: Allegheny

Phone: (412) 682-1624
Fax: (412) 622-0655

Nonprofit operator of a full-service cemetery offering cremation, bronze memorials, vaults, crypts, niches and urns. The Cemetery claims to be the oldest institution of its kind west of the Allegheny Mountains and the sixth incorporated cemetery in the United States. Over 120,000 members of Pittsburgh's families are now resting in the Cemetery, including 16 Pittsburgh Mayors who are interred throughout its grounds. One of the largest cemeteries in the country, it spreads across 300 acres and has 15 miles of paved roadways. A guardhouse, arched gates, chapel, several historical mausoleums and a four-story bell and clock tower stand on the property, which is listed on the National Register of Historic Places. Perpetual care funds, now exceeding $8 million, ensure the Cemetery's protection and constant vigilance in maintenance.

Officers: Thomas G. Roberts *P*

Human Resources: Barbara Wirkowski *AST to P*

Total Employees	45	Regional Employees	45
Year Established	1844	SIC Code	6553

Allegheny Child Care Academy, Inc.

940 Penn Ave.
Pittsburgh, PA 15222
County: Allegheny

Phone: (412) 281-9928
Fax: (412) 281-9925

Provider of day care services at five sites in Pittsburgh (including the above address) and one each in East Liberty and Robinson Township, PA. The Company is licensed to serve 640 children with a current enrollment of 510 children, from six weeks to age six. Each day care center has a large gym area with mats and exercise equipment. Multimedia computer systems are used in preschool classrooms. The day care centers are open Monday through Friday from 6:30 a.m. to 6:30 p.m., with breakfast and lunch served at all of the sites and dinner served at four of them. The Company also operates a kindergarten at its 10 Wood St. site in Pittsburgh.

Officers: Melissa Kania Henry *P (Human Resources)*
Tim Kust *VP*
David Henry *SEC*

Purchasing: Frank Popowski *TRS*

Total Employees 110	**Regional Employees** 110
Year Established 1992	**SIC Code** 8351
Annual Revenues ($000) 2-3,000	

Allegheny Computer Services, Inc.

1231 Banksville Rd.
Pittsburgh, PA 15216
County: Allegheny

Phone: (412) 561-1300
Fax: (412) 341-0249

Provider of computer sales, service and parts for Apple, Compaq, DEC, Hewlett-Packard, IBM and NEC, as well as custom-built clones and all other major brands. The Company also markets computer-related supplies, furniture and accessories. In addition, it offers custom software, conversions, data entry services, business forms, memory and system upgrades, parts and pre-developed software. The Company is an authorized sales and service provider for Apple, Compaq, Hewlett-Packard, IBM and Novell.

Officers: Ronald L. Seamons *P*
James Baxter, Jr. *SEC & TRS*

Human Resources: Marian Dailey

Total Employees 34	**Regional Employees** 34
Year Established 1972	**SIC Code** 7374
Annual Revenues ($000) 2,700	

Allegheny Container L.P.

Rte. 910 W.
P.O. Box 111428, Pittsburgh, PA 15238
Cheswick, PA 15024
County: Allegheny

Phone: (412) 826-1040
Fax: (412) 826-8442

Designer and manufacturer of corrugated sheets, shipping cartons and folding cartons. The Company serves a variety of clients throughout the Tri-State area. It operates an additional plant in New Kensington, PA.

Officers: Ronald W. Hawkins *CEO*

Human Resources: Darlene Szalanczy

Purchasing: Mark J. Magister

Total Employees	60	**Regional Employees**	60
Year Established	1978	**SIC Code**	2653
Annual Revenues ($000)			6,000

Allegheny Council to Improve Neighborhoods

Two Gateway Center, 18th Fl.
Pittsburgh, PA 15222
County: Allegheny

Phone: (412) 281-2102
Fax: (412) 391-4512

Nonprofit developer and manager of affordable housing for homeless families and individuals, women and children in crisis, frail elderly, individuals with physical and mental disabilities, and low- and moderate-income families. The Organization also operates a major weatherization program serving Allegheny, Greene and Washington Counties, PA. In addition, it operates a program to help public housing residents secure expanded educational and employment opportunities, and unemployed people to save their homes from foreclosure. The Organization's subsidiary, AHI Development, Inc. (AHI), is a developer of housing. AHI operates Supportive Housing Management Services, a manager of low-income housing. Both operations are located in Clairton, PA. The Organization is also known as ACTION-Housing, Inc.

Officers: Jonathan E. Zimmer *EDIR*
Terri Gould *DIR-Human Services & Community Affairs*
Larry Swanson *DIR-Housing & R&D*
Kathy Szwarc *CON*

Total Employees	62	**Regional Employees**	62
Year Established	1957	**SIC Code**	8399
Annual Revenues ($000)			5-7,000

Allegheny County Bar Assn., The

Koppers Bldg., 436 Seventh Ave., Ste. 400
Pittsburgh, PA 15219
County: Allegheny

A

Phone: (412) 261-6161
Fax: (412) 261-3622
Internet Address: www.acba.org

Nonprofit service organization composed of more than 67 substantive law sections and active committees in which its membership of approximately 8,000 lawyers participate. The Association publishes three communications vehicles consisting of the daily Pittsburgh Legal Journal, the official Court publication, which is a newspaper that prints the Court calendar, schedules, legal notices, a variety of official news items and legal advertising; the PLJ magazine, the official Association magazine which publishes legal decisions, court opinions, points of information of interest to the legal community, articles on timely legal topics, announcements about the Association's educational programs and other activities; and The Allegheny Lawyer, the official newsletter of the Association which focuses on the accomplishments of individual members and Association activities. In addition to the services provided members, the Association provides several services to the public. Among the most popular are "Fairy Tales & Nursery Rhymes", a program for grade school children which teaches them about the legal system, the Lawyer Referral Service which assists the public by identifying lawyers who practice in specific areas of law and the Pro Bono Project which assists people who meet the income criteria for free legal assistance by assigning their cases to volunteer attorneys.

Officers: W. Christopher Conrad *P*
Barry M. Simpson *President-Elect (1998)*
James I. Smith III *EDIR*
James E. Abraham *TRS*
Kim Berkeley Clark *SEC*

Human Resources: David A. Blaner *AST-EDIR*

Total Employees	72	**Regional Employees**	72
Year Established	1870	**SIC Code**	8699
Annual Revenues ($000)	3,200		

Allegheny County Sanitary Authority

3300 Preble Ave.
Pittsburgh, PA 15233
County: Allegheny

Phone: (412) 766-4810
Fax: (412) 734-8715

Nonprofit governmental authority operating one of the larger wastewater treatment facilities in the Ohio Valley, also known as ALCOSAN. The Authority serves almost 320,000 residential, commercial and industrial accounts, comprising a population of approximately 900,000 in 83 communities, including the City of Pittsburgh. Its facility occupies 56 acres along the Ohio River on the Northside, processing an average of 200 million gallons of wastewater daily 24 hours a day, 365 days a year.

Officers: Joseph Katarincic *CH*
Joseph W. Lengyel *EDIR*

Human Resources: Jim Tolbert *MGR-Human Resources*

Purchasing: Harry Owens *MGR-Purchasing*

Total Employees............................296	**Regional Employees** 296
Year Established 1946	**SIC Code** 4911

Allegheny East Mental Health/Mental Retardation Center, Inc.

712 South Ave.
Pittsburgh, PA 15221
County: Allegheny

Phone: (412) 243-3400
Fax: (412) 244-4781

Nonprofit organization providing a full range of services to mentally retarded and mentally ill children and adults. The Organization's mental health services include outpatient care, case management, partial hospitalization, residential care, and vocational training and socialization. Its mental retardation services include residential care, vocational training, day treatment and socialization. The Organization provides care to approximately 2,900 clients primarily in Allegheny County through over 60 facilities, including contract inpatient services with hospitals, individual homes, and children and youth services. Its primary satellite sites are located at 10 Duff Rd., Ste. 301, in Pittsburgh, PA; One Monroeville Center, Ste. 475, in Monroeville, PA; and 510 Seco Rd. in Monroeville, PA.

Officers: Barbara Conniff *EDIR*
Flo W. Can Cara, Ph.D. *DIR-Mental Health Services*
Daniel Conniff *Fiscal DIR*
David Gigliotti *DIR-Planning & Community Relations*
Karen Madden *DIR-Base Service Unit*
Edward Picchiarini *DIR-Mental Retardation Services*
Paul I. Weiss, M.D. *Medical DIR*
Ken Wood *Program DIR-Mental Health Services*
Mark Waggoner *Business MGR*

Human Resources: Kerri McMaster *DIR-Human Resources*

Total Employees............................260	**Regional Employees** 260
Year Established 1969	**SIC Code**.....................................8093

Allegheny Financial Group, Ltd.

3000 McKnight East Dr.
Pittsburgh, PA 15237
County: Allegheny

Phone: (412) 367-3880
Fax: (412) 367-8353

Registered investment advisor offering asset management, financial planning and retirement plans to individuals and businesses. The Firm provides its services on a fee-only or a fee and commission basis. The Firm is an affiliate of Allegheny Investments, Ltd. with which it shares its office. (Refer to the Allegheny Investments, Ltd. profile for additional information.)

Officers: James J. Browne *P*
Joseph M. DiCarlo *EVP*
Philip M. Gallagher *EVP*
Karl G. Smrekar, Jr. *SVP*
James D. Hohman *SEC & TRS*

Total Employees.............................40	**Regional Employees** 40
Year Established 1974	**SIC Code**.....................................6282

Allegheny Foundry Co.

1100 Penn Center Blvd.
Pittsburgh, PA 15235
County: Allegheny

Phone: (412) 243-1445
Fax: (412) 829-8183

Manufacturer of gray iron castings for municipalities, utilities and the construction industry. The Company's plant is located in Bolivar, PA.

Officers: Steven S. Wolfberg *P*

Total Employees	35	**Regional Employees**	35
Year Established	1880	**SIC Code**	3321
Annual Revenues ($000)	2,500		

Allegheny Health, Education and Research Foundation

Fifth Avenue Place, 120 Fifth Ave.
Pittsburgh, PA 15212
County: Allegheny

Phone: (412) 359-6000
Fax: (412) 359-5192
Internet Address: www.allhealth.com

Nonprofit, statewide, integrated academic health system with a total of 4,683 beds, also known as AHERF. The Organization's charitable mission is to learn, to teach, to heal the sick and to conserve health. This mission is accomplished through the delivery of a comprehensive range of health-care services, the education and training of health care professionals and research. Its clinical focus is on providing adult and pediatric primary, secondary and tertiary referral services to residents of Pittsburgh and Southwestern Pennsylvania in the western part of the state, and Philadelphia and the Delaware Valley in the eastern part of the state. For selected tertiary services, broader regional, national and international areas are also served. The Organization is comprised of Allegheny General Hospital at 320 E. North Ave. in Pittsburgh, PA; Allegheny Integrated Health Group in Philadelphia and Pittsburgh, PA; Allegheny University Hospitals in Philadelphia, PA, which includes Allegheny University Hospitals—Bucks County, Elkins Park, Hahnemann and MCP; Allegheny University Hospitals-Centennial in Philadelphia, PA, which includes City Avenue, Graduate, Mt. Sinai and Parkview Hospitals; Allegheny University Hospitals-New Jersey, which includes Rancocas in Riverside, NJ; Allegheny University Medical Centers at 500 Finley St. in Pittsburgh PA, which includes Alleghency Valley Hospital (1301 Carlisle St. in Natrona Heights, PA), Forbes Hospice (6655 Frankstown Ave.), Forbes Metropolitan Hospital (225 Penn Ave.), Forbes Nursing Center (6655 Frankstown Ave.) and Forbes Regional Hospital (2570 Haymaker Rd. in

Monroeville, PA); Allegheny University of the Health Sciences in Philadelphia, PA, which includes MCP•Hahnemann School of Medicine, School of Health Professions, School of Nursing and School of Public Health; and St. Christopher's Hospital for Children in Philadelphia, PA. The Organization's hospitals provide adult and pediatric clinical services for more than 96,000 inpatient and 2 million outpatient visits each year. In addition, its more than 4,000 faculty teach 3,200 students enrolled in educational programs at Allegheny University of the Health Sciences, which was formerly known as the Medical College of Pennsylvania and Hahnemann University.

Officers: Sherif Abdelhak *P & CEO*

Human Resources: Dwight Kasperbauer *EVP & Chief Human Resources Officer*

Total Employees	31,550	**Regional Employees**	11,370
Year Established	1988	**SIC Code**	8062
Annual Revenues ($000)	3,219,886		

Allegheny Investments, Ltd.

3000 McKnight East Dr.
Pittsburgh, PA 15237
County: Allegheny

Phone: (412) 367-3880
Fax: (412) 367-8353

Investment banking firm and provider of financial advisory services. In addition to providing access to all major stock exchanges, the Firm offers a variety of financial advisory services, including risk management and estate planning, retirement planning, education funding, income tax planning and asset allocation. The Firm is an affiliate of Allegheny Financial Group, Ltd. with which it shares its office. (Refer to the Allegheny Financial Group, Ltd. profile for additional information.)

Officers: James D. Hohman *P*
   N. John Marinack *SVP*

Total Employees	210	**Regional Employees**	202
Year Established	1976	**SIC Code**	6211

Allegheny Metalworking Corp.

17 Leonburg Rd.
Cranberry Township, PA 16066
County: Butler

Phone: (412) 776-2177
Fax: (412) 776-0755
Internet Address: www.almetco.com

Provider of precision metal fabricating and machining services for a wide range of industries, including telecommunications and electronic equipment, medical equipment, industrial control and automation, transportation systems, motion control and laboratory instruments. The Company serves clients nationwide.

Officers: Donald F. Insley *P*
              Warren J. Mercer *VP*

Human Resources: Sally Fennell

Purchasing: Mark Wiegand

Total Employees............................94	**Regional Employees** 94
Year Established 1967	**SIC Code**..................................3444
Annual Revenues ($000) 12,000	

Allegheny Paper Shredders Corp.

Old William Penn Hwy E.
P.O. Box 80
Delmont, PA 15626
County: Westmoreland

Phone: (412) 468-4300
Fax: (412) 468-5919

Designer and manufacturer of paper shredders. The Company claims that it offers the widest range of paper shredders available, from office models to high volume shredding systems that can destroy up to 10 tons of paper per hour. In addition to offering equipment, the Company can assist clients in setting up a complete document destruction program—developing the most efficient means of collecting confidential materials, processing them through the shredding system and recycling the shredded paper for a profit. The Company also offers sorting, in-floor and metering conveyors; hydraulic loading systems; auto-feed systems; book shredders; component shredders; tire shredders; plastic bottle and metal container shredders; and a complete line of powerful horizontal balers. Its clients include banks, insurance companies, hospitals, government agencies and other organizations, as well as the majority of the Fortune 1000. Through a division, Allegheny Records Destruction Service in New Alexandria, PA, the Company operates a commercial shredding service catering to clients in Western Pennsylvania. Also located at the above address is a sister company, Allegheny

Metals Corp., which provides metal products to the Company and fabricates tension furniture for correctional facilities.

Officers: John W. Wagner *P*
Judith L. Golock *VP*
Thomas A. Wagner *SAL MGR*

A

Human Resources: Robert E. Wagner *DIR-MKT*

Purchasing: Tim Graham

Total Employees	45	Regional Employees	40
Year Established	1968	SIC Code	3579
Annual Revenues ($000)	7,000		

Allegheny Plastics, Inc.

17 Avenue A
Leetsdale, PA 15056
County: Allegheny

Phone: (412) 749-0700
Fax: (412) 749-9530

Diversified manufacturer of commercial plastic products operating through three divisions with separate plant locations. The Performance Plastics Division at 24 Chadwick St. in Sewickley, PA, is a supplier of advanced thermoplastic components used by OEMs in industries such as aerospace, mechanical power transmission, electrical/electronic, chemical process equipment and business equipment. The plant, with precision injection molding and machining capability, specializes in processing high performance composites with properties exceeding those of traditional materials. The Printed Plastics Division at 1224 Freedom Rd. in Cranberry Township, PA, manufactures products such as plastic cards, technical goods and advertising items for a variety of industries, including finance, health care, retail, advertising, aviation, training and education. The Process Equipment Division, which is located at the above address, is a supplier of environmentally safe specialty surface treatment systems to the steel, wire, plating, chemical, aerospace and other industries. Its turnkey systems include fume abatement and wastewater plants, tanks and covers, material handling and structural support systems, process control and automation installation, commissioning and after sales service.

Officers: Walter M. Yost *P*

Human Resources: Dennis Hoffman

Total Employees	210	Regional Employees	210
Year Established	1936	SIC Code	3089
Annual Revenues ($000)	20,000		

Allegheny Power System, Inc.

800 Cabin Hill Dr.
Greensburg, PA 15601
County: Westmoreland

Phone: (412) 837-3000
Fax: (412) 838-6009
Internet Address: www.alleghenypower.com

Provider of electric service to nearly 1.4 million customers in an area serving 29,000 square miles in portions of Maryland, Ohio, Pennsylvania, Virginia and West Virginia, with a population of about 3 million. In Pennsylvania, the Company serves an area of approximately 9,900 square miles in all or parts of 23 counties in the Southwestern and Central parts of the Commonwealth, estimated to have a population of 1.4 million. The counties served include Armstrong, Butler, Cameron, Centre, Clarion, Elk, Fayette, Franklin, Fulton, Greene, Washington and Westmoreland. The Company also serves customers in small parts of Adams, Allegheny, Bedford, Clinton, Indiana, Lycoming, McKean, Potter and Somerset Counties. In addition, minute areas of Huntington and Jefferson Counties are also served. The Company, which is headquartered in Hagerstown, MD, is listed on the NYSE.

Officers: Alan J. Noia *CH, P & CEO*
Michael P. Morrell *SVP & CFO*
Jay S. Pifer *SVP*
Peter J. Skrgic *SVP*

Human Resources: Ronald A. Magnuson *DIR-Human Resources*

Total Employees..........................4,995	**Regional Employees** 1,586
Year Established 1916	**SIC Code** 4911
Annual Revenues ($000) 2,327,649	

Allegheny Steel Distributors, Inc.

Rte. 910
P.O. Box 837
Indianola, PA 15051
County: Allegheny

Phone: (412) 767-5000
Fax: (412) 767-5007
Internet Address: asd910@aol.com

Carbon flat rolled steel service center specializing in cut lengths, sheared bundles and slit coils. The Company supplies a variety of industrial manufacturers throughout the nation.

Officers: Robert W. Wickerham *P*
Timothy P. Brady *EVP*
Robert J. MacZura *VP-OPR & SAL*

Total Employees............................65	**Regional Employees** 63
Year Established 1972	**SIC Code**....................................5051

A

Allegheny Valley School

1996 Ewings Mill Rd.
Coraopolis, PA 15108
County: Allegheny

Phone: (412) 299-7777
Fax: (412) 299-6701

Nonprofit, private organization operating residential facilities and educational programs for children and adults with mental retardation, many of whom are physically handicapped. The Organization operates more than 60 facilities serving over 725 individuals throughout Pennsylvania in the counties of Allegheny, Beaver, Butler, Dauphin and Mercer and Philadelphia. Its mission is to provide programs and facilities that help the individuals with mental retardation entrusted to the Organization's care to live with purpose and dignity, and to provide opportunities for its clients to function at their full potential as independently as possible.

Officers: Regis G. Champ *CEO*
Mickey L. Coleman *Administrator-Pittsburgh Campus*
Carol G. Erzen *Administrator-Patricia Hillman Miller Campus*
Gary L. Hoffman *Administrator-Western Region Single Family Residences*
Matt Nerone *Administrator-Eastern Region Single Family Residences*
Jim E. Ulinski *Administrator-Eastern Region OPR*
Theo A. Lasinski *DIR-Program DEV & Quality Assurance*
Robin A. Mieczkowski *DIR-Social Services*
Jerry L. Parfitt *DIR-FIN*
John F. Police *DIR-Maintenance*
M. Clare Weaver *DIR-Health Services*
Diane M. Barna *Executive AST & Chief DEV Officer*
Paula L. Nerone *AST Administrator-Eastern Region OPR*

Human Resources: Richard R. Rizzutto *DIR-Personnel Services*

Total Employees........................1,600	**Regional Employees** 900
Year Established 1960	**SIC Code**....................................8299
Annual Revenues ($000) 52,000	

Allen Chevrolet Co., Don

5315 Baum Blvd.
Pittsburgh, PA 15224
County: Allegheny

Phone: (412) 681-4800
Fax: (412) 681-4914

Automobile dealership selling Chevrolet and Geo vehicles. The Company offers a full line of new and used cars, trucks and vans, and provides parts and service for automobiles. Its affiliate, Don Allen Motors Ltd., also located at the above address, markets Buick, Mazda and Pontiac vehicles.

Officers: Charles J. Voelker *CH & CEO*
David K. Voelker *P; VP-Don Allen Motors Ltd.*
Richard Voelker *VP; P-Don Allen Motors Ltd.*
Cynthia W. Frohlich *SEC & TRS*
James Fitzpatrick *AST-SEC*

Total Employees............................102	**Regional Employees** 102
Year Established 1951	**SIC Code** 5511
Annual Revenues ($000) 36,000	

Allied Electric Supply Co.

1201 Forbes Ave.
Pittsburgh, PA 15219
County: Allegheny

Phone: (412) 391-0205
Fax: (412) 391-3463

Distributor of electrical supplies in the Tri-State area operating 12 full-service branch sites within a 90-mile radius of Pittsburgh. These are located in Allison Park, Butler, Canonsburg, Castle Shannon, Cranberry Township, Indiana, Natrona Heights, Pittsburgh (at the above address), Washington, Waynesburg and West Liberty, PA; and Morgantown, WV. The Company's major suppliers include 3M, GE (both distribution and lamp equipment), Hubbell, Klein, Leviton, Lightolier, Milwaukee, NuTone, Panduit and Wiremold. Its primary customers are industrial, commercial and institutional facilities and small- to medium-sized electrical contractors. The Company's salespeople are trained to assist in the layout and design of distribution equipment and lighting.

Officers: Edward Berman *P*
John Pugliese *VP-SAL*
Robert Umbel *VP & GMGR*

Human Resources: James R. Bunn *VP-FIN*

Purchasing: Douglas Miller

Total Employees...............................85	**Regional Employees** 75
Year Established 1922	**SIC Code**......................................5063
Annual Revenues ($000) 25,000	

A

Alling and Cory

2920 New Beaver Ave.
Pittsburgh, PA 15233
County: Allegheny

Phone: (412) 734-2000
Fax: (412) 734-0994

Distributor of paper and packaging products claiming to be the oldest and one of the largest independent paper merchants in the United States. The Company is a distributor of printing papers; industrial products and packaging, including packaging materials, equipment, janitorial supplies and other industrial products; envelopes; office products, including computer and word processing supplies, copier papers, toners and developers, and tapes and tools for business machines and postage meters; and publishing papers. It operates 16 distribution centers located in Maryland, New York, Ohio, Pennsylvania and West Virginia. The Company also operates 21 Paper Shops, which are warehouse outlets selling a variety of the Company's products. Alcor Envelope Co., Hamburg, NY, is the Company's envelope subsidiary. It is capable of producing up to 3 million envelopes a day. The Company is a subsidiary of Union Camp Corp., which is headquartered in Wayne, NJ, and listed on the NYSE.

Officers: Paul C. Carney *Regional P*

Total Employees........................1,150	**Regional Employees** 105
Year Established 1819	**SIC Code** 5111
Annual Revenues ($000) 800,000	

ALLTEL Pennsylvania, Inc.

201 N. Jefferson St.
P.O. Box 300
Kittanning, PA 16201
County: Armstrong

Phone: (412) 543-9300
Fax: (412) 543-1580

Provider of local and long distance telephone service and telephone equipment such as PBX switches and key telephone systems. The Company serves the Allegheny, Armstrong, Beaver, Washington and Westmoreland Counties in the Pittsburgh metropolitan area as well as Blair, Cambria, Cameron, Carbon, Centre,

Clarion, Clearfield, Crawford, Elk, Erie, Forest, Greene, Huntingdon, Indiana, Jefferson, Lawrence, Lycoming, McKean, Northumberland, Schuylkill, Union, Venango and Warren Counties, PA. The Company is a subsidiary of ALLTEL Corp. (AC), which is headquartered in Little Rock, AR, and listed on the NYSE, and part of its ALLTEL Northeast Region, which is headquartered in Hudson, OH. ALLTEL Information Services, Inc., also a subsidiary of AC, has an office at Fourth Ave. and Wood St. in Pittsburgh.

Officers: David L. Thomas *P*
Frederick Griech *EVP*
Americo Cornacchione *VP*
Andrew F. Coulter *VP*
John Forringer *VP*
Charles Galloway *VP*
Clark Hoffman *VP*
Jim Kimzey *VP*
John Kuhns *VP*
Jack Mitchell *VP*
Jeffrey W. Reynolds *VP*
Will Staggs *VP*
Francis X. Frantz *SEC*
Jerry M. Green *TRS*
David Cameron *AST-SEC*
Gary DeBore *AST-SEC*

Regional Employees....................542
Year Established 1964   **SIC Code**....................................4813

Almes & Assoc., Inc.

Four Triangle Dr., Ste. 200
Export, PA 15632
County: Westmoreland

Phone: (412) 327-5200
Fax: (412) 327-5280

Consulting engineering firm specializing in civil, environmental, geotechnical, mining and investigative engineering. The Firm's services include ash handling/management, coal mine permitting, coal refuse permitting and design, construction management, construction monitoring and construction quality assurance, dam design, environmental site assessments, geotechnical engineering, hydrogeologic/groundwater studies, industrial waste disposal design, investigative engineering, soil and groundwater remediation, solid waste landfill design, storm water management, underground storage tanks and wetlands services. The Firm serves clients in the industrial, commercial, governmental and residential sectors. It maintains a Carolina Regional Office in Raleigh, NC, and a Mid-Atlantic Regional Office in Beckley, WV.

Officers: Richard G. Almes *P*
Charles B. Gillian *SVP*
Randy Wood *VP*
Claudio Yon *VP*
Dave Olson *DIR & MGR-Environmental ENG*
Fred Vass *DIR & MGR-Mine Services*
Thomas Eld *MGR-Contract Services*
Lewis Ernest *MGR-Business DEV*
Blaise Genes *MGR-Geotechnical ENG*
Chester Smolenski *MGR-Investigative ENG*

Human Resources: Laura Mauser *ADM MGR*

Total Employees............................80	**Regional Employees** 30
Year Established 1986	**SIC Code**......................................8711
Annual Revenues ($000) 5,800	

Alon Surface Technologies, Inc.

Grantham St.
P.O. Box 231
Tarentum, PA 15084
County: Allegheny

Phone: (412) 226-1677
Fax: (412) 226-8411

Manufacturer of a range of engineered surface modifications for various metals to resist most forms of corrosion caused by oxidation, sulfidation, abrasion, erosion and hydrogen permeation. In addition to a plant located at the above address, the Company operates a plant in Leechburg, PA, and a sales office in Houston, TX. The Company is an affiliate of NUKEM GmbH, which is a subsidiary of RWE AG, both of which are headquartered in Alzenau, Germany. RWE is listed on the Frankfurt Stock Exchange.

Officers: James S. Herb *P & CEO*
George Kwiatek *CON*
Sermin Caola *DIR-Quality*

Total Employees............................34	**Regional Employees** 32
Year Established 1960	**SIC Code**......................................3479

Alpern, Rosenthal & Co.

Warner Centre, 332 Fifth Ave., Ste. 400
Pittsburgh, PA 15222
County: Allegheny

Phone: (412) 281-2501
Fax: (412) 471-1996

Certified public accounting firm providing audit, accounting, tax and business consulting services to clients primarily located in Western Pennsylvania. The Firm's specialized services include management and human resource consulting, management information systems, mergers and acquisitions, financing assistance, and succession and strategic planning. It serves a diversified client base in a variety of industries, including manufacturing, construction, retail, wholesale, distribution, health care, professional services, real estate and energy. The Firm's subsidiary, ARC Capital, L.P., is engaged in mergers and acquisitions and business dispositions. Its affiliate, ARC Technologies Group, Inc., is engaged in information systems consulting. Both of these operations are located at the above address.

Officers: Fred J. Morelli, Jr. *CH*
Sean M. Brennan *Shareholder*
Emanuel V. DiNatale *Shareholder*
Keith D. Horn *Shareholder*
Michael H. Levin *Shareholder*
Thomas J. Menk *Shareholder*
Alexander Paul *Shareholder*
Harvey A. Pollack *Shareholder*
Fred M. Rock *Shareholder*
Edward F. Rockman *Shareholder*
Irving P. Rosenthal *Shareholder*
Joel M. Rosenthal *Shareholder*
Deborah H. Wells *Shareholder*

Human Resources: Michael L. DeLargy *DIR-OPR*
James T. Martin *Resources MGR*

Total Employees............................120	**Regional Employees** 120
Year Established 1961	**SIC Code**.....................................8721

Alpha Carb Enterprises

691 Hyde Park Rd.
P.O. Box 528
Leechburg, PA 15656
County: Armstrong

Phone: (412) 845-2500
Fax: (412) 845-2846

A

Designer and manufacturer of high-speed progressive carbide dies. The Company's dies produce high-volume precision stampings for the electronics, electrical and various other industries. The Company maintains complete in house capabilities. It can design a die from client part prints or build from their drawings, and can produce replacement parts for existing dies.

Officers: Louis W. Leibert *P*

Purchasing: Russell K. Mundy *General OPR MGR*

Total Employees	110	**Regional Employees**	110
Year Established	1974	**SIC Code**	3544

Alternative Program Assoc.

6117 Broad St.
Pittsburgh, PA 15206
County: Allegheny

Phone: (412) 362-9300
Fax: (412) 362-9807

Nonprofit organization providing community-based alternatives to institutional placement for at-risk children. The Organization provides home-like treatment services within highly creative, noninstitutionalized environments. Whenever possible, the Organization uses the family as the primary treatment and placement resource for the children it serves. The Organization's goal is to make every attempt to assist clients and families to control their destiny while ensuring each family member's right to safety. It currently provides in-home family therapy and family-based mental health services to 500-600 families with almost 1,500 children per year. An additional 75 children each year receive foster care services. Residential programs operated by the Organization serve 50 children per year.

Officers: Hank Lipinski *CEO*
    Peggy Harris *COO*

Human Resources: Albie Shempp *DIR-Human Resources*

Total Employees	125	**Regional Employees**	125
Year Established	1978	**SIC Code**	8322
Annual Revenues ($000)	7,000		

Altmeyer Home Stores, Inc.

Central City Plaza
New Kensington, PA 15068
County: Westmoreland

Phone: (412) 339-6628
Fax: (412) 339-1166

Owner and operator of a 14-store retail chain selling a variety of textile-related home furnishings, including bed and bath linens, curtains and draperies. The Company's stores are all located within a 75-mile radius of Pittsburgh, PA.

Officers: Rod Altmeyer, Sr. *P*

Human Resources: Judith Altmeyer *SEC & TRS*

Total Employees............................175	**Regional Employees** 125
Year Established 1941	**SIC Code**......................................5719

American Airlines, Inc.

Pittsburgh International Airport
P.O. Box 12362
Pittsburgh, PA 15231
County: Allegheny

Phone: (412) 472-5001
Internet Address: www.amrcorp.com

Commercial airline operating three daily nonstop flights from Pittsburgh to Dallas, TX. The Company is headquartered at the Dallas/Ft. Worth Airport. It is a subsidiary of AMR Corp., which is also headquartered at the Dallas/Ft. Worth Airport, and listed on the NYSE. American Eagle, another subsidiary of the Company, operates four daily nonstop flights from Pittsburgh to JFK Airport in New York, NY. The Company's reservations/information number is (800) 433-7300.

Officers: Don Doyle *GMGR*

Regional Employees.......................55	
Year Established 1934	**SIC Code**......................................4512

American Auto-Matrix, Inc.

One Technology Dr.
Export, PA 15632
County: Westmoreland

Phone: (412) 733-2000
Fax: (412) 327-6124
Internet Address: www.auto-matrix.com

Developer, manufacturer, distributor and supporter of microprocessor-based networkable systems for the control and monitoring of building environments. The Company's product applications include direct digital temperature, light process, fume hood and laboratory control, as well as energy, integrated fire and security management. Its products feature direct digital control, open architecture, generation-to-generation compatibility, distributed control and object-oriented programming. The Company's products and its Auto-Flow divisions' systems are sold, installed and maintained worldwide through a network of more than 130 authorized dealers, distributors and representatives. The Company maintains international sales offices in England, the People's Republic of China and Thailand. The Company is a subsidiary of the Silvermines Group Plc, which is headquartered in Leicester, England, and listed on the London Stock Exchange.

A

Officers: Robert P. Schwab *P & CEO*
Charles F. Farina *VP-SAL & MKT*
Jeffrey L. Phelps *VP-FIN & ADM*
Robert J. Lofgren *DIR-ENG & Customer Support Services*
Christine M. Rendulich *DIR-MKT Communications*

Human Resources: Lee Christie

Purchasing: Rich Tibbens

Total Employees.............................60
Year Established 1979

Regional Employees 57
SIC Code......................................3823

American Beverage Corp.

One Daily Way
Verona, PA 15147
County: Allegheny

Phone: (412) 828-9020
Fax: (412) 828-8876

Producer of fruit juice, fruit drinks and cocktail mixes, doing business as Daily Juice Products. The Company's brand names include Big Juicy and Little Hug. It is a subsidiary of Bolswessanen USA, Inc., which is a subsidiary of Bolswessanen Holdings, Inc., which is a subsidiary of Konincklijke Bols Wessanen N.V., which is headquartered in Amsterdam, The Netherlands, and listed on the Amsterdam Stock Exchange.

Officers: David Bober *P*
Tony Battaglia *VP-FIN*
Paul Beranek *VP-SAL & MKT*
Don Bonaroti *VP-OPR*

Regional Employees....................350
Year Established 1960

SIC Code......................................2033

American Bridge Co.

Three Gateway Center, Ste. 1100
Pittsburgh, PA 15222
County: Allegheny

Phone: (412) 562-4400
Fax: (412) 562-4411

General contractor with capabilities in heavy, civil, industrial and commercial construction. The Company operates branch offices in Los Angeles, CA; Orlando, FL; Chicago, IL; and New York, NY. The Company is a subsidiary of CEC Investment Corp.

Officers: Robert H. Luffy *P & CEO*
           Alex Fattaleh *SVP-Western Region*
           Michael D. Flowers *SVP*
           Mike Cegelis *VP*
           Lanny Frisco *VP*
           Les Snyder *VP*
           Pamela A. Bena *CON*

Human Resources: Tonilynn Parks *Human Resources Administrator*

Total Employees 1,500	**Regional Employees** 65	
Year Established 1874	**SIC Code** 1600	
Annual Revenues ($000) 165,000		

American Business Center, Inc.

Frick Bldg., 437 Grant St., Ste. 520
Pittsburgh, PA 15219
County: Allegheny

Phone: (412) 281-6255
Fax: (412) 281-6262
Internet Address: www.abciba.com

Employment agency providing personnel and human resource services. The Company's American Business Center division provides permanent employment placement services for the clerical and entry-level markets. Three Rivers Interim Personnel and IBA Temps serve the temporary employment market. International Business Assoc., Inc. provides permanent employment placement services for technical, administrative, information systems, accounting and financial professionals, and offers executive recruitment. The Agency places more than 1,600 people annually within Pittsburgh's business community.

Officers: Jeffrey B. Lange *P*
           Kathleen Tucci *VP-SAL*

Total Employees 30	**Regional Employees** 30
Year Established 1966	**SIC Code** 7361

American Express Financial Advisors, Inc.

5700 Corporate Dr., Ste. 650
Pittsburgh, PA 15237
County: Allegheny

A

Phone: (412) 366-7300
Fax: (412) 366-0346
Internet Address: www.americanexpress.com/advisors

Provider of a variety of financial planning and investment services. The Company, which is headquartered in Minneapolis, MN, operates more than 700 offices throughout the United States, with additional regional offices in the North Hills and South Hills areas of Pittsburgh, and in Monroeville, McMurray and Murrysville, PA. The Company is a subsidiary of American Express Co., Inc., which is headquartered in New York, NY, and listed on the NYSE. The Company has approximately 125 financial advisors (independent contractors) in the Pittsburgh metropolitan area.

Officers: Daniel E. Martin *GVP*

Human Resources: Chad Lewis *Recruiting Coordinator*

Regional Employees 70
Year Established 1894   **SIC Code** 6211

American Express Travel Related Services Co., Inc.

Six PPG Place, Ste. 850
Pittsburgh, PA 15222
County: Allegheny

Phone: (412) 471-7140
Fax: (412) 471-0956

Provider of corporate travel services. The Company fulfills the travel and reporting needs of several major national corporations as well as those of many other businesses in the Pittsburgh metropolitan area. Its Pittsburgh Business Travel Center along with its American Express Travel Management Services, is part of an extensive network offering a full range of products and services, including reservation placement, account management and consultation, travel and entertainment expense, and management information reporting and consultation as well as card inquiry assistance. The local facility is a branch office, with the Company's headquarters located in New York, NY. It is a subsidiary of the American Express Co., Inc., which is also headquartered in New York, NY, and listed on the NYSE.

Officers: Ronald F. Lane *Senior DIR*

Regional Employees....................135
Year Established 1985   **SIC Code**....................................4724

American Glass Inc.

1900 Liberty St.
P.O. Box 963
Mount Pleasant, PA 15666
County: Westmoreland

Phone: (412) 547-3544
Fax: (412) 547-2077
Internet Address: www.lesmith@trib.infi.net

Owner and operator of an all handmade glass factory, doing business as the L. E. Smith Glass Co. The Company manufactures a wide variety (over 700 units) of giftware, tabletop and industrial lighting pieces. Its glass artisans are third and fourth generation skilled glass makers producing 12 colors of glass, including lead-free crystal. The Company claims that it also is the leading domestic (hand-made glassware) private label manufacturer. The Company's giftware products are sold primarily to traditional specialty retailers, manufacturers/wholesalers and the food service market. Its lighting fixture products are sold to manufacturers and retailers. The Company is a subsidiary of NBI, Inc., which is headquartered in Longmont, CO, and listed on the OTC market.

Officers: Jay H. Lustig *CH*
Michael C. Miller *P*
Forrest L. Kastner *Plant MGR*
Norm Pennington *NATL SAL MGR-Lighting*
Pamela Steitz *NATL SAL MGR-Giftware*

Human Resources: Sammy E. King *CON*

Total Employees...........................150   **Regional Employees** 150
Year Established 1907   **SIC Code**....................................3229
Annual Revenues ($000) 12,000

American Home Improvement Products, Inc., The

9001 Rico Rd., Bldg. 9
Monroeville, PA 15146
County: Allegheny

Phone: (412) 858-3500
Fax: (412) 858-3495

Manufacturer, marketer and installer of residential home remodeling products under license to Sears, Roebuck and Co. The Company's major products include replacement windows; siding, soffit and fascia; kitchen cabinet refacing; and exterior paint coatings. The Company's corporate, Eastern Division and Kitchen Cabinet Division headquarters are all located at the above address. Its other facilities include Central Division headquarters in Elk Grove Village, IL; Western Division headquarters in Hayward, CA; a window and door manufacturing plant in Delmont, PA; three kitchen cabinet refacing manufacturing plants (one in each operating region); 80 sales offices throughout the U.S.; 18 installation sites throughout the U.S.; and 8 telemarketing centers throughout the U.S. The products not manufactured by the Company (i.e., vinyl siding and paint coatings) are outsourced.

Officers: Gary J. Iskra *P & CEO*
Mark A. Aloe *EVP & CFO*
Mel J. Feinberg *EVP & COO*

Human Resources: Charles W. Klinzing *DIR-Human Resources*

Purchasing: Karen Smay *Purchasing MGR*

Total Employees........................2,183	**Regional Employees** 300
Year Established 1945	**SIC Code**....................................3442
Annual Revenues ($000) 111,000			

American International Forwarding, Inc.

5177 Campbells Run Rd.
Pittsburgh, PA 15205
County: Allegheny

Phone: (412) 787-5370
Fax: (412) 788-6500

  Provider of moving services focusing exclusively on the international shipment of household goods for corporate employees and their families. The Company operates branch offices in Huntington Beach, CA; Ridgefield, CT; and Houston, TX. All of its offices have received ISO 9002 certification.

Officers: James L. Putt *P*
Bryan S. Putt *GMGR-Pittsburgh, PA*

Human Resources: Robert Smouse

Purchasing: Jeff Carraway

Total Employees.............................67	**Regional Employees** 38
Year Established 1981	**SIC Code**....................................4731
Annual Revenues ($000) 36,363			

American Micrographics Co., Inc.

4112 Monroeville Blvd.
Monroeville, PA 15146
County: Allegheny

Phone: (412) 856-6900
Fax: (412) 856-7688

Provider of document management systems, including microfilm, digital imaging and online retrieval. The Company specializes in the conversion of records to its MASS-IV™ System, an automated records management system that combines the mass storage capabilities of micrographics with the quick access time of computerized indexing. All records are converted to microfilm and digital images and cross-referenced in a key word index database. The system is designed for random access storage and quick retrieval of records. The system increases productivity by having fewer people handle information while providing document control with total file integrity. The Company's Digital Imaging System converts paper records and microfilm (16mm, 35mm or microfiche) for storage on electronic media. Using a custom-built database, images can be retrieved electronically, printed or transmitted over a customer's LAN, WAN or the Internet. It also offers an apprenticeship program for certifying micrographic technicians and has trained more than 200 people as equipment operators and micrographic technicians. The Company has provided services to an extensive customer base of Fortune 100 enterprises, small businesses and local governments as well as Department of Energy and Department of Defense prime contractors. A branch office is located in Orlando, FL.

Officers: I. N. Rendall Harper, Jr. *P*
Elizabeth J. Harper *GMGR*

Total Employees	30	**Regional Employees**	20
Year Established	1977	**SIC Code**	3861

American Photocopy Equipment Co. of Pittsburgh, Inc.

181 Bateman Rd.
Imperial, PA 15126
County: Allegheny

Phone: (412) 695-7391
Fax: (412) 695-1118
Internet Address: amcom-pgh@worldnet.att.net

Provider of sales, service and leasing of Mita and Panasonic photocopiers, facsimile machines and electronic white boards. The Company also offers cost per copy plans. Its products range from digital copiers to high-speed duplicators, full color digital imaging systems, fax networks, internet-ready fax and multi-functional machines. The Company, which does business as AMCOM Office

Systems, serves both large and small clients in Allegheny, Beaver, Butler, Washington and Westmoreland counties. It is a subsidiary of Global Imaging Systems, Inc., which is headquartered in Tampa, FL.

Officers: Matthew G. Swider *P*
Donald Fink *VP-Service*

Human Resources: Teresa N. Dunn *VP*

Purchasing: James Falcon

Total Employees............................65	**Regional Employees** 65
Year Established 1978	**SIC Code**....................................5044
Annual Revenues ($000) 8,000	

American Refining Group, Inc.

2010 William Pitt Way
Pittsburgh, PA 15238
County: Allegheny

Phone: (412) 826-3000
Fax: (412) 826-3015

Independent refiner and marketer of petroleum products claiming to be the largest re-processor of pipeline interface in the United States. The Company serves all of the major pipeline companies, reconverting diesel fuel and gasoline mixtures back into the high quality fuel products that first entered their pipeline systems. It controls in excess of 750,000 barrels of petroleum storage. The Company provides products to three primary marketing segments of its industry: the wholesale rack customer, the commercial end user and the retail customer. The Company sells its products via an established wholesale rack business, as well as on a direct, delivered, basis to meet customer needs. While a large portion of its customer base is the independent marketer and reseller, it also serves many commercial and industrial accounts such as manufacturing operations, hospitals, municipalities, transportation and trucking companies, fire and police departments. The Company markets to end users through four 'ROUND*TOWN gasoline stations in the Pittsburgh metropolitan area and supports fleet operators through its COMM*PLAN commercial fueling gasoline station in Warrendale, PA. The Company operates pipeline interface re-processing refineries in St. Louis, MO, and Indianola, PA, and a lube oil refinery in Bradford, PA. It also operates a fleet of delivery vehicles. The Company is headquartered in West Conshohockten, PA.

Officers: Harry R. Halloran, Jr. *CH*
Donald E. Schupp *P & COO*
John C. Trinkl *SVP & TRS*
Thomas F. Halloran *VP*
Richard Halloran *SEC*

Human Resources: Jill Hadley

Total Employees............................221   **Regional Employees** 50
SIC Code 2911

American Roller Bearing Co.

150 Gamma Dr.
Pittsburgh, PA 15238
County: Allegheny

Phone: (412) 781-1190
Fax: (412) 963-0616

Manufacturer of roller bearings, including ball rollers, tapered rollers and cylindrical rollers, for heavy applications. The Company's plants are located in Hiddenite and Morganton, NC. It serves industrial clients nationwide.

Officers: Lawrence N. Succop II *CEO*
Frank C. Dickson *P*
J. William C. Succop *VP*

Human Resources: Bernadine Sturm

Purchasing: Carl Succop *VP-SAL*

Total Employees............................300   **Regional Employees** 30
Year Established 1911   **SIC Code**......................................3562

American Textile Co.

49th & Harrison Sts.
P.O. Box 4006
Pittsburgh, PA 15201
County: Allegheny

Phone: (412) 681-9404
Fax: (412) 681-3582

Manufacturer of protective covers for mattresses and pillows, among other things. The Company's primary business is manufacturing utility bedding products, including mattress covers, pads and pillow coverings. Its newest item is an allergy protective product marketed under the name Aller-Ease, which is made of 3M Propore™ fabric, an effective barrier against dust, dust mites and moisture. The Company has an exclusive agreement with 3M for the use of this fabric in mattress covers, pillow covers, featherbed and comforter covers. The Company sells its products to most major retailers in the U.S., including Kmart, Sears, Target and WalMart.

Officers: Reid W. Ruttenberg *CH & CEO*
John R. (Jack) Ouellette *P*
C. Lance Ruttenberg *VP-OPR*
Robert Van Jones *VP-SAL*

Human Resources: John L. Riccio *VP-FIN*

Purchasing: Ron Kline

Total Employees............................180	**Regional Employees** 180
Year Established 1925	**SIC Code**......................................2392
Annual Revenues ($000) 23,000	

A

American Thermoplastic Co.

106 Gamma Dr.
Pittsburgh, PA 15238
County: Allegheny

Phone: (412) 967-0900
Fax: (412) 967-9990
Internet Address: www.binders.com

Manufacturer of ring binders, index tabs and related loose-leaf products for business and education. The Company specializes in custom-imprinting of its products. Four Point Products, a division of the Company, is also located at the above address.

Officers: Steven Silberman *P*

Total Employees............................145	
Year Established 1954	**SIC Code**......................................2782

American Video Glass Co.

777 Technology Dr.
Mt. Pleasant, PA 15666
County: Westmoreland

Phone: (412) 696-6000
Fax: (412) 696-6406

Manufacturer of glass for color television picture tubes sold solely to Sony television manufacturing facilities. The Company is a joint venture between Corning Asahi Video Products Co. in State College, PA; Corning, Inc. in Corning, NY; and Sony Electronics, Inc. in Park Ridge, NJ. The Company is located at the Sony Technology Center-Pittsburgh (STCP), which is, physically, the largest Sony facility in the world encompassing 800 acres. The STCP also houses operations of Sony Chemicals Corp. of America and Sony Electronics, Inc. (see separate profiles).

Officers: Don Dicken *P*
Fred Ishii *Deputy P*
Hiroshi Takagi *VP-Technology Integration*
Tim Agnew *DIR-Business DEV*
Goro Sekiya *DIR-MFG*
Nancy Oja *MGR-MRO Materials*

Human Resources: Dan Lhota *MGR-Human Resources*

Total Employees ....500+   **Regional Employees** ....500+
SIC Code 3211

AMG Sign Co.

1928 Forbes Ave.
Pittsburgh, PA 15219
County: Allegheny

Phone: (412) 391-9578
Fax: (412) 391-9583

Designer, manufacturer, installer and servicer of signs, electronic displays, neon signs and plaques. As a full-service custom sign company, it serves clients throughout Eastern Ohio, Western Pennsylvania and West Virginia. The Company also supplies a variety of computerized electronic displays for interior and exterior use, which can be used for advertising, employee communications or safety programs. These units can be programmed using a hand-held infrared remote keypad, computer or telephone modem. Other products manufactured by the Company include illuminated signs and letters, architectural signage, interior and exterior signage systems, directories, metal letters and plaques, post and panel systems, vinyl graphics, coordinated interior and exterior signage systems, and neon displays. The Company has complete manufacturing capabilities, a neon fabrication plant and a design department. Its recent clients have included the Federal Home Loan Bank, Fifth Avenue Place, Heinz, Marriott, National City Bank, PNC Bank and PPG Place.

Officers: Gilbert Mendelson *CH*
         Stephen Gerson *P*

Human Resources: Susan Taylor *CON*

Total Employees.............................40   **Regional Employees** 40
Year Established 1970   **SIC Code**....................................3993
Annual Revenues ($000) 3,000

Amore Management Co.

4130 Monroeville Blvd., Ste. 1
Monroeville, PA 15146
County: Allegheny

Phone: (412) 373-3300
Fax: (412) 856-8671

Real estate management firm specializing in apartment rentals. The Company owns and manages apartment communities in the eastern, southern and western suburban areas of Greater Pittsburgh. Its apartment complexes include Linden Brooke in Bethel Park; York Square in Chippewa; Churchill Square in Churchill;

Edgewood Court in Edgewood; Heritage Hills in Jefferson Borough; Stonecliffe in Monroeville; Pine Ridge in Oakdale; and Beacon Hill and Pennwood Square in Wilkinsburg. The Company also owns and manages properties in North Carolina and Ohio consisting of Lakemont in Greensboro, NC, and Heatherwood in Ravenna, OH.

A

Officers: Vincent Amore *P*
Robert Amore *SEC*
Leonard Bizyak *CON*
Frank Berceli *GMGR*

Human Resources: Bill Ardini *Area MGR (Purchasing)*

Total Employees..............................65
Year Established 1968

Regional Employees 62
SIC Code.......................................6531

Anchor Hocking Packaging Co.

1840 Baldridge St.
Connellsville, PA 15425
County: Fayette

Phone: (412) 626-0120
Fax: (412) 626-3214

Manufacturer of metal closures. The Company is headquartered in Cincinnati, OH. It is a subsidiary of Crown Cork & Seal Co., Inc., which is headquartered in Philadelphia, PA, and listed on the NYSE.

Officers: Jerry Gresco *DIR-OPR*

Regional Employees....................440
Year Established 1941

SIC Code.......................................3466

Anchor Hocking Specialty Glass Co.- Phoenix Glass Plant

400 Ninth St.
Monaca, PA 15061
County: Beaver

Phone: (412) 775-0010
Fax: (412) 773-3363

Manufacturer of glass, components, industrial lighting, floral vases, table top glassware, jars and bakeware. The Company operates two additional plants in Bremen and Lancaster, OH. It is a division of Newell Co., which is headquartered in Freeport, IL, and listed on the NYSE.

Officers: George Hamilton *P*
Daniel Bruggeman *VP & CON*

Ben Johansen *VP-MER*
Steve Lynch *VP-SAL*
Harry Ruska *VP-OPR*

Human Resources: Joe Filimon *VP-Human Resources*

Total Employees........................1,000
Year Established........................1880
Annual Revenues ($000)..65,000

Regional Employees..................740
SIC Code....................................3229

Andersen Consulting L.L.P.

One PPG Place, Ste. 2100
Pittsburgh, PA 15222
County: Allegheny

Phone: (412) 232-3113
Fax: (412) 232-0693
Internet Address: www.ac.com

Provider of business integration services, offering a range of capabilities, from designing and installing computer systems to simplifying and automating a company's processes to reshaping the way an organization operates its business. The Firm helps clients to align their people, processes and technology to meet the rapidly changing demands of their competitive marketplace. Headquartered in Chicago, IL, the Firm is a business unit of Andersen Worldwide, which has dual headquarters in Chicago, IL, and Geneva, Switzerland. It operates 152 offices located in 47 countries.

Officers: Michael P. Sullivan *MPTR-Pittsburgh Office*
Kurt H. Miller *PTR*
Robert L. Totterdale *PTR*
Newell I. Troup, Jr. *PTR*

Human Resources: Ann D. South

Total Employees......................45,000
Year Established........................1913
Annual Revenues ($000)....................................4,800,000+

Regional Employees..................130
SIC Code....................................8742

Antech Ltd.

One Triangle Dr.
Export, PA 15632
County: Westmoreland

Phone: (412) 733-1161
Fax: (412) 327-7793

Full-service environmental laboratory providing organic and inorganic analytical services through the following service areas: Comprehensive

Environmental Response, Compensation & Liability Act/Resource Conservation & Recovery Act, corrective action, drinking water analysis, groundwater monitoring, national pollutant discharge elimination system monitoring, remediation support, site assessment/characterization/treatability studies, underground storage tank cleanups, waste characterization and nuclear services. The Company is a subsidiary of American Waste Services, Inc., which is headquartered in Warren, OH, and listed on the NYSE.

Officers: David M. Miller *P*
          Edward V. Forrai *EVP*
          Joseph A. Lanoy *VP-Analytical SAL*

Human Resources: Marylee Murrin *CAO*

Purchasing: Robert R. Latoche *VP-FIN*

Total Employees	42	**Regional Employees**	42
Year Established	1982	**SIC Code**	8734
Annual Revenues ($000)	3,000		

Anthony Crane Rental L.P.

1165 Camp Hollow Rd.
West Mifflin, PA 15122
County: Allegheny

Phone: (412) 469-3700
Fax: (412) 469-0691

Renter of cranes and heavy construction equipment for applications in the oil refining and construction industries. The Company operates additional facilities in Arizona, California, Florida, Georgia, South Carolina, Texas and West Virginia, as well as in Mercer, Monroeville and Philadelphia, PA.

Officers: Ray G. Anthony *P*
          Samuel R. Anthony *VP*
          David Mahokey *SEC & TRS*

Total Employees	800-900	**Regional Employees**	100
Year Established	1966	**SIC Code**	7353

Apollo Bancorp, Inc.

201 N. Warren Ave.
P.O. Box 247
Apollo, PA 15613
County: Armstrong

Phone: (412) 478-3151
Fax: (412) 478-1118

Bank holding company for its subsidiary, Apollo Trust Co., a community bank located 35 miles east of Pittsburgh. The Bank's market area includes Southern Armstrong and Northern Westmoreland Counties, PA. It operates branch offices in Allegheny Township, North Apollo, North Washington and Spring Church, PA.

Officers: Helen J. Clark *CH & P*
Raymond E. Muth *EVP & SEC*
R. Scott Brunermer *AVP & Compliance Officer*
Richard Dixon *AVP*
James C. Mondale *TRS*
Shirley Colwell *Office MGR & AST-TRS*
Victor J. Rossi *Loan Officer & Branch MGR*
Melissa L. Walker *Trust Officer*

Total Employees............................70 **Regional Employees** 70
Year Established ....1871 **SIC Code**....................................6712
Annual Revenues ($000) ....105,000 (Assets)

Applied Industrial Materials Corp.

Edgetowne Commons, 1009 Beaver Grade Rd., Ste. 300
Coraopolis, PA 15108
County: Allegheny

Phone: (412) 264-4311
Fax: (412) 264-4326

Manufacturer and marketer of a variety of ferroalloys, metals, minerals and specialty materials that are used primarily as alloying agents, fluxing agents and/or performance improvement additives in the production of metal castings, carbon steel and specialty steels by the North American steel and foundry industries. The Company's corporate headquarters are located in Denver, CO. Located at the above address is the headquarters of its Metals Group (MG). The MG is comprised of four distinct but related businesses which manufacture and market the following intermediary metals and materials: ferrosilicon, ferrovanadium, ferromolybdenum, metallurgical process materials, fluorspar and various other ferroalloys. The MG consists of AIMCOR Metallurgical Process Materials in Aurora, IN, which produces a variety of materials that enable steel manufacturers to improve product quality and increase productivity through processing in the steel ladle; Masterloy Products, Ltd. in Gloucester, Ontario, Canada, which produces ferrovanadium and ferromolybdenum—alloying agents that impart a number of desirable properties to steel and cast iron to enhance their performance; Tennessee Alloys Co. in Bridgeport, AL, which produces ferrosilicon—used in steel production as a deoxidizer to impart strength, machinability and special conductivity properties to steel and cast iron; and a Southeast Regional Office in Birmingham, AL. In addition, its Agency and Trading Products business unit, located at the above address, acts as an agent for foreign suppliers of metals and alloys seeking North American distribution and also buys and resells related alloys and materials.

Officers: Charles W. Kopec *P*
Larry Byrnes *VP-SAL & MKT*
Doug Katt *VP-OPR*
John Straka *VP & CON*

Human Resources: Linda Rumberg

Purchasing: Debbie Williams

Total Employees	133	**Regional Employees**	21
Year Established	1986	**SIC Code**	3313
Annual Revenues ($000)	75,000		

Applied Science Assoc., Inc.

245 Pittsburgh Rd.
Butler, PA 16001
County: Butler

Phone: (412) 284-7300
Fax: (412) 285-8884

Provider of custom-designed performance improvement and multimedia solutions. The Company's products and services solve problems for growth-oriented organizations with people-intensive, complex requirements such as those found in the telecommunications, health care, manufacturing and financial industries. It has extensive experience in the support and implementation of process improvement strategies, new technology and equipment, new product development and launches, and government mandate compliance. The Company's multimedia development experience dates back to the mid-1970s and includes the completion of thousands of hours of finished multimedia that have been applied to training, trade show/information kiosks, on-line reference systems, sales presentation tools and performance support systems. Its client list includes a host of national and international companies as well as every branch of the federal government and many state and local governments. The Company is a subsidiary of Analysis & Technology, Inc., which is headquartered in North Stonington, CT, and listed on the NASDAQ.

Officers: John G. Drugo, Ph.D. *SVP & Division MGR*
John T. McCoy *SVP & CFO*

Human Resources: Pamela J. Semler *Human Resources Administrator*

Purchasing: Arlene Forsthoffer

Total Employees	55	**Regional Employees**	55
Year Established	1961	**SIC Code**	8748
Annual Revenues ($000)	4,000		

Applied Test Systems, Inc.

348 New Castle Rd.
P.O. Box 1529, Butler, PA 16003
Butler, PA 16001
County: Butler

Phone: (412) 283-1212
Fax: (412) 283-6570
Internet Address: www.atspa.com

Designer and manufacturer of materials testing equipment, laboratory and production furnaces and ovens, electric heating elements and nondestructive testing standards. The Company serves clients worldwide, including governments, universities and other manufacturers. It operates two subsidiaries, Electro Heat Systems, Inc. in Saxonburg, PA, and Single Source Computers at RIDC Park in Pittsburgh, PA.

Officers: Ken Zillmer *GMGR*
             Floyd R. Ganassi *VP*

Total Employees..............................70	**Regional Employees** 70
Year Established 1965	**SIC Code**.......................................3829

Aquatech International Corp.

One-Four Coins Dr.
P.O. Box 150
Canonsburg, PA 15317
County: Washington

Phone: (412) 746-5300
Fax: (412) 746-5359

Designer, manufacturer, installer and servicer of custom-built water and wastewater treatment systems for a variety of industrial applications. The Company supplies engineered systems which incorporate a wide range of process equipment including clarification; filtration; sludge handling; softening, demineralization, condensate polishing and selective ion exchange; degasification; reverse osmosis, ultrafiltration and electrodialysis; wastewater treatment systems; and chemical feed equipment. The Company's experience encompasses all facets of water treatment and its diverse industrial users, including the automotive and electronics industry, and cogeneration facilities, fertilizer plants, petrochemical plants and refineries, pharmaceutical manufacturers, pulp and paper mills, resource recovery projects, steel producers and utilities. The Company's subsidiary, Aquatech Systems (Asia) Private, Ltd. (ASAPL), which is headquartered in Bangalore, India, with an engineering office in Pune, India, was established to support the Company's mission in the Middle East and Far East. ASAPL has complete support and stand-alone capabilities. The Company also operates a sales office in Bednall, Straffordshire, England.

Officers: Chandra Sharma *CH & CEO*
V. N. Sharma *P*
J. N. Sharma *VP*
James Dobos *DIR-Technical Services*
Dennis Gray *DIR-OPR*
F. Bryan Popp *DIR-Corporate Planning*

A

Human Resources: Kimberly Tennant

Purchasing: Deepa Sharma

Regional Employees.....................100
Year Established 1981   **SIC Code**....................................3589
Annual Revenues ($000) 20,000

ARC-Allegheny

1001 Brighton Rd.
Pittsburgh, PA 15233
County: Allegheny

Phone: (412) 322-6008
Fax: (412) 322-3710

Nonprofit human service agency providing a full range of supports for children and adults with retardation and other developmental disabilities. These supports include early intervention and assessments for infants and toddlers; family-like homes and apartments with varying degrees of supervision for teens and adults; respite/sitter care; parent education and support networks; leisure and recreational activities; training and employment—both facility-based and competitive work opportunities in the community; advocacy; and ongoing education and awareness activities. The Agency serves more than 6,000 children and adults with retardation–and their families–in Allegheny County, PA, each year. It operates approximately 34 sites located in Allison Park, Avalon, Bridgeville, Brighton Heights, Coraopolis, Emsworth, Greentree, Hampton Township, Hill District, McCandless Township, McKeesport, Ross Township, Sharpsburg, South Park, Strip District, Tarentum and Zelienople. ARC-Allegheny is one of 1,150 chapters of The Arc, a national organization on mental retardation located in states across the country.

Officers: Marsha S. Blanco *EDIR*
Human Resources: Debra Lynch *Human Resource DIR*

Total Employees..........................400   **Regional Employees** 400
Year Established 1955   **SIC Code**....................................8331
Annual Revenues ($000) 18,000

Ardex, Inc.

1155 Stoops Ferry Rd.
Coraopolis, PA 15108
County: Allegheny

Phone: (412) 264-4240
Fax: (412) 264-1622
Internet Address: www.ardex.com

Manufacturer of self-leveling toppings, underlayments, mortars and grouts for fast-track commercial and retail renovation. The Company operates sales offices in Garden Grove, CA; Washington, D.C.; Atlanta, GA; Chicago, IL; Paramus, NJ; and Dallas, TX.

Officers: Herbert Goller *P*

Regional Employees ....45+
SIC Code 3241

ARIN Intermediate Unit 28

Rte. 422 E.
P.O. Box 175
Shelocta, PA 15774
County: Armstrong

Phone: (412) 463-5300
Fax: (412) 463-5315

Nonprofit regional educational service agency serving education in Armstrong and Indiana Counties and one of 29 intermediate units in Pennsylvania. The Agency, also known as Armstrong-Indiana Intermediate Unit 28, works in partnership with the 11 school districts, two area vocational-technical schools, nonpublic schools, area businesses and human resource agencies in the two-county region to offer cost-effective, high-quality programs to students of all ages, teachers, support staff and administrators. It operates over 75 programs, providing instructional and related services for over 2,000 children with special needs as well as education, training and career counseling for approximately 1,000 adults.

Officers: Thomas P. Carey, Ed.D. *EDIR*
Robert H. Coad, Jr., Ed.D. *AST-EDIR*
John T. Smith, Jr., Ph.D. *DIR-Special Education*
Derrick A. Mergen *Coordinator of Technology Services*

Human Resources: Gary R. Munsch *Business MGR*

Total Employees...........................220
Year Established 1971

Regional Employees 50
SIC Code.....................................8331

Aristech Chemical Corp.

USX Tower, 600 Grant St.
Pittsburgh, PA 15219
County: Allegheny

A

Phone: (412) 433-2747
Fax: (412) 433-7721

Manufacturer of intermediate and industrial chemicals, polypropylene resins and acrylic sheet. The Company operates chemical plants in Haverhill, OH, Neville Island, PA, and Pasadena, TX; polypropylene plants in LaPorte, TX, and Neal, WV; and an acrylic sheet plant in Florence, KY. In addition, a research facility is located in Monroeville, PA. The Company is a subsidiary of Mitsubishi Corp., which is headquartered in Tokyo, Japan, and listed on the Tokyo Stock Exchange.

Officers: Jiro Kamimura *CH & CEO*
Charles W. Hamilton *P & COO*
Michael J. Egan *CFO*
Mark K. McNally *SVP & GC*

Human Resources: John Guna

Total Employees........................1,400	**Regional Employees** 470
Year Established 1986	**SIC Code**....................................2821
Annual Revenues ($000) 1,000,000	

ARL, Inc.

238 Moon Clinton Rd.
P.O. Box 836
Coraopolis, PA 15108
County: Allegheny

Phone: (412) 264-6996
Fax: (412) 264-1470

Provider of domestic and international transportation services. The Company transports a range of products, including food, beer, frozen food, steel, machinery, import/export plastics, and liquid and dry bulk goods.

Officers: Ronald J. Faherty *CEO*
Ronald K. Faherty, Jr. *P*

Human Resources: John Lioi

Total Employees...........................40	
Year Established 1980	**SIC Code**....................................4731
Annual Revenues ($000) 40,000	

Armstrong County Memorial Hospital

One Nolte Dr.
Kittanning, PA 16201
County: Armstrong

Phone: (412) 543-8191
Fax: (412) 543-8535

Nonprofit hospital serving residents of Armstrong, Butler, Clarion, Indiana and Venango Counties, PA. Staffed with 100 physicians, the Hospital provides a wide range of care, including a psychiatric care program, the Richard G. Laube Cancer Center, home health services (including home IV therapy), nuclear medicine, laser surgery, cardiac catheterization, occupational therapy services, occupational health care program, magnetic resonance imaging services, physical therapy (including aquatic therapy/sports medicine), and information and referral case management. Its facilities include 14 intensive/coronary care units, 26 psychiatric care units, four drug and alcohol detoxification beds, 22 obstetrics/gynecology units (including four birthing rooms) and 22 bassinets for newborns, 128 medical/surgical units, six pediatric beds and 17 skilled nursing unit beds. Additional services include pre-admission testing, inpatient and outpatient cardiac rehabilitation program, ambulatory surgery center, outpatient nutrition counseling, organ and tissue donor program, family support group psychiatry, physician referral service, rural health clinics/primary care and sleep disorders lab. The Hospital also offers community education programs covering a wide range of health issues, such as an Alzheimer's disease support group, a diet-free weight loss program and emergency medical technician classes. Its two subsidiaries, Armstrong Health & Education Foundation, the fund-raising arm of the Hospital, and ArmsCare, Inc., a supplier of durable medical equipment, are also located at the above address. In addition, the Hospital operates Armstrong Primary Care Center outpatient facilities in Elderton, Leechburg and Sarver, PA.

Officers: Jack Hoard *P & CEO*
Dianne Emminger *VP-Information Services*
Richard B. O'Connell *VP-ADM*
Mona Rupert *VP-Clinical Services*
Joyce Shanty *VP-Nursing Services*
Richard Szymkowski *VP-FIN & CFO*

Total Employees............................845
Year Established 1898   **SIC Code**....................................8062

Armstrong/Kover Kwick, Inc.

401 Sproul St.
P.O. Box 337
McKees Rocks, PA 15136
County: Allegheny

Phone: (412) 771-2200
Fax: (412) 771-5777

Manufacturer of felts, cloth wipers, and furnace, oiling and mill processing rolls. The Company also distributes disposable paper wipers and disposable clothing, cheesecloth, flannel, cotton and wool waste, and sorbent products, including rugs, booms, pads and socks. Its brand names include TOHO Non-Tex Rolls, Arm Wipes, Kwicksaddles and Kwickboards.

Officers: Robert H. Wolf *P*
Kenneth L. Simon *VP-MFG*
Nancy L. Simon *VP*
Martin C. Sloan *VP-SAL*
Susan L. Wolf *VP*
Richard S. Simon *SEC & TRS*
Robert J. Esplen *CON*
Jeff Klinkner *Plant MGR*
William McAleer *SAL MGR*

Total Employees............................34
Year Established 1926
Annual Revenues ($000) 6-8,000
Regional Employees 32
SIC Code 2299

Artcraft Blazers, Inc.

7502 Thomas Blvd.
Pittsburgh, PA 15208
County: Allegheny

Phone: (412) 242-0266
Fax: (412) 242-2068

Manufacturer of blazers for men, women and children. The Company produces Polartec brand outerwear, school blazers, and police and fire blazers and pants. It markets its products throughout the United States and Canada.

Officers: Robert P. Lazar *OWN & P*
Audrey Lazar *SEC & TRS*

Human Resources: Dorothy Hill *CON*

Total Employees............................50
Year Established 1950
Annual Revenues ($000) 2,000
Regional Employees 50
SIC Code 2389

Arthur Andersen LLP

One PPG Place, Ste. 2100
Pittsburgh, PA 15222
County: Allegheny

Phone: (412) 232-0600
Fax: (412) 232-0693

Provider of professional services in the areas of audit, tax, business advisory and business, economic and financial consulting. Headquartered in Chicago, IL, the Firm is a business unit of Andersen Worldwide, which has dual headquarters in Chicago, IL, and Geneva, Switzerland. The Firm serves clients through 361 offices located in 76 countries. The local office serves clients throughout Western Pennsylvania and West Virginia.

Officers: Thomas J. Balestreire *MPTR*
Timothy G. Daigle *Partner-In-Charge-Business Consulting Services*
John W. Higbee *Partner-In-Charge-Audit & Business Advisory Services*
Scott W. Reid *Partner-In-Charge-Tax & Business Advisory Services*
William H. Rooney *Partner-In-Charge-Economic & Financial Consulting Services*

Human Resources: Gregory R. McFaden *DIR-ADM*

Total Employees	44,000	**Regional Employees**	180
Year Established	1913	**SIC Code**	8721
Annual Revenues ($000)	4,500,000		

Arthurs, Lestrange & Co., Inc.

Two Gateway Center
Pittsburgh, PA 15222
County: Allegheny

Phone: (412) 566-6800
Fax: (412) 263-2788

Investment banking firm providing a full range of investment services to clients across the country. The Company claims to be one of the largest locally owned and managed investment banking firms in Western Pennsylvania. It offers a variety of general investment products, including common stocks, preferred stocks, corporate bonds and notes, tax free bonds and notes, convertible securities, precious metals, mutual funds, money funds, tax free trusts, insurance products, new issues, government bonds and certificates of deposit. The Company also provides a variety of specialized investment products and services including tax deferred investments, fixed income services, investment research and portfolio analysis. Its Municipal Finance Department has acted as the financial advisor and managing underwriter for over $4.5 billion in various public enterprises. The Company operates a retail branch office in McKeesport, PA, and two investment banking offices located in Harrisburg and Philadelphia, PA.

Officers: Robert A. Woeber *P & CEO*
Michael P. Bova *EVP & COO*
George G. Sofis *SVP & TRS*

Human Resources: Kenneth W. Pegher *SVP & CON*

Total Employees............................42	**Regional Employees** 40
Year Established 1947	**SIC Code** 6211
Annual Revenues ($000) 3,732	

AS Acquisition Corp.

2840 Library Rd.
Pittsburgh, PA 15234
County: Allegheny

Phone: (412) 884-2636
Fax: (412) 884-6915

Provider of security products and services through its subsidiary, Allied Security Inc. (ASI), which is also located at the above address. The majority of ASI's revenue comes from uniformed security guard services. Other services include specific loss investigations, privacy sweeps and consulting services related to loss reduction. The Company's customer base includes organizations of all types and sizes in both the public and private sectors, from all levels of government to manufacturers, institutions, research and development parks, utilities and residential complexes. It operates approximately fifty offices in major markets across the United States.

Officers: Neal H. Holmes *CH & CEO*
Steven B. Stein *COO*
Mark Desrosiers *SVP*
Dick Finley *SVP-MKT & SAL*
Tom Fogle *SVP*
Glenn A. Pifer *SEC & TRS*

Human Resources: Phil Schugar

Total Employees........................8,000	**Regional Employees** 600
Year Established 1957	**SIC Code** 7381
Annual Revenues ($000) 160,000	

Ashdown Corp.

4100 Steubenville Pike
P.O. Box 4547
Pittsburgh, PA 15205
County: Allegheny

Phone: (412) 922-9888
Fax: (412) 922-2380
Internet Address: www.bruceplastics.com

Holding company engaged in the manufacturing of molded plastic parts through its subsidiary, Bruce Plastics, Inc., which is also located at the above address. The Company is a full-service injection molder of both proprietary and custom-molded parts. Its proprietary products include handles, feet, bumpers, grommets, fasteners, suction cups, thread protectors and fan blades. The Company's custom-molding services include in-house design, engineering and tool building services, utilizing molding machines ranging from 39 to 500 tons; hot stamping, sonic sealing and riveting machines; drills; and hand assembly.

Officers: Bipin Khimasia *P*
Dhiren S. Shah *EVP; P & CEO-Bruce Plastics, Inc.*
Barry Roos *NATL SAL & MKT MGR-Bruce Plastics, Inc.*

Human Resources: Pat Palmisano *Administrative AST (Purchasing)*

Total Employees............................90	**Regional Employees** 90	
Year Established 1952	**SIC Code**......................................3089	

ASKO, Inc.

501 W. Seventh Ave.
P.O. Box 355
Homestead, PA 15120
County: Allegheny

Phone: (412) 461-4110
Fax: (412) 461-5400

Manufacturer of shear knives, saw blades and circular saws. Through Sintermet, Inc., a subsidiary located in Kittanning, PA, the Company produces tungsten carbide wear parts. Other divisions include Asko, Inc. in South Holland, IL, and CKC, Inc. in Rock Hill, SC; and a subsidiary, Asko BV in Amsterdam, The Netherlands. All of the Company's products are for the steel making industry.

Officers: William H. Rackoff *P*
Timothy J. Giegel *VP & CFO*

Human Resources: M. Robert Thomas

Purchasing: Tom Songer

Total Employees............................400	**Regional Employees** 150	
Year Established 1933	**SIC Code**......................................3425	

Aspen Systems Corp.

411 Seventh Ave., 4th Fl.
Pittsburgh, PA 15219
County: Allegheny

Phone: (412) 391-7553
Fax: (412) 391-8741

Employee-owned provider of customized document management services and systems to the legal community. The Company's computerized litigation support enables clients to accurately, quickly and efficiently pinpoint and access needed documents. Its litigation support services include project planning/system design, project management, discovery management, document screening, document imaging/OCR/ICR processing, document indexing/coding, depository/facilities management, systems support and customer support. The Company has successfully performed on more than 1,000 litigation support projects for many of the major law firms and corporations in the United States. The Company, which operates offices nationwide, is headquartered in Rockville, MD.

Officers: Albert Lampert *P*
Mel J. Goldenberg *SVP & GMGR-Legal Information MGT Services Group*
Ron McHugh *VP-Commercial Litigation Support Division*
Chris Olsson, Jr. *MGR-Document Processing-Pittsburgh, PA*

Purchasing: Linda J. Dybiec *VP & CON-FIN & Accounting (Rockville, MD)*

Total Employees	1,800	**Regional Employees**	200
Year Established	1959	**SIC Code**	7379
Annual Revenues ($000)			85,000

Assad Iron & Metals, Inc.

Albany Rd.
P.O. Box 76
Brownsville, PA 15417
County: Fayette

Phone: (412) 785-6000
Fax: (412) 785-8991

Processor of scrap iron and nonferrous metals. The Company also provides containers for fabrication shops and machine shops to discard of their scrap materials.

Officers: James Snyder *P*
Daniel R. Snyder *VP*

Total Employees	41	**Regional Employees**	41
Year Established	1972	**SIC Code**	3341

Associated Cleaning Consultants & Services, Inc.

431 Davidson Rd.
Pittsburgh, PA 15239
County: Allegheny

Phone: (412) 795-9200
Fax: (412) 795-9204

Provider of contract janitorial services to commercial and industrial clients throughout the eastern U.S., including clients in Florida, Georgia, Maryland, North Carolina, Ohio, Pennsylvania, Rhode Island, South Carolina and Virginia.

Officers: Jerome Riems *P*
Jeffrey Riems *SEC & TRS*

Purchasing: Sandy Fornicoia

Total Employees 1,000-2,000
Year Established 1970   **SIC Code**....................................7349

Associated Graphics, Inc.

1441 Metropolitan St.
Pittsburgh, PA 15233
County: Allegheny

Phone: (412) 321-2506
Fax: (412) 321-8227

Manufacturer of presentation folders, literature packaging, CD/disk packaging and video packaging customized to client specifications. The Company's products are sold through a network of independent dealers to a variety of corporate end users.

Officers: George R. Siegel *P*
Jeffrey Siegel
Christine Siegel-Cruny

Total Employees.............................35   **Regional Employees** 35
Year Established 1972   **SIC Code**....................................2782
Annual Revenues ($000) 4,200

Associated Occupational Therapists, Inc.

401 Locust St., Ste. 2A
Coraopolis, PA 15108
County: Allegheny

Phone: (412) 299-0704
Fax: (412) 299-0716
Internet Address: www.eagletherapy.com

Provider of comprehensive occupational therapy services in 12 outpatient clinics, school districts, acute care and home health settings, businesses, developmental disability/mental health centers and geriatric rehabilitation facilities throughout Pittsburgh and the Tri-State area. The Company offers full-time, part-time and temporary on-site contractual services. It also offers consulting services for injury management, job accommodation, injury prevention, safety and compliance with the Americans with Disabilities Act. The Company's outpatient services are provided at clinics operated by Eagle Physical Therapy and Physical Rehabilitation Enterprises, located in Allison Park, Baden, Bellevue, Bradford Woods, Butler, Export, Mars, Monroeville, Moon Township, Mt. Lebanon, Robinson and Zelienople, PA.

Officers: Hanna Gruen *P*
Carol King-Etzel *VP & SEC*
Cynthia C. Thomas *VP & TRS*

Total Employees	70+	**Regional Employees**	70+
Year Established	1980	**SIC Code**	8099
Annual Revenues ($000)			2,500

Associates Litho, Inc.

325 32nd St.
P.O. Box 4008
Pittsburgh, PA 15201
County: Allegheny

Phone: (412) 281-2773
Fax: (412) 471-6640

Full-service commercial printer providing complete preparation, printing, finishing and distribution services. The Company produces one- to six-color books, catalogs, product sheets and promotional/advertising sheets. Its clients include advertising agencies, universities, hospitals and print brokers throughout the Northeastern U.S.

Officers: Owen T. Cook *P*
John D. Trexel *VP-SAL*
John A. Zahorchak *Plant Superintendent*

Human Resources: Thomas G. Cook *VP & GMGR (Purchasing)*

Total Employees	30	**Regional Employees**	30
Year Established	1962	**SIC Code**	2752
Annual Revenues ($000)			3,000

Astorino & Assoc., Ltd., L. D.

227 Fort Pitt Blvd.
Pittsburgh, PA 15222
County: Allegheny

Phone: (412) 765-1700
Fax: (412) 765-1711

   Multidisciplinary architectural and engineering firm. The Company is a provider of architectural services, offering construction management, interior design, landscaping, graphics and project management services. Its subsidiaries, also located at the above address, are Astorino Branch Engineers, Inc., a mechanical, civil, structural and electrical engineering firm; and Astorino Branch Environmental, Inc., a full service environmental engineering, industrial hygiene and safety consulting firm. The Company's staff includes architects, engineers, cost estimators, construction managers, interior designers, graphic designers and even an archivist. The Company has designed and supervised the construction of sports facilities, prisons, public and private housing, hospitals and medical centers, government facilities, churches, educational facilities, corporate offices, banks, shopping centers, restaurants, commercial and industrial developments, and warehouse and distribution facilities. It serves clients worldwide.

Officers: Louis D. Astorino *CH*
Dennis L. Astorino *P*
Patrick I. Branch *EVP*
Bernard J. Quinn *P-Astorino Branch Environmental, Inc.*

Human Resources: Janis D. Babich

Purchasing: James Kohl

Total Employees............................120	**Regional Employees**...................119
Year Established 1972	**SIC Code**......................................8712
Annual Revenues ($000) 10,000	

AT&T Corp.

Commerce Ct., Four Station Sq., Ste. 400
Pittsburgh, PA 15219
County: Allegheny

Phone: (412) 642-7000
Fax: (412) 642-7260

   Provider of communications and information services, claiming to run the world's largest, most sophisticated communications network and to be the leading provider of long-distance and wireless services. The Company also offers Internet access and hosting services and access to home entertainment, and has begun to deliver local telephone service. In addition, it offers outsourcing, consulting, systems integration and customer care services to large businesses and manages one of the world's largest credit card programs. The Company, which is headquartered in New York, NY, is listed on the NYSE. Its Pittsburgh metropolitan area employees work at approximately 20 different office sites, with major locations at 635 Grant St. (AT&T Operations and Billing); 2400 Penn Ave. (AT&T Wireless Services Sales and Service); 2630 Liberty Ave. (AT&T Wireless Services Administration and Customer Care); and 5500 Corporate Dr. (McCandless Township) (AT&T Customer Care). The facility located at the above address handles AT&T Business Sales and AT&T Customer Care. The local sites encompass almost every phase of the Company's operations and business units.

Officers: Stan Hays *Global Business Services*
Janet Martha *Midmarkets Business Services*
Linda Rayland *Small Business Services*
Lenora Vesio *Public Relations*

Total Employees....................130,000   **Regional Employees** 2,000
Year Established 1885   **SIC Code**....................................4812
Annual Revenues ($000)..................................52,000,000+

Atlas Group, Inc., The

311 Rouser Rd.
P.O. Box 611
Coraopolis, PA 15108
County: Allegheny

Phone: (412) 262-2830
Fax: (412) 262-2820

Employee-owned holding company engaged in the exploration, production and marketing of natural gas and oil through its subsidiaries, consisting of Atlas Energy Corp. (gas and oil exploration), Atlas Gas Marketing, Inc. (gas marketing) and Mercer Gas Gathering, Inc. (natural gas gathering and transportation), all located at the above address; Atlas Resources, Inc. (driller) in Jackson Center, PA; and Atlas Energy Group, Inc. (driller) in Masury, OH. The Company is active in natural gas and oil exploration, production and marketing, primarily in the Appalachian region, and more recently has engaged in exploratory drilling throughout the continental United States. The Company operates in excess of 1,200 wells. To help fund its drilling activity, the Company forms partnerships to solicit individual investors through a nationwide network of brokers/dealers and then acts as managing general partner for subscribers to the partnerships. Since 1985, it has sponsored five public and twenty private drilling programs. The Company has drilled about 100 wells per year over the last several years in the Appalachian Basin and typically owns about 25% interest in each well through one of its operating affiliates. The Company also produces in excess of nine billion cubic feet of natural gas annually, purchases an additional 10 billion cubic feet of natural gas from local and southwest producers, and sells gas to approximately 150 customers. To facilitiate the delivery of natural gas to its customers, the Company has constructed over 600 miles of gas gathering and transmission facilities.

Officers: Charles T. Koval *CH*
James R. O'Mara *P & CEO*
Tony C. Banks *VP & CFO*
Frank P. Carolas *VP-Geology*
James J. Kritzo *VP-Land*
Bruce M. Wolf *GC & SEC*

Human Resources: James M. Ogan *DIR-Human Resources (Purchasing)*

Total Employees............................101	**Regional Employees** 37
Year Established 1972	**SIC Code**.....................................1381
Annual Revenues ($000) 75,000	

Atlas Industries, Inc.

530 Bell Ave.
P.O. Box 470
Carnegie, PA 15106
County: Allegheny

Phone: (412) 276-9221
Fax: (412) 276-9222

Employee-owned organization serving commercial and industrial construction markets in Kentucky, Ohio, Western Pennsylvania, Virginia and West Virginia. The Company is a contractor specializing in industrial insulation and cold storage projects, with a branch site in New Martinsville, WV. Its subsidiaries include ARC-Spec, Inc., located at the above address, a manufacturers' representative group for construction products; Atlas Wholesale Supply, Inc., located at the above address, a wholesale distributor of construction products; ATS Construction, Inc., located at the above address, an industrial insulation contractor; ATL Construction & Supply, Inc. in New Martinsville, WV, a wholesale distributor of construction products; Atlas Scaffold & Supply, Inc. in South Charleston, WV, a scaffold contractor and distributor and wholesale distributor of construction products; and Atlas Properties, Inc. in Meadville, PA, an operator of a recreational campground facility.

Officers: William A. Bayer *P*
Mark S. Lock *EVP*
Debra L. Harding *TRS*
Charles Bayer *SEC*

Total Employees............................200	**Regional Employees** 75
Year Established 1962	**SIC Code**.....................................1742

Atlas Railroad Construction Co.

2153 State Rte. 519
P.O. Box 8
Eighty Four, PA 15330
County: Washington

Phone: (412) 228-4500
Fax: (412) 228-3183

Provider of engineering, construction and maintenance services for railroad and mass transit facilities. The Company serves clients nationwide.

Officers: William M. Stout *P*
　　　　　Mark A. Stout *VP*

Human Resources: William M. Kerns *CON (Purchasing)*

Total Employees	200	**Regional Employees**	100
Year Established	1954	**SIC Code**	1622
Annual Revenues ($000)	10,000+		

Atlas Resource Management, Inc.

2153 State Rte. 519
P.O. Box 355
Eighty Four, PA 15330
County: Washington

Phone: (412) 228-8400
Fax: (412) 228-3183

Contractor providing engineering and heavy construction for infrastructure, roadway, bridge, drainage, environmental protection, low-rise building and site work projects. The Company serves public and private clients nationwide.

Officers: William M. Stout *P*
　　　　　Mark A. Stout *VP*

Human Resources: William M. Kerns *CON (Purchasing)*

Total Employees	100	**Regional Employees**	25
Year Established	1988	**SIC Code**	1622
Annual Revenues ($000)	5,000		

Auberle

1101 Hartman St.
McKeesport, PA 15132
County: Allegheny

Phone: (412) 673-5800
Fax: (412) 673-5805

Nonprofit provider of services to at-risk children and families in Western Pennsylvania. While the Organization began as a home for mistreated and neglected teenage boys, who still make up the majority of its clients, the Organization now also serves teenage girls, children age 7 through 12 years and families receiving crisis intervention. The Organization's primary goal is to return children to their homes if possible; foster care and independent living skills are provided when this is not feasible. Its staff helps kids to get in touch with their feelings, work with authority figures and discipline themselves as well as assist them with living skills and academic work. The Organization serves over 1,500 children and youth each year, with 145 children currently in its physical care and 125 families through in-home services. The Organization operates four boys programs in the McKeesport area; two group homes for girls in Mt. Pleasant; a group home for girls in Wilmerding; a shelter in Duquesne; and in-home offices in McKeesport and Monessen.

Officers: Lynn Knezevich *EDIR*
Jean O'Connell Jenkins *Associate DIR*
Jerry Meyer *AST-DIR*

Total Employees 230	**Regional Employees** 230
Year Established 1952	**SIC Code** 8361
Annual Revenues ($000) 6,100	

AUMA Actuators, Inc.

Four Zesta Dr.
Pittsburgh, PA 15205
County: Allegheny

Phone: (412) 787-1340
Fax: (412) 787-1223

Manufacturer of electric motor valve actuators and gear boxes. The Company operates regional sales offices located in Los Angeles, CA; Chicago, IL; Annapolis, MD; Charlotte, NC; and Houston, TX. It is a subsidiary of AUMA Riester GmbH & Co. KG, which is headquartered in Muellheim, Baden, Germany.

Officers: Samuel A. Bennardo *P*
Russell Matthis *ENG MGR*
Richard Oaks *MKT MGR*
Anthony Pecora *SAL MGR*
Thomas Perkins *CON*

Human Resources: Bonnie Hostetler

Purchasing: Myron Kowalski

Total Employees..............................50	Regional Employees 45
Year Established 1976	SIC Code....................................3625

A

Austin Co., James

115 Downieville Rd.
P.O. Box 827
Mars, PA 16046
County: Butler

Phone: (412) 625-1535
Fax: (412) 625-3288

Manufacturer of household and industrial cleaning products, including bleaches, ammonias, fabric softeners, glass cleaners, all-purpose cleaners, windshield washer fluid, dish and laundry products, hand soaps and degreasers. The Company's major brand names are A-1 Bleach, A-1 Fluff, Austin's and Wipe Away. Its products are marketed within the geographic area east of the Mississippi River. The Company also offers contract packaging services. It operates additional manufacturing plants in Deland, FL; Merrimack, NH; and Statesville, NC.

Officers: Harry G. Austin, Jr. *CH*
John T. Austin, Sr. *P*
Harry G. Austin III *VP-NATL SAL*
John T. Austin, Jr. *VP-Regional SAL*
Robert Downie *VP-FIN*

Human Resources: Denny Baird

Purchasing: Frank Bjalobok

Total Employees............................165	Regional Employees 145
Year Established 1889	SIC Code....................................2842
Annual Revenues ($000) 30,000	

Automated Healthcare, Inc.

261 Kappa Dr.
Pittsburgh, PA 15238
County: Allegheny

Phone: (412) 967-2690
Fax: (412) 967-3599

Manufacturer of automated pharmaceutical dispensing equipment for use by health care institutions. The Company is a subsidiary of McKesson Corp., which is headquartered in San Francisco, CA, and listed on the NYSE.

Officers: Sean McDonald *P*
Robert Kachur *VP-OPR*
Matthew Marshall *VP-SAL*
Manoj Wangu *VP-ENG*
Tami Chinchor *CON*

Total Employees..............................95
Year Established 1987

Regional Employees 95
SIC Code....................................3841

Automatic Data Processing, Inc.

100 Commerce Dr.
Pittsburgh, PA 15275
County: Allegheny

Phone: (412) 788-1530
Fax: (412) 747-7753

Provider of fully integrated human resources, benefits and payroll solutions, offering data processing and computing services to a broad range of clients in the Tri-State area. The Company's services include payroll processing and tax filing, and it markets time clocks. The Company, which is also known as ADP, is headquartered in Roseland, NJ, and listed on the NYSE.

Officers: Bob King *GMGR*

Human Resources: Kara Yeager *Division Recruiter*

Total Employees.....................27,000
Year Established 1949
Annual Revenues ($000) 4,300,000

Regional Employees 225
SIC Code....................................7374

Automotive Ignition Co., Inc.

301 Meade St.
P.O. Box 91039
Pittsburgh, PA 15221
County: Allegheny

Phone: (412) 243-3080
Fax: (412) 241-8843

Distributor of diesel and electrical products primarily for trucks and construction equipment. The Company operates a branch facility, Blair Diesel & Electric Co., which is located in Altoona, PA.

Officers: Paul V. Logue *P*
Joseph J. Duffy *VP*

Total Employees..............................30
Year Established 1926
Annual Revenues ($000) 5,000

Regional Employees 25
SIC Code....................................5013

Avalotis Painting Company, Inc.

519 2nd St.
P.O. Box 6
Verona, PA 15147
County: Allegheny

Phone: (412) 828-9666
Fax: (412) 828-6599

Contractor providing commercial and industrial painting, lining, fireproofing, rubber roofing, corrugated sheeting, wallpapering and waterproofing services. The Company operates branch offices located in Tampa, FL; Chicago, IL; and Philadelphia, PA. It serves clients throughout the United States and is expanding internationally.

Officers: Aristotle Aivaliotis *P*
Chris Aivaliotis *VP*

Total Employees............................200	**Regional Employees** 100
Year Established 1966	**SIC Code**......................................1721
Annual Revenues ($000) 22,000	

Axiom Real Estate Management, Inc.

Six PPG Place, Ste. 600
Pittsburgh, PA 15222
County: Allegheny

Phone: (412) 281-0801
Fax: (412) 281-7455

Provider of property and facility management services managing more than 80 million square feet in over 500 properties around the country. The Company maintains 15 branch offices located in Denver, CO; Stamford, CT; Washington, D.C.; Tampa, FL; Atlanta, GA; Chicago, IL; Boston, MA; Detroit, MI; West Orange, NJ; New York, NY; Cincinnati and Cleveland, OH; Philadelphia, PA; and Dallas and Houston, TX. It is a subsidiary of Grubb & Ellis Co., which is headquartered in Northbrook, IL, and listed on the NYSE.

Officers: Ronald M. Puntil *P*
Philip B. Rogers *SVP*
James G. Sterling *SVP*
James B. White *SVP*
Blake W. Harbaugh *VP & CON*
Terry Paterni *VP & TRS*

Human Resources: Vince Ristucci

Total Employees........................1,500	**Regional Employees** 75
Year Established 1992	**SIC Code**......................................6500

Babcock Florida Co.

2220 Palmer St.
Pittsburgh, PA 15218
County: Allegheny

Phone: (412) 351-3515
Fax: (412) 351-1522

Owner and operator of the Crescent B Ranch, a 90,000-acre ranch located near Ft. Meyers and Punta Gorda, FL, and one of the largest in Florida. The Company performs a number of business activities at this site, including cattle breeding, vegetable farming and limestone mining. It also offers wilderness tours through Babcock Wilderness Adventures and hunting for wildlife. In addition, the Company owns and operates a Holiday Inn in Punta Gorda, FL.

Officers: Richard S. Cuda *P*
Carl P. Stillitano *TRS*

Total Employees 110	**Regional Employees** 5
Year Established 1915	**SIC Code** 212
Annual Revenues ($000) 8,000

Babcock Lumber Co.

2220 Palmer St.
P.O. Box 8348
Pittsburgh, PA 15218
County: Allegheny

Phone: (412) 351-3515
Fax: (412) 351-1522
Internet Address: www.babcockenterprises.com

Wholesale distributor of lumber products and specialty building materials, including hardwood and softwood lumber, Formica and Wilsonart laminates, Armstrong ceilings, Hardie fiber cement sidings, Masonite exterior sidings and engineered flooring. The Company also produces kiln-dried hardwoods, finished moldings, furniture panels, stair parts and other millwork, which is marketed domestically throughout the U.S. and exported primarily to Europe. The Company predominantly serves independent dealers. Its distribution facilities are located in Ruskin, FL; Buffalo and Rochester, NY; Columbus and Youngstown, OH; Altoona, PA; and Clarksburg and Gassaway, WV. Its manufacturing facilities are located in Donegal, Ebensburg and St. Marys, PA; and Elkins, WV.

Officers: Carl P. Stillitano *P*
Joseph M. Churak *VP*

Total Employees 503	**Regional Employees** 245
Year Established 1887	**SIC Code** 2431
Annual Revenues ($000) 143,000

Babst, Calland, Clements & Zomnir, P.C.

Two Gateway Center, 8th Fl.
Pittsburgh, PA 15222
County: Allegheny

Phone: (412) 394-5400
Fax: (412) 394-6576

Provider of legal services with 54 attorneys. The Firm's practice areas include environmental, energy, construction, corporate, commercial and litigation. It operates a branch office in Philadelphia, PA.

Officers: Chester R. Babst III *P*
Dean A. Calland *VP*
Frank J. Clements *VP & SEC*
Richard M. Zomnir *VP & TRS*
Dennis M. Yates *EDIR*

Human Resources: Sharon A. Kolesar

Total Employees............................122
Year Established 1986

Regional Employees...................119
SIC Code 8111

Bacharach, Inc.

625 Alpha Dr.
Pittsburgh, PA 15238
County: Allegheny

Phone: (412) 963-2000
Fax: (412) 963-2091
Internet Address: www.bacharach-inc.com

Manufacturer of analytical, combustion and environmental measurement and detection instruments. The Company's product line includes sensors and instruments for combustion analysis, emissions monitoring and temperature, humidity and ventilation measurement for the HVAC, commercial and industrial markets. The Company's gas detection product lines utilize infrared, catalytic and electrochemical technologies for monitoring oxygen, combustibles and toxic gases. The Fixed Systems line includes controllers, transmitters, sensors and systems components for facility monitoring. The Portable Instrument line includes single and multi-gas instruments for personal safety in the workplace. The GMD Systems line specializes in the monitoring of highly toxic gases. The Company also states that it is a leading domestic manufacturer of instruments used to tune and maintain diesel engine fuel injection systems. The Company operates branch sales and service centers in Garden Grove, CA; Merrillville, IN; Pennsauken, NJ; Houston, TX; Markham, Ontario, Canada; and Christiansfeld, Denmark.

Officers: Paul M. Zito *P & CEO*
Edward J. Startari *SVP-OPR*
William P. Raible *VP-FIN*

Human Resources: Bernard Dombrosky

Purchasing: Pat Sims

Total Employees	300	Regional Employees	275
Year Established	1909	SIC Code	3823

Bailey Engineers, Inc.

Southpointe Industrial Park, 125 Technology Dr.
P.O. Box 401
Canonsburg, PA 15317
County: Washington

Phone: (412) 745-6200
Fax: (412) 745-6292

Provider of design engineering, supply and installation services for iron and steel desulfurization stations, steel ladle treatment stations, and basic oxygen furnace mixed gas blowing and secondary combustion systems, with complete fabricating, machining and assembly facilities available. The Company's products include electromechanical clay guns, hydraulic clay guns, tap hole drills (conventional and soaking bar), single and double shaft pub mills, stationary wheel pig casting machines, ladle cleaning stations, metallic and nonmetallic expansion joints, tuyeres, plate coolers and a broad range of valves, as well as repair and conditioning services for all of these products. The Company also offers electronic document management system services, including scanning, indexing, retrieving, reviewing and editing. In addition, the Company leases its excess office space at the Southpointe Industrial Complex. The Company's corporate offices as well as its product and real estate divisions are located at the above address; and the engineering division is located at 135 Technology Dr. in Canonsburg, PA. It also maintains offices in Hammond, IN, and Richfield, OH.

Officers: Richard A. Barcelona *P & CEO*
Emil A. Galis *EVP*
George Missiriotis *VP-ENG*
Frank Rollo *VP-SAL*
Richard K. Miller *CON*

Human Resources: Jack Barcelona *VP-ADM*

Purchasing: John Ihnat

Total Employees	100+	Regional Employees	40+
Year Established	1928	SIC Code	8711

Baptist Homes Society, Inc.

489 Castle Shannon Blvd.
Pittsburgh, PA 15234
County: Allegheny

B

Phone: (412) 563-6550
Fax: (412) 572-8253

Nonprofit provider of long-term care for the elderly offering independent housing, personal care/assisted living, skilled nursing care and related services, such as rehabilitative therapies, housing, meals and nutrition. The Company, doing business as Baptist Homes of Western Pennsylvania, has three operating subsidiaries all located at the above address on its Mt. Lebanon campus. Baptist Homes Nursing Center provides skilled and intermediate nursing services to 126 residents and participates in the Medicare and Medicaid programs. The facility includes a 41-bed special care unit providing specialized services for persons with Alzheimer's disease and related forms of dementia. The Baptist Homes Residence is a licensed personal care facility providing assisted living services to 60 older adults. The Baptist Manor is a HUD 202/8 apartment complex offering 100 apartments for low- and moderate-income seniors and persons who are mobility impaired.

Officers: Kathleen S. Anderson *P & CEO*
Nancy E. Detwiler *Executive Administrator*
Stan J. Walasik *CFO*

Human Resources: Cynthia L. Sinopoli *Human Resources MGR*

Total Employees............................215   **Regional Employees** 215
Year Established 1910   **SIC Code**.....................................8051

Bardan, Inc.

5724 Curry Rd.
Pittsburgh, PA 15236
County: Allegheny

Phone: (412) 655-7541
Fax: (412) 655-0887

Owner and operator of Daniel's Discount, a full-line hardware store selling a variety of products, including namebrand major appliances, power tools, paint and plumbing supplies. The Company also operates Bardan Appliance Outlet, located at 5681 Horning Rd. in Pittsbugh, PA, which is a scratch and dent depot for General Electric major appliances.

Officers: Irvin M. Beck *P (Purchasing)*
Joe Horowitz *SEC*
Abe Horowitz *TRS*

Total Employees............................50	**Regional Employees** 50
Year Established 1940	**SIC Code**.....................................5251
Annual Revenues ($000)...10,000+	

BASF Corp.

370 Frankfort Rd.
Monaca, PA 15061
County: Beaver

Phone: (412) 728-6900
Fax: (412) 728-1870
Internet Address: www.basf-corp.com

Manufacturer of styrene-butadiene and acrylic latices for the domestic and international paper coatings, adhesive raw materials, carpet backing, textile coatings and architectural coatings industries. The Company is headquartered in Mt. Olive, NJ. The facility located at the above address is a part of its Dispersions & Paper Chemicals business group. The Company is a subsidiary of BASF AG, which is headquartered in Ludwigshafen, Germany, and listed on the Frankfurt Stock Exchange.

Officers: Joseph Breunig *DIR-MFG*

Human Resources: Robynne Sherrill

Purchasing: Joyce Kerr

Total Employees.......................15,000	**Regional Employees** 100
Year Established 1940	**SIC Code**.....................................2822
Annual Revenues ($000).......................................6,200,000	

Bayer Corp.

100 Bayer Rd.
Pittsburgh, PA 15205
County: Allegheny

Phone: (412) 777-2000
Fax: (412) 778-4430

International research-based company with major businesses in health care, chemicals and imaging technologies. The Company consists of nine divisions: Agfa in Ridgefield Park, NJ, produces graphic systems, printing plates and medical, technical and photo imaging systems; Agriculture in Kansas City, MO, produces crop protection, specialty products and animal health products; Consumer Care in Morristown, NJ, produces nonprescription antacids,

B

analgesics, cold and cough medicines, aspirin, vitamins and feminine care products; Diagnostics in Tarrytown, NY, produces diagnostic testing systems consisting of instruments and associated reagents for clinical chemistry, diabetes, hematology, immunodiagnostics, blood proteins and urine chemistry; Fibers, Additives and Rubber, at the above address, produces synthetic fibers, synthetic rubber and rubber chemicals, additives and adhesive raw materials, specialty additives, and aroma chemicals, food ingredients, flavors and fragrances; Industrial Chemicals, at the above address, produces iron oxides and other inorganic pigments, porcelain enamel and ceramic frits, organic and inorganic chemicals, custom-made fine and specialty chemicals, tantalum alloys and niobium powders; Performance Products, at the above address, produces coatings and raw materials, organic pigments and dyes for coatings and plastics, detergent optical brighteners, leather tanning agents and dyes, textile processing chemicals, and dyes, pigments and brighteners for the paper industry; Pharmaceutical in West Haven, CT, produces pharmaceuticals, biological products and biotechnologically derived therapeutics; and Polymers, at the above address, produces polyurethanes and plastics. The Company has several subsidiaries: ChemDesign Corp. in Fitchburg, MA; Deerfield Urethane, Inc. in South Deerfield, MA; H&R Florasynth in Teterboro, NJ; Rhein Chemie Corp. in Trenton, NJ; H. C. Starck Inc. in Newton, MA; and Wolff Walsrode in Burr Ridge, IL. In addition, it maintains an office in Washington, D.C. and an Automotive Products Center in Auburn Hills, MI. The Company is a member of the worldwide Bayer Group, a $32.4 billion chemical and pharmaceutical organization. Led by Bayer AG, which is headquartered in Leverkusen, Germany, and listed on the Frankfurt Stock Exchange, the Bayer Group is one of the world's 50 largest industrial companies. The Bayer Corp. is the largest subsidiary of Bayer AG. In 1996, the Company invested $621 million in research and development.

Officers: Helge H. Wehmeier *P & CEO*
Gary S. Balkema *EVP; P-Consumer Care Division*
Rolf A. Classon *EVP; P-Diagnostics Division*
Nicholas T. Cullen *EVP; P-Performance Products Division*
David R. Ebsworth, Ph.D. *EVP; P-Pharmaceutical Division*
E. L. Foote *EVP; P-Industrial Chemicals Division*
Ronald D. Fuchs *EVP & CTO*
Gerd D. Mueller *EVP, CAO & CFO*
H. Lee Noble *EVP; P-Polymers Division*
Erhard Rittinghaus *EVP; P-Agfa Division*
Hermann R. Werner *EVP; P-Agriculture Division*
Richard L. White *EVP; P-Fibers, Additives & Rubber Division*
Frank Wenzel, Ph.D. *CON*
Leslie F. Nute *GC & SEC*
Jon R. Wyne *TRS*
Margo L. Barnes, Ph.D. *Corporate Communications*
Bernhard Opitz, Ph.D. *ENG*
David C. Owens *Corporate Health, Environment & Safety*
Helmut F. Porkert, Ph.D. *Materials MGT*
John J. Tremse *Information Systems*

Human Resources: Howard W. Reed *Human Resources*

Total Employees......................24,000	Regional Employees 1,900
Year Established 1884	SIC Code....................................2819
Annual Revenues ($000) 9,019,600	

Beaconsfield Financial Services, Inc.

101 W. Mall Plaza, Ste. 204
Carnegie, PA 15106
County: Allegheny

Phone: (412) 276-5600
Fax: (412) 276-5070

Full-service brokerage firm offering stocks, bonds, mutual funds, tax-free municipal bonds, life insurance, and fixed and variable tax sheltered annuities. The Company specializes in "no fee" financial planning. It operates branch offices in Kalamazoo, MI, and at 115 Evergreen Heights Dr. in Pittsburgh, PA.

Officers: King Rainier *P & CEO*
            Betty Rainier *SEC & TRS*

Total Employees.............................70	Regional Employees 65
Year Established 1983	SIC Code....................................6211
Annual Revenues ($000) 3,000	

Bearing Service Co. of Pennsylvania

500 Dargan St.
Pittsburgh, PA 15224
County: Allegheny

Phone: (412) 621-7300
Fax: (412) 621-7125

Manufacturer and distributor of ball and roller bearings. The Company is also a distributor of power transmission products. Its major lines include FAG, Rexnord/Linkbelt, Sealmaster, SNR, Timken and Torrington. The Company operates branch offices in Decatur, AL; LaSalle, IL; Griffith, IN; and Canton, Cleveland, Columbus and Warren, OH. In addition, it operates a heat-treating and repair facility in Donora, PA.

Officers: Jacob W. Banks *CH*
            William J. Banks *P*
            Meredith Rose *CON*

Total Employees...........................130	Regional Employees 65
Year Established 1933	SIC Code....................................3562
Annual Revenues ($000) 35,000	

Beaver Newspapers, Inc.

400 Fair Ave.
Beaver, PA 15009
County: Beaver

Phone: (412) 775-3200
Fax: (412) 775-7212

B

Publisher of the Beaver County Times, a daily newspaper with a daily circulation of 44,882 and a Sunday circulation of 53,588 distributed in Beaver County and the outlying counties. The Company is a subsidiary of Calkins Newspapers, Inc., which is headquartered in Levittown, PA.

Officers: Grover J. Friend *P*
Charles P. Smith *EVP*
Edward J. Birch *SVP*
Shirley C. Ellis *VP & SEC*
Stanley M. Ellis *VP*
F. Wallace Gordon *VP & Publisher*
Sandra C. Hardy *VP*
Carolyn C. Smith *VP*

Total Employees............................320
Year Established 1900   **SIC Code** 2711
Annual Revenues ($000)...15,000+

Beaver Valley Geriatric Center

246 Friendship Cir.
Beaver, PA 15009
County: Beaver

Phone: (412) 775-7100
Fax: (412) 775-2290

Nonprofit operator of a 672-bed skilled, intermediate and acute care long-term nursing facility. The Facility is located on a 96-acre campus in the heart of Beaver County. It offers 12 clinical service programs, including dental, ophthalmology, orthopedic, radiology, psychiatry and podiatry under the direction of the center's staff physicians serving residents of Beaver County and the surrounding communities. The Facility is owned by Beaver County and managed by the Medical Center of Beaver County, which is also located in Beaver, PA.

Officers: William R. Jubeck *Administrator*
John Antoline *Commissioner*
Nancy Loxley *Commissioner*
Bea Schulte *Commissioner*

Human Resources: Melanie Szurley

Regional Employees ....700+
Year Established 1959   **SIC Code** 8059
Annual Revenues ($000) 30,000

Beckwith Machinery Co.

4565 William Penn Hwy.
P.O. Box 8718, Pittsburgh, PA 15221
Murrysville, PA 15668
County: Westmoreland

Phone: (412) 327-1300
Fax: (412) 327-9318

Distributor and servicer of Caterpillar earthmoving equipment and supplies. As an authorized dealer for Caterpillar equipment, the Company handles both new and used equipment for rent, lease or sale, including backhoes, tractors, motor graders, loaders, scrapers, hydraulic excavators, paving equipment, engines and generators. It also distributes Toyota lift trucks. In addition, it maintains a full line of Caterpillar and Toyota parts. The Company operates branch facilities in Altoona, Clarion, Clearfield, Cranberry Township, Erie and Somerset, PA, and Clarksburg, WV; a fabrication facility in Blawnox, PA; a remanufacturing facility in Indiana, PA; a parts distribution and field service facility in Delmont, PA; and a material handling facility and the power systems division in North Versailles, PA.

Officers: James S. Beckwith III *CH*
G. Nicholas Beckwith III *P & CEO*

Total Employees ....700+   **Regional Employees** 250
Year Established 1907   **SIC Code** 3599
Annual Revenues ($000) ....170,000+

Behrenberg Glass Co.

57 Mark Dr.
P.O. Box 100
Delmont, PA 15626
County: Westmoreland

Phone: (412) 468-4181
Fax: (412) 468-8861

Manufacturer of bent and decorated glass products including trays, candy dishes, platters, serve ware, snack servers and sandblasted pieces. The Company also produces bent and decorated fixtures glass, including flat fire, phosphorescent signs, lower-end bent lighting, channels, diffusers and lantern glass in clear, textured, sandblasted and printed styles.

Officers: John P. Behrenberg, Sr. *P & CEO*
John P. Behrenberg, Jr. *Production MGR*

Total Employees	35	**Regional Employees**	35
Year Established	1923	**SIC Code**	3231
Annual Revenues ($000)	1,750		

B

Bell Atlantic NYNEX Mobile

5700 Corporate Dr., Ste. 700
Pittsburgh, PA 15237
County: Allegheny

Phone: (412) 635-2000
Fax: (412) 369-8151
Internet Address: www.banm.com

Provider of wireless service claiming to be the largest such provider on the East Coast and the second largest in the United States. Headquartered in Bedminster, NJ, the Company was formed in July 1995 by combining the mobile cellular operations of Bell Atlantic Corp. and NYNEX Corp. The Company owns and operates a wireless network covering 111,000 square miles and a chain of wireless retail outlets, offering a full range of wireless personal communications services, including voice, data and paging. The Company's local facilities include its regional headquarters located at the above address; switching office/engineering sites in Bridgeville and Pittsburgh, PA; and 16 retail stores throughout Western Pennsylvania along with two sales kiosks in Wal-Mart stores in St. Mary's, PA, and Weston, WV. The Company planned to relocate to a new facility during the Fall of 1997, at 200 Allegheny Dr. in Warrendale, PA 15086.

Officers: Jerald Fountain *Regional VP-Pittsburgh*

Human Resources: Dana Keefer

Purchasing: Joseph Reilly

Total Employees	6,500+	**Regional Employees**	275
Year Established	1983	**SIC Code**	4812
Annual Revenues ($000)	2,500,000		

Bell Atlantic-Pennsylvania, Inc.

201 Stanwix St.
Pittsburgh, PA 15222
County: Allegheny

Phone: (412) 633-3248
Fax: (412) 633-2672
Internet Address: www.bell-atl.com

Provider of telecommunications and related services to customers throughout Pennsylvania. The Company, which is headquartered in Philadelphia, PA, is an operating segment of Bell Atlantic Corp., which is also headquartered in Philadelphia, PA, and listed on the NYSE. The Company operates numerous facilities located throughout the Pittsburgh metropolitan area.

Officers: Olive M. Bell *VP & GMGR-Greater Pittsburgh District*

Total Employees	63,000	**Regional Employees**	3,800
Year Established	1878	**SIC Code**	4813
Annual Revenues ($000)	13,081,400		

Bell Federal Savings and Loan Assn. of Bellevue

532 Lincoln Ave.
Pittsburgh, PA 15202
County: Allegheny

Phone: (412) 734-2700

Customer-oriented savings and loan association engaged in attracting retail deposits from the general public and investing those funds primarily in fixed-rate, owner-occupied, single-family conventional mortgage loans and, to a much lesser extent, residential construction loans, multifamily loans and consumer loans. The Bank's revenues are derived from interest on conventional mortgage loans, interest and dividends on investment securities and short-term investments, and other fees and service charges. Its primary source of funds is deposits and borrowings from the Federal Home Loan Bank. The Bank's primary market area is the territory surrounding its offices, while its lending activities extend throughout Allegheny County and bordering towns located in Armstrong, Beaver, Butler, Washington and Westmoreland Counties, PA. In addition to its principal office in Bellevue located at the above address, the Bank operates six other retail offices, all of which are located in Allegheny County (Mt. Lebanon, Oakland, downtown Pittsburgh, Ross Township, Sewickley and Wexford). The Bank is a subsidiary of First Bell Bancorp, Inc., which is headquartered in Wilmington, DE, and listed on the NASDAQ.

Officers: Albert H. Eckert II *P & CEO*
Jeffrey M. Hinds *EVP & CFI*
William D. Adams *VP*

Human Resources: Jeffrey A. Spindler *MGR-Human Resources*

Total Employees 65	**Regional Employees** 65		
Year Established 1891	**SIC Code** 6035		
Annual Revenues ($000) 709,000			

B

Berkley Surgical Corp.

Barton Mill Rd.
P.O. Box 1127
Uniontown, PA 15401
County: Fayette

Phone: (412) 438-3000
Fax: (412) 438-3046

Manufacturer of surgical masks marketed to domestic and international markets, including hospitals and dentists' offices. The Company is a division of Berkley Medical Resources, Inc., which is headquartered in West Palm Beach, FL.

Officers: John Berkley *OWN & P*
Ted Michaelis *EVP*
Dom Tommarello *VP & GMGR*

Human Resources: Ron Victor *Human Resources MGR*

Regional Employees 100	
Year Established 1997	**SIC Code** 3842

Berry Metal Co.

2408 Evans City Rd.
Harmony, PA 16037
County: Butler

Phone: (412) 452-8040
Fax: (412) 452-4115

Manufacturer of lances used to refine molten metal for nonferrous steelmaking applications. The Company's products include water cooled oxygen lances, double flow lances, post combustion lances, sensor lances, special purpose lances, combined blowing lances, and solids/oxygen injection lances for basic oxygen furnaces, electric arc furnaces and Q-BOP. It also provides steelmakers with engineering, and technical support and service. In addition to the Company's main plant which is located at the above address, it operates repair shops in LaPorte, IN, and Charleston, SC.

Officers: Theodore J. Leczo *P*
Nick Rymarchyk, Jr. *VP*

Human Resources: Richard L. McCafferty

Purchasing: Judith L. Kelly

Total Employees............................106   Regional Employees 91
Year Established 1965   SIC Code.....................................3443

Best Feeds & Farm Supplies, Inc.

106 Seminary Ave.
P.O. Box 246
Oakdale, PA 15071
County: Allegheny

Phone: (412) 693-9417
Fax: (412) 693-8101

Manufacturer of pet foods for dogs and cats marketed under the brand names Demand and Joy to customers throughout the United States, Canada, Iceland, Japan and Mexico. The Company operates plants at 100 Union Ave. in Oakdale, PA, and in West Plains, MO.

Officers: Russell N. Kohser II *P*

Human Resources: Frank Dean *Plant MGR*

Total Employees............................100
Year Established 1945   SIC Code.....................................2047

Bethel Bakery, Inc.

5200 Brightwood Rd.
Bethel Park, PA 15102
County: Allegheny

Phone: (412) 835-6658
Fax: (412) 835-7084

Bakery offering a broad range of baked goods, including bread and rolls, muffins, danish rolls, sweet rolls, cookies, a variety of sweets and desserts, danish dough coffeecakes, sweet dough coffeecakes, pan rolls, donuts, pudding cakes and pies.

Officers: John S. Walsh *P*

Human Resources: Christine T. Walsh *VP & SEC*

Purchasing: Chuck Jury

Total Employees............................50   Regional Employees 50
Year Established 1955   SIC Code.....................................5461

Betsy Ann Chocolates, Inc.

322 Perry Hwy.
Pittsburgh, PA 15229
County: Allegheny

Phone: (412) 931-4288
Fax: (412) 931-9777

Producer, wholesaler and retailer of chocolates and a line of truffles for the consumer and corporate gift markets. Its candy is sold by mail order and through retail stores, including five Company-owned stores located throughout the Pittsburgh metropolitan area and one franchised store located in the South Hills area of Pittsburgh. To a smaller extent, the Company also markets its products to a network of wholesalers in Illinois, Maryland, Michigan, New York, Ohio and West Virginia.

Officers: James D. Paras *P*
              Daniel Paras *VP*

Human Resources: Karen Paras

Total Employees............................100	**Regional Employees** 100
Year Established 1938	**SIC Code**.....................................2064
Annual Revenues ($000) 2,500	

Bev-O-Matic Corp.

127 E. Seventh Ave.
Homestead, PA 15120
County: Allegheny

Phone: (412) 461-6400
Fax: (412) 461-4120

Manufacturer and operator of vending machines.

Officers: Leslie Frank *P*

Total Employees............................150
SIC Code 3581

Blattner/Brunner, Inc.

One Oxford Centre, 301 Grant St., 6th Fl.
Pittsburgh, PA 15219
County: Allegheny

Phone: (412) 263-2979
Fax: (412) 263-2126

Full-service advertising, marketing and public relations firm specializing in fully integrated communications programs for a variety of business-to-business, consumer and health care clients. The Agency also offers data base marketing, sales promotion and interactive communications services.

Officers: Joseph Blattner *CEO*
Michael J. Brunner *P (Purchasing)*

Human Resources: Rick Booth

Total Employees............55	**Regional Employees**..........55
Year Established..........1979	**SIC Code**..........7311
Annual Revenues ($000) ....35,000 (Billings)	

Blazer Diamond Products, Inc.

7650 Rte. 30
Irwin, PA 15642
County: Westmoreland

Phone: (412) 863-2249
Fax: (412) 864-6460
Internet Address: www.blazerdiamond.com

Manufacturer of diamond saw blades, core bits, saws and core drilling machines. The Company's products are primarily sold to construction supply distributors for a variety of applications, including highway work, building renovation, and concrete testing and sampling.

Officers: Paul E. Merlin *P*
Joe Budyka *VP-OPR*
Christopher P. Merlin *VP-MKT*
Jim Osborne *Customer Service*

Human Resources: Nancy Merlin

Purchasing: Phil Kochasic

Total Employees............30	**Regional Employees**..........30
Year Established..........1981	**SIC Code**..........3545
Annual Revenues ($000)..........5,000+	

Bloom Engineering Co., Inc.

5460 Horning Rd.
Pittsburgh, PA 15236
County: Allegheny

Phone: (412) 653-3500
Fax: (412) 653-2253
Internet Address: www.bloomeng.com

Designer and manufacturer of industrial gas and oil-fired burners and related equipment, including Ka-Weld® custom-designed insulation shapes used to insulate water-cooled parts in reheat furnaces. The Company operates sales offices in San Francisco, CA; Chicago, IL; Cleveland, OH; Philadelphia, PA; and Carrollton, TX. Its subsidiaries include Process Combustion Corp., which is also located at the above address, a designer and manufacturer of air pollution equipment, such as thermal oxidizers; and Bloom Engineering (Europa) GmbH, in Dusseldorf, Germany, a manufacturer of burners and related equipment, with sales offices in Paris, France, and Genoa, Italy. The Company is a subsidiary of Sterling Industries Plc, which is headquartered in Somerset, England, and listed on the London Stock Exchange.

B

Officers: James E. Johns *P & CEO*
Harry P. Finke *VP-Technical Services*
John P. Watkins *VP-SAL*
Joseph M. Mazzetti *Plant Superintendent*
W. Philip Goodboy *MGR-ENG*

Human Resources: David G. Todd

Purchasing: William D. Quattro

Total Employees............................150	**Regional Employees** 135
Year Established 1934	**SIC Code**......................................3433

Blumcraft of Pittsburgh

460 Melwood Ave.
Pittsburgh, PA 15213
County: Allegheny

Phone: (412) 681-2400
Fax: (412) 681-6840

   Manufacturer of tempered glass doors and related hardware, and railings for fine buildings. While the majority of the Company's clients are in the U.S., it does receive orders from other parts of the world.

Officers: Harry P. Blum *PTR*
Louis Blum *PTR*
Max Blum *PTR*

Purchasing: Joseph Locascio

Total Employees.............................70	**Regional Employees** 70
Year Established 1914	**SIC Code**......................................3231

Bobby J's, Inc.

5935 Broad St.
Pittsburgh, PA 15206
County: Allegheny

Phone: (412) 363-5261
Fax: (412) 363-5266

Provider of cosmetology, educational training and video production services operating through three divisions. Bobby J's Hair Fashion Studios, at 404 Wood St. and 9725 Frankstown Rd. in Pittsburgh, offer cosmetology services. Bobby J's The Academy, at 205 N. Highland Ave. in Pittsburgh, is a licensed and certified school offering a cosmetology program. Bobby J's Video Productions, also located at the above address, offers video production, editing and duplication services.

Officers: Bobby J. Hunt *P*
Kelly Allen *AST-Systems MGR*

Human Resources: Stephanie R. Jackson *Systems MGR (Purchasing)*

Total Employees............................55	**Regional Employees** 55
Year Established 1984	**SIC Code**.....................................7231

Bohlin Cywinski Jackson

307 Fourth Ave., Ste. 1300
Pittsburgh, PA 15222
County: Allegheny

Phone: (412) 765-3890
Fax: (412) 765-2209

Provider of architectural services including site and master planning, feasibility studies, programming, interior design and historic preservation/restoration. The Firm's clients range from individual residences to major corporate, institutional and public facilities. Other offices are located in Philadelphia and Wilkes-Barre, PA; and Seattle, WA.

Officers: Peter Bohlin *Principal*
Bernard Cywinski *Principal*
Frank Grauman *Principal*
Dan Haden *Principal*
Jon Jackson *Principal*

Total Employees..............................65	**Regional Employees** 29
Year Established 1965	**SIC Code**.....................................8712

Bon Tool Co.

4430 Gibsonia Rd.
Gibsonia, PA 15044
County: Allegheny

Phone: (412) 443-7080
Fax: (412) 443-7090

Manufacturer and distributor of construction hand tools and light equipment for the building trades. The Company's product line includes more than 3,000 items for masonry, concrete, drywall, tile setting, roofing, flooring and plastering purposes. Its products are sold nationally.

Officers: Carl Bongiovanni *P*
John Wight *SAL*

Purchasing: Sean Helman

Total Employees	35	**Regional Employees**	35
Year Established	1957	**SIC Code**	3423

Bowman, Inc., E. W.

Pittsburgh Rd.
P.O. Box 849
Uniontown, PA 15401
County: Fayette

Phone: (412) 438-0503
Fax: (412) 439-5880

Manufacturer of annealing lehrs, decorating lehrs, TV lehrs, bending lehrs and kilns. The Company's 56,000 square foot factory was designed specifically for the fabrication and assembly of its product line used in the manufacture of TV glass, glass bottles, light bulbs and tableware. More than 1,200 of the Company's lehrs and kilns are in service on six continents around the world.

Officers: James A. Ulmer *P*
Richard C. Standish *CFO*
Leo Mangold *Plant MGR*
Fred K. Davis *Chief ENG*
Martha F. Korona *Executive SEC*

Human Resources: Barry S. Mortichesky *VP-ADM*

Purchasing: William R. Ulmer *Purchasing DIR*

Total Employees	133	**Regional Employees**	133
Year Established	1950	**SIC Code**	3567

Bradley Center, The

522 Saxonburg Rd.
Pittsburgh, PA 15238
County: Allegheny

Phone: (412) 767-5460
Fax: (412) 767-5620

Nonprofit charitable organization providing treatment for abused, neglected and troubled children and families. The Organization's services include residential treatment, therapeutic foster care, supervised independent living, home-based treatment services, a partial hospitalization program, school-based support services, child and family therapy, and a therapeutic summer day program. The Organization operates two other facilities in Pittsburgh at 1789 S. Braddock Ave. (foster care services) and 135 Cumberland Rd. (day treatment for adolescents).

Officers: Walter H. Goedeke *EDIR*
Dawn Comorat *DIR-Outpatient Services*
Henry F. Gonsowski *DIR-Residential Treatment Facility*
Bernadette Hughes *DIR-Therapeutic Foster Care*
Daniel P. Hunt *DIR-OPR*
Kathleen A. Lynch *DIR-DEV & Community Relations*
Gary S. Phillips *DIR-Residential Treatment Center*

Human Resources: Christine M. Steinle

Purchasing: Christine Klingensmith

Total Employees............................163	**Regional Employees** 163
Year Established 1905	**SIC Code**......................................8361

Braeburn Alloy Steel

101 Braeburn Rd.
New Kensington, PA 15068
County: Westmoreland

Phone: (412) 224-6900
Fax: (412) 224-1958

Provider of toll conversion services to the specialty steel and metals market. The Company presses, forges and hot rolls customers' materials into various shapes and forms. The Company claims that it is the sole "conversion-only" metals facility successfully in operation in the U.S. today. The Company is a division of C. C. X., Inc., which is headquartered in Charlotte, NC.

Officers: Richard A. Rinaldi *P & CEO*
Barry Anderson *VP-MFG*
Morris Kubitz *VP & CON*
Clem F. Templeton *VP-SAL & MKT*

Human Resources: Tom Evanowski

Purchasing: Rosemarie Bielata

Total Employees	100	**Regional Employees**	100
Year Established	1897	**SIC Code**	3462
Annual Revenues ($000)	10-20,000		

B

Brayman Construction Corp.

3503 Gibsonia Rd.
Gibsonia, PA 15044
County: Allegheny

Phone: (412) 443-1533
Fax: (412) 443-8733

General contractor providing heavy highway construction services. The Company specializes in bridges, reinforced concrete box culverts, reinforced concrete arch culverts and demolition. Its Foundation Division constructs caissons, piling, sheet piling and cofferdams. The Company's customers include the Pennsylvania Department of Transportation, Pennsylvania Turnpike Commission, Conrail, various county and city governments, and other private firms. Its Foundation Division provides services to the building construction sector, as well as the heavy highway market. The Company's service area comprises Eastern Ohio, Western Pennsylvania and Northern West Virginia.

Officers: Stephen M. Muck *P & CEO*
John F. Hughes *VP*
Deborah G. Muck *SEC*
Michael K. Bechtold *CON*
William E. Hanlon *AST-TRS & AST-SEC*
Francis A. Mannella *Foundation Division*

Total Employees	70-125	**Regional Employees**	70-125
Year Established	1958	**SIC Code**	1622
Annual Revenues ($000)	15-25,000		

Bricmont, Inc.

Southpointe Industrial Park, 500 Technology Dr.
Canonsburg, PA 15317
County: Washington

Phone: (412) 746-2300
Fax: (412) 746-9420
Internet Address: www.bricmont.pgh.pa.us.com

Provider of engineering and design/build services. The Company's engineering services consist of feasibility/planning studies, furnace optimization studies, layout/conceptual design studies, field engineering, start-up assistance, cost estimating, furnace inspection/evaluation and energy audits. Its design/build services consist of complete engineering for design and construction of industrial furnaces and related equipment; project engineering and detailed design of furnaces and mechanical handling equipment; project management, cost control, detailed schedule control, procurement/purchasing, expediting/inspection and construction management; and turnkey installation of continuous processing lines, thin cast strip facilities, walking hearth and walking beam furnaces, continuous pusher furnaces, coil annealing furnaces, rotary hearth furnaces, roller hearth, and batch type furnaces for reheating and heat treating of ferrous and nonferrous metals. The Company also provides analysis and consulting services consisting of applied finite element analysis, including heat transfer and thermal stress, thermodynamic analysis, failure analysis, structural analysis, high temperature materials technology and heating process development. In addition, it provides training, which consists of maintenance and operations training for blast furnaces and stoves, electric arc furnaces, continuous casters, soaking pits, reheat furnaces, heat treat furnaces, boilers and rolling mills. The Company is a subsidiary of Inductotherm, Inc., which is headquartered in Rancocas, NJ.

Officers: William M. Goodlin *CEO*
David C. Gilbert *SVP-MKT & SAL*
F. Lang Marks *SVP-OPR*

Human Resources: Robert M. Amic *CFO*

Purchasing: Van Stragand

Total Employees..................100	**Regional Employees** 100
Year Established 1966	**SIC Code**.........................8711
Annual Revenues ($000) 40,000	

BRIDGES pbt

1300 Brighton Rd.
Pittsburgh, PA 15233
County: Allegheny

Phone: (412) 321-5400
Fax: (412) 321-9823

General contractor providing design/build, construction management and project development services. The Company performs new construction and renovation work for such sectors as commercial, retail, light industrial, nonresidential and health care (hospitals, nursing homes, elderly housing and personal care facilities). It serves clients within a 300-mile radius of Pittsburgh, PA.

Officers: Paul R. Bridges *CH*
Glenn A. Gates *P*
Mark A. Davis *VP*

Total Employees..................150	**Regional Employees** 150
Year Established 1983	**SIC Code**.........................1542
Annual Revenues ($000) 24,000	

Brookside Lumber & Supply Co., Inc.

500 Logan Rd.
P.O. Box 327
Bethel Park, PA 15102
County: Allegheny

Phone: (412) 341-3600
Fax: (412) 835-8672
Internet Address: www.cyberyard.com

Retailer of building products including kitchen and bath cabinets, windows, patio doors, interior and entrance doors, moldings, a variety of plywoods, deck lumber, interior stair railing and accessories, siding (vinyl and wood) and lumber. The Company also offers professional installation services for many of its products.

Officers: Bruce Edwards *P*

Total Employees	82	**Regional Employees**	82
Year Established	1926	**SIC Code**	5211

Broudy Printing, Inc.

223 Auburn St.
P.O. Box 5248
Pittsburgh, PA 15206
County: Allegheny

Phone: (412) 362-6700
Fax: (412) 362-7788

Commercial printer offering direct mail, in-house color scanning, media conversion, electronic image retouch, page make-up, desktop publishing and in-house bindery services. The Company also provides fulfillment services. Its clients include universities, health care organizations and major corporations as well as designers and marketing communication professionals.

Officers: Adrienne Mallet *P*
Herbert Mallet *VP*

Total Employees	46	**Regional Employees**	46
Year Established	1958	**SIC Code**	2759
Annual Revenues ($000)	10,200		

Brown & Root Environmental

Foster Plaza VII, 661 Andersen Dr.
Pittsburgh, PA 15220
County: Allegheny

Phone: (412) 921-7090
Fax: (412) 921-7152
Internet Address: www.halliburton.com/bar/barinfo.htm

Provider of engineering design and construction management services; remediation design and implementation; regulatory assessment, negotiation support and permitting; subsurface investigations and feasibility studies; risk assessment and multi-media modeling; comprehensive industrial hygiene and safety consulting and training services; and air quality management services. The Company's total environmental services include investigations, assessments, development of alternatives, design and construction management for civil and environmental projects. The Company, which is headquartered in Houston, TX, operates a number of branch offices serving clients throughout the U.S. and the world. It is a division of Brown & Root, Inc. (B&RI), which is also headquartered in Houston, TX. B&RI is a subsidiary of Halliburton Co., which is headquartered in Dallas, TX, and listed on the NYSE.

Officers: Robert Warters *P*
Donald Senovich, Sr. *SVP & Regional MGR*
Sally Dines *MGR-FIN & Accounting*
Jon Heitmeier *MGR-Business DEV*
Donald Nusser *MGR-Industrial Programs*

Human Resources: Marilyn Diethorn

Purchasing: Shawn Scaff

Total Employees	1,000	**Regional Employees**	140
Year Established	1960	**SIC Code**	8711

Browning-Ferris Industries Pennsylvania, Inc.

W. Noblestown Rd.
P.O. Box 448
Carnegie, PA 15106
County: Allegheny

Phone: (412) 429-2600
Fax: (412) 429-8867
Internet Address: www.bfi.com

Provider of refuse collection, refuse recycling and disposal of medical waste services to hospitals, doctors' offices, malls and restaurants in the Tri-State area. The Company, doing business as BFI Pittsburgh, operates the BFI Recyclery on

28th and Smallman Sts. in Pittsburgh and a recyclery at the above address, as well as the BFI Imperial Landfill in Imperial, PA. The Company is a subsidiary of Browning-Ferris Industries, Inc., which is headquartered in Houston, TX, and listed on the NYSE.

B

Officers: Jeff Sanislo *Disrict VP*

Total Employees	185	**Regional Employees**	185
Year Established	1969	**SIC Code**	4953
Annual Revenues ($000)	22,000		

Brownsville Health Services Corp.

125 Simpson Rd.
Brownsville, PA 15417
County: Fayette

Phone: (412) 785-7200
Fax: (412) 785-1888

Nonprofit operator of the Brownsville General Hospital, a 119-bed facility with over 100 physicians representing 30 medical specialties. The hospital, also located at the above address, offers a full range of inpatient services including acute adult and pediatric care, a skilled nursing unit and a geriatric psychiatric unit; outpatient services; same day surgery; and state-of-the-art diagnostic and therapeutic services. The Company's for-profit subsidiary, West Point Health Corp., also located at the above address, operates a medical office complex, physician billing service, and an off-site laboratory and health education center.

Officers: Richard D. Constantine, Jr. *CEO*
Joy Z. Zeiner *CFO*
Karen L. Dei Cas *DIR-MKT & Public Relations*
Darlene Ferguson *DIR-Nursing*

Human Resources: Alvin W. Allison, Jr. *Associate Administrator & DIR-Human Resources*

Purchasing: Edward Kaczmarczyk

Total Employees	350	**Regional Employees**	325
Year Established	1916	**SIC Code**	8062
Annual Revenues ($000)	40,300		

Bryan Mechanical, Inc.

339 Rochester Rd.
Pittsburgh, PA 15237
County: Allegheny

Phone: (412) 364-3400
Fax: (412) 367-4979

Mechanical contractor providing new construction in heating, ventilation and air conditioning, as well as process piping and underground pipe work. The Company also offers repair and maintenance services, and operates a pipe fabrication shop. It maintains a branch office in Greensburg, PA. The Company serves commercial, industrial and institutional clients in Maryland, Ohio, Pennsylvania, Virginia and West Virginia.

Officers: Nancy M. Bryan *CEO*
John J. Sirc *P*
Gregory A. Jack *Division VP*
Barry K. Litman *Division VP*
Brian R. McKay *Division VP*

Human Resources: Mark M. Connor *VP & CFO*

Purchasing: William Reichenecker

Total Employees	125	**Regional Employees**	125
Year Established	1984	**SIC Code**	1711
Annual Revenues ($000)	25,000		

BT Office Products International, Inc.

79 N. Industrial Park
P.O. Box 9339, Pittsburgh, PA 15225
Sewickley, PA 15143
County: Allegheny

Phone: (412) 741-6494
Fax: (412) 749-8728
Internet Address: www.btopi.com

Distributor of a full-range of office products, including traditional office supplies, office furniture, computer supplies and accessories, copiers and office equipment, business forms, and advertising specialty and promotional products. The Company, which is headquartered in Buffalo Grove, IL, is listed on the NYSE. The Pittsburgh Division, located at the above address, serves clients in the Tri-State area. It operates a branch office in Cleveland, OH. The Pittsburgh Division is a part of the Company's Midwest Region.

Officers: John R. Kennedy *P*
Joseph Aiello *VP-OPR*
Michael Malone *VP-SAL & MKT*

Human Resources: Jeanne L. Beers *Human Resources MGR*

Purchasing: David E. O'Malley *Distribution Center DIR*

Total Employees	6,600	**Regional Employees**	165
Year Established	1933	**SIC Code**	5112
Annual Revenues ($000)			1,412,500

B

BTI Americas, Inc.

The Law & Finance Bldg., 429 Fourth Ave., Ste. 604
Pittsburgh, PA 15219
County: Allegheny

Phone: (412) 255-6181
Fax: (412) 255-0336

Full-service travel agency, primarily dealing with corporate clients. The Firm's specialties include single-source global management, consultative management services, information technology and business meetings. The Company is headquartered in Northbrook, IL. It operates several other offices in the Pittsburgh metropolitan area located on-site at the facilities of major customers.

Officers: Louise T. Miller *VP*

Total Employees	3,000	**Regional Employees**	80
Year Established	1970	**SIC Code**	4724
Annual Revenues ($000)			4,000,000

Buchanan Ingersoll P.C.

One Oxford Centre, 301 Grant St., 20th Fl.
Pittsburgh, PA 15219
County: Allegheny

Phone: (412) 562-8800
Fax: (412) 562-1041
Internet Address: www.bipc.com

Provider of legal services with more than 250 attorneys. The Firm claims that it is one of the two oldest large commercial law firms in continuous practice in Pennsylvania and among the largest law firms in the mid-Atlantic region. The Firm provides counsel in these areas: beverage industry, broadcasting and cable television, commercial transactions, computer law, construction industry law, corporate law and finance, creditors' rights and bankruptcy, energy, environmental law, ERISA and employee benefits, family law, financial institutions, franchising, government relations, health care, insurance regulation, intellectual property, international transactions, labor and employment, litigation, mergers and acquisitions, municipal law, natural resource law, public finance, real estate, security alarm, tax and estate planning, technology law, trade regulation, trade secret litigation, transportation law and venture capital. The

Firm's clients range from individuals and start-up companies to private and publicly held institutions and multinational conglomerates, including over 50 of the Fortune 500 industrial corporations. It operates branch offices in Miami and Tampa, FL; Lexington, KY; Princeton, NJ; Buffalo, NY; and Harrisburg and Philadelphia, PA. In addition, affiliate offices are located in Belgium and England.

Officers: William R. Newlin *MDIR*
Thomas L. VanKirk *Administrative DIR*

Total Employees............................582	**Regional Employees** 365
Year Established........................1850	**SIC Code** 8111

Buck Consultants, Inc.

USX Tower, 600 Grant St., Ste. 4918
Pittsburgh, PA 15219
County: Allegheny

Phone: (412) 281-2506
Fax: (412) 394-4094
Internet Address: www.buckconsultants.com

Employee-owned employee benefit, actuarial and compensation consulting firm servicing 5,000 pension and other benefit plans for employers in all 50 states and throughout the world. The Firm's services include actuarial consulting, health and welfare consulting, defined contribution plan recordkeeping, outsourcing and administrative functions, communication consulting and compensation consulting. Its clients range from some of the world's largest utilities and industrial corporations to small businesses, and include not-for-profit organizations, a large number of state and local government retirement systems, and several national and international quasi-governmental organizations. Together, the plans served by the Firm cover more than 10 million active and retired employees and have assets totaling over $400 billion. The Firm, which is headquartered in New York, NY, operates more than 60 offices worldwide.

Officers: William E. Giegerich, Jr. *CH*
Joseph A. LoCicero *P & CEO*
William Daniels *Consulting Actuary-Pittsburgh*

Human Resources: M. Michael Brackley

Purchasing: William Daniels

Total Employees ....2,500+	**Regional Employees** 75
Year Established 1916	**SIC Code**....................................8748
Annual Revenues ($000) 228,000	

Buhl Optical Co.

1009 Beech Ave.
Pittsburgh, PA 15233
County: Allegheny

Phone: (412) 321-0076
Fax: (412) 322-2640

Manufacturer of projection lenses and other optical equipment. The Company's products include projection lenses for LCD video projectors, 35mm slide projectors and custom lenses; custom overhead projectors for corporate boardrooms, meeting and conference centers, and military briefing rooms; and radiographic projectors for hospitals and the medical industry. It operates an additional manufacturing site in St. Petersburg, FL. In March 1997, the Company was acquired by Navitar Optical Inc., which is headquartered in Rochester, NY.

Officers: Frank Caracciolo *P*

Total Employees..............................35
Year Established 1935

Regional Employees 35
SIC Code 3827

Buncher Co., The

5600 Forward Ave.
P.O. Box 81930
Pittsburgh, PA 15217
County: Allegheny

Phone: (412) 422-9900
Fax: (412) 422-1298

Developer and lessor of business facilities for use as administrative offices, data and technical centers, distribution, warehousing and light manufacturing. These facilities range from 20,000 to 350,000 square feet blocks of existing, customizable and built-to-suit business space. In Southwestern Pennsylvania, the Company's properties include full-service industrial/commercial parks and stand-alone facilities within the City of Pittsburgh, including the Strip District, Allegheny, Beaver and Westmoreland counties. The Company's branch offices are located in the Buncher Industrial District in Leetsdale, PA; Buncher Youngwood Commerce Park in Youngwood, PA; and the Tri-County Commerce Park in New Sewickley Township, PA. Through its two subsidiaries, Multi-Service RR Supply Co. in Leetsdale, PA, and Buncher Rail Car Services Co. in Lynchburg, VA, the Company provides railcar repair services and remanufactured brake system components for railcars and locomotives.

Officers: Jack G. Buncher *CH*
Herbert S. Green *VCH*
Thomas J. Balestrieri *P*

Human Resources: Ruth H. Neff *Administrative MGR*

Regional Employees....................100
Year Established 1918   **SIC Code**....................................6552

Bunting Inc.

409 W. Warrington Ave.
Pittsburgh, PA 15210
County: Allegheny

Phone: (412) 481-0445
Fax: (412) 481-1506

Provider of products and services for the industrial identification market. The Company manufactures pipe and valve identification, engraved and stamped metal tags, etched products, nameplates, bar-coded labeling systems, safety signs, software for asset, inventory and tool tracking, safety signs and tags, as well as rubber stamping products. Its custom services include art, layout and design, screen printing, etching, and engraving and stamping. The Company's affiliate, Bunting Graphics, Inc. at 20 River Rd. in Verona, PA, with approximately 15 employees, produces exterior and interior signage for commercial, educational and institutional facilities such as hotels, hospitals, universities, parking garages, arenas, theaters, restaurants and office buildings. It also provides signage consultation services to determine sign specifications and locations, and Americans With Disabilities Act requirement analysis of each facility.

Officers: Jody P. Bunting *P*
Andrew W. Bunting *VP*

Purchasing: Kim Morris

Total Employees...........................100   **Regional Employees** 100
Year Established 1869   **SIC Code**....................................3993

Burns and Roe Services Corp.

P.O. Box 18288
Pittsburgh, PA 15236

County: Allegheny

Phone: (412) 892-4701
Fax: (412) 892-4736
Internet Address: 206.3.152.100/products.htm

Principal support service contractor to the U.S. Department of Energy's Federal Energy Technology Center, a facility that conducts and manages research projects to develop advanced technologies applicable to fossil energy and the environment. The Company provides engineering, computer systems, public relations and maintenance support services to the facility. The Company, which is headquartered in Oradell, NJ, is a subsidiary of Burns and Roe Enterprises, Inc. (BREI), which is also headquartered in Oradell, NJ. BREI is a full-service engineering and construction organization with a worldwide customer base.

B

Officers: Donald P. Daley *Project DIR*

Human Resources: Michael Lynch *(Oradell, NJ)*

Purchasing: Michael Clark *(Oradell, NJ)*

Total Employees .... 2,000+	**Regional Employees** 100
Year Established 1932	**SIC Code** 8711

Burns International Security Services

Parkway Center Inn, Ste. 785
Pittsburgh, PA 15220
County: Allegheny

Phone: (412) 922-2331
Fax: (412) 928-9435

   Provider of an array of security-related services, ranging from contract security personnel for patrolling all types of facilities to drug screening kits, criminal records checks, credit checks, driver's license reports, social security verification and security analysis/surveys. The Company also offers temporary and emergency services and strike coverage. In addition, it provides mail room services. The Company, which is headquartered in Parsippany, NJ, operates branch offices throughout the nation. It is a unit of Borg-Warner Protective Services Corp. (BWPSC), which is also headquartered in Parsippany, NJ. BWPSC is a subsidiary of Borg-Warner Security Corp., which is headquartered in Chicago, IL, and listed on the NYSE. The local office serves clients in the Tri-State area.

Officers: Michael Kochan *GMGR*

Regional Employees 515	
Year Established 1909	**SIC Code** 7381

Burns, White & Hickton

Fifth Avenue Place, 120 Fifth Ave., Ste. 2400
Pittsburgh, PA 15222
County: Allegheny

Phone: (412) 394-2500
Fax: (412) 281-1352

   Provider of legal services with 40 attorneys. The Firm's practice areas include general litigation, workers' compensation, corporate, labor and employment, energy, estates and trusts, domestic relations, municipal law, contract negotiations and alternative dispute resolution. It maintains branch offices located in San Francisco, CA, and Wheeling, WV.

Officers: David A. Damico *Executive MEM*
David J. Hickton *Executive MEM*
Lisa Pupo Lenihan *Executive MEM*
David B. White *Executive MEM*
Steven P. Franckhauser *MEM*
Randy K. Hareza *MEM*
Charles G. Manoli, Jr. *MEM*
Robert J. Ray *MEM*
Robert L. Schneider *MEM*

Human Resources: Michael W. Burns *Executive MEM*

Purchasing: Pat Goheen

Total Employees............................110	**Regional Employees** 100
Year Established 1987	**SIC Code** 8111

Burson-Marsteller

One Gateway Center, Ste. 2000
Pittsburgh, PA 15222
County: Allegheny

Phone: (412) 471-9600
Fax: (412) 394-6610
Internet Address: www.bm.com

Provider of a full-range of advertising, public relations and public affairs services, including strategy development, corporate communications, marketing communications, employee relations, public affairs/government relations, media relations, issues management, crisis preparedness and management, and corporate and business-to-business advertising. These disciplines are carried out through the Agency's eight practice areas: advertising, corporate ,government & emerging markets, health care, marketing, media, public affairs and technology. It serves a diverse body of clients ranging from major corporations, business associations and professional organizations to governmental entities and nonprofit institutions. The Agency, which is headquartered in New York, NY, operates offices in more than 35 countries. It is a subsidiary of Young & Rubicam, L.P., which is also headquartered in New York, NY.

Officers: Harold Burson *CH*
Thomas D. Bell, Jr. *P & CEO*
Laura J. Gongos *EVP & MDIR-Pittsburgh*
Donna L. Evans *SVP & Client Service MGR*
Jody Lange *SVP & Creative DIR*
Robert A. Sprague *SVP & DIR-Communications Services*

Human Resources: Patricia Langowski *(Chicago, IL)*

Total Employees...................2,200	**Regional Employees** 35	
Year Established 1953	**SIC Code** 7311	
Annual Revenues ($000) 261,000		

B

Burt Hill Kosar Rittelmann Assoc.

650 Smithfield St., Ste. 2600
Pittsburgh, PA 15222
County: Allegheny

Phone: (412) 394-7000
Fax: (412) 394-7880
Internet Address: www.burthill.com

Architectural, engineering and interior design firm specializing in commercial office, retail, health care, high-tech and educational facilities, as well as historic renovation and adaptive reuse. With additional offices located in Washington, D.C., and Butler and Philadelphia, PA, the Firm has staff of approximately 58 registered architects, 21 licensed engineers and 13 certified interior designers.

Special Designations: ENR_{500}

Officers: John E. Kosar *DIR*
Frank G. McCurdy *DIR*
Peter H. Moriarty *DIR*
P. Richard Rittelmann *DIR*
Paul W. Scanlon *DIR*
William P. Brennan *Managing Principal-Pittsburgh, PA*
John E. Brock *Managing Principal-Butler, PA*
Harry T. Gordon *Managing Principal-Washington, D.C.*
Stephen Jones *Senior Associate-Philadelphia, PA*

Human Resources: Cecil J. Tranquill, Ph.D.

Total Employees...................246	**Regional Employees** 191	
Year Established 1936	**SIC Code** 8712	
Annual Revenues ($000) 22,800		

Business Forms, Inc.

1610 Fourth St.
P.O. Box 611
Monongahela, PA 15063
County: Washington

Phone: (412) 258-7200
Fax: (412) 258-8548
Internet Address: www.bforms.com

Producer of custom-printed forms and checks in continuous, unit set and laser cut sheet format. The Company provides full in-house composition, typesetting and high resolution imagesetting from a variety of graphic software packages. It also offers warehouse distribution services, including pick-and-pack distribution to reselling customers. The Company operates six web offset presses with up to four colors.

Officers: Jonathan W. Shirer *Principal OWN & P*
David K. Stroup *VP & GMGR*

Human Resources: Susan Hartman

Purchasing: Theresa Ninchak

Total Employees............................41	**Regional Employees** 41
Year Established 1951	**SIC Code**....................................2761
Annual Revenues ($000) 4,000	

Business Records Management, Inc.

1018 Western Ave.
Pittsburgh, PA 15233
County: Allegheny

Phone: (412) 321-0600
Fax: (412) 321-5152

Provider of business information management services for all forms of information media. The Company's services include hard copy document storage, computer media storage and rotation, optical imaging (scanning), confidential destruction of all media, information restoration, disaster recovery and business resumption services, on-site training and records management audit services, records management software, and inventory tracking by container, cost allocation, destruction, etc. The Company's disaster recovery services are offered through its BRM/Gateway division, which provides facilities, computer systems and other equipment needed to recover from an unplanned business interruption. The Company serves over 500 companies and organizations from every business sector, including accounting and law firms, health care providers, insurance companies and manufacturers. It operates seven facilities strategically located around Pittsburgh.

Officers: James C. Roddey *P*
George M. Elish *SVP*
Steven B. Wright *VP*

Human Resources: Bill Duke

Purchasing: Cheryl Leicher

Total Employees..............................60	**Regional Employees** 60
Year Established 1985	**SIC Code**......................................4225
Annual Revenues ($000) 5,000	

Butler County Children's Center, Inc.

131 Homewood Dr.
Butler, PA 16001
County: Butler

Phone: (412) 287-2761
Fax: (412) 287-4205

Nonprofit private provider of a variety of child care programs for children from birth through 15 years. The Center's mission is to provide quality child care services which contribute to the well-being of the family. Child care is available for infants, toddlers and preschool children. Licensed as a private academic school, the Center offers a certified kindergarten program and nursery school curriculum. It also offers a before- and after-school program for children in the Butler area and Chicora School Districts; and a summer fun care program and a Teen Trippers program during the summer for children ages 6 through 15. In addition, the Center's Head Start program provides comprehensive educational, nutrition and health services to 233 children, and social and parent involvement services to their parents.

Officers: David P. Baum *P*
Alice Nunes *Program MGR*

Human Resources: Marilyn E. Albert *EDIR*

Purchasing: Marcia Brain Salsbury *CON*

Total Employees...........................100	**Regional Employees** 100
Year Established 1973	**SIC Code**......................................8351
Annual Revenues ($000) 3,000	

Butler County Community College

250 Executive Dr.
Butler, PA 16003
County: Butler

Phone: (412) 287-8711
Fax: (412) 285-6047

Nonprofit, comprehensive two-year college granting the Associate's degree in Arts, Science and Applied Science. The College offers 16 business programs, 16 technology programs, 10 transfer programs and six health and human service programs. Transfer agreements enable students to transfer credits to 27 senior level institutions. The campus consists of 13 buildings situated on 328 acres, one mile south of Butler, PA. In addition, off-campus centers are located in Cranberry Township, Ford City and New Castle, PA. The College enrolls approximately 3,100 students.

Officers: Fred F. Bartok, Ph.D. *P*
Robert J. Chick, Ph.D. *Dean-FIN*
M. Karen Deichert *Dean-ADM*
Robert M. Sanderson, Ph.D. *Dean-Instruction*
Melvin Waisanen, Ph.D. *Dean-Students*
William D. Speidel III *EDIR-Butler County Community College Foundation*
Scott W. Briggs *AST to P*

Total Employees............................280	**Regional Employees** 280
Year Established 1965	**SIC Code**......................................8222
Annual Revenues ($000) 11,300	

Butler Health System

911 E. Brady St.
Butler, PA 16001
County: Butler

Phone: (412) 283-6666
Fax: (412) 284-4645

Nonprofit health care delivery system comprised of four divisions. Butler Health Care Providers consists of Butler Memorial Hospital, which is also located at the above address, and is a 302-bed acute care hospital offering inpatient and outpatient health care services, with 19 skilled nursing beds and 30 bassinettes; Butler Health Trax in Butler, PA, provides physical rehabilitation, wellness and weight management services; Butler Regional Recovery, with facilities at the above address, and in Cranberry Township and Natrona Heights, PA, provides drug and alcohol treatment services; Community Diagnostics, with two facilities in Butler, PA, provides lab testing, urine collection and radiology services; and Family Services of Butler Memorial Hospital, with facilities in Butler, Karns City, Moniteau and Slippery Rock, provides family services. The System's other three divisions, Butler Medical Providers, consists of Butler Medical Assoc., which operates physician practices in Butler, Chicora, Cranberry Township, Evans City and Saxonburg, PA; Butler Memorial Hospital Foundation is the fund-raising arm of the System; and Community Health Planning focuses on planning for the health needs of the community.

B

Officers: Joseph A. Stewart *P & CEO*
Patrick C. Burns *VP-FIN*
Joseph Dado *VP-Information Systems*
John I. Lewis *VP-OPR*
John J. Righetti *VP-Communications*

Human Resources: James C. McManus *VP-Human Resources*

Purchasing: Paul Eberhardt

Total Employees........................1,255	**Regional Employees**................1,255
Year Established 1898	**SIC Code**....................................8062
Annual Revenues ($000) 75,677	

Butler Motor Transit, Inc.

210 S. Monroe St.
P.O. Box 1602, Butler, PA 16003
Butler, PA 16001
County: Butler

Phone: (412) 282-1000
Fax: (412) 282-3080

Operator of a fleet of 33 motorcoaches providing charter service, scheduled escorted tours and sightseeing. The Company, doing business as Butler Motor Tours, offers an array of scheduled escorted tours, ranging from one-day tours to three-week circle tours, to destinations from Alaska and California to Montreal, Quebec, Canada and Washington D.C. It can also customize tours to meet the needs of individual groups, clubs, organizations or conventions. The Company operates a tour division office, doing business as Gad-About Tours of Ohio, in Columbiana, OH, and a branch office in New Kensington, PA. The Company serves clients throughout Eastern Ohio and Western Pennsylvania.

Officers: William G. Kaylor *P*
Thomas M. Kaylor *VP*
Robert M. Kaylor *SEC & TRS*

Total Employees............................79	**Regional Employees** 68
Year Established 1941	**SIC Code**....................................4142

Byrnes & Kiefer Co.

131 Kline Ave.
Callery, PA 16024
County: Butler

Phone: (412) 538-9200
Fax: (412) 538-9292

Manufacturer and distributor of food products for bakeries, institutions, supermarkets and restaurants. The Company's products include food coloring and Reymer's Blennd, an orange-lemon noncarbonated beverage concentrate. Its plant, located at the above address, produces cookie mixes, fillings, icings and bread mixes for industrial baking customers in New York, Ohio, Pennsylvania and West Virginia. Another plant, located in Laguna Hills, CA, produces lemon juice and Chefmaster's brand food color for the home and the baking industry. The Company also maintains a warehouse in Syracuse, NY.

Officers: Edward G. Byrnes, Jr. *P*
Tom Byrnes *VP*
J. Jay Thier *VP-FIN*

Total Employees............................80	**Regional Employees** 45
Year Established 1902	**SIC Code**..2051
Annual Revenues ($000) 18,000

C. H. and D. Enterprises, Inc.

R.D. 1
P.O. Box 334-H
New Stanton, PA 15672
County: Westmoreland

Phone: (412) 925-9832
Fax: (412) 925-9833

Highway contractor providing a variety of services, including excavation, drainage, clearing, grubbing, small bridge construction, paving and sidewalks for clients throughout Southwestern Pennsylvania. An affiliate, Hall Enterprises, Inc., also located at the above address, is engaged in the leasing and rental of equipment.

Officers: Carol H. Brady *P, SEC & TRS (Human Resources & Purchasing)*
Harry H. Brady *VP-OPR*

Total Employees 12-70	**Regional Employees** 12-70
Year Established 1984	**SIC Code** 1611
Annual Revenues ($000) 5,000

C. R. H. Catering Co., Inc.

1600 Morrell Ave.
P.O. Box 757
Connellsville, PA 15425
County: Fayette

Phone: (412) 628-8545
Fax: (412) 628-8523
Internet Address: www.crh-catering.com

Provider of vending machines and food service to commercial, institutional, manufacturing, educational and medical facilities. The Company's operating divisions are located in Cumberland, MD; Greensboro, NC; Altoona, Connellsville and Pittsburgh, PA; Norfolk, VA; and Morgantown, WV.

Officers: Joseph M. Cordaro *P*
John Berardinelli *SAL MGR*

Human Resources: Derwood Bollinger *AST to P (Purchasing)*

Total Employees............................250	**Regional Employees** 60
Year Established 1968	**SIC Code**.....................................3581
Annual Revenues ($000) 26,000	

C. U. E., Inc.

11 Leonberg Rd.
Cranberry Township, PA 16066
County: Butler

Phone: (412) 772-5225
Fax: (412) 772-5280

Manufacturer of liquid-cast, thermoset, polyurethane products including sheet, bar, rod and tube stock. The Company molds polyurethane for customers in a wide range of industries, including aerospace, corrugated, metal forming, mining, packaging, paper and pulp, and transportation. Its proprietary product lines include Timesaver™ and Snap-Lock™ brand rotary die cutter blankets plus Dura-Latch™ and Cor-Lock™ brand free wheeling anvil covers for the corrugated industry; and Hardliner® impact/abrasion resistant polyurethane sheets for mining and aggregate wear lining applications. The Company's production capabilities range from low-volume prototype work through high-volume production runs.

Officers: Joseph C. Scaletta *P*
Donald L. Fiscus *VP-MFG*

Human Resources: Jacque Dawson *Office MGR*

Purchasing: David Jamison

Total Employees............................84	**Regional Employees** 84
Year Established 1986	**SIC Code**.....................................3089

C-K Composites, Inc.

5000 Bridgeport St. Extension
P.O. Box 1087
Mt. Pleasant, PA 15666
County: Westmoreland

Phone: (412) 547-4581
Fax: (412) 547-2890

Engineer, manufacturer and marketer of products, components and structures made with technical plastics and composite materials. The Company manufactures three basic lines of materials: filament-wound reinforced plastic tubes; cast and molded epoxy resin; and densified, resin-impregnated and laminated wood. The products are used in a variety of electrical, mechanical and military applications. With a few exceptions, the Company's products are custom-engineered to meet the requirements of its customers.

Officers: Gene Carlisle *CH*
F. Patrick Kozbelt *P*

Total Employees	49	**Regional Employees**	49
Year Established	1955	**SIC Code**	3089
Annual Revenues ($000)	5,000		

Calgon Corp.

5400 Campbells Run Rd.
P.O. Box 1346, Pittsburgh, PA 15230
Pittsburgh, PA 15205
County: Allegheny

Phone: (412) 494-8000
Fax: (412) 494-8927
Internet Address: www.calgon.com

Producer and supplier of specialty chemicals and related technical services and equipment, principally for water treatment and papermaking applications. The Company's other chemical products include surface treatment, specialty biocides and cosmetic ingredients, all linked by its core technologies. The Company provides its customers with formulated products based on the proprietary development, manufacture and blending of specialty polymers and other chemicals that are marketed together with detection, monitoring, dosing and metering equipment. It operates seven manufacturing plants, six of which are for chemicals and one for related monitoring/feed equipment, and has sales offices throughout the world. The Company is a subsidiary of English China Clays Plc, which is headquartered in Theale, England, and listed on the London Stock Exchange.

Officers: James H. Heagle *P & COO*
Rick P. Markle *VP-SAL & MKT, Americas*
Richard G. Varsanik *VP-Idea to Commercialization*

Human Resources: George M. Rickus, Jr. *VP-Human Resources*

Total Employees......................1,000	**Regional Employees** 375
Year Established 1918	**SIC Code**....................................2899
Annual Revenues ($000) 281,000	

California University of Pennsylvania

250 University Ave.
California, PA 15419
County: Washington
Phone: (412) 938-4000
Fax: (412) 938-1500

Nonprofit educational institution offering more than 100 associate's, bachelor's, master's and certification programs through the College of Education and Human Services, the College of Liberal Arts, the Eberly College of Science and Technology, the School of Graduate Studies and Research, and the Continuing Education program. The University is located thirty miles south of Pittsburgh. Its 80-acre main campus contains 38 buildings. The 104-acre Roadman Park contains athletic fields and courts, running facilities and a stadium. The University's student body is comprised of approximately 5,200 undergraduates and 1,000 graduate students. It is part of the Pennsylvania State System of Higher Education.

Officers: Angelo Armenti, Jr., Ph.D. *P*
 Curtis Smith, Ph.D. *Provost & VP-Academic Affairs*
 Paul Burd, Ph.D. *VP-Student Growth & DEV*
 Allan Golden, Ph.D. *VP-ADM & FIN*
 Richard H. Webb, Ph.D. *VP-Advancement*

Human Resources: Penny Stanick

Purchasing: Carl Maurer

Total Employees...........................750	**Regional Employees** 750
Year Established 1852	**SIC Code**....................................8221
Annual Revenues ($000) 57,000	

Calig Steel Drum Co.

1400 Fleming Ave.
P.O. Box 418
McKees Rocks, PA 15136
County: Allegheny

Phone: (412) 771-6440
Fax: (412) 771-6211
Internet Address: www.calig.com

Manufacturer of lined and unlined steel drums. The Company's product line consists of 44- through 60-gallon steel drums in gauges 22 through 16; 55-gallon plastic and steel salvage (overpak) drums; 55-gallon ISO drums for export; steel drum with agitator insert for product agitation; FDA-approved interior drum linings; drums (pans) manufactured for steel band instruments; and a wide range of drums to meet various United Nations performance capabilities. The Company's unique capabilities include a five-stage cleaning and zinc phosphatizing process, custom silk screening on drum exterior, a triple seam drum chime manufacturing process, custom-fabricated designs to customer specifications and ink jet or label markings on drum exterior. It supplies the specialty chemicals, soaps and cosmetics, flavor and fragrance, pharmaceuticals, petroleum, oils (food grade), and coatings, resins and adhesives industries.

Officers: Elliot Calig *VP*
Lee Calig *VP*
Jeffrey Calig *QA MGR*

Purchasing: Richard Rote *Purchasing MGR*

Total Employees..............................90
Year Established.........................1910
Annual Revenues ($000)...15-20,000
Regional Employees 90
SIC Code....................................3412

Campos Market Research

216 Blvd. of the Allies, 3rd Fl.
Pittsburgh, PA 15222
County: Allegheny

Phone: (412) 471-8484
Fax: (412) 471-8497

Full-service marketing research company providing both consumer and business-to-business research. The Company has expertise in qualitative and quantitative research. It is equipped with two focus group suites and a 40-line telephone bank and provides in-house focus group moderators and research analysts to complete any size job. The Company serves clients nationwide.

Officers: Yvonne Campos *P*
René Campos *VP*

Human Resources: Rosa Hassett *(Purchasing)*

Total Employees.............................61	Regional Employees 61	
Year Established 1986	SIC Code...................................8732	
Annual Revenues ($000) 2,100		

C

Campus Dimensions, Inc.

200 Seco Rd.
Monroeville, PA 15146
County: Allegheny

Phone: (412) 372-8300
Fax: (412) 372-1008

Developer and implementor of event marketing programs that target college students. The Company reaches over 2,000 campuses in all 50 states on behalf of clients such as ABC Television, AT&T, Coca-Cola, Ford, Pepsi and Procter & Gamble. Its College Credit Card Corp. division specializes in the marketing of credit cards and other financial products for clients such as Discover Card. The Company is headquartered in Philadelphia, PA.

Officers: Edward Solomon *P*
Diane Brady *VP*
Nancy Law *VP*
Jay Muchnick *VP*

Human Resources: Sissy Habura

Purchasing: Michael Torterete *DIR-OPR*

Total Employees............................150	Regional Employees 78
Year Established 1976	SIC Code...................................8742

Cannon Boiler Works, Inc.

Schreiber Industrial Park, Bldg. Nine
P.O. Box 1
New Kensington, PA 15068
County: Westmoreland

Phone: (412) 335-8541
Fax: (412) 335-6511
Internet Address: www.boilerroom.com

Designer, manufacturer and marketer of boiler room and heat recovery equipment for industrial markets in the U.S. and Canada. In addition, the Company services boiler room equipment. The Company's affiliate, Cannon Technology, Inc., is also located at the above address and employs four people.

Officers: Arthur P. Skelley *P & CEO*
John M. Koltick, Jr. *VP*

Madonna J. Flinn *CON*
Dean R. Mohn *Service MGR*
John V. Radion *SAL MGR*
Robert Roycroft *Production MGR*

Human Resources: Sharette Ciccocioppo

Purchasing: Margaret Knosky

Total Employees	55	**Regional Employees**	55
Year Established	1972	**SIC Code**	3443
Annual Revenues ($000)	6-7,000		

Cannon U.S.A., Inc.

1235 Freedom Rd.
Cranberry Township, PA 16066
County: Butler

Phone: (412) 772-5600
Fax: (412) 776-1070
Internet Address: www.cannonusa.com

Producer of plastics processing equipment for polyurethanes, composites and thermoforming for North American manufacturers of plastic products in the appliance, automotive and recreational industries. The Company's equipment is used for a wide variety of applications, from manufacturing foam insulation for refrigerators to instrument panels for automobiles to insulation in skis. The Company is a subsidiary of Cannon S.p.A., which is headquartered in Milan, Italy.

Officers: R. Brooks Hammer *P & CEO*
Robert W. Fortwangler *EVP*
Mark A. Clark *VP-ENG*
John V. Ellis *VP-MFG*
William M. Worms *VP-SAL*

Human Resources: Linda Kirschler

Purchasing: Karen Fuller

Total Employees	70	**Regional Employees**	70
Year Established	1977	**SIC Code**	3559
Annual Revenues ($000)	30,000		

Canonsburg General Hospital

100 Medical Blvd.
Canonsburg, PA 15317
County: Washington

Phone: (412) 745-6100
Fax: (412) 873-5876

Nonprofit 120-bed hospital, with 92 acute care beds and 28 subacute/skilled beds, providing primary and selected secondary levels of care to residents of northern Washington and southern Allegheny Counties, PA. The Hospital has a medical staff of 160 physicians in 30 specialties, emphasizing primary health care that is community based. The Hospital provides a broad spectrum of services, including emergency medicine, subacute/skilled care, general medicine and intensive care/cardiac care. Its surgical services include general, orthopedic, gynecological, ophthalmological and ENT surgery. Its diagnostic capabilities include CT scanner, mammography, nuclear medicine, MRI, noninvasive cardiology and chemotherapy. Crossroads Physical Rehabilitation, Inc., located in McMurray, PA, is a joint venture of the Hospital and its physical therapy service.

Recent Events: On June 3, 1997, the Hospital announced its plans to merge with Allegheny University Medical Centers, a subsidiary of Allegheny Health, Education and Research Foundation.

Officers: Barbara A. Bensaia *EVP & COO*
Richard C. Chesnos *CFO*

Human Resources: Martha L. Clister *DIR-Human Resources*

Total Employees	425	**Regional Employees**	425
Year Established	1903	**SIC Code**	8062

Canterbury Place

310 Fisk St.
Pittsburgh, PA 15201
County: Allegheny

Phone: (412) 622-9000
Fax: (412) 622-9249

Nonprofit skilled nursing care center. The 190-bed Facility provides independent living support, personal care, Alzheimer's care, skilled and intermediate nursing care, respite care and in-home case management for older adults. It operates under a management contract with the University of Pittsburgh Medical Center (UPMC), whereby the UPMC provides management for the nursing home.

Officers: Edmund S. Ruffin III *CH*

Human Resources: Lisa Fair *DIR-Support Services*

Total Employees	140	**Regional Employees**	140
Year Established	1859	**SIC Code**	8059

Cap Gemini

Two Gateway Center, Ste. 390
Pittsburgh, PA 15222
County: Allegheny

Phone: (412) 394-6460
Fax: (412) 394-6466
Internet Address: www.capgemini.com

Provider of information technology consulting services. As one of 50 branch operations nationwide, the local office offers a variety of services including, but not limited to, strategic systems planning, systems integration, business process reengineering, operational improvements and year 2000 readiness assessments. The local office is a part of the Company's Eastern Division, which is based in Hudson, OH. The Company, headquartered in New York, NY, is a subsidiary of Cap Gemini Sogeti of Paris, France, which is listed on the Paris Stock Exchange.

Officers: William Euller *SVP-Eastern Division MGR*
Richard B. Black *Senior Client Services Executive*

Human Resources: Denise Longo *(Purchasing)*

Total Employees ....25,000+	**Regional Employees** ....30+
Year Established 1968	**SIC Code** 7379
Annual Revenues ($000) 3,200,000	

Carbidie Corp.

R.D. 3, 425 Arona Rd.
P.O. Box 509
Irwin, PA 15642
County: Westmoreland

Phone: (412) 864-5900
Fax: (412) 864-2443

Manufacturer of a wide variety of preformed and unfinished tools, dies, parts and components made from tungsten carbide, including grades with submicron size particles. The Company's preforms are pressed, shaped and sintered to meet each customer's requirements and specifications. Its major markets are the beverage, electronic stamping, automotive, fluid handling and powder metal, with clients in 40 countries. The Company is also engaged in a manufacturing and sales joint venture, Carbidie Asia Pacific Pte. Ltd., in Singapore. The Company is a division of Greenfield Industries, Inc., which is headquartered in Augusta, GA, and listed on the NASDAQ.

Officers: Edward S. Cline *GMGR*
Jack Harris *Plant MGR*
Ven Krutz *Plant MGR*

Human Resources: Rob R. Barto

Total Employees............................210	**Regional Employees** 210	
Year Established 1953	**SIC Code**....................................3544	
Annual Revenues ($000) 25,000		

C

Cardiac Fitness, Inc.

5438 Centre Ave.
Pittsburgh, PA 15232
County: Allegheny

Phone: (412) 681-8123
Fax: (412) 681-8744

Provider of management and staffing services for two Cardiac Care Centers located in Erie and Pittsburgh, PA. In addition, the Company owns 82% of Main Medical, Inc. (MMI), which is also headquartered at the above address. MMI provides mobile ultrasound services to clients in the Pittsburgh metropolitan area. MMI also manages 13 outpatient diagnostic testing centers through its Mid-Atlantic Imaging Network, located in Coraopolis (2), Cranberry, Monroeville, North Charleroi, Pittsburgh (4), Upper St. Clair, Washington, West Mifflin and Wexford, PA. C. F. Nuclear Medicine Services L.P., a 90%-owned subsidiary of MMI, offers mobile nuclear diagnostic services in Pittsburgh, as well as New York, North Carolina and West Virginia.

Officers: John R. Tomayko, Ph.D. *P & CEO*
   Annette McPeek *VP & CON*

Human Resources: Elizabeth M. Sullivan *EDIR-Human Resources*
   Susan Buys *MGR-Human Resources*

Purchasing: Jeffrey Krivan *EDIR-Technical Services*

Total Employees............................154	**Regional Employees** 150	
Year Established 1985	**SIC Code**....................................8099	
Annual Revenues ($000) 8,000		

Care Connection, Inc.

1386 Old Freeport Rd.
Pittsburgh, PA 15238
County: Allegheny

Phone: (412) 963-6737
Fax: (412) 963-1466

Provider of community-based home health care services to clients in a variety of settings, including private homes, hospitals and nursing homes. The Company supplies private duty and supplemental staffing personnel to clients throughout Western Pennsylvania. For work ranging from light housekeeping to qualified around-the-clock skilled nursing, the Company can provide registered nurses, licensed practical nurses and vocational nurses, physical, occupational and speech therapists, certified home health aides and companions/homemakers or sitters for homebound patients. Its services include home care for children, infusion therapy, respite care, home ventilation care, bath visits, medical transport staffing, and hospital and nursing home staffing. Branch offices are located in Butler, Fox Chapel and the South Hills area of Pittsburgh, all in Pennsylvania.

Officers: Phil Warman *OWN*
   David Cottington *EDIR*

Total Employees............................300   **Regional Employees** 300
Year Established 1985   **SIC Code**....................................8082
Annual Revenues ($000) 2,500

Care Unlimited, Inc.

3288 Babcock Blvd.
Pittsburgh, PA 15237
County: Allegheny

Phone: (412) 367-3620
Fax: (412) 367-3769

   Provider of nursing and home health care services to clients in Allegheny and the surrounding counties. The Company's personnel include registered nurses, licensed practical nurses, nurse's aides/home health aides, companions, sitters, live-ins, escort-transportation personnel, therapists (speech, physical, occupational and respiratory), medical social workers and developmental/child life specialists. Its nursing specialties service provides pediatric nurses, ventilator nurses, obstetrical nurses, maternal/child care nurses, I.V. nurses, oncology nurses and rehabilitation nurses. The Company also provides supplemental staffing for hospitals, nursing facilities, mental health and mental retardation facilities, medical offices and industrial facilities. Additional offices are located in Butler, Erie, Greensburg and Meadville, PA.

Officers: Laurye Feller *P & CEO*
   Dean White *Administrator*

Regional Employees 200-300
Year Established 1984   **SIC Code**....................................8082

Carlow College

3333 Fifth Ave.
Pittsburgh, PA 15213
County: Allegheny

C

Phone: (412) 578-6053
Fax: (412) 578-6265

Nonprofit, Catholic, liberal arts college, primarily for women. The College offers more than 30 majors, nine pre-professional programs, eight certification programs and six certificate programs in Allied Health. It awards the Bachelor of Arts, Bachelor of Science, Bachelor of Science in Nursing, Bachelor of Social Work, Masters of Education, Masters of Art Education, Masters of Science in Nursing and Masters of Science in Professional Leadership degrees. The student body is comprised of approximately 2,300 students with an average class size of 15-20. The College operates off-site locations in Beaver, Cranberry Township and Greensburg, PA. In addition, various courses and workshops are offered through Distance Learning, using interactive television, and through the Internet.

Officers: Grace Ann Geibel, RSM, Ph.D. *P*

Human Resources: Barbara Farnsworth

Total Employees	375	**Regional Employees**	375
Year Established	1929	**SIC Code**	8221

Carlson Wagonlit Travel

Two Gateway Center., Ste. 250
Pittsburgh, PA 15222
County: Allegheny

Phone: (412) 391-1650
Fax: (412) 261-9033

Provider of a full range of travel-related business services, including travel reservations, travel expense management and payment systems. The Company is headquartered in Minnetonka, MN. It is a part of the Carlson Travel Group, a segment of Carlson Cos., Inc., which is also headquartered in Minnetonka, MN. The local branch office serves corporate clients in the Pittsburgh metropolitan area.

Officers: Joanne Reagan-Tate *Branch MGR*

Total Employees	20,000	**Regional Employees**	32
Year Established	1888	**SIC Code**	4724
Annual Revenues ($000)	33,000 (Pittsburgh)		

Carnegie Institute

4400 Forbes Ave.
Pittsburgh, PA 15213
County: Allegheny

Phone: (412) 622-3131
Fax: (412) 622-1970
Internet Address: www.clpgh.org

Nonprofit operator of the Carnegie Museum of Art (located at the above address), the Carnegie Museum of Natural History (located at the above address), the Carnegie Science Center (located at One Allegheny Ave. in Pittsburgh), The Andy Warhol Museum (located at 117 Sandusky St. in Pittsburgh) and the Carnegie Music Hall (located at the above address), which together constitute the Carnegie Institute. Established at the turn of the century as a museum focused on contemporary art, the Carnegie Museum of Art has a distinguished collection of American and European paintings. Over the expanse of a century the collection has amplified in scope to include European and American decorative arts, architectural objects, Asian art, African art, and film and video. Known as the "home of the dinosaurs," the Carnegie Museum of Natural History features 10 complete dinosaur skeletons, including T. rex; ancient Egyptian and Inuit artifacts; world-class minerals and gems; African and North American wildlife; and a hands-on Discovery Room. It also offers a schedule of changing exhibits, lectures, classes and tours for all ages. The Carnegie Science Center houses more than 250 hands-on science exhibits for visitors of all ages; the Rangos Omnimax Theater; The Henry Buhl Jr. Planetarium and observatory; and a World War II decommissioned submarine. It also offers informal science and computer classes for children and adults, professional development workshops for educators, outreach programs, high school science apprenticeships and other specialized science programs. The Andy Warhol Museum is the most comprehensive single-artist museum in the world with more than 40,000 square feet of exhibition space. Art and archives spanning Warhol's career are displayed as well as related temporary exhibitions. The Carnegie Music Hall and the Lecture Hall are home to numerous performing groups with national and international reputations including the River City Brass Band, the Y Music Society and the International Poetry Forum.

Officers: Frank Brooks Robinson *CH*
Ellsworth H. Brown *P*
Dolores F. Ellenberg *VP-Planning & DEV*
William Stein *VP-MKT*
Henry P. Hoffstot, Jr. *SEC*
Nancy A. Paradise *AST-SEC*
Robert F. Fallgren *AST-TRS*
William F. Neil *CON*
Lorene D. Vinski *AST to P-Corporate Affairs*
Richard Armstrong *The Henry J. Heinz II DIR-Carnegie Museum of Art*
Diane C. Becherer *DIR-Public Programs & Services*

Seddon L. Bennington *DIR-Carnegie Science Center*
Terrence P. O'Horo *Acting DIR-Financial Services*
James B. Richardson *Acting DIR-Carnegie Museum of Natural History*
Thomas Sokolowski *DIR-The Andy Warhol Museum*
Doris Carson Williams *DIR-Office of Business Enterprises*

Human Resources: Jim Bender *Acting DIR-General Services & Human Resources*

Total Employees............................942   **Regional Employees**...................942
Year Established........................1895   **SIC Code**....................................8412
Annual Revenues ($000)...36,000

Carnegie Library of Pittsburgh, The

4400 Forbes Ave.
Pittsburgh, PA 15213
County: Allegheny

Phone: (412) 622-3114
Fax: (412) 622-6278

Nonprofit public institution dedicated to the free and equal access of information to all the people it serves. Through its role as a local library for residents and organizations of Pittsburgh and Allegheny County, as a District Center for Allegheny County public libraries and as a resource for the Commonwealth of Pennsylvania, the Library serves a broad and diverse audience within the state. Since it is a member of an international bibliographic network, its collections are used by libraries serving people throughout the world. As a free public library, it provides collections, programs and services through a network that includes the Main Library (located at the above address) and 18 branch libraries, the Bookmobile Center and three bookmobiles, and the Library for the Blind and Physically Handicapped. In addition, deposit collections comprised of books of selected titles for long-term loan are available in community agencies, senior centers, public housing centers and recreation centers. During 1996, the Library's staff answered 1.7 million questions and hosted a variety of programs for over 217,000 people. In the same year, the Library circulated over 3 million items.

Officers: Robert B. Croneberger *DIR*
Loretta O'Brien *Deputy DIR*

Total Employees.......................550+   **Regional Employees**................550+
Year Established.......................1895   **SIC Code**....................................8231
Annual Revenues ($000)...17,991

Carnegie Mellon University

5000 Forbes Ave.
Pittsburgh, PA 15213
County: Allegheny

Phone: (412) 268-2000
Fax: (412) 268-6929
Internet Address: www.cmu.edu

Nonprofit, private university with programs encompassing the areas of engineering, technology, science, liberal arts, fine arts, and public and private management. The University includes four undergraduate colleges consisting of the College of Engineering, the College of Fine Arts, the College of Humanities and Social Sciences, and the Mellon College of Science. Its three graduate schools are comprised of the Graduate School of Industrial Administration, the H. John Heinz III School of Public Policy and Management, and the School of Computer Science. The University's many research centers, exploring fields such as biotechnology, computer-aided design, computer science, creative inquiry, data storage, economic development, engineering design, international management, light microscope and magnetic resonance imaging, robotics, scientific literacy and writing, and software engineering, receive funding from government and corporate sponsors. It enrolls approximately 4,700 undergraduates and 2,300 graduate students. The campus has 59 buildings situated on 103 acres in the Oakland section of Pittsburgh. During the 1995-1996 school year, the University granted 1,001 Bachelor's degrees, 796 Master's degrees and 193 Doctor's degrees.

Officers:　Jared L. Cohon, Ph.D.　*P*
　　　　　　Paul Chistiano　*Provost*
　　　　　　Jeff Bolton　*VP-Planning & Budgets*
　　　　　　William F. Elliott　*VP-Enrollment*
　　　　　　Don Hale　*VP-University Relations*
　　　　　　Eric Johnson　*VP-DEV*
　　　　　　Patrick J. Keating　*VP-Business & CFO*

Human Resources:　Barbara Smith

Purchasing:　David Hamlin

Total Employees................3,616	**Regional Employees**...........3,616
Year Established................1900	**SIC Code**.................8221
Annual Revenues ($000)................505,198	

Carriage House Children's Center, Inc.

5604 Solway St.
Pittsburgh, PA 15217
County: Allegheny

Phone: (412) 421-0300
Fax: (412) 421-1327

Nonprofit provider of child care services and preschool for children ages six weeks to six years with an enrollment of approximately 190. The Center also manages an affiliate of Magee-Womens Hospital, The Children's Center of Pittsburgh, located at 327 Craft Ave. in Pittsburgh, PA. It, too, provides care for children ages six weeks to six years with an enrollment of approximately 130.

Officers: Natalie A. Kaplan *EDIR (Human Resources)*
Fred Serino *P*

Purchasing: Tina Schron

Total Employees............................100	**Regional Employees** 100
Year Established 1974	**SIC Code**....................................8361

Carson Industries, Inc.

189 Foreman Rd.
Freeport, PA 16229
County: Armstrong

Phone: (412) 295-5147
Fax: (412) 295-4033

Manufacturer of a variety of products made of Statesmetal™, an aluminum alloy. The Company's product line includes dinnerware and accessories; wind chimes; gifts for the garden, including bird feeders, hose holders, garden signs and sundials; and giftware, including candle jar holders, sachet frames, potpourri burners, minilites, hooks and Christmas ornaments. It also produces custom-made products with corporate or group logos. The Company's products are marketed nationwide through manufacturers' representatives, gift stores and, to a small extent, directly to customers.

Officers: Harry G. Carson, Sr. *CEO*
Harry G. Carson, Jr. *P*
Jeffrey L. Carson *VP*
Pamela A. Carson-Keller *VP-PDEV*
Bob Gray *VP-SAL*
Barry Moore *VP-MKT*
Albert Musloe *VP-MFG*
J. Carter Tackett *CFO*

Human Resources: Kelly Bricker

Purchasing: Eric Hoffman

Total Employees 170-200	**Regional Employees** 170-200
Year Established 1970	**SIC Code**....................................3365

Case, Sabatini & Co.

470 Streets Run Rd.
Pittsburgh, PA 15236
County: Allegheny

Phone: (412) 881-4411
Fax: (412) 881-4421

Regional certified public accounting firm providing auditing, tax preparation, litigation support, and estate, financial and computer consulting services. The Firm's clients include construction, real estate, manufacturing, health care and retail companies. It operates a branch office in Greensburg, PA.

Officers: Charles Case *MPTR*

Total Employees	35	**Regional Employees**	35
Year Established	1971	**SIC Code**	8721

Castle Rubber Co.

1003 Railroad St.
P.O. Box 589, Butler, PA 16003
East Butler, PA 16029
County: Butler

Phone: (412) 287-5791
Fax: (412) 287-1784

Manufacturer of custom industrial rubber components, seals, gaskets, automotive parts, slitter rings, bellows and vibration dampeners, and provider of industrial roll covering services to the steel and related industries. The Company also provides complete rubber compounding, engineering and mold design in addition to lathe cutting and rubber to metal bonding. It is a subsidiary of Park-Ohio Industries, Inc., which is headquartered in Cleveland, OH, and listed on the NASDAQ.

Officers: Kent Roberts *Plant MGR*
Ross Conley *MIS MGR*
Bill Greenawalt *SAL & MKT MGR*
Kevin Robinson *CON*

Human Resources: Jim Rathbun *Human Resources MGR*

Purchasing: Irving Halsted *Purchasing Agent*

Total Employees	150	**Regional Employees**	150
Year Established	1923	**SIC Code**	3069
Annual Revenues ($000)	10-15,000		

Castriota Chevrolet, Inc.

1701 W. Liberty Ave.
Pittsburgh, PA 15226
County: Allegheny

Phone: (412) 343-2100
Fax: (412) 343-9353

Automobile dealership selling Chevrolet vehicles. The Company offers a full line of new cars, light trucks and sport utility vehicles. It also sells late model used cars and trucks. In addition, it operates a service department and body shop and maintains a substantial GM parts inventory.

Officers: Anthony J. Castriota *P & CEO*
Mary Lou Castriota *SEC & TRS*
Wayne Mullin *GMGR*

Human Resources: Robert E. Yaggi *CON (Purchasing)*

Total Employees............................56	**Regional Employees** 56
Year Established 1979	**SIC Code** 5511
Annual Revenues ($000) 75,000	

Catholic Charities of the Diocese of Pittsburgh

212 Ninth St.
Pittsburgh, PA 15222
County: Allegheny

Phone: (412) 456-6999
Fax: (412) 456-6970
Internet Address: www.trfn.clpgh.org/cathchar

Nonprofit organization operating as an independent unit within the Diocese of Pittsburgh. Through six county offices and various program sites, the Organization provides services that include adoption, counseling, family day care, parish social ministry, neighborhood-based services, information and referral as well as services for refugees and the elderly. The Organization claims to be one of the largest social service agencies in Southwestern Pennsylvania. Its funding is provided through government grants, the United Way, the Diocese of Pittsburgh, fees for service, and private contributions from individuals, corporations and foundations. The Organization operates offices in Allegheny, Beaver, Butler, Greene, Lawrence and Washington Counties, PA. Many of its programs operate out of the Organization's headquarters facility at the address listed above. Other Pittsburgh program sites include the Ozanam Cultural Center, Roselia Center and St. Joseph's House of Hospitality.

Officers: Sister Patricia Cairns *EDIR*
Violeta Antelman *DIR-Professional Services*
Eugene Bokor *DIR-FIN*
Ron Cichowicz *DIR-Public Relations & DEV*
Anthony Turo *DIR-Community Outreach Services*

Human Resources: Patricia DiGiovine *DIR-Human Resources*

Total Employees...........................165   **Regional Employees**..................112
Year Established ....,1910   **SIC Code**....................................8322

Catholic Diocese of Pittsburgh-Pastoral Center

111 Blvd. of the Allies
Pittsburgh, PA 15222
County: Allegheny

Phone: (412) 456-3000
Fax: (412) 456-3168

Nonprofit religious organization whose mission is to continue the ministry of Christ. Through its administrative offices located at the above address in the Pastoral Center, the Organization assists 218 member parishes in conducting educational, pastoral and social programs.

Officers: Donald Wuerl *Bishop*
William Winter *Auxiliary Bishop*
David Zubik *Auxiliary Bishop*

Human Resources: Darlene Holzer

Total Employees...........................150
Year Established 1843   **SIC Code**....................................8661

Cauley Detective Agency, Inc.

5777 Baum Blvd.
Pittsburgh, PA 15206
County: Allegheny

Phone: (412) 661-6000
Fax: (412) 661-7939

Provider of contract security guard services to clients throughout the Tri-State area.

Officers: James P. Cauley, Jr. *P & CEO*
                 Sarah W. Cauley *VP*
                 John W. Hall *VP*

Human Resources: Roger Rees *VP*

Total Employees............................560	**Regional Employees** 560
Year Established 1937	**SIC Code**......................................7381

CB Commercial/Arnheim & Neely

The Law & Finance Bldg., 429 Fourth Ave., Ste. 200
Pittsburgh, PA 15219
County: Allegheny

Phone: (412) 391-1800
Fax: (412) 391-1146
Internet Address: www.cbcommercial.com

Diversified commercial real estate firm providing a variety of asset, brokerage, corporate, financial, institutional and research services for office, industrial and retail properties. The Firm's services include property management, facilities management, tenant representation, landlord representation, transaction management, multi-market planning, strategic planning, financial planning, asset acquisition and disposition, consultation, market analysis and econometric forecasting. It serves clients throughout ten counties in Southwestern Pennsylvania. CB Commercial, which is headquartered in Los Angeles, CA, is a partial equity owner of the Firm.

Officers: Leonard Silk *CEO*
                 Jeffrey B. Ackerman *P*
                 Andrew Stewart *COO*
                 Edward Zehfuss *EVP*

Purchasing: Linda Zehfuss

Total Employees.............................31	**Regional Employees** 31
Year Established 1933	**SIC Code**......................................6531

Cegelec AEG Automation Systems Corp.

701 Technology Dr.
Canonsburg, PA 15317
County: Washington

Phone: (412) 873-9300
Fax: (412) 873-9416
Internet Address: www.cegelec-asc.com

Supplier of complete automation solutions and services, including assembly systems for automotive components, electronics products, medical devices, consumer products and other small- to medium-size parts; and automated paint finishing and sealing systems for automobiles and commercial vehicles. The Company also offers high technology services to dramatically reduce a manufacturer's time, cost and risk to develop, introduce and produce new products. These services include advanced computer tools to analyze, simulate and optimize product design and manufacturing process alternatives. In addition, the Company furnishes project management and members of the product development team, and an assembly system constructed of proven hardware and software modules. Its Paint Finishing Systems Division is located in Rochester Hills, MI. The Company is a subsidiary of Cegelec AEG Systems and Automation GmbH, which is headquartered in Frankfurt, Germany, and a division of Alcatel Alsthom (AA). AA is headquartered in Paris, France, and listed on the New York and Paris Stock Exchanges.

Officers: Wayne L. Huff *P & CEO*
William S. McDougall *VP-FIN*

Human Resources: Robert P. Percival *VP-Human Resources*

Purchasing: James D. Sagan

Total Employees	280	Regional Employees	225
Year Established	1989	SIC Code	3569
Annual Revenues ($000)	80-100,000		

Cellone Bakery, Inc.

193 Chartiers Ave.
P.O. Box 16288, Pittsburgh, PA 15242
Pittsburgh, PA 15205
County: Allegheny

Phone: (412) 922-5335
Fax: (412) 922-6940

Baker of Italian breads and rolls, including rye bread and hoagie buns. The Company primarily serves supermarket chains, as well as some institutional clients, in the Tri-State area.

Officers: Jay Cellone *P*

Total Employees	90	Regional Employees	90
Year Established	1950	SIC Code	2051

CellSource, Inc.

5001 Baum Blvd., Ste. 430
Pittsburgh, PA 15213
County: Allegheny

Phone: (412) 683-4080
Fax: (412) 683-4078

Acquirer, marketer and distributor of medical device technology in the surgical market, specializing in body sculpting and plastic surgery instruments and products. The Company's products are marketed to plastic and cosmetic surgeons, hospitals and patients. These include its patented "Tulip" liposuction syringe system for body sculpting surgery and supportive post-operative garments. Additionally, through its sponsorship of research programs into tissue engineering possibilities, the Company has positioned itself to add tissue engineering technology products to its catalog as that industry develops and products are produced. Within two years, the Company plans to launch another project—an obesity treatment program. The Company operates a garment manufacturing facility in Mesa, AZ.

Officers: John M. Johnson *CH, P & CEO*
Marcille Pilington *DIR & EVP*
J. William Futrell, M.D. *DIR-RES & Chief-U of Pittsburgh-Division of Plastic Surgery*

Human Resources: Debora J. Mitchell *(Purchasing)*

Total Employees	43	**Regional Employees**	13
Year Established	1990	**SIC Code**	5047
Annual Revenues ($000)	2,500		

Cemline Corp.

Freeport Rd.
P.O. Box 55
Cheswick, PA 15024
County: Allegheny

Phone: (412) 274-5430
Fax: (412) 274-5448

Manufacturer of ASME code pressure vessels, heat exchangers, replacement tube bundles and packaged water heaters used in the construction of commercial buildings, including hospitals and other institutional structures, and for renovation and replacement parts. The Company serves clients nationwide.

Officers: Charles L. Chappell *P*
Hugh K. Chappell *VP*

Total Employees	50	**Regional Employees**	50
Year Established	1936	**SIC Code**	3443

Center for Hazardous Materials Research

320 William Pitt Way
Pittsburgh, PA 15238
County: Allegheny

Phone: (412) 826-5320
Fax: (412) 826-5552
Internet Address: www.chmr.org

Nonprofit organization dedicated to technology commercialization, research and development, waste minimization and pollution prevention. The Organization operates three nationally renowned centers, all of which are located at the above address. The National Environmental Technology Applications Center supports the commercialization of innovative environmental technologies. The Bioremediation Product Evaluation Center encourages the application of bioremediation products for a variety of oil spill and hazardous waste cleanups. The Ground-Water Remediation Technologies Analysis Center promotes innovative technologies to clean up contaminated groundwater. The Organization primarily serves small businesses, as well as government agencies and academia.

Officers: Samuel Schulhof *CH*
Edgar Berkey *P*
David Glaser *VP*
Robb Lenhart *VP*

Human Resources: Diane Ragan *VP*

Purchasing: Linda Kelley

Total Employees.............................48
Year Established 1986
Annual Revenues ($000) 3,200
Regional Employees 47
SIC Code.....................................8731

Centerline Engineering Corp.

12450 Perry Hwy.
P.O. Box 249
Wexford, PA 15090
County: Allegheny

Phone: (412) 935-6020
Fax: (412) 935-9620
Internet Address: www.lg.com

Provider of consulting engineering services, including design, design/build, construction engineering, automation and controls design, and environmental and construction management services for the metals industry, including steel, aluminum and nonferrous metals. The Company primarily serves clients in

North and South America. It is a subsidiary of Lockwood Greene Engineers, Inc., headquartered in Spartanburg, SC, which is majority owned by Philipp Holzmann USA Ltd. (PHUL). PHUL, which is headquartered in Charlotte, NC, is a wholly owned subsidiary of Philipp Holzmann AG, headquartered in Frankfurt, Germany.

Officers: William J. Hakos *VCH*
Andrew Kapusta *P*
Steven W. Cummings *VP & CFO*
Malcolm (Mike) G. Milligan *Business DEV MGR*

Human Resources: Ellen L. Fleming

Purchasing: Bob Platt

Total Employees............................140	**Regional Employees** 140
Year Established 1975	**SIC Code** 8711
Annual Revenues ($000) 17,000	

Centimark Corp.

12 Grandview Cir.
Canonsburg, PA 15317
County: Washington

Phone: (412) 743-7777
Fax: (412) 743-7790

Commercial roofing contractor providing roof construction and repair and floor work. The Company also owns and operates Superior Travel Co., a travel agency located in Cleveland, OH.

Officers: Edward Dunlap *P & CEO*
John Rudzik *VP & CFO*

Human Resources: Richard Gunther

Purchasing: Joe Scarmazzi

Total Employees........................1,900	**Regional Employees** 900
Year Established 1968	**SIC Code** 1761
Annual Revenues ($000) 174,000	

Central Electric Cooperative, Inc.

Rte. 368 E.
P.O. Box 329
Parker, PA 16049
County: Armstrong

Phone: (412) 399-2931
Fax: (412) 399-2300
Internet Address: www.csonline.net/cec

Member-owned rural electric system that serves approximately 22,684 members in portions of Allegheny, Armstrong, Butler, Clarion, Forest, Mercer and Venango Counties, PA. The Company has approximately 2,993 miles of distribution line. It is one of 14 rural electric cooperatives in New Jersey and Pennsylvania, and claims to be the second largest in Pennsylvania. All of the co-ops belong to the Pennsylvania Rural Electric Assn., their statewide organization which is headquartered in Harrisburg, PA. They are also members of the National Rural Electric Cooperative Assn., which is headquartered in Washington, D.C. The Company buys wholesale power from Allegheny Electric Cooperative, Inc., a generation and transmission co-op organized by Pennsylvania rural electric cooperatives to acquire wholesale power at reasonable rates. The Company borrows 70% of its money from the Rural Utilities Service and the remaining 30% from the National Rural Utilities Cooperative Finance Corp. to build its lines and is repaying the loans at current interest rates.

Officers: Lloyd G. McClintock *P*
Larry S. Adams *GMGR*
Kenneth J. Clark *AST-GMGR & MGR-Member Services*
Dennis W. Beggs *MGR-FIN & MKT*
Susan A. Redmond *MGR-Administrative Services*
Fred E. Terwilliger *MGR-ENG*

Human Resources: James F. Marron

Purchasing: George F. Becker

Total Employees...........................71	**Regional Employees** 21
Year Established........................1937	**SIC Code**....................................4911
Annual Revenues ($000) 21,301	

Central Maintenance & Service Co., Inc.

61 E. Crafton Ave.
Pittsburgh, PA 15205
County: Allegheny

Phone: (412) 922-4131
Fax: (412) 922-1963

Provider of contract janitorial services to commercial and industrial clients in Southwestern Pennsylvania.

Officers: David R. Duffy *P*
Terrance R. Duffy *VP*
W. Lee Cassidy *VP*

Total Employees............................300
Year Established 1960   **SIC Code**......................................7349

Central Property Services, Inc.

The Law & Finance Bldg., 429 Fourth Ave., Ste. 1308
Pittsburgh, PA 15219
County: Allegheny

Phone: (412) 261-0210
Fax: (412) 471-3346

Provider of commercial cleaning and maintenance services in Pittsburgh and surrounding areas. The Company services commercial office space, university space, airport space, industrial space, recreational facilities, food service areas and retail establishments. It specializes in cleaning medical office space.

Officers: George Whalen *P*
Louis G. DiNardo *VP & GMGR*
James Booze *DIR-OPR*
Kellie Kreiser *DIR-MKT & SAL*

Purchasing: Tony Letiziz

Total Employees............................750   **Regional Employees** 750
Year Established 1989   **SIC Code**......................................7349

Central Tax Bureau of Pennsylvania, Inc.

300 Mt. Lebanon Blvd.
Pittsburgh, PA 15234
County: Allegheny

Phone: (412) 343-9611
Fax: (412) 343-4660

Provider of tax collection and administrative services to municipalities and school districts throughout the Commonwealth of Pennsylvania. The Company operates additional offices in Aston, Belle Vernon, Berwick, Burgettstown, Dubois, Ellwood City, Franklin, Girard, Greensburg, Johnstown, Kittanning, Lewisburg, McKees Rocks, Norristown, Penn Hills, Uniontown, Verona, Waynesburg and Wilkinsburg, PA. Its subsidiary, Don Wilkinson Agency in Forty Fort and Hazleton, PA, provides tax collection and administration for local municipalities and school districts, and personal property tax administration to county governments in Pennsylvania.

Officers: Don E. Wilkinson *P*
Robert J. Villella *EVP*
Linda Gerlach *TRS*

Human Resources: Dena M. Wengert *SEC*

Total Employees	175	Regional Employees	50
Year Established	1927	SIC Code	7389

Century Steel Erectors, Inc.

1125 Camp Hollow Rd.
West Mifflin, PA 15122
County: Allegheny
Phone: (412) 469-8800
Fax: (412) 469-0813

Provider of specialty subcontractor services consisting of steel erection, rigging, crane rental and industrial maintenance services.

Officers: Donn R. Taylor *P*
David Mahokey *SEC & TRS*

Human Resources: Darlaine L. Taylor

Total Employees	100	Regional Employees	100
Year Established	1983	SIC Code	1791
Annual Revenues ($000)			13,500

Cerdec Corp.—Drakenfeld Products

W. Wylie Ave.
P.O. Box 519
Washington, PA 15301
County: Washington
Phone: (412) 223-5900
Fax: (412) 229-5602

Manufacturer of ceramic pigments, inorganic pigments, glass enamels, precious metal products and ceramic glaze systems. The Company is a subsidiary of Cerdec AG, which is headquartered in Frankfurt, Germany. It maintains international sales, marketing and manufacturing facilities in Brazil, China, France, Germany, Indonesia, Italy, Japan, Korea, Mexico and Spain. Cerdec AG is a joint venture between CIBA Ltd. in Basel, Switzerland, which is listed on the Zurich Stock Exchange, and Degussa AG in Frankfurt, Germany, which is listed on the Frankfurt Stock Exchange.

Officers: Robert Martel *P & CEO*
Gerald Heider *VP*
Tom Kearns *VP*
Charles Neff *VP*
Mirek Novotny *VP*
Ronald Sorice *VP*
Betty Lee *SEC*
J. Michael Scureman *AST-SEC*

C

Human Resources: Dave Bocchini

Total Employees........................1,600   **Regional Employees** 310
Year Established 1869   **SIC Code**.....................................2851
Annual Revenues ($000) 60,000

Ceridian Employer Services

2025 Greentree Rd.
Pittsburgh, PA 15220
County: Allegheny

Phone: (412) 572-8050
Fax: (412) 343-7692
Internet Address: ces.ceridian.com

Provider of integrated human resources management systems, outsourced payroll processing, tax filing, training and other consulting services to mid-sized and large employers. The Company, which is headquartered in Minneapolis, MN, operates more than 30 branch offices throughout the U.S. It is a division of Ceridian Corp., which is also headquartered in Minneapolis, MN, and listed on the NYSE. The local facility serves clients in Western Pennsylvania and West Virginia.

Officers: Frank J. Ravella *VP & GMGR-Pittsburgh Region*
Scott Hersh *District VP-Client Services*

Total Employees........................8,000   **Regional Employees** 30
Year Established 1932   **SIC Code**.....................................7374
Annual Revenues ($000) 1,500,000

Certified Carpet Distributors, Inc.

6901 Lynn Way
Pittsburgh, PA 15208
County: Allegheny

Phone: (412) 441-2700
Fax: (412) 441-9038

Wholesaler of floor covering products, including commercial and residential carpet, padding, ceramic floor and wall tile, vinyl tile, commercial sheet vinyl, rubber and carpet cove base, and wood flooring. The Company also offers flooring adhesives, mortars and grout; flooring underlayment; and miscellaneous installation supplies. Its clients include contractors and retail dealers in parts of Maryland, Ohio, Pennsylvania and West Virginia.

Officers: Robert Eisner *P*

Human Resources: Nancy Georges

Purchasing: Linda Holmes

Total Employees............................34	Regional Employees 29	
Year Established 1965	SIC Code....................................5023	

Champ Printing Co., Inc.

730 Fourth Ave.
Coraopolis, PA 15108
County: Allegheny

Phone: (412) 269-0197
Fax: (412) 269-0473

Provider of full-service commercial printing and typesetting to the public and to businesses in Western Pennsylvania.

Officers: Robert D. Champ *P*

Human Resources: Bernie Opatick *GMGR (Purchasing)*

Total Employees............................42	Regional Employees 42
Year Established 1979	SIC Code....................................2752
Annual Revenues ($000) 5,500	

Chancellor Broadcasting Co.

One Allegheny Sq.
Pittsburgh, PA 15212
County: Allegheny

Phone: (412) 323-5300
Fax: (412) 323-5313
Internet Address: www.3wsradio.com

Owner and operator of radio station WWSW simulcasting on AM 970 and FM 94.5. The Station broadcasts 24 hours per day, with an oldies format geared to the 25-54 year old, baby boom generation. The Company is headquartered in Dallas, TX, and listed on the NASDAQ.

Officers: Steven Dinetz *P & CEO*
George Toulas *EVP*
Michael Frohm *VP & GMGR*

Human Resources: Charles Weaver *(Purchasing)*

Total Employees............................37	Regional Employees 37
Year Established 1929	SIC Code...................................4832
Annual Revenues ($000) 9,000	

C

Chapman Corp.

331 S. Main St.
Washington, PA 15301
County: Washington

Phone: (412) 228-1900
Fax: (412) 228-4311

Provider of engineering and construction services to industrial customers, institutions and commercial ventures. The Company offers civil, structural, mechanical, electrical and instrumentation services on "greenfield" projects and upgrades to existing facilities. It also performs commercial and industrial fabrication of pipe, sheet, duct and plate. The Company's engineers and project managers have design, planning, scheduling, estimating, procurement and construction experience in various industries such as glass, steel and specialty metals, chemical, utility, paper, beverage and mining. Its Imaging and Engineering Technology Division offers electronic document management systems which transform various paper-based processes into one automated program. The Company serves clients across the nation.

Officers: John W. Chapman *CEO*
Art W. Hathaway *P*
Joan A. Chapman *VP-Systems*
Robert J. Macedonia *VP-FIN & ADM*
Richard D. Tomsic *VP-SAL & MKT*

Human Resources: R. Gene Chapman

Purchasing: Michael Aloe

Total Employees............................500	Regional Employees 300
Year Established 1945	SIC Code....................................8711
Annual Revenues ($000) 70,000	

Charapp Ford, Inc., Babe

637 Eden Park Blvd.
McKeesport, PA 15132
County: Allegheny

Phone: (412) 751-2130
Fax: (412) 751-4007

Automobile dealership selling a full line of Ford vehicles. The Company offers new and used cars and trucks, as well as leasing, parts, service and body work. Its affiliates include Charapp Ford North at 110 Rte. 908 in Natrona Heights, PA; Charapp Ford South at 2840 Washington Rd. in Pittsburgh, PA; and Charapp Freeport Dodge at 559 Freeport Rd. in Freeport, PA. The Company and its affiliates have a total of 240 employees.

Officers: Babe Charapp *C-OWN*
Ron Charapp *C-OWN*
Richard Bercik *GMGR-Natrona Heights, PA*
Paul Letso *GMGR-Pittsburgh, PA*
Joe Lucchetti *GMGR-McKeesport, PA*
Henry Rudzki *GMGR-Freeport, PA*

Total Employees	75	**Regional Employees**	75
Year Established	1979	**SIC Code**	5511

Chatham College

Woodland Rd.
Pittsburgh, PA 15232
County: Allegheny

Phone: (412) 365-1100
Fax: (412) 365-1609
Internet Address: www.chatham.edu

Nonprofit, private educational institution. The College offers 35 undergraduate departmental majors and 6 graduate programs of study. Its undergraduate program enrolls only female students while its graduate program is coeducational. The College's total enrollment consists of approximately 821 undergraduate, graduate and continuing education students.

Officers: Esther Barazzone *P*
G. Timothy Bowman *VP-FIN & ADM*
Lou Anne Caligiuri *VP-Student DEV*
Mary Kay Poppenberg *VP-Institutional Advancement*
Anne Steele *VP-Academic Affairs*
Annette Giovengo *Dean-Enrollment MGT*

Human Resources: Frank Greco *DIR-Human Resources*

Total Employees	284	**Regional Employees**	284
Year Established	1869	**SIC Code**	8221
Annual Revenues ($000)	15,500		

Chatwins Group, Inc.

300 Weyman Plaza, Ste. 340
Pittsburgh, PA 15236
County: Allegheny

Phone: (412) 885-5501
Fax: (412) 885-5512

Designer, manufacturer and marketer of a broad range of fabricated and machined industrial parts and products, primarily for OEMs in a variety of industries. The Company's principal fabricated and machined products include large, seamless pressure vessels for highly pressurized gases; steel and aluminum grating; industrial hydraulic and pneumatic cylinders; industrial cranes; large mill equipment; cold-rolled steel leaf springs; and roll-formed storage racks. Its divisions include Alliance, which designs, engineers and manufactures cranes used in a wide range of steel and aluminum mill applications, and large special purpose cranes used in marine and aerospace applications and heavy industrial plants; Auto-Lok, which manufactures and markets roll-formed storage racks for industrial and commercial handling systems and general storage applications; CP Industries (CPI), which specializes in manufacturing large, seamless pressure vessels for above ground storage and transportation of highly pressurized gases such as natural gas, hydrogen, nitrogen, oxygen and helium; Europa, which holds interests in a small number of leases for oil and gas properties, investing in low-risk gas exploration and managing a portfolio of oil and gas participations; Hanna, which designs and manufactures a broad line of hydraulic and pneumatic cylinders, actuators, accumulators and manifolds; Klemp, which is a diversified manufacturer of steel and aluminum bar grating products in a variety of sizes, configurations and finishes, and also custom fabricates bar grating products for specialized applications; and Steelcraft, which manufactures and markets cold-rolled steel leaf springs. The Company operates a variety of facilities located in Georgia, Illinois, Missouri, Ohio, Oklahoma, Texas, Utah and Wisconsin. In addition to its corporate headquarters located at the above address, CPI's manufacturing plant is located in McKeesport, PA.

Officers: Charles E. Bradley *CH*
Joseph C. Lawyer *P & CEO*
Kimball J. Bradley *VP & Division P-Auto-Lok*
Russell S. Carolus *VP & SEC*
Jack T. Croushore *VP & Division P-CPI*
John M. Froehlich *VP, CFO & TRS*
Gerald W. McClure *VP & Division P-Klemp*
Robert L. Rakstang *VP & Division P-Hanna*
Christopher Sause *VP & Division P-Alliance*
Alan S. Wippman *VP & Division P-Steelcraft*
Thomas J. Vogel *Division P-Europa*

Total Employees 1,112   **Regional Employees** 131
Year Established 1980   **SIC Code** 6719
Annual Revenues ($000) 160,000

Chelsea Building Products, Inc.

565 Cedar Way
Oakmont, PA 15139
County: Allegheny

Phone: (412) 826-8077
Fax: (412) 826-8096

Designer and extruder of rigid vinyl lineals for window and door systems. The Company claims to be the nation's leading supplier of vinyl window and door systems to both the new construction and remodeling and replacement markets and, through its network of window manufacturers throughout the United States, produces the greatest number of custom-sized and shaped vinyl windows annually. The Company's brands include Poly-Tex and Custom Gard vinyl windows, Chelsea Windows and Patio Doors and a variety of proprietary window programs. Its extrusions produce over 350 different window products. The Company is a subsidiary of the Tessenderlo Group, which is headquartered in Brussels, Belgium, and is listed on the Brussels Stock Exchange.

Officers: Ted Kridler *P*
Bob Conway *DIR-FIN*
Bob Longfellow *DIR-Strategic Business Planning*
E. L. Walker, Jr. *DIR-MKT*
Paul Brestelli *VP-MFG*
Ronald J. Lynch *VP-PDEV*
Tom Morrow *VP-SAL & MKT*

Human Resources: Ray Walkowski

Total Employees ....300+	**Regional Employees** ....300+
Year Established 1975	**SIC Code** 3082

ChemTech Consultants, Inc.

1370 Washington Pike, 4th Fl.
Bridgeville, PA 15017
County: Allegheny

Phone: (412) 221-1360
Fax: (412) 221-5685

Provider of process and project engineering services with expertise in chemical process design, instrumentation and control, materials handling, boiler and power generation, environmental control systems, capital planning and feasibility, and plant operations and optimization. The Company serves a variety of industries nationwide, including the coal tar processing, chemicals, metals, coke making, food processing, pharmaceuticals and manufacturing applications industries.

Officers: Anthony Foster *P*
Thurman A. Wilson *VP-ENG*

Human Resources: John H. Palmer *VP-FIN*

Purchasing: Richard T. Budzowski *MGR-SAL*

Total Employees ....50+	**Regional Employees** ....50+
Year Established 1988	**SIC Code** 8711

Chestnut Ridge Foam, Inc.

Rte. 981 N.
P.O. Box 781
Latrobe, PA 15650
County: Westmoreland

Phone: (412) 537-9000
Fax: (412) 537-9004

Manufacturer and fabricator of fire-resistant and other specialty (including molded polyurethane) foam cushioning products. The Company serves a variety of markets worldwide, including aviation, surface transportation (bus and rail) and institutional (detention facilities, universities, health care and the military). Additional markets include contract furniture and products for the inking and stenciling industry. The Company's brand names include Prevent, Safguard, Saflite II and Vonar. It operates a regional sales office in Orlando, FL.

Officers: G. Scott Baton *CH*
Dennis R. Robitaille *P*
Larry Garrity *VP-FIN*
Bob Leccia *VP-MFG*
Carl Ogburn *VP-SAL & MKT*
Dan Myers *Technical DIR*

Human Resources: Vickie Glasser

Purchasing: Fred Shine

Total Employees...........................150	**Regional Employees** 149
Year Established 1986	**SIC Code**.....................................3086
Annual Revenues ($000)..16,000+	

Chick Workholding Solutions, Inc.

500 Keystone Dr.
Warrendale, PA 15086
County: Allegheny

Phone: (412) 772-1644
Fax: (412) 772-1633

Manufacturer of Chick Multi-Lok and Qwik-Lok workholding systems for vertical and horizontal computer and numerically controlled milling machines. The Company's products are utilized by a wide variety of industries in producing machine parts.

Officers: G. Rex Swann *CEO*
        Paul Swann *P*
        Cal Macomber *NATL SAL MGR*

Purchasing: Judy Damico

Total Employees..............................50   Regional Employees 50
Year Established 1989   SIC Code....................................3545

Children's Home of Pittsburgh, The

5618 Kentucky Ave.
Pittsburgh, PA 15232
County: Allegheny

Phone: (412) 441-4884
Fax: (412) 441-0167

   Nonprofit provider of children's services serving the needs of infants and their families. The Agency offers two programs. Throughout the history of its Infant Adoption program, the Agency has placed almost 7,000 infants and young children in permanent, adoptive homes. Through the Agency's Transitional Infant Care (TIC) program, it operates a specialty hospital (located at the above address) which provides care for premature and high-risk infants who require continued hospitalization following prolonged stays in traditional neonatal intensive care units. Since the inception of the TIC program in 1984, the Agency has treated over 1,000 premature and high-risk infants.

Officers: Pamela R. Schanwald *CEO*
        Marilyn Caye *DIR-DEV*
        Nancy Kennedy *Clinical Administrator-Transitional Infant Care*
        Kristin Morris *Clinical Administrator-Adoption*

Human Resources: Lynne DiBucci

Total Employees..............................67   Regional Employees 67
Year Established 1894   SIC Code....................................8069

Children's Hospital of Pittsburgh

3705 Fifth Ave.
Pittsburgh, PA 15213
County: Allegheny

Phone: (412) 692-5325
Internet Address: www.chp.edu

   Nonprofit regional referral center, 235-bed hospital committed to routine through tertiary pediatric care, education and advanced research. The Hospital was ranked seventh among pediatric hospitals across the nation by U.S. News & World Report. Its staff of 672 physicians provide a wide range of care, including adolescent medicine, neurology and neurosurgery, the Benedum pediatric trauma program, transplantation, critical care medicine, cardiology, diabetes care, orthopaedics and otolaryngology (ear, nose and throat). The Hospital also operates satellite facilities providing specialty outpatient services at Children's East in Monroeville, PA; Children's South in the South Hills area of Pittsburgh, PA; and Children's North in Wexford, PA.

Officers: Paul S. Kramer *P*

Human Resources: Todd Purvis *DIR-Human Resources*

Total Employees..........................2,298	**Regional Employees** 2,298
Year Established 1890	**SIC Code**.....................................8069
Annual Revenues ($000) 181,174	

Chiz Bros. Inc.

R.D. 4, Box 40A, Glassport-Elizabeth Rd.
Elizabeth, PA 15037
County: Allegheny

Phone: (412) 384-5220
Fax: (412) 384-2358

Refractory contractor engaged in the design and installation of industrial furnace linings such as forge furnaces, heat-treat furnaces, stress-relieving furnaces, kilns and lehrs. The Company maintains a vast in-house stock of brand name materials from conventional refractories to ceramic fiber. The Company claims to be one of the largest distributor/installers of Unifrax Fiberfrax Ceramic Fiber products in the world. In addition, its installation crew is available 24 hours a day to assist clients nationwide. The Company serves the iron and steel, glass and ceramics, aluminum, power and coal, forge and foundry, and petrochemical industries as well as providing for industrial boilers and incinerators. It operates branch offices in Alliance, OH, and Erie, PA.

Officers: Edward S. Chiz *P*
Randy A. Pingree *VP-FIN*
Mark A. Rhoa *SAL MGR*

Human Resources: George A. Chiz *SEC & TRS*

Purchasing: Raymond M. Chiz *VP*

Total Employees...............................34	**Regional Employees** 32
Year Established 1967	**SIC Code**.....................................3255

Chris Candies, Inc.

1557 Spring Garden Ave.
Pittsburgh, PA 15212
County: Allegheny

Phone: (412) 322-9400
Fax: (412) 322-9402

Contract private label manufacturer serving the confectionery industry. The Company supplies its services throughout the United States to the major chocolate manufacturers and marketers. The Company's products include candy bars, chocolate novelties, organic chocolates and baking products, which are sold through a national brokerage network. In addition, it has a licensing agreement with the comic strip character Ziggy & Friends.

Officers: Timothy J. Rogers *P*
Mark E. McDonel *SEC & TRS*
Karl W. Lex *Plant MGR*

Human Resources: Keith W. Jackson *CON*

Total Employees	30-70	**Regional Employees**	40
Year Established	1947	**SIC Code**	2064

Christopher M's Hand Poured Fudge

2840 Liberty Ave.
Pittsburgh, PA 15222
County: Allegheny

Phone: (412) 338-0400
Fax: (412) 338-0401

Producer of fudge, including chocolate, vanilla and fruit flavors. The Company's confectioneries are sold through retail stores.

Officers: Christopher Warman *P*

Total Employees	15-50		
Year Established	1988	**SIC Code**	2066

Chubb & Son Inc.

Fifth Avenue Place, 120 Fifth Ave.
Pittsburgh, PA 15222
County: Allegheny

Phone: (412) 391-6585
Fax: (412) 456-8979

Provider of commercial and personal property and casualty insurance to individuals and businesses. The Company, which is headquartered in Warren, NJ, is a subsidiary of The Chubb Corp., which is also headquartered in Warren, NJ, and listed on the NYSE. It maintains more than 100 offices worldwide, with branch offices located throughout the United States, Canada, Europe, Latin America and Asia. The Company operates a number of insurance companies known as the Chubb Group of Insurance Cos., including Federal Insurance Co., Great Northern Insurance Co., Pacific Indemnity Co. and Vigilant Insurance Co.

Officers: Linda A. Kortlandt *Pittsburgh Branch MGR*

Human Resources: Gary Tierney *Pittsburgh Branch Human Resources MGR*

Total Employees	9,000	**Regional Employees**	84
Year Established	1882	**SIC Code**	6331
Annual Revenues ($000)	5,680,000		

CIBER, Inc.

1500 Ardmore Blvd., Ste. 402
Pittsburgh, PA 15221
County: Allegheny

Phone: (412) 243-9020
Fax: (412) 243-9030

Provider of custom computer application software consulting, development, integration and implementation services. The Company, which is headquartered in Englewood, CO, and listed on the NASDAQ, works with clients to implement new information technology, to refine and integrate existing information software and to build new, open systems that replace or supplement legacy systems. Its services include strategic analysis and design, development and integration of hardware and software systems, time and material consulting, packaged software migration implementation and project outsourcing management. The local branch office serves clients in Western Pennsylvania.

Officers: Christine R. Locklin *Branch MGR*
           Scott Barnyak *Account MGR*
           Christy Maruca *Account MGR*
           Barbara Steinour *Account MGR*

Total Employees	2,500	**Regional Employees**	180
Year Established	1974	**SIC Code**	7379
Annual Revenues ($000)	156,873		

CID Assoc., Inc.

730 Ekastown Rd.
Sarver, PA 16055
County: Butler

Phone: (412) 353-0300
Fax: (412) 353-0308

Designer and manufacturer of all types of modular facilities through three divisions. The Contract Construction Division handles pre-engineered buildings and high-tech construction such as RF-shielded enclosures, nuclear medicine rooms, computer centers, clean rooms, in-plant offices and turnkey interior retrofit packages. The Steel Fabrication Division manufactures modular buildings mainly for the steel industry, expandable to three stories high, in unlimited widths and lengths. The Company will design and build to client specifications liftable and modular pulpits, computer centers, crane cabs, electrical enclosures and motor control centers. This same concept is used by the Haz-Safe Division in the manufacture of secondary containment enclosures for hazardous storage and medical waste. The Company serves commercial, industrial, institutional, government and military clients worldwide.

Officers: Marlene J. Docherty *CEO, SEC & TRS*
            Charles D. Docherty *P*
            Scott S. Docherty *VP*

Human Resources: Casey S. Docherty *OPR MGR*

Purchasing: Ray Simon *Purchasing Agent*

Total Employees............................50	**Regional Employees** 50
Year Established 1972	**SIC Code**....................................1541
Annual Revenues ($000) 7,000	

Citizens General Hospital

651 Fourth Ave.
New Kensington, PA 15068
County: Westmoreland

Phone: (412) 337-3541
Fax: (412) 339-7449

Nonprofit 214-bed hospital providing medical and surgical care. The Hospital's facilities and services include an ambulatory surgery center, a birthing center, a skilled nursing facility, a school of nursing, an angio-interventional center, chemotherapy, physical and occupational therapy, an emergency department, endoscopy, a heart station, laboratory, a paramedic response unit, respiratory care, HealthPLACE and PhysicianFind Referral Service.

Officers: Robert E. Marino *EDIR*

Total Employees............................755	**Regional Employees** 755
Year Established 1912	**SIC Code**....................................8062

Citizens, Inc.

204 S. Jackson St.
Evans City, PA 16033
County: Butler

Phone: (412) 538-3410
Fax: (412) 538-2228

Bank holding company for the Citizens National Bank of Evans City (Bank), an independent bank providing both traditional and nontraditional banking services for individuals, organizations and businesses, including a full-service trust department, an indirect loan center for car dealers and other retailers, commercial loan services (including a complete U.S. Small Business Administration Loan Program), residential mortgage programs, desktop banking through Citizens Link™, corporate cash management services, group banking (a benefit program that enables employers to provide discounted financial services to their employees) and one-hour turnaround on consumer loans. The Bank operates 13 additional branch offices in Butler (3), Chicora, Cranberry Township, Evans City, Lyndora, Parker, Petrolia, Saxonburg, Wexford (2) and Zelienople, PA.

Officers: Samuel J. Irvine III *CH & CEO*
Donald S. Shamey *P*
Margaret Irvine Weir *EVP*

Human Resources: Susan Todd

Purchasing: Angie Banyay

Total Employees............................180	**Regional Employees** 180
Year Established 1878	**SIC Code**......................................6712
Annual Revenues ($000) 280,135	

Citizens Transport, Inc.

204 S. Jackson St.
P.O. Box 268
Evans City, PA 16033
County: Butler

Phone: (412) 538-4400
Fax: (412) 538-2228

Provider of armored car services and courier delivery to clients throughout Western Pennsylvania.

Officers: Dennis R. Moody *P*

Total Employees.............................42	**Regional Employees** 25
Year Established 1971	**SIC Code**......................................7381
Annual Revenues ($000) 1,000	

Civil & Environmental Consultants, Inc.

601 Holiday Dr., Foster Plaza 3
Pittsburgh, PA 15220
County: Allegheny

Phone: (412) 921-3402
Fax: (412) 921-1815
Internet Address: www.cecinc.com

   Provider of environmental consulting and engineering services to private- and public-sector clients nationwide. The Firm offers such services as site assessment and characterization, environmental audits and hazard assessment, solid and hazardous waste management, hydrogeology and groundwater modeling, site remediation and waste treatment, wetlands management and surface water resource engineering. Additional services are offered in the areas of underground storage tank closure and remediation, geotechnical engineering, civil engineering and site development, and construction phase services and management. The Firm operates a branch office located in Cincinnati, OH.

Special Designations: ENR$_{500}$

Officers: James M. Roberts, Ph.D. *P*
               Kenneth R. Miller *VP*
               James P. Nairn *VP*

Human Resources: Gregory P. Quatchak *VP*

Purchasing: Terry Roberts

Total Employees	80	**Regional Employees**	60
Year Established	1989	**SIC Code**	8744
Annual Revenues ($000)	10,500		

Clark Bar America, Inc.

RIDC Industrial Park, 610 Alpha Dr.
Pittsburgh, PA 15238
County: Allegheny

Phone: (412) 963-7540
Fax: (412) 963-7741
Internet Address: www.clarkbar.com

   Manufacturer of candy and confectionery products. The Company's product line includes Bun bars in caramel, maple and vanilla flavors; Clark chocolate-coated peanut butter bars; and Yoo-hoo chocolate-coated nugget bars. It also markets Everlast endurance and energy bars. The Company's products are distributed nationally through food and confectionery brokers.

Officers: Archie Strimel *CEO*
               Jim Clister *OWN & P*

Gary Evans *VP-SAL & MKT*
George McBriar *COO*

Human Resources: Debbie Tutak

Purchasing: Kevin Brown

Total Employees 100-150

Year Established 1886

Regional Employees 100-150

SIC Code 2064

Clean Textile Systems, L.L.P.

51st & Allegheny Valley Railroad
Pittsburgh, PA 15201
County: Allegheny

Phone: (412) 681-7600
Fax: (412) 687-5490

Provider of linen and laundry services and medical uniforms to hospitals, extended care facilities, clinics and others. The Company's Clean Textile division serves the hospitality industry; its Clean Care division, at 128 N. Lexington in Pittsburgh, PA, serves the health care industry. The Company's clients are located in Maryland, Ohio, Pennsylvania, Virginia and West Virginia. It operates a depot in Washington, PA.

Officers: Douglas H. Ostrow *P*
Dennis Collins *CON*

Total Employees...........................160

Year Established 1934

Regional Employees 160

SIC Code 7213

Cleaning Services Corp.

1330 Wall Ave.
Pitcairn, PA 15140
County: Allegheny

Phone: (412) 373-1440
Fax: (412) 372-1859

Provider of a wide range of commercial and residental cleaning services, including janitorial, carpet and upholstery cleaning, wall washing, ultrasonic blind cleaning and floor maintenance. The Company's subsidiaries include ServiceMaster Professional Building Maintenance Co., which is also headquartered at the above address and serves clients throughout the Pittsburgh metropolitan area; ServiceMaster of Tri-County in Lancaster, PA; and ServiceMaster Services in Exton, PA. The Company is a franchisee of The ServiceMaster Co. L.P., which is headquartered in Downers Grove, IL. It operates through their Residential/Commercial Division, which is headquartered in Memphis, TN.

Officers: Frank C. Gibson *P*

Human Resources: Deborah Gibson *SEC*

Purchasing: Tom Jordan *OPR MGR*

Total Employees............................350	Regional Employees 200
Year Established 1973	SIC Code......................................7349

Cleveland Motion Controls, Inc.

2600 Liberty Ave.
Pittsburgh, PA 15222
County: Allegheny

Phone: (412) 261-8600
Fax: (412) 261-8609

   Manufacturer of motion control products such as amplifiers to a variety of industries worldwide, including the glass, auto, plastic, printing and medical sectors. The facility located at the above address is the Servo Controls and Systems Division of the Company, which is headquartered in Cleveland, OH. The Company is a subsidiary of International Motion Controls, Inc., which is headquartered in Buffalo, NY.

Officers: Paul Rowan *GMGR*
        Frederick Mackey *MFG MGR*
        Himanshu Shah *MKT MGR*

Regional Employees....................100
Year Established 1968   **SIC Code**......................................3625
Annual Revenues ($000) 12,000

Club One, Inc.

6325 Penn Ave.
Pittsburgh, PA 15206
County: Allegheny

Phone: (412) 362-4806
Fax: (412) 362-9056

   Owner and operator of Club One, a 50,000 square foot health and fitness facility located in the East Liberty/Shadyside area of Pittsburgh. The facility offers indoor swimming, racquetball, group exercise programs, spinning, yoga, weight training, indoor track, treadmills, stairmasters, exercise bikes, Nordic Tracks, personal trainers, physical therapy and spa facilities, and includes a restaurant, nursery and hair salon.

Officers: James Rosenbloom *P*
        Donald Doyle *GMGR*

Total Employees............................105	Regional Employees 105
Year Established 1979	SIC Code......................................7991

Codo Manufacturing Corp.

Seven Ave. B, Buncher Industrial District
Leetsdale, PA 15056
County: Allegheny

Phone: (412) 741-2010
Fax: (412) 741-2785

Manufacturer of office reprographic products including carbon papers and films, word and data processing ribbons, laser toner printer cartridges, one-time multi-write carbons, and thermal ribbons and labels for the bar coding industry.

Officers: Gilbert F. Dadowski *P*
                 Jeffrey G. Dadowski *VP-MKT*
                 Daniel C. Homich *VP-SAL*
                 William J. Kennedy *VP-FIN*

Purchasing: Inez McHaffie

Total Employees	50	**Regional Employees**	50
Year Established	1928	**SIC Code**	3955

Cohen & Grigsby, P.C.

2900 CNG Tower, 625 Liberty Ave.
Pittsburgh, PA 15222
County: Allegheny

Phone: (412) 394-4900
Fax: (412) 391-3382
Internet Address: www.cohenlaw.com

General business law firm with approximately 70 attorneys. The Firm is organized into three major departments consisting of business/tax, labor and employment, and litigation. Within these three departments, individual practice groups have been organized by specific industry or type of law. The Firm has experience in a broad range of legal disciplines, including banking, bankruptcy, creditors' rights, commercial and public finance, commercial litigation, environmental law, estate planning and administration, health care, immigration, international transactions, labor and employment law, real estate, securities regulation and taxation. It serves private and public, domestic and multinational corporations in a variety of industrial sectors as well as financial and service organizations, hospitals and other health care providers, nonprofit corporations, government agencies and individuals.

Officers: Charles C. Cohen *CH*
                 Charles R. Brodbeck *P & CEO*
                 Dennis J. Lewis *CH-Litigation Practice Group*
                 John L. Lyncheski *CH-Labor/Employment & Health Care Practice Group*
                 Hugh W. Nevin *CH-INTL Business Practice Group*

Human Resources: Allan J. Todesco *(Purchasing)*

Total Employees............................150	**Regional Employees** 150
Year Established 1981	**SIC Code** 8111

Columbia Energy Services Corp.

121 Hillpointe Dr., Ste. 100
Canonsburg, PA 15317
County: Washington

Phone: (412) 873-1300
Fax: (412) 873-1310

Nonregulated natural gas marketing company providing an array of supply, fuel management and transportation-related products and services to a diverse customer base, including distribution companies, independent power producers, large industrial plants, commercial businesses, joint marketing partners and individual homeowners throughout the Northeast, Midwest and Gulf Coast regions of the U.S. The Company operates offices in Lexington, KY; Canton, Cleveland, Columbus and Toledo, OH; York, PA; Houston, TX; Reston, VA; and Charleston, WV. It is a subsidiary of Columbia Gas System, Inc., which is headquartered in Reston, VA, and listed on the NYSE.

Officers: Anthony Trubisz, Jr. *P*
Greg Davis *VP-Day Trading*
Marshall D. Lang *VP-MKT*
Pamela R. Murphy *VP-OPR*

Human Resources: Robert Gustafson

Total Employees..............................97	**Regional Employees** 60
Year Established 1989	**SIC Code**......................................4923
Annual Revenues ($000) 750,000	

Columbia Gas of Pennsylvania, Inc.

650 Washington Rd.
Pittsburgh, PA 15228
County: Allegheny

Phone: (412) 344-9800
Fax: (412) 572-7165
Internet Address: www.columbiaenergy.com

Natural gas utility providing services to residential, commercial and industrial customers in 455 communities located throughout 26 counties in Pennsylvania. The Company operates service centers in Bethel Park, Bradford, Emlenton, Gettysburg, Glenfield, Jeannette, New Bethlehem, New Castle, Rochester, Somerset, State College, Uniontown, Warren, Washington and York. The Company also operates a customer service center in Smithfield to provide centralized customer service for all of its 387,000 customers. The Company is a subsidiary of Columbia Gas System, Inc., which is headquartered in Wilmington, DE, and listed on the NYSE.

Officers: Gary J. Robinson *P & CEO*
Terrence J. Murphy *SVP-Public Policy & Corporate Communications*

Human Resources: Sally Hobbs *DIR-Human Resource Programs*

Purchasing: Richard Rupp

Total Employees	1,000	**Regional Employees**	657
Year Established	1885	**SIC Code**	4924
Annual Revenues ($000)	432,623		

Commercial Stone Co., Inc.

2200 Springfield Pike
Connellsville, PA 15425
County: Fayette

Phone: (412) 626-0080
Fax: (412) 626-8543

Manufacturer and wholesaler of asphalt products and provider of state-approved aggregates. The Company's facilities include an underground mine: the Springfield Pike Quarry, in Connellsville, PA; two surface mines: the Belle Vernon Quarry in Belle Vernon, PA, and the Rich Hill Quarry in Connellsville, PA; and three asphalt plants: the Connellsville Asphalt Plant in Connellsville, PA, the Irwin Asphalt Plant in Adamsburg, PA, and the Washington Asphalt Plant in Dunningsville, PA. The Company's products are used in a variety of construction-related projects, including road construction, serving clients throughout Southwestern Pennsylvania.

Officers: Joseph H. Shearer *CH & CEO*
R. Scott Shearer *P & COO*
Richard Young *EVP*
Scott Turer *CON*

Human Resources: Leah Treille *MGR-ADM*

Purchasing: Theodore DiNardo *General Superintendent*

Total Employees	110	**Regional Employees**	110
Year Established	1972	**SIC Code**	2951

Commonwealth Land Title Insurance Co.

Frick Bldg., 437 Grant St., Mezzanine Level
Pittsburgh, PA 15219
County: Allegheny

Phone: (412) 471-1492
Fax: (412) 471-8167

Provider of a title-related services, including searches and insurance. The Company is headquartered in Philadelphia, PA. The local branch office serves clients in Western Pennsylvania and West Virginia, with an additional small branch office located in Washington, PA. The Company is a subsidiary of Reliance Group Holdings, Inc., which is headquartered in New York, NY, and listed on the NYSE.

Officers: Gerald E. Shelpman *VP & Division MGR*
Charles J. Keffer *VP & Pittsburgh Branch MGR*
Barbara Milnarcik *VP & Agency MGR*
Ronald J. Shelpman *AVP & Washington, PA, Branch MGR*

Human Resources: William Block *(Philadelphia, PA)*

Purchasing: David Spangler *(Philadelphia, PA)*

Total Employees	5,000	**Regional Employees**	44
Year Established	1876	**SIC Code**	6361

Community Bancorp, Inc.

2681 Mosside Blvd.
Monroeville, PA 15146
County: Allegheny

Phone: (412) 856-8410
Fax: (412) 856-4330

Bank holding company for its sole direct subsidiary, Community Savings Bank (CSB). CSB is a Pennsylvania-chartered savings bank with twelve locations throughout Allegheny, Washington and Westmoreland Counties, PA. The Company was acquired in 1992 by USBANCORP, Inc., which is headquartered in Johnstown, PA, and listed on the NASDAQ. Traditionally, CSB originated and held fixed-rate residential mortgage loans, which were funded primarily by certificates of deposit and offered a few fee-based services. CSB has begun the process of expanding its product offerings through the introduction of commercial lending and expanded consumer lending and deposit gathering in order to position it as a full-service community bank. In addition to the Company's main banking office which is also located at the above address, branch offices are located in Bethel Park, Coraopolis, Finleyville, Jeannette, New Kensington, North Versailles and Pittsburgh (5).

Officers: W. Harrison Vail *P & CEO*
Thomas J. Chunchick *SVP-ADM*
Harry G. King *SVP-Retail Banking*
Vincent Locher *SVP-Commercial Lending*

Human Resources: Richard Barron *VP-Human Resources*

Total Employees...............................96	**Regional Employees** 96	
Year Established 1890	**SIC Code**.....................................6712	
Annual Revenues ($000)...........................426,386 (Assets)		

Community College of Allegheny County

800 Allegheny Ave.
Pittsburgh, PA 15233
County: Allegheny

Phone: (412) 237-3100
Fax: (412) 237-3195
Internet Address: www.ccac.edu

Nonprofit, public comprehensive two-year college offering programs to meet a wide range of educational needs. The College offers numerous academic programs leading to the Associate's degree in Arts, the Associate's degree in Science, the Associate's degree in Applied Sciences and numerous Certificates. These programs train students for employment and enable the student to transfer to four-year institutions. The College also offers Continuing Education programs to enrich the personal and professional lives of the people of the community. These programs are offered at the college's four campuses, at the eight major off-campus centers and at over 400 off-campus sites. The College claims to be the largest community college in Pennsylvania, enrolling one of every four students attending a community college in the state. The 18th-largest multicampus community college in the nation, it compares in size to the undergraduate enrollment of the University of Pittsburgh and the Pennsylvania State University. The College enrolls approximately 90,000 students, with around 23,000 in academic programs and about 67,000 in community service and continuing education. In addition to the Allegheny Campus, located at the above address, the College is comprised of the Boyce Campus, which is situated 15 miles east from Pittsburgh's Golden Triangle and adjacent to Boyce Park and the Monroeville community; the North Campus, which can be found at 8701 Perry Hwy. in McCandless; and the South Campus, which is located in West Mifflin, on a 200-acre site near Century III Mall. The College is an instrumentality of the Commonwealth of Pennsylvania.

Officers: John M. Kingsmore, Ph.D. *P*
J. David Griffin, Ph.D. *VP-Student Services*
James Holmberg, Ph.D. *VP-Academic Affairs*
Patricia McDonald, Ph.D. *VP-Continuing Education*
Jacqueline Taylor, Ph.D. *VP-Institutional DEV*

Human Resources: Jeanne Shader

Purchasing: Joseph Pugliano

Total Employees	4,773	Regional Employees	4,773
Year Established	1966	SIC Code	8221
Annual Revenues ($000)			69,500

Community College of Beaver County

One Campus Dr.
Monaca, PA 15061
County: Beaver

Phone: (412) 775-8561
Fax: (412) 775-4055

Nonprofit, public, two-year college offering the Associate's degree, certificate and diploma programs in 38 areas of study. The College also operates the Aviation Sciences Center at 125 Cessna Dr. in Beaver Falls, PA. In addition to offering aviation education, it claims to be the only school to own an air traffic control tower, equipped, staffed and operated by the College's faculty and students. The College enrolls 1,238 full-time students and 1,114 part-time students.

Officers: Margaret Williams-Betlyn, Ph.D. *P*
　　　　　　　Judy A. Garbinski *VP-Planning, Assessment & DEV*
　　　　　　　Michael J. Macon *VP-Student Services*
　　　　　　　James H. Thomas, Jr., Ed.D. *VP-Academic Services*

Human Resources: David Albanese *DIR-Human Resources*

Purchasing: John A. Rizzo *VP-Business & CON*

Total Employees	300	Regional Employees	290
Year Established	1966	SIC Code	8222
Annual Revenues ($000)			12,000

Community Playthings

New Meadow Run, Rte. 40
P.O. Box 240
Farmington, PA 15437
County: Fayette

Phone: (412) 329-8573
Fax: (412) 329-1270

Manufacturer and retailer of children's wooden toys and furniture. The local plant provides plywood panel processing, assembly and finishing of wooden products, and steel fabrication including powder coating and welding, for the

Company's products. The plant is owned and operated by Bruderhof Communities International (BCI), which is headquartered in Rifton, NY. BCI operates additional facilities in Norfolk, CT; Elka Park and Ulster Park, NY; and two locations in England.

Officers: Harry Kleinsasser *GMGR*
Mike Pappas *SEC & TRS*

C

Human Resources: Randy Gauger

Total Employees	300	**Regional Employees**	80
Year Established	1950	**SIC Code**	3944
Annual Revenues ($000)	6,000		

Composidie, Inc.

101 Rte. 380 W.
Apollo, PA 15613
County: Armstrong

Phone: (412) 727-3466
Fax: (412) 727-3788

Designer and manufacturer of progressive carbide dies for high speed volume production related to electronics and semiconductors and other industries. In addition to building stamping tools related to connector and/or contact tools, the Company stamps parts from the tools it produces for clients such as AMP, Bic Corp., Levolor, Lucent, Northern Telecom and Texas Instruments. The facility located at the above address contains the Company's corporate headquarters, as well as its Lead Frame and Connector Divisions. Its other operations include the EDM Services Division in Greensburg, PA, a wire electronic discharge machining facility, and the Toolex Division in Leechburg, PA, a grinding facility.

Officers: L. Ted Wohlin *P*
Chester A. Jonczak *VP*
Priscilla Slagle *CON*

Purchasing: Shari McCutcheon

Total Employees	270	**Regional Employees**	270
Year Established	1971	**SIC Code**	3469
Annual Revenues ($000)	40,000+		

Compunetics, Inc.

Monroeville Industrial Park, 700 Seco Rd.
Monroeville, PA 15146
County: Allegheny

Phone: (412) 373-8110
Fax: (412) 373-2720
Internet Address: www.compunetics.com

Operating through its Printed Circuit Boards Division and Engineering Services Division, the Company provides complete board design and prototyping. Through its Compunetix, Inc. (CI) subsidiary, located at 2000 Eldo Rd. in Monroeville, PA, the Company specializes in telecommunications technology and related services. It has designed, developed and installed digital voice conferencing systems that can support a new generation of high-performance teleconferencing capabilities. These systems are successfully functioning in a number of operationally critical conferencing environments, including government mission-oriented systems for NASA and the FAA, and commercial service bureau application environments. CI consists of the Communications Systems Division, the Federal Systems Division, the Instrumentation Systems Division and a subsidiary, Chorus Call, Inc., which operates a branch office in Lugano, Switzerland (Compunetix SA).

Officers: Giorgio Coraluppi *P*
Constance Michael *CON*
Ansel Schwartz *SEC*
Terry Zimmerman *OPR MGR*
Keith Marcon *CON-Compunetix, Inc.*
Joe Kasunich *MGR-Instrumentation Systems Division*
John Lawrence *MGR-Teleconferencing Services*
Gerard Pompa *MGR-Communications Systems Division*

Human Resources: Aimee Miller *Human Resources Administrator*

Total Employees............................225
Year Established 1968
Annual Revenues ($000) 27,000
Regional Employees 220
SIC Code.....................................3661

Computer Assoc. International, Inc.

2000 Park Lane
Pittsburgh, PA 15275
County: Allegheny

Phone: (412) 494-2500
Fax: (412) 494-9301
Internet Address: www.cai.com

Provider of mission-critical software that runs businesses. The Company develops, licenses and supports more than 500 integrated products for applications that include enterprise management, database and application development, Internet/Intranet, financial, manufacturing and human resources. Its clients include major industrial, government, educational and research organizations, as well as small- to mid-sized businesses. The Company has partnerships and alliances with virtually every leading hardware and software vendor. From its headquarters in Islandia, NY, the Company operates 130 offices in 40 countries around the globe and is listed on the NYSE. The local office serves clients throughout the Commonwealth of Pennsylvania.

Officers: Robert Marcoux *Divisional VP-SAL*
David Molinaro *Regional VP-Service*

Human Resources: Kelly Clarke

Total Employees	9,000	**Regional Employees**	150
Year Established	1976	**SIC Code**	7372
Annual Revenues ($000)	3,900,000		

Computerm Corp.

111 Wood St.
Pittsburgh, PA 15222
County: Allegheny

Phone: (412) 391-7804
Fax: (412) 391-4964

Provider of computer products to Fortune 500 data centers that connect IBM mainframe computers to remote devices. The Company connects IBM mainframes with remote peripherals in any location, without using additional CPUs. The system uses integral data compression to maximize throughput and reduce communication costs. It supports native frame relay for alternative path routing. Applications supported include disaster recovery, printing, tape vaulting, check imaging and data center consolidation. The Company has over 1,200 systems installed in a variety of networking environments and industries. A branch office is located in England.

Officers: Richard Madden *CEO*
Doug Goodall *P*
Sharon Evankovich *Public Relations*

Human Resources: Barbara Young *Personnel DIR & CON*

Total Employees	97	**Regional Employees**	96
Year Established	1969	**SIC Code**	3600

COMPUTERPEOPLE, Inc.

4400 Campbells Run Rd.
Pittsburgh, PA 15205
County: Allegheny

Phone: (412) 494-9800
Fax: (412) 494-9890
Internet Address: www.compeople.com

Provider of software consulting services and computer systems design, analysis and programming to more than 500 corporations nationwide. In addition to mainframe support, the Company specializes in client-server technology support including SAP, Oracle and Powersoft consulting practices. The Company has operations in 38 states including regional offices in Sacramento, CA; Cincinnati and Columbus, OH; Portland, OR; and Pune, India. Its divisions are COMPUCOM, which provides records management, imaging and microfiche services, and RPM Systems, which provides client-server assistance.

Officers: Lewis P. Wheeler *P*
Paul Freudenberg *P-RPM Systems Division*
Tom Sweeney *P-COMPUCOM Division*
Terry A. Serafini *EVP*
Tom Pascale *VP-MKT*
Joe Reljac *VP-ADM*

Total Employees........................1,000   **Regional Employees**..................260
Year Established........................1968   **SIC Code**......................................7379
Annual Revenues ($000)...70,000

ComTrol Corp.

500 Pennsylvania Ave.
P.O. Box 306
Irwin, PA 15642
County: Westmoreland

Phone: (412) 864-3800
Fax: (412) 864-9358

Designer and manufacturer of mining, industrial and utility voice communication systems. The Company's industrial audio equipment is designed for use in explosive, corrosive and high noise areas. Its mining communication units are approved by the Mine Safety and Health Administration for use in methane atmospheres. Its industrial and utility communication units are approved by Factory Mutual for use in explosive environments. All of the Company's equipment is designed for easy system expansion and interconnection to other systems such as telephones and handheld radios.

Officers: Thomas I. Agnew *P*
Dennis Freda *SAL MGR*
Richard J. Kuhn *Chief ENG*

Human Resources: Jack Parfitt *Production Supervisor*

Purchasing: Perry Cotherman

Total Employees...............................36	**Regional Employees** 36	
Year Established 1976	**SIC Code**....................................3669	
Annual Revenues ($000) 2,500		

C

Comunale Co., Inc., S. A.

305 23rd St.
Pittsburgh, PA 15215
County: Allegheny

Phone: (412) 782-5840
Fax: (412) 782-3202

Full-service fire protection contractor, providing sales, design, fabrication and installation of all types of fire protection systems. The Company also offers 24-hour emergency service as well as inspection and maintenance of fire protection equipment. The Company is headquartered in Akron, OH. It operates additional branch offices in Detroit, MI; Cincinnati, Cleveland, Columbus and Fremont, OH; and Johnstown and Philadelphia, PA.

Officers: Stephen A. Comunale *P*
Michele G. Comunale *VP*
Martha A. Comunale *SEC & TRS*

Human Resources: Joseph May

Purchasing: Mark J. Comunale *VP & Pittsburgh Branch MGR*

Total Employees...........................320	**Regional Employees** 45	
Year Established 1973	**SIC Code**....................................1799	
Annual Revenues ($000) 45,000		

Conair Group, Inc., The

100 Wall St.
Pittsburgh, PA 15202
County: Allegheny

Phone: (412) 261-3488
Fax: (412) 261-3482

Manufacturer of auxiliary equipment primarily for the plastics industry, including material handling equipment, temperature control equipment, robots, granulators, pelletizers and downstream extrusion equipment. The Company's principal plant is located in Franklin, PA.

Officers: G. Watts Humphrey, Jr. *CH & CEO*
E. Niles Kenyon *P & COO*
Eugene O'Sullivan *CFO*

Total Employees............................600	**Regional Employees** 150
Year Established 1955	**SIC Code** 3559
Annual Revenues ($000) 125-150,000	

Conco Systems, Inc.

530 Jones St.
Verona, PA 15147
County: Allegheny

Phone: (412) 828-1166
Fax: (412) 826-8255

Provider of off-line mechanical tube cleaning products and services. The Company manufactures a complete line of tube cleaning tools and systems used to clean condensers and heat exchanger tubes in nuclear and fossil power generation stations worldwide. Its Service Division provides specialized services incorporating state-of-the-art equipment for SF6 and helium leak detection, as well as eddy current testing, tube cleaning and plugging. Heat transfer testing, condenser performance evaluation software and on-line deposition and corrosion monitoring systems are exclusive products of its Consulting Division. Studies are also performed. The Company operates a manufacturing facility at 135 Sylvan St. in Verona, PA.

Officers: Edward G. Saxon *P*
George E. Saxon, Jr. *VP-SAL & MKT*
Gregory J. Saxon *VP-MFG*

Human Resources: Regina Saxon-Godish
Purchasing: Richard Blumette

Total Employees............................50	**Regional Employees** 50
Year Established 1923	**SIC Code** 7699

Connelly Assoc., Inc., J. Edward

2180 Noblestown Rd.
Pittsburgh, PA 15205
County: Allegheny

Phone: (412) 920-4066
Fax: (412) 920-4070

Full-service incentive marketing company. It supplies marketing strategies to meet or exceed clients' objectives for their various needs, including account acquisition, loan generation, ad specialty, business/gift service awards, and film and video production. Three of the Company's divisions are located at the above address: J. Edward Connelly Assoc. provides marketing programs for the banking and savings and loan industry; Performance Improvement focuses on a high-impact employee involvement process designed to help corporations develop cost-containment strategies; and Treasures, Inc. distributes replica artifacts and art reproductions from the Vatican Museum and the Sistine Chapel. The Company's other divisions consist of International Marketing Solutions in Clearwater, FL, which designs and develops programs for all types of businesses, and the Service Marketing Group in Garden City, NY, which serves the supermarket industry.

C

Officers: John E. Connelly *CH*
Regis McGrady *P*
Alan Bernthaler *VP & TRS*
Audree Wirginis *SEC*

Human Resources: Bernard Meinert *CON*

Purchasing: Ray Doyle

Total Employees............................175
Year Established 1958

Regional Employees 90
SIC Code....................................7389

Conomos, Inc., John B.

Coulter & Station Sts.
P.O. Box 279
Bridgeville, PA 15017
County: Allegheny

Phone: (412) 221-1800
Fax: (412) 221-4641

Provider of industrial painting services primarily serving the steel, chemicals, petrochemicals and power generating industries. The Company's industrial painting projects include highway and rail bridges and trestles; stacks, precipitators and ductwork; chemical process facilities, piping and equipment; power generation facilities, boilers and precipitators; material handling equipment, conveyors, unloaders and screening plants; blast furnaces, coke plants and steel mill facilities; tanks, vessels and standpipes; pollution equipment, dust collectors and cleaning plants; cranes, runways and unloaders; heavy and light industrial buildings; process lines, heat treating furnaces and mill equipment; dams, penstocks and hydro-facilities; offices, welfare facilities and commercial buildings; roofing, siding and metal decking; and pulp and papermaking facilities. The Company also offers hazardous materials abatement, fireproofing, specialty coating systems, roofing and decking, construction services and maintenance, and managed maintenance programs. It operates field offices in Chesterton, IN; Baltimore, MD; Lackawanna, NY; and Charleston, WV.

Officers: John B. Conomos *P*
Stephen Dobrosielski *Estimating MGR*
Damon Halkias *SAL MGR*
Denver Haught *Production MGR*

Human Resources: James R. King *CON & SEC*

Purchasing: Jan Prendergast

Total Employees 350-500	**Regional Employees** 50
Year Established 1968	**SIC Code**.....................................1721

CONSOL, Inc.

Consol Plaza, 1800 Washington Rd.
Pittsburgh, PA 15241
County: Allegheny

Phone: (412) 831-4000
Fax: (412) 831-4916

Provider of management and other related services to a group of coal producing companies, often referred to as the CONSOL Coal Group. The Company is a subsidiary of CONSOL Energy, Inc. (CEI), which is headquartered in Wilmington, DE. CEI is jointly owned by E. I. Du Pont De Nemours & Co., which is headquartered in Wilmington, DE, and listed on the NYSE, and Rheinbraun AG of Germany, which is headquartered in Cologne, Germany. In 1996, the CONSOL Coal Group produced 71.6 million tons of coal from 26 mining complexes and related facilities located in six states and Alberta, Canada. It possesses five billion tons of reserves. The CONSOL Coal Group companies include Consol Pennsylvania Coal Co., with operations in Southwestern Pennsylvania; Consolidation Coal Co., with operations in Illinois, Ohio, Pennsylvania, Virginia and West Virginia; and Fairmont Supply Co., a supplier of industrial equipment operating out of Washington, PA.

Officers: B. R. Brown *CH*
William G. Karis *P & CEO*
Ronald J. FlorJancic *EVP-MKT*
C. Wes McDonald *EVP-OPR*
Ronald E. Smith *EVP-ENG Services, Environmental Affairs & Exploration*

Human Resources: Buck V. Hyler *VP-Human Resources*

Total Employees..........................8,206	**Regional Employees** 745
Year Established 1860	**SIC Code**.....................................1222
Annual Revenues ($000) 2,400,000			

Consolidated Health Corp. of Pittsburgh

215 S. Negley Ave.
Pittsburgh, PA 15206
County: Allegheny

Phone: (412) 661-0814
Fax: (412) 661-0230

Owner and operator of the Podiatry Hospital of Pittsburgh, an acute care hospital with 13 beds, specializing in diseases and injuries of the foot and ankle offering inpatient and outpatient treatment. The hospital's services include comprehensive examination and management of foot and ankle injuries, gait analysis, noninvasive vascular testing, physical therapy, orthotic development and surgery. The Company is a subsidiary of Rx Medical Services Corp., which is headquartered in Ft. Lauderdale, FL, and listed on the OTC.

Officers: Joseph Noviello *CEO*
Randolph Speer *P*

Human Resources: Carol Hilyard *DIR-Human Resources*

Total Employees	76	**Regional Employees**	76
Year Established	1942	**SIC Code**	8069

Construction Engineering Consultants, Inc.

2018 Waverly St.
Pittsburgh, PA 15218
County: Allegheny

Phone: (412) 351-6465
Fax: (412) 351-6401

Provider of materials testing and inspection services in the field as well as in the laboratory. The Company performs geotechnical test borings and engineering design and aggregate, asphalt, cement, concrete, grout, soils, masonry, fireproofing and structural steel testing and inspection services for construction projects. It serves clients throughout the Tri-State area.

Officers: Joseph F. Artuso *CEO*
Ralph J. Artuso *P*

Human Resources: George R. Wargo

Purchasing: John E. Artuso *VP*

Total Employees	40	**Regional Employees**	40
Year Established	1976	**SIC Code**	8734
Annual Revenues ($000)	2,000		

Consumers Produce Co., Inc. of Pittsburgh

One 21st St.
Pittsburgh, PA 15222
County: Allegheny

Phone: (412) 281-0722
Fax: (412) 281-6541

Wholesale distributor of fresh fruits and vegetables to supermarkets, fruit markets and suppliers of restaurants. The Company serves clients throughout the Tri-State area.

Officers: Alan L. Siger *P*

Total Employees	85	**Regional Employees**	85
Year Established	1952	**SIC Code**	5148
Annual Revenues ($000)	51,000		

Continental Clay Co.

260 Oak Ave.
P.O. Box 1013
Kittanning, PA 16201
County: Armstrong

Phone: (412) 543-2611
Fax: (412) 545-9659

Manufacturer of acid-resistant brick, paving brick and radial chimney brick for industrial and commercial applications nationwide. The Company is a subsidiary of International Chimney Corp., which is headquartered in Buffalo, NY.

Officers: Richard T. Lohr *P*
    Eugene Brand *SEC*

Total Employees	34	**Regional Employees**	34
Year Established	1896	**SIC Code**	3251

Continental Design and Management Group

Southpointe Industrial Park, 160 Technology Dr.
Canonsburg, PA 15317
County: Washington

Phone: (412) 873-4700
Fax: (412) 873-4734

Provider of engineering and professional services consisting of all disciplines of construction engineering, detail design engineering, feasibility studies, automation and control engineering, project management, construction management, procurement, shop inspection and expediting, estimating, quality assurance/quality control and design/construct projects. The Company serves the metals, glass, food and beverage, and chemical sectors of the industrial construction market. It operates a branch office in North Royalton, OH. The Company is a subsidiary of Stevens Painton Corp., which is headquartered in Middleburg Heights, OH, with its Eastern Division operations located in Pittsburgh. An affiliated company, Chemsteel Construction Co., Inc., is also located at the above address. It provides design, installation and maintenance of acid-proof and corrosion-resistant systems, servicing the metals and chemical sectors of the industrial construction marketplace. It has 24 employees. (Refer to the Stevens Painton Corp. profile for additional information.)

Officers: Harry Albrecht *CH*
Thomas Snyder *P*

Total Employees	110	**Regional Employees**	105
Year Established	1991	**SIC Code**	8711
Annual Revenues ($000)			6,000

Contraves Brashear Systems, L.P.

615 Epsilon Dr.
Pittsburgh, PA 15238
County: Allegheny
Phone: (412) 967-7700
Fax: (412) 967-7973
Internet Address: www.contraves.com

Designer, developer and manufacturer of electro-optical systems, including astronomical equipment, telescopes, tracking systems, fire control systems and large optical components. The Company's customers include Lockheed Martin, Mitsubishi Electric, TRW and various branches of the U.S. Department of Defense. It operates an additional production facility located in Wampum, PA. The Company was created on May 30, 1997 when it purchased the Fire Control and Surveillance Systems Divisions from Contraves, Inc. The Company's general partner is Optics Acquisition Co., L.L.C. in McLean, VA, and its individual partners are William E. Conway, Jr. and Joanne Barkett Conway.

Officers: William E. Conway, Jr. *P & CEO*
Nicki T. Baldini *EVP & CFO*
Dawn S. Rucker *EVP & COO*

Human Resources: Kathy Moretti *DIR-Human Resources & ADM*

Purchasing Director: David Delozier

Total Employees	125	**Regional Employees**	125
Year Established	1881	**SIC Code**	3812
Annual Revenues ($000)			15,000

Contraves, Inc.

Keystone Commons Bldg. S. 700 Braddock Ave.
East Pittsburgh, PA 15112
County: Allegheny

Phone: (412) 829-4800
Fax: (412) 829-4804
Internet Address: www.contraves.com

Provider of turnkey contract manufacturing, assembly, precision machining, prototyping and high volume, repair and modernization of all build-to-print, design-to-cost, design/engineer-to-manufacturability of electronics, electrical, electro-mechanical, electro-optical, opto-mechanical, precision motion control systems and components for OEM and medical systems applications. The Company operates a simulation and training division in Tampa, FL. The Company is a subsidiary of Oerlikon-Buhrle Holding AG, which is headquartered in Zurich, Switzerland.

Officers: Joseph Pandl *CON*

Human Resources: Kathryn L. Zacks *DIR-Human Resources & ADM*

Total Employees............................275	**Regional Employees** 200
Year Established 1974	**SIC Code**......................................3827

Cook Vascular™ Inc.

Rte. 66, River Rd.
P.O. Box 529
Leechburg, PA 15656
County: Armstrong

Phone: (412) 845-8621
Fax: (412) 845-2848

Designer, manufacturer and marketer of medical products for interventional, therapeutic and diagnostic vascular applications, including lead extraction devices, electrophysiology catheters and various vascular access devices. The Company is a part of the Cook Group, which is headquartered in Bloomington, IN.

Officers: Louis B. Goode *P*
Teresa Cecchetti *OPR MGR*
Barry Norlander *MKT MGR*
Victor Sheaffer *NATL & INTL SAL MGR*

Human Resources: Vicki Myers *Personnel MGR*

Regional Employees....................120	
Year Established 1981	**SIC Code**......................................3845

Coopers & Lybrand L.L.P.

USX Tower, 600 Grant St., 35th Fl.
Pittsburgh, PA 15219
County: Allegheny

Phone: (412) 355-8000
Fax: (412) 355-8089
Internet Address: www.colybrand.com

Professional services firm providing a full range of client services, including basic accounting, auditing, tax, health care regulatory services, computer assurance services, human resource advisory services and financial advisory services both domestically and internationally. The Firm, which is headquartered in New York, NY, operates in 100 cities nationwide and has approximately 750 offices in over 140 countries.

Officers: Louis L. Testoni *MPTR*

Total Employees	68,000+	Regional Employees	200
Year Established	1898	SIC Code	8721
Annual Revenues ($000)	6,000,000+		

Coordinated Group of Cos., Inc.

200 Fleet St., 5th Fl.
Pittsburgh, PA 15220
County: Allegheny

Phone: (412) 920-2200
Fax: (412) 920-2279

Holding company providing employee benefit consulting services, third-party administration and brokerage services. The Company's subsidiaries, Benefit Coordinators Corp. (fee-based service organization) and Coordinated Benefits Corp. (commission-based licensed brokerage), are both located at the above address. Its other subsidiaries, Coordinated Benefits of California, Inc. and Coordinated Consulting Group, Inc., are both located in San Diego, CA. A division, Benefit Coordinators of Warren, is located in Warren, PA.

Officers: John D. Babb, Jr. *P*
          Tim Buzbee *VP*
          Mike Lawton *VP*
          Robert Rokicki *SEC & TRS*

Human Resources: Steve Adams

Purchasing: Annamarie Shannon

Total Employees	58	Regional Employees	45
Year Established	1968	SIC Code	8742
Annual Revenues ($000)	4,000		

Copperweld Corp.

Four Gateway Center, Ste. 2200
Pittsburgh, PA 15222
County: Allegheny
Phone: (412) 263-3200
Fax: (412) 263-6995

Manufacturer of mechanical and structural tubing. The Company also claims to be the world's largest producer of bimetallic wire products. Its Copperweld Shelby Division produces drawn-over-mandrel and seamless mechanical steel tubing at two plants in Shelby, OH. This tubing is used in the manufacture of hydraulic cylinders and mechanical parts for automobiles, trucks, construction equipment and in many other applications. Its Copperweld Miami Division operates a manufacturing facility in Piqua, OH, near Dayton. This division supplies custom-engineered welded mechanical steel tubing to primary OEM markets, such as automotive, office furniture, store fixtures, construction and recreational equipment producers, and is also a significant supplier to service centers. Its Copperweld Chicago Division and Copperweld Birmingham Division, which operate plants located in Chicago, IL, and Birmingham, AL, produce structural tubing. Its Copperweld Fayetteville Division, located in Fayetteville, TN, produces bimetallic wire and strand products for cable TV, telephone, electronic, electric utility and other applications. Its Canadian subsidiary, Copperweld Canada, Inc., owns Sonco Steel Tube (SST) and Standard Tube (ST). SST operates three manufacturing facilities in the Toronto area, and claims to be Canada's largest producer of structural tubing. ST, with plants in Brantford and Woodstock, Ontario, and Winnipeg, Manitoba, claims to be one of Canada's two largest producers of drawn-over-mandrel tubing and has extensive capabilities for the fabrication of tubing components for the auto industry. The Company markets its products throughout the United States, Canada and overseas. The Company is a subsidiary of Imetal, S.A., which is headquartered in Paris, France, and listed on the Paris Stock Exchange.

Officers: John D. Turner *P & CEO*
G. Basil Davies *SVP-MKT & SAL*
Douglas E. Young *SVP & CFO*

Human Resources: Eugene R. Pocci *VP-Human Resources*

Total Employees......................2,500	**Regional Employees** 70
Year Established 1915	**SIC Code**....................................3317
Annual Revenues ($000) 700,000	

Cordage Papers/Pittsburgh

55 Sexton Rd.
McKees Rocks, PA 15136
County: Allegheny

Phone: (412) 771-3515
Fax: (412) 771-4092

Independent wholesaler and distributor of fine printing and writing paper to printers, graphic designers and other end users. The Company is one of 10 divisions of The Cincinnati Cordage and Paper Co., which is headquartered in Cincinnati, OH.

Officers: Richard A. Jarvis, Jr. *GMGR*

Human Resources: Anne Hennen *(Cincinnati, OH)*

Purchasing: Bob Welch *(Cincinnati, OH)*

Total Employees	225	**Regional Employees**	30
Year Established	1892	**SIC Code**	5111
Annual Revenues ($000)			150,000

CORE Network LLC

625 Walnut St.
McKeesport, PA 15132
County: Allegheny

Phone: (412) 673-5005
Fax: (412) 673-6673

Owner and operator of 33 rehabilitation facilities located throughout Allegheny, Beaver, Cambria, Fayette, Washington and Westmoreland Counties, PA. The Company also manages eight inpatient facilities in hospitals and nursing homes. It specializes in providing physical, occupational and speech therapies, and industrial rehabilitation, and offers a variety of specialty programs. The Company plans to continue to expand into other communities and counties in the coming years. It participates in many of the region's insurance plans, HMOs, PPOs and other managed care plans. CORE stands for Centers for Outpatient Rehabilitation and Evaluation.

Officers: Richard W. Bowling *CEO*
Brendan D'Andrea *VP*
Dino Rovito *VP*

Human Resources: Paul Rockar *VP-Human Resources*

Total Employees	368		
Year Established	1986	**SIC Code**	8049

Cornelius Architectural Products, Inc.

30 Pine St.
Pittsburgh, PA 15223
County: Allegheny

Phone: (412) 781-9003
Fax: (412) 781-7840

Manufacturer of custom architectural products for the construction industry, specializing in aluminum, stainless steel, brass and bronze fabrication. The Company's architectural products include sign systems, exterior pylons, interior signs, directories, etched products, dimensional letters, metalwork, bronze entrances, grilles, kiosks, street lights, planters, elevator interiors, light fixtures, door pulls and building accessories. The Company markets its products directly to international owners, developers, general contractors and end users. All products are installed and serviced by the Company's personnel. Its manufacturing plant is located in Etna, PA.

Officers: J. Rogers Flannery *CH*
Rick J. Kline *P*

Total Employees............................134	**Regional Employees**...................110
Year Established 1980	**SIC Code**......................................3446

Cornerstone TeleVision, Inc.

Signal Hill Dr.
Wilmerding, PA 15148
County: Allegheny

Phone: (412) 824-3930
Fax: (412) 824-3759

Nonprofit owner and operator of the television station WPCB channel 40. The station broadcasts Christian religious programming 24-hours a day, airing over 80 different programs weekly. The station also produces three daily programs and seven weekly programs with a limited production crew plus numerous special spots and promos. Four of the programs are syndicated nationally. The Company also owns and operates television stations WKBS in Altoona, PA, and W50BF in Sharon, PA.

Officers: R. Russell Bixler *CEO*
Blake Richert *VP*
David Skeba *VP*

Human Resources: Dee Richert *SEC*

Purchasing: Oleen Eagle *P*

Total Employees............................108	**Regional Employees** 105
Year Established 1970	**SIC Code**......................................4833
Annual Revenues ($000) 6,000	

Corning Consumer Products Co.

100 Eighth St.
Charleroi, PA 15022
County: Washington

Phone: (412) 483-6531
Fax: (412) 489-2211

Manufacturer of consumer glass products including Corelle dinnerware, Pyrex bakeware, Visions cookware, and Corningware and Suprema commercial tableware. The Company is a division of Corning, Inc., which is headquartered in Corning, NY, and listed on the NYSE.

Officers: Paul M. Topichak *Plant MGR*

Total Employees	650	**Regional Employees**	650
Year Established	1893	**SIC Code**	3229

Corporate Information Systems, Inc.

Penn Center West Two, Ste. 430
Pittsburgh, PA 15276
County: Allegheny

Phone: (412) 787-9600
Fax: (412) 787-3070
Internet Address: www.ciscorp.com

Provider of software integration consulting services. The Company, doing business as CISCORP, offers a full range of services, from information systems planning to custom application design and development to staff augmentation. Its services are organized into process-related activities, including requirements analysis; information system and technology planning; architecture and development approach; business process reengineering; design, including graphical user interface design; systems development and implementation; systems integration; on-going maintenance and support; performance and tuning; knowledge transfer; project management; and staff augmentation. The Company also offers network consulting services, which consists of network planning and design; network installation; on-going maintenance and support; and management, performance and tuning. The Company's other facilities include a sales office in Philadelphia, PA, and a combination sales office and technology center in Santa Clara, CA.

Officers: Joseph Ogrodnik *OWN & CEO*
Robert Martin *VP*

Human Resources: George Preisendorfer *DIR-Human Resources*

Total Employees	235	**Regional Employees**	150
Year Established	1981	**SIC Code**	7373
Annual Revenues ($000)	19,000		

Couch/Mollica Travel Ltd.

300 Trimont Plaza, 1301 Grandview Ave.
Pittsburgh, PA 15211
County: Allegheny

Phone: (412) 381-8888
Fax: (412) 381-2103
Internet Address: www.astanet.com/get/couchmlica

Corporate travel agency specializing in cost control and international reservations. The Company serves clients nationwide.

Officers: Vicki L. Couch *Principal*
Sheila Mars Mollica *Principal*

Total Employees............................34	**Regional Employees** 34	
Year Established 1985	**SIC Code**....................................4724	
Annual Revenues ($000) 32,672		

Covato/Lipsitz, Inc.

Manor Oak II, 1910 Cochran Rd., Ste. 633
Pittsburgh, PA 15220
County: Allegheny

Phone: (412) 341-1144
Fax: (412) 341-5563

Full-service broker-dealer offering an array of investment services at discounted rates, including investment advisory services and venture capital.

Officers: Alfred I. Lipsitz *P*
Ned E. Siegel *VP*
Georgene G. Hickton *SEC*
Susan Holmes *Financial OPR*

Total Employees............................31	**Regional Employees** 31
Year Established 1980	**SIC Code**....................................6211

Coy Co., A. C.

1061 Waterdam Plaza, Ste. 201
P.O. Box 1262
Canonsburg, PA 15317
County: Washington

Phone: (412) 941-2220
Fax: (412) 942-9140

Provider of temporary personnel specializing in supplying employees with information and engineering expertise. The Company provides staff on a contract or full-time basis. Its areas of concentration include system integration, WAN, user support, training, technical writing, programming, design and analysis. A branch office is located in Columbus, OH.

Officers: Frank J. Yocca *P*
John Yocca *OPR MGR*

Human Resources: Barbara Young

Total Employees............108	**Regional Employees**..............98
Year Established...........1984	**SIC Code**...............8742
Annual Revenues ($000)..............6,200		

Cranberry Manufacturing Co., Inc.

800 Commonwealth Dr.
Warrendale, PA 15086
County: Allegheny

Phone: (412) 776-5350
Fax: (412) 776-3566

Contract manufacturing facility which provides precision machining and assembly services. The Company primarily serves clients in the Tri-State area.

Officers: Peter R. Swann *CEO*
Nils T. Swann *P*
John Ashbaugh *VP*
John Latz *SEC & TRS*

Human Resources: Betty N. Harris *Personnel MGR*

Total Employees............78	**Regional Employees**...............78
Year Established...........1964	**SIC Code**...............3599
Annual Revenues ($000)..............8,000	

Crawford Realty Co.

4117 Old William Penn Hwy.
Murrysville, PA 15668
County: Westmoreland

Phone: (412) 733-2933
Fax: (412) 733-1233

Real estate broker, land developer, residential home builder and commercial builder. The Company provides its services throughout the Pittsburgh metropolitan market area. The Company is affiliated with Parkway Assoc., Inc., a holding company for rental properties located at the same address.

Officers: Calvin D. Crawford *P*
Richard C. Crawford *VP*

W. Harvey Steele *VP*
Robert C. Verona *VP*
Paul Capezzuto *SEC & TRS*

Total Employees............................35
Year Established 1953
Annual Revenues ($000) 7,000

Regional Employees 35
SIC Code......................................1521

Crossgates, Inc.

3555 Washington Rd.
Canonsburg, PA 15317
County: Washington

Phone: (412) 941-9240
Fax: (412) 941-4339

Developer and marketer of real estate and manager of property. The Company is primarily involved in retail, office, warehouse and distribution, multifamily and medical projects in Maryland, Ohio, Pennsylvania and West Virginia. Its operating units, all of which are based at the above address, include Crossgates Construction Management; Crossgates Realty, Inc.; Spectrum Services, Inc.; and Crossgates Management, Inc., which provides asset management services for multifamily, commercial and light industrial properties. The Company maintains a regional office in Mechanicsburg, PA.

Officers: Arthur C. Schwotzer *CH*
Gregg A. Schwotzer *P*
Donald Smith *EVP-DEV*
Christopher P. Fitting *VP-MKT*
James Fusco *VP & CFO*
Robert Lewis *VP-Crossgates Management, Inc.*
David Schumacher *VP-Construction*

Human Resources: Diane Voda

Total Employees...........................150
Year Established 1959

Regional Employees 45
SIC Code......................................6552

Crossroads Speech & Hearing, Inc.

205 E. McMurray Rd.
Canonsburg, PA 15317
County: Washington

Phone: (412) 941-4434
Fax: (412) 941-4714

Provider of speech, hearing and language services to nursing facilities, hospitals, schools, home care agencies, day cares and specialized programs on a contractual basis. The Company operates a branch office at 100 McKnight Park Dr. in

Pittsburgh, PA, and maintains therapists throughout Maryland, Ohio, Pennsylvania and West Virginia.

Officers: Christie Ann Conrad *C-OWN*
Kathryn L. Rector *C-OWN*

Human Resources: Nancy Gualazzi

Total Employees	110	**Regional Employees**	75
Year Established	1981	**SIC Code**	8049

Crouse, Inc., Wayne

3370 Stafford St.
P.O. Box 4349
Pittsburgh, PA 15204
County: Allegheny

Phone: (412) 771-5176
Fax: (412) 771-2357

Provider of mechanical contracting and engineering services specializing in plumbing, process piping and wastewater treatment plants. The Company serves markets in Maryland, New York, North Carolina, Ohio, Pennsylvania, South Carolina, Virginia and West Virginia.

Officers: William P. Lugaila *P*

Human Resources: Kenneth R. Marino *SEC & TRS*

Purchasing: Vincent DiClaudio

Total Employees	200	**Regional Employees**	125
Year Established	1937	**SIC Code**	1711
Annual Revenues ($000)	23,000		

Crown Buick GMC Truck, Inc.

Nine Clairton Blvd.
Pittsburgh, PA 15236
County: Allegheny

Phone: (412) 653-7800
Fax: (412) 653-0223

Automobile dealership selling new Buick automobiles and GMC trucks. The Company also sells used cars and trucks, provides parts and service, and operates a body shop.

Officers: Carl J. Pecoraro *P*
Ronald Yannazzo *General SAL MGR*

Human Resources: Patricia A. Fedak *SEC & TRS*

Purchasing: Ronald Cain

Total Employees............................60	**Regional Employees** 60
Year Established 1986	**SIC Code** 5511
Annual Revenues ($000) 35,000	

Crown Communications

Penn Center West, Bldg. III, Ste. 229
Pittsburgh, PA 15276
County: Allegheny

Phone: (412) 788-0906
Fax: (412) 788-0908
Internet Address: www.crowncomm.net

Owner and operator of what the Company claims is one of the largest independent communications tower networks in the United States. The Company's extensive tower network enables it to offer wireless coverage to all types of wireless users, including 2-way radio, cellular paging, PCS, broadcast and microwave. The Company's Crown Network Systems, Inc. subsidiary is divided into two separate divisions. The Crown Network Systems Construction Division is a complete turnkey construction business, with experience in project management, site acquisition, site design, engineering, heavy construction, tower, shelter, antenna and line installation. The Crown Network Systems Engineering Division offers engineering services, including network management, system design consulting, system performance analysis, RF management and consulting, maintenance and installation services, and antenna system design. The Company's Crown Mobile Systems, Inc. subsidiary claims to be one of the largest authorized Motorola and Kenwood 2-way radio dealers in the U.S. as well as a fully staffed 2-way radio service and installation business. The Company provides service to such businesses as Airtouch Paging, Arch Communications, AT&T Wireless, Bell Atlantic NYNEX Mobile, Federal Bureau of Investigation, Federal Express, IBM, Internal Revenue Service, MobileComm, Sprint Spectrum and the U.S. Postal Service. It also provides site management, tower rentals and consulting services for both Company-owned and third party communications facilities. The Company operates additional offices in Columbus, OH; and Carnegie, Fort Washington and Jeanette, PA.

Officers: Robert A. Crown *P*
Barbara A. Crown *SEVP*
Giuseppe A. Floro *EVP*
Mark A. Uminski *VP-ENG*

Human Resources: Ron Tancreti *Human Resources MGR*

Purchasing: Kevin Conroy *Property MGR*

Total Employees............................220	**Regional Employees** 190
Year Established 1981	**SIC Code** 1623

CSE Corp.

600 Seco Rd.
Monroeville, PA 15146
County: Allegheny

Phone: (412) 856-9200
Fax: (412) 856-9203

Manufacturer of gas detection equipment and breathing apparatus, including Explorer Multi-Gas monitors and the SR-100 Self-Contained Self Rescuer, an escape only breathing apparatus. The Company is also a national distributor of health and safety products.

Officers: Sam Shearer *OWN & P*
Guy B. Carson *VP-OPR*
Scott A. Shearer *VP-SAL & MKT*

Human Resources: Ron Kerston

Purchasing: Nick Orell

Total Employees............................70	**Regional Employees** 63	
Year Established 1964	**SIC Code**.....................................3823	
Annual Revenues ($000)...8-12,000		

CTR Systems, Inc.

555 Keystone Dr.
Warrendale, PA 15086
County: Allegheny

Phone: (412) 772-2400
Fax: (412) 772-3750

Provider of time and attendance systems, photo identification equipment and data collection devices, such as electronic time clocks, and developer of software to support and enhance these systems. The Company also provides access control and parking revenue control equipment, which monitor and control fee collection at parking facilities. In addition, it provides technical support and systems maintenance for its products. The Company operates sales and service offices located in Rochester and Syracuse, NY; Kent, OH; and Erie, Philadelphia, Pittsburgh and Wilkes-Barre, PA.

Officers: Dru Duffy *P*
Dan Duffy *VP-SAL*
Doug Duffy *VP-OPR*
Bob Wilkie *CFO*

Human Resources: Leisha Friedman

Total Employees..........................130	**Regional Employees** 90	
Year Established 1964	**SIC Code**.....................................5046	
Annual Revenues ($000)...15-20,000		

Cummins Power Systems, Inc.

Three Alpha Dr.
Pittsburgh, PA 15238
County: Allegheny

Phone: (412) 820-8300
Fax: (412) 820-8308

Marketer and distributor of Cummins Diesel engines and parts and engine-driven Onan generator sets, and a servicer of vehicles with Cummins engines. The Company, which is headquartered in Bristol, PA, operates an additional sales and service branch in Harrisburg, PA. It serves clients throughout Pennsylvania and parts of Maryland, New Jersey and West Virginia. The Company was previously named Cummins Diesel Engines, Inc. It is an independent distributor for Cummins Engine Co., Inc., which is headquartered in Columbus, IN, and listed on the NYSE.

Officers: Lynn R. Coy *P*
Sam A. Washburn *EVP*

Human Resources: Kathy C. Hopkins *(Bristol, PA)*

Total Employees............................250	**Regional Employees** 60
Year Established 1937	**SIC Code**......................................3519

Cunningham Co., M. E.

Rochester Rd.
P.O. Box 307
Ingomar, PA 15127
County: Allegheny

Phone: (412) 369-9199
Fax: (412) 366-3048

Manufacturer of Mecco safety indent industrial marking equipment for the identification of metal, plastic and wood products. The Company's product line includes a range of hand stamps, numbering heads, computer controlled marking systems and bar code systems. Its products are marketed primarily to the metalworking industry. The Company is affiliated with Mecco Machine Ltd., which is also located at the above address, at P.O. Box 222.

Officers: Edwin W. Speicher *P*
Franklin S. Speicher *AST-SEC*

Human Resources: John R. Jackson *TRS*

Purchasing: Warren K. Speicher *VP & SEC*

Total Employees............................30	**Regional Employees** 30
Year Established 1889	**SIC Code**......................................3953
Annual Revenues ($000) 3,200	

Custom Printed Graphics, Inc.

2933 Mary St.
P.O. Box 42330
Pittsburgh, PA 15203
County: Allegheny

Phone: (412) 381-5700
Fax: (412) 381-5738

Screen printer specializing in the production of signs, decals and textiles. The Company operates fully automated screen printing machines, with computerized facilities in their art department. It has the capability to print up to 12 colors on T-shirts.

Officers: Larry N. Ennis *P*
Kenneth A. Ennis *VP*

Total Employees..............................38
Year Established........................1962
Annual Revenues ($000)..3,100

Regional Employees 38
SIC Code......................................3993

Cutler-Hammer, Inc.

Five Parkway Center
Pittsburgh, PA 15220
County: Allegheny

Phone: (412) 937-6100
Fax: (412) 937-6696

Manufacturer of electrical distribution and control systems and equipment such as circuit breakers, motor control, switchgear and load centers to domestic and international markets. The Company operates offices and plants across the United States, including a Technology Center near the Pittsburgh airport and a manuacturing plant in Beaver, PA. It is a subsidiary of Eaton Corp., which is headquartered in Cleveland, OH, and listed on the NYSE.

Officers: Joseph L. Becherer *SVP*

Regional Employees..................1,500
Year Established 1979

SIC Code......................................3613

D. X. I., Inc.

200 Hightower Blvd.
Pittsburgh, PA 15205
County: Allegheny

Phone: (412) 788-2466
Fax: (412) 788-4230

Provider of automation software and services to the international ocean transportation industry. The Company provides automated documentation systems to handle tariff and bill of lading transactions for shippers, ocean carriers and carrier conferences.

Officers: Robert M. Ryan *CH & CEO*
Pritam M. Advani *CFO*
Renard L. Biltgen *CTO*
Peter J. Karlovich *CIO*
Kevin M. Foy *VP-Business DEV*
Edward Ryan *VP-SAL*

Human Resources: Jennifer L. Stambaugh

Total Employees	110	**Regional Employees**	106
Year Established	1987	**SIC Code**	7372
Annual Revenues ($000)	10,000		

D&L, Inc.

Four Gateway Center, 12th Fl.
Pittsburgh, PA 15222
County: Allegheny

Phone: (412) 765-3643
Fax: (412) 765-0905

Provider of project and construction management and engineering services to a wide range of industrial and public sector clients both domestically and internationally. The Firm's services include design engineering, feasibility studies, funding estimates and claims management. Its advanced management systems provide cost control to capital projects. Branch offices are located in Birmingham, AL; Gary, IN; and Philadelphia, PA.

Special Designations: ENR$_{100}$

Officers: Dominick J. DeSalvo *Principal*
Joseph J. Liptak *Principal*

Total Employees	150	**Regional Employees**	120
Year Established	1982	**SIC Code**	8711
Annual Revenues ($000)	15,600		

Daily News Publishing Co., Inc., The

409 Walnut St.
P.O. Box 128
McKeesport, PA 15134
County: Allegheny

Phone: (412) 664-9161
Fax: (412) 664-3972

Publisher of The Daily News, a daily newspaper published six days a week with a circulation of approximately 26,600. The newspaper is distributed in Allegheny, Westmoreland and Fayette Counties, PA.

Officers: Patricia Mansfield Miles *Publisher*

Total Employees............................100	**Regional Employees** 100
Year Established 1884	**SIC Code** 2711

Dandy Service Corp.

916 Brush Creek Rd.
Warrendale, PA 15086
County: Allegheny

Phone: (412) 935-1920
Fax: (412) 772-3622

Provider of contract truckload carrier services transporting general commodities. The Company serves states in the Central and Eastern time zones. It operates a fleet of approximately 48 tractors and 85 trailers.

Officers: Daniel W. Lang *P (Purchasing)*
Michael A. Bradshaw *TRS*

Human Resources: Larry L. Sieff

Total Employees..............................55	**Regional Employees** 26
Year Established 1981	**SIC Code** 4213
Annual Revenues ($000) 5,500	

Danieli United

400 Holiday Dr.
Pittsburgh, PA 15220
County: Allegheny

Phone: (412) 808-5400
Fax: (412) 808-5480

Designer and engineer of hot- and cold-rolled sheet rolling mill equipment. The Company is a division of Danieli Corp. (DC), which is headquartered in Youngstown, OH, and supplies the equipment, engineering expertise and turnkey plants for ferrous and nonferrous hot and cold strip and plate production, and downstream conditioning and finishing lines. DC is a subsidiary of Danieli and C., S.p.A., which is headquartered in Buttrio, Italy, and listed on the Italian Stock Exchange.

Officers: Sidney R. Snitkin *VP & GMGR*
Margartis Batis *DIR-SAL*
Steven Demase *DIR-Major Projects/Project Control*

Human Resources: Ronald Weisenstein

Total Employees............................77	Regional Employees 77
Year Established 1994	SIC Code 8711
Annual Revenues ($000) 20,367	

Danka Office Imaging

Foster Plaza VI, 681 Andersen Dr.
Pittsburgh, PA 15222
County: Allegheny

Phone: (412) 928-1831
Fax: (412) 928-1850
Internet Address: www.danka.com

Provider of sales and service for high volume photocopiers, selling Kodak copiers and servicing a variety of different brands. The local facility is a branch office of Danka Office Systems Plc, which is headquartered in St. Petersburg, FL, with executive offices in London, England. It is listed on the NASDAQ. The local office serves clients in Western and Central Pennsylvania, as well as portions of New York, Ohio and West Virginia.

Officers: Joseph E. Trdinich *GMGR-SAL & Service*

Human Resources: Cindy Durning

Regional Employees......................40	
Year Established 1977	SIC Code 3861

Danka Office Products

409 Beatty Rd.
Monroeville, PA 15146
County: Allegheny

D

Phone: (412) 373-4500
Fax: (412) 373-4530
Internet Address: www.danka.com

Independent marketer of automated office equipment and provider of related service, parts and supplies to wholesale and retail customers. The Company's principal operating headquarters are located in St. Petersburg, FL, with executive offices in London, England. It is listed on the NASDAQ. The facility located at the above address is an administrative and service center for clients in Allegheny, Fayette, Greene, Washington and Westmoreland Counties in Pennsylvania. A sales office is located at 2030 Ardmore Blvd. in Pittsburgh, PA. The Company's local product offerings include Ascom Hasler mailing equipment, Lexmark printers and typewriters, Mita copiers and facsimile equipment and Riso duplicating machines.

Officers: Richard Organ *Area Administrative MGR*
Kevin Graham *Major Markets MGR*

Regional Employees....................100
Year Established........................1977   **SIC Code**.....................................5044

Datatel Resources Corp.

1729 Pennsylvania Ave.
Monaca, PA 15061
County: Beaver

Phone: (412) 775-5300
Fax: (412) 775-0688

Producer of custom, manifold and continuous business forms. The Company also provides document design services, promotional products and direct mail services. It operates two Muller Martinl progress presses with interstage UV curing and a maximum of eight offset colors. The Company also has a plant in Indianapolis, IN.

Officers: Allen J. Simon *P*

Total Employees...........................95
Year Established........................1955   **SIC Code**.....................................2761
Annual Revenues ($000) 22,000

Davies, McFarland & Carroll, P.C.

One Gateway Center, 10th Fl.
Pittsburgh, PA 15222
County: Allegheny

Phone: (412) 281-0737
Fax: (412) 261-7251

Provider of legal services with 18 attorneys The Firm's areas of concentration include business and commercial litigation, product litigation, workers' compensation and employers' liability, toxic and environmental law, business and estate planning, medical malpractice and professional negligence, and criminal defense.

Officers: Ralph A. Davies *MDIR*
                Lynn E. Bell-Carroll *DIR*
                Edward A. McFarland *DIR*

Human Resources: Marshall J. Tindall

Purchasing: William D. Mech *Business MGR*

Total Employees	38	**Regional Employees**	38
Year Established	1983	**SIC Code**	8111
Annual Revenues ($000)	3,500		

Davis & Warde, Inc.

704 Second Ave.
Pittsburgh, PA 15219
County: Allegheny

Phone: (412) 261-1904
Fax: (412) 261-1917

Provider of computerized typesetting, computerized graphics, commercial printing and an imagesetting service bureau. Through Dawar Technologies, a division of the Company also located at the above address, it provides screen-printing on polycarbonate film for graphic overlays, nameplates, pressure sensitive labels, membrane switches, urethane encapsulation and roll labels.

Officers: James F. Ocskay *P*
                H. Gene Baumgarten *VP-OPR*

Human Resources: Susan S. Ocskay

Purchasing: Greg Luginski

Total Employees	40	**Regional Employees**	40
Year Established	1926	**SIC Code**	2759
Annual Revenues ($000)	3,000		

Davison Sand & Gravel Co.

400 Industrial Blvd.
New Kensington, PA 15068
County: Westmoreland

D

Phone: (412) 362-4900
Fax: (412) 335-6745

Producer of ready-mix concrete, crushed limestone, sand and gravel. The Company serves the construction industry of Western Pennsylvania and Northern West Virginia. It is a subsidiary of Pioneer Concrete of America Co., Inc., which is headquartered in Houston, TX.

Officers: Terry Young *P*
David Clement *SVP & Regional MGR*
David W. Humphreys *VP-SAL*

Human Resources: Marilynn Swank

Regional Employees.....................250
Year Established 1854   **SIC Code**....................................3273

Daxus Corp.

915 Penn Ave.
Pittsburgh, PA 15222
County: Allegheny

Phone: (412) 577-4100
Fax: (412) 577-4141
Internet Address: www.daxus.com

Provider of software products and systems integration services. The Company designs, implements and manages manufacturing and distribution technology, specifically factory automation and information systems, for the metals, chemical, consumer packaged goods, foodservice and manufacturing industries. Its team of software professionals focuses on helping clients solve their problems using the appropriate mix of the Company's proprietary core application products, purchased hardware and software, and software and integration services. Recent applications of technology include lap-top and pen-based sales force automation tools, production data warehousing, voice-based solutions for both returned goods and warehouse distribution, FDA-compliant Electronic Batch Records Systems and intranet-based Product Data Management Systems, material tracking systems for steel and other industrial materials manufacturers, and client server integration. The Company maintains branch offices in Chicago, IL; Munster, IN; and Philadelphia, PA.

Officers: William S. Brown IV *P & CEO*
Daniel W. Busse *VP-Consumer Products*
Thomas W. Jurecko *VP-Metals*
Daniel J. McDermott *VP-OPR*
Patricia M. Rogan *CFO*

Human Resources: Keith Young *MGR-DEV & Continuous Improvement*
Purchasing: Rick Lettieri *VP-SAL*

Total Employees............................100	**Regional Employees** 80
Year Established 1962	**SIC Code**......................................7373
Annual Revenues ($000) 10,000	

Deaktor/Sysco Food Service Co.

One Whitney Dr.
P.O. Box 1000
Harmony, PA 16037
County: Butler

Phone: (412) 452-2100
Fax: (412) 452-1033

Wholesaler of grocery products, dairy products, frozen foods, and food service equipment and supplies to restaurants, schools, hospitals and related institutions in Western Pennsylvania and parts of Ohio and West Virginia. The Company is a subsidiary of Sysco Corp., which is headquartered in Houston, TX, and listed on the NYSE.

Officers: Barry Friends *P*

Human Resources: Ray Wimple

Purchasing: Dave Kirkpatrick

Total Employees............................325	**Regional Employees** 325
Year Established 1986	**SIC Code**......................................5142

Dean Witter Reynolds, Inc.

One Oxford Centre, 301 Grant St., 43rd Fl.
Pittsburgh, PA 15219
County: Allegheny

Phone: (412) 434-8500
Fax: (412) 434-8461

Full-service broker-dealer and investment banking firm. The Company, which is headquartered in New York, NY, operates approximately 400 branch offices throughout the United States. It is a subsidiary of Morgan Stanley, Dean Witter, Discover & Co., which is also headquartered in New York, NY, and is listed on the NYSE.

Officers: Jeff Grier *FVP & Branch MGR*

Regional Employees......................60	
Year Established 1924	**SIC Code**......................................6211

Deklewa & Sons, Inc., John

1273 Washington Pike
P.O. Box 158
Bridgeville, PA 15017
County: Allegheny

Phone: (412) 257-9000
Fax: (412) 257-4486

Provider of general construction and construction management services, specializing in commercial, institutional, municipal and industrial facilities, and foundation and specialty work.

Officers: Richard T. Deklewa *P*
David J. Deklewa *VP*
James R. Deklewa *VP & TRS*
John E. Deklewa *VP & SEC*
Donald W. Dempsey *VP-Business DEV*

Total Employees..........................200	**Regional Employees** 200
Year Established........................1918	**SIC Code**.....................................1541
Annual Revenues ($000) 45,000	

Dellovade, Inc., A. C.

108 Cavasina Dr.
Canonsburg, PA 15317
County: Washington

Phone: (412) 873-8190
Fax: (412) 873-8187

Supplier and installer of preformed metal siding, roofing and accessories. Affiliates of the Company include Dellovade Fabricators, Inc. and Greenmoor, Inc., both located in Avella, PA, and Sunbelt Erectors, Inc., located at the above address.

Officers: Armand C. Dellovade *P*
Dennis Dellovade *VP*
Carl L. Smith III *VP-FIN*
Peter J. Dellovade *SEC*

Purchasing: Rick Chapman

Total Employees..........................250	**Regional Employees** 175
Year Established 1973	**SIC Code**.....................................1761
Annual Revenues ($000) 35,000	

Deloitte & Touche LLP

One PPG Place, Ste. 2500
Pittsburgh, PA 15222
County: Allegheny
Phone: (412) 338-7200
Fax: (412) 338-7380

Provider of professional services in the areas of accounting, auditing, taxation and management consulting. The Firm serves large corporate and middle market organizations in a wide variety of industries, including manufacturing, health care, construction, higher education, retail, real estate, communications, higher education and public sector clients. It offers many special services, including business and financial advisory services, computer assurance services, information systems consulting, litigation support, valuation services, and actuarial and employee benefits consulting. Headquartered in Wilton, CT, the Firm operates more than 100 offices throughout the United States. It is a part of Deloitte Touche Tohmatsu International, which is headquartered in New York, NY, and operates 692 offices in 125 countries.

Officers: Stanley G. Russell, Jr. *Office MPTR*
Glen Feinberg *MGT Solutions & Services Partner-in-Charge*
Alan E. Kesler *Accounting & Auditing Partner-in-Charge*
Allan C. Lucchini *Tax Partner-in-Charge*
David Johnson *MDIR-Consulting Group*

Human Resources: Sydney Snyder

Total Employees	63,000	**Regional Employees**	480
Year Established	1895	**SIC Code**	8721
Annual Revenues ($000)	6,500,000		

Delta Air Lines, Inc.

Pittsburgh International Airport
P.O. Box 12328
Pittsburgh, PA 15231
County: Allegheny
Phone: (412) 472-5370
Fax: (412) 472-5374

Commercial airline operating 13 daily flights out of the Pittsburgh International Airport, consisting of six to Atlanta, GA; one to Buffalo, NY; and six to Cincinnati, OH. The Company, which is headquartered in Atlanta, GA, is listed on the NYSE. Its reservations/information number is (800) 221-1212.

Officers: Bob Miller *Station MGR*

Total Employees	70,000	**Regional Employees**	34
Year Established	1929	**SIC Code**	4512

Delta Furniture Rentals & Sales, Inc.

101 Wood St.
Pittsburgh, PA 15222
County: Allegheny

Phone: (412) 765-0165
Fax: (412) 765-3465

Retailer and renter of both office and residential furniture and furnishings through both retail showrooms and an outside sales force. While anyone can buy or rent residential furniture at the Company's showrooms, the vast majority of its business is done through leasing agreements with rental properties throughout the Pittsburgh metropolitan area. The Company specializes in designing rental packages that fit a variety of lifestyles, from executive lines to economical lines ideal for students or recent graduates, and even model homes. When the furniture rental contracts expire, the furniture is shipped to its Clearance Warehouse at 2231 Sawmill Run Blvd. in Pittsburgh, PA. The Company's also operates a Contract Group that specializes in providing office furniture and designs for corporate clients. In addition, DELTA Corporate Suites provides short-term furnished housing in the Tri-State area. The Company maintains an inventory in excess of $4 million and operates a fleet of eight delivery trucks. Its other facilities include an operations and distribution center at 1201 Brighton Rd. in Pittsburgh, PA; a regional office and retail showroom in Cleveland, OH; and retail showrooms in Pittsburgh at 4625 Campbells Run Rd. and at the above address.

Officers: William J. Eggert *P & CEO*

Human Resources: Christine Harbison

Total Employees............................80	**Regional Employees** 70
Year Established 1987	**SIC Code** 5712
Annual Revenues ($000) 18,000	

Delta International Machinery Corp.

246 Alpha Dr.
Pittsburgh, PA 15238
County: Allegheny

Phone: (412) 963-2400
Fax: (412) 963-2489

Manufacturer, marketer and servicer of a line of general purpose woodworking machinery, including table saws, band saws, planers, jointers, grinders, drill presses, shapers, lathes, and other tools and accessories. The Company sells its products in the U.S., Canada and other foreign countries under its Biesmeyer and Delta brand names through a network of independent and mail order distributors, hardware stores and home centers. The Company's markets include do-it-yourself/homeshop craftsmen; commercial, residential and industrial construction; remodeling; and cabinet manufacturing, case goods and furniture makers.

The Company operates production facilities in Mississippi, Tennessee and Taiwan. It is a subsidiary of Pentair, Inc., which is headquartered in St. Paul, MN, and listed on the NASDAQ.

Officers: Nevin J. Craig *P*
Mark Strahler *VP-SAL & MKT*

Total Employees............................600   **Regional Employees** 90
SIC Code 3542

Deluxe Check Printers, Inc.

615 McMichael Rd.
P.O. Box 2852, Pittsburgh, PA 15230
Pittsburgh, PA 15205
County: Allegheny

Phone: (412) 788-2105
Fax: (412) 788-1236

Printer of checks for regional financial institutions. The Company is a division of Deluxe Corp., which is headquartered in Shoreview, MN, and listed on the NYSE.

Officers: Phil Gentry *GMGR*

Regional Employees ....350+
Year Established 1920   **SIC Code** 2759

Demor & Sons, Inc., A. J.

2150 Eldo Rd.
Monroeville, PA 15146
County: Allegheny

Phone: (412) 242-6125
Fax: (412) 372-5818

Mechanical contractor specializing in plumbing, HVAC and process piping in the multifamily housing, commercial, institutional, industrial and water treatment plant segments of the market. The Company also operates a facility located in Throop, PA.

Officers: David A. Demor *P*
John A. Bianco *VP-Construction*
Joan T. Cology *SEC & TRS*

Total Employees............................45   **Regional Employees** 35
Year Established 1925   **SIC Code** 1711
Annual Revenues ($000)..6-7,500

Detroit Switch, Inc.

1025-33 Beaver Ave.
Pittsburgh, PA 15233
County: Allegheny

Phone: (412) 322-9144
Fax: (412) 321-1997

Manufacturer of pressure switches and temperature switches for a variety of clients, including General Electric, General Motors and the U.S. Navy. The Company also produces aluminum clad wood windows under its Trimline brand name that are primarily sold to builders and remodelers in Allegheny County, PA.

Officers: Gregory A. Stein *P (Human Resources)*
Robert A. Stein *TRS*
Rick C. Stein *SEC*
Mark T. Kosar *AST SEC*

Purchasing: Linda DeFalco

Total Employees..............................37   **Regional Employees** 37
SIC Code 3613

Development Dimensions International, Inc.

1225 Washington Pike
Bridgeville, PA 15017
County: Allegheny

Phone: (412) 257-0600
Fax: (412) 257-0614
Internet Address: www.ddiworld.com

International human resources company that specializes in helping clients improve their business performance by aligning people strategies with business strategies. The Company, which is also known as DDI, works in close partnership with clients to assess their organization and people, develop and implement practical strategies, and achieve measurable improvements in organizational and individual performance. It helps clients create high-involvement cultures and integrated human resource systems where selection, training and development, and performance management are all linked and working together. The Company serves more than 12,000 organizations each year, including 400 of the Fortune 500 and a wide range of businesses—manufacturing, retail, service and government. Its programs have been translated into 20 languages, including Cantonese and Mandarin Chinese, French, German, Japanese, Portuguese and Spanish. The Company operates more than 70 offices and affiliates worldwide.

Officers: William C. Byham *P & CEO*
         Robert W. Rogers *COO*

Total Employees .... 1,100+	**Regional Employees** 500
Year Established 1970	**SIC Code** 8742

DialAmerica Marketing, Inc.

Seven Parkway Center, 875 Greentree Rd., Ste. 700
Pittsburgh, PA 15220
County: Allegheny

Phone: (412) 921-3425
Fax: (412) 921-8019

Telemarketer of magazine titles to U.S. households for major publishers, including Conde Nast, McGraw-Hill and Time. The Company, which is headquartered in Mahway, NJ, operates 52 call centers in 27 states.

Officers: Bill Griffin *Divisional SAL MGR*

Regional Employees 650	
Year Established 1957	**SIC Code** 7389
Annual Revenues ($000) .... 200,000+	

Diamond Wire Spring Co.

1901 Babcock Blvd.
Pittsburgh, PA 15209
County: Allegheny

Phone: (412) 821-2703
Fax: (412) 821-2743

Designer and manufacturer of custom precision industrial springs. The Company produces springs and wire forms for every conceivable industry in countless varieties of shapes from straight lengths to the most intricate assemblies. The Company's Catalog Division at 1903 Babcock Blvd. in Pittsburgh, PA, offers a stock catalog of its more than 3,000 parts, all ready to ship. The Company operates additional manufacturing facilities in Taylors, SC, and Tyler, TX. It serves clients in the U.S. and Canada.

Officers: Donald G. Fazio *P*
         Frank E. Fazio *VP-SAL*

Purchasing: Paul T. Fazio

Total Employees 75	**Regional Employees** 45
Year Established 1939	**SIC Code** 3495

Dick Corp.

900 Rte. 51
P.O. Box 10896, Pittsburgh, PA 15236
Clairton, PA 15025
County: Allegheny

Phone: (412) 384-1000
Fax: (412) 384-1215

Provider of construction, construction management and design/build services to a wide spectrum of local, regional, national and international clients. The Firm is divided into three operating units—Bridge & Highway Division, Building Division and Power & Industrial Division. Its Building Division projects in the Pittsburgh region include the Blue Cross Primary Care Facility/Monroeville, A. J. Demor Elderly High-rise, Marshall University Library, Point Park Library, Bobby Rahal Mercedes Benz Dealership, St. Francis Hospital Surgery Tower, University of Pittsburgh Medical Center and West Penn Hospital. The Firm operates regional project offices in Washington, D.C.; Las Vegas, NV; Charleston, WV; and Guaynabo, Puerto Rico.

Special Designations: ENR_{400} $FB-P_{500}$

Officers: David E. Dick *C-OWN & CEO*
David E. Dick *C-OWN & CEO*
Douglas P. Dick *C-OWN & P*
George Harakal *P-Building Division*
John Kudrna *P-Bridge & Highway Division*
Dan Martin *P-Power & Industrial Division*
Ken Burk *CFO*

Human Resources: Andrew Peters

Total Employees	2,000	**Regional Employees**	452
Year Established	1922	**SIC Code**	1600
Annual Revenues ($000)	475,000		

Dickie, McCamey & Chilcote, P.C.

Two PPG Place, Ste. 400
Pittsburgh, PA 15222
County: Allegheny

Phone: (412) 281-7272
Fax: (412) 392-5367

Full-service law firm with 118 attorneys serving business entities and individuals. The Firm's practice areas include civil litigation, general corporate, workers' compensation, probate, trusts and estates, tax, real estate, bankruptcy, environmental, employment law and white-collar crime. It operates a branch office located in Wheeling, WV.

Officers: Wilber McCoy Otto *P*

Charles W. Kenrick *MDIR*
Thomas P. Latz *SEC & TRS*

Human Resources: Patricia Seward *Human Resources MGR*

Total Employees............................300	**Regional Employees** 295
Year Established 1906	**SIC Code** 8111

Dietrich Industries, Inc.

One Mellon Bank Center, 500 Grant St., Ste. 2226
Pittsburgh, PA 15219
County: Allegheny

Phone: (412) 281-2805
Fax: (412) 281-2965

Manufacturer of light metal framing and stainless steel products through 18 plants across the country.

Officers: William S. Dietrich *P*

Total Employees.........................1,900	**Regional Employees** ....
Year Established 1959	**SIC Code**......................................3312

Digital Equipment Corp.

1500 Ardmore Blvd.
Pittsburgh, PA 15221
County: Allegheny

Phone: (412) 244-7200
Fax: (412) 244-7450
Internet Address: www.digital.com

Provider of computer systems, software and integration services, including network integration, systems integration and multivendor computing. The Company, which is headquartered in Maynard, MA, is listed on the NYSE.

Officers: Steve Sugarman *SAL MGR*
Steve Wolf *SAL MGR*

Regional Employees ....100+
Year Established 1957   **SIC Code**......................................3571
Annual Revenues ($000) ....

Direct Mail Service Inc.

930 Penn Ave.
Pittsburgh, PA 15222
County: Allegheny

D

Phone: (412) 471-6300
Fax: (412) 471-8059

Provider of services helping clients to implement mailing, marketing and advertising plans. The Company offers mailing services, printing, packaging/shipping, warehousing, inquiry fulfillment, media distribution, data processing and project planning services. Its capabilities range from assembling a multi-component package, to printing, labeling and mailing 200 to 400,000 direct mail pieces on a short turn-around. The Company's clients include corporations, small and large businesses, advertising and public relations agencies, and non-profit organizations.

Officers: David L. Marconi *P*

Total Employees..............................65	**Regional Employees**....................65
Year Established........................1918	**SIC Code**....................................2759

Diskriter, Inc.

3257 W. Liberty Ave.
Pittsburgh, PA 15216
County: Allegheny

Phone: (412) 344-9700
Fax: (412) 344-4834

Provider of systems integration equipment and services to customers in the Tri-State area. The Company represents a variety of manufacturers and products in the systems integration and office automation industry, including Novell networks; Apple, Compaq and IBM computers; Optika Image Processing; Lanier, Olympus and Philips dictation products; Lanier and Murata fax machines; and Lexmark printers and typewriters. Its network systems group of certified Novell/Banyan engineers provide network consultation, planning, installation, training and support. The Company has installed LANs and WANs in most environments, including health care, legal, banking, education, retail and government. It also offers a range of services, including professional consulting services and contracted services (temporary help for a specific project or for a specific time frame). In addition, the Company's Diskriter Health Care Solutions division provides consulting, outsourcing and turnkey solutions for the health care industry with a specialization in the medical records department and transcription services; and its two subsidiaries located at 505 McNeilly Rd. in Pittsburgh, PA, Diskriter Communications, Inc., provides Internet and Intranet consulting, design and implementation, and Diskriter Office Works, Inc., provides reconditioned brand-name office furniture at a discount. The Company is employee-owned.

Officers: Willard S. Hull *P*
Richard A. Roupe *VP-FIN*
Rick Toth *VP & CTO*
Damian Kush *Commercial SAL MGR*
Donna Smykla *Health Care SAL MGR*
Andrew Krolick *P-Diskriter Communications, Inc.*
Hank Pizoli *P-Diskriter Office Works, Inc.*

Total Employees	155	**Regional Employees**	155
Year Established	1947	**SIC Code**	7373
Annual Revenues ($000)	15,000		

Diversified Group Administrators, Inc.

311 S. Central Ave.
P.O. Box 330
Canonsburg, PA 15317
County: Washington

Phone: (412) 746-8700
Fax: (412) 746-8628

Provider of insurance-related services for group benefit plans. The Company's services include third-party claims administration, benefit plan consulting, group insurance brokerage, PPO/PHO/IPA network administration, utilization management and sundry services. The Company is a subsidiary of Medical Control, Inc., which is headquartered in Dallas, TX, and listed on the NASDAQ.

Officers: J. Ward Hunt *CH*
David C. Bramer *P & CEO*
Michele L. Peindl *SVP*
Teresa G. Brinkman *VP*

Human Resources: Daniel Riston *CFO, SEC & TRS (Purchasing)*

Total Employees	260	**Regional Employees**	85
Year Established	1982	**SIC Code**	6411
Annual Revenues ($000)	4,500 (Pennsylvania)		

Doepken Keevican & Weiss, P.C.

USX Tower, 600 Grant St., 37th Fl.
Pittsburgh, PA 15219
County: Allegheny

Phone: (412) 355-2600
Fax: (412) 355-2609
Internet Address: www.dkwlaw.com

Provider of legal services in all areas of corporate and commercial law, including mergers and acquisitions, securities, banking, creditors' rights and bankruptcy, franchising, complex civil litigation, labor and employment relations, environmental law, tax, estates and trusts, employee benefits and real estate. The Firm, with approximately 65 attorneys, operates branch offices located in Detroit, MI, and Harrisburg, PA.

Officers: Michael Weiss *P-Board of DIR*

Total Employees	151	**Regional Employees**	145
Year Established	1988	**SIC Code**	8111

Dollar Bank, Federal Savings Bank

Three Gateway Center
Pittsburgh, PA 15222
County: Allegheny

Phone: (412) 261-4900
Fax: (412) 261-8535

Federally chartered mutual savings bank with 46 offices throughout Southwestern Pennsylvania and Northeastern Ohio. In addition to its full-service branches, the Bank operates five loan centers in the Pittsburgh area. As a regional full-service bank, it provides a broad range of financial services to individuals and businesses in the Pittsburgh and Cleveland markets. In the commercial banking area, clients may choose from lines of credit and term loans as well as equipment leasing and real estate financing for all types of income, commercial and industrial properties. Business checking, cash management services, custom certificates and government-sponsored loans round out its mix of business services. The Bank's line of retail banking services includes money market accounts, individual retirement accounts and certificates of deposit. It also offers personal and home equity loans, mortgages, secured and unsecured lines of credit, auto and boat loans, and VISA. The Bank's subsidiaries include Security Savings Mortgage Corp. in Canton, OH; and Dollar Bank Leasing Corp. in Pittsburgh, PA.

Officers: Stephen C. Hansen *P & CEO*
Jeffrey Morrow *EVP*
Robert Oeler *EVP*
John Anderson *SVP-Corporate Banking*
Edward Brown *SVP-Branch ADM*
Andrew Devonshire *SVP-Private Banking*
Thomas Kobus *SVP & TRS*
Abraham Nader *SVP-Data Services/OPR*
Jack Shelley *SVP-Real Estate*
Joseph Smith *SVP-MKT*

Human Resources: Bruce Nagle *VP-Human Resources*

Total Employees	1,048	**Regional Employees**	782
Year Established	1855	**SIC Code**	6035
Annual Revenues ($000)	2,594,000 (Assets)		

Donnelley Financial, R. R.

600 River Ave.
P.O. Box 6766
Pittsburgh, PA 15212
County: Allegheny

Phone: (412) 321-0440
Fax: (412) 323-7862

Provider of financial printing services to clients in the Tri-State area. The Company is headquartered in New York, NY. It is a business unit of R. R. Donnelley & Sons Co., which is headquartered in Chicago, IL, and listed on the NYSE.

Officers: Joseph Bundick *Division MGR*

Human Resources: Barb Kachurik

Purchasing: Joe Suriano

Regional Employees......................75
Year Established 1972   **SIC Code** 2782

Dotter Services, Inc., D.

329 Forest Grove Rd.
Coraopolis, PA 15108
County: Allegheny

Phone: (412) 771-2990
Fax: (412) 771-3016

Owner and operator of adult care centers throughout the Pittsburgh metropolitan area. The Company's Autumn Lane Assisted Living Homes in Bellevue, Monroeville, Moon Township and Robinson Township provide assisted living in small eight-bed homes. Its Autumn Lane Personal Care facilities in Aliquippa (62 beds) and Coraopolis (46 beds) provide Alzheimer's care. All of the sites offer adult day care services.

Officers: Barbara Dotter *P*
Jane Dotter *EVP*
Edward Dotter *SEC*

Total Employees..............................70   **Regional Employees** 70
Year Established 1971   **SIC Code** 8051

DoubleTree Hotel Pittsburgh

1000 Penn Ave.
Pittsburgh, PA 15222
County: Allegheny

Phone: (412) 281-3700
Fax: (412) 227-4500

Full-service hotel featuring 616 guest rooms and 42 suites, 18 meeting rooms that can be converted into approximately 30,000 square feet of banquet/convention space, the Orchard Cafe, Motions lounge, a fitness center and a business center. The Hotel is owned by Forest City Ventures in Cleveland, OH, and operated by DoubleTree Hotels. The Hotel was formerly known as the Pittsburgh Vista Hotel.

Officers: Joe Kane *GMGR*
Doug Copeland *DIR-MKT*
Coleman Hughes *DIR-OPR*
Frank Taylor *DIR-Food & Beverage*

Human Resources: Pat Sherr *DIR-Human Resources*

Total Employees ....500+
Year Established 1970

Regional Employees ....500+
SIC Code 7011

Downtown Motors of Pittsburgh, Inc.

2001 W. Liberty Ave.
Pittsburgh, PA 15226
County: Allegheny

Phone: (412) 561-4500
Fax: (412) 561-2256

Automobile dealership, doing business as Downtown Pontiac, selling a full line of new Pontiac vehicles. The Company also offers used cars, as well as parts, service and a body shop.

Officers: Bernard M. Alpern *P*

Human Resources: Lorraine Carroll

Purchasing: Richard K. Alpern *VP*

Total Employees 30
Year Established 1924

Regional Employees 30
SIC Code 5511

Du-Co Ceramics Co.

155 S. Rebecca St.
P.O. Box 568
Saxonburg, PA 16056
County: Butler

Phone: (412) 352-1511
Fax: (412) 352-1266

Manufacturer of technical ceramic insulators, technical porcelain and steatite for electrical and refractory applications used by appliance manufacturers worldwide.

Officers: Reldon W. Cooper *CEO*
Nicholas J. Norante *VP-SAL*
Lora Cooper Saiber *GMGR & TRS*
Linda Cooper Knapp *SEC*

Human Resources: Bert T. Drum

Purchasing: Kenneth P. McGee

Total Employees............................185	**Regional Employees** 185
Year Established 1949	**SIC Code**......................................3264

Ductmate Industries, Inc.

R.D. 3, Rte. 136
Box 113
Monongahela, PA 15063
County: Washington

Phone: (412) 258-0500
Fax: (412) 258-3619
Internet Address: www.ductmate.com

Manufacturer of HVAC ductwork connectors and accessories. The Company supplies six types of duct connector systems and over two dozen related products and machines to the sheet metal industry. Its product line includes connector systems; access doors; hangers and reinforcements; turning vane and rail; gaskets, sealants and adhesives; hardware; T.D.C./T.D.F. corners, cleats and gasket; and various machines. The Company's products are sold through a nationwide distributor network and direct to residential and commercial duct cleaning businesses. Its other facilities include a manufacturing site in Lodi, CA; manufacturing and sales in Melbourne, Australia (Ductmate PTY., LTD.); manufacturing and sales in Stoney Creek, Ontario, Canada (Ductmate Canada, LTD.); sales in London, England (Ductmate Europe, LTD.); and manufacturing and sales in Dundee, Scotland (Ductmate Europe, LTD.).

Officers: Frederick J. Arnoldt *P*
Raymond W. Yeager *EVP*
Bruce Arnoldt *VP-OPR*
Tim Omstead *VP*

Human Resources: Carole Guido

Total Employees	125	**Regional Employees**	80
Year Established	1977	**SIC Code**	3444
Annual Revenues ($000)	23,000		

D

Duerr Packaging Co., Inc.

892 Steubenville Pike
Burgettstown, PA 15021
County: Washington

Phone: (412) 947-1234
Fax: (412) 947-4321

Manufacturer of packaging products including thermoformed plastics (vacuum forming and pressure forming), transparent plastic lids and boxes, rigid paper boxes and decorative heart boxes. The Company's products are marketed to a variety of manufacturers, including producers of confectionery, bakery goods, office products, giftware and china. It also operates a paper box plant located in Imperial, PA.

Officers: Samuel A. Duerr, Jr. *CEO*
Samuel A. Duerr III *P*
David C. Duerr *VP.*

Human Resources: Lorraine T. Duerr *SEC & TRS*

Purchasing: Wayne Albright

Total Employees	66	**Regional Employees**	66
Year Established	1953	**SIC Code**	2652

Dun & Bradstreet Corp.

790 Holiday Dr., 3rd Fl.
P.O. Box 1406, Pittsburgh, PA 15230
Pittsburgh, PA 15220
County: Allegheny

Phone: (412) 920-6909
Fax: (412) 920-6939
Internet Address: www.dnb.com

Provider of business, commercial-credit and business-marketing information services. The Company maintains a worldwide database covering more than 44 million businesses. It can integrate client infomation with the Company's database to develop customized reports for an array of applications. The Company, which is headquartered in Murray Hill, NJ, is listed on the NYSE. The local office serves clients in Western Pennsylvania, Eastern New York and Ohio, and West Virginia.

Officers: Thomas V. Acquaviva *District MGR-SAL*
Katherine Eighmy *District MGR-Information Resources*

Human Resources: Peggy Ders

Total Employees..........................2,300	**Regional Employees** 30
Year Established 1841	**SIC Code**....................................7323
Annual Revenues ($000) 2,100,000	

Duquesne Club

325 Sixth Ave.
Pittsburgh, PA 15222
County: Allegheny

Phone: (412) 391-1500
Fax: (412) 391-2540

Nonprofit private club offering social and business programming for its approximate 2,400 members. The Club's facilities include a fitness and health center, 30 overnight rooms and a dining room.

Officers: Melvin D. Rex *GMGR*

Total Employees ....300+	**Regional Employees**................300+
Year Established 1890	**SIC Code**....................................8699

Duquesne University

600 Forbes Ave.
Pittsburgh, PA 15282
County: Allegheny

Phone: (412) 396-6050
Fax: (412) 396-4334
Internet Address: www.duq.edu

Nonprofit, private Catholic coeducational institution offering more than 150 programs on the bachelor's, master's and doctoral levels in its nine schools: the College and Graduate School of Liberal Arts, and the Schools of Business Administration, Education, Health Sciences, Law, Music, Natural and Environmental Sciences, Nursing and Pharmacy. The University is situated on a 40-acre campus in downtown Pittsburgh. Its student body is comprised of approximately 5,750 undergraduates and 3,650 graduate students from all over the United States and 90 countries.

Officers: John E. Murray, Jr., J.D., S.J.D. *P*
Michael P. Weber, D.A. *Provost & VP-Academic Affairs*
Rev. Sean Hogan *EVP-Student Life*
Isadore R. Lenglet *EVP-MGT & Business*

Human Resources: Richard Williamson *DIR-Human Resource MGT*

Total Employees	2,224	Regional Employees	2,224
Year Established	1878	SIC Code	8221
Annual Revenues ($000)			115,439

Dura-Bond Industries, Inc.

2658 Jefferson St.
P.O. Box 518
Export, PA 15632
County: Westmoreland

Phone: (412) 327-0280
Fax: (412) 327-0113

Holding company for three subsidiary corporations. Dura-Bond Coating, Inc., with facilities at 3200 Youghiogheny River Rd. in McKeesport, PA, and in Steelton, PA, coats steel pipe used in the transmission of oil and natural gas. It also distributes products used in the installation and maintenance of these pipelines. Dura-Bond Steel Corp., which is located at the above address, fabricates structural steel used for the marine industry and industrial applications. Turtle Creek Industrial Railroad, Inc., which is also located at the above address, operates an eleven mile shortline railroad serving the Company and several clients along its route.

Officers: Wayne Norris *P & SEC*
Bradley Norris *VP*
James A. Norris *TRS*

Human Resources: Sandi Moses

Purchasing: Jason Norris

Total Employees	201	Regional Employees	160
Year Established	1959	SIC Code	3441
Annual Revenues ($000)			16,000

Dura-Metal Products Corp.

447 Arona Rd.
P.O. Box 680
Irwin, PA 15642
County: Westmoreland

Phone: (412) 864-9770
Fax: (412) 864-9896

Fabricator and finisher of wear-resistant and corrosion-resistant parts and tooling constructed from ultrahard materials such as tungsten carbide and industrial ceramics. The Company is also a fabricator of powder compaction press tooling for the powder metal, magnet and battery industries.

Officers: Joseph B. Freiland *P & CEO*

John P. Graham *SAL MGR*
Jay Jamison *ENG & Quality MGR*
Robert Kettering *MFG MGR*

Human Resources: David Kubiak *CON*

Purchasing: Michael J. Fetchen *Resource MGR*

Total Employees............................93	**Regional Employees** 93
Year Established 1971	**SIC Code**......................................3599
Annual Revenues ($000) 7,000	

Duraloy Technologies, Inc.

120 Bridge St.
P.O. Box 81
Scottdale, PA 15683
County: Westmoreland

Phone: (412) 887-5100
Fax: (412) 887-5224
Internet Address: www.duraloy.com

Manufacturer of products and components made with high alloy, heat-resistant and corrosion-resistant materials using centrifugal and static casting processes. The Company casts a wide variety of austentic, ferritic, nickel-based and cobalt-based alloys for heat and/or corrosion resistant service. Its products include steel mill furnace rolls, heat treating fixtures, petrochemical reformer tube assemblies and ethylene coils. The Company is a subsidiary of the Park Corp., which is headquartered in Cleveland, OH.

Officers: Vince Schiavoni *P*
Rick McIntyre *VP-FIN*
Rick Kauffman *MGR-SAL & MKT*
Roman Pankiw *Technical MGR*
Paul Rokosz *GMGR-OPR*

Human Resources: Pati Adams

Purchasing: Alan Kite

Total Employees...........................135	**Regional Employees** 135
Year Established 1923	**SIC Code**......................................3369
Annual Revenues ($000) 21,000	

Dyna-Craft Industries, Inc.

4060 Norbatrol Ave.
Murrysville, PA 15668
County: Westmoreland

Phone: (412) 325-2000
Fax: (412) 325-2298

Manufacturer of metal stampings and tooling. The Company is headquartered in Penang, Malaysia. It is a subsidiary of the Heong Leong Group, which is head-quartered in Kuala Lumpur, Malaysia.

Officers: Donald A. Grandmont *GMGR*

Total Employees........................1,800	**Regional Employees** 270
Year Established 1960s	**SIC Code**....................................3469

Dynamet Inc.

195 Museum Rd.
Washington, PA 15301
County: Washington

Phone: (412) 228-1000
Fax: (412) 228-2087

Producer of titanium metals and powder metal alloys. The Company hot rolls and finishes titanium and nickel-based alloys into coils, bar, shapes and wire; forges and makes components for the medical and aerospace industries; and makes powder alloys for the aerospace and tooling industries. It operates additional facilities in Clearwater, FL, and Bridgeville, PA, as well as a service center in Stanton, CA. The Company is a subsidiary of Carpenter Technology Corp., which is headquartered in Reading, PA, and listed on the NYSE.

Officers: Robert J. Torcolini *P*
  Robert Dickson *SVP & CFO*
  Louis L. Lherbier *VP & Technical DIR*

Total Employees............................270	
Year Established 1967	**SIC Code**....................................3356

Dyno Nobel, Inc.

Scott St. & Gillifa Dr.
P.O. Box 192
Donora, PA 15033
County: Washington

Phone: (412) 379-8100
Fax: (412) 379-4770

Manufacturer of ammonium nitrate. The product is marketed to distributors primarily within the Tri-State area to be utilized in highway construction, coal strip mining and quarry work. It is also used as raw material for one of the processes in manufacturing nitric oxide. The facility located at the above address is one of the Company's production plants. The Company is headquartered in Salt Lake City, UT. It is a subsidiary of Dyno Industrier A.S., which is headquartered in Oslo, Norway, and listed on the Oslo Stock Exchange.

Officers: Douglas J. Jackson *P (Salt Lake City, UT)*
Steven K. Burgin *Plant MGR*

Human Resources: Earl J. Banner

Purchasing: Jeris C. Johnson

Total Employees..........................2,343	**Regional Employees** 48	
Year Established 1968	**SIC Code**......................................2873	
Annual Revenues ($000) 26,000		

Eagle Printing Co., Inc.

114 W. Diamond St.
P.O. Box 271, Butler, PA 16003
Butler, PA 16001
County: Butler

Phone: (412) 282-8000
Fax: (412) 282-1280

Publisher of the Butler Eagle, a newspaper with a daily circulation of 31,310 and a Sunday circulation of 32,587 primarily to residents of Butler County and also to East Brady, Grove City, Rimersburg and Worthington, PA. The Company also publishes five weekly newspapers: Cranberry Eagle, with a circulation of 12,000; Sunday Cranberry Eagle, with a circulation of 15,000; The News Weekly, with a circulation of 8,000; Slippery Rock Eagle, with a circulation of 10,000; and Hampton-Richland Eagle, with a circulation of 12,000. The Company also operates a full-service pre-press shop and bindery serving outside clients.

Officers: Vernon L. Wise, Jr. *P & Publisher*
John L. Wise III *VP & SEC*
Vernon L. Wise III *VP & TRS*

Human Resources: Ronald A. Vodenichar *GMGR (Purchasing)*

Total Employees..........................180	**Regional Employees** 180	
Year Established 1869	**SIC Code** 2711	
Annual Revenues ($000)..10,000+		

Earth Sciences Consultants, Inc.

One Triangle Dr.
Export, PA 15632
County: Westmoreland

Phone: (412) 733-3000
Fax: (412) 325-3352

Provider of environmental sciences and engineering consulting services to a variety of clients, including light and heavy manufacturers, energy and utility companies, natural resources organizations, professional services firms, waste management companies and public administration organizations. The Firm offers services in air quality, construction management, corrective action, engineering design, geologic services, industrial compliance, liability management, litigation support, radiological services, solid waste management, and water quality and industrial wastewater. It employs specialists in a number of disciplines, including geology; geochemistry; hydrogeology; biology; chemistry; civil, chemical, environmental and agricultural engineering; health and safety; construction; and soil science. The Firm operates branch offices in Denver, CO; Akron, OH; and Blue Bell, PA. It is a subsidiary of American Waste Services, Inc., which is headquartered in Warren, OH, and listed on the NYSE.

Special Designations: ENR$_{500}$

Officers: Scott C. Blauvelt *P*
Joseph M. Harrick *EVP*
Robert C. Hendricks *EVP*
Thomas C. Slavonic *EVP*
Marcel D. Tourdot *EVP*
David S. Hess *VP-Technical SAL*

Human Resources: Marylee Murrin *CAO*

Purchasing: Robert R. Latoche *VP-FIN*

Total Employees	106	**Regional Employees**	79
Year Established	1979	**SIC Code**	8711
Annual Revenues ($000)			14,000

East Liberty Electroplating, Inc.

1126 Butler Plank Rd.
Glenshaw, PA 15116
County: Allegheny

Phone: (412) 961-0517
Fax: (412) 487-1807

Provider of metal finishing services including anodizing (chrome, sulphuric and hard anodize), barrel plating, electroless nickel (high and medium phosphorus baths), nickel, nickel/chrome, tin, zinc, zinc-nickel alloy (cadmium substitute), black oxide, chromate conversion (iridite), degreasing, passivation, buffing/polishing, bright dipping (copper alloys) and vibratory finishing.

Officers: Thomas Drozd *P*
Robert Bugel *VP*
Thomas Bugel *VP*

Vincent Kovalik *VP & SEC*
Joseph Thimons *VP & TRS*

Total Employees............................60	**Regional Employees**...................60
Year Established........................1920	**SIC Code**......................................3471
Annual Revenues ($000) 3,500	

Easter Seal Society of Western Pennsylvania

632 Ft. Duquesne Blvd.
Pittsburgh, PA 15222
County: Allegheny

Phone: (412) 281-7244
Fax: (412) 281-9333

Nonprofit organization providing programs and services which assist individuals with disabilities (infants, children and adults) in achieving physical, social and economic independence. The Society operates four licensed private schools in Allegheny County offering customized educational programs to children with disabilities between the ages of two and eight. A similar type program is also offered for infants and toddlers with disabilities. Adult services focus on vocational rehabilitation, including assessment, on-the-job training, employment and community job placement assistance. The Society trains and employs individuals with disabilities in the manufacturing process such as machine operations, hand assembly and packaging skills; training is also provided in areas such as food preparation, clerical, janitorial and building maintenance. It markets Daymax office products (calendars, desk pads and personal organizers) to government agencies and corporations with as many as 4 million products being manufactured per year. In addition, it operates and maintains a number of Pennsylvania Department of Transportation Driver License Centers where individuals with disabilities are employed as camera operators and janitorial staff. The Society consists of the Allegheny Division located at the above address; the Cambria/Somerset Division in Johnstown, PA; the Fayette Division in Uniontown, PA; and the Venango Division in Franklin, PA. It also operates the Clarion/Jefferson Site in Punxsutawney, PA; and the Somerset Site in Somerset, PA. The Society provides services to residents of 20 counties throughout Western Pennsylvania. It is affiliated with the National Easter Seal Society, which is headquartered in Chicago, IL.

Officers: Lawrence P. Rager, Jr. *P & CEO*
James G. Bennett *EVP*
Eleanor K. Lieb *CFO*

Human Resources: Debra L. Chesney *DIR-Human Resources*

Total Employees............................198	
Year Established........................1934	**SIC Code**......................................8322
Annual Revenues ($000) 7,605	

Eat 'N Park Restaurants, Inc.

100 Park Manor Dr.
Pittsburgh, PA 15205
County: Allegheny

Phone: (412) 788-1600
Fax: (412) 787-1771

E

Owner and operator of a chain of family restaurants. The Company has 69 restaurants in Ohio (5), Pennsylvania (61) and West Virginia (3), including approximately 45 located throughout the Pittsburgh metropolitan area.

Officers: James Broadhurst *CEO*
Basil Cox *P*
David L. Wohleber *EVP & CFO*

Total Employees.........................7,023	**Regional Employees** 4,236
Year Established 1949	**SIC Code**.....................................5812
Annual Revenues ($000) 150,000	

EBARA Solar, Inc.

811 Rte. 51 S.
Clairton, PA 15025
County: Allegheny

Phone: (412) 382-1254
Fax: (412) 382-1251

Developer, manufacturer and marketer of unique solar photovoltaic technology. While the Company is primarily engaged in research and development, it markets solar modules for applications in residential power generation, remote water pumping and other remote power requirements. The Company is a subsidiary of EBARA Corp., which is headquartered in Tokyo, Japan, and listed on the Tokyo Stock Exchange.

Officers: Richard Rosey *P*
John Easoz *VP*
Robert Brenneman *MGR-Process OPR*
Edgar Kochka *MGR-Process DEV*
Richard Sprecace *MGR-Facility OPR*
Robert Lazzari *CON*
Daniel Meier *Chief Scientist*

Human Resources: Dana Corey

Purchasing: Debbie Tomalski

Total Employees.............................70	**Regional Employees** 70
Year Established 1991	**SIC Code**.....................................3674
Annual Revenues ($000)..5-7,000	

Eckert Seamans Cherin & Mellott, LLC

USX Tower, 600 Grant St., 42nd Fl.
Pittsburgh, PA 15219
County: Allegheny

Phone: (412) 566-6000
Fax: (412) 566-6099

Full-service national law firm with more than 240 attorneys in 10 cities throughout the eastern United States. The Firm serves a wide variety of clients, including multinational corporations, professional sports teams, small businesses, nonprofit institutions, municipalities, government agencies and individuals. It has substantial experience in many fields of law, including antitrust, appellate, bankruptcy, construction, corporate and finance, creditors' rights, education, employee benefit/ERISA, energy, environmental, estate planning and administration, government contracts, government relations, health care, immigration, information technology, insurance, intellectual property, international business and trade, labor and employment, land use, litigation, municipal and municipal finance, product liability, real estate, securities, sports and entertainment, taxation, toxic tort litigation, transportation, trusts and white-collar criminal defense. The Firm's branch offices are located in Washington, D.C.; Boca Raton, Ft. Lauderdale, Miami and Tallahassee, FL; Boston, MA; and Allentown, Harrisburg and Philadelphia, PA. Its affiliated companies, which are also located at the above address, consist of Cathay Mason Group, a China-U.S. investment counseling group; and Main Street Capital Holdings L.L.C., a private investment firm.

Officers: LeRoy S. Zimmerman *CH-Executive Comm.*
Thomas D. Wright *CH-OPR Comm.*
Stephen R. Delinsky *OPR Comm.*
Charles C. Papy *OPR Comm.*

Total Employees............................510	**Regional Employees** 250
Year Established 1958	**SIC Code** 8111

Edgar Services, Inc.

3047 Industrial Blvd.
Bethel Park, PA 15102
County: Allegheny

Phone: (412) 831-3925
Fax: (412) 831-3916

Provider of cleaning services doing business as The Maids. With three other satellite offices located in Pittsburgh at 59 Penn Circle W., 101 Rodi Rd. and 2015 Babcock Blvd., the Company offers cleaning services to homes, apartments and small offices throughout the Pittsburgh metropolitan area. It operates with four-person supervised cleaning teams using environmentally preferred cleaning products. The Company is a franchisee of The Maids International, which is head-quartered in Omaha, NE, and it claims to be the largest volume producing franchise of that organization.

Officers: Harry Edgar *P*

Total Employees............................90	**Regional Employees** 90	
Year Established 1985	**SIC Code**....................................7349	

Edwards & Sons, Inc., A. G.

600 William Penn Place, Ste. 100
Pittsburgh, PA 15219
County: Allegheny

Phone: (412) 281-3800
Fax: (412) 281-2221
Internet Address: www.agedwards.com

Full-service broker-dealer and investment banking firm offering a broad range of products and services, including stocks, bonds, mutual funds, IRAs, annuities, life insurance and professional money management. Other Pittsburgh area offices are located in Beaver, Butler, Greensburg, Greentree and Peters Township, PA. From its headquarters in St. Louis, MO, the Company operates more than 550 branch offices throughout the United States. It is a subsidiary of A. G. Edwards, Inc., which is also headquartered in St. Louis, MO, and listed on the NYSE.

Officers: Tom Rieck *MGR-Greentree Office*
David Spatig *MGR-Pittsburgh Office*

Total Employees........................12,784 **Regional Employees** 103
Year Established ....1887 **SIC Code**....................................6211
Annual Revenues ($000) 1,454,467

Eichleay Holdings, Inc.

6585 Penn Ave.
Pittsburgh, PA 15206
County: Allegheny

Phone: (412) 361-0200
Fax: (412) 363-9018

Holding company providing engineering and industrial construction services nationwide through its operating companies, including Eichleay Corp., Eichleay Engineers, Inc. (PA) and Eichleay Engineers, Inc./Peter F. Loftus Division, all located at the above address, and Eichleay Engineers, Inc. of California, which is based in Concord, CA.

Special Designations: ENR_{400} ENR_{500}

Officers: George F. Eichleay *P & CEO*

Theodore W. Nelson, Jr. *EVP & COO*
John G. Borman *VP-FIN*

Total Employees.........................2,000	**Regional Employees** 600	
Year Established 1875	**SIC Code** 8711	
Annual Revenues ($000) 200,000		

Eidemiller, Inc., Adam

1003 E. Pittsburgh St.
Greensburg, PA 15601
County: Westmoreland

Phone: (412) 242-0100
Fax: (412) 837-0765

Owner and operator of three hotels in Greensburg, PA, consisting of the 145-room Four Points Hotel Greensburg by Sheraton located at 100 Sheraton Dr., the 57-room Holiday Inn Express Greensburg located on Rte. 30 E. and the 65-room Super 8 Motel located at 111 Sheraton Dr.

Officers: Wilmer P. Eidemiller *P*

Total Employees............................275	
Year Established 1925	**SIC Code** 7011
Annual Revenues ($000)..9,000+	

Electric M&R, Inc.

2025 Milford Dr.
P.O. Box 326
Bethel Park, PA 15102
County: Allegheny

Phone: (412) 831-6101
Fax: (412) 831-1160

Manufacturer of lighting fixtures and repairer of electric motors operating through two divisions: Pittsburgh Reflector Co. (PRC) and Electric Manufacturing & Repair Co. (EM&RC). PRC, which is located in Irwin, PA, manufactures and markets commercial fluorescent lighting fixtures and specialty display lighting. The principal markets for its lighting fixtures are firms engaged in the installation of electrical fixtures in construction projects and firms installing new or replacement electrical fixtures in their own facilities. EM&RC, which is located at the above address, repairs AC/DC industrial motors and magnetic chucks, markets new industrial motors, and provides dynamic balancing and vibration analysis. It serves a market located primarily in Western Pennsylvania. As of December 31, 1996, the Company changed its status from that of a public corporation to that of a private corporation.

Officers: Gretchen Oswald *OWN, P & CEO (Purchasing)*
Ray Croushore *CFO*

Purchasing: Scott Stanley *VP & COO*

Total Employees............................46	**Regional Employees** 46
Year Established 1915	**SIC Code**....................................3646
Annual Revenues ($000)..2-3,000	

Electro-Glass Products, Inc.

Rte. 981
P.O. Box 157
Mammoth, PA 15664
County: Westmoreland

Phone: (412) 423-5000
Fax: (412) 423-7955
Internet Address: www.electro-glassprod.com

Manufacturer of glass insulators using the pressed powdered process. The Company's products include glass for all types of hermetic seals; glass for optic attachment of lasers, night vision and evacuation tubes; ground and screened glass powders; granulated glass powders ready to press; long-length preforms for high pressure requirements; and Military Armor Glass, which controls miniscus climb. These products are used for such applications as rectifiers, transistors, mercury switches and diodes in the space, defense and automotive industry. The Company also provides on-site melting, grinding and spray drying, and operates an in-house machine shop.

Officers: James K. Schmidt *OWN, P & GMGR*
Donald G. Shirer *VP*
Kevin J. Tamblyn *VP-MFG*
John E. Reed *SEC*

Human Resources: Twila M. Schmidt
Sharyn Jackson

Purchasing: Stephen Puskar

Total Employees............................53	**Regional Employees** 53
Year Established 1973	**SIC Code**....................................3229
Annual Revenues ($000) 2,500	

Elizabeth Carbide Die Co., Inc.

601 Linden St.
P.O. Box 95
McKeesport, PA 15132
County: Allegheny

Phone: (412) 751-3000
Fax: (412) 754-0755
Internet Address: www.eliz.com

Manufacturer of rotary and single-station press tooling serving the pharmaceutical industry in North and South America, Europe, Asia and Australia. The Company is also a major source of tooling for hundreds of customers in the powdered metal, ceramic, chemical, electronics and confectionery industries. The Company's corporate headquarters and main manufacturing facility are located at the above address. Its divisions include Elizabeth Carbide Components in Latrobe, PA, which produces carbide and tool steel wear parts for many industries; Elizabeth Carbide Europe SA in Brussels, Belgium, which sells and services tooling and specialty tableting presses throughout the European continent; Elizabeth Carbide of North Carolina in Lexington, NC, which specializes in the manufacture of round tooling; Elizabeth-Hata International in Irwin, PA, which provides sales and service for Hata tableting presses and is a manufacturer of control systems, tablet testing systems and various auxiliary equipment; and Elizabeth-Hata Japan Ltd. in Osaka, Japan, the liaison organization for tooling and presses serving Asia and the Pacific Rim.

Officers: Richard A. Pagliari *C-OWN, CH & CEO*
David A. Keefer *C-OWN & P*
Wayne A. Sanderson *VP & GMGR*
Larry D. Landini *SAL MGR*

Human Resources: Philip Davis *Personnel MGR*

Purchasing: Paul Marlowe *Purchasing Agent*

Total Employees............................230	**Regional Employees** 190
Year Established 1954	**SIC Code**......................................3544
Annual Revenues ($000) 30,000	

Eljer Manufacturing, Inc.

1301 Eljer Way
Ford City, PA 16226
County: Armstrong

Phone: (412) 763-1621
Fax: (412) 763-6277

Manufacturer of vitreous china plumbing fixtures and accessories. The Company is a division of Eljer Industries, Inc. (EII), which is headquartered in Dallas, TX. EII is a subsidiary of Zurn Industries, Inc., which is headquartered in Erie, PA, and listed on the NYSE.

Recent Events: Zurn Industries, Inc. recently announced its intent to relocate its headquarters to Addison, TX.

Officers: Ronald C. Grafton *Plant MGR*

Human Resources: Leroy M. Harnish, Jr. *MGR-Human Resources*

Regional Employees....................500
Year Established 1904   **SIC Code**.....................................3261

Elkem Metals Co. L.P.

P.O. Box 266
Pittsburgh, PA 15230
County: Allegheny

Phone: (412) 299-7200
Fax: (412) 299-7225

Diversified producer of manganese, silicon and chromium ferroalloys and metals; several specialty ferroalloys; and calcium carbide and lime. Each meets the precise requirements of its steel, foundry, aluminum, superalloy, silicones, electronics and acetylene customers. The Company operates five strategically located plants to provide just-in-time truck and rail deliveries to U.S. and Canadian customers, as well as shipments by sea to customers worldwide. Its plants are located in Ashtabula and Marietta, OH; Alloy, WV; and Hamilton, Ontario, and Chicoutimi, Quebec, Canada. It also has a joint venture facility in Salt Lake City, UT. Overall financial and administrative support is provided from the local facility. The Company is a subsidiary of Elkem A/S, which is headquartered in Oslo, Norway, and listed on the Oslo Stock Exchange.

Officers: Anthony C. LaRusso *P; SVP-Elkem A/S-North America*
Geir I. Kvernmo *DIR-MKT & Customer Service*
Richard O. Aa *CON*

Human Resources: Jerry W. Jenkins *(Marietta, OH)*

Total Employees........................1,500   **Regional Employees** 40
Year Established 1980   **SIC Code**.....................................3313

Elmhurst Corp.

One Bigelow Sq., Ste. 630
Pittsburgh, PA 15219
County: Allegheny

Phone: (412) 281-8731
Fax: (412) 281-9463

Investment holding company engaged in the hospitality, real estate and security industries. The Company owns and operates the Ramada Plaza Suites & Conference Center, which is also located at the above address. The hotel features

311 suites, a full-service restaurant and lounge, banquet/meeting facilities, health club, indoor pool, hair stylist, travel agency, valet, self-service laundry, convenience store and floral shop. Through its Elmhurst Hospitality division, the Company is a consulting manager to the Hotel Brunswick in Lancaster, PA. In addition, it is engaged in the security industry through an investment in an alarm service provider serving clients in the Southwestern U.S.

Officers: William E. Hunt *CH*
               Dan Altman *P & CEO*

Human Resources: Jill Campbell

Total Employees............................275	**Regional Employees** 175
Year Established 1974	**SIC Code** 7011
Annual Revenues ($000) 23,000	

Embassy Suites Hotel-Pittsburgh International Airport

550 Cherrington Pwy.
Coraopolis, PA 15108
County: Allegheny

Phone: (412) 269-9070
Fax: (412) 262-4119
Internet Address: www.embassy-suites.com

Hotel featuring 223 suites, the Foggy Bottom Grill & Lounge and Horsefeathers Bar. The Hotel's meeting facilities can accommodate 700 for banquets and 1,000 for meetings, with more than 10,000 square feet of space. The Hotel is owned and operated by the Davidson Hotel Co., which is headquartered in Memphis, TN.

Officers: Chick Hill *OWN & P*
               Tom Spoto *GMGR*
               Scott Greenwood *Food & Beverage DIR*
               Julie Unitas *DIR-SAL*

Human Resources: Penny Allyn *DIR-Human Resources*

Total Employees............................250	**Regional Employees** 250
Year Established 1991	**SIC Code** 7011

EMC International, Inc.

11 Parkway Center, Ste. 100
Pittsburgh, PA 15220
County: Allegheny

Phone: (412) 921-4010
Fax: (412) 921-1099

Engineer and supplier of steelmaking equipment, such as electric arc furnaces, ladle metallurgy facilities, ladle furnaces, vacuum degassing facilities, process control systems, alloy materials handling systems, lime/carbon/flux materials handling systems, auxiliary equipment and systems and spare parts. The Company also offers consulting engineering services, process technology, turnkey project management, personnel training involving technology transfer, field service maintenance assistance and maintenance programs. Its engineering and technology services enable steelmakers to efficiently start-up, operate and maintain their facilities. The Company is a subsidiary of MIDREX Corp. (MC), which is headquartered in Charlotte, NC. MC is a subsidiary of Kobe Steel, Ltd., which is headquartered in Tokyo, Japan, and listed on the Tokyo Stock Exchange.

Officers: Ken D. Matthews *P*
Ron D. Gray *VP-Technology*
Rand H. Kane *VP-ENG*
James C. Simmons *VP-SAL*
William L. Davidson *CON*

Human Resources: D. Roy Shaffer

Total Employees.............................36
Year Established 1987

Regional Employees 36
SIC Code....................................3567

Employee Benefit Data Services, Inc.

One Gateway Center
Pittsburgh, PA 15222
County: Allegheny

Phone: (412) 394-6300
Fax: (412) 394-9669

Full-service employee benefit service center established to provide the data intensive services of employee benefit plans. The Company's services can be limited to a single product like COBRA administration, however, most clients access its expanded services for complete support of active and retiree benefit administration. Services available include computer integrated telephonic participant enrollment, full flexible benefit administration, eligibility maintenance, premium reconciliation, carrier reporting, integrated COBRA service, student dependent certification, spending account administration, pension benefit calculations, pension application processing, retiree benefit administration and pension payments. The Company provides comprehensive service levels for organizations of all sizes and types with a total of more than 500,000 covered participants. It operates a branch office in Harrisburg, PA.

Officers: Paul A. Mockenhaupt *P*
David A. Borra *VP*
David A. Howes *VP*
Daniel D. Stumpf *VP*

Human Resources: Bonnie Gruemken

Purchasing: Arlene Paris

Total Employees	57	**Regional Employees**	56
Year Established	1980	**SIC Code**	8748

Ensinger, Inc.

365 Meadowlands Blvd.
Washington, PA 15301
County: Washington

Phone: (412) 746-6050
Fax: (412) 746-9078

Manufacturer of engineering plastic stock shapes, profiles and finished parts utilizing proprietary extrusion, casting, injection and compression molding processes. The Company offers a complete range of reinforced and unreinforced base materials ranging from standard engineering plastics such as acetals and nylons to high performance materials such as polyimides. It has an ISO 9002 certification. The Company is responsible for the U.S. operations of Ensinger GmbH + Co., which is headquartered in Nufringen, Germany. The Company's subsidiaries include Ensinger Special Polymers, Inc. in Houston, TX; Ensinger Vekton, Inc. in Hawthorne, NJ; HP Polymer, Inc. in Dallas, TX; and Putnam Precision Molding, Inc. in Putnam, CT. It also maintains a warehouse and sales office in Placentia, CA.

Officers: Rick Phillips *P*
Larry Resavage *VP & GMGR*

Human Resources: Deborah Burk *Human Resource MGR*

Total Employees	50+		
Year Established	1986	**SIC Code**	3082

ENTEX Information Services, Inc.

5313 Campbells Run Rd.
Pittsburgh, PA 15205
County: Allegheny

Phone: (412) 788-7575
Fax: (412) 788-7585
Internet Address: www.entex-is.com

Employee-owned provider of a complete range of computer hardware and software products and services, including consulting, distribution, configuration, installation, systems engineering, maintenance, asset management and help desk support. The Company is also a reseller of Apple, Compaq, Hewlett Packard, IBM, Microsoft, NEC and more than 1,500 other manufacturers. It primarily serves larger corporate clients. The Company, which is headquartered in Rye Brook, NY, operates approximately 60 branch offices throughout the nation. The local facility serves clients in Western Pennsylvania, and portions of Ohio and West Virginia.

Officers: Christopher W. Caruso *GMGR-Pittsburgh*

Human Resources: Theodore Ritenour

Total Employees........................8,000	**Regional Employees** 85
Year Established 1993	**SIC Code**....................................7373
Annual Revenues ($000) 2,500,000	

Envirotrol, Inc.

432 Green St.
P.O. Box 61
Sewickley, PA 15143
County: Allegheny

Phone: (412) 741-2030
Fax: (412) 741-2670
Internet Address: www.envirotrol.com

Recycler of activated carbon and provider of carbon products and services, including adsorption systems, virgin carbon and reactivated carbon, custom segregated reactivation, bulk transportation and field services. The Company markets its products and services to a variety of industries, particularly those involved in environmental remediation activities that utilize activated carbon, including wastewater treatment centers, petroleum companies, chemical companies, municipalities and air quality management operations. The Company's facilities include plants in Beaver Falls and Darlington, PA, and a warehouse in Rochester, PA.

Officers: Carl W. Tobias *C-OWN*
Renee W. Tobias *C-OWN*
Keith G. Tobias *C-OWN*

Human Resources: Carolyn B. Cadman *MGR-Human Resources*

Total Employees...........................100	**Regional Employees** 98
Year Established 1970	**SIC Code**....................................2819
Annual Revenues ($000) 17-20,000	

Epic Metals Corp.

11 Talbot Ave.
Braddock, PA 15104
County: Allegheny

Phone: (412) 351-3913
Fax: (412) 351-2018
Internet Address: www.epicmetals.com

Manufacturer of Epicore and Wideck composite floor and roof deck ceiling systems, acoustical security ceiling systems and Maxspan stay-in-place bridge forms. The Company's clients include architects, engineers and contractors nationwide.

Officers: Donald H. Landis *P*
Robert Ault *VP-ENG*
Tom Hartman *VP-SAL*
David F. Landis *VP*
David A. Mancosh *VP*

Total Employees 80-100
Year Established 1968

Regional Employees 80-100
SIC Code 3441

Epstein, Tabor & Schorr

Centre City Tower, 650 Smithfield St., Ste. 1600
Pittsburgh, PA 15222
County: Allegheny

Phone: (412) 261-2245
Fax: (412) 261-5609

Certified public accounting and consulting firm providing a variety of services. These include accounting and auditing services; tax compliance and planning services; management advisory services; management information, accounting and billing systems services; and marketing and business communications services. The Firm primarily serves small- and mid-sized businesses, including wholesale/retail operations, new business start ups, professional practices and nonprofit entities in Western Pennsylvania, Ohio and West Virginia. Its staff of 24 professionals is certified in the disciplines of accounting, law and management information systems.

Officers: Harold I. Schorr *MPTR*

Total Employees 37
Year Established 1930

Regional Employees 37
SIC Code 8721

Equipco Division of Phillips Corp.

Phillips Industrial Park, Mayview Rd.
P.O. Box 338
Bridgeville, PA 15017
County: Allegheny

E

Phone: (412) 221-2800
Fax: (412) 257-3109
Internet Address: www.equipco.com

Distributor of material handling equipment doing business as Equipco. The Company markets forklift equipment, rail car movers, side loaders, tow tractors, personnel carriers, sweeper/scrubbers, hand pallet jacks, racking, lift stackers and tables, vertical and horizontal carousels, and dock levelers, boars and plates. It carries a variety of brand names including Baumann, Boschman, Cascade, Drexel, E-Z-Go, Factory Cat, Hyster, Jet, Kent, Lift Rite, Powerboss, Presto, Remstar, Sellick, Swingshift, Trackmobile, Unarco and United Tractor. The Company also rents forklifts and offers aftermarket parts and service support for all of its products. A branch office is located in Meadville, PA. In addition, it operates service sites in Belpre, OH, and Altoona and Lock Haven, PA.

Officers: Carl H. Swanson, Jr. *P*
Thomas B. Rush *VP*

Human Resources: Anthony M. Angotti *Personnel MGR*

Total Employees	96	**Regional Employees**	86
Year Established	1944	**SIC Code**	5084
Annual Revenues ($000)			20,000

Equipment Corp. of America

Station St.
P.O. Box 306
Coraopolis, PA 15108
County: Allegheny

Phone: (412) 264-4480
Fax: (412) 264-1158
Internet Address: www.ecanet.com

Distributor of new and reconditioned equipment for the heavy commercial, civil and marine construction, mining and material handling industries. The Company maintains a complete inventory, for purchase, rental or rent-to-purchase, of air compressors, air hoists, augers, clamshell buckets, concrete buckets, demolition hammers, derricks, dragline buckets, generator sets, grapples, hoisting machinery, locomotive cranes, pile driving accessories, pile extractors, pile hammers air/steam, pile hammers diesel, pile threaders and shackles, rigging equipment, taglines, tieback drills, vibratory pile equipment, winches, and wire rope blocks and fittings. It also offers equipment service and rebuilding, and maintains an extensive parts inventory. The Company operates branch sales, warehouse and service facilities in Upper Marlboro, MD, and Aldan, PA.

Officers: Alfred R. Kern *P*
A. Roy Kern, Jr. *VP*
William E. Rose *VP*

Total Employees	30	**Regional Employees**	12
Year Established	1918	**SIC Code**	5082
Annual Revenues ($000)	5,000		

Ernst & Young LLP

One Oxford Centre, 301 Grant St.
Pittsburgh, PA 15219
County: Allegheny

Phone: (412) 644-7800
Fax: (412) 644-0533
Internet Address: www.ey.com

Worldwide public accounting and consulting firm with audit, tax and consulting practice groups serving a wide range of Pittsburgh area businesses. The Firm serves clients in virtually all industry groups, including aerospace and defense, consumer products, energy, financial services, health care, information, communications and entertainment, insurance, life sciences, manufactruing, real estate and construction. The Firm, which is headquartered in New York, NY, operates more than 600 offices in over 100 countries, including 89 U.S. offices employing 23,000 people and generating $3.57 billion in revenues. The Pittsburgh regional office oversees part of New York and West Virginia, along with Western Pennsylvania with additional offices located in Buffalo and Syracuse, NY; Erie, PA; and Charleston, WV.

Officers: James A. Williams *Area MPTR*
Frank J. Gori *Area DIR-Assurance & Advisory Business Services*
Mark L. Sullivan *Area DIR-Tax*

Human Resources: Cheryl Weinrich *Area DIR-Human Resources*

Total Employees	71,500	**Regional Employees**	355
Year Established	1915	**SIC Code**	8721
Annual Revenues ($000)	7,800,000		

ESA, Inc.

311 Thomson Park Dr.
Cranberry Township, PA 16066
County: Butler

Phone: (412) 776-2870
Fax: (412) 776-4452

Provider of computer consulting and recruiting services to the engineering industry. The Company, which is also known as Eclectic System Architectures, provides contract software engineers for factory automation and embedded control projects. It serves a diverse range of industries, including defense, transportation, nuclear, chemical, medical, food processing, metals, furnace, test and measurement, plastics, manufacturing, communications and glass. A branch office is located in Cleveland, OH.

E

Officers: Andrew J. Kalnas III *P*
James W. Kalnas *VP-SAL & MKT*
Connie E. Shaw *CON*

Human Resources: Bruce D. Draganjac *Consulting Services Resource MGR*

Total Employees............................90		**Regional Employees** 68	
Year Established 1988		**SIC Code** 8748	
Annual Revenues ($000) 6,000			

ESB Bank, F.S.B.

1060 Freeport Rd.
Pittsburgh, PA 15238
County: Allegheny

Phone: (412) 758-5584
Fax: (412) 758-0576

Provider of banking services, including commercial loans, education loans, installment loans, auto loans, home equity loans, mortgage loans, second mortgage loans, refinance loans, overdraft protection on checking, discount brokerage service, savings accounts, regular checking accounts, commercial checking accounts, certificates of deposit, IRA/Keough accounts, Christmas club savings, vacation club savings, safety deposit boxes, Visa and MasterCard, U.S. savings bonds, money orders and traveler's checks. The Bank is headquartered at 600 Lawrence Ave. in Ellwood City, PA. It is a subsidiary of PennFirst Bancorp, Inc., which is also headquartered at 600 Lawrence Ave. in Ellwood City, PA, and listed on the NASDAQ. The Bank operates eight additional branch offices in Aliquippa, Ambridge, Coraopolis, Ellwood City, Monaca, New Castle, Pittsburgh and Zelienople, PA. (Although the Bank's headquarters are located out of the Pittsburgh Business Directory's defined seven-county Pittsburgh metropolitan area, six of its branch banks are within these parameters. The choice of the Pittsburgh branch at the above address was an arbitrary selection. For additional information regarding the Bank, contact the corporate office.)

Officers: Charlotte A. Zuschlag *P & CEO*
Charles P. Evanoski *SVP & CFO*
Robert C. Hilliard *SVP-Audit & Compliance*
Frank O. Martz *SVP-OPR*
Todd F. Palkovich *SVP-Lending*

Human Resources: John T. Stunda *SVP-ADM*

Purchasing: David Barletta

Total Employees............................130	**Regional Employees** 50
Year Established 1915	**SIC Code**......................................6035

Extrude Hone Corp.

8075 Pennsylvania Ave.
P.O. Box 527
Irwin, PA 15642
County: Westmoreland

Phone: (412) 863-5900
Fax: (412) 863-8759
Internet Address: www.extrudehone.com

Inventor, developer and refiner of nontraditional processes that machine, finish and measure complex shapes in both conventional and advanced materials. The Extrude Hone process selectively "hones" the edges and surfaces of passages that restrict the flow of pliable abrasive media extruded through workpiece and tooling. It allows manufacturers to deburr, radius and polish in one operation, even inaccessible areas; produce true round radii, even on complex edges; reduce surface roughness by 75% to 90% on cast, machined or electrical discharge machined surfaces; hold close tolerances due to the selectivity and easy controllability of the process; process dozens of holes or parts simultaneously; and maintain flexibility—the same machine can do a variety of jobs just by changing tooling, process settings and, if necessary, media. The Extrude Hone process was originally invented for deburring and finishing critical aircraft hydraulic and fuel system components. Presently more than 1,200 Extrude Hone installations are utilized in 40 countries. The equipment ranges from small machines polishing precision one-of-a-kind dies with no special tooling to fully automated systems processing over a thousand automotive components per hour, day after day. The Extrude Hone process is used to manufacture critical components for aerospace, nuclear and medical applications; precision dies and molds; and high production components for automotive, industrial and consumer products. The Company operates additional facilities in Paramount, CA; and in England, France, Germany, Ireland, Japan and the People's Republic of China.

Officers: Larry Rhoades *OWN & P*
Tom Kohut *VP-SAL*

Human Resources: C. Gary Dinsel *VP*

Total Employees............................260	**Regional Employees** 200
Year Established 1966	**SIC Code**......................................3541

Fagen's, Inc.

9000 Brooktree Rd.
P.O. Box 658
Wexford, PA 15090
County: Allegheny

Phone: (412) 935-3700
Fax: (412) 935-2240
Internet Address: www.fagens.com

F

Owner and operator of five Fagen's Building Centers which retail building materials. The Company's product line includes lumber, drywall, roofing and siding, windows, prehung doors, millwork, trusses, wall panels and hardware. Approximately 90% of its customer base consists of contractors and professional builders. The Company's stores are located in Hudson and Panama City, FL; Canton and East Liverpool, OH; and Verona, PA. Its manufacturing facilities are located in North Jackson, OH (truss components), and Pittsburgh, PA (door shop). The Company is a subsidiary of Fagen's Holding, Inc., which is headquartered in Wilmington, DE.

Officers: Jack Fagen *P*
Lou Massaglia *VP-Purchasing*
Herb Werner *Credit MGR*
Dan Whitacre *Accounting MGR*

Human Resources: Dolores Porter *Human Resources MGR*

Purchasing: John Fagen *Senior Buyer*

Total Employees	400	**Regional Employees**	85
Year Established	1985	**SIC Code**	5211
Annual Revenues ($000)	60,000		

Family Health Council, Inc.

960 Penn Ave., Ste. 600
Pittsburgh, PA 15222
County: Allegheny

Phone: (412) 288-2130
Fax: (412) 288-9036
Internet Address: www.trfn.clpgh.org/fhc/

Nonprofit organization whose mission is to improve the health and well-being of individuals, the quality of family life, and to promote an informed acceptance of human sexuality and a lifestyle of responsible parenthood. The Organization administers a network of health services in 23 western Pennsylvania counties. It claims to be the largest direct provider of family planning services in Pennsylvania and directly operates 25 offices and provides family planning funding to another 50 sites. The Organization's services include family planning, comprehensive gynecological care, prenatal care, pediatric care, testing and treatment for sexually transmitted diseases, breast and cervical cancer screening, nutrition counseling, the WIC (Women, Infants and Children) nutrition program, adoption, health education and comprehensive teen pregnancy prevention. It serves more than 65,000 women each year who make more than 156,000 visits for care ranging from contraception to cancer screening. The Organization is supported by a variety of state and federal grants, patient fees and contributions from corporations, foundations and individuals.

Officers: Frank A. Bonati, Ph.D. *P*
　　　　　　Richard Baird *VP*
　　　　　　Cheryl Sills *VP-DEV & Communications*

Human Resources: Lori Freedlander *VP-Human Resources*

Purchasing: Chris Young

Total Employees	240	**Regional Employees**	148
Year Established	1971	**SIC Code**	8399
Annual Revenues ($000)			16,000

Family Resources

141 S. Highland Ave., Ste. 201
P.O. Box 11009, Pittsburgh, PA 15237
Pittsburgh, PA 15206
County: Allegheny

Phone: (412) 363-1702
Fax: (412) 363-1724

Nonprofit agency devoted to the prevention and treatment of child abuse through the strengthening of families and neighborhoods. The Agency's mission is carried out through a comprehensive set of services grouped into three divisions. Community services programs promote positive family interaction and work to prevent child abuse by reducing stress in families and providing opportunities for support, education and recreation to families and community groups. Treatment services include specialized mental health services that work to heal wounds of violence in families where child abuse has occurred. The Professional Training and Consultation division offers workshops, conferences and consultation to improve professional competence in addressing intra-familial abuse and neglect. The Agency operates additional facilities in Mars, McKeesport and Pittsburgh (downtown and the South Side), PA.

Officers: Walter H. Smith, Jr., Ph.D. *EDIR*

Human Resources: Paul Dwornick *DIR-OPR*

Total Employees	190	**Regional Employees**	190
Year Established	1986	**SIC Code**	8322
Annual Revenues ($000)			4,000

Family Services of Western Pennsylvania

921 Penn Ave., 4th Fl.
Pittsburgh, PA 15222
County: Allegheny

Phone: (412) 261-3623
Fax: (412) 261-6245
Internet Address: www.nb.net/~fswp

Nonprofit agency providing social, behavioral and other human services to adults, children, families and communities in Western Pennsylvania. The Agency operates three major divisions. The Family Service Division offers counseling, an employee-assistance program and community building, with sites at the above address, and in McKeesport and Tarentum, the North Hills and South Hills areas of Pittsburgh, and at 14 family centers in various communities. The Foster Care Division offers family foster care at 46th and Hatfield St. in Lawrenceville. The Allegheny Valley Mental Health and Mental Retardation Division offers an extensive range of mental health and mental retardation services, operating from 3230 William Pitt Way in Pittsburgh, and eight major sites in Greensburg, New Kensington and Tarentum.

Officers: Virginia T. Fragale *Interim EDIR*
Dennis Mitchell *Interim CFO*
Susan L. Collins *Foster Care DIR*
Robert J. Feikema *Family Service DIR*
Patricia L. Valentine *DIR-Allegheny Valley Mental Health/Mental Retardation Program*

Human Resources: Linda R. Steffey *Human Resources MGR*

Purchasing: Jennette Rue *Purchasing CLK*

Total Employees	400	**Regional Employees**	400
Year Established	1948	**SIC Code**	8322
Annual Revenues ($000)	16,000		

Fansteel Inc.—Hydro Carbide Division

Rte. 30 & Rte. 982
P.O. Box 363
Latrobe, PA 15650
County: Westmoreland

Phone: (412) 539-9701
Fax: (412) 539-8140

Supplier of pre-formed tungsten carbide compositions for a wide variety of markets. The Company is a division of Fansteel Inc., which is headquartered in

North Chicago, IL, and listed on the NYSE. The Division produces tungsten carbide rod, die parts, rolls and other products for the metalworking market, and nozzles, studs and substrates, valve parts, bearings and other wear parts for the oil and energy industries. The 37,000 square foot plant located at the above address blends tungsten carbide powders with cobalt or nickel binders to create 28 grades of materials that are then pressed and machined for the rotary tool and die fabricating markets. The Division operates an additional plant in Gulfport, MS, and warehouses in Los Angeles, CA; Gladwin, MI; Bergerac, France; Stuttgart, Germany; and Singapore.

Officers: Thomas McLaren *Group GMGR*
Joe Campbell *Quality Control MGR*
Ron Rollinger *SAL MGR*
Henry Patts, Ph.D. *Technical DIR*
William Wager *CON*

Human Resources: Cathy O'Brien

Purchasing: Paul Kuhns

Total Employees	160	**Regional Employees**	100
Year Established	1967	**SIC Code**	3544

Fayette Bank

58 W. Main St.
P.O. Box 2088
Uniontown, PA 15401
County: Fayette

Phone: (412) 438-4531
Fax: (412) 437-1403
Internet Address: www.citipage.com/fayettebank

   Full-service bank offering a broad range of checking, savings, loans and lines of credit to businesses and individuals. The Bank also provides cash management services to businesses. It operates 11 branch offices located in Fairchance, Jefferson, McMurray (Donaldson's Crossroads); Pittsburgh (Brookline, Brentwood, Mt. Oliver, Pleasant Hills and the South Side); Uniontown (Cherry Tree and a Giant Eagle); and Waynesburg, PA. The Company is a subsidiary of BT Financial Corp., which is headquartered in Johnstown, PA, and listed on the NASDAQ.

Officers: Andrew J. Duran *P*
James T. Matysik *EVP*
Ben E. Wright, Jr. *SVP*

Total Employees	106	**Regional Employees**	91
Year Established	1947	**SIC Code**	6022
Annual Revenues ($000)	355,000 (Assets)		

Federal Home Loan Bank of Pittsburgh

601 Grant St.
Pittsburgh, PA 15219
County: Allegheny

Phone: (412) 288-3400
Fax: (412) 288-2861

Bank serving as a central source of credit to housing lenders in Delaware, Pennsylvania and West Virginia. It also provides correspondent banking, investment and safekeeping services to financial institutions. The Bank is a strong advocate for community development and contributes financing for affordable housing. An equity investment by purchasing stock is required for financial institutions to access its varied credit programs, but is not required of those solely interested in noncredit services. Membership is open to savings institutions, commercial banks, insurance companies and credit unions with at least 10% of their assets in residential mortgages. Members are required to own stock in the Bank in proportion to their qualified mortgage assets and earn an attractive rate of return on their investment. The Bank is part of the Federal Home Loan Bank System, a national network of more than 6,100-member financial institutions, 12 Federal Home Loan Banks and the Federal Housing Finance Board in Washington, D.C.

Officers: James D. Roy *P & CEO*
William G. Batz *EVP & COO*
James C. Chaney *SVP & DIR-Community Investment*
Jerold L. Dambaugh *SVP & DIR-Information Systems*
Jane P. Duffy *SVP & DIR-MKT*
Craig C. Howie *SVP & Chief Credit Officer*
Lawrence F. Kirchner *SVP*
Arthur R. Love *SVP & Chief Investment Officer*
Eric J. Marx *SVP & CFO*
Dana A. Yealy *SVP & GC*

Human Resources: Linda M. Kimak *SVP-Human Resources & ADM*
Lynn S. Villani *DIR-Human Resources*

Regional Employees....................234
Year Established........................1932   **SIC Code**....................................6019
Annual Revenues ($000)......................23,900,000 (Assets)

Federal Reserve Bank of Cleveland, Pittsburgh Office

717 Grant St.
P.O. Box 867
Pittsburgh, PA 15219
County: Allegheny

Phone: (412) 261-7800

Regional Reserve Bank that, along with 11 other Reserve Banks and the Board of Governors in Washington, D.C., comprise the Federal Reserve System. As the nation's central bank, the Federal Reserve System formulates monetary policy, regulates banks, and provides banking services to financial institutions and to the U.S. government. With an additional branch office in Cincinnati, OH, and a check processing center in Columbus, OH, the Federal Reserve Bank of Cleveland serves the Fourth Federal Reserve District, which includes Ohio, Eastern Kentucky, Western Pennsylvania and the northern panhandle of West Virginia. The Pittsburgh office distributes currency and coin to area depository institutions, collects and clears checks, supervises local banks and provides services to the U.S. Treasury. The Pittsburgh office is one of only five "Fed" offices nationwide that process savings bonds, and one of two offices that print and mail bonds.

Officers: Raymond L. Brinkman *AVP*
Kimberly B. Ray *AVP*
Robert B. Schaub *AVP*

Regional Employees....................400
Year Established 1918   **SIC Code** 6011

Federated Investors

Federated Investors Tower, 1001 Liberty Ave.
Pittsburgh, PA 15222
County: Allegheny

Phone: (412) 288-1900
Fax: (412) 288-1982
Internet Address: www.federatedinv.com

Provider of investment management and financial services, including a wide array of investment products that are sold to individual and institutional investors, and mutual funds services to the industry, including fund administration and distribution. The Company states that it ranks as one of the 10 largest mutual fund companies in the United States with assets under management and administration totaling $115.8 billion as of March 31, 1997. Of this total, $39.5 billion were funds advised, distributed or administered by the Company. It provides investment advisory and administrative services to more than 348 mutual funds offering over 506 share classes. With more than $8 billion in assets in growth, growth and income, equity income, indexed and asset allocation funds, the

Company claims to rank in the top 7% of all equity money managers. It also claims to rank in the top 1% of money market fund managers and the top 5% of bond fund managers. In the fixed-income bond and money market funds, the Company manages more than $68 billion in assets. These investments capitalize on portfolio management strength in cash, government, investment-grade corporate, mortgage-backed, municipal and high-yield products. The Company's New York based global investment subsidiary, Federated Global Research, was launched in 1995. It currently manages 10 funds with over $775 million in assets. The Company's Federated Services Co. subsidiary is a major provider of administrative and distribution services to mutual fund providers. It develops and markets systems, software and technology products and mutual fund services for fund administration, marketing and distribution, transfer agency, portfolio accounting and management, clearing and 401(k) recordkeeping. The Company has offices in five downtown Pittsburgh locations as well as offices in Boston, MA, and New York, NY.

Officers: John F. Donahue *CH & CEO*
Edward C. Gonzales *VCH*
J. Christopher Donahue *P & COO*
Richard B. Fisher *CH-Federated Securities Corp.*
Arthur L. Cherry *P & CEO-Federated Services Co.*
James F. Getz *P-Federated Securities Corp.*
John W. McGonigle *P & CEO-Federated Investors Management Co.*
William D. Dawson II *EVP & Chief Investment Officer-Domestic Fixed Income*
Henry A. Frantzen *EVP & Chief Investment Officer-Global Equity & Fixed Income*
J. Thomas Madden *EVP & Chief Investment Officer-Domestic Equity, High-Yield & Asset Allocation*

Human Resources: Terry Kelly *VP & DIR-Human Resources*

Purchasing: Maroon DeVito *MGR-Corporate Planning*

Total Employees.........................2,045 **Regional Employees** 1,860
Year Established ....1955 **SIC Code**......................................6722

Ferrari Importing Co.

200 Waterfront Dr.
Pittsburgh, PA 15222
County: Allegheny

Phone: (412) 323-0335
Fax: (412) 323-0317
Internet Address: www.gammasports.com *or* www.atssports.com

Manufacturer, wholesaler and distributor of sporting goods and related products doing business as Gamma Sports. The Company is primarily engaged in the racquet sports segment of the sporting goods industry. Its product line consists of more than 5,000 items, including racquets and racquet strings, balls, grips, racquet accessories, vibration dampeners, stringing machines, ballhopper baskets, tennis nets and posts, windscreens, water removers, court equipment, apparel and accessories. The Company has recently expanded to two other sports—golf and baseball—producing golf balls and radar guns. The Company's clients include all of the nation's largest sporting good retailers such as Oshman's, Sports and Recreation, The Sports Authority and most tennis specialty pro-shops and teaching pros. In addition, it exports to more than 45 countries. The Company claims that its ATS Total Sports mail order catalog, which includes the products of a variety of manufacturers, is the world's largest supplier of racquet strings, stringing machines, grips, court equipment and accessories.

Officers: Harry M. Ferrari, Ph.D. *P*
Ray Harrington *EVP*
Ron Carr *R&D MGR*
Matt Sherman *NATL SAL MGR*
Chuck Vietmeier *Export MGR*

Human Resources: Harry Ingram *GMGR*

Purchasing: Scot Fischer

Total Employees 50-55	**Regional Employees** 34
Year Established 1974	**SIC Code**....................................3949
Annual Revenues ($000) 15,000		

Ferri Enterprises, Inc.

Town Square Professional Bldg.
Murrysville, PA 15668
County: Westmoreland

Phone: (412) 327-0921
Fax: (412) 733-7594

Operator of various businesses and developer of real estate. The Company's businesses include a supermarket, Ferri's Fine Foods; a pharmacy, Ferri Pharmacy; two hardware stores, True Value Hardware; and a restaurant, Lamplighter Restaurant. The restaurant is located in Delmont, PA; the other businesses are located in Murrysville, PA. The Company also owns and operates Creekside Shops Shopping Center, Franklin Plaza Shopping Center, Village of Murrysville Shopping Center and Town Square Professional Building, all located in Murrysville, PA.

Officers: Edward J. Ferri *P*

Total Employees...........................200	**Regional Employees** 200
Year Established 1954	**SIC Code** 5411
Annual Revenues ($000) 16,000		

F

Ferro Corp.

60 Greenway Dr.
P.O. Box 4332
Pittsburgh, PA 15204
County: Allegheny

Phone: (412) 331-3550
Fax: (412) 331-3553
Internet Address: www.ferro.com

Manufacturer of glass enamels used in the automotive, appliance, glass container, architectural and lighting industries. The Company also produces organic polymer coatings for glass and plastic applications. The Company, which is headquartered in Cleveland, OH, is listed on the NYSE. It has operations in 21 countries. The plant located at the above address is a part of the Company's Coatings, Colors and Ceramics business segment.

Officers: Cliff Ruderer *GMGR*
Bruce Brackbill *SAL & MKT MGR*

Purchasing: Don Watson

Total Employees ....7,000+	**Regional Employees** ....70+
Year Established 1919	**SIC Code** 2816
Annual Revenues ($000) 1,400,000	

Ferry Electric Co.

250 Curry Hollow Rd.
Pittsburgh, PA 15236
County: Allegheny

Phone: (412) 892-2100
Fax: (412) 892-2107

Electrical contractor specializing in design build and value engineering for commercial, industrial and institutional projects. The Company also maintains a division to focus on special projects and residential services. It serves clients throughout the Tri-State area.

Officers: James R. Ferry *P*
Gerald P. Comber *VP*
James J. Ferry II *VP*

Human Resources: Jill J. Yeager *Corporate SEC*

Purchasing: Robert P. Doerfler

Total Employees 100	**Regional Employees** 100
Year Established 1926	**SIC Code** 1731

Few Assoc., Inc., Bill

Frick Bldg., 437 Grant St., Ste. 1025
Pittsburgh, PA 15219
County: Allegheny

Phone: (412) 281-1025
Fax: (412) 281-1874
Internet Address: www.billfew@earthlink.net

Provider of investment management and financial counseling services. The Firm's specific services include private investment management of mutual fund accounts, private investment management of individual securities accounts, estate and business planning, retirement counseling and 401(k) plan management. A branch office is located at 711 E. Pittsburgh St. in Greensburg, PA.

Officers: William E. Few, Jr. *P & CEO*
John R. Brown III *EVP & CFO*
Stuart M. Miller *EVP*
Barbara L. Perfetta *EVP*
Joseph A. Scarpo, Jr. *EVP*
Michael Kauffelt II *SVP*
Veronica Steinkirchner *SVP*

Human Resources: W. Timothy Few *EVP & COO*

Purchasing: Howard S. Gittens *SVP*

Total Employees	48	**Regional Employees**	48
Year Established	1987	**SIC Code**	8742
Annual Revenues ($000)			5,800

Fibercon International, Inc.

100 S. Third St.
Evans City, PA 16033
County: Butler

Phone: (412) 538-5006
Fax: (412) 538-9118
Internet Address: www.fibercon.com.au

Manufacturer of carbon steel fibers that reinforce concrete and replace traditional wire mesh and rebar in the concrete and stainless steel fibers for high temperature refractory reinforcement. The Company's steel fiber reinforcement products and technology are used in a wide variety of new construction and renovation projects around the globe, including industrial flooring, roads, bridges, parking facilities, airports and buildings. Its joint venture holdings include Fibercon Australia PTY., Ltd. in Perth, Australia (sales office); Fibercon U.K., Ltd. in Chelmsford, England (sales office); and Fiberconcrete Malaysia in Klang, Malaysia (manufacturing plant).

Officers: Nicholas C. Mitchell, Sr. *CEO*
George N. Mitchell *P*
Nicholas C. Mitchell, Jr. *SVP*
Frank Adams *VP-ENG*
Keith Foley *VP-SAL*

Human Resources: Stacy Gamble

Purchasing: Monica Perry

Total Employees............................30	Regional Employees 28
Year Established 1972	SIC Code......................................3315

Fike & Sons Dairy, Inc., R. Bruce

47 W. Craig St.
Uniontown, PA 15401
County: Fayette

Phone: (412) 438-8581
Fax: (412) 438-1197

Producer of fluid milk products, including fruit drinks, teas and milk. The Company also produces ice cream in half-gallon and five-quart cartons under private labels. It serves a variety of customers, ranging from convenience stores to supermarkets, in Maryland, Eastern Ohio, Western Pennsylvania and parts of West Virginia. The Company is a subsidiary of the Protein Holding Co., which is headquartered in Laurel, MD.

Officers: Jack Sherman *SVP & GMGR*
Ed Evans *VP-SAL*
Tim Griglack *VP-OPR*
Ralph Cavalcante *CON*

Human Resources: Mike Shanaberger

Purchasing: Leslie Locke

Total Employees............................170	Regional Employees 170
Year Established 1913	SIC Code......................................2026

Filmet Color Laboratories, Inc.

7436 Washington St.
Pittsburgh, PA 15218
County: Allegheny

Phone: (412) 351-3510
Fax: (412) 351-4326
Internet Address: www.filmet.com

Provider of on-demand digital and offset printing, large format color output, electronic prepress, interior and exterior signage, photographic imaging and full color fleet graphics. The Company operates branch offices in Brook Park, OH, and Lancaster, PA.

Officers: Rick Bachelder *P*
Dennis Chapple *VP-FIN*
Michael Hoffay *VP-SAL & MKT*
Ernie Scholze *VP & GMGR*

Human Resources: Heather Wallace

Purchasing: Steve Bird

Total Employees............................265	**Regional Employees** 205
Year Established 1910	**SIC Code**.....................................7384

First Bank of Leechburg

152 Market St.
P.O. Box 566
Leechburg, PA 15656
County: Armstrong

Phone: (412) 842-1181
Fax: (412) 845-6373

Provider of banking services, offering a complete range of basic loan and deposit products and services. The Bank also offers special programs including Banclub, a packaged checking program with accidental death and dismemberment insurance coverage; Senior Accent, a club for customers over 50 years old; American Dream savings, which offers higher rates with relationship accounts; 2 Good 2 Be True mortgage, for first-time home owners; Sentry CD, which offers higher rates for Senior Accent members; Check Card, a combination ATM and debit card; and Business Revitalization Loans, offering below prime rate loans for storefront and side renovations to small businesses. The Bank operates three additional branch offices in Leechburg, near the border of Armstrong and Westmoreland Counties, PA. The Bank is a subsidiary of First Commonwealth Financial Corp. (FCFC), which is headquartered in Indiana, PA, and listed on the NYSE. FCFC provides trust services for the Bank.

Officers: William P. Malloy *P*
Larry Baudino *VP-Support Services*
Mark Maszgay *VP-Credit ADM*
Donald Tallarom *VP*

Human Resources: Carrie Riggle *Human Resources Representative*

Total Employees............................58	**Regional Employees** 58
Year Established 1900	**SIC Code**.....................................6021
Annual Revenues ($000)............................225,000 (Assets)

First Impression Printing Co., Inc.

One Federal St.
Pittsburgh, PA 15212
County: Allegheny

Phone: (412) 321-5800
Fax: (412) 321-5806

Commercial printer offering in-line aqueous coating. The Company also provides electronic prepress services, including scanning, imagesetting, digital dot generated contract proofs, computer-to-plate and in-house bindery services.

Officers: Gary Pandolfo *P*
Glenn Means *CON*
Mike Minyon *Plant MGR*

Human Resources: Ellen Pandolfo

Total Employees............................34	**Regional Employees** 34
Year Established 1981	**SIC Code**......................................2759

Fiserv, Inc.

Fiserv Center, 912 Ft. Duquesne Blvd.
Pittsburgh, PA 15222
County: Allegheny

Phone: (412) 577-3000
Fax: (412) 577-3994
Internet Address: www.fiserv.com

Provider of financial data processing systems and related information management services and products to more than 5,000 banks, credit unions, mortgage firms and savings institutions worldwide. The Company, which is headquartered in Brookfield, WI, is listed on the NASDAQ. It operates full-service offices in more than 70 cities. The Company's Pittsburgh business unit has three primary offerings. The Custom Outsourcing Solution is a package of financial data processing systems and services tailored to match the strategic objectives of mid-sized to large financial institutions. The Custom Outsourcing Solution provides highly-automated account and transaction processing, advanced delivery systems, sophisticated operations automation and related services that attract and retain customers, boost retail and commercial sales, improve operational efficiency and reduce ongoing expenses. The InformEnt Data Warehouse Solution is a complete data warehouse solution that gives financial institution decision makers and analysts a single source for current, accurate and consistent information on profitability, customers and marketplace activity. The Backroom Systems back-office automation products is a complete line of systems for financial institutions of any size, designed to automate call center sales and quality service delivery, eliminate manual tasks and reduce the time required to correct proof errors, automate incoming and outgoing check and item returns, reduce the backlog of research requests and improve the timeliness, control and security of wire transfers.

Officers: James C. Puzniak *P-Pittsburgh*

Human Resources: Terrie Baker *VP*

Total Employees.........................8,590	**Regional Employees** 400	
Year Established 1978	**SIC Code**....................................7374	
Annual Revenues ($000) 798,268		

Fisher Scientific Co.

2000 Park Lane
Pittsburgh, PA 15275
County: Allegheny

Phone: (412) 490-8300
Fax: (412) 490-8930
Internet Address: www.fisher1.com

Provider of more than 245,000 scientific products and services to research, health care, industrial, educational and governmental markets in 145 countries. The Company serves scientists engaged in biomedical, biotechnology, pharmaceutical, chemical and other fields of research and development and is a supplier to clinical laboratories, hospitals, health care alliances, physicians' offices, environmental testing centers, remediation companies, quality-control laboratories and many other customers. It offers scientific instruments, equipment, supplies, workstations and research chemicals to laboratories; diagnostic instruments, test materials and related products to health care diagnostics centers; and a comprehensive offering of teaching aids for science education. It also supplies occupational health and safety products and maintenance, repair and operating materials. The Company's services range from an electronic mall on the Internet and software for high-performance transaction processing to the design, construction and equipping of turnkey laboratories. It also serves customers as a third-party purchaser of supplies and as an integrator of some 6,000 independent suppliers. The Company, which is headquartered at the above address, is a subsidiary of Fisher Scientific International Inc., which is headquartered in Hampton, NH, and listed on the NYSE. In addition to the facility located at the above address that provides administrative support to all of the Company's U.S. operations, it maintains several other local sites—an electrochemistry facility at 1610 Parkway View Dr. in Pittsburgh, PA; the Fisher Technology Group at 600 Business Center Dr. in Pittsburgh, PA; an instrument manufacturing plant at 1410 Wayne Ave. in Indiana, PA; and a distribution center at 585 Alpha Dr. in Pittsburgh, PA.

Officers: Michael J. Quinn *P*
Charles Amidon *P-Fisher OPR & Logistics Division*
Joseph Kletzel *P-Fisher RES Division*
James Osborn *P-Fisher Health Care Division*
Charles Wozniak *P-Fisher Safety Division*

Human Resources: Thomas Rea *SVP-Human Resources*
Joseph D'Alessandro *VP-Human Resources*

Purchasing: Robert Forte

Total Employees.........................4,090	**Regional Employees** 650
Year Established 1902	**SIC Code**.....................................5169
Annual Revenues ($000) 2,144,000	

Fluor Daniel GTI, Inc.

637 Braddock Ave.
East Pittsburgh, PA 15112
County: Allegheny

Phone: (412) 823-5300
Fax: (412) 824-7215

Provider of environmental, consulting, engineering and remediation services to a variety of commercial and industrial customers and to federal, state and local government agencies. The principal services provided by the Company are detailed, scientific environmental assessment and remediation programs, which combine elements of hydrogeology, geochemistry, chemistry, biochemistry and engineering. A typical program generally includes interaction with the appropriate governmental regulatory agencies, detailed site assessment that may include installation of a series of monitoring wells, design and implementation of a cost-effective remediation system, construction management services and ongoing monitoring and maintenance of the system for the duration of the program. These assessments and remediation programs are generally in response to regulatory programs adopted by state agencies as well as U.S. Environmental Protection Agency programs, such as the Resource Conservation and Recovery Act and the Comprehensive Environmental Response, Compensation and Liability Act. The Company, which is headquartered in Norwood, MA, is listed on the NASDAQ.

Officers: Michael Mann *District MGR (Philadelphia, PA)*
Robert Anderson *OPR MGR*

Human Resources: Anne M. Nolan *VP-Human Resources (Norwood, MA)*

Purchasing: Warren Bryant *(Norwood, MA)*

Total Employees.........................1,400	**Regional Employees** 45
Year Established 1975	**SIC Code**.....................................8748
Annual Revenues ($000) 180,000	

FNH Corp.

First Financial Center, 98 Wendel Rd.
Irwin, PA 15642
County: Westmoreland

Phone: (412) 864-7776
Fax: (412) 864-7636
Internet Address: www.fnhbank.com

Bank holding company for its wholly owned subsidiary, The First National Bank of Herminie (Bank), which provides a full range of banking and bank-related services. The Bank serves communities located in Allegheny and Westmoreland Counties, PA, with branch offices in Greensburg (8), Herminie, Irwin and North Huntingdon. In addition, the Bank operates an office in the Shop N' Save, located on East Pittsburgh St. in Greensburg, which is open seven days a week.

Officers: James R. Lauffer *CH, P & CEO*
Jay A. Miller *VCH*
Kerry M. Anthony *COO & EVP-Cashier*
Sharon Migliozzi *AVP-ADM & Investments, & AST-SEC*
Samuel E. Hopkinson *SEC & TRS*

Human Resources: Anthony P. Zello, Jr. *Human Resources Officer*

Total Employees............................96		**Regional Employees** 96
Year Established 1912		**SIC Code**....................................6712
Annual Revenues ($000)...........................224,085 (Assets)			

Foerster Instruments, Inc.

R.I.D.C. Park W., 140 Industry Dr.
Pittsburgh, PA 15275
County: Allegheny

Phone: (412) 788-8976
Fax: (412) 788-8984
Internet Address: www.foerstergroup.com

Manufacturer and distributor of nondestructive testing instrumentation. The Company is also a provider of integrity testing services, using eddy current and ultrasonic technology. It serves the automotive industry; the bar, tube and wire industry; and the aerospace industry. Its clients are primarily located in the United States and Canada. The Company operates a sales and service center in Birmingham, AL, and a manufacturing subsidiary, Foerster Systems, Inc., in Salem, OH. The Company is a subsidiary of Institut Dr. Forster, which is headquartered in Reutlingen, Germany.

Officers: Robert D. Shaffer *P*
Timothy L. Brown *NATL SAL MGR*

Human Resources: Carey Ferrali

Purchasing: Jack May

Total Employees...............................61	Regional Employees 49
Year Established 1978	SIC Code.....................................3829
Annual Revenues ($000) 12,000	

Food Services Management Assoc.

235 Alpha Dr.
Pittsburgh, PA 15238
County: Allegheny

Phone: (412) 963-1695
Fax: (412) 963-7586

Owner and operator of three restaurants with eight facilities, all located in the Pittsburgh metropolitan area. Abate Italian & Seafood Restaurant, located at the Waterworks Mall, serves seafood and Italian specialties. Dingbats restaurants serve a variety of dishes, including salads, sandwiches, prime rib, hamburgers and barbecue ribs, with locations at One Oxford Centre, Robinson Township Center, Ross Park Mall, Waterworks Mall and in Butler, PA. Juno Trattoria serves regional Italian cuisine, with restaurants located at One Oxford Centre and Ross Park Mall.

Officers: Dominic C. Abbott *P, CEO & MPTR*

Human Resources: Victor D. Son, Jr. *VP & CFO*

Purchasing: Joseph DeMartino *EVP, COO & MPTR*

Total Employees............................700	Regional Employees 700
Year Established 1982	SIC Code.....................................5812
Annual Revenues ($000)..15,000+	

Forbes Travel Service, Inc.

5835 Forbes Ave.
Pittsburgh, PA 15217
County: Allegheny

Phone: (412) 521-7300
Fax: (412) 422-3885

Owner and operator of a travel agency providing corporate and leisure travel services as well as convention and meeting planning services. The Agency operates a branch office in Pittsburgh at 1116 Freeport Rd.

Officers: Larry Maloney *P*
Ed Siegel *SEC & TRS*

Total Employees...............................50	Regional Employees 50
Year Established 1954	SIC Code.....................................4724
Annual Revenues ($000) 26,000	

Foreman Architects Engineers, Inc.

525 W. New Castle St.
P.O. Box 189
Zelienople, PA 16063
County: Butler

Phone: (412) 452-9690
Fax: (412) 452-0136

Provider of architectural and engineering services, including architectural design, master planning, interior design, landscape architecture, structural engineering, mechanical engineering, electrical engineering, energy management, building utilization studies, construction management, and voice, video and data distribution systems. The Firm's affiliate, Foreman Program and Construction Managers, Inc. (FPCMI), also located at the above address, is a multiple prime construction manager. FPCMI provides the following services to clients during the pre-construction phase: building utilization/feasibility studies, cost estimating, schedule control, value engineering and constructability review, bid packaging, communication and project reporting. During the construction phase, it provides contractor coordination, change order control, quality control and safety. FPCMI provides services on a wide range of projects, including public elementary, middle and high schools; university projects; hospital projects (i.e., LDRP, C-section, pharmacy and ambulatory surgery); and retail facilities (i.e., distribution facilities and hospitality facilities). Both firms share a branch office in Manheim, PA. While FPCMI employs 25 people, some of their staff overlaps with the Firm's.

Officers: Clifford G. Foreman *P; VP-Foreman Program and Construction Managers, Inc.*
David E. Foreman *VP; VP-Foreman Program and Construction Managers, Inc.*
Phillip G. Foreman *SEC & TRS; P-Foreman Program and Construction Managers, Inc.*

Human Resources: Kay Yohn *Accounts Payable*

Total Employees	75	**Regional Employees**	65
Year Established	1956	**SIC Code**	8712

Forman Enterprises, Inc.

178 Thorn Hill Rd.
Warrendale, PA 15086
County: Allegheny

Phone: (412) 779-2170
Fax: (412) 779-2181

Owner and operator of a chain of retail apparel stores doing business as American Outpost and American Eagle Outlet. The Company is the former American Eagle Outlet Division of American Eagle Outfitters, Inc., which is headquartered in Warrendale, PA. The Company was established in November 1995, when 32 of the original American Eagle Outlet stores were acquired. The Company's merchandise emphasis is on certain basic categories of fashionable casual apparel for men and women with an increasing emphasis on women's apparel. Standard store inventory includes denim jeans and chinos, sweaters, casual shirts (polos, flannels, rugbys and t-shirts), outerwear and accessories. The Company's marketing strategy is to provide quality casual lifestyle apparel at value price points translating into a savings of 20% to 70% off those charged by specialty clothing retail stores. As of May 21, 1997, the Company operated 54 stores located in 29 states. The Company intends to open additional traditional mall stores, outlet stores and power strip locations in both existing and new markets, with a goal of opening a minimum of 15 sites per year.

Officers: Sam Forman *CH*
Howard Katcher *EVP & COO*
Wendy Forn *VP-Ladies*
Gary Geramita *VP & CFO*
Robert O'Connell *VP-OPR*
Amaz Zivony *VP-MER*
Steven Stern *DIR-Stores*

Purchasing: Ronald Macklin *DIR-MER & MKT*

Total Employees............................534	**Regional Employees** 70	
Year Established 1995	**SIC Code**......................................5621	

Forum, Inc.

214 N. Lexington Ave.
Pittsburgh, PA 15208
County: Allegheny

Phone: (412) 244-8780
Fax: (412) 244-9032

Manufacturer of fluorescent and high intensity discharge lighting fixtures for commercial applications. The Company's subsidiary, Samco Inc., also located at the above address, is a manufacturers' representative organization marketing lighting-related products. It represents over 15 companies and covers markets in Western Pennsylvania.

Officers: Norman Garret *P*
Don Dziubaty *VP*

Purchasing: Linda Jones

Total Employees............................72	**Regional Employees** 72	
Year Established 1963	**SIC Code**......................................3646	
Annual Revenues ($000) 10,000		

Franklin Interiors, Inc.

The Landmarks Bldg., One Station Sq., Ste. 500
Pittsburgh, PA 15219
County: Allegheny

Phone: (412) 261-2525
Fax: (412) 255-4089

Distributor of office furnishings and a provider of facilities planning, facilities services and office environment consulting services. The Company's products range from work stations to desks, seating, filing systems and a full complement of accessories. Its facilities planning services consist of programming, schematic design/space planning, interior design development, budget development for interiors, project management and maintenance of computerized databases. Its facilities services include painting, systems furniture refurbishing, cleaning, fabric protection, reconfiguration and asset management. Its office environment consulting services provide education and solutions for productive work environments. The Company also operates a warehouse located at 1360 Island Ave. in McKees Rocks, PA.

Officers: Ralph J. Dallier *P*
Garry Pyles *DIR-SAL & MKT*
Denise Robinson *DIR-Design*

Human Resources: Linda E. King *DIR-Human Resources*

Total Employees............................60	**Regional Employees** 60
Year Established 1945	**SIC Code**....................................5021
Annual Revenues ($000) 17,000	

Frazier-Simplex, Inc.

436 E. Beau St.
P.O. Box 493
Washington, PA 15301
County: Washington

Phone: (412) 225-1100
Fax: (412) 225-3114
Internet Address: www.frazier-simplex.com

Provider of engineering, design, consulting and construction services to the worldwide glass-making industry. The Company's sister firm, Frazier-Simplex Machine Co., which is located at 1720 N. Main St. in Washington, PA, fabricates batch chargers and suspended refractory walls for the Company and provides a variety of fabrication services for other clients.

Officers: John E. Frazier II *CH*
Ronald D. Argent *P*
Karl Kleinert *VP-SAL*

Human Resources: Joyce J. Smith

Purchasing: Jack Smaroff

Total Employees...............................50   **Regional Employees** 50
Year Established 1918   **SIC Code** 8711

Freeport Transport, Inc.

1200 Butler Rd.
Freeport, PA 16229
County: Armstrong

Phone: (412) 295-2181
Fax: (412) 295-1280

Property holder leasing land and building/office space. In addition, the Company operates an affiliate and two divisions. Freeport Transport Industries, Inc. (FTII), an affiliate headquartered at the above address and with additional locations in New Eagle, PA, and Niagara Falls, Ontario, Canada, is a common carrier of general commodities throughout the United States and Canada. While it specializes in dry and liquid bulk commodities, it also hauls packaged materials. FTII operates 80 power units and 145 trailers out of its three terminals. Lyndon's Market, a division located in Freeport, PA, operates a 24-hour convenience store featuring hot and cold deli foods, a bakery and catering service, gift items, and gas and diesel fuel. Eagle Rock Products, also located at the above address, manufactures ornamental stone for homes, fireplaces, walks, gardens and lawns. It also produces gift items such as planters, stone frogs, rabbits and turtles for the lawn and garden.

Officers: Don L. Smetanick *C-OWN & P*
Lynne H. Smetanick *C-OWN*
Greg A. Westendorf *VP*

Human Resources: Linda M. Scheier *SEC & TRS*

Total Employees...........................130   **Regional Employees** 105
Year Established 1959   **SIC Code** 4200
Annual Revenues ($000) 12,000

Frick Health System

508 S. Church St.
Mt. Pleasant, PA 15666
County: Westmoreland

Phone: (412) 547-1500
Fax: (412) 547-1266

Nonprofit operator of the Frick Hospital & Community Health Center located at the above address. The 163-bed general medical and surgical care hospital provides a full range of inpatient and diagnostic outpatient testing and treatment services. These services include cancer care, cardiac services, diabetes care, emergency care, health education and community outreach programs, imaging/radiology services, laboratory services, nursing care, pulmonary rehabilitation services, rehabilitation services, support services, surgical services and women/infant care. Frick Diversified Services Corp., a subsidiary of the Company also located at the above address, provides support services for the entire organization. The hospital is affiliated with the University of Pittsburgh Medical Center.

Officers: Rodney L. Gunderson *CEO & EDIR*
Arlene Assey *DIR-Physician & Clinical Services*
Kevin B. May *DIR-Fiscal Services & CFO*
Patricia Painter *DIR-ADM Services*
Margaret Tepper *DIR-Nursing Services*

Human Resources: Linda Pietrzak *DIR-Human Resources & Support Services*

Total Employees............................725	**Regional Employees** 725
Year Established 1902	**SIC Code**......................................8062
Annual Revenues ($000) 42,123	

Friedman, Inc., Harold

530 Fairground Hill
Butler, PA 16001
County: Butler

Phone: (412) 283-6030
Fax: (412) 287-5549

Owner and operator of full-line retail supermarkets ranging from 18,000 to 55,000 square feet. The Company's stores feature bakeries, delis, fresh seafood departments, floral sections, video stores, restaurants, take-out foods, bulk foods, one-hour photo labs, ATMs, fruit and food baskets, and catering services. Its supermarkets operate under the names Friedman's Supermarkets and BiLo Foods. Friedman's Supermarkets are located in Butler (3), Chicora and Saxonburg, PA. BiLo Foods are located in Butler, PA, and Morgantown, WV.

Officers: Carole F. Bitter, Ph.D. *P*
Dale Eichenlaub *VP & GMGR*
David Crater *CON*

Human Resources: Patricia DiTullio

Total Employees............................500	**Regional Employees** 500
Year Established 1900	**SIC Code** 5411

F

FSS Airholdings, Inc.

15 Allegheny County Airport
West Mifflin, PA 15122
County: Allegheny

Phone: (412) 466-2500
Fax: (412) 466-1978
Internet Address: www.corpjet.com

Provider of full-service aviation management and support services specializing in corporate, medical and government aviation programs. The Company offers services in the areas of aircraft sales and leasing, charter service, major airframe and engine maintenance, management consulting and general aviation support for the business traveler. Its subsidiaries include Corporate Jets, Inc., located at the above address and in Scottsdale, AZ; CJ Airport Management, Inc. in Cumberland, MD, and Charlottesville, VA; and Heli-Dyne Systems, Inc. in Hurst, TX.

Officers: Fred S. Shaulis *CH & CEO*
Thomas M. Ramirez *P & COO*
John Frevola *SVP & GMGR (Scottsdale, AZ)*
Larry Pietropaulo *SVP*
Bob Titus *SVP-FIN*

Human Resources: Dawn Chambers *DIR-Human Resources*

Total Employees............................625	**Regional Employees** 153
Year Established 1968	**SIC Code** 4522
Annual Revenues ($000) 81,000	

Fuhrer Holdings, Inc., Frank B.

3100 E. Carson St.
Pittsburgh, PA 15203
County: Allegheny

Phone: (412) 488-8844
Fax: (412) 488-0195

Wholesaler of malt beverage products, doing business as Frank B. Fuhrer Wholesale Co. The Company is a master distributor of Anheuser-Busch, Coors and several import products. It serves beer distributors and taverns in Allegheny and outlying counties.

Officers: Frank B. Fuhrer, Jr. *CH*
            David M. Fuhrer *P*
            Frank B. Fuhrer III *VP-OPR*

Human Resources: Jack L. Miller *VP-FIN & ADM*

Total Employees............................130	**Regional Employees** 130
Year Established 1982	**SIC Code**......................................5181
Annual Revenues ($000) 84,000	

Future-All, Inc.

Hammond & Gregg Sts.
P.O. Box 528
Carnegie, PA 15106
County: Allegheny

Phone: (412) 279-2670
Fax: (412) 279-2682

Operator of a machining, fabricating and assembly facility comprising 60,000 square feet of manufacturing space. The Company is primarily engaged in the manufacture of blast furnace and steelmaking equipment. It provides its services to the steel industry, including major producers and engineering concerns.

Officers: Charles R. King *P*

Purchasing: C. Richard King, Jr.

Total Employees..............................42	**Regional Employees** 42
Year Established 1979	**SIC Code**.......................................3599

G&G Investments, Inc.

3140 William Flynn Hwy.
Glenshaw, PA 15116
County: Allegheny

Phone: (412) 486-9100
Fax: (412) 487-0390

Holding company with investments primarily in the North American glass packaging industry. The Company's glass container and bottle making related businesses include a 63% controlling interest in Consumers Packaging, Inc. (CPI), which is headquartered in Toronto, Ontario, Canada, and listed on the Toronto Stock Exchange. CPI maintains a 58% interest in Anchor Glass Container Corp., which is headquartered in Tampa, FL, and operates 11 plants including a facility at 1926 Baldridge St. in Connellsville, PA. The Company's additional glass container and bottle making businesses include Glenshaw Glass Co., Inc., which is also headquartered at the above address, with a plant on Rte. 8 in Glenshaw, PA; Hillsboro Glass Co. in Hillsboro, IL; Fabrica de Envases de Vidro, S.A. de C.V. in

Mexicali, Mexico (25% interest); and Imtec, Inc. in Tulsa, OK, a producer of equipment used to manufacture glass containers and bottles. The Company's other holdings include Break Bulk Distributors, Inc., Bristol Consolidators, Inc. and Executive Warehouse, Inc., all of which provide warehousing services in the Pittsburgh metropolitan area; Delta Properties Management, Inc. in Shaler Township, PA, a lessor of apartment and office buildings; Federal Equipment Leasing, Inc. in Indianola, PA, a lessor of automobiles; Ghaznavi Investments, Inc. in Shaler Township, PA, an investment firm; J&S, Inc. in Indianola, PA, a trucking company; National Equipment Leasing in Shaler Township, PA, an equipment lessor; and Today's Express, Inc. in Indianola, PA, a trucking company.

Officers: John J. Ghaznavi *CH & P*

Total Employees......................10,000			
Year Established.........................1895	**SIC Code**.....................................6719		
Annual Revenues ($000)...1,300,000			

GA Industries, Inc.

9025 Marshall Rd.
Cranberry Township, PA 16066
County: Butler

Phone: (412) 776-1020
Fax: (412) 776-1254

Manufacturer of automatic valves primarily for water and wastewater applications, including Golden Anderson automatic valves, Rodney Hunt sluice gates and Tru-Tech valves, as well as Allis Chalmers-type cone and butterfly valves. The Company serves clients worldwide. It operates an additional facility in Mars, PA, and a combination foundry, fabrication and machine shop in Orange, MA.

Officers: John H. Kilmer *CH*
Grant A. Colton, Jr. *P*
Michael L. Colton *SEC*

Purchasing: Wayne R. Prem *VP-Purchasing*

Total Employees............................300	**Regional Employees**...................100
Year Established.........................1890	**SIC Code**.....................................3494
Annual Revenues ($000)...35-40,000	

Gage Co., The

3000 Liberty Ave.
P.O. Box 1168, Pittsburgh, PA 15230
Pittsburgh, PA 15201
County: Allegheny

Phone: (412) 471-6600
Fax: (412) 255-6953

   Wholesale distributor of pipes, valves, fittings, plumbing and heating equipment, water systems and industrial supplies. The Company's customers include tradespeople, industrial users, master plumbers and contractors. It operates 40 branch sales offices located throughout Indiana, Maine, Maryland, Massachusetts, Michigan, New Hampshire, Ohio, Pennsylvania and Virginia.

Officers: Robert A. Chute *OWN, CH & P*
Gary Van Luven *CFO*
Allen J. Faulhaber *VP-Central OPR*
Thomas Mullen *VP-New England OPR*
Thomas Tomczak *VP-Michigan OPR*
Tom Wright *VP-SAL*

Human Resources: Betty Curto

Purchasing: Stuart Kosal *VP-Purchasing/Supplier Relations*

Total Employees	600	**Regional Employees**	100
Year Established	1892	**SIC Code**	5085
Annual Revenues ($000)	200,000		

GAI Consultants, Inc.

570 Beatty Rd.
Monroeville, PA 15146
County: Allegheny

Phone: (412) 856-6400
Fax: (412) 856-4970
Internet Address: www.gaiconsultants.com

   Engineering consultants providing a comprehensive range of planning, permitting and design services in the areas of civil, environmental, geotechnical and structural engineering; mining; water resources; industrial and hazardous waste management; municipal and industrial landfill design; archaeological surveys; transportation; risk assessments; environmental site assessments; site development; and construction monitoring. The Company operates branch offices in Ft. Wayne, IN; King of Prussia, PA; Charleston, WV; and Vina del Mar, Chile. Its affiliate, GAI Consultants-Southeast, maintains offices in Orlando, FL, and Raleigh, NC. Both companies are subsidiaries of Affiliated GAI Cos., Inc., which is a holding company also headquartered at the above address.

Special Designations: ENR$_{500}$

Officers: Anthony M. DiGioia, Jr. *P*
Richard E. Gray *SVP*
Henry A. Salver *SVP*
Thomas D. Donovan *VP*
John A. Hribar *VP*
James E. Niece *VP*

Human Resources: Mark J. Pavlik

Total Employees	438	**Regional Employees**	270
Year Established	1958	**SIC Code**	8711
Annual Revenues ($000)	31,000		

Galbreath-Middle Atlantic

USX Tower, 600 Grant St., Ste. 4300
Pittsburgh, PA 15219
County: Allegheny

Phone: (412) 471-9500
Fax: (412) 471-0995
Internet Address: www.galbreath.com

Provider of real estate and real estate-related services, including asset and property/facilities management, leasing, tenant representation, investment sales, consulting, construction services, development and redevelopment. The general partnership, doing business as The Galbreath Co., manages and leases more than 6.3 million square feet of office and industrial properties in New York, Ohio, Pennsylvania, Virginia and West Virginia. Its local properties include the CNG Tower and USX Tower. It is also involved in the development of the South Side Works, a 130-acre mixed-use project taking form on the former LTV Steel site, along the Monongahela River.

Officers: Jack R. Norris *P-Mid-Atlantic Region*

Total Employees	150	**Regional Employees**	100+
Year Established	1921	**SIC Code**	6531

Gallatin Home Care, Inc., Albert

20 Highland Park Dr., Ste. 203
Uniontown, PA 15401
County: Fayette

Phone: (412) 438-6660
Fax: (412) 438-4468

Provider of home health care services, including skilled nursing, mental health nursing, restorative nursing, physical therapy, occupational therapy, enterostomal therapy, speech-language therapy, medical social work, home health aide care and hospice services for the terminally ill. The Company, doing business as Albert Gallatin Home Care & Hospice, operates branch offices in Butler, Brownsville, Connellsville, Cranberry Township, Greensburg, Masontown, Monongahela, Uniontown and Washington, PA; and in Bridgeport, Morgantown and New Martinsville, WV. It serves clients in all of Butler, Fayette, Greene, Washington and Westmoreland Counties, PA; Harrison, Marion, Marshall, Monongalia, Preston, Taylor and Wetzel Counties, WV; and part of Allegheny and Beaver Counties, PA. The Company is a division of Staff Builders, Inc., which is headquartered in Lake Success, NY, and listed on the NASDAQ.

Officers: Gerald L. Shuttlesworth *EDIR*
Patricia Altman *DIR-ADM*
Bonita Campbell *DIR-OPR*
Chris Constantine *DIR-Hospice ADM*
Frank Ovial *DIR-FIN*
Craig Falkenstine *Communications MGR*

Human Resources: Donna Grote *DIR-Human Resources*

Total Employees...........................861   **Regional Employees** 700
Year Established 1979   **SIC Code**....................................8082

GalvTech

300 Mifflin Rd.
Pittsburgh, PA 15207
County: Allegheny

Phone: (412) 464-1900
Fax: (412) 464-2018

Manufacturer of hot dip galvanized (zinc-coated) steel coils for applications in residential and commercial construction, HVAC, appliances, agricultural products, construction products and service centers.

Officers: G. Watts Humphrey, Jr. *CH*
Wilson J. Farmerie *P*
Edwin H. Gott, Jr. *GPTR*
Thomas Grudovich *AST to CH*

Human Resources: Robert W. Riordan *GPTR*

Total Employees............................80   **Regional Employees** 80
Year Established 1996   **SIC Code**....................................3479

Ganassi Oldsmobile-Pontiac-GMC Truck, Inc., Annette

1750 Rte. 8
Glenshaw, PA 15116
County: Allegheny

Phone: (412) 487-8500
Fax: (412) 486-5627

Owner and operator of an automobile and truck dealership. The Company sells new and used vehicles, offers leasing, and provides parts and service. It also sells and leases commercial trucks up to 56,000 GVW (Gross Vehicle Weight) and provides parts and service. The dealership offers Oldsmobile, Pontiac and GMC Trucks.

Officers: Annette D. Ganassi *P*

Human Resources: Amy L. Neff

Total Employees............................45	**Regional Employees** 45
Year Established 1989	**SIC Code** 5511
Annual Revenues ($000) 17,000	

Gannett Fleming, Inc.

Two Parkway Center, 875 Greentree Rd., Ste. 211
Pittsburgh, PA 15220
County: Allegheny

Phone: (412) 922-5575
Fax: (412) 922-3717
Internet Address: www.gannettfleming.com

Provider of engineering and planning services. These include transportation—highways, bridges/structures, transit, railroads and traffic/parking; water management—water, wastewater, dams and flood protection; waste management—hazardous materials and solid wastes; planning—transportation, water and waste management, community planning, public participation, and privatization and joint development; land development—residential subdivisions, industrial parks, commercial complexes, site analysis, master plans, and public and agency coordination; specialized services—architectural, structural, geotechnical, mechanical/electrical, and management and financial; and industrial services. The Company also provides impact statements and assessments, geotechnical laboratory analyses, environmental laboratory analyses, management information services, printing and reprographic services, and construction management and inspection. The Company is headquartered in Camp Hill, PA. It is a subsidiary of Gannett Fleming Affiliates, Inc., which is also headquartered in Camp Hill, PA. The office located at the above address oversees projects within an approximate 200-mile radius of Pittsburgh, PA, in Ohio, Pennsylvania and West Virginia.

Officers: Ron J. Drnevich *CH & P*
Chester L. Allen *VP*
Roger J. Banks *VP*
Robert J. Dietz *VP*
William C. Ehresman *VP*
Richard Hergenroeder *VP*
F. James Knight *VP*
James J. Long *VP*
Walter Marriott III *VP*
David L. Sheridan *VP*
John J. Frye *Regional Office MGR*

Human Resources: Roderick A. Savidge *(Camp Hill, PA)*

Purchasing: David M. Liddick *(Camp Hill, PA)*

Total Employees..................1,450	**Regional Employees** 70
Year Established 1915	**SIC Code**..............................8711
Annual Revenues ($000) 113,000	

Gannett Satellite Information Network, Inc.

One Monroeville Center, Ste. 800
Monroeville, PA 15146
County: Allegheny

Phone: (412) 373-4000
Fax: (412) 373-4010

Regional circulation and distribution center for the USA Today newspaper. The Company is headquartered in Arlington, VA. It operates regional circulation and distribution centers nationwide. The local office is responsible for servicing Western Pennsylvania, and portions of Maryland, Ohio and West Virginia. The Company is a subsidiary of Gannett Co., Inc., which is also headquartered in Arlington, VA, and listed on the NYSE.

Officers: Lee E. Caylor *GMGR-Pittsburgh*
Jeff Teasdale *CON-Pittsburgh*

Human Resources: Jonny Valente

Purchasing: Valerie Daniels

Total Employees..................2,029	**Regional Employees** 32
Year Established 1982	**SIC Code**..............................2711

Gardner Displays Co., Inc.

7500 Thomas Blvd.
Pittsburgh, PA 15208
County: Allegheny

Phone: (412) 731-8500
Fax: (412) 731-7859

Manufacturer and supplier of industrial exhibits and displays for trade shows and conventions. The Company does business as Creative Productions. It serves clients nationwide.

Officers: Clifford W. Hellberg   *P*
Steve Hellberg   *VP-SAL*
Mark Sullivan   *TRS*

Purchasing: Marvin Aron

Total Employees............................100	**Regional Employees** 100
Year Established 1935	**SIC Code**......................................3993

Gatan, Inc.

780 Commonwealth Dr.
Warrendale, PA 15086
County: Allegheny

Phone: (412) 776-5260
Fax: (412) 776-3360

Manufacturer of electron microscope equipment and parts. The Company's headquarters are located in Pleasanton, CA.

Officers: Bill Weigand   *DIR-MFG*

Total Employees............................170	**Regional Employees** 80
SIC Code 3827	

Gateway Clipper, Inc.

Nine Station Square Dock
Pittsburgh, PA 15219
County: Allegheny

Phone: (412) 355-7980
Fax: (412) 355-7987

Owner and operator of six riverboats touring the Allegheny, Monongahela and Ohio Rivers. The Company's fleet sails year-round, offering passengers the opportunity to sightsee and relax, or to enjoy on-board entertainment and dining. It also offers charters for corporate and social events.

Officers: Terry Wirginis   *P*

Ronald S. Shively *GMGR*
Joseph D'Amico *DIR-Service OPR*
Suzanne M. Gradisek *DIR-MKT*
Maria A. Grimm *DIR-OPR Systems*
Daniel Lacek *DIR-Fleet OPR*
Deborah A. Yednak *DIR-SAL*

Total Employees............................100	**Regional Employees** 100
Year Established 1958	**SIC Code**......................................4489
Annual Revenues ($000) 10,000	

Gateway Engineers, Inc., The

1011 Alcon St.
Pittsburgh, PA 15220
County: Allegheny

Phone: (412) 921-4030
Fax: (412) 921-9960

Provider of consulting engineering services, including surveying, inspection, mapping, hydrology and a variety of municipal services. The Firm's municipal engineers specialize in hydrology, hydraulics, sanitary sewers, planning and surveying. It serves clients in Allegheny, Butler and Washington Counties, PA.

Officers: Donald W. Hannegan *CEO*
Ruthann L. Omer *P*
Daniel S. Deiseroth *VP*
Joseph D. Lavrich, Jr. *VP-Construction Inspection*
Paul J. Gaus *SEC & TRS*
Kevin P. Hannegan *DIR-Surveys*
Thomas R. Hudzema *DIR-OPR*

Human Resources: Rosemarie Griffin *DIR-ADM (Purchasing)*

Total Employees.............................65	**Regional Employees** 65
SIC Code 8711	

Gateway Rehabilitation Center

Moffett Run Rd.
Aliquippa, PA 15001
County: Beaver

Phone: (412) 766-8700
Fax: (412) 375-8815

Nonprofit health care organization that offers comprehensive treatment for individuals, youth and families with alcohol and other substance abuse problems. The Organization, which claims to be the largest addiction treatment system in Southwestern Pennsylvania, is a network of nine community-based rehabilitation centers. Its services include detoxification, residential treatment, day intensive outpatient treatment, morning and evening outpatient programs, individual therapy and halfway house care. Youth and young adults receive treatment in separate inpatient and afterschool programs. The Organization also offers a six-week educational program for young people who are experiencing legal problems as a result of their use of alcohol or other drugs. It operates additional facilities in Aliquippa, Cranberry Township, Greensburg, Greentree, McMurray, Monroeville, Pittsburgh and Sewickley, PA.

Officers: Kenneth S. Ramsey, Ph.D. *P & CEO*
James L. Aiello *VP-Treatment Programs*
Pamela J. Hughes *VP-Nursing & Clinical Support Services*
Stephen B. Roman *VP-ADM*

Human Resources: Paige Kaufman *DIR-Human Resources*

Purchasing: Sherry L. Kerr *CFO*

Total Employees............................230
Year Established........................1972
Annual Revenues ($000)...10,000
Regional Employees..................230
SIC Code......................................8399

GBC Materials Corp.

580 Monastery Dr.
Latrobe, PA 15650
County: Westmoreland

Phone: (412) 537-7991
Fax: (412) 537-4910
Internet Address: www.gbc-bgp-team.thomasregister.com

Manufacturer of subminiature high volume glass and ceramic components utilizing a pressing and firing process. The Company's glass products are used in high volume production of hermetic glass-to-metal seals where preformed frames, multi-hole parts and rings permit the introduction of a finite amount of sealing glass into the automatic seal process. These parts are typically used in hermetic packages, fuses, fiber-optic connectors and integrated circuit packages. The Company's ceramic parts are used in cellular phones, thermostats, semiconductor packages, automotive braking systems, air bag restraint systems, microwave varactors, thermocouples, medical implants and more for industries such as automotives, electronics, electrical, appliance, aircraft and instruments. The Company's subsidiary, Basic Glass Products Corp. in Lone Grove, OK, manufactures glass preforms and tubing using direct draw and redraw technology. These products are typically used in miniature fuse bodies, lenses for photo transistors, glass-to-metal seals used in integrated circuit packages, erasable, programmable, Read-Only-Memory (EPROM), Read-Only-Memory (ROM), glass lenses and more.

Officers: William R. Golya *P & CEO*
                J. Richard Karr *VP & GMGR*

Purchasing: Carol T. Barackman

Total Employees...........................120   **Regional Employees** 100
Year Established 1958   **SIC Code**....................................3259

GE Lighting-Bridgeville Glass Plant

540 Mayer St.
Bridgeville, PA 15017
County: Allegheny

Phone: (412) 221-9100
Fax: (412) 257-7396

   Manufacturer of leaded glass tubing including exhaust, flair, fluorescent and germicidal tubing. The Plant is a part of GE Lighting (GEL), which is headquartered in Cleveland, OH. GEL is a business unit of the General Electric Co., which is headquartered in Fairfield, CT, and listed on the NYSE. Components produced at the Plant are shipped to other GE facilities for assembly into finished products for applications in the electronics and lighting industries.

Officers: Tony Smith *Plant MGR*

Human Resources: Dan Carey

Regional Employees.....................200
SIC Code 3229

GENCO Distribution System

100 Papercraft Park
Pittsburgh, PA 15238
County: Allegheny

Phone: (412) 820-3700
Fax: (412) 826-0856
Internet Address: www.genco.com

   Provider of reverse logistics management, customized software solutions, asset recovery management, product rework/remanufacturing, reclamation, recycling, transportation management, contract distribution, airport concession distribution, and consulting and product management services. The Company claims that its operational expertise and technological solutions reduce costs and improve efficiency for retailers, manufacturers and distributors in a variety of industries, including mass merchandising retail, grocery retail, specialty retail, health and personal care products, cosmetic and fragrance, home computer/electronics, home improvement, small appliance, sporting goods and auto parts. The Company maintains a worldwide network of over 1,000 after-market buyers and dealers in more than 20 countries around the world for the disposition of returned merchandise. Its system is made up of over 40 facilities across the United States and Canada comprising more than 5 million square feet of space. These include return centers for Elizabeth Arden in Roanoke, VA; Kmart in Atlanta, GA, Chicago, IL, Reno, NV, and Allentown, PA; Procter & Gamble in Columbus, OH; Sears in Woodland, CA, Atlanta, GA, and Allentown, PA; Target in Indianapolis, IN; United Grocers in Portland, OR; and Whirlpool in Garland, TX. Its distribution centers include the Airport Distribution Center in Pittsburgh, PA; Chelsea Building Products in Trafford, PA; and PICB/OK Grocery in Blawnox, PA.

Officers: Herb S. Shear *P & CEO*
Jerry A. Davis *COO*
Larry Schoenberger *CFO*
Curtis Greve *SVP-Customer Service*
Frank Kaiser *SVP-Teammate Services*
Dan Eisenhuth *VP-Asset Recovery*
Frank Koch *VP-Systems*
Steve South *VP-GENCO Logistics*

Human Resources: Jim Quinn

Purchasing: John Bender

Total Employees.........................2,100	**Regional Employees** 300
Year Established 1898	**SIC Code**.....................................4225
Annual Revenues ($000) 90,000	

GenCorp Inc.

Chambers Ave.
Jeannette, PA 15644
County: Westmoreland

Phone: (412) 523-5441
Fax: (412) 523-7306

   Manufacturer of polymer products including vinyl film and sheeting for producers of office supplies, stereo components and ceiling tiles, and for the wood and steel industries. The plant located at the above address is a part of the Decorative and Building Products Division of the Company, which is headquartered in Fairlawn, OH, and listed on the NYSE.

Officers: Steve Pcolka *GMGR*

Total Employees.........................8,950	**Regional Employees** 270
Year Established 1945	**SIC Code**.....................................3081

General Carbide Corp.

Greensburg-Hempfield Business Park
P.O. Box C
Greensburg, PA 15601
County: Westmoreland

Phone: (412) 836-3000
Fax: (800) 547-2659
Internet Address: www.generalcarbide.com

Manufacturer of cemented tungsten carbide wear and metal forming parts for various industrial corporations around the world. The Company's carbide components are manufactured in a wide range of grades, sizes, shapes and quantities. An affiliate and licensee of the Company, General Carbide Europe, Ltd., located in Daventry, Northants, England, markets the Company's products overseas.

Officers: Premo J. Pappafava *CEO*
Mona L. Pappafava *P*
Edwin A. McKinnon *VP-Technology*

Human Resources: Sharon A. DePree

Purchasing: Janis Selway

Total Employees...........................150	Regional Employees 150
Year Established 1968	SIC Code....................................3544
Annual Revenues ($000) 15,000

General Cleaning, Inc.

101 E. Seventh Ave.
Homestead, PA 15120
County: Allegheny

Phone: (412) 461-6181
Fax: (412) 461-6161

Provider of contract cleaning services. The Company offers janitorial service, floor maintenance, carpet cleaning, wall washing, window cleaning and light fixture cleaning for commercial, financial and medical institutions. It primarily serves clients in Allegheny County.

Officers: Lois W. Riske *P (Human Resources & Purchasing)*
John P. Riske, Jr. *VP & TRS*

Total Employees...........................150	Regional Employees 150
Year Established 1934	SIC Code....................................7349
Annual Revenues ($000) ....1,000+

General Motors Corp., Metal Fabricating Division-Pittsburgh Plant

1451 Lebanon School Rd.
P.O. Box 158, McKeesport, PA 15134
West Mifflin, PA 15122
County: Allegheny

Phone: (412) 469-6500
Fax: (412) 469-6705

Fabricator of automotive metal parts producing a variety of components for General Motors automobiles, including fenders, doors, roofs, deck lids and hoods. The Plant is a unit of the Metal Fabricating Division of the General Motors Corp., which is headquartered in Detroit, MI, and listed on the NYSE.

Officers: Alfonzo Hall *Plant MGR*
James Pazehoski *OPR MGR*
Guy Volponi *Resident CON*

Human Resources: Daniel Praschan

Regional Employees.................1,000
Year Established 1949   **SIC Code** 3711
Annual Revenues ($000) 81,000

General Press Corp.

Allegheny Dr.
P.O. Box 316
Natrona Heights, PA 15065
County: Allegheny

Phone: (412) 224-3500
Fax: (412) 224-3934
Internet Address: www.gpc.lm.com

Provider of commercial printing services. The employee-owned company produces advertising and direct mail offset lithography, specializing in food and beverage labels for national accounts. The Company operates two 8-color presses and offers its clients full-service prepress, printing and bindery technology.

Officers: James V. Wolff *P & CEO*
David M. Wolff *VP*

Human Resources: Terrence L. Conroy *VP (Purchasing)*

Total Employees..............................60   **Regional Employees** 60
Year Established 1937   **SIC Code**....................................2752
Annual Revenues ($000) 8,500

General Wire Spring Co.

1101 Thompson Ave.
McKees Rocks, PA 15136
County: Allegheny

Phone: (412) 771-6300
Fax: (412) 771-2771
Internet Address: www.generalwirespring.com/springs/

Manufacturer of custom industrial springs, including compression, extension, torsion and wire forms. The Company also produces a full line of industrial sewer and drain cleaning machinery to clear clogged lines, from 1 1/4" to 10" in diameter.

Officers: Art Silverman *CEO*
Lee Silverman *P*
Steve Glick *CFO*
Bob Gelman *SAL MGR-Drain Cleaners*
Bob Silverman *SAL MGR-Springs*

Human Resources: Jeff Silverman

Purchasing: Jack Yankowski

Total Employees ....100+
Year Established 1930   **SIC Code**....................................3589

Geneva College

3200 College Ave.
Beaver Falls, PA 15010
County: Beaver

Phone: (412) 846-5100
Fax: (412) 847-5017
Internet Address: www.geneva.edu

Nonprofit, Christian, coeducational college whose mission is to educate and minister to a diverse community of students through biblically based programs and services that are anchored in the historic evangelical and reformed Christian faith. The College awards the Associate in Business Administration, Associate in Biblical Studies and Associate in Engineering; the Bachelor of Arts, Bachelor of Science, Bachelor of Science in Engineering, Bachelor of Science in Education; and the Master of Arts in Professional Psychology, Master of Arts in Higher Education and Master of Science in Organizational Leadership. The campus spans more than 55 acres overlooking the Beaver River, approximately 30 miles northwest of Pittsburgh. The College enrolls approximately 1,750 men and women. It also operates the Center for Urban Theological Studies, which is located in Philadelphia, PA, and degree completion programs throughout Western Pennsylvania.

Officers: John H. White, D.Min. *P*
James N. Boelkins, Ph.D. *Provost & VP-Academic Affairs*
Joy Jewell *VP-Student DEV*
William J. Katip *VP-Enrollment Services*
James MacDonald *VP-Business & FIN*
Charles N. O'Data *VP-DEV*

Human Resources: Donald McBurney

Purchasing: Nancy Graham

Total Employees...........................390	**Regional Employees** 380
Year Established 1848	**SIC Code**......................................8221
Annual Revenues ($000) 24,250		

Geo-Con, Inc.

Corporate One, Bldg. II, 4075 Monroeville Blvd., Ste. 400
Monroeville, PA 15146
County: Allegheny

Phone: (412) 856-7700
Fax: (412) 373-3357
Internet Address: www.wcc.com

Provider of capabilities in hazardous waste site remediation and specialty geo-technical contracting. The Company's services include total waste site remediation, construction of vertical barriers for groundwater control, insitu soil mixing and treatment, landfill construction and closure, and ground improvement technologies. It operates branch offices in Rancho Cordova, CA; Tampa, FL; Voorhees, NJ; and Denton, TX. The Company is a subsidiary of Woodward-Clyde International-Americas, which is a subsidiary of the Woodward-Clyde Group, Inc., both of which are headquartered in Denver, CO.

Officers: Peter J. Nicholson *P*
Steven R. Day *VP-ENG*
Brian H. Jasperse *VP-OPR*
Donald Merz *TRS*
Linda W. Ward *Business DEV*

Human Resources: Gina M. Burns

Purchasing: Dale O. Ringer

Total Employees...........................100	**Regional Employees** 70
Year Established 1979	**SIC Code**......................................1794
Annual Revenues ($000) 33,000		

Geoffrey Boehm Chocolates

One Chocolate Sq., 91 43rd St.
Pittsburgh, PA 15201
County: Allegheny

Phone: (412) 687-3370
Fax: (412) 687-7523

Manufacturer of confectionery products, specializing in fund-raising activities, executive gift services and retail markets. The Company also operates two retail stores that sell its products, located at 1705 E. Carson St. and 4717 Liberty Ave. in Pittsburgh. The Company is a division of Boyer Candy Co., Inc., which is headquartered in Altoona, PA.

Officers: Anthony Forgione *P & CEO*
Roger Raybuck *VP & CFO*
Linggawaty Irawan *CON*

Total Employees	125	**Regional Employees**	125
Year Established	1914	**SIC Code**	2066

GeoSonics, Inc.

359 Northgate Dr.
P.O. Box 779, Warrendale, PA 15095
Warrendale, PA 15086
County: Allegheny

Phone: (412) 934-2900
Fax: (412) 934-2999
Internet Address: www.iglou.com/VibraTech/geosonics

Provider of vibration and sound consulting, blasting seismology and instrument manufacturing. The Company's offerings include vibration and noise measurement services, telemonitoring systems, seismograph leasing and sales, seismograph calibration and repair, vibration phase control program, blast summary service, pre-blast and pre-construction inspections, damage claim assessments, authoritative testimony, noise surveys, geophysical surveys, seismic monitoring seminars, public relations programs and marketing services. Its staff consists primarily of geologists, physicists, geophysicists and mining engineers whose experience spans all aspects of vibration and noise control. The Company operates additional facilities in Cheshire, CT; Pembroke Pines, FL; Westford, MA; and Raleigh, NC. Its seismograph equipment manufacturing plant is located in St. Petersburg, FL. The Company's affiliate, Vibra-Tech (VT), which is headquartered in Hazelton, PA, employs 76 people with five at the above address. VT provides services similar to the Company but does not do any manufacturing.

Officers: D. T. Froedge *P & CEO*
Marion B. Henry *CFO*

Human Resources: Alvin L. Budd *Administrative AST to P & CEO*

Total Employees............................59		**Regional Employees** 29	
Year Established 1971		**SIC Code**....................................3829	

Gerome Manufacturing Co., Inc.

G

Oliver Rd.
P.O. Box 1089
Uniontown, PA 15401
County: Fayette

Phone: (412) 438-8544
Fax: (412) 437-5608

Manufacturer of enclosures for the electric and electronic industry, magnetic shields and specialities for electronic instruments, and power supplies and hardware for the cathodic protection of pipelines and underground metallic structures. The Company also operates a plant in Newberg, OR, similar in size and capability to the Uniontown, PA plant, to serve customers on the West Coast.

Officers: Henry M. Gerome *P*
Henry Mark Gerome *VP*

Total Employees...........................135	**Regional Employees** 93
Year Established 1957	**SIC Code**....................................3499
Annual Revenues ($000) 10,000	

Geyer Printing Co., Inc.

3700 Bigelow Blvd.
Pittsburgh, PA 15213
County: Allegheny

Phone: (412) 682-3633
Fax: (412) 682-4856

Provider of commercial lithography, specializing in full-color printing, dimensional printing and direct mail projects. The Company also offers complete desktop/prepress and bindery services. It serves clients throughout the Pittsburgh metropolitan area, ranging from corporations to advertising agencies and designers.

Officers: Bruce P. McGough *P*
Thomas E. Samuels *VP*
Don Fritz *CON*

Total Employees............................85	**Regional Employees** 85
Year Established 1909	**SIC Code**....................................2752
Annual Revenues ($000) 13,000	

Giant Eagle, Inc.

RIDC Industrial Park, 101 Kappa Dr.
Pittsburgh, PA 15238
County: Allegheny

Phone: (412) 963-6200
Fax: (412) 963-0374

Owner, operator and franchiser of a regional chain of 142 supermarkets located throughout Ohio, Pennsylvania and West Virginia, including 56 Company-owned stores, with an average store size of 55,000 square feet. The Company's subsidiaries include OK Grocery Co., also located at the above address, which supplies its supermarkets; and Butler Refrigerated Meats, Inc. in Harmony, PA, which is a wholesaler of meat, fish and seafood products to 246 outlets located in the Tri-State area.

Recent Events: On 5/14/97, Riser Foods, Inc. (RFI), which is headquartered in Cleveland, OH, and listed on the ASE, announced that it had reached a definitive agreement to merge with Giant Eagles under which the Company was to acquire all of RFI's outstanding Class A and Class B stock. The combined companies will have retail stores in Ohio, Pennsylvania and West Virginia, and wholesale operations in both Ohio and Pennsylvania, with combined sales expected to be $4 billion in 1998. The transaction was subject to required regulatory approvals and other customary terms and conditions, and also subject to shareholder approval.

Special Designations: FB-P$_{500}$

Officers: David Shapira *CH & CEO*
Raymond J. Burgo *P & COO*

Human Resources: Ray Huber *VP*

Total Employees......................12,700
Year Established........................1931
Annual Revenues ($000) 2,300,000

SIC Code 5411

Giffin Interior & Fixture, Inc.

500 Scotti Dr.
Bridgeville, PA 15017
County: Allegheny

Phone: (412) 221-1166
Fax: (412) 221-3745

Interior contracting firm specializing in the fabrication, finishing and installation of custom casework and architectural millwork. The Company's products include custom display fixtures, showcases, cashwraps, retail perimeter systems and restaurant casework; furniture, including conference tables and desks; hospital and institutional casework; moulding, trims, panels and decor systems; entertainment centers and custom residential cabinetry; and solid surface fabrication. Its interior contracting services include drywall, ceilings, carpentry and subcontracting.

Officers: Gordon D. Giffin *P*
              Russell R. Schlaegle *EVP*

Human Resources: Donna Jean Horton

Total Employees..........................125	**Regional Employees** 125
Year Established 1980	**SIC Code**....................................2541
Annual Revenues ($000) 11,300	

Gilson Engineering Sales, Inc.

535 Rochester Rd.
P.O. Box 101099
Pittsburgh, PA 15237
County: Allegheny

Phone: (412) 369-0100
Fax: (412) 366-1728

Manufacturers' representative and distributor of industrial control equipment. The Company markets pressure, temperature, and level and flow measurement and control instruments to utilities and chemical, steel and other industries. Its other products include recorders, annunciators, and pH and conductivity sensors. The Company also represents manufacturers of automation control products such as timers, counters and photoelectric, proximity and programmable controllers. It maintains sales offices in Orlando, FL; Cleveland, Columbus and Toledo, OH; and Charleston, WV.

Officers: Cletus O. Gilson *P*
              Pat N. Patchen *VP*

Human Resources: Fran Kramer

Total Employees............................37	**Regional Employees** 22
Year Established 1964	**SIC Code**....................................3824
Annual Revenues ($000) 18,000	

Girl Scouts of Southwestern Pennsylvania

606 Liberty Ave.
Pittsburgh, PA 15222
County: Allegheny

Phone: (412) 566-2570
Fax: (412) 391-4413

Nonprofit organization dedicated to inspiring girls with the highest ideals of character, conduct, patriotism and service that they may become happy and resourceful citizens. The Organization is a chartered council of Girl Scouts of the U.S.A., which is headquartered in New York, NY. It claims to be the 16th largest council in the nation out of 320. The Organization serves girls between the ages of five and 17, with approximately 23,000 participants and more than 6,400 volunteers. Its geographic boundaries encompass all of Garrett County, MD; Allegheny, Fayette, Greene and Washington Counties, PA; Monongalia and Preston Counties, WV; and portions of Somerset and Westmoreland Counties, PA.

Officers: Martha D. Smith *P*
Marlene Szary *EDIR*
Diane Doyle *AST-EDIR*
Terri Agnew *DIR-Membership*
Michael W. Murray *DIR-DEV*
Ted Bakota *CON*

Purchasing: Bernadette Kniedler *Product SAL Program DIR*

Total Employees.............................50
Year Established.........................1919   SIC Code....................................8699
Annual Revenues ($000)..3,200

Glassmere Fuel Service, Inc.

1967 Saxonburg Blvd.
Tarentum, PA 15084
County: Allegheny

Phone: (412) 224-0880
Fax: (412) 265-3588

Wholesaler and retailer of petroleum products. The Company is a wholesale distributor of BP and Citgo gasolines and diesel fuels, and a wholesale and retail distributor of Citgo, Gulf and Mobil bulk and packaged lubricants. It also delivers home heating oil to residential customers as well as bulk gasoline and diesel fuel to service stations and farm, commercial and industrial markets. In addition, the Company owns and operates 11 "Glassmart" convenience and gasoline stations located in Apollo (2), Brackenridge, Bradenville, Greensburg, Latrobe, Murrysville, Saltsburg, Sarver, Saxonburg and Tarentum (at the above address), PA; one "Glassmere" truck stop in Blairsville, PA; and a warehouse in Sarver, PA.

Officers: Dell M. Cromie *P*
Linda J. Cromie *VP*
William Kolish *SEC*

Human Resources: Dave Kaniecki

Purchasing: Dave Talmage

Total Employees...........................154   Regional Employees...................154
Year Established.........................1941   SIC Code.....................................5172
Annual Revenues ($000)...35,000

Goldberg, Persky, Jennings & White, P.C.

1030 Fifth Ave., 3rd Fl.
Pittsburgh, PA 15219
County: Allegheny

G

Phone: (412) 471-3980
Fax: (412) 471-8308
Internet Address: www.gpjw@sgi.net

Provider of legal services with 24 attorneys. The Firm's practice areas include litigation, occupational and environmental disease, personal injury, property damage, product liability, workers' compensation and social security disability. Its branch offices are located in Saginaw, MI; Greensburg and Johnstown, PA; and Huntington, WV.

Officers: Theodore Goldberg *P*
Joel Persky *VP*
Robert L. Jennings, Jr. *TRS*
Thomas W. White *AST-TRS*

Human Resources: William C. Rose *Administrator (Purchasing)*

Total Employees............................120	**Regional Employees** 104
Year Established 1984	**SIC Code** 8111

Golden Eagle Construction Co., Inc.

North Gallatin Extension
P.O. Box 945
Uniontown, PA 15401
County: Fayette

Phone: (412) 437-6495
Fax: (412) 437-5788

Contractor providing heavy highway road construction and paving services in Southwestern Pennsylvania. The Company has a number of subsidiaries and affiliates, including B&L Trucking, Inc., BSC Construction, Inc., Phantom Transport, Inc. and SLS Construction, Inc., all of which are engaged in the hauling of crushed stone, asphalt, coal, salt and dirt and are also located at the above address; Coolspring Stone Supply, Inc. in Uniontown, PA, a producer of crushed stone and asphalt; Golden Eagle Asphalt, Inc. in Washington, PA, a producer of asphalt; and Mineral Transport, Inc. in Fairmont, WV, a hauler of asphalt and aggregates.

Officers: William R. Snoddy, Sr. *P*
William R. Snoddy, Jr. *VP*

Human Resources: Jesse T. Wallace III

Purchasing: Roger Glover

Total Employees............................250
Year Established 1970   SIC Code 1611

Golden Triangle Construction Co., Inc.

40 Pattridge Lane
Imperial, PA 15126
County: Allegheny

Phone: (412) 695-1600
Fax: (412) 695-1611

Provider of heavy, highway, utility and structural construction services. The Company performs projects ranging from $250,000 to $28 million primarily within a 100-mile radius of Pittsburgh. Its projects include sewer/water, street/utility, and interstate highway rehabilitation and reconstruction. The Company produces its own concrete for its construction projects. The Company's clients include Allegheny County, the City of Pittsburgh and the Pennsylvania Department of Transportation. The Company's affiliates, all located at the above address, are Eagle Pointe Community, Inc.; Golden Triangle Enterprises, Inc.; and Imperial Surplus Sales, Inc.

Officers: Umbert Sciulli *P*
Gilbert E. Bucci, Sr. *SEC & TRS*
Charles J. Nedermitter *General Supervisor*

Human Resources: Gail Felton

Purchasing: Gilbert E. Bucci, Jr. *VP*

Total Employees............................115   Regional Employees...................115
Year Established 1952   SIC Code 1611
Annual Revenues ($000) 18,974

Goldschmidt Industrial Chemical Corp.

941 Robinson Hwy.
P.O. Box 279
McDonald, PA 15057
County: Washington

Phone: (412) 796-1511
Fax: (412) 922-6657

Manufacturer and marketer of tin chemical products used in metal finishing and glass coating processes or as chemical intermediates and catalysts in chemical industries. The Company is a subsidiary of Th. Goldschmidt AG, which is headquartered in Essen, Germany.

Officers: Richard Paterson-Jones *P*
Sharon Holzhauer *Business MGR*
Charles Zimmerman *OPR MGR*
Fred Gilley *SEC*

Human Resources: Susan Schuler

Purchasing: Vince Gianello

Total Employees............................30	**Regional Employees** 30
Year Established 1935	**SIC Code**....................................5169
Annual Revenues ($000)..10,000+	

Golf Digest Information Systems, Inc.

RIDC Industrial Park, 639 Alpha Dr.
Pittsburgh, PA 15238
County: Allegheny

Phone: (412) 963-8888
Fax: (412) 963-9028

Developer and marketer of a nationwide golf tee-time reservation system software. The system allows golf courses, hotels and travel reservation centers to book tee-times at any participating golf courses, one year or more, in advance. Future plans anticipate allowing golfers to connect via the Internet and make their own tee-time reservations. The Company is a division of The New York Times Co. Magazine Group, which is headquartered in Trumbull, CT. The Magazine Group is a unit of The New York Times Co., which is headquartered in New York, NY, and listed on the ASE.

Officers: Jay Fitzgerald *CEO*
Bob Sauerberg *VP & CFO*
John H. Stafford *VP & COO*
Jay Troutman *VP-Network SAL*

Human Resources: Robin Mentzinger

Total Employees............................65	**Regional Employees** 45
Year Established 1995	**SIC Code**....................................7372

Goodwill Industries of Pittsburgh

2600 E. Carson St.
Pittsburgh, PA 15203
County: Allegheny

Phone: (412) 481-9005
Fax: (412) 481-2091
Internet Address: www.goodwillpitt.org

Nonprofit business that manages a wide array of human service, residential and social outreach programs which serve thousands of people each year. The Organization's Workforce Development Center provides a comprehensive menu of employment-related services to help people with disabilities and disadvantages, including evaluation and testing, training and education, job placement and ongoing support. The Organization also operates several businesses to help fund its various programs and to provide training and job opportunities for its clients. The Organization sells donated clothing and household items at 14 retail stores throughout the region. It also runs a weekly motor vehicle auction, a computer recycling business and book store. In addition, it operates a commercial bulk mail presort service, the largest recycling center in Fayette county and one of the region's largest workshop facilities employing people with disabilities. The Organization is part of an international organization that includes 180 autonomous Goodwill agencies throughout the United States as well as 50 foreign affiliates. Under a franchise-like agreement with Goodwill Industries International, which is headquartered in Washington, D.C., the Organization serves all of Southwestern Pennsylvania and manages two affiliate units, Goodwill Industries of Fayette County in Uniontown, PA, and Goodwill Industries of North Central West Virginia, Inc. in Morgantown, WV.

Officers: Robert S. Foltz, Ph.D. *P*
Peter J. Travisano *SVP-OPR*
Thomas M. McNamara *VP-SAL*
Patricia L. Petrosky *VP-Human Services*
Michael J. Smith *VP & DIR-Goodwill Industries of Fayette County*

Human Resources: Tina Lynch *DIR-Human Resources*

Purchasing: Jacqueline Joyce *CON*

Total Employees............................700	**Regional Employees** 630
Year Established 1919	**SIC Code**......................................8331
Annual Revenues ($000) 19,000	

Grant, Inc., Louis A.

R.R. 2, Rte. 66
Box 264A
Export, PA 15632
County: Westmoreland

Phone: (412) 468-4700
Fax: (412) 468-8188

Designer, manufacturer and marketer of mill maintenance equipment for the steel, aluminum and cement industries. The Company has developed equipment and techniques for the removal of refractory linings and slag accumulations from open hearth furnaces, blast furnaces, soaking pits, basic oxygen furnaces, hot stoves, torpedo cars, ladles, AOD, reheat furnaces, blast furnace mixers, open hearth mixers and spray chambers, blast/furnace/runners, induction furnaces and tar tanks. Its equipment is also available for rental, with the option of an operator provided. The Company has a manufacturing plant in Delmont, PA, as well as service centers in Kentucky, Michigan, Ohio and Texas. A subsidiary, Furnace Services, Inc., is located in Hammond, IN.

Officers: Ruth M. Grant *P*
Louis A. Grant, Jr. *EVP*

Total Employees............................150	**Regional Employees** 80
Year Established 1951	**SIC Code**.....................................7353
Annual Revenues ($000) 15,000	

Graphic Arts Color Corp.

422 First Ave.
Pittsburgh, PA 15219
County: Allegheny

Phone: (412) 391-4350
Fax: (412) 391-4686

Provider of printing services, including desktop publishing, digital retouching, electronic prepress, multicolor conventional printing, multicolor on-demand digital printing, bindery and shipping services.

Officers: Frank Rastetter *P*
James Rastetter *VP*

Total Employees..............................45	**Regional Employees** 45
Year Established 1950	**SIC Code**.....................................2759
Annual Revenues ($000) 5,500	

Graphic Arts Technical Foundation

200 Deer Run Rd.
Sewickley, PA 15143
County: Allegheny

Phone: (412) 741-6860
Fax: (412) 741-2311

Nonprofit, member-supported, scientific, technical and educational foundation dedicated to the advancement of graphic communications industries worldwide. The Foundation provides members and nonmembers with technical and training information to improve quality, reduce waste and enhance productivity. Its Technical Center houses extensive facilities, including classrooms, laboratories, and prepress and press facilities valued at over $20 million. Its recently opened Center for Imaging Excellence includes advanced workshops in digital production as well as workshops on desktop publishing, preflighting and color reproduction. The Foundation also offers hands-on workshops on sheetfed and web press operating. The Foundation has a long tradition of applied technical research committed to finding solutions to the technical problems experienced by its industry. Its technical inquiry desk received nearly 4,000 inquiries from around the world last year and its technical staff conducted 326 audits for member companies. The Foundation's boards and committees direct its programs. Over 200 industry representatives give of their time and experience on these boards and committees. The Foundation has nearly 7,900 members in 61 countries. develops technologies and practices for printing

Officers: George Ryan *P*
John Sweeney *VP-SAL & MKT*
Richard Warner *VP & DIR-RES*
Barry Faigen *CON*

Human Resources: Beth Bennett *(Purchasing)*

Total Employees 76	**Regional Employees** 72
Year Established 1924	**SIC Code** 8733
Annual Revenues ($000) 7,054	

Greater Pittsburgh Convention & Visitors Bureau, Inc.

Four Gateway Center, 18th Fl.
Pittsburgh, PA 15222
County: Allegheny

Phone: (412) 281-7711
Fax: (412) 644-5512
Internet Address: www.pittsburgh-cvb.org

Nonprofit civic organization established to create revenue and jobs in Allegheny County and the City of Pittsburgh by generating convention, trade show and leisure travel business. The Bureau's mission remains intact today as the official tourist promotion agency of Allegheny County and as an independent organization serving its memberhsip of approximately 700 businesses. The Bureau is funded by business membership investments and by two of the five percent Allegheny County Hotel/Motel Room Tax. It also receives support from the Commonwealth of Pennsylvania's Tourism Matching Grant program, other state grants and the donation of in-kind services. The Bureau operates visitor information service centers at the Pittsburgh International Airport, University of Pittsburgh, 315 Grandview Ave. and at the above address.

G

Officers: Joseph R. McGrath *P & CEO*
Robert P. Imperata *EVP*

Total Employees...............61	**Regional Employees** 61	
Year Established 1935	**SIC Code**......................................8743	
Annual Revenues ($000) 5,711		

Green Acres Contracting Co., Inc.

Pennsylvania Ave.
P.O. Box 463
Scottdale, PA 15683
County: Westmoreland

Phone: (412) 887-8096
Fax: (412) 887-8111

Specialty contractor providing highway construction and highway maintenance-related services. These include installing and maintaining guide rails, ground-mounted and overhead signs, right-of-way fences, impact attenuators and concrete jersey barriers, and landscaping. The Company's services are primarily contracted by state highway departments. It maintains a shipping and storage facility in Winslow Township, PA.

Officers: Thomas M. Pisula *P*
Paul F. Humberston *VP & TRS*
Gregory M. Pisula *SEC*
Dennis Schavolt *Head Estimator*

Human Resources: Anna H. Sabbers *Payroll Supervisor*

Purchasing: Douglas Riley *Equipment MGR*

Total Employees...........................150	**Regional Employees** 90	
Year Established 1975	**SIC Code**......................................1799	
Annual Revenues ($000) 20,000		

Green Valley Packing Co.

2992 Green Valley Rd.
Claysville, PA 15323
County: Washington

Phone: (412) 225-2176

Processor and packer of meat.

Officers: George Weiss *P*

Total Employees............................60	**Regional Employees** 60
Year Established 1958	**SIC Code** 2011

Greif Bros. Corp.

Five Grable Rd.
Washington, PA 15301
County: Washington

Phone: (412) 222-8300
Fax: (412) 222-0210

Manufacturer of corrugated boxes for a wide variety of packaging applications. The Company operates a second facility at 901 Vermont Ave. in Washington, PA, which provides value-added items for the corrugated boxes, including labels and partitions. The Company, which is headquartered in Delaware, OH, is listed on the NASDAQ. The local plant is a part of its Corrugated Products Division, which is headquartered in Zanesville, OH.

Officers: Geoffrey K. Landry *GMGR*

Purchasing: Lou Marinkovich

Regional Employees....................100	
Year Established 1877	**SIC Code** 2653

Grogan, Graffam, McGinley & Lucchino, P.C.

Three Gateway Center, 22nd Fl.
Pittsburgh, PA 15222
County: Allegheny

Phone: (412) 553-6300
Fax: (412) 642-2226

Provider of legal services with 30 attorneys. The Firm handles almost all forms of adversary proceedings, including jury and nonjury trials in state and federal courts, administrative hearings before state and federal agencies, and statutory and common law arbitration hearings, including, but not limited to, environmental law, general and complex civil litigation, legal malpractice and medical malpractice defense, general tort and casualty defense, collections and recoveries, general corporate law, municipal law, real estate, and tax and estate planning.

Officers: John R. McGinley, Jr. *P*

Human Resources: Ronald A. Soncini *EDIR*

Total Employees............................74
Year Established 1971

Regional Employees 74
SIC Code 8111

Ground Improvement Techniques, Inc.

460 Old Frankstown Rd.
Monroeville, PA 15146
County: Allegheny

Phone: (412) 798-2220
Fax: (412) 798-0114

Provider of geotechnical specialty construction services. The Company is a heavy construction contractor engaged in the building of sanitary landfills and slurry trench cut-off walls. It also provides specialized services to heavy industry, including the metals, coal and petroleum sectors. The Company designs and constructs systems to provide water intrusion control; grouting cement/chemical; epoxy applications flexible/rigid; foundation stabilization storage tanks, tunnels, arches and mill equipment foundations; mine subsidence control; dam renovations and restorations; soil remediation; and concrete rehabilitation. The Company provides its services nationwide to commercial, industrial and government clients. Branch offices are located in Kissimmee, FL, and Woodland, WA.

Officers: Theodore L. Hoey *P*
Robert T. Coneybeer *VP*
Robert E. Kinghorn *VP*
John D. Cooper *SEC & TRS*

Total Employees............................250
Year Established 1984
Annual Revenues ($000) 35,000

Regional Employees 30
SIC Code 1629

Ground Technology, Inc.

275 Center Rd.
Monroeville, PA 15146
County: Allegheny

Phone: (412) 856-9440
Fax: (412) 856-9535
Internet Address: www.dappolonia.com

Provider of civil, geotechnical and environmental engineering services to utilities, heavy industry, contractors, architectural and engineering firms, and commercial enterprises. The Company does business as the D'Appolonia Engineering Division of Groundwater Technology, Inc. Its services include subsurface exploration; foundation design; ground subsidence mitigation; design of dams, tunnels and retaining walls; geotechnical instrumentation; slope and rock face stabilization; dam inspection and emergency action planning; site grading design; storm water management; design of municipal and industrial waste containment facilities; environmental site assessment; remediation design; and construction monitoring. The Company has provided engineering services, scientific evaluations and construction management for projects in more than 40 countries. It operates branch offices in Mt. Pleasant, SC, and Cordoba, Argentina.

Officers: Eugene C. Palmer *P & Principal*
Robert E. Snow *Principal*
James L. Withiam *Principal*

Total Employees............................35   **Regional Employees** 33
Year Established 1956   **SIC Code** 8711

Grubb & Ellis Co.

Six PPG Place, Ste. 600
Pittsburgh, PA 15222
County: Allegheny

Phone: (412) 281-0100
Fax: (412) 281-8814

Provider of full-service commercial real estate services, including brokerage and property and facilities management. The Company also offers mortgage brokerage, appraisal, consultation and asset management services. It claims to lease and manage more office buildings in metropolitan Pittsburgh than any other firm. The Company, which is headquartered in Northbrook, IL, is listed on the NYSE. It operates branch offices throughout the United States and has representation in a number of other countries. Axiom Real Estate Management, Inc., a subsidiary of the Company, shares the above address. (Refer to the Axiom Real Estate Management, Inc. profile for additional information.)

Officers: George H. Kingsley III *EVP & District MGR*
Edward P. Doran *SVP*
Michael W. Hendrickson *SVP*
Thomas B. McChesney *SVP*
Gerard M. McLaughlin *SVP*
A. Keith Staso *SVP*

Total Employees........................3,000   **Regional Employees** 53
Year Established 1958   **SIC Code** 6500

Guardian Industries Corp.

300 Glass House Rd.
Clairton, PA 15025
County: Allegheny

Phone: (412) 384-3400
Fax: (412) 384-5530

Manufacturer of float glass primarily for the automotive industry. The Company is headquartered in Auburn Hills, MI.

Officers: Gary Cochran *Plant MGR*

Regional Employees....................160	
Year Established 1982	**SIC Code** 3211

Guardian Protection Services, Inc.

650 Ridge Rd.
Pittsburgh, PA 15205
County: Allegheny

Phone: (412) 788-2580
Fax: (412) 788-2592

Marketer, installer and monitor of 24-hour security systems protecting against burglary, fire and emergency. The Company claims to be one of the nation's largest distributors of First Alert Professional Products and Bose® sound systems. It markets to the residential, commercial, industrial and institutional sectors. In addition to its corporate headquarters, the Company's 24-hour monitoring station is also located at the above address. The Company operates branch sales and service offices in Newark, DE; Atlanta, GA; Indianapolis, IN; Baltimore and Rockville, MD; Livingston and Mt. Laurel, NJ; Buffalo and Rochester, NY; Cincinnati, Cleveland, Columbus, Dayton and Youngstown, OH; Philadelphia and Pittsburgh (4955 Steubenville Pike), PA; Charleston, SC; and Lorton, VA. The Company is a subsidiary of the Armstrong Group of Cos., which is headquartered in Butler, PA.

Officers: Russell L. Cersosimo *P*
Lawrence Wargo *EVP & GMGR*
David Phillips *CFO*
Joseph Colosimo *VP-OPR*
William Graham *VP-SAL & MKT*

Human Resources: Dave Rosswog

Purchasing: Michael Szulkowski

Total Employees...........................600	**Regional Employees** 350
Year Established 1950	**SIC Code**.....................................7382

Gumberg Co., J. J.

1051 Brinton Rd.
Pittsburgh, PA 15221
County: Allegheny

Phone: (412) 244-4000
Fax: (412) 244-9133

Real estate management and development firm, specializing in the development and ownership of top-tiered real estate and professionally managed, institutionally owned properties. The Company has holdings and manages properties from Maine to Florida and west of the Mississippi River.

Officers: Stanley R. Gumberg *CH*
Ira J. Gumberg *P & CEO*
John E. Kramer *EVP*

Human Resources: Lawrence N. Gumberg *VCH & COO*

Total Employees...........................250
Year Established.........................1923 **SIC Code**.....................................6512

Gupta Permold Corp.

234 Lott Rd.
Pittsburgh, PA 15235
County: Allegheny

Phone: (412) 793-3511
Fax: (412) 793-1055
Internet Address: www.nb.net/gupta.com

Manufacturer operating through two divisions. The Casting division produces customized aluminum permold castings to client specifications. The Rail Transit division produces a variety of equipment for the rail transit industry, including braking resistor assemblies, traction gear assemblies, and AC and DC motors and components. The Company also produces wood products for its industrial packaging needs. In addition, the Company rehabilitates original equipment for transit systems nationwide. An additional manufacturing site is located in Pittsburg, CA.

Officers: Lakshmi P. Gupta *P*

Human Resources: Devendra Kumar

Total Employees..............................90 **Regional Employees**....................70
Year Established.........................1980 **SIC Code**.....................................3365

Guttman Group, The

200 Speers St.
Belle Vernon, PA 15012
County: Fayette

G

Phone: (412) 483-3533
Fax: (412) 483-3697

Owner and operator of a variety of businesses through its member companies, all of which are based at the above address. The Guttman Oil Co. (GOC) is a distributor of a complete line of branded and unbranded fuels, lubricants and related products. These products are marketed from retail terminals in Maryland, Ohio, Pennsylvania, Virginia and West Virginia. GOC also owns and operates pipelines, barge terminals and bulk plants throughout its marketing area, as well as 26 Crossroads Food Mart convenience stores and gas stations located across Western Pennsylvania. In addition, GOC operates 14 card-access fueling (card-lock) sites for commercial vehicles under a franchise arrangement with Pacific Pride. Other members of the Group include Mon River Towing, Inc., a towboat and barge operator with a fleet of 14 towboats and 250 barges, and the Guttman Realty Co.

Officers: Alan R. Guttman *CEO*
Richard M. Guttman   *P*
Ivan I. Melnick *VP-FIN*
Dolores Harper *SEC*
James L. Guttman *P-Mon River Towing, Inc.*
Keith C. Kyle *VP-Transportation-Mon River Towing, Inc.*
Fred J. Perino *VP-Supply & OPR-Guttman Oil Co.*
Donald F. Smith *VP-SAL & MKT-Guttman Oil Co.*

Total Employees............................650	**Regional Employees** 600
Year Established 1931	**SIC Code**......................................5172
Annual Revenues ($000)...100,000+	

H&H Distributors, Inc.

5101 Baum Blvd.
Pittsburgh, PA 15224
County: Allegheny

Phone: (412) 621-8444
Fax: (412) 621-7124

Retailer, wholesaler and installer of products for the automotive aftermarket, including automobile sound and alarm systems, sun roofs and other accessories. The Company recently added spoilers and light truck accessories to its product line. The Company has also expanded its involvement in the cellular phone business and states that it currently is one of the largest agents for Bell Atlantic NYNEX Mobile Systems in the Pittsburgh market, selling portable cellular phones as well as installing phones in cars. In addition to selling direct to the general public and to business, it supplies accessories to automobile dealers and provides installation services for such products. The Company, doing business as the Harry Survis Auto Center, operates branch sales and service sites in Greensburg, McMurray and West Mifflin, PA. The Company is a subsidiary of Oakhurst Co., Inc., which is headquartered in Grand Prairie, TX, and listed on the NASDAQ Small Cap.

Officers: Harold Garfinkel *P*
James E. Stein *VP*

Purchasing: Mark Doman *MER MGR*

Total Employees 50		**Regional Employees** 50
Year Established 1937		**SIC Code** 5013
Annual Revenues ($000) 4,500			

H-Tech, Inc.

208 Bursca Dr.
P.O. Box 436
Bridgeville, PA 15017
County: Allegheny

Phone: (412) 221-5920
Fax: (412) 221-2193

Provider of technically oriented temporary personnel and support personnel to clients throughout the Pittsburgh metropolitan area. The Company maintains an active file of more than 5,000 resumes of CAD operators, drafters, designers, engineers and technical support people capable of serving industrial construction projects and machinery. It also provides welders, fitters, machinists and assembly technicians for industry.

Officers: Frank J. Paolicelli *P (Purchasing)*
K. Dean Strucker *VP*
Richard Hall *MGR-SAL & Recruiting*

Human Resources: Carol Paolicelli

Total Employees 130		**Regional Employees** 125
Year Established 1981		**SIC Code** 8711
Annual Revenues ($000) 5,800			

Hagan Consulting Group, Inc.

Benedum-Trees Bldg., 223 Fourth Ave., Ste. 1100
Pittsburgh, PA 15222
County: Allegheny

Phone: (412) 355-5000
Fax: (412) 355-5094

Provider of personal financial planning services and business financial consulting. The Company has three affiliated companies, two of which are located at the above address. The Hagan Accounting Group, Inc. is a certified public accounting firm providing tax, accounting and auditing services, and financial statements. The American HealthCare Group, Inc. is a management services organization that provides services to physician networks, including managed care contract negotiations, utilization management programs, information systems and network development. Medical Group Management, Inc. at 730 River Ave. in Pittsburgh, PA, provides computer systems management, educational classes, medical billing, computer equipment and custom software.

Officers: Robert E. Hagan, Jr. *P*

Human Resources: Linda M. Sekely *DIR-Personal Financial Services*

Total Employees	52	**Regional Employees**	52
Year Established	1973	**SIC Code**	8721
Annual Revenues ($000)	4,500		

Halco Co.

Five Belle Vernon Hwy.
P.O. Box 108
Belle Vernon, PA 15012
County: Fayette

Phone: (412) 929-7300
Fax: (412) 929-7301

Operator of a sewing factory producing a variety of novelty and Christmas-related products. The Company's merchandise includes Santa Claus suits, stockings, tree skirts, hats, wigs and beards, jingle bells, Mrs. Santa costumes, bunny costumes, elf costumes and other related items.

Officers: Allen M. Hoffman *P*
                Terri H. Greenberg *VP-SAL & MKT*

Human Resources: Kevin J. Henry *OPR MGR*

Total Employees	45	**Regional Employees**	45
Year Established	1977	**SIC Code**	2389

Hallmark/Tassone, Inc.

Four Gateway Center, 10th Fl.
Pittsburgh, PA 15222
County: Allegheny

Phone: (412) 471-5300
Fax: (412) 471-3308

Provider of full-service integrated marketing and communications services to clients as an agency or as a consultant. The Firm's services include advertising; public relations; direct marketing and sales promotion; strategic planning; research; interactive and Internet marketing; and major event marketing for consumer, business-to-business, industrial, corporate, health care and financial service clients. The Firm's full-service agency subsidiaries include Frayley-Wilson/Hallmark in Orlando, FL; Pearson-Thomas/Hallmark in Tampa, FL; and Winner-Koenig/Hallmark in Tampa, FL. Also located at the above address is a business affiliate, Caplan/Capozzi, engaged in event marketing; and a joint venture partner, DDF&M, Inc., a full-service agency.

Officers: William S. Binstock *CH & CEO*
Timothy L. Tassone *P & COO*
Susan Brooke *SVP & MGT Supervisor*
Louis Lasday *SVP*
Stan Muschweck *SVP & MGT Supervisor*
Steve Alber *VP-Creative*
Phil Lityin *VP-Creative*
Steve Smith *VP-Creative*

Human Resources: A. Scott Arthur *VP-FIN (Purchasing)*

Total Employees............................78	**Regional Employees** 48
Year Established 1995	**SIC Code** 7311
Annual Revenues ($000) 32,000	

Hallmor Machine, Inc.

531 McMurray Rd.
Bethel Park, PA 15102
County: Allegheny

Phone: (412) 835-8320
Fax: (412) 835-6041

Operator of machining job shop providing design/build and design/print services, which include tooling and repairs for manufacturers of machinery, steel mill manufacturing equipment, pumps and coal mining equipment. The Company's areas of expertise include the ability to repair, rebuild and replace expanding mandrels and segments, fabricate rolls and generally repair or replace a variety of parts. It primarily serves clients in the Tri-State area.

Officers: James R. Cousins *P*

Human Resources: Richard R. Cousins *VP (Purchasing)*

Total Employees................................32	**Regional Employees** 32
Year Established 1941	**SIC Code**.......................................3599
Annual Revenues ($000) 2,250	

H

Hamill Manufacturing Co.

500 Pleasant Valley Rd.
Trafford, PA 15085
County: Westmoreland

Phone: (412) 744-2131
Fax: (412) 744-3121

Operator of machine shop utilizing computer and numerically controlled technology. The Company specializes in the design and manufacturing of critical components for a number of applications, including nuclear and fossil power generation, steel making, glass and plastic mold manufacturing, and space exploration. It provides precision machining, welding and fabrication of difficult-to-machine metals such as inconel and other nickel-based alloys, stainless steel and titanium. The Company also provides engineering services such as drafting, tool design, structural analysis and metallurgical evaluation.

Officers: Jeffrey S. Kelly *P*
Yessayi Mardirossian *VP-ENG*
James W. DeGoey *MKT DIR*
Larry M. Taylor *MFG DIR*

Human Resources: Evelyn L. Stahl

Purchasing: Stephen C. Pohlman

Total Employees................................87	**Regional Employees** 87
Year Established 1952	**SIC Code**.......................................3599
Annual Revenues ($000) 8,500	

Hanlon Electric Co.

530 Old Frankstown Rd.
Monroeville, PA 15146
County: Allegheny

Phone: (412) 795-6100
Fax: (412) 795-9541

Electrical contractor providing a variety of services, including project budgeting assistance, design and build project development, energy management audits, power quality studies, project cost estimating, project development assistance/consultation, project management, project scheduling, quality control, service and maintenance, and value engineering. The Company services commercial facilities, hospitals and institutions, and colleges and universities throughout Southeastern Pennsylvania. It maintains a fleet of approximately 15 service trucks.

Officers: Thomas P. Hanlon, Jr. *P*
Michael R. Hanlon *VP-ENG*
Thomas P. Hanlon III *VP*
Terrence E. Hanlon *TRS*

Human Resources: Cindy Hill

Total Employees	50	**Regional Employees**	50
Year Established	1930	**SIC Code**	1731

Harbison-Walker Refractories Co.

USX Tower, 600 Grant St.
Pittsburgh, PA 15219
County: Allegheny

Phone: (412) 562-6200
Fax: (412) 562-6421
Internet Address: www.hwr.com

Supplier of refractory products and technologies. The Company mines and processes certain minerals, and manufactures over 200 refractory products in various shapes, sizes and forms. Refractories, which are made principally from magnesite, graphite, bauxite, quartzite and fire clays, are used in virtually every industrial process requiring heating or containment of a solid, liquid or gas at a high temperature. Iron and steel producers use the Company's products in various types of furnaces, in coke ovens and in iron and steel handling and steel finishing operations. Industrial markets for its products include non-ferrous metals producers (aluminum, copper and zinc), mineral processors (cement and lime), glass producers, fossil-fueled power plants, chemical and petroleum processing plants and general industry. The Company operates 10 manufacturing plants and two raw materials processing sites throughout the U.S. and Canada, as well as a research laboratory located in West Mifflin, PA. The Company is a subsidiary of Global Industrial Technologies, Inc., which is headquartered in Dallas, TX, and listed on the NYSE.

Officers: Juan M. Bravo *P*
William K. Brown *VP-Minerals & Mining OPR*
Gerry J. Gustas *VP-U.S./Canada OPR*
Jeff P. Hutchinson *VP-INTL*
John S. Miller *VP-Technology*
Steve S. Ross *VP-ADM*

Human Resources: Larry J. Gorski *DIR-Human Resources*

Purchasing: Melvin G. Wees *Procurement & Logistics MGR*

Total Employees	1,750	**Regional Employees**	300
Year Established	1865	**SIC Code**	3255

Harley Hotel of Pittsburgh

699 Rodi Rd.
Pittsburgh, PA 15235
County: Allegheny

Phone: (412) 244-1600
Fax: (412) 829-2334

Operator of a suburban 152-room hotel with meeting and banquet facilities that can accommodate up to 300 people. The Hotel's recreational amenities include indoor and outdoor heated pools, saunas, whirlpool and tennis courts. It also contains the River Three Restaurant and Lounge. The Hotel is owned by Harley Hotels, Inc., located in Middleburg Heights, OH, which is a subsidiary of Helmsley-Spear, Inc., based in New York, NY.

Officers: John F. Mild *GMGR-Harley Hotel of Pittsburgh*

Human Resources: Elma Pugliese *Executive SEC*

Total Employees............................105	Regional Employees 105
Year Established 1968	SIC Code 7011
Annual Revenues ($000) 4,000	

Harmony Castings, Inc.

251 Perry Hwy.
P.O. Box 230
Harmony, PA 16037
County: Butler

Phone: (412) 452-5811
Fax: (412) 452-0118
Internet Address: www.harmonycastings.com

Manufacturer of aluminum castings for high-tech medical and process instrumentation applications.

Officers: Donald Weil *P*
              Dennis Smith *VP*

Total Employees............................136	Regional Employees 136
Year Established 1980	SIC Code 3365
Annual Revenues ($000) 12,000	

Harris Cleaning Service, Inc.

601 Pennsylvania Ave.
P.O. Box 133
Rochester, PA 15074
County: Beaver

Phone: (412) 775-0533
Fax: (412) 775-9805

Provider of contract janitorial services to commercial, industrial and residential clients. The Company also cleans acoustical ceilings and upholstery, and shampoos carpeting. It operates throughout Allegheny, Beaver and Butler Counties, PA.

Officers: William H. Harris, Jr. *P (Human Resources & Purchasing)*

Total Employees............................40	**Regional Employees** 40
Year Established 1957	**SIC Code**....................................7349
Annual Revenues ($000) 275		

Harris Masonry, Inc.

420 Greentree Rd.
Pittsburgh, PA 15220
County: Allegheny

Phone: (412) 922-7276
Fax: (412) 922-1761

Provider of masonry services including brick, block and stonework. The Company serves both commercial and industrial clients throughout the Ohio, Pennsylvania and West Virginia region.

Officers: Lee Harris *P*
Scott Harris *VP*

Total Employees 100-250	
Year Established 1962	**SIC Code**....................................1741

Harry Products, Inc.

495 Pittsburgh Rd.
Butler, PA 16002
County: Butler

Phone: (412) 586-9411
Fax: (412) 586-2132

Owner and operator of a chain of discount stores, doing business as Trader Horn and Warehouse Sales. The Company brings a low-overhead, no-frills approach to selling its large in-depth inventory of plumbing, hardware, automotive, paint, sporting goods, lawn and garden, appliances and hardware. The larger Trader Horn stores also feature the product lines of vinyl flooring, carpet remnants, wallpaper, finished and unfinished furniture, home improvements, lamps, toys, crafts and giftware. Each store is unique as it carries goods based on the needs of the customers in the particular area. The Company claims that it is the largest independent and locally owned chain of discount houses in the area. The Company's Trader Horn stores are located in Butler, Clarion, Ellwood City, Grove City, Indiana, Kittanning and Wexford, PA. Its Warehouse Sales stores are located in Butler (2), Eau Claire and New Castle, PA.

Officers: Robert M. Greenberger *P*
Judith M. Greenberger *VP*

Human Resources: Barbara Hollack

Purchasing: Frank Schutzman

Total Employees...........................450   **Regional Employees** 187
SIC Code 5399
Annual Revenues ($000) 38,000

Hartford Financial Services Group, Inc., The

One PPG Place, Ste. 1700
Pittsburgh, PA 15222
County: Allegheny

Phone: (412) 281-8833
Fax: (412) 281-8038

Provider of all lines of commercial and personal insurance as well as life, group and various financial services, unbundled loss control services and managed care. The Company, which is headquartered in Hartford, CT, is listed on the NYSE. The local office serves clients in Western Pennsylvania and West Virginia.

Officers: Barbara Smiley *GMGR*
James Bober *Quality Training & SAL MGR*
Patricia Dickey *Commercial Business Unit MGR*
Patrick Fredella *Claims*
George Donovan *Group SAL*
Ronald Herrmann *Life SAL*
Harry Fuehrer *DIR-Structured Settlements*
Charles Sheehy *Staff Counsel*

Human Resources: Samuel J. Prentice *MGR-Customer Services*

Total Employees......................22,000   **Regional Employees** 130
Year Established 1810   **SIC Code** 6400

Haser Trucking, Inc.

1023 North Ave.
Pittsburgh, PA 15209
County: Allegheny

Phone: (412) 821-1395
Fax: (412) 821-6201

Provider of rental trucks and professional drivers for hauling activities. The types of equipment include flatbed, extendible and dry van trailers; flatbed, box and tilt body straight trucks; drop frame trailers; detachable neck trailers; semi tractors; and pickup trucks. The Company also manages two companies, both headquartered at the above address. Mueller Trucking Co. is a licensed and bonded property broker for both interstate and intra-Pennsylvania commerce, specializing in working with customers to match their freight with licensed and insured motor carriers looking for backhauls. Reinsfelder, Inc. is a motor carrier authorized by the Pennsylvania Public Utilities Commission and the Interstate Commerce Commission to transport property within the boundaries of Pennsylvania and to points within the United States.

Officers: Edward P. Haser *P & CEO*
Paul A. Haser *VP*

Total Employees	47	**Regional Employees**	47
Year Established	1918	**SIC Code**	4212
Annual Revenues ($000)			7,000+

Haskell of Pittsburgh, Inc.

231 Haskell Lane
Verona, PA 15147
County: Allegheny

Phone: (412) 828-6000
Fax: (412) 828-6262

Manufacturer of a full-line of steel office furniture including desking systems/workstations, files and storage, seating and tables. The Company sells its products throughout the U.S. and Canada. In addition to the Company's headquarters and manufacturing facility which is located at the above address, it operates 16 regional distribution centers throughout the U.S. and Canada, including a site in New Kensington, PA.

Officers: Joseph F. Wojdak *P*
Jack Boyle *VP-FIN*
Pamela A. Grove *VP-SAL & MKT*
Greg Lintelman *NATL SAL MGR*

Human Resources: Christine A. Thurston

Purchasing: Kevin Maloney

Total Employees	425	Regional Employees	400
Year Established	1947	SIC Code	2522
Annual Revenues ($000)	40,000		

Haus Co., F. L.

921 Ridge Ave.
Pittsburgh, PA 15212
County: Allegheny

Phone: (412) 231-7700
Fax: (412) 231-7709
Internet Address: www.flhaus.com

Provider of reprographics products and services to the architectural, engineering and construction fields, including engineering copiers and plotters; design, plotting and duplicating media; and drafting and plotter supplies. The Company has recently expanded its offerings to provide full-service document solutions, including commercial print management, business forms management, technically advanced documents such as electronic forms, cold technology and imaging, multimedia development of web sites and CD-Rom. It has also established a promotions department that features in-house silk screening and embroidery in addition to ad specialties.

Officers: Frances L. Haus, Jr. *CEO*
Frances L. Haus III *P*
Jeffrey Haus *VP*

Total Employees	33	Regional Employees	33
Year Established	1964	SIC Code	2752

Hayes Large Architects

606 Liberty Ave.
Pittsburgh, PA 15222
County: Allegheny

Phone: (412) 391-3086
Fax: (412) 391-7280
Internet Address: www.hayeslarge.com

Provider of planning, architecture, landscape architecture, interior architecture and structural engineering services to schools, colleges and universities, health care, life care, and corporate and commercial facilities. The Company operates branch offices in Altoona and Harrisburg, PA.

Officers: J. Richard Fruth *PTR*
G. Randolph Hudson *PTR*
Richard L. Karcher *PTR*
S. Dwight Knouse *PTR*
Vern McKissick *PTR*
Robert E. Wedge *PTR*
James Schmidt *DIR-Production*

Human Resources: John A. Missell *Senior Associate*

Purchasing: Jason A. Fournier *DIR-Business DEV*

Total Employees...........................104   **Regional Employees** 17
Year Established 1922   **SIC Code**....................................8712

HDR Engineering, Inc.

Three Gateway Center
Pittsburgh, PA 15222
County: Allegheny

Phone: (412) 497-6000
Fax: (412) 497-6080
Internet Address: www.hdrinc.com

Employee-owned provider of engineering services specializing in bridges, highways, water, wastewater, municipal advocacy and a variety of geotechnical services. The Company is headquartered in Omaha, NE, and operates 41 offices nationwide. The Pittsburgh office, which serves clients in the Tri-State area, is presently working on the rehabilitation of the Ft. Pitt Bridge and tunnels; the ALCOSAN capital improvements project; the Mon-Fayette expressway; the rehabilitation of the Glenwood Bridge; the Boston Central Artery in Boston, MA; a bridge replacement in Chelyan, WV; and people mover designs and support to ADtranz. The Company is a subsidiary of HDR, Inc., which is also headquartered in Omaha, NE.

Officers: Ralph W. Gilbert, Jr. *SVP*
Arthur W. Hedgren, Jr. *SVP*
James M. Sheahan *VP*
Mark J. Sikora *VP*

Human Resources: Susan K. Philipp *(Purchasing)*

Total Employees........................1,600   **Regional Employees** 80
Year Established 1917   **SIC Code** 8711
Annual Revenues ($000)........................7,000 (Pittsburgh)

HealthAmerica-Pennsylvania Corp.

Five Gateway Center
Pittsburgh, PA 15222
County: Allegheny

Phone: (412) 553-7300
Fax: (412) 553-7384

Provider of HMOs, PPOs, Point-of-Service plans, a custom-designed Small Business managed care product and traditional indemnity products. These plan designs are offered on both a "fully insured" and "self-insured" basis. The Company also offers a Medicare "risk" HMO product. The Company has 570,000 members enrolled in Pennsylvania, with 340,000 in the Pittsburgh region. Its managed care network includes over 4,000 physicians and 60 hospitals, including Allegheny General Hospital, Children's Hospital, Magee-Womens Hospital, St. Francis Hospital and West Penn Hospital. Over 10,000 employers offer the Company's managed care programs. Some of its largest accounts are ALCOA, Carnegie Mellon University, CNG, Kaufmann's, Mellon Bank, Penn State University, PPG, USAirways, USX and Wheeling-Pittsburgh Steel. The Company also operates in Steubenville and Youngstown, OH, and Clarksburg, Morgantown, Weirton and Wheeling, WV, under the name HealthAssurance. Another major office, independent of the Pittsburgh facility, is located in Harrisburg, PA, and services clients in the central portion of Pennsylvania. The Company is a subsidiary of Coventry Corp., a national managed care firm which is headquartered in Nashville, TN, and listed on the NASDAQ.

Officers: Robert Mayer *P & CEO*

Human Resources: Robert Mientus *DIR-Human Resources*

Total Employees........................1,420
Year Established 1975   **SIC Code**......................................6324

HEALTHSOUTH of Pittsburgh, Inc.

2380 McGinley Rd.
Monroeville, PA 15146
County: Allegheny

Phone: (412) 856-2400
Fax: (412) 856-2437
Internet Address: www.gprh.org

Owner and operator of the HEALTHSOUTH Rehabilitation Hospital of Greater Pittsburgh (Hospital), an 89-bed comprehensive medical rehabilitation facility which is also located at the above address. The Hospital provides inpatient and outpatient medical rehabilitation programs and services, including head injury, spinal cord injury, ventilator independence, orthopaedics and trauma, stroke and young stroke, amputation, arthritis, pain management, general rehabilitation, driver retraining occupational health, outpatient therapy, return-to-work therapy, rehabilitation engineering and aquatic therapy. In addition, the Hospital offers WORKperfect, a Coordinated Care Organization. Outpatient facilities are located in Cranberry Township, Monroeville (2) and Pittsburgh (3), PA. The Company is a subsidiary of HEALTHSOUTH Corp., which is headquartered in Birmingham, AL, and listed on the NYSE.

Officers: Faith A. Deigan *CEO*
Justin Armstrong *DIR-Therapeutic Services*
Geno Bonetti *DIR-Business DEV*
Amber Stanko *DIR-Nursing*
Albert Mirarchi *CON*

Human Resources: Teresa Stranko

Total Employees	400	**Regional Employees**	400
Year Established	1987	**SIC Code**	8093

Heckett MultiServ

612 N. Main St.
Butler, PA 16001
County: Butler

Phone: (412) 283-5741
Fax: (412) 283-3578

Provider of large volume metal reclamation from steelmaking slag. The Company also offers materials handling and environmental services for the worldwide steel industry. The Company is a division of Harsco Corp., which is headquartered in Camp Hill, PA, and listed on the NYSE. The local facility oversees the Company's North and South American operations, with 69 plants located throughout Argentina, Brazil, Canada, Chile, Mexico, Trinidad, Venezuela and the United States. The Company's office in London, England, is responsible for the balance of its worldwide operations consisting of an additional 64 plants located in 20 countries.

Officers: Richard E. Chapla *P*
Edward G. Jaicks *VP-MKT & SAL*

Human Resources: Robert A. Imhof *VP-Human Resources*

Total Employees	6,400	**Regional Employees**	180
Year Established	1939	**SIC Code**	3312
Annual Revenues ($000)	500,000+ (Heckett MultiServ)		

Help-Ur-Self, Inc.

2301 Duss Ave., Ste. 19
Ambridge, PA 15003
County: Beaver

Phone: (412) 251-2100
Fax: (412) 251-2108

H

Retailer of candy and snacks, operating 13 stores under the names, Icky, Sticky and Goo, and Help-Ur-Self. The Company's products are sold primarily from bulk bins. It also sells packaged candy and snacks, and gift items such as containers and bubble gum machines. The Company's stores are located in Auburn, Holyoke and Lanesborough, MA; Nashua, NH; Albany, Niagara Falls and Poughkeepsie, NY; Cincinnati, OH; and Harrisburg and Lancaster, PA; and three Pittsburgh area stores located in Monroeville, Ross Park Mall and the South Hills.

Officers: Stephen M. Silverman *P*

Total Employees............................135	**Regional Employees** 45
Year Established 1989	**SIC Code** 5411
Annual Revenues ($000) 5,500	

Hempfield Foundries Co.

1075 S. Main St.
P.O. Box 69
Greensburg, PA 15601
County: Westmoreland

Phone: (412) 834-6060
Fax: (412) 834-6052

Producer of gray and ductile iron castings for a wide range of end users. The Company's products include flanged pipe fittings in sizes from 6" to 60"; valve bodies from 10" to 54"; automotive die castings for stamping auto body parts to 20,000 lb.; slag pots to 40,000 lb.; and general engineered gray and ductile iron castings from 500 lb. to 40,000 lb.

Officers: Charles O. Rall *CH*
Robert L. Patterson, Jr. *P & CEO*
Donald Hackman *SAL MGR*
Timothy Barnhart *AST-Superintendent*

Human Resources: Paul M. Dominick *Foundry Superintendent*

Purchasing: Rebecca Ann Reiner

Total Employees.............................36	**Regional Employees** 36
Year Established 1907	**SIC Code** 3321

Henderson Bros., Inc.

The Gulf Tower, 707 Grant St., Ste. 2300
Pittsburgh, PA 15219
County: Allegheny

Phone: (412) 261-1842
Fax: (412) 261-4149

Full-service insurance agency representing most major insurance companies and handling all types of insurance products. The Company operates branch offices in Bethel Park and Charleroi, PA, and Weirton, WV, serving clients throughout the Tri-State area. While all of its facilities offer commercial lines of coverage, only the Bethel Park branch also offers personal lines of coverage.

Officers: Daniel P. Grealish *P (Purchasing)*
Thomas B. Grealish *VP & SEC*

Human Resources: Pamela A. Dmitrzak

Total Employees............................66	**Regional Employees** 64
Year Established 1893	**SIC Code** 6411

Henry Printing Co., Chas. M.

Maple Ave. & Tunnel St.
P.O. Box 68
Greensburg, PA 15601
County: Westmoreland

Phone: (412) 834-7600
Fax: (412) 836-7759

Provider of graphic design services, desktop publishing and commercial printing. The Company's specialties include book manufacturing (paperback), large format sheet printing (up to 36" x 49" sheets), foil stamping and embossing, die cutting and gluing. Its specialty products include die-cut pocket folders, full-color art reproductions and high resolution film imaging.

Officers: William M. Henry *CH & TRS*
Charles E. Henry *P & CEO*
Louise H. Boyle *SEC*

Total Employees............................50	**Regional Employees** 50
Year Established 1898	**SIC Code** 2752
Annual Revenues ($000) 4,000	

Hercules, Inc.

Rte. 837
P.O. Box 567
West Elizabeth, PA 15088
County: Allegheny

Phone: (412) 384-2520
Fax: (412) 384-7311

H

Manufacturer of hydrocarbon resins for use in the adhesives, plastics, paint and rubber markets. The Company, which is headquartered in Wilmington, DE, is listed on the NYSE. The local production facility is known as the Jefferson Plant.

Officers: Joseph P. Ziegler *Plant MGR*
Louis R. Sliman *Plant CON*

Human Resources: Jennifer B. Jevens

Purchasing: Jerry P. Lazor

Total Employees........................7,300	**Regional Employees** 300
Year Established 1973	**SIC Code**....................................2821
Annual Revenues ($000)......100,000 (West Elizabeth, PA)	

Herrmann Printing & Litho, Inc.

1709 Douglass Dr.
Pittsburgh, PA 15221
County: Allegheny

Phone: (412) 243-4100
Fax: (412) 731-2268

Provider of professional technical assistance and manufacturing support for the production of marketing literature and other forms of printed communications. The Company's services include consulting, training and technical support for desktop publishing software applications; hardware and software system design and installation support for in-house desktop publishing departments; retouching, cloning and outlining electronic images; and the conversion of digital files into multicolor printed materials such as sales support materials, house organs, magazines, point-of-sale displays and annual reports.

Officers: Eugene V. Herrmann, Jr. *P (Human Resources)*
Jay Migliozzi *VP-SAL*
Jerry Migliozzi *VP-Printing Production*
Rodney A. Herrmann *GMGR*

Purchasing: Tony Iovino

Total Employees............................37	**Regional Employees** 37
Year Established 1956	**SIC Code**....................................2752
Annual Revenues ($000) 5,000	

Hewlett-Packard Co.

111 Zeta Dr.
Pittsburgh, PA 15238
County: Allegheny

Phone: (412) 782-0400
Fax: (412) 784-3340

Manufacturer of computer products, electronic test and measurement instrumentation, medical electronic equipment, analytical instrumentation and electronic components. The Company also provides service and support for its products. The facility at the above address is one of approximately 130 sales offices located across the United States, with many others abroad. The Company, which is headquartered in Palo Alto, CA, is listed on the NYSE.

Officers: Linda Kaufman *Branch Business MGR*

Total Employees....................105,000	Regional Employees 100
Year Established 1939	SIC Code....................................3825
Annual Revenues ($000) 32,000,000	

Heyl & Patterson, Inc.

Three Penn Center W., Ste. 320
P.O. Box 36, Pittsburgh, PA 15230
Pittsburgh, PA 15276
County: Allegheny

Phone: (412) 788-6900
Fax: (412) 788-6913

Manufacturer of bulk material handling equipment, including train car positioners, train car dumpers, barge unloaders and ship loaders. The Company also produces thermal processing equipment such as dryers, coolers, mixers, calciners and pollution control equipment. It operates additional facilities and joint ventures in Sao Paulo, Brazil; Iquique, Chile; Calcutta, India; Queretaro and Tlalnepantla, Mexico; and Lima, Peru. The Company is affiliated with Bridge & Crane Inspection Co., Minneapolis, MN, and Pittsburgh, PA; CCLX Management, Pittsburgh, PA; and Fore Testing Laboratories, Miamisburg, OH.

Officers: Robert M. Turbeville *P & CEO*
  John Edelman *EVP*
  Richard E. Salnick *VP-ENG*

Human Resources: Linda A. Kaczmorski

Total Employees...........................300	Regional Employees 70
Year Established 1887	SIC Code....................................3559
Annual Revenues ($000) 25,000	

Highmark, Inc.

Fifth Avenue Place, 120 Fifth Ave.
Pittsburgh, PA 15222
County: Allegheny

Phone: (412) 255-7000
Fax: (412) 255-5318
Internet Address: www.highmark.com

Nonprofit provider of managed care and indemnity health care services and employee benefits. The Company was created by consolidating the businesses and best practices of Blue Cross of Western Pennsylvania and Pennsylvania Blue Shield. The Company offers managed care programs and traditional indemnity coverage for groups and individuals. Group products include traditional fee-for-service and managed care; SelectBlue (POS); KeystoneBlue (HMO); PreferredBlue (PPO); and SecurityBlue (Medicare HMO). It also offers coverage for older adults and special programs for individuals and families with low to moderate incomes. Individual products include Preferred (reduced rate); Preferred (standard rate); Special Care; Security 65; KeystoneBlue (HMO); SecurityBlue (Medicare HMO); BlueCHIP (HMO); Caring Program (HMO); and Gateway Health Plan (Medicaid HMO). In addition, the Company provides managed care products and networks for supplemental services, including dental, vision and mental health, and offers life, casualty and employee benefits programs. Within the 29 counties of Western Pennsylvania, the Company conducts its health care insurance business as Highmark Blue Cross Blue Shield. In the rest of the state, the Company uses the name Pennsylvania Blue Shield and continues to work with the state's other Blue Cross plans—Capital Blue Cross, which serves 21 counties in Central Pennsylvania; Independence Blue Cross, which serves the five-county Philadelphia area; and Blue Cross of Northeastern Pennsylvania, which serves 13 counties in the Scranton/Wilkes-Barre area. Highmark Blue Cross Blue Shield is an independent licensee of the Blue Cross and Blue Shield Assn. The Company maintains dual operating centers, located at the above address and in Camp Hill, PA, with regional offices in Erie and Johnston, PA. It serves a total of 20.6 million people nationwide under its managed care, medical-surgical, dental, vision, Medicare and medigap programs. The Company's subsidiaries include Alliance Ventures, Inc.; Davis Vision, Inc.; HealthGuard; Keystone Health Plan West, Inc.; Trans-General Life and Casualty Group, Inc.; and United Concordia Cos., Inc.

Officers: Samuel D. Ross, Jr. *CH*
John N. Shaffer *VCH*
William M. Lowry *CEO*
John S. Brouse *P*

Total Employees 12,000	**Regional Employees** 4,060
Year Established 1937	**SIC Code** 6324
Annual Revenues ($000) 6,300,000	

Hilb, Rogal & Hamilton Co. of Pittsburgh, Inc.

333 Forbes Ave.
Pittsburgh, PA 15222
County: Allegheny

Phone: (412) 281-3353
Fax: (412) 281-3276

Provider of risk management, benefit consulting and corporate insurance brokerage services. The local facility is one of approximately 60 branch offices of Hilb, Rogal & Hamilton Co., which is headquartered in Glen Allen, VA, and listed on the NYSE.

Officers: Jack McGrath *P*

Regional Employees......................90
SIC Code 6311

Hill House Assn., The

1835 Centre Ave.
Pittsburgh, PA 15219
County: Allegheny

Phone: (412) 392-4400
Fax: (412) 392-4462
Internet Address: www.hillhouse.ckp.edu

Nonprofit community service organization in the Hill District of Pittsburgh. The Association provides day care; support for the elderly; educational and cultural services for all ages; job training, vocational training, parenting and life skills for young adults; and neighborhood development. Its facilities include the Kay Program Center at 1908 Wylie Ave. in Pittsburgh, PA, providing boxing and other fitness programs for residents of the Hill District community; Senior Service Center at 2038 Bedford Ave. in Pittsburgh, PA, providing services and programs for senior citizens; and Youth Fair Chance at 2851 Bedford Ave. in Pittsburgh, PA, providing services to high school-aged children and young adults. The Association also manages the Hill House Center, a collaboration of 19 independent social, health, educational and housing agencies.

Officers: William H. Isler *P*
James F. Henry *EDIR*
Carl Redwood, Jr. *AST-DIR*

Total Employees............................125
Year Established 1964

Regional Employees 125
SIC Code......................................8322

Hillman Co., The

Grant Bldg., 310 Grant St., Ste. 1900
Pittsburgh, PA 15219
County: Allegheny

Phone: (412) 281-2620
Fax: (412) 338-3520

Investment holding company engaged in a variety of diversified investments and operations, including hospital supplies, biotechnology and energy-related businesses.

Officers: Henry L. Hillman *CH-Executive Comm.*
Carl G. Grefenstette *CH*
Lawrence M. Wagner *CEO & P*
H. Vaughan Blaxter III *VP & GC*
Richard M. Johnston *VP-Investments*
Charles H. Bracken, Jr. *TRS*

Total Employees ....1,500+	**Regional Employees** ....90+
Year Established 1946	**SIC Code** 6719
Annual Revenues ($000) ....1,000,000+	

Hinkel-Hofmann Supply Co., Inc.

1200 Western Ave.
Pittsburgh, PA 15233
County: Allegheny

Phone: (412) 231-3131
Fax: (412) 231-4404

Wholesale distributor of building products, including roofing and ceiling materials, and floor coverings, including carpeting, hardwood flooring, and ceramic and resilient floor tiles. The Company also manufactures vinyl windows. Its products are marketed through a variety of channels, including building supply retailers, carpet dealers and contractors, primarily in the Tri-State area.

Officers: Edgar W. Michaels *P*

Human Resources: Arnold Sopko

Total Employees..............................40	**Regional Employees** 40
Year Established 1927	**SIC Code** 3442

Hipwell Manufacturing Co.

831 W. North Ave.
Pittsburgh, PA 15233
County: Allegheny

Phone: (412) 231-7310
Fax: (412) 231-4456

Manufacturer and marketer of flashlights and lanterns. The Company's products are sold to a variety of industrial accounts and retailers (primarily the hardware market). It also manufactures products for clients under their private labels.

Officers: Harry H. Hipwell, Sr. *P*
Harry H. Hipwell, Jr. *VP*

Human Resources: John Siemon *Plant MGR (Purchasing)*

Total Employees............................40	**Regional Employees** 40
Year Established 1887	**SIC Code**....................................3648
Annual Revenues ($000)...<5,000		

HJM Enterprises, Inc.

4030 William Flynn Hwy. (Rte. 8)
Allison Park, PA 15101
County: Allegheny

Phone: (412) 487-3332
Fax: (412) 487-3401

Contractor specializing in insurance repair and restoration, doing business as FireDEX of Pittsburgh. The Company has the staff, equipment and facilities to handle the restoration of any residential or commercial property, including structure cleaning, contents cleaning and complete construction services. The Company also offers 24-hour emergency service, which enables it to respond immediately to any property claims in Southwestern Pennsylvania. The facility located at the above address includes over 12,500 square feet of warehouse space. This enables the Company to provide on-site deodorization and cleaning. Furthermore, its warehouse contains a three-story bay and overhead crane which provide storage space large enough for the contents of up to 12 average size homes at any time. The Company operates a branch facility off Rte. 286 on Old Frankstown Rd. in Murrysville, PA.

Officers: Steven J. Manley *P*
David M. Hood *VP & GMGR*

Human Resources: Margaret A. Lefebvre

Total Employees............................58	**Regional Employees** 58
Year Established 1987	**SIC Code**....................................1542

HMR Communications, Inc.

10 Communications Way
West Newton, PA 15089
County: Westmoreland

Phone: (412) 872-8220
Fax: (412) 872-8721

Manufacturer of electronic and electromechanical products, including highway distance measuring instruments, highway survey systems, computer-controlled small parts casting machines and musical instrument tuners. The Company has the facilities for complete in-house production, including a plant for the manufacture of blank printed circuit boards, a production shop used for printed circuit assembly and a machine shop for mechanical parts fabrication. It also offers a design group to assist clients with new product designs.

Officers: Henry Robbins, Jr. *P*

Total Employees 45	**Regional Employees** 45
Year Established 1974	**SIC Code** 3829
Annual Revenues ($000) 2,373	

Hoechstetter Printing Co.

218 N. Braddock Ave.
Pittsburgh, PA 15208
County: Allegheny

Phone: (412) 241-8200
Fax: (412) 242-3835

Provider of commercial printing services which claims to be the largest full-service commercial printer in Western Pennsylvania. The Company operates a fully electronic prepress with scanning, photo retouching and desktop publishing capabilities, a DuPont Waterproof color proofing system, and offers customer workshops and training. It also operates four-, five-, six- and seven-color (with in-line aqueous coater) Heidelberg sheetfed presses and a six-color Miller half-web press complete with finishing equipment for in-line die-cutting, perforating, gluing, folding and trimming. Its bindery services include perfect binding, saddle stitching, pocket folder gluing, foil stamping, embossing and die-cutting. The Company serves clients in more than 30 states. It is a subsidiary of Graphic Industries, Inc., which is headquartered in Atlanta, GA, and listed on the NASDAQ.

Officers: Robert Hreha *P*
          Jake Zoller *VP-MFG*

Human Resources: Sheree Hutter-Lucas *Human Resources DIR*

Purchasing: Don Flory

Total Employees............................215	**Regional Employees** 215
Year Established 1963	**SIC Code**......................................2752
Annual Revenues ($000) 30,000	

Holiday Inn Green Tree

401 Holiday Dr.
Pittsburgh, PA 15220
County: Allegheny

Phone: (412) 922-8100
Fax: (412) 922-6511

Hotel featuring 200 guest rooms. Its facilities include an outdoor heated swimming pool and pool bar, an exercise room, and Harlan T. Longnecker's Original Saloon and Eatery. With the recent addition of a new ballroom, the Hotel now offers more than 11,000 square feet of function space. It is owned by Servico, Inc., which is headquartered in West Palm Beach, FL, and listed on the ASE.

Officers: Thomas J. Becek *GMGR*
David J. Keenan *DIR-SAL*

Human Resources: Jackie Adams

Total Employees............................130	**Regional Employees** 130
Year Established 1972	**SIC Code** 7011
Annual Revenues ($000) 7,000	

Holiday Inn Pittsburgh South

164 Fort Couch Rd.
Pittsburgh, PA 15241
County: Allegheny

Phone: (412) 833-5300
Fax: (412) 833-7520

Hotel featuring 202 guest rooms and 8 suites. It also contains banquet and meeting facilities totaling 6,600 square feet with a 500-person capacity for sitdown dinners, Georgine's restaurant, the Silhouette Lounge, a gift shop and an outdoor pool. The Hotel is owned by S.M.I.S. and is operated by Suburban Lodging Corp. The Hotel was formerly known as the Sheraton Inn-South Hills.

Officers: Donald F. Bagnato *P*
Frank A. Rota *GMGR*
Chris Bagnato *OPR AST*

Human Resources: Matt Veres

Total Employees..........................145	Regional Employees 145	
Year Established 1967	SIC Code 7011	
Annual Revenues ($000)...5,000+		

Holiday Inn Select University Center H

100 Lytton Ave.
Pittsburgh, PA 15213
County: Allegheny

Phone: (412) 682-6200
Fax: (412) 682-5745
Internet Address: www.fosterselect.com

Hotel featuring 251 guest rooms and three suites. Its facilities include an indoor pool, 15 meeting rooms, banquet and exhibit space, and Foster's Bar & Grill. The Hotel is owned by the Schenley Hotel Assoc. and is managed by Bristol Hotels & Resorts.

Officers: Dennis Burrell *GMGR*

Human Resources: Daniele Crisi

Purchasing: Dave Matzie

Total Employees..........................217	Regional Employees 217
Year Established 1988	SIC Code 7011
Annual Revenues ($000)...10,000	

Holiday Travel International

12239 Rte. 30
Irwin, PA 15642
County: Westmoreland

Phone: (412) 863-7500
Fax: (412) 863-7590
Internet Address: cyberburg.com/holiday

Travel agency providing a variety of travel-related services for corporate clients and individuals. The Agency also offers wholesale programs for other travel agencies nationwide and consulting services. It states that it is the official travel agency for the Commonwealth of Pennsylvania. The Agency operates branch offices in Belle Vernon, Bethel Park, Harrisburg, Indiana, Pittsburgh and West Mifflin, PA.

Officers: Philip Petrulli *P*
Dorothy Petrulli *VP*

Total Employees..........................36	
Year Established 1971	SIC Code 4724
Annual Revenues ($000) 16,000	

Holy Family Institute

8235 Ohio River Blvd.
Pittsburgh, PA 15202
County: Allegheny

Phone: (412) 766-4030
Fax: (412) 766-5434

Nonprofit provider of support, care and professional treatment services to abused and neglected children and families in crisis. The Institute offers a variety of programs, including teen parenting, family preservation, youth counseling, parent education, family counseling, specialized foster care, group foster care and partial hospitalization. It also contracts with school districts to provide school-based mental health services; operates the Alternative Learning Center, an alternative special education school to rehabilitate children identified with social, emotional and learning difficulties; operates a summer day camp in Homewood, PA, for inner-city youth; and helped establish the Institute for Learning Disabilities in 1996. In addition, it operates a 10-acre residential facility in Emsworth, PA, which serves as a temporary home for approximately 85 abused and neglected children between the ages of six and 18. The Institute helps more than 2,000 families and 600 children each year throughout Southwestern Pennsylvania by the organization's programs and services. Its other community offices are located at 422 Third Ave. in Ford City, PA; 605 E. 10th Ave. in Homestead, PA; 324 Munson Ave. in McKees Rocks, PA; and 211 N. Whitfield St. in Pittsburgh, PA. The Institute is a non-denominational organization that is owned and operated by the Sisters of the Holy Family of Nazareth.

Officers: Sister Linda Yankoski *EDIR*
Frederick A. Massey, Jr. *CAO*
Deborah Gooden *Program Services Administrator*
Larry McKinney *Community Initiative Administrator*
Melissa A. Walls *DIR-DEV*

Human Resources: Kim Radler-Smith *DIR-Human Resources*

Total Employees............................300	**Regional Employees** 300
Year Established 1900	**SIC Code**.....................................8361
Annual Revenues ($000) 11,330	

Honeywell Home and Building Controls

1005 S. Bee St.
Pittsburgh, PA 15220
County: Allegheny

Phone: (412) 928-4217
Fax: (412) 928-4266

Provider of controls for heating, ventilating, humidification and air-conditioning equipment; security and fire alarm systems; energy-efficient lighting controls; and building management systems and devices. A key component of the Company's local service organization is its Comprehensive Technical Services (CTS) program. The CTS program focuses on upgrading the plant infrastructure and managing facilities of industry and manufacturers to increase efficiency, productivity and quality while reducing energy costs and process scrap. The CTS program makes every effort to preserve and upgrade each plant's existing equipment and introduces new technologies as needed. The local facility is a branch office of Honeywell Home and Building Controls (HHBC), which is headquartered in Minneapolis, MN. HHBC is a division of Honeywell, Inc., which is also headquartered in Minneapolis, MN, and listed on the NYSE. Other regional branch offices are located in Harrisburg, Wilkes-Barre and Valley Forge, PA, as well as various locations in major cities across the United States.

Officers: Rich J. Majcher *Pittsburgh GMGR*

Regional Employees....................105
Year Established........................1885   **SIC Code**....................................3822

Hoogovens Technical Services, Inc.

200 Fleet St., Ste. 6000
Pittsburgh, PA 15220
County: Allegheny

Phone: (412) 937-0183
Fax: (412) 937-0187

Provider of engineering and contracting services, offering a variety of technologies and services to the coke, iron, steel and aluminum manufacturing industries. The Company also provides related technological and operational assistance, rolling mill technology, energy and environmental services and feasibility studies. The Company is a subsidiary of Koninklijke Hoogovens B.V., which is headquartered in Ijmuiden, The Netherlands. The Company is the U.S. headquarters of the Hoogovens Technical Services companies. It serves clients in the United States and Latin America and works in cooperation with the other Hoogovens Technical Services companies to serve clients worldwide. It operates additional full-service offices in Merrillville, IN; Burlington and Sault Ste. Marie, Ontario, Canada.

Officers: Nico G. J. Bleijendaal *P & CEO*
David Marshall *COO*
Glenn MacDonald *CFO*
Mark Brandon *VP-OPR*

Human Resources: Cheryl Lukaszewicz

Purchasing: Thomas R. Levenson

Total Employees..........................265   **Regional Employees** 67
Year Established........................1989   **SIC Code**....................................8711
Annual Revenues ($000)...58,000

Horix Manufacturing Co.

1384 Island Ave.
P.O. Box 9324, Pittsburgh, PA 15225
McKees Rocks, PA 15136
County: Allegheny

Phone: (412) 771-1111
Fax: (412) 331-8599
Internet Address: www.sgi.net/horix

Designer, manufacturer, tester and servicer of filling systems used to package free-flowing liquids into bottles, jars and cans. The Company's products include container unscramblers, rinsers, fillers, labelers, packers, wrappers, coolers and warmers. Its machines have packaged millions of gallons of sauces, juices, wines, distilled spirits, detergents, pharmaceuticals, ketchup, cooking oils, chemicals, automotive products and countless other materials. Its systems are operating in major manufacturing and processing plants in over 45 countries. The Company maintains branch sales offices in Clearwater, FL, and Atlanta, GA.

Officers: Frank B. Fairbanks *OWN*
Robert G. Hodinko *P*
Robert P. Semich *TRS*

Human Resources: John L. Brown

Purchasing: Bruce H. Large

Total Employees..............................44	Regional Employees 42
Year Established 1922	SIC Code.....................................3565
Annual Revenues ($000) 6,000	

Horovitz, Rudoy & Roteman

Lawyers Bldg., 428 Forbes Ave., Ste. 900
Pittsburgh, PA 15219
County: Allegheny

Phone: (412) 391-2920
Fax: (412) 391-4703
Internet Address: www.hrrcpa.com

Certified public accounting firm serving closely held businesses and high technology, manufacturing and nonprofit organizations. The Firm provides a variety of professional services including business valuation and litigation support. It primarily serves clients located in the Pittsburgh metropolitan area.

Officers: Israel J. Rudoy *MPTR*

Total Employees..............................48	Regional Employees 48
Year Established 1956	SIC Code.....................................8721

Hospital Council of Western Pennsylvania, The

500 Commonwealth Dr.
Warrendale, PA 15086
County: Allegheny
Phone: (412) 776-6400
Fax: (412) 776-6969

Nonprofit membership organization providing its members with representation and advocacy, information, education, shared resources and management assistance in the health care field. The Organization serves 88 of the region's acute care and specialty hospitals, long-term care facilities and rehabilitation centers as well as 40 allied and associate members from throughout the 30 counties comprising Western Pennsylvania. The Organization has several affiliate companies, which are all located at the above address. Administrative Resources, Inc. (ARI) has been providing services to health care and community organizations for more than 10 years to facilitate cost reduction, income production, management effectiveness, educational opportunities and quality improvement. Through ValuCare, ARI provides its 690-participating member facilities with the most comprehensive and competitive group purchasing program available to nonacute care facilities in the nation. Healthcare Information Corp. (HIC), the Organization's only for-profit subsidiary, focuses its resources and efforts on fulfilling the growing information and technological needs of the council, its family of companies and their members. Hospital Shared Services (HSS) serves the needs of its members, which are more than 510 hospitals located in 13 states. As a founding partner of AmeriNet, one of the largest hospital group purchasing organizations in the nation, HSS continues to position itself as a leading resource for its participating organizations through cost-reducing contracts and programs, management services and educational opportunities. Other affiliates include Health and Hospitals, Inc. and Health Knowledge Systems.

Officers: Ian G. Ranson, Ph.D. *P*
John Laslavic *EVP-Hospital Shared Services*
Neil Bohnent *VP*
Debbie Ference *VP-Center for Health Careers*
Lynne Robinson *VP-Public Affairs*
Vic Samalovitch *VP-MKT*
Walter Wayne *VP-FIN*

Human Resources: Marc Cammarata *VP-Human Resources*

Purchasing: William Poutous

Total Employees............................150	**Regional Employees** 150	
Year Established 1941	**SIC Code**......................................7389	

Houston Harbaugh, P.C.

Two Chatham Center, 12th Fl.
Pittsburgh, PA 15219
County: Allegheny

Phone: (412) 281-5060
Fax: (412) 281-4499
Internet Address: www.hh-law.com

Provider of legal services with 30 attorneys. The Firm's practice areas include general corporate, commercial litigation, insurance defense, health law, estate planning and administration, labor and employment law, municipal law and finance, pension and benefits, creditors' rights, tax and environmental.

Officers: Gregory A. Harbaugh *P*
Michael J. Dempster *SEC*
John D. Houston II *TRS*

Human Resources: Keith Cameron *EDIR (Purchasing)*

Total Employees	62	**Regional Employees**	62
Year Established	1975	**SIC Code**	8111

Huckestein, Inc., James E.

200 Poplar St.
Pittsburgh, PA 15223
County: Allegheny

Phone: (412) 781-5750
Fax: (412) 781-9562

Provider of mechanical construction services, including process piping, heating, refrigeration, mechanical maintenance, plumbing, ventilating, temperature control, sheet metal, air conditioning, lighting control, security access and energy management through direct digital control (facility automation specialist for Andover Control Co.). The Company serves commercial, institutional and industrial clients in the Pittsburgh metropolitan area.

Officers: James E. Huckestein *CH*
James K. Jennings *C-OWN & P*
Blanche B. Huckestein *C-OWN, SEC & TRS*
Jerry Markovich *CON*

Total Employees	75	**Regional Employees**	75
Year Established	1977	**SIC Code**	1711
Annual Revenues ($000)			11,000

Hunter's Truck Sales & Service, Inc.

101 E. Main St.
Eau Claire, PA 16030
County: Butler

Phone: (412) 791-2525
Fax: (412) 791-2837

Full-service truck dealer claiming to be the largest of its kind in the Tri-State area. The Company is positioned to be a one stop shopping center for any types of medium or heavy truck needs. It sells new International and Peterbilt heavy and medium duty trucks; performs all types of repair work, including major and minor repairs, warranty work, collison work, repainting and full-service maintenance; and offers leasing programs and daily truck rentals. The Company is an authorized dealer for Caterpillar Diesel, Cummins Diesel, Dana, Detroit Diesel, Eaton, Fuller, Horton, Jacobs Brake and Rockwell products and carries a $2.5 million parts inventory. Other corporate facilities include Hunter Idealease in Butler, PA; Hunter's Truck Center in Butler, PA; and Hunter's Truck Sales in Butler and Uniontown, PA.

Officers: Homer J. Hunter *P*
Harry J. Hunter *VP*
Robert L. Hunter *SEC & TRS*

Human Resources: Nancy J. Hunter

Total Employees............................170	**Regional Employees** 170
Year Established 1938	**SIC Code** 5511
Annual Revenues ($000) 95,000	

Hussey Copper Ltd.

100 Washington St.
Leetsdale, PA 15056
County: Allegheny

Phone: (412) 251-4200
Fax: (412) 251-4243

Producer of copper and copper alloys.

Officers: Roy Allen *P*

Total Employees............................500	
Year Established 1848	**SIC Code** 3351

IA Construction Corp.

158 Lindsey Rd.
P.O. Box 248
Zelienople, PA 16063
County: Butler

Phone: (412) 452-8621
Fax: (412) 452-0514

Provider of highway and bridge construction services primarily to state and local government entities. The Company also markets bituminous asphalt to a variety of users. It serves customers throughout Delaware, Maryland and Pennsylvania as well as portions of Virginia. The Company, which is headquartered in Concordville, PA, operates a number of branch offices throughout its coverage area.

Officers: Robert Field *EVP*
              George Ausseil *VP-Pennsylvania OPR*
              Jack Rutter *VP*
              Eric Sussman *VP-FIN & TRS*

Total Employees............................850		**Regional Employees** 100	
Year Established 1924		**SIC Code** 1611	
Annual Revenues ($000) 150,000			

ICF Kaiser Engineers, Inc.

Gateway View Plaza, 1600 W. Carson St.
Pittsburgh, PA 15219
County: Allegheny

Phone: (412) 497-2000
Fax: (412) 497-2212
Internet Address: www.icfkaiser.com

Provider of fully integrated engineering, construction and consulting services in the market areas of environment, industry, infrastructure and energy. The Firm, which is headquartered in Fairfax, VA, operates 70 offices around the world. The Pittsburgh facility is a regional office. The Firm is a subsidiary of ICF Kaiser International, Inc., which is also headquartered in Fairfax, VA, and listed on the NYSE. Locally, the Firm's environmental services include audits and assessments, engineering, permitting, pollution control and waste management, contaminated site investigations, site remediation and construction management. Its major environmental projects include construction management for the demolition of the old terminal at Greater Pittsburgh International Airport; air permitting and environmental remediation for PPG Industries; and engineering and construction of an industrial wastewater treatment plant for Aristech Chemical Corp. The Firm provides a full spectrum of process and design engineering, project management, construction and construction management services for domestic and foreign facilities, including those for the iron and steel, coal processing, chemical, nitric acid and aluminum industries. Its major industrial projects include coke-oven and byproducts plant consulting for LTV Steel; on-going engineering, construction and maintenance services for AK Steel; and engineering, design, procurement and construction services for four new nitric acid plants. The Firm's infrastructure services include studies, design and construction management for mass/rapid transit, highway, advanced intelligent transportation systems and public facilities. Its infrastructure projects include architectural and engineering design services for the Airport Busway tunnels and for Phase I of the Martin Luther King Jr. East Busway Extension for the Port Authority of Allegheny County; and ADA updates to 10 key stations for the Greater Cleveland Regional Transit Authority. Locally, the Firm is not presently engaged in any energy-related projects.

Officers: James O. Edwards *CH & CEO*
David Watson *Group P*
Michael F. Gaffney *Group EVP*
Casey E. McGeever *Group SVP-U.S. Eastern OPR*
Paul J. DeCoursey *Group VP-Business DEV*

Human Resources: Geraldine N. Rupert *Human Resources MGR*

Purchasing: Patti J. Andritz *Facility MGR*

Total Employees ....5,000+	**Regional Employees** 260
Year Established 1914	**SIC Code** 8711
Annual Revenues ($000) 1,250,000	

ICM Acquisition Corp.

10 Wood St.
Pittsburgh, PA 15222
County: Allegheny

Phone: (412) 261-2647
Fax: (412) 261-4588
Internet Address: www.icmschool.com

Private, coeducational school, doing business as the ICM School of Business & Medical Careers. The School, which is located in downtown Pittsburgh, reports that its mission is to provide adult students with a quality education necessary for them to enter and succeed in their chosen careers. The School awards the Associate in Specialized Business Degree or Diploma upon the successful completion of the academic requirements for the computer, accounting, business management, fashion merchandising, office administration, travel and tourism, medical assisting and occupational therapy assistant programs. The degree and diploma are approved by the Pennsylvania Department of Education, Division of Academic Program Approval. The School is one of 17 owned by Educational Medical, Inc., which is headquartered in Roswell, GA, and listed on the NASDAQ.

Officers: Gerry Kosentos *EDIR*
Carla M. Ryba *DIR-Education*
Ginger Serafini *DIR-Admissions*

Human Resources: Patty Salopek *DIR-Career Center*

Purchasing: Denise Ringer-Fisher *DIR-FIN*

Total Employees...........................70	Regional Employees 70
Year Established 1963	SIC Code...................................8299
Annual Revenues ($000) 6,000		

IKG Greulich

R.D. 2, Rte. 910
P.O. Box 295
Cheswick, PA 15024
County: Allegheny

Phone: (412) 828-2223
Fax: (412) 828-4103

Manufacturer and marketer of grid-reinforced concrete deck and open grid deck for bridge surfaces. Both product lines offer lightweight, high-strength, high-durability decking that can be quickly and easily installed with reduced on-site labor. The precast and prefabricated panels arrive at the job site ready to be installed, minimizing traffic disruption. The Company is a division of Harsco Corp., which is headquartered in Camp Hill, PA, and listed on the NYSE.

Officers: Fred Beatty *P (Clark, NJ)*
Kurt W. Rorick *GMGR*

Purchasing: Jay Mutschler

Total Employees...........................80	Regional Employees 80
Year Established 1955	SIC Code...................................3441
Annual Revenues ($000) 10,000		

IKM, Inc.

One PPG Place
Pittsburgh, PA 15222
County: Allegheny

Phone: (412) 281-1337
Fax: (412) 281-4639

Provider of architectural, engineering and interior design services, including master planning, new construction, rehabilitation and historic preservation. In addition, the Firm offers services such as facilities operations/maintenance analysis and outsourcing, project development, computer-aided facilities management and sophisticated laboratory design (and related animal quarters). More than

90% of its work is generated by repeat clients, including commercial entities, developers, educational institutions, government, health care, long-term care, manufacturing, and research and development. The Firm has designed classrooms; computer facilities; conference centers with advanced audio-visual and teleconferencing equipment; fitness centers; offices; medical clinics and advanced medical spaces for emergency departments, trauma units, diagnostic imaging, transplant units and special procedures operating rooms; parking garages; and others. Its notable projects include the Pittsburgh Board of Education, Buhl Planetarium, South Side Hospital, a diagnostic/treatment center for the University of Pittsburgh Medical Center and a state-of-the art trauma center for Allegheny General Hospital.

Officers: Mihai Marcu *P & CEO*
Alan Fishman *VP*
Bob Moro *VP*

Human Resources: John Schrott *VP*

Purchasing: Marion Zentarsky *SVP & CFO*

Total Employees..............................49
Year Established 1908
Annual Revenues ($000) 6,000

Regional Employees 49
SIC Code....................................8712

IKON Office Solutions of Western Pennsylvania

Foster Plaza Three, 601 Holiday Dr.
Pittsburgh, PA 15220
County: Allegheny

Phone: (412) 922-5042
Fax: (412) 922-2085
Internet Address: www.ikon.com

Diversified retailer and servicer of office equipment doing business as IKON. The Company's brand names include Canon, Hewlett-Packard, Microsoft, Novell, Oce and Xerox. The Company also offers training for all the products that it carries as well as systems integration and facilities management services. The Company's territory covers Western Pennsylvania, with branch offices in Clarion, Erie and Export, PA, and a service center at 2250 Noblestown Rd. in Pittsburgh, PA. The Company is a marketplace of IKON Office Solutions, Inc., which is headquartered in Valley Forge, PA, and listed on the NYSE.

Officers: Guy Mattola *CH*
Steve Fedell *P*
Pete Bringe *VP-SAL*
Nelson Nemes *VP-Service*

Human Resources: Victor Maciak

Purchasing: Shawn Watkins *DIR-FIN OPR*

Total Employees......................30,000	**Regional Employees**..................215	
Year Established........................1975	**SIC Code**....................................5044	
Annual Revenues ($000)..40,000		

INDSPEC Chemical Corp.

411 Seventh Ave., Ste. 300
Pittsburgh, PA 15219
County: Allegheny

Phone: (412) 765-1200
Fax: (412) 765-0439

Producer of resorcinol, a chemical used primarily as a bonding and stiffening agent in the manufacture of tires and tread rubber. Resorcinol is also used in the manufacture of high performance wood adhesives, ultraviolet light stabilizers, sunscreens, dyestuffs, pharmaceuticals, agrichemicals, carbonless paper and fire-retardant plastic adhesives. The Company claims to be the largest resorcinol producer in the world and the sole producer in the United States, having supplied approximately 90% of the resorcinol sold in the domestic market in 1996. It is also a leading supplier of resorcinol and resorcinol-based products in Europe and Asia. Resorcinol and resorcinol-based products accounted for approximately 96% of the Company's sales in fiscal 1996. The Company markets its products in approximately 50 countries throughout Europe, Asia, Africa and the Near East. It operates a plant in Petrolia, PA, and a sales office in Rotterdam, The Netherlands. The Company is a wholly owned subsidiary of INDSPEC Technologies, Ltd., a Pennsylvania Business Trust, which, in turn, is wholly owned by INDSPEC Holding Corp.

Officers: Frank M. Spinola *P & CEO*

Human Resources: Larry Hines

Total Employees..........................380	**Regional Employees**..................370	
Year Established........................1988	**SIC Code**....................................2869	
Annual Revenues ($000)..131,627		

Industrial Gasket and Shim Co., Inc.

200 Country Club Rd.
P.O. Box 368
Meadow Lands, PA 15347
County: Washington

Phone: (412) 222-5800
Fax: (412) 222-5898

Custom, precision job shop specializing in the manufacture of shims, gaskets and sealants. The Company's metals group produces its Pre-Cut™ brand of tab shims, as well as custom shims, metal stampings, specialty washers and laminated shims out of metals such as aluminum, brass, bronze, copper, carbon steel, stainless steel and zinc. Its processes include laser cutting, computer and numerically controlled turret presses and conventional stamping presses, with capabilities ranging from five tons to 200 tons. The Company's gasket group fabricates such brands as Armstrong, Frenzelit, Garlock and Klinger gaskets from a broad range of materials using hand-cut, die-cut and kiss-cut processes. The Company's sealant group produces its Seal It!™ brand of industrial sealants, operative from -60°F up to 2,950°F, as well as packings, O-rings, V-rings, lathe cuts and four-square cuts. The Company serves clients worldwide.

Officers: Kaye R. Desch *P*
Kinsley M. Desch *VP-OPR*
John W. Hulme *VP-SAL*

Human Resources: Jim Garet

Purchasing: Dave Sphar

Total Employees	110	**Regional Employees**	110
Year Established	1961	**SIC Code**	3053
Annual Revenues ($000)			10,000+

Industrial Rubber Products Co.

726 Trumball Dr.
Pittsburgh, PA 15205
County: Allegheny

Phone: (412) 276-6400
Fax: (412) 276-4900

Distributor of industrial rubber products including hose, conveyor belts, seals, O-rings and metal hose assemblies. The Company's subsidiaries include Rubber Rolls, Inc. in Meadow Lands, PA, which manufactures rubber and polyurethane roll covers, metal roll cores and molded items, and offers metal core repair and replacement; and The Lordstown Corp. in Bessemer, PA, which is an applicator of rubber tank lining materials.

Officers: Frank J. Kelly *CH*
Frank J. Kelly, Jr. *CEO*
Michael C. Kerestes *P*

Human Resources: David W. Schnupp *TRS*

Purchasing: Jack Baird

Total Employees	80	**Regional Employees**	72
Year Established	1954	**SIC Code**	3069

Innovative Carbide, Inc.

11099 Rte. 993
P.O. Box 389
Irwin, PA 15642
County: Westmoreland

Phone: (412) 863-6900
Fax: (412) 863-2573

Manufacturer of tungsten carbide blanks and preforms. The Company sells its products worldwide to finishers in the automotive, oil, computer and can industries, among others.

Officers: Byron Wardropper *P*
Ronald Geckle *VP*

Human Resources: Bethany Wardropper

Purchasing: Richard Bussard

Total Employees	46	**Regional Employees**	46
Year Established	1988	**SIC Code**	2819
Annual Revenues ($000)	7-10,000		

Innovative Systems, Inc.

790 Holiday Dr.
Pittsburgh, PA 15220
County: Allegheny

Phone: (412) 937-9300
Fax: (412) 937-9309
Internet Address: www.innovgrp.com

Provider of integrated client information solutions to the financial industry. With the Company's help, organizations can market and service their clients more effectively by leveraging massive amounts of data on customers, contacts, prospects and suspects. Its solutions incorporate database products that define and organize client data for customer service, profitability analysis and for marketing activities focused on selected individuals, households and other relationship groupings; data quality tools that work with data extract tools to load and maintain data from existing systems; and professional services that include technical consulting, systems integration and outsourcing, and that use methods developed from multiple projects in relevant industries to ensure smooth, dependable implementation. The Company maintains a branch office in London, England.

Officers: Robert J. Colonna *P*
Gary W. Fiedler *COO*

Human Resources: Frank Ruggieri *VP-Human Resources*

Total Employees	120	**Regional Employees**	113
Year Established	1968	**SIC Code**	7371

Institute for Transfusion Medicine, The

3636 Blvd. of the Allies
Pittsburgh, PA 15213
County: Allegheny

Phone: (412) 622-7251
Fax: (412) 687-0787

Nonprofit operator of the Central Blood Bank (CBB). The CBB serves more than 40 hospitals in Western Pennsylvania and Northern West Virginia, providing complete transfusion medicine services, specialized laboratory support and blood center management. It operates as the region's provider of blood through the support of volunteer donors at mobile blood drives and community donor centers in Butler, Coraopolis, Cranberry Township, Grove City, Greenville, McKeesport, McMurray, Monroeville, Natrona Heights, New Kensington, O'Hara Township, Pittsburgh (Downtown, North Hills, Oakland, South Hills and Upper St. Clair) and Washington, PA; and Fairmont and Weirton, WV. The Institute's Centralized Transfusion Services division is a network of integrated transfusion services that supports eight major hospitals in the Pittsburgh area. The Institute's Diagnostics is an entity comprised of the Coagulation Laboratory and the Molecular Immunodiagnostics Laboratory that provides comprehensive diagnostic, consultative and educational services in the areas of coagulation, viral serology and molecular immunodiagnostics. The Institute also operates LifeSource Blood Services in Chicago, IL.

Officers: William H. Portman *P*

Human Resources: Carolyn Barone

Total Employees............................480
Year Established 1950   **SIC Code** 8099

Instrumentation Industries, Inc.

2990 Industrial Blvd.
Bethel Park, PA 15102
County: Allegheny

Phone: (412) 854-1133
Fax: (412) 854-5668

Manufacturer of respiratory care and anesthesia products for hospitals, home care facilities and nursing facilities worldwide. The Company also services critical care equipment and refrigeration systems for hospitals and industry in the Tri-State area.

Officers: Edward C. Horey, Jr. *P*
           Robert Bauer *SAL & MKT MGR*
           Donald Delaney *Production MGR*
           Lori Zuravleff *QA/RA MGR*

Human Resources: Lillian R. Horey

Purchasing: Robert Fargo

Total Employees............................41   **Regional Employees** 41
Year Established 1967   **SIC Code**....................................3841
Annual Revenues ($000) 2,000

Integrated Health Services, Inc.

890 Weatherwood Lane
Greensburg, PA 15601
County: Westmoreland

Phone: (412) 837-8076
Fax: (412) 837-3152
Internet Address: www.ihs-inc.com

Owner and operator of a 120-bed skilled nursing facility, doing business as Integrated Health Services of Greater Pittsburgh. The facility specializes in the subacute care, respiratory therapy (including ventilators) and inpatient rehabilitation. The Company, which is headquartered in Owings Mill, MD, is listed on the NYSE. It operates additional facilities in the Pittsburgh metropolitan area.

Officers: Jim Palmer *EDIR*

Regional Employees....................150
SIC Code 8051

Integration Technology Systems, Inc.

271 Westch Dr.
Mount Pleasant, PA 15666
County: Westmoreland

Phone: (412) 696-3000
Fax: (412) 696-3333
Internet Address: www.icestations.com

Manufacturer and distributor of industrial computer enclosures for use in harsh industrial environments. These include locations with extreme ambient temperatures, airborne dusts or mists, splashing or spraying liquids, dangerous gases, vapors or combustible dusts. The Company claims that its ICE/STATIONS (internally contained environment) are used in most of the top industrial companies in the world and that it is the world's largest manufacturer of computer enclosures.

Officers: Charles J. Matone, Jr. *P*
John T. Spangler *EVP*
James S. Pastierik *VP-SAL & MKT*

Total Employees............................100	**Regional Employees** 100
Year Established 1985	**SIC Code**......................................3572

InterCare Health Systems Ltd.

2575 Boyce Plaza Rd.
Pittsburgh, PA 15241
County: Allegheny

Phone: (412) 257-2290
Fax: (412) 257-0374

Provider of behavioral health care services through two mental health hospitals. The Company operates the 50-bed Southwood Hospital, located at the above address, and the 40-bed Lakewood Hospital, in North Strabane, PA, both of which provide inpatient and outpatient services. These services include residential treatment, day treatment, mental health groups, adventure-based challenge programs, consultation to businesses and schools, in-service training, summer camps for children, speakers' bureau and family-based treatment. The Company also operates InterCare Psychiatric Services, which provides outpatient psychiatric services, and InterCare Options, which is a managed care company, both located at the above address.

Officers: Alan A. Axelson, M.D. *P & Medical DIR; P-Southwood Hospital*
Lynn Struble *Administrator & COO*
Elaine Axelson *SEC & TRS-Southwood Hospital*

Human Resources: Mark Capone

Total Employees............................285	**Regional Employees** 285
Year Established 1979	**SIC Code**......................................8063

Interform Corp.

1901 Mayview Rd.
P.O. Box A
Bridgeville, PA 15017
County: Allegheny

Phone: (412) 221-3300
Fax: (412) 221-6222

Manufacturer of business forms and provider of printing services. The Company, doing business as Interform Solutions, produces business forms, including cut sheets, continuous forms, mailers and unit sets; commercial and direct mail products; and data mailers. It also offers a full-service electronic pre-press department, commercial and direct mail printing, security feature printing to protect valuable documents from fraudulent reproduction, envelope printing, electronic variable imaging, stock tab products, mailing services, affixed-on cards and labels, printing management and warehousing. The Company markets its products through a network of independent distributors concentrated in Eastern Pennsylvania, New Jersey and metropolitan New York, and directly through its Consolidated Graphics Communications division, which is a distributor of graphic printing products, with 14 sales sites in the Tri-State area. The Company is a subsidiary of Champion Industries, Inc., which is headquartered in Huntington, WV, and listed on the NASDAQ.

Officers: David G. Pilcher *P*
Clifford J. Bright *VP-FIN & ADM*
Kark Karch *VP-MFG*
Ted Nowlen *VP-Information Technology*

Human Resources: Tony Nicastro

Purchasing: Jan Potisek

Total Employees	245	**Regional Employees**	220
Year Established	1962	**SIC Code**	2761
Annual Revenues ($000)			34,000

International Business Machines Corp.

Four Allegheny Center
Pittsburgh, PA 15212
County: Allegheny

Phone: (412) 237-7700
Fax: (412) 237-4013

Multinational manufacturer and marketer of information technologies, providing advanced information services and solutions to its clients. The Company, which is also known as IBM, is headquartered in Armonk, NY, and listed on the NYSE. Its local facility offers sales, technical support and a variety of services.

Officers: Theodore Roberts, Jr. *Services Office Executive*

Total Employees	240,000	**Regional Employees**	300
Year Established	1917	**SIC Code**	3577
Annual Revenues ($000)			76,000,000

International Communication Materials, Inc.

Rte. 119 S.
P.O. Box 716
Connellsville, PA 15425
County: Fayette

Phone: (412) 628-1014
Fax: (412) 628-1214

Manufacturer of toners, developers and specialty products that are used in laser printers, copiers and other related imaging equipment. The Company, which does business as ICMI, also produces monocomponent toners, dual component toners, magnetic toners, ionographic toners, high resolution toners, color toners and developers, and ancillary consumable products. In addition, it produces ink jet supplies, remanufactured cartridges, media supplies, ink rolls, photoreceptors, film and fabric ribbons, and thermal transfer ribbons. The Company is a subsidiary of Nu-Kote Holding, Inc., which is headquarterted in Dallas, TX, and listed on the NASDAQ.

Officers: Robert L. Leonard, Jr. *VP-SAL*

Regional Employees.....................135
Year Established 1978   **SIC Code**...................................3861

International Staple & Machine Co.

629 E. Butler Rd.
P.O. Box 629, Butler, PA 16003
Butler, PA 16001
County: Butler

Phone: (412) 287-7711
Fax: (412) 287-2811

Manufacturer of fasteners, such as nails, staples and wire products, for industrial and construction markets nationwide. Also located at the above address are two divisions, Carton Closing Co., a producer of industrial packaging equipment, and Naw Specialty Wire Co., a manufacturer of wire. The Company's other divisions include Air Nail Co. in Southgate, CA, and Container Stapling Co. in Herrin, IL, both of which produce fasteners. The Company is a subsidiary of Atro Industriale S.p.A., which is headquartered in Milan, Italy.

Officers: John Dean *CEO*
            Bill Been *VP-Production*
            Vince Fritz *VP-SAL & MKT*

Human Resources: Mark Kania *CFO*

Purchasing: Paul Lucas

Regional Employees ....120+
Year Established 1938   **SIC Code**...................................3315

Interpose Group, Inc.

326 Center Ave.
Verona, PA 15147
County: Allegheny

Phone: (412) 826-1220
Fax: (412) 826-9224

Provider of managed care consulting services to employers, insurance carriers and third-party administrators in workers' compensation, and short- and long-term disability programs. The Company's services include early telephone case management intervention, on-site field case management, vocational assessments, medical bill and case review, independent medical evaluations, legal nurse consulting, life care plans on catastrophic injuries, liability claim consulting and transitional duty programs for employers. It also offers professional consultants, nurses and vocational counselors at 15 locations throughout Pennsylvania and West Virginia. The Company is an affiliate of Amerisys, which is headquartered in Orlando, FL.

Officers: Mark L. Heckman *C-OWN & P*
Sharon L. Mains *C-OWN & EVP*
Deborah Fauth *Certified Case MGR*
Jackie Lentz *Certified Case MGR*
Ann Riemenschneider *Certified Case MGR*

Human Resources: Charlotte Chesler *(Purchasing)*

Total Employees..............................38
Year Established.........................1982

Regional Employees 25
SIC Code......................................8742

Interstate Brands Corp.

1700 Island Ave.
Pittsburgh, PA 15233
County: Allegheny

Phone: (412) 231-2000
Fax: (412) 231-7242

Bakery producing bread and baked goods marketed under the brand names Hostess Cake, Towntalk Bread and Wonder Bread. The Company wholesales its products to supermarkets, grocery stores and convenience stores in the Tri-State area. The Company is headquartered in Kansas City, MO. It is a subsidiary of Interstate Bakeries Corp., which is also headquartered in Kansas City, MO, and listed on the NYSE.

Officers: Jeffrey Nutt *GMGR*

Human Resources: Marilynn Brown *Human Resource MGR*

Regional Employees....................200
SIC Code 2051

Interstate Paper Supply Co., Inc.

103 Good St.
P.O. Box 670
Roscoe, PA 15477
County: Washington

Phone: (412) 938-2218
Fax: (412) 938-3415

Manufacturer of converted packaging products. The Company is also known as IPSCO.

Officers: Bart R. Raitano *P*
Robert Milinski *VP & GMGR*
Edwin J. Raitano *VP & TRS*
Mark B. Raitano *VP & SEC*

Total Employees..............................85
Year Established 1950   **SIC Code**....................................2679

Intex Corp.

931 Rte. 51 & Worthington Ave.
P.O. Box 18509, Pittsburgh, PA 15236
Clairton, PA 15025
County: Allegheny

Phone: (412) 384-3310
Fax: (412) 384-3240

Provider of diversified computer related services. The Company offers data entry services to an expanding network of clients in several states as well as in the Pittsburgh metropolitan area, currently serving over 40 organizations. These services include document scanning; input and verification of all business documents, surveys, medical records, inventories, payrolls and data for Internet; output to tape, diskette, data communications to customer, computer or transmission via Internet; quality control of documents coupled with balancing routines; litigation support; data conversions and data base input; and courier service. The Company also offers AS/400 computer outsourcing services, networking products and services, and application software and hardware, PC networking products and installation services. It maintains a data entry branch facility at 170 Bilmar Dr. in Kennedy Township, PA.

Officers: Louis R. Funaiock *P*
Albert J. Suess *VP-OPR*

Human Resources: Joyce Bernard

Purchasing: Pamela Hill

Total Employees..............................50   **Regional Employees** 50
Year Established 1995   **SIC Code**....................................7374
Annual Revenues ($000) 1,000

Ionics, Inc.

3039 Washington Pike
Bridgeville, PA 15017
County: Allegheny

Phone: (412) 257-2029
Fax: (412) 221-7110
Internet Address: www.ionics.com

Manufacturer of water treatment equipment and provider of stainless steel fabrication services. The Company's consumer and household water products include water softeners, reverse osmosis filters and silver carbon filters. Its custom-fabricated products include separators, fans and wheels for commercial nuclear, navy nuclear, Department of Energy and Department of Defense applications. The Company, which is headquartered in Watertown, MA, is listed on the NYSE.

Officers: Joseph M. Loftis, Sr. *VP*

Human Resources: James Melani *(Purchasing)*

Regional Employees....................150
Year Established 1941   **SIC Code** 3589
Annual Revenues ($000) 300,000

Iron Age Holdings Corp.

Robinson Plaza Three, Ste. 400
Pittsburgh, PA 15205
County: Allegheny

Phone: (412) 787-4100
Fax: (412) 787-8112

Holding company engaged in the manufacturing and marketing of footwear through its subsidiary operations. Iron Age Corp. (IAC), which is also headquartered at the above address, claims to be one of the oldest and largest suppliers of industrial safety footwear in North America. Its line of more than 280 styles includes sport boots, work boots, casuals, dress, hikers, waterproof boots and slip-resistant footwear. All IAC safety footwear is manufactured in accordance with ANSI Z41 1991 standards in all six categories of shoe protection—impact and compression, metatarsal, electrical hazard, puncture-resistant, conductive and electrostatic dissipative. IAC's footwear is sold through a nationwide Company-owned distribution network of 74 regional retail/distribution centers, 115 shoemobiles and a factory direct mail-order operation. In addition, it distributes products through in-plant safety shoe stores to workers at large industrial corporations. IAC's other segments include Iron Age Canada, Iron Age Mexico and the Iron Age Branded Wholesale Division. The Company's other businesses include the Dunham Shoe Co. in Lewiston, ME; Falcon Shoe Manufacturing Co. in Lewiston, ME; and the Knapp Shoe Co. in Penn Yan, NY, which includes the

Knapp Retail Shoe Division and the Knapp Direct Marketing Footwear Division. The Company's products are manufactured at its two plants in Lewiston, ME, or are produced through an international network of manufacturers of industrial footwear both in the U.S. and off-shore. The Company also maintains a warehouse and distribution center in Penn Yan, NY. Its brand names include Armor 75 X-tra Lite, Dunham, Duraflex, Grabber, Iron Age, Knapp, Knapp Two-Shot, Mighty Tough, Sport Work and Wide-Trak.

Officers: Donald R. Jensen *CH, P & CEO*
William J. Mills *EVP*
Max Rush *SVP*
Keith McDonough *VP-FIN & CFO*
Donald Stella *VP-MKT*
Ted Johanson *P-MFG*

Human Resources: Patti Boyle

Purchasing: Willie Taaffe *Corporate VP-OPR & Distribution*

Total Employees	729	**Regional Employees**	89
Year Established	1817	**SIC Code**	5139
Annual Revenues ($000)	125,000		

Iron City Industrial Cleaning Corp.

6640 Frankstown Ave.
P.O. Box 5361
Pittsburgh, PA 15206
County: Allegheny

Phone: (412) 661-2001
Fax: (412) 661-9356

Provider of uniform rental and service programs for all types of businesses and industries. The Company also offers an entrance and safety mat rental service. Its Dust Control Services and Iron City Uniform Rental divisions operate out of the above address and at a facility located in Delmont, PA, and its Industrial Uniform Rental division operates out of Tipton, PA. The Company serves clients throughout the Tri-State region.

Officers: Arthur Sonnenklar *CH*
Jed Zidell *P*

Human Resources: Steve Lazur

Purchasing: James Bell

Total Employees	150	**Regional Employees**	120
Year Established	1928	**SIC Code**	7218
Annual Revenues ($000)	9,000		

Iron City Sash & Door Co.

631 Iron City Dr.
Pittsburgh, PA 15205
County: Allegheny

Phone: (412) 928-2850
Fax: (412) 922-3480

Wholesale distributor of windows and doors to building supply retailers. The Company operates distribution centers in Baltimore, MD; Rochester, NY; Massillon, OH; and Sandy Lake and Windber, PA. Its manufacturing division, Triad Door Co., is located in North Lima, OH. The Company serves customers throughout Maryland, New York, Ohio, Pennsylvania and West Virginia.

Officers: Gary D. Brown *P*

Human Resources: Jane Dixon *CFO*

Purchasing: Frank Lalama

Total Employees	400	Regional Employees	45
Year Established	1952	SIC Code	5031
Annual Revenues ($000)	130,000		

Isiklar Brick, Inc.

602 Morris St.
P.O. Box 346
Darlington, PA 16115
County: Beaver

Phone: (412) 827-2700
Fax: (412) 827-2974

Manufacturer of brick operating through two subsidiaries. Darlington Brick and Clay Products Co., which is also located at the above address, manufactures and distributes face brick and paving brick, and imports and distributes marble from Turkey. Powell & Minnock Brick Works, Inc. in Coeymans, NY, manufactures and distributes face brick, molded brick and paving brick. The Company primarily serves clients east of the Mississippi River.

Officers: Glen O. Hein *P*
                Edward Adams *CON*
                Alan Buglione *SAL MGR*

Total Employees	160	Regional Employees	75
Year Established	1896	SIC Code	3251

Itam Techint Italimpianti, Inc.

Cherrington Corporate Center, 100 Corporate Center Dr.
Coraopolis, PA 15108
County: Allegheny

Phone: (412) 262-2240
Fax: (412) 262-3064

Designer and builder of industrial plants and equipment for the iron and steel-making industry. The Company's product line includes reheat and heat treating furnaces, computer process controls, material handling equipment, and strip processing lines, including galvanizing, pickling, electrolytic tinning, annealing, cleaning, coil preparation and tension leveling lines. Its services include technical and economic feasibility studies, computerized operational simulation studies, engineering, process control by computer, erection and installation, training of personnel, and start-up and operational assistance. The Company primarily serves clients in North America. It is a subsidiary of Techint, which is headquartered in Milan, Italy.

Officers: Gianluigi Nova *P & CEO*
Giuseppe Facco *VP & DIR-FIN Department*
Norman T. Ferguson *VP-SAL & Technology*

Human Resources: Martin Clancy

Purchasing: Anthony Celli

Total Employees............................100	**Regional Employees** 100
Year Established 1979	**SIC Code** 8711

J. V. Manufacturing Co., Inc.

1603 Burtner Rd.
Natrona Heights, PA 15065
County: Allegheny

Phone: (412) 224-1704
Fax: (412) 224-7728
Internet Address: www.salsgiver.com/jvmfgco

Designer and builder of carbide progressive stamping dies for the metalworking industry.

Officers: John C. Vecchi *P*
Samuel A. Gruber *VP*
Alan M. Vecchi *Plant MGR*

Human Resources: Richard Celecki *(Purchasing)*

Total Employees..............................92	**Regional Employees** 92
Year Established 1975	**SIC Code** 3544

J. W. Steel Fabricating Co.

Mars Industrial Park
P.O. Box 174, Evans City, PA 16033
Mars, PA 16046
County: Butler

Phone: (412) 625-1355
Fax: (412) 625-2966

Fabricator of structural and specialty steel for a variety of applications, including platework, tanks, bins, conveyors, platforms, handrails, ductwork and heat exchangers, to customer specifications. The Company primarily serves clients in the eastern U.S. in a variety of industries, including steel and coal, as well as contractors. Its affiliate, Fey Steel Fabricating Co., is also located at the above address.

Officers: James H. Watts *P (Purchasing)*
       Robert J. Fey *VP*

Human Resources: Ginette M. Novak *CON*

Total Employees............................50	**Regional Employees** 50	
Year Established 1985	**SIC Code**....................................3441	
Annual Revenues ($000) 100,000		

J&L Structural, Inc.

111 Station St.
Aliquippa, PA 15001
County: Beaver

Phone: (412) 378-6490
Fax: (412) 378-6493

Manufacturer of lightweight hot-rolled structural shapes, junior I-beams and channels along with limited standard beam sections. The Company's products are used in a variety of applications, including manufactured housing, truck trailers and highway guard rail systems. It operates two divisions, the Ambridge division in Ambridge, PA, and the Brighton Electric division in Beaver Falls, PA. The Company is a subsidiary of CPT Holdings, Inc., which is headquartered in New York, NY.

Officers: Howell A. Breedlove *P & CEO*
       James E. Howe *VP & SEC*
       Carl A. Snyder *VP & TRS*

Human Resources: M. Edward Murphy *MGR-Human Resources*

Purchasing: Robert L. Mulholland

Total Employees...........................260	**Regional Employees** 260	
Year Established 1987	**SIC Code**....................................3325	
Annual Revenues ($000) 120,000		

Janney Montgomery Scott, Inc.

Koppers Bldg., 436 Seventh Ave., Ste. 2800
Pittsburgh, PA 15219
County: Allegheny

Phone: (412) 565-3219
Fax: (412) 565-3223

Full-service regional securities investment firm. The Company claims to be the oldest and largest of its kind headquartered in Pennsylvania. It provides an array of products and services for individuals, institutions, corporations and the public sector, offering such services as research, money management, investment advisory, personal financial planning, insurance, mutual funds, syndicates and new issue sales, venture capital and public finance. The Company is a subsidiary of Penn Mutual Life Insurance Co., both of which are headquartered in Philadelphia, PA. It operates more than 40 full-service investment offices throughout Connecticut, Delaware, Massachusetts, New Jersey, New York, Ohio, Pennsylvania, Rhode Island, Virginia and Washington, D.C. Other Pittsburgh area offices are located in Ligonier and McMurray, PA.

Officers: Rudolph Sander *CH*
Norman T. Wilde, Jr. *P*
James Wolitarsky *CFO*
Lawrence Hunt *VP & Branch MGR-McMurray, PA*
Philip A. Kontul *VP & Branch MGR-Pittsburgh, PA*
Walter Saling, Jr. *VP & Branch MGR-Ligonier, PA*

Human Resources: Mary Ann Melchiorre

Total Employees.........................1,500   **Regional Employees** 60
Year Established 1832   **SIC Code** 6211

Jarrell & Rea, Inc.

1422 Smallman St.
Pittsburgh, PA 15222
County: Allegheny

Phone: (412) 261-1420
Fax: (412) 642-2826

Wholesale distributor of seafood products sold primarily to restaurants and grocery stores within the Pittsburgh region. The Company operates a branch office, Silver Sea Sales, in Baltimore, MD.

Officers: James M. Rea, Jr. *P & CEO (Purchasing)*
Thomas R. Rea *EVP*
Mark Maehling *VP*

Human Resources: Harriett M. Rea *SEC*

Total Employees............................70 Regional Employees 35
Year Established ....1932 SIC Code....................................5146
Annual Revenues ($000) 20,000

JDS Fashions, Inc.

601 Hansen Ave.
Butler, PA 16001
County: Butler

Phone: (412) 282-1111
Fax: (412) 282-1135

Manufacturer of knit and woven active wear and work clothing. The Company produces apparel under contract for other enterprises and under its own label, Chameleon, for distribution to retailers nationwide.

Officers: James B. Rice *P*
Steven Sloboda *VP*

Total Employees............................50 Regional Employees 50
Year Established ....1987 SIC Code....................................2326
Annual Revenues ($000) 1,000

Jeannette Healthpace Corp.

600 Jefferson Ave.
Jeannette, PA 15644
County: Westmoreland

Phone: (412) 527-3551
Fax: (412) 527-9430

Nonprofit operator of the Jeannette District Memorial Hospital which is also located at the above address and is a full-service community hospital with 181-beds and over 200 physicians. The hospital's specialized services include acute care; the Ambulatory Outpatient Center, which provides personalized care for all outpatient procedures; The Family Birth Place, which offers complete single room maternity care; The Rehabilitation Center, a 16-bed inpatient unit; The Skilled Nursing Center, an 11-bed transitional care unit; Joslin Diabetes Center Satellite facility; and The Sleep Disorders Center. Satellite sites include the All About Health Resource and Education Center, in Greensburg, PA; Norwin HealthCare Center, in North Huntingdon, PA; and Outpatient Therapies Center, in Jeannette, PA.

Officers: Paul Smiy *CH*
Robert J. Bulger *P; P-Jeannette District Memorial Hospital*
John Lapina *TRS; CH-Jeannette District Memorial Hospital*
Robert A. MacGregor *VP-Diagnostic/Support Services-Jeannette*

District Memorial Hospital
Justin G. Rushin, Jr. *VP-Financial Services-Jeannette District Memorial Hospital*
Margaret Walters *VP-Nursing Services-Jeannette District Memorial Hospital*

Human Resources: Patti Sunder *VP-Human Resources*

Total Employees	712	**Regional Employees**	712
Year Established	1959	**SIC Code**	8062
Annual Revenues ($000)	40,669		

Jeannette Shade & Novelty Co.

N. 4th St.
P.O. Box 99
Jeannette, PA 15644
County: Westmoreland

Phone: (412) 523-5567
Fax: (412) 523-0123

Manufacturer of glass, specializing in pressed borosilicate glass parts primarily for the indoor, outdoor, architectural and industrial lighting industries. The Company also produces aircraft and airport lighting glass; traffic signal glass-pedestrian signal lenses; scientific glass (for scientific applications); and lenses for theatrical, motion picture and television lighting. In addition, it is a specialist in pressed and tempered heavy duty explosion proof/hazardous location lenses. The Company recently installed a state-of-the-art continuous glass furnace, along with automatic glass making equipment. The Company does business as Jeannette Specialty Glass Co.

Officers: Theodore Sarniak III *CEO*
Norman Weinstein *VP-SAL & MKT*
Robert C. Johnston *CON*

Human Resources: J. Theodore Yester *P & COO (Purchasing)*

Total Employees	61	**Regional Employees**	61
Year Established	1903	**SIC Code**	3229
Annual Revenues ($000)	6,100		

Jeansports, Inc.

822 Anderson St.
New Kensington, PA 15068
County: Westmoreland

Phone: (412) 339-8555
Fax: (412) 339-3785

Contract manufacturer of women's and misses' sportswear.

Officers: Charles Hoch *P*

Total Employees..............................75	**Regional Employees** 75
SIC Code 2339	

Jefferson Memorial Park, Inc.

401 Curry Hollow Rd.
Pittsburgh, PA 15236
County: Allegheny

Phone: (412) 655-4500
Fax: (412) 655-7758

Operator of Jefferson Memorial Cemetery and Jefferson Memorial Funeral Home. The nonsectarian cemetery has lot owners in excess of 59,000 and includes a funeral home on its premises. The Company also operates a concrete burial vault plant that manufactures and markets wholesale vaults to other cemeteries. L&M Lawncare, a division of the Company, offers fertilization, weed and insect control, and composting services for residential and commercial lawns. It provides lawn care for approximately 4,000 customers in the South Hills area of Pittsburgh, PA.

Officers: John D. Neel *CH*
                Harry C. Neel *P & CEO*

Total Employees..............................75	**Regional Employees** 75
Year Established 1929	**SIC Code**......................................6553
Annual Revenues ($000) 5,000	

Jendoco Construction Corp.

2000 Lincoln Rd.
Pittsburgh, PA 15235
County: Allegheny

Phone: (412) 361-4500
Fax: (412) 361-4790

General contractor engaged in a variety of industrial construction projects throughout the Tri-State area. The Company's range of experience includes research facilities and laboratories, retail and commercial projects, hospital and medical facilities, housing facilities, schools, and water and wastewater treatment plants. Its current jobs in process include Asbury Place (Alzheimer's facility), Astor Place, the Cambria County Prison and Weinberg Village/Menorah Heights.

Officers: Peter C. Dozzi *CH*
Fred P. Fanto *CEO*
Thomas J. Murphy *P*

Purchasing: Dwight E. Kuhn *VP*

Total Employees..........................100	**Regional Employees** 100
Year Established........................1957	**SIC Code**.....................................1542
Annual Revenues ($000) 33,300	

Jenny Lee Bakery, Inc.

620 Island Ave.
McKees Rocks, PA 15136
County: Allegheny

Phone: (412) 331-8900
Fax: (412) 331-8903

Bakery producing a full line of more than 225 different products, including pies, cakes, cookies, candies, breads, coffee cakes, danish, birthday cakes and wedding cakes. The Company sells its baked goods through its four retail stores located in Ingram, Kennedy Township, downtown Pittsburgh and at the above address. The Company also operates an outlet store in downtown Pittsburgh. In addition, its products are sold in four Shop-N-Save supermarkets located in Emsworth, Heidelberg, Pittsburgh and West Mifflin, PA.

Officers: Bernard R. Baker *C-OWN & P*
Beverly M. Baker *C-OWN & VP*

Human Resources: Nancy C. Lindenfelser *SAL MGR & DIR-Human Resources*

Purchasing: Larry Bill

Total Employees..........................110	**Regional Employees**...................110
Year Established........................1938	**SIC Code**.....................................2051
Annual Revenues ($000) 4,000	

JetNet Corp.

Keystone Dr.
P.O. Box 451
Carnegie, PA 15106
County: Allegheny

Phone: (412) 923-1440
Fax: (412) 279-7470
Internet Address: www.jetnetcorp.com

Manufacturer and supplier of food processing equipment and accessories. The Company produces JetNet brand netting in both cotton and polyester materials in over 300 different styles and sizes. It also produces the applicators that apply the netting in a variety of meat and poultry applications. In addition, the Company sells other products such as thermoplastic cutting boards, safety gloves and cotton gloves. Its clients include meat processors and packers worldwide.

Officers: Donald G. Sartore *P & CEO*
William Sartore *VP-MFG*
Thomas P. Gates *CON*

Human Resources: William Lowery

Purchasing: Joseph Sico *VP-SAL*

Total Employees............................82
Year Established........................1966

Regional Employees....................77
SIC Code....................................2399

Jewish Family & Children's Service of Pittsburgh

5743 Bartlett St.
Pittsburgh, PA 15217
County: Allegheny

Phone: (412) 422-7200
Fax: (412) 422-1162

Nonprofit social service agency providing a myriad of services to all persons in the community. The Agency's services include care management and direct services to help the elderly maintain their independence and dignity; skilled compassionate counseling for individuals and families in trouble; support groups to provide emotional assistance through trying times; special needs services such as guardianship; career and vocational services to help the unemployed and the underemployed; family life and adoption programs to enhance Jewish families; services to families with children with special needs; and resettlement services for refugees from the former Soviet Union. In 1996, the Agency provided support to more than 5,000 community members. Its Career Development Center (CDC) claims to be one of only a limited number of nonprofit career counseling agencies in the area. Each year, the CDC provides career counseling, testing, placement and other career services to more than 1,000 Pittsburgh area residents.

Officers: Dan B. Frankel *P*
Norman R. Keane *EDIR*
Linda Ehrenreich *DIR-Career Development Center*

Human Resources: Jonathan Budd *AST-DIR*

Total Employees...........................51	**Regional Employees** 51
Year Established 1937	**SIC Code**....................................8322
Annual Revenues ($000) 2,200	

JH Water Systems, Inc.

183 Eisaman Rd.
Irwin, PA 15642
County: Westmoreland

Phone: (412) 863-0435
Fax: (412) 863-5498

Marketer and installer of impervious geomembrane liner systems for pollution control. The Company's products are used in reservoirs, landfills, sewage treatment plants, wastewater treatment plants, water treatment plants, leachate collection basins and decontamination pads. It serves clients worldwide.

Officers: John C. Hutchins *P*
Richard C. Gangle *VP*
John W. Hutchins *SEC & TRS*

Human Resources: Carol Ann Hutchins *(Purchasing)*

Total Employees...........................35	**Regional Employees** 35
Year Established 1981	**SIC Code**....................................3089
Annual Revenues ($000) 15,000	

Johnson Controls Network Integration Services, Inc.

101 Ewing Rd.
Carnegie, PA 15106
County: Allegheny

Phone: (412) 279-1700
Fax: (412) 279-2901
Internet Address: www.johnsoncontrols.com

Provider of network design and installation services. The Company consults, designs, engineers, furnishes, installs, tests, documents and maintains wireless and cabling-related network systems (LANs and WANs) for voice, data, video and image communications. Its capabilities include expertise with all forms of network cabling (twisted pair, fiber-optic, coaxial, copper, etc.), electronics (hubs, routers, bridges, switches, etc.), hardware (file servers, workstations, uninterruptible power supplies, etc.), software (network management, network operating systems, etc.) and accessories (network interface cards, modems, connectors, patch panels, etc.). The scope of its projects range from small turnkey cabling solutions to large national LAN/WAN installations, physical and logical layers designs, multifloor design/builds for voice and data networks, and complex campus communications projects. The Company operates branch offices in Los Angeles and San Francisco, CA; Washington, D.C.; Miami, FL; Atlanta, GA; Indianapolis, IN; Baltimore, MD; Detroit and Grand Rapids, MI; Buffalo and Schenectady, NY; Cleveland, OH; and Philadelphia, PA. The Company is a subsidiary of Johnson Controls, Inc., which is headquartered in Milwaukee, WI, and listed on the NYSE.

Officers: Bruce Jacobs *P & COO*
Richard W. Suminski *Regional GMGR-East*
Dennis P. Muir *Regional SAL MGR-East*
Timothy D. Sauer *Regional MKT MGR-East*

Human Resources: Jack Bebernes *DIR-Human Resources*

Total Employees	400	**Regional Employees**	70
Year Established	1979	**SIC Code**	1731

Johnson & Higgins of Pennsylvania, Inc.

Six PPG Place, Ste. 300
Pittsburgh, PA 15222
County: Allegheny

Phone: (412) 391-5350
Fax: (412) 391-4631
Internet Address: www.jh.com

Insurance brokerage and human resource consulting company that claims to be the largest of its kind in the world. The facility located at the above address is a branch office of Johnson & Higgins (J&H), which is headquartered in New York, NY. The local office serves clients throughout Western Pennsylvania and West Virginia. The Company's global network, UNISON, is comprised of 74 J&H offices in the United States and Canada, 50 J&H offices overseas and exclusive relationships with UNISON partners in over 140 additional cities around the world.

Officers: Michael C. Barbarita *Pittsburgh Branch MGR*

Human Resources: Dorothy Hunkele

Total Employees	8,600	**Regional Employees**	130
Year Established	1845	**SIC Code**	6411
Annual Revenues ($000)	1,008,000		

Johnson/Schmidt and Assoc.

Parkway West & Rte. 60
P.O. Box 15508
Pittsburgh, PA 15244
County: Allegheny

Phone: (412) 788-1500
Fax: (412) 787-5960

Provider of architectural, strategic facility planning, engineering and interior design services. The Firm specializes in total building technology for corporate, industrial, financial, retail, health care, material handling, educational and government-related institutions. Its architectural and planning services range from feasibility studies to system performance evaluation. The Firm's in-house engineering design segment provides energy management, process, electrical and control, power, fire protection, plumbing and renewable energy source systems. Its architects, engineers, interior designers and space planners provide a variety of interior design and facility management services to design dynamic working environments. The Firm is also known as JSA Architects.

Officers: James B. Johnson *P*
Thomas W. Schmidt *EVP*
James V. Eckles *SVP*
M. Timothy Lawler, Ph.D. *SVP*

Human Resources: Edward A. Shriver, Jr. *VP & Office MGR*

Total Employees 53		**Regional Employees** 53	
Year Established 1930		**SIC Code** 8712	

Johnston the Florist, Inc.

14179 Lincoln Way
P.O. Box 100, McKeesport, PA 15134
Irwin, PA 15642
County: Westmoreland

Phone: (412) 751-2821
Fax: (412) 751-2961

Owner and operator of 24 Johnston the Florist retail stores located throughout Southwestern Pennsylvania. The Company markets flowers and related floral supplies and maintains its own five acres of greenhouses. It also operates 12 seasonal garden centers and three year-round garden centers. During the autumn harvest season, the Company offers pony rides, a haunted hayride, pumpkins and more as part of their fall festival at the Country Place location.

Officers: Earle S. Guffey *CEO*
Mark J. Guffey *P*

Human Resources: Karen Sheridan

Purchasing: Sandi Cielieska

Total Employees...........................170
Year Established 1898   SIC Code....................................5992

Jones Brewing Co.

254 Second St.
P.O. Box 746
Smithton, PA 15479
County: Westmoreland

Phone: (412) 872-6626
Fax: (412) 872-6538
Internet Address: www.stoneysbeer.com

Operator of a brewery producing a variety of beers. "Stoney's Beer," an all-grain beer without any sugar, artificial ingredients or additives heads the Company's line of flagship beers which includes Stoney's Light, Stoney's N/A (a nonalcoholic beer), Esquire, Fort Pitt, Fort Pitt Light and Gold Crown. It also markets a line of Hand-Crafted beers under the "Eureka" label including Black & Tan, Red Irish Amber, Gold Lager and Gold Light. In addition, the Company performs private label brewing under contracts with the Johnstown Brewing Co. in Johnstown, PA (Morley's Red Beer); Mayer Bros. in West Seneca, NY (The Rebel-Draft Cider); Pennsylvania Brewing Co. in Pittsburgh, PA (Penn Pilsner & Penn Dark); and World Wide Beverage in Philadelphia, PA (Manayunk's Main Street Beer).

Officers: Gabriel M. Podlucky, Jr. *OWN & P (Human Resources)*
Sandra M. Podlucky *VP*
Diana Henry *Accounting MGR*

Purchasing: Al Kitz *Plant MGR*

Total Employees............................50   Regional Employees 50
Year Established 1907   SIC Code....................................2082

Jones & Brown, Inc.

2515 Preble Ave.
Pittsburgh, PA 15233
County: Allegheny

Phone: (412) 323-2100
Fax: (412) 323-9509

Distributor of wholesale building products, primarily for residential and commercial remodeling. The Company's products include roofing, siding, soffit/fascia, gutters, windows, doors, kitchens and baths. It operates branch offices in Livonia, MI; Harrisburg, Johnstown and Washington, PA; and Parkersburg, WV.

Officers: Barry Snyder *P*

Total Employees............................190	**Regional Employee** 150
Year Established 1927	**SIC Code**....................................5033
Annual Revenues ($000) 40,000	

Jones, Day, Reavis & Pogue

One Mellon Bank Center, 500 Grant St., 31st Fl.
Pittsburgh, PA 15219
County: Allegheny

Phone: (412) 391-3939
Fax: (412) 394-7959

International law firm with 19 additional offices located throughout the world. The Firm handles a wide range of legal matters ranging from single plaintiff cases and small transactions to large, complex transactions, multi-jurisdictional litigation, and a broad range of regulatory matters. It is an integrated partnership that operates as one firm worldwide and is organized into four practice groups: Business Practice, Government Regulations, Litigation and Tax. The groups are complemented by Specialized Industry Practices that provide interdisciplinary services to legally intensive and highly regulated industries, including energy, health care and financial institutions. The Firm's main office is located in Cleveland, OH. It has more than 1,000 attorneys worldwide, with 45 attorneys working in the Pittsburgh office.

Officers: Paul M. Pohl *PTR-in-Charge-Pittsburgh Office*

Total Employees........................2,600	**Regional Employees** 106
Year Established 1893	**SIC Code** 8111

Jones, Gregg, Creehan & Gerace, LLP

Grant Bldg., 310 Grant St., Ste. 3000
Pittsburgh, PA 15219
County: Allegheny

Phone: (412) 261-6400
Fax: (412) 261-2652

Provider of legal services with approximately 20 attorneys. The Firm's practice areas include arson, insurance fraud, product liability, general liability, fidelity and surety, general insurance coverage, construction law, business and commercial law, labor and employment, Federal Employment Liability Act, environmental and toxic tort, workers' compensation, bankruptcy, wills and estate planning, personal injury, real estate, and state, federal and local tax.

Officers: Samuel P. Gerace *MPTR*

Human Resources: David L. Wittig *DIR-ADM (Purchasing)*

Total Employees............................40	**Regional Employees** 40
Year Established 1935	**SIC Code** 8111

Joy Technologies Inc.

Thorn Hill Industrial Park, 177 Thorn Hill Dr.
Warrendale, PA 15086
County: Allegheny

Phone: (412) 779-4500
Fax: (412) 779-4509

Developer, manufacturer, distributor and servicer of underground mining machinery for the extraction of coal and other bedded materials. The Company, doing business as Joy Mining Machinery, produces complete longwall systems (longwall shearers, roof supports and face conveyors), continuous miners, batch haulage (shuttle cars and articulated haulers), continuous haulage systems (chain haulage and flexible conveyor trains) for use in longwall and room and pillar mining operations. It claims to be the only manufacturer that offers a complete longwall system to the industry. In addition to the Company's global headquarters located at the above address, it operates facilities in Australia, South Africa, the United Kingdom and across the United States, as well as sales offices in India, the People's Republic of China, Poland, Russia and Slovenia. Its U.S. manufacturing facilities are located in Cleveland and Solon, OH; and Franklin and Reno, PA. Other regional operations are located in Homer City and Meadow Lands, PA. The Company is a subsidiary of Harnischfeger Industries, Inc., which is headquartered in St. Francis, WI, and listed on the NYSE.

Officers: John N. Hanson *CH & CEO*
Mark E. Readinger *P & COO*

Human Resources: Frank E. Joyce *VP-Human Resources*

Total Employees........................5,300	**Regional Employees** 434
Year Established 1919	**SIC Code**....................................3532
Annual Revenues ($000) 1,400,000	

Kaufmann's

400 Fifth Ave.
Pittsburgh, PA 15219
County: Allegheny

Phone: (412) 232-2000
Fax: (412) 232-2662

Operator of 47 department stores located in New York (13), Ohio (20), Pennsylvania (13) and West Virginia (1) with Pittsburgh metropolitan area stores in Greensburg, Monaca, Monroeville, Pittsburgh (Downtown at the above address, North Hills and South Hills) and West Mifflin, PA. The Company is a subsidiary of The May Department Stores Co., which is headquartered in St. Louis, MO, and listed on the NYSE.

Officers: Clarence Reynolds *CH*
              Richard Bennet III *P & CEO*

Human Resources: Ronald Grzymkowski *SVP-Human Resources*

Purchasing: Jennifer Kolesar

Total Employees......................16,000	**Regional Employees** 6,625
Year Established 1871	**SIC Code** 5311
Annual Revenues ($000) 1,300,000	

KCS Computer Services, Inc.

777 Penn Center Blvd., Ste. 600
Pittsburgh, PA 15235
County: Allegheny

Phone: (412) 823-8632
Fax: (412) 823-8821
Internet Address: www.kcscomp.com

Provider of a range of technology-specific systems integration services, including information technology solutions, client/server consulting, Microsoft consulting, custom software development and technical training. The Company hosts its training at its two Training Development Centers in Pittsburgh or at client sites. The Company also provides industry-specific consulting services in the industries of banking and health care and maintains a bank consulting services division in Cleveland, OH. The Company serves clients nationwide.

Officers: James S. Kelly, Jr. *P & CEO*
              Ronald J. Pearce *COO & EVP*

Human Resources: F. Theodore Wolsko *VP-Resource MGT*

Total Employees...........................150	**Regional Employees** 120
Year Established 1985	**SIC Code** 7379
Annual Revenues ($000) 12,000	

Keibler-Thompson Corp.

130 Entrance Dr.
New Kensington, PA 15068
County: Westmoreland

Phone: (412) 335-9161
Fax: (412) 335-6189

Manufacturer of machinery for steel mills serving customers worldwide. The Company's main sales office is located in New Kensington, PA. It maintains branch offices in Birmingham, AL; Gary, IN; Baltimore, MD; Cleveland and Middletown, OH; and Philadelphia, PA.

Officers: Mern Kemble *CEO*
Donald Hilty *P*
Terry Kemble *VP-OPR*
Matt Mancuso *VP-ENG & INTL SAL*
Cary Rigatti *VP & Plant MGR*

Total Employees............................200
Year Established 1973   **SIC Code**.....................................3559

Kendi Enterprises, Inc.

330 Mt. Pleasant Rd.
Scottdale, PA 15683
County: Westmoreland

Phone: (412) 887-5520
Fax: (412) 887-5526

Provider of heavy construction services, including excavating and seal coating, paving and site development for residential and commercial clients in Southwestern Pennsylvania. The Company also manufactures and markets asphalt and distributes asphalt sealer.

Officers: Paul W. Kendi, Jr. *P*

Total Employees.............................35   **Regional Employees** 35
Year Established 1968   **SIC Code**.....................................2951
Annual Revenues ($000)...2,000+

Kennywood Entertainment Co., Inc.

4800 Kennywood Blvd.
West Mifflin, PA 15122
County: Allegheny

Phone: (412) 461-0500
Fax: (412) 464-0719
Internet Address: www.kennywood.com

Owner and operator of two amusement parks, Idlewild Park in Ligonier, PA, and Kennywood Park in West Mifflin, PA; and a waterpark, Sandcastle, in West Homestead, PA.

Officers: Harry W. Henninger *P*
              Jerome Gibas   *GMGR-Idlewild*
              Scott Mackay *GMGR-Sandcastle*
              Peter J. McAneny *GMGR-Kennywood*

Human Resources: Joseph J. Barron

Total Employees........................2,000	**Regional Employees** 2,000
Year Established 1898	**SIC Code**....................................7996

Kensington Windows Inc.

One Kiski Valley Industrial Park, R.D. 1
Vandergrift, PA 15690
County: Westmoreland

Phone: (412) 845-8133
Fax: (412) 845-9151

Manufacturer of high performance custom-sized vinyl replacement windows for residential applications, including picture windows, slider windows, casement windows, awning windows, hopper windows, bow windows, bay windows, garden windows and patio doors. The Company markets its products to building contractors and through professional dealers east of the Rockies. The Company is a unit of Jannock, Inc. in Greentree, PA, which is a subsidiary of Jannock Ltd. (JL). JL is headquartered in Toronto, Ontario, Canada, and is listed on the NASDAQ and Toronto Stock Exchanges.

Officers: G. Ronald Thomson *P*
              Jay Cooper *VP-MKT*
              Jim Cosharek *VP-FIN*
              Brian Hammerbacher *VP-MFG*
              Al Simeone *VP-SAL*

Human Resources: Cindee McDermott

Purchasing: Jeff Mangini

Total Employees...........................200	**Regional Employees** 200
Year Established 1971	**SIC Code**....................................3442
Annual Revenues ($000)...20,000+	

Kerotest Manufacturing Corp.

5500 Second Ave.
Pittsburgh, PA 15207
County: Allegheny

Phone: (412) 521-4200
Fax: (412) 521-2160

Manufacturer of valves and pipe fittings including steel gate valves, strainers, weld-end insulators, lubricated plug valves, plastic distribution valves, weldball valves and electrofusion systems. The Company operates a branch facility located in Mansura, LA.

Officers: Larry Lenarz *CEO*
Robert G. Visalli *P*
Bernard P. Hilterman *SVP, SEC & TRS*

Human Resources: Richard B. Lorantas

Total Employees............................115	**Regional Employees** 90
Year Established 1909	**SIC Code**......................................3494

Ketchum Advertising Pittsburgh, Inc.

Six PPG Place, 13th Fl.
Pittsburgh, PA 15222
County: Allegheny

Phone: (412) 456-3500
Fax: (412) 456-3700

Full-service advertising agency, doing business as Ketchum Advertising, specializing in consumer product, business-to-business, retail and service clients. The Agency serves a diverse base of national and international marketers, including Harris Semiconductor, Highmark Blue Cross/Blue Shield, Nationwide Insurance and PNC Bank. It operates a branch office in San Francisco, CA. The Agency is a division of Omnicom Group Inc. (OGI), which is headquartered in New York, NY, and listed on the NYSE. In June 1996, it merged into OGI.

Officers: James V. Ficco *P*
David S. Egan *EVP & DIR-Account MGT*
Cliff Miller *EVP & Executive Creative DIR*
Petra Arbutina *SVP & Media DIR*
Michael F. Walsh *SVP & DIR-OPR & FIN*

Human Resources: Mavis Ellek

Purchasing: Brice Bickerton

Total Employees............................230	**Regional Employees**...................118
Year Established 1923	**SIC Code** 7311
Annual Revenues ($000) ....255,000 (Billings)	

Ketchum Public Relations Pittsburgh, Inc.

Six PPG Place, Ste. 1111
Pittsburgh, PA 15222
County: Allegheny

Phone: (412) 456-3885
Fax: (412) 456-3900

Full-service public relations agency offering specialized counsel in a number of practice areas, including business-to-business marketing, labor and workplace relations, crisis communications, consumer lifestyles marketing and public affairs. The Agency, doing business as a branch office of Ketchum Public Relations Worldwide (KPRW), claims to be the largest public relations agency in Pittsburgh and the largest agency between New York and Chicago. Its client roster includes the American Iron & Steel Institute, Commonwealth of Pennsylvania, Del Monte Foods, General Nutrition Centers, H. J. Heinz, MCI, Mine Safety Appliances, Nationwide Insurance and SmithKline Beecham Consumer Healthcare. The Agency is headquartered in New York, NY, and claims to be the seventh-largest public relations firm in the world. It has 12 North American offices as well as offices around the globe. The Agency is a division of Omnicom Group Inc. (OGI), which is headquartered in New York, NY, and listed on the NYSE. In June 1996, KPRW merged into OGI.

Officers: Lawrence R. Werner *EVP & DIR*
L. Michael Kelly *Associate DIR*
Kelley Murray Skoloda *SVP*
Gerald P. Thompson *SVP*

Human Resources: Joyce M. Adler

Purchasing: Brice Bickerton

Total Employees 600	**Regional Employees** 50	
Year Established 1923	**SIC Code** 7311	
Annual Revenues ($000) ....39,573 (Billings)		

Key Bellevilles, Inc.

100 Key Lane
Leechburg, PA 15656
County: Armstrong

Phone: (412) 295-5111
Fax: (412) 295-2570

Manufacturer of disc springs claiming to be the largest such producer in North America. The Company manufactures disc springs from 1/2" to 36" outside diameter, 2" thick. It also claims to carry the largest stock of finished inventory and raw material of any manufacturer in the world, with more than 9,000 different sizes and types of disc springs in stock.

Officers: Robert J. Key *P*

Purchasing: Tim Blake

Total Employees............................60	**Regional Employees** 60
Year Established 1967	**SIC Code**......................................3493
Annual Revenues ($000)...5,000+	

Keystone Aluminum, Inc.

126 Myoma Rd.
P.O. Box 807
Mars, PA 16046
County: Butler

Phone: (412) 538-3940
Fax: (412) 789-9600

Manufacturer of Aluminum Deox, a critical ingredient utilized in the manufacturing of steel which is marketed to customers worldwide.

Officers: Brendan O'Connor *P*
Arthur Greenberg *CFO*

Total Employees............................31	**Regional Employees** 31
Year Established 1979	**SIC Code**......................................3341
Annual Revenues ($000) 2,000	

Keystone Brewers, Inc.

3340 Liberty Ave.
Pittsburgh, PA 15201
County: Allegheny

Phone: (412) 682-7400
Fax: (412) 682-2379
Internet Address: www.pittsburghbrewingco.com

Owner and operator of a brewery, doing business as the Pittsburgh Brewing Co., offering approximately 20 brands of beer and malt products. These products are marketed under the Company's brand names along with at least a dozen beverages bottled under contract. In a typical year, the Company produces enough brew to fill almost half a million kegs as well as 250 million bottles and nearly 100 million cans. Its brand names include American, American Light, I.C. ICE, I.C. Light, Iron City, Keene's, Mustang, Old German and J.J. Wainwright's.

Officers: Thomas Gephart *CH*
Joseph R. Piccirilli *P*
James Gehrig   *CFO*
James Kraynik *VP-SAL*
Tim McAleer *VP-MKT*

Human Resources: Nancy Bowers *Human Resources DIR*

Purchasing: Kevin Morgan

Total Employees	275	**Regional Employees**	275
Year Established	1861	**SIC Code**	2082
Annual Revenues ($000)			45,000

K

Keystone Foam Corp.

Rte. 982 N.
P.O. Box 355, Loyalhanna, PA 15661
Derry, PA 15627
County: Westmoreland

Phone: (412) 694-8833
Fax: (412) 694-8519

Fabricator of flexible foam products, including polyurethane, polyester, polyethylene and polystyrene. The Company serves clients in the upholstered furniture, bedding and packaging industries, primarily located in the Northeastern U.S. It also distributes carpet cushion.

Officers: Gerald P. Quinn, Sr. *P*

Human Resources: Lynn Bumar

Purchasing: Alecia Quinn

Total Employees	50	**Regional Employees**	50
Year Established	1983	**SIC Code**	3086
Annual Revenues ($000)			9,000

Keystone Mailing Service, Inc.

4777 Streets Run Rd.
Pittsburgh, PA 15236
County: Allegheny

Phone: (412) 881-5000
Fax: (412) 881-0135

Provider of direct mail services processing more than one million pieces of commercial mail per day. The Company assists its customers to target specific demographic markets and provides a complete mailing process that includes coast-to-coast tracking. The Company's services include ink jet labeling, Cheshire labeling, laser printing, metering and stamping, letter inserting, bursting, folding, sealing, collating, bar coding, presorting, data services, list management, demographics and data files. The Company also operates Keystone Alternate Delivery, which offers door-to-door delivery services.

Officers: Lois S. Kaufman *CEO*
William Hoellein *GMGR*

Human Resources: Randy A. Baker *DIR-Human Resources (Purchasing)*

Total Employees............................225   **Regional Employees** 225
Year Established 1930   **SIC Code**......................................7331

Keywell L.L.C.

890 Noble Dr.
P.O. Box 18289, Pittsburgh, PA 15236
West Mifflin, PA 15122
County: Allegheny

Phone: (412) 462-5555
Fax: (412) 462-3894

Processor of stainless steel scrap and high temperature alloys and wholesaler of various grades of specialty alloys including nickel, chrome, molybdenum, cobalt and tungsten. The Company, which is headquartered in Chicago, IL, operates an additional local facility in Midland, PA, with other processing sites in Atlanta, GA; Baltimore, MD; Detroit, MI; Frewsburg, NY; Monroe, NC; and Houston, TX. The Company claims to be one of the three largest processors of its kind in the world and the largest high-temperature alloy processor in the world. The Company markets its products to the steel and specialty metal industries as well as the automotive and aircraft industries in the United States and abroad.

Officers: Bob Halloran *VP*
               Mike Levy *VP*

Total Employees............................320   **Regional Employees** 45
Year Established 1924   **SIC Code**......................................5093

Killam Assoc.

100 Allegheny Dr.
Warrendale, PA 15086
County: Allegheny

Phone: (412) 772-0200
Fax: (412) 772-1955
Internet Address: www.killam.com

Provider of environmental consulting and engineering services, including planning, investigation, design and management services. The Firm's areas of expertise include municipal and industrial wastewater, water supply and stormwater management, municipal and site engineering, coastal resource management and hazard mitigation, hazardous and solid waste, environmental site assessments, wetlands and ecology, storage tanks and hydrogeology, air quality and facilities contract operations. It serves both public and private sector clients. The Firm is headquartered in Millburn, NJ. It is a subsidiary of Thermo TerraTech, Inc., which is headquartered in Waltham, MA, and listed on the ASE. Branch offices located in Dublin, OH, Somerset, PA, and Danville, WV, report to the facility located at the above address.

Officers: Emil C. Herkert *P*
Thomas L. Hartwig *SVP & GMGR*
Sean C. Isgan *VP*
James G. Ryan *VP*

Human Resources: Lillian R. Henry *DIR-ADM*

Purchasing: Virginia A. Deily

Total Employees............................573   **Regional Employees** 66
Year Established 1937   **SIC Code** 8711

Kinney Engineers, Inc., S. P.

143 First Ave.
P.O. Box 445
Carnegie, PA 15106
County: Allegheny

Phone: (412) 276-4600
Fax: (412) 276-6890

Provider of design engineering, manufacturing, consulting and maintenance services to the steel industry. The Company's manufactured products include blast furnace valves and accessories, and pipeline straining equipment. It operates an additional manufacturing plant in Colonial Heights, VA.

Officers: Rol F. Kinney *CH*
R. Kerry Trachok *CFO*
Craig S. Kinney *VP & GMGR*
W. Chris Dempster *SAL MGR*

Total Employees..............................65   **Regional Employees** 40
Year Established 1945   **SIC Code** 3569

Kipin Industries, Inc.

4194 Green Garden Rd.
Aliquippa, PA 15001
County: Beaver

Phone: (412) 495-6200
Fax: (412) 495-2219

Provider of a complete range of commercial and industrial environmental services, ranging from waste identification and site analysis to recycling and processing, from demolition and property remediation to recapturing hidden assets and revenues through sale of property and processed materials. The Company's support services include custom fabrication, tank removal, tank cleaning and decontamination, decommissioning, lead and asbestos removal, materials screening and assay, waste briquetting, water and sandblasting, excavation, water treatment and dewatering services. Since its inception, the Company has recycled and remediated over 1 million cubic yards of coal tar materials. It recycles hazardous and nonhazardous coal tars in coke plants on a daily basis. The Company maintains recycling facilities in Birmingham, AL; Baldwin and Chicago, IL; Indianapolis, IN; Ashland, KY; and Pittsburgh, PA.

Officers: Peter Kipin, Sr. *P*
Duane Ready *CON*

Purchasing: Peter Kipin, Jr.

Total Employees............................70	**Regional Employees** 20
Year Established 1978	**SIC Code**.....................................2999
Annual Revenues ($000)..10,000+	

Kirkpatrick & Lockhart L.L.P.

Oliver Bldg., 535 Smithfield St., Ste. 1500
Pittsburgh, PA 15222
County: Allegheny

Phone: (412) 355-6500
Fax: (412) 355-6501
Internet Address: www.kl.com

Provider of legal services with more than 400 attorneys. The Firm serves large corporations and small business enterprises, families and individuals, colleges and schools, health care organizations and hospitals, governmental agencies and nonprofit foundations. Its practice areas include antitrust; banking and financial institutions; bankruptcy and business restructurings; construction; corporate; energy; environmental; ERISA, ESOP and executive compensation issues; government contracts; governmental affairs and legislation; health care; insurance coverage; intellectual property; international trade and finance; investment companies and investment advisers; labor and employment law; litigation; media and entertainment law; mergers and acquisitions; nonprofit organizations; product liability; real estate; securities; tax; technology; transportation; trusts and estates; and white collar crime. The Firm operates branch offices in Washington, D.C.; Miami, FL; Boston, MA; New York, NY; and Harrisburg, PA.

Officers: Sanford B. Ferguson *CH-MGT Comm.*
Donald E. Seymour *Administrative PTR*

Human Resources: Clare Westwood

Total Employees..........................979	**Regional Employees** 482
Year Established 1946	**SIC Code** 8111

Kleen All of America, Inc.

1036 William Flynn Hwy.
Glenshaw, PA 15116
County: Allegheny

Phone: (412) 487-1400
Fax: (412) 487-2090

Provider of asbestos and lead paint removal services to commercial and industrial clients in 14 states in the eastern half of the U.S., including Connecticut, Florida, Georgia, Indiana, Kentucky and Pennsylvania.

Officers: Randall McMillan *P*
Victor Lisotto *SEC & TRS*

Total Employees............................120	**Regional Employees** 40
Year Established 1978	**SIC Code**....................................1799
Annual Revenues ($000)...9-10,000		

Klett Lieber Rooney & Schorling

One Oxford Centre, 301 Grant St., 40th Fl.
Pittsburgh, PA 15219
County: Allegheny

Phone: (412) 392-2000
Fax: (412) 392-2128

Provider of legal services with more than 90 attorneys. The Firm has a broad commercial practice, representing corporations and other business entities in matters of corporate and public finance, including venture capital; corporate acquisitions and mergers; real estate development and financing; federal, state and local taxation; labor and employment relations; litigation before state and federal courts and administrative agencies; health care; environmental law; bankruptcy and creditors' rights; estate planning and probate; executive compensation and employee benefits; and entrepreneurial development of high technology or emerging companies. The Firm has branch offices located in Wilmington, DE; and Harrisburg and Philadelphia, PA.

Officers: Arthur J. Rooney II *P*
John A. Barbour *VP & DIR*
Robert T. Harper *CH-Corporate Department & MEM-OPR Comm.*
Edwin L. Klett *CH-Litigation Department & DIR*
William A. K. Titelman *CH-Harrisburg Office, SEC & DIR*

Human Resources: Robert J. Tyler, Jr. *Administrator*

Purchasing: Kathleen Glatz *MKT & Recruiting Coordinator*

Total Employees............................180	**Regional Employees** 125
Year Established 1902	**SIC Code** 8111

Kline, Keppel & Koryak, P.C.

One Gateway Center, 7th Fl.
Pittsburgh, PA 15222
County: Allegheny

Phone: (412) 281-1901
Fax: (412) 281-1884

Certified public accounting firm providing a variety of services, including tax and estate planning, business evaluations and retirement planning. The Firm operates a branch office in Boardman, OH.

Officers: L. Stephen Kline *MPTR*
Edward J. Keppel *Senior PTR*
Craig A. Koryak *Senior PTR*

Human Resources: Jacquelyn Brinker

Total Employees............................30	**Regional Employees** 25
Year Established 1978	**SIC Code**....................................8721

Knepper Press Corp.

1120 Robb Hill Rd.
Oakdale, PA 15071
County: Allegheny

Phone: (412) 788-2550
Fax: (412) 788-4491

Commercial printer providing a variety of services, including direct mail, electronic prepress, imaging, color scanning and digital color proofing. The Company produces catalogs, brochures, magazines, booklets and inserts.

Officers: William Knepper *P*
Edward Ford *VP-SAL & MKT*

Total Employees............................51	**Regional Employees** 51
Year Established 1873	**SIC Code**....................................2759
Annual Revenues ($000) 7,250	

Knickerbocker Russell Co., Inc.

4759 Campbells Run Rd.
Pittsburgh, PA 15205
County: Allegheny

Phone: (412) 494-9233
Fax: (412) 787-7991

Distributor of construction equipment and materials to contractors, municipalities and industry within an approximate 100-mile radius of Pittsburgh. The

Company's equipment includes water pumps, pressure washers, sand blasters, concrete equipment, hand tools, welders, scaffolding, blazers and generators. Its materials include grouts, insulation, caulking, geotextiles, polyplastics and polydrains. The Company also offers service and rentals. It has twelve salespeople covering Ohio, Western Pennsylvania and West Virginia.

Officers: Howard Creese *P*
Tim Ellison *VP*
Wesley Hathaway *SAL MGR-Construction Materials*

Purchasing: Mark Harbaugh

Total Employees..............................38	**Regional Employees** 38
Year Established 1956	**SIC Code**.....................................5082
Annual Revenues ($000) 11,000			

Kop-Coat, Inc.

Koppers Bldg., 436 Seventh Ave., Ste. 1850
Pittsburgh, PA 15219
County: Allegheny

Phone: (412) 227-2700
Fax: (412) 227-2618

Manufacturer of pleasure marine coatings and compounds and wood treatment products. The Company's products are marketed through mass merchandisers, home centers and hardware stores in North America. It operates additional facilities in Los Angeles (2), CA; Chicago, IL; Rockaway, NJ; Cleveland (4), OH; Belgium; and a research facility in Harmarville, PA. The Company is a subsidiary of RPM, Inc., which is headquartered in Medina, OH, and listed on the NASDAQ.

Officers: Charles G. Pauli *P & COO*
Richard F. Kelly *VP-FIN*
Suzanne Meyer *CON*

Human Resources: Mary Grasha Houpt

Purchasing: William Rhea

Total Employees...........................350	**Regional Employees** 60
Year Established 1989	**SIC Code**.....................................2851
Annual Revenues ($000) 120,000			

Kopp Glass, Inc.

2108 Palmer St.
Pittsburgh, PA 15218
County: Allegheny

Phone: (412) 271-0190
Fax: (412) 271-4103

Manufacturer of hand-formed industrial glassware from pot-melted glass. The Company's products are sold exclusively to OEMs worldwide for use in aircraft glassware, airport lighting glassware and traffic signal lenses. The Company can customize its products to meet the clarity and color specifications of each client.

Officers: James D. Stephens *P*
Bruce A. McNally *VP-SAL*
Joseph J. Pavlik *VP, SEC & TRS*
Bruce D. Stephens *VP-MFG*
David Dutt, Ph.D. *ENG MGR*

Human Resources: Laurel Diana

Purchasing: Charles Rudek

Total Employees	125	**Regional Employees**	125
Year Established	1926	**SIC Code**	3229
Annual Revenues ($000)	9,000		

Koppel Steel Corp.

Sixth Ave. & Mount St.
P.O. Box 750, Beaver Falls, PA 15010
Koppel, PA 16136
County: Beaver

Phone: (412) 843-7100
Fax: (412) 847-6385

Manufacturer of seamless tubular products, special bar quality products and semi-finished steel products. The Company operates plants in Ambridge and Koppel, PA, and in Baytown, TX. The Ambridge plant is a seamless tube making facility; the Koppel plant's operations consist of a melting and casting facility and bar mill. The Company is a subsidiary of NS Group, Inc., which is headquartered in Newport, KY, and listed on the NYSE.

Officers: Paul C. Borland, Jr. *P*

Total Employees	805	**Regional Employees**	715
Year Established	1990	**SIC Code**	3312

Koppers Industries, Inc.

Koppers Bldg., 436 Seventh Ave.
Pittsburgh, PA 15219
County: Allegheny

K

Phone: (412) 227-2001
Fax: (412) 227-2935

Integrated producer of carbon compounds and treated wood products for use in a variety of markets, including the chemical, railroad, aluminum and steel industries. The Company operates through three divisions. The Carbon Materials & Chemicals division distills coal tar into a variety of intermediate products, including carbon pitch, phthalic anhydride and creosote, which are basic materials necessary in the production of aluminum, polyester resins and plasticizers, and the pressure treatment of wood, respectively. The Coke Products division converts coal into foundry and furnace coke for sale to steel mill blast furnaces and foundries; and coke by-products, including coal tars, gases, oils and chemicals are sold to other industrial operations. The Railroad & Utility Products division treats railroad crossties, utility poles and pilings with preservatives for various uses and sells other products and services to the railroad and utility industries. The company operates 22 production facilities in the U.S. and maintains indirect ownership interests in 21 facilities overseas. The Company's voting stock is owned, in approximately equal proportions, by Cornerstone-Spectrum, Inc., Koppers Australia Proprietary Ltd. and 120 management investors and directors.

Officers: Robert K. Wagner *CH & Acting CEO*
Randall D. Collins *VP & SEC*
Donald E. Davis *VP & CFO*
William R. Donley *VP & GMGR-Utility & Construction Products*
Lawrence F. Flaherty *VP & MGR-Total Quality & Technical Resources*
Thomas D. Loadman *VP & GMGR-Railroad Products & Services*
Walter W. Turner *VP & GMGR-Carbon Materials & Chemicals*
Timothy J. Wojtowicz *GMGR-Coke Products*
M. Claire Schaming *TRS*

Human Resources: Joseph E. Boan *VP-Human Resources*

Total Employees........................1,933	**Regional Employees** 400
Year Established 1988	**SIC Code**.....................................2491
Annual Revenues ($000) 588,544	

Kopsack Assoc., Inc.

174 Virginia Ave.
Rochester, PA 15074
County: Beaver

Phone: (412) 775-6400
Fax: (412) 775-4386

Owner and operator of the Rochester Manor & Rehabilitation Center, a 122-bed facility providing long- and short-term skilled nursing care. The Company's affiliate, Rochester Villa, Inc., also located at the above address (employing approximately 20), owns and operates the Rochester Villa, a personal care and assisted living facility with 105 units.

Officers: Robert E. Kopsack *OWN, P & CEO*
Kathryn D. Kopsack *Administrator*

Purchasing: Edie Bryan

Total Employees............................120	**Regional Employees** 120
Year Established 1990	**SIC Code**......................................8051

Kosmos Cement Co.

200 Neville Rd.
Pittsburgh, PA 15225
County: Allegheny

Phone: (412) 771-5513
Fax: (412) 777-6054

Manufacturer of portland cement and masonry. The Company primarily markets its products to ready-mix contractors and supply businesses in the Tri-State area. The Company is joint venture between Southdown, Inc. (SI) (75%), which is headquartered in Houston, TX, and listed on the NYSE, and Lone Star Industries, Inc. (25%), which is headquartered in Stamford, CT, and listed on the NYSE. The joint venture operates another plant in Louisville, KY. The Company's facilities are operated by SI.

Officers: Robert A. Prisby *VP-SAL*

Regional Employees.......................85	
Year Established 1930s	**SIC Code**......................................3241
Annual Revenues ($000) 126,000	

Kossman Development Co.

11 Parkway Center, Ste. 300
Pittsburgh, PA 15220
County: Allegheny

Phone: (412) 921-6100
Fax: (412) 921-0913

Provider of architectural design, real estate development, management and leasing services. The Company also provides real estate and brokerage services for owners and users of other properties. It owns, manages and has developed over 3 million square feet of retail and office space. The Company has designed and built special purpose buildings for Dun & Bradstreet and Westinghouse Electric Co., and retailers such as Whitlock Auto Supply, Warehouse Club, KMart, Dunham's Sporting Goods and others.

Officers: Paul Kossman *OWN & P*
   W. Anthony Dunn *VP-Leasing*
   Dennis A. Ross *VP-Construction*
   Richard A. Christy *CON*
   James C. Podomik *Property MGT*

Total Employees...............................35	**Regional Employees** 35
Year Established 1950	**SIC Code**......................................6500

KPMG Peat Marwick LLP

One Mellon Bank Center, Ste. 2500
Pittsburgh, PA 15219
County: Allegheny

Phone: (412) 391-9710
Fax: (412) 391-8963
Internet Address: www.us.kpmg.com

International professional services firm providing a broad array of consulting, assurance, tax and process management services in five markets: financial services; manufacturing, retailing and distribution; health care and life sciences; information, communications and entertainment; and public services. The Pittsburgh office serves as the headquarters for the financial services practice for the area encompassing Kentucky, Michigan, Western New York, Ohio, Western Pennsylvania and West Virginia. In addition to providing accounting, assurance and consulting services, the local office focuses on taxation, particularly state and local tax, employee benefit, not-for-profit and international tax. The Firm's local clients include the City of Pittsburgh, C&K Coal, Elliott Corp., Mellon Bank Corp., Northwest Savings Assn., Petroleum Development Corp., Presbyterian Assn. of Aging, Thrift Drug, Union Carbide, United Refining and the University of Pittsburgh. Headquartered in New York, NY, the Firm is a part of Klynveld Peat Marwick Goerdeler's worldwide operations, which is headquartered in Amsterdam, The Netherlands. It operates more than 1,100 offices in 147 countries.

Officers: Stephen G. Butler *CH*
Roger S. Siboni *Deputy CH*
Francis J. Lison *MPTR-Pittsburgh*

Human Resources: Carla Kassabian

Total Employees......................77,850	**Regional Employees** 160
Year Established 1902	**SIC Code**....................................8721
Annual Revenues ($000) 8,100,000	

KRC Holdings, Inc.

11250 Rte. 30
Irwin, PA 15642
County: Westmoreland

Phone: (412) 863-9000
Fax: (412) 864-7810

Owner and operator of automobile dealerships retailing new and used cars. The Company's facilities also provide parts, service and body shop repairs. Its operations consist of Kenny Ross & Sons Chevrolet, Inc. in North Huntingdon, PA; Kenny Ross Chevrolet-Geo-Buick North, Inc. in Zelienople, PA; Kenny Ross Chevrolet-Oldsmobile-Cadillac, Inc. in Somerset, PA; Kenny Ross Development in Pittsburgh, PA; and Kenny Ross Ford in Adamsburg, PA.

Officers: Kenny Ross *CEO*
James Ross *P*
Dennis R. Kral *VP*

Total Employees..........................510	**Regional Employees** 510
Year Established 1954	**SIC Code**....................................5511
Annual Revenues ($000) 204,309	

KTA-Tator, Inc.

115 Technology Dr.
Pittsburgh, PA 15275
County: Allegheny

Phone: (412) 788-1300
Fax: (412) 788-1306
Internet Address: www.kta.com

Provider of engineering consulting services specializing in protective coatings and linings. The Company provides comprehensive coatings consulting services, including coatings inspection, training, materials/design engineering and structural evaluations, expert witness, coatings failure analysis, laboratory testing and contract management, as well as a complete line of coatings inspection instrumentation. The Company operates regional sales and service centers located in Los Angeles, CA; Honolulu, HI; Chicago, IL; Lexington, KY; Boston, MA; Clinton, NJ; Houston, TX; and Seattle, WA.

Officers: Kenneth B. Tator *P & CEO*
Daniel P. Adley *VP*
Eric S. Kline *VP*
Kenneth A. Trimber *VP*
Dwight G. Weldon *VP*

Human Resources: Wendy D. Williams *Administrative AST*

Purchasing: John C. Konopka *CFO*

Total Employees ....200+   **Regional Employees** 100
Year Established 1949   **SIC Code** 8711
Annual Revenues ($000) 15,000

Kvaerner Metals

One Oliver Plaza
Pittsburgh, PA 15222
County: Allegheny

Phone: (412) 566-4500
Fax: (412) 566-3229
Internet Address: www.kvaerner.com/metals

Provider of metals engineering technology, specializing in the iron and steel, nonferrous and precious metals industries. The Company has the capability to manage projects from concept through to start-up; from project finance to operator training. Its main project services include project management; project financing; planning; estimating and cost control; process development and design; multidiscipline engineering; procurement; expediting, inspection and shipping; installation and construction management; and testing, commissioning and start-up. The Company's support services include consulting; technical and economic feasibility studies; technology transfer; environmental audits; energy audits; environmental and safety risk management; test work (laboratory and pilot scale); and specialty design services. The Company, which is headquartered in London, England, maintains its U.S. headquarters at the above address. It operates sales offices in Evansville and Merrillville, IN, and Eastlake, OH. The Company is a division of Kvaerner ASA, a Norwegian company which is also headquartered in London, England, and listed on the London and Oslo Stock Exchanges.

Recent Events: The Company will be relocating to a new corporate headquarters facility in the Spring of 1998 in the Penn Liberty Plaza at 12th and Liberty in the Strip District of Pittsburgh, PA.

Officers: John Wilson *CEO*
James J. McGrath *P*
James Boughton *SVP-Equipment*
Mike Grumet *SVP-Automation*
Dave Meehan *SVP-ENG & Construction*

Human Resources: Juanita Russell

Total Employees........................1,350   Regional Employees 970
Year Established 1830   SIC Code....................................8711
Annual Revenues ($000) 325,000

L. & E. T. Co., Inc., The

1061 Third St.
North Versailles, PA 15137
County: Allegheny

Phone: (412) 829-8240
Fax: (412) 829-8243

   Subcontractor providing a variety of construction-related services including lath and plaster work, computer floors, exterior finish systems, acoustic ceilings and drywall, fireproofing and demolition. The Company serves commercial and industrial customers throughout Pittsburgh and the outlying region.

Officers: Richard A. Zottola *P*

Human Resources: Linda J. Smith

Total Employees............................45   Regional Employees 45
Year Established 1960   SIC Code....................................1742

L. K. Graphic Communications

R.D. 5, Box 7
Belle Vernon, PA 15012
County: Fayette

Phone: (412) 684-6330
Fax: (412) 684-6442

   Provider of commercial printing and graphic design services. The Company offers logo design, display ads, brochures, advertising inserts and business cards. Its capabilities include sheet-fed printing, web offset printing and full-color printing.

Officers: Cindy Assad *EDIR*

Total Employees............................35   Regional Employees 35
Year Established 1989   SIC Code....................................2752
Annual Revenues ($000) 2,500

La Roche College

9000 Babcock Blvd.
Pittsburgh, PA 15237
County: Allegheny

Phone: (412) 367-9300
Fax: (412) 367-9277
Internet Address: www.laroche.edu

Nonprofit, Catholic coeducational institution. The liberalarts college offers 37 majors and 18 minors of study, including graphic design, interior design, human resources management, nursing, administration and management, applied mathematics, English education and environmental studies. Its student body is comprised of approximately 1,340 undergraduates and 300 graduate students from 15 states and 25 countries.

Officers: Monsignor William A. Kerr *P*
Sister Carolyn Winschel, Ph.D. *EVP*

Human Resources: George Zaffuto

Purchasing: Art Shuker

Total Employees............................180
Year Established........................1963

Regional Employees...................180
SIC Code.....................................8221

Ladbroke Racing Corp.

Foster Plaza Nine, 750 Holiday Dr.
Pittsburgh, PA 15220
County: Allegheny

Phone: (412) 937-4410
Fax: (412) 937-4418

Owner and operator of three racing and wagering entertainment operations, Ladbroke Detroit Race Course in Livonia, MI; Ladbroke Golden Gate Fields in Albany, CA; and Ladbroke Racing Pennsylvania (LRP) on Racetrack Rd. in Meadow Lands, PA. The Company also owns and operates Casino San Pablo, a card club in San Pablo, CA. LRP is comprised of seven facilities in Western Pennsylvania: Ladbroke at The Meadows in Meadow Lands; Ladbrokes-Greensburg in Greensburg; Ladbrokes-Harmar Township in Pittsburgh; Ladbrokes-Johnstown in Johnstown; Ladbrokes-Moon Township in Coraopolis; Ladbrokes-New Castle in New Castle; and Ladbrokes-West Mifflin in West Mifflin. LRP's facilities offer off-track racing, wagering and dining, featuring live simulcasting (via satellite) from racetracks across the country. Each site averages approximately 20,000 square feet in size and has over 200 television monitors. In addition, each site contains bars and lounges, teletheatres and cafes, and offers full-service dining. Ladbroke at The Meadows also offers live harness racing. The Company is the U.S. subsidiary of Ladbroke Group PLC, which is headquartered in London, England, and listed on the London Stock Exchange.

Officers: John R. Long *P & COO*
John J. Ford *VP & GC*
George P. Harbison *VP & CFO*
Mike Jeannot *VP-OPR-Ladbroke Racing Pennsylvania*
John M. Swiatek *VP-OPR*
Vita Marie Fontana *DIR-FIN*
Joe Michels *DIR-Construction & Property*
Tom Chaffee *DIR-Programming & Simulcasting-Ladbroke Racing Pennsylvania*
Jeff Harmon *DIR-FIN-Ladbroke Racing Pennsylvania*
Tony Mediate *DIR-MKT & Communications-Ladbroke Racing Pennsylvania*
Randy Edmonds *GMGR-Ladbroke at The Meadows*

Human Resources: Ruth Honacki *DIR-Human Resources*

Total Employees........................2,000   **Regional Employees** 1,100
Year Established 1985   **SIC Code**...................................7948

Lampus Co., R. I.

816 R. I. Lampus Ave.
P.O. Box 167
Springdale, PA 15144
County: Allegheny

Phone: (412) 362-3800
Fax: (412) 274-4033

Manufacturer and marketer of concrete masonry units for the construction industry in the Pittsburgh area; concrete landscaping products (paving units and retaining wall systems) for markets in Western Pennsylvania and Eastern Ohio; and metal alloys throughout the United States.

Officers: Donald L. Lampus *CEO*
Richard R. Jucha *P*
Jack Blake *VP*
T. E. Kelley *VP*
Robert Welling *VP*

Human Resources: Shelly Rudli

Purchasing: Patrick Zalepa

Total Employees...........................50   **Regional Employees** 50
Year Established 1924   **SIC Code**...................................3271
Annual Revenues ($000) 25,000

Landau Building Co.

9855 Rinaman Rd.
Wexford, PA 15090
County: Allegheny

Phone: (412) 935-8800
Fax: (412) 935-6510

General contractor specializing in commercial and institutional buildings, hospitals, health care facilities and nursing homes, warehouse and distribution centers, and financial institutions. The Company works primarily for private owners and negotiates much of the work. Its clients include Allegheny General Hospital, Keebler, Mellon Bank, Mercy Hospital, PPG Industries, USAirways, Westinghouse and Xerox. The Company has won awards for quality craftsmanship for work on Dollar Bank, the Student Union at Washington & Jefferson College, the D. T. Watson Rehabilitation Facility and the Pittsburgh Children's Zoo. It serves clients in the Tri-State area.

Officers: Roy N. Landau *CH & CEO*
Thomas A. Landau *P*
Edward E. Hughes *VP*
Jeff C. Landau *VP*

Total Employees............................60	**Regional Employees** 60	
Year Established 1891	**SIC Code**....................................1542	
Annual Revenues ($000) 15,000		

Lane, Inc., Angelo

12 W. Noblestown Rd.
Carnegie, PA 15106
County: Allegheny

Phone: (412) 279-1234
Fax: (412) 276-6522

Manufacturer and marketer of concrete blocks. The Company also sells ready-mix concrete and concrete-related products. It serves a variety of clients within an approximate 60-mile radius of its facility, including commercial and residential builders and some do-it-yourselfers. The Company operates a fleet of 10 trucks.

Officers: John G. Lane *P*
Vincent J. Lane *VP*
Velma R. Lane *SEC & TRS*

Total Employees............................36	**Regional Employees** 36	
Year Established 1933	**SIC Code**....................................3271	
Annual Revenues ($000) 7,000		

Laser Drive, Inc.

5318 Ranalli Dr.
Gibsonia, PA 15044
County: Allegheny

Phone: (412) 443-7688
Fax: (412) 444-6430

Manufacturer of high-voltage power supplies for applications in the electro-optics market. The Company offers power supply product lines for helium neon lasers, argon lasers and CO2 lasers, as well as arclamp, flashlamp and deuterium to clients worldwide.

Officers: Anthony Pavlik *P*

Human Resources: Pam Morgan

Purchasing: Barb Clark

Total Employees	75	**Regional Employees**	75
Year Established	1976	**SIC Code**	3679
Annual Revenues ($000)			8,000

Laso Contractors, Inc.

R.D. 4, Box 174
P.O. Box 660
Ligonier, PA 15658
County: Westmoreland

Phone: (412) 238-6578
Fax: (412) 238-2721

Interior finish subcontractor primarily providing labor and materials for union shop construction of metal framing, drywall, sprayed-on fireproofing, exterior insulation finish systems, lath and plaster, and acoustical installations. The Company performs work on commercial projects throughout Western Pennsylvania.

Officers: Betsy F. Norris *C-OWN & P*
Amy P. Graham *C-OWN, SEC & TRS (Human Resources & Purchasing)*

Total Employees	50	**Regional Employees**	50
Year Established	1971	**SIC Code**	1742

Latrobe Area Hospital

121 W. Second Ave.
Latrobe, PA 15650
County: Westmoreland

Phone: (412) 537-1000
Fax: (412) 532-6900
Internet Address: www.lah.com

Nonprofit 260-bed community hospital providing a wide range of general medical and surgical services, including cancer treatment, cardiology, obstetrics, pediatrics, mental health, a family practice residency program, special care units, family planning, emergency and home health services. The Hospital operates a variety of off-site facilities, including family practice medical offices in Blairsville, Mt. View, Norvelt and Saltsburg, PA; diagnostic testing centers for conducting blood work, x-rays and lab specimens in Blairsville, Hannastown, Latrobe, Ligonier, Mt. View, Norvelt and Saltsburg, PA; outpatient mental health services in Mt. Pleasant, PA; and Latrobe Area Hospital Home Health Services, offering home care in Blairsville, Latrobe, Ligonier, Mt. Pleasant, Mt. View and Saltsburg, PA.

Officers: Douglas A. Clark *EDIR*
Robert Thornton *CFO*
John Gray *Associate DIR*
Shirley Stasiowski *Associate DIR*
Marie Zanotti *Associate DIR*
Thomas Gessner, M.D. *Medical DIR*

Human Resources: Jeryl L. Gates *DIR-Human Resources*

Purchasing: Marsha Walter

Total Employees........................1,400	**Regional Employees** 1,400
Year Established 1910	**SIC Code**......................................8062
Annual Revenues ($000) 104,725	

Latrobe Assoc.

135 Gertrude St.
P.O. Box 29
Latrobe, PA 15650
County: Westmoreland

Phone: (412) 539-1612
Fax: (412) 539-1191

Injection and compression molder of plastic products, doing business as Westmoreland Plastics Co. Approximately 80% of the Company's resins are thermoset and 20% are thermoplastic. It also produces a proprietary line of plastic knobs and handles.

Officers: John Adams *C-OWN*
Dave Bittner *C-OWN*
Mike Sullivan *C-OWN*
Thomas J. Casey *P*
Fred Crocker, Jr. *VP*

Human Resources: Regina Aniballi

Purchasing: Nancy Marts

Total Employees..............................45	**Regional Employees** 45
Year Established 1950	**SIC Code**....................................3089
Annual Revenues ($000) 3,000	

Latrobe Printing & Publishing Co., Inc.

1211 Ligonier St.
P.O. Box 111
Latrobe, PA 15650
County: Westmoreland

Phone: (412) 537-3351
Fax: (412) 537-0489

Publisher of the Latrobe Bulletin, a daily newspaper published Monday through Saturday serving residents of Latrobe, PA, and surrounding communities. The newspaper has approximately 8,500 subscribers.

Officers: Thomas M. Whiteman II *P*
Hazel D. Whiteman *VP*
Marie McCandless *Head Editor*

Human Resources: Carl A. DePasqua *Business MGR (Purchasing)*

Total Employees..............................30	**Regional Employees** 30
Year Established 1873	**SIC Code** 2711

Latrobe Steel Co.

2626 Ligonier St.
P.O. Box 31
Latrobe, PA 15650
County: Westmoreland

Phone: (412) 537-7711
Fax: (412) 532-6316

Producer of high-speed tool and die steel and vacuum-melted, high-strength specialty steels and alloys. The Company's products include high-strength alloy steels for aerospace components and other critical applications; high-speed steels for metal cutting and punching tools; corrosion-resistant, high-strength alloys for hostile environments and exotic applications; tool steels; and high performance bearing steels for aircraft engine bearings. It also performs conversion of titanium, nickel-based, heat-resistant and stainless alloys for other metal producers. The Special Products division produces machined parts and components, forgings, blanks and cut lengths. The Koncor Industries division, located in Wauseon, OH, produces drill bits, drill rod, flat ground, premium finish bar and plate. The Company also operates the Sandycreek Service Center, which is located in Franklin, PA. Tool steels customers include manufacturers of high-speed steel cutting tools and tool and die shops producing both hot and cold work dies and molds. Customers of the vacuum-melted steels and alloys produced include manufacturers and subcontractors (large forge shops) for components used in aircraft, missile, defense, medical, energy exploration and other critical applications. The Company's distribution subsidiaries are Houghton & Richards Corp. in Marlborough, MA; Ohio Alloy Steels, Inc. in Youngstown, OH; and Sanderson Special Steels Ltd. in Sheffield, England. The Company is a subsidiary of The Timken Co., which is headquartered in Canton, OH, and listed on the NYSE.

Officers: Hans J. Sack *P & CEO*
Brad W. Crozier *GMGR-OPR & ENG*
John W. Dillon *GMGR-MKT & Technology*
Joseph A. Visconti *GMGR-SAL*
R. Scott White *GMGR*

Human Resources: R. Thomas Okonak *MGR-Associate Services*

Purchasing: Gene F. Zurawsky *MGR-Procurement & Administrative Services*

Total Employees........................1,000
Year Established 1913

Regional Employees 650
SIC Code......................................3312

Latronics Corp.

1001 Lloyd Ave.
Latrobe, PA 15650
County: Westmoreland

Phone: (412) 539-1626
Fax: (412) 539-2540

Manufacturer of ceramic-to-metal seals for the high power semiconductor industry. The Company also operates a sales office located in Chippenham, England.

Officers: Nancy S. Robbins *CH*
James S. Robbins *VP-OPR*
Ron J. Yurko *VP-ENG*
David Bowers *DIR-SAL*

Human Resources: Eleanor Smith

Total Employees............................200   Regional Employees 200
Year Established 1958   SIC Code......................................3679
Annual Revenues ($000) 16,000

Laurel Highlands River Tours, Inc.

P.O. Box 107
Ohiopyle, PA 15470
County: Fayette

Phone: (800) 472-3846
Fax: (412) 329-8532
Internet Address: www.primepage.com/laurel

Outdoor recreation company located in the heart of the Ohiopyle State Park. The Company offers a variety of professionally guided rafting tours on the Cheat and Youghiogheny Rivers; guided fishing tours; instructional courses in kayaking and canoeing; team building sports (Capture the Flag); and rentals of rafts, canoes, duckies, kayaks, shredders and bicycles. The Company also offers lodging at its two guest houses, the Ferncliff Guest House and the Ohiopyle Guest House, and operates a retail store. While the Company's business office is open year round, its recreational services are seasonal.

Officers: Linda McCarty *C-OWN*
            Mark McCarty *C-OWN*

Total Employees............................100   Regional Employees 100
Year Established 1965   SIC Code......................................7999

Lazarus

100 South Hills Village
Pittsburgh, PA 15241
County: Allegheny

Phone: (412) 854-2955
Fax: (412) 854-2965

Department store offering a full line of apparel for men, women and children, and merchandise for the home. The Company is a segment of Rich's/Lazarus/Goldsmith's (RLG), which is headquartered in Atlanta, GA. RLG is a division of Federated Department Stores, Inc., which is headquartered in Cincinnati, OH, and listed on the NYSE. Lazarus operates 50 stores located in Indiana, Kentucky, Ohio, Pennsylvania and West Virginia. Pittsburgh area stores are located in Beaver, Greensburg, Monroeville, Natrona and West Mifflin, PA, as well as in the North Hills and South Hills areas of the City. A new downtown Pittsburgh store isscheduled to open during the Fall of 1998 at Fifth Ave. and Wood St.

Officers: Russell Stravitz *CH & CEO-Rich's/Lazarus/Goldsmith's Division*
Susan Kronick *P & COO-Rich's/Lazarus/Goldsmith's Division*
Malcom Roseman *Regional VP-Pittsburgh*

Human Resources: Lee Ann Rohan

Regional Employees.................2,000
Year Established 1851   **SIC Code** 5311

LCI International, Inc.

The Landmarks Bldg., One Station Sq., Ste. 600
Pittsburgh, PA 15219
County: Allegheny

Phone: (412) 355-0400
Fax: (800) 860-1018
Internet Address: www.lcii.com

Worldwide, full-service, facilities-based telecommunications company offering a broad range of business and residential transmission services, including switched and dedicated inbound and outbound services, card services, data services and international services. The Company, which is headquartered in McLean, VA, is listed on the NYSE. The local office is one of many sales offices the Company operates throughout the United States. It serves clients in the Tri-State area.

Officers: John Truxell *SAL MGR*

Total Employees........................2,400   **Regional Employees** 30
Year Established 1983   **SIC Code**....................................4813
Annual Revenues ($000) 1,100,000

Learning Tree Assn. of Pittsburgh, The

907 West St., 3rd Fl.
Pittsburgh, PA 15221
County: Allegheny

Phone: (412) 247-4900
Fax: (412) 247-0535
Internet Address: tree1975@ix.netcom.com

Owner and operator of private academic nursery schools. The Company's facilities, known as The Learning Tree Schools, are licensed by the Pennsylvania Department of Education and the Department of Public Welfare. Its centers are located in California, Jeannette, Monroeville and Pittsburgh (the above address and in the South Side).

Officers: Jamie M. Southworth, Ph.D. *C-OWN & CEO*
Horton C. Southworth, Ph.D. *C-OWN & TRS*
Michele Antol *DIR-Instruction*

Human Resources: Alexandra Southworth *DIR-FIN (Purchasing)*

Total Employees.............................70   Regional Employees 70
Year Established 1975   SIC Code....................................8351

LeaseTek, Inc.

300 Penn Center Blvd., Ste. 500
Pittsburgh, PA 15235
County: Allegheny

Phone: (412) 829-3080
Fax: (412) 829-0840
Internet Address: www.leasetek.com

Provider of lease/loan accounting software for the asset-based finance industry. The Company's products include the LeaseManag-r, which assists in payment quotations, daily operations and data management, daily accounting and taxation, and management reporting; the Maintenance Track-r, which assists in tracking maintenance and operating expenses; and the Quote-r, which assists in tracking sales prospects, pricing vehicles, quoting payments and measuring sales staff performance. The Company operates branch offices in London, England, and Stockholm, Sweden.

Officers: Michael J. Pochan *CEO*
Anthony Petroy *CFO*
Robert F. Culbertson III *EVP*
Mark J. Wallace *DIR-New Business DEV*

Human Resources: Donna Salmane *(Purchasing)*

Total Employees.............................45   Regional Employees 40
Year Established 1983   SIC Code....................................7372
Annual Revenues ($000) 5,000

Leco & Assoc., Inc., M.

61 McMurray Rd.
Pittsburgh, PA 15241
County: Allegheny

Phone: (412) 833-7853
Fax: (412) 833-9450

Provider of revenue enhancement/recovery services to hospitals, health care institutions and group medical practices. The Company maintains on-site staff at client facilities. Its client list includes more than 250 hospitals throughout the east coast and midwest, ranging from 30-bed rural hospitals to many of the nation's largest medical centers.

Officers: Robert J. Galasso *PTR*
Michael Leco *PTR*
William J. Poole *PTR*

Human Resources: Anne M. Leco

Total Employees............................100   **Regional Employees** 40
Year Established 1982   **SIC Code**......................................8742

Lee Group, Inc., R. J.

350 Hochberg Rd.
Monroeville, PA 15146
County: Allegheny

Phone: (412) 325-1776
Fax: (412) 733-1799
Internet Address: www.rjlg.com

Provider of contract research, analytical services and applications development in various fields of materials characterization. In addition to traditional materials studies, the Company's capabilities include environmental analyses, industrial hygiene applications, indoor air quality services and specialized contract research projects that utilize optical and electron microscopy, microprobe analysis, x-ray diffraction, and wet and instrumental chemical techniques. The Company operates a sales office in Richland, WA, and additional laboratories in San Leandro, CA; Houston, TX; and Manassas, VA.

Officers: Richard J. Lee, Ph.D. *P*
Fred C. Schwerer *VP-Technology Coordination*
Ian M. Stewart *VP-Analytical Services*

Human Resources: Herminia B. Strickland

Purchasing: Kathy Gustafson

Total Employees............................125   **Regional Employees** 100
Year Established 1980   **SIC Code**......................................8731

LeFebure Corp.

220 Executive Dr., Ste. 2
Cranberry Township, PA 16066
County: Butler

Phone: (412) 776-4994
Fax: (412) 776-2370

Manufacturer of banking automation systems, such as automatic teller machines, and physical security equipment, such as vaults, safes and drive-ups. The Company is headquartered in Cedar Rapids, IA. It is a division of De La Rue Plc, which is headquartered in London, England, and listed on the London Stock Exchange. The local facility provides sales, service and installations.

Officers: Matt Cayuela *Regional SAL MGR*
Linda Smoot *Regional Service MGR*

Human Resources: Neil Fallon *Human Resources DIR (Cedar Rapids, IA)*

Total Employees........................8,000	**Regional Employees** 50
Year Established 1892	**SIC Code**....................................3578

Legg Mason Wood Walker, Inc.

CNG Tower, 625 Liberty Ave., Ste. 2500
Pittsburgh, PA 15222
County: Allegheny

Phone: (412) 261-7300
Fax: (412) 261-5399

Full-service broker-dealer and a member of all major stock exchanges. The Company, headquartered in Baltimore, MD, operates approximately 100 offices throughout the United States, including branches in Butler and Upper St. Clair, PA. It is a subsidiary of Legg Mason, Inc., which is also headquartered in Baltimore, MD, and is listed on the NYSE.

Officers: Carl Hohnbaum *SVP & Regional MGR*
Steve Fischetti *MGR-Upper St. Clair Office*
Howie Pentony *MGR-Butler Office*

Total Employees........................2,900	**Regional Employees** 70
Year Established 1899	**SIC Code** 6211
Annual Revenues ($000) 625,000	

Lender's Service, Inc.

Cherrington Corporate Center, 700 Cherrington Pwy.
P.O. Box 90, Pittsburgh, PA 15230
Coraopolis, PA 15108
County: Allegheny

Phone: (412) 299-4000
Fax: (412) 299-4067
Internet Address: www.lendersservice.com

Provider of real estate information, products and services, and claims to be the nation's largest independent title agency. The Company serves more than 1,300 lending and real estate investing clients, including the industry's leading mortgage banks, government agencies, mortgage brokers and consumer finance companies. It offers appraisal and collateral assessment products nationwide, and title and closing services in 33 jurisdictions. It also manages a network of nearly 6,000 independent fee appraisers, abstractors and closing agents. The Company has significant relationships with nine of the top 10 mortgage banks and 18 of the 25 largest consumer finance companies, as well as with Fannie Mae, Freddie Mac and ALLTEL, formerly known as CPI. The Company is a subsidiary of Merrill Lynch & Co., Inc., which is headquartered in New York, NY, and listed on the NYSE.

Officers: Michael A. Johnston *CH & CEO*
Joseph J. Murin *P & COO*
Steven G. Cohen *CFO*
Thomas M. Frunzi *EVP-MKT*
C. William Griffin *EVP-Client Services*
Leonard C. Splane *EVP-Client Services*

Human Resources: Diane Book

Purchasing: Robert Zapko

Total Employees............................500	**Regional Employees** 480
Year Established 1967	**SIC Code**......................................6541

Lenox, Inc.

Lenox Rd. & Rte. 31 E.
Mt. Pleasant, PA 15666
County: Westmoreland

Phone: (412) 547-4541
Fax: (412) 547-4549

Manufacturer of fine crystal stemware and some small giftware. The Company is headquartered in Lawrenceville, NJ. It is a subsidiary of Brown-Forman Corp., which is headquartered in Louisville, KY, and listed on the NYSE. The local plant also includes a retail store and factory outlet store.

Officers: Ross Houser *Plant MGR*
Regional Employees ....200+
Year Established 1965   **SIC Code** 3229

Leopold Co., Inc., The F. B.

227 S. Division St.
Zelienople, PA 16063
County: Butler

Phone: (412) 452-6300
Fax: (412) 452-1377
Internet Address: www.fbleopold.com

Manufacturer of water and wastewater treatment equipment for municipalities and industries. The Company also operates two plants located in Zelienople, PA. It is a subsidiary of Thames Water Plc, which is headquartered in London, England, and listed on the London Stock Exchange.

Officers: Robert Wimmer *P*
Michael J. Ulizio *GMGR*

Human Resources: Richard Matz

Purchasing: Francis Daugherty

Total Employees............................130   **Regional Employees** 130
Year Established 1924   **SIC Code** 3589

LePage's, Inc.

120 Delta Dr.
Pittsburgh, PA 15238
County: Allegheny

Phone: (412) 967-0250
Fax: (412) 967-0255

Manufacturer of pressure-sensitive tapes and adhesive products, including invisible and transparent tape, commercial tape and dispensers, removable note pads and removable, reusable adhesive putty. The Company also offers printed tape products, including Looney Tunes licensed fun tape and holiday gift tag tape. It offers all of its products in either private label or LePage's branded packaging. The Company operates a manufacturing plant in Gloucester, MA.

Officers: Gary L. Dean *COO*
Edward P. Kennedy *EVP-SAL*

Human Resources: Anita L. Knize *MGR-Benefits & ADM*
Purchasing: Marsha St. Peter *Purchasing MGR*

Total Employees	200	Regional Employees	24
Year Established	1876	SIC Code	2891
Annual Revenues ($000)		25,000	

Lesker Co., Kurt J.

1515 Worthington Ave.
Clairton, PA 15025
County: Allegheny

Phone: (412) 233-4200
Fax: (412) 233-4275
Internet Address: www.lesker.com

Manufacturer of vacuum systems and components for a wide range of applications. The Company operates branch offices in Livermore, CA; Sherman, TX; Toronto, Ontario, Canada; Julich, Germany; and Budapest, Hungary; and a branch office and manufacturing site in Hastings, England.

Officers: Kurt J. Lesker III *P*
Allen Demetrius *EVP*
Michele Migliuolo *VP-Technology*

Purchasing: Michael Sadusky

Total Employees	160	Regional Employees	140
Year Established	1954	SIC Code	3545
Annual Revenues ($000)		30,000	

Levin, Inc., Sam

600 W. Main St.
Mt. Pleasant, PA 15666
County: Westmoreland

Phone: (412) 547-3521
Fax: (412) 547-5158

Owner and operator of retail furniture stores under the name Levin Furniture. The Company operates six stores in the Pittsburgh metropolitan area and four in Ohio.

Officers: Robert Levin *CEO*
Howard Slavin *P*

Total Employees	300		
Year Established	1929	SIC Code	5712

Levinson Steel Co., The

110 Roessler Rd., Ste. 300-C
Pittsburgh, PA 15220
County: Allegheny

Phone: (412) 572-3400
Fax: (412) 572-3406

Owner and operator of five steel service centers in the Eastern U.S., stocking a variety of carbon steel structurals, bars, tubing and plate. The Company provides sawing, shearing, flame-cutting and just-in-time delivery of carbon steel products to manufacturers, fabricators, construction companies and other service centers throughout the U.S. and Canada. The Company's steel service centers are located in Greenville, KY; Seekonk, MA; Camden, NJ; and Ambridge and York, PA. It also maintains sales offices in Birmingham, AL, and Bethlehem, PA.

Officers: Bill Bennett *P & CEO*
Ken Thomas *VP, TRS & SEC*

Human Resources: Claire Thompson

Total Employees............................160	**Regional Employees** 21
Year Established 1902	**SIC Code**......................................5051
Annual Revenues ($000) 57,000	

Lewis-Goetz and Co., Inc.

650 Washington Rd., Ste. 510
Pittsburgh, PA 15228
County: Allegheny

Phone: (412) 341-7100
Fax: (412) 341-7192

Distributor of industrial rubber products including above ground and underground conveyor belting, industrial hose products, gaskets and packing, and a full range of molded and extruded rubber parts. The Company's inventory includes approximately 30,000 items representing more than 500 primary and secondary suppliers. The Company is comprised of 11 divisions consisting of Central Valley Rubber Services Co. in Roanoke, VA; Colonial-Republic Rubber Co. in Mount Laurel, NJ; Gooding & Shields Rubber Co. at 4915 Campbells Run Rd. in Pittsburgh, PA; Gooding Rubber Co. in Beckley, WV; Haynes Rubber & Supply Co. in Rocky Mount, NC; Richmond Rubber Co. in Richmond, VA; Shields & Wright Rubber Co. in Brooklyn Heights, OH, with a branch site in Findlay, OH; Shields Industrial Rubber Co. in Clearwater, FL; Shields Rubber Co. in Dolton, IL; Shields Rubber Co. in Baltimore, MD; and Shields Rubber Co. in Erie, PA.

Officers: Andrew B. Lewis *CH & CEO*
David R. Goetz, Sr. *P, COO & CFO*
Howard E. Neff *EVP*

Ronald H. Petronio *VP*
Joann Capan *SEC & TRS*

Human Resources: Kelly A. Garvey *DIR-Human Resources*

Total Employees............................265
Year Established 1935
Annual Revenues ($000) 65,500

Regional Employees 60
SIC Code....................................5085

Leybold Vacuum Products, Inc.

5700 Mellon Rd.
Export, PA 15632
County: Westmoreland

Phone: (412) 327-5700
Fax: (412) 733-1217
Internet Address: www.leybold-vacuum.com

Manufacturer, importer and exporter of industrial vacuum pumps and pumping systems for the semiconductor processing; food and packaging; air conditioning; automotive; paper, film and foil converting; and research, instrumentation and medical device manufacturing industries. The company distributes its parts and provides services worldwide. The Company operates sales offices in Boston, MA, and Austin, TX; and sales and service offices in San Jose, CA, and Dallas, TX. It is a subsidiary of Leybold AG, which is headquartered in Cologne, Germany.

Officers: Richard T. Heglin *P-Trade Americas*
Ken K. Kalia *P-Semiconductor Solutions*

Human Resources: Valerie Mooney

Purchasing: John Mance

Total Employees............................300
Year Established 1962
Annual Revenues ($000) 100,000

Regional Employees 200
SIC Code....................................7699

Lico, Inc.

929 Fifth Ave.
McKeesport, PA 15132
County: Allegheny

Phone: (412) 422-7786
Fax: (412) 664-0940

Manufacturer and distributor of janitorial cleaning products. The Company manufactures more than 120 liquid and powdered cleaning chemicals, including disinfectants, industrial degreasing products, hand soaps, carpet cleaning chemicals, restroom care products, warewashing and laundry products, all-purpose cleaners, floor finishers/sealers, sewage and water plant treatments, vehicle cleaners and environmentally friendly dilution control systems. Its manufacturing division serves clients east of the Mississippi River, including Puerto Rico. The Company distributes Rubbermaid commercial products, paper towels and toilet tissue, restaurant supplies, garbage bags, industrial floor and carpet cleaning equipment, Eureka industrial vacuums, grounds and pest control products, Kimberly-Clark wiping products, Go-Jo hand care products and industrial matting systems. Its janitorial distribution division serves clients throughout the Tri-State area.

Officers: Helen Lichtenstein *P*
　　　　　　 Stan Lichtenstein *EVP*

Human Resources: Sam Lichtenstein *VP (Purchasing)*

Total Employees............................35	**Regional Employees** 35
Year Established 1922	**SIC Code**....................................2819

Lighthouse Electric Co., Inc.

1957 Rte. 519 S.
Canonsburg, PA 15317
County: Washington

Phone: (412) 873-3500
Fax: (412) 873-3510

　　Provider of electrical contracting services to commercial, industrial and institutional customers throughout the Tri-State area.

Officers: Anthony Mikec *P*
　　　　　　 Todd Mikec *VP*

Total Employees...........................140	**Regional Employees** 140
Year Established 1984	**SIC Code**....................................1731
Annual Revenues ($000) 20,000	

Limbach Holdings, Inc.

Four Northshore Center
Pittsburgh, PA 15212
County: Allegheny

Phone: (412) 359-2100
Fax: (412) 321-3809

　　Provider of heating and air conditioning contracting services nationwide through several subsidiaries, all of which are headquartered at the above address. Affiliated Building Services, Inc. offers on-site maintenance services to large commercial and industrial property owners throughout the United States. Limbach Constructors, Inc. offers commercial and industrial heating, air conditioning and process piping services. It claims to be the fourth-largest mechanical contractor in the United States. LINC Corp. is a franchiser of a mechanical service management system. It has over 100 franchisees both nationally and internationally. The Company is a subsidiary of Anjou International Co., Inc. (AICI), which is head-quartered in New York, NY. AICI is a subsidiary of Generale Des Eaux Cie Sa, which is headquartered in Paris, France.

L

Officers: Joseph E. Earle *MDIR & COO*
Charles L. Boyd *VP; P & COO-Limbach Constructors, Inc.*
George A. Fechter *VP; CH-Affiliated Building Services, Inc.*
Martin A. Keyser *VP, SEC & GC; VP-Law & SEC-Affiliated Building Services, Inc.; VP, GC & SEC-Limbach Constructors, Inc.; SEC & GC-LINC Corp.*
Robert C. Miele *VP-FIN & ADM, & TRS; VP & COO-Limbach Constructors, Inc.; TRS-Affiliated Building Services, Inc. & LINC Corp.*
Stephen B. Wurzel *VP; CH & CEO-Limbach Constructors, Inc.*
William Eichner *CON*
John S. Pattillo, Jr. *P-Affiliated Building Services, Inc.*
Kenneth A. Piercy *P & CEO-LINC Corp.*

Total Employees..........................2,481
Year Established..........................1986   **SIC Code**......................................1711
Annual Revenues ($000)..319,170

Lincoln Financial Group, Inc.

Koppers Bldg., 436 Seventh Ave., Ste. 600
Pittsburgh, PA 15219
County: Allegheny

Phone: (412) 288-3950
Fax: (412) 288-3955

Provider of insurance, investment and pension products, and financial, business and estate planning services to individuals and commercial clients. The facility at the above address is one of 38 regional sales offices located throughout the United States and in five countries that market the products and services of the Company's affiliate, the Lincoln National Life Co., which does business as Lincoln Life. The Company and its affiliate are subsidiaries of Lincoln National Corp., which is listed on the NYSE. All of the companies are headquartered in Ft. Wayne, IN.

Officers: Albert E. Heiles, Jr. *P & Regional CEO*

Human Resources: Jill A. McArdle *Office MGR*

Total Employees..........................4,000   **Regional Employees**....................50
Year Established..........................1905   **SIC Code**......................................6411
Annual Revenues ($000)..15,000

Lincoln Hydraulics, Inc.

20 Museum Rd.
Washington, PA 15301
County: Washington

Phone: (412) 222-2700
Fax: (412) 222-9888

Job shop providing custom machining, fabricating, and hydraulic manufacturing and repair services primarily for steel mills and coal mines

Officers: Walter V. Spotte *P*

Purchasing: Robert Hall

Total Employees............................31	**Regional Employees** 31
Year Established 1972	**SIC Code**....................................3569
Annual Revenues ($000) 2,500	

Lind-Burt, Inc.

Gatehouse Bldg., Station Square
Pittsburgh, PA 15219
County: Allegheny

Phone: (412) 391-8800
Fax: (412) 391-8488
Internet Address: www.pc-solutions.com

Provider of information systems consulting and integration services doing business as PC Solutions. The Company's services consist of strategic consulting and project management; complex LAN/WAN network design and installation; client/server consulting and implementation; relocation planning and services; client help desk consulting, planning and augmentation; facilities cabling engineering and installation; technical writing and network documentation; server-based hardware maintenance support; customized network software support; and dedicated training. The Company primarily serves clients in the Ohio, Pennsylvania and West Virginia area.

Officers: Louis J. Lind *P & CEO*
Steven Wirth *EVP*
Tom Garvin *VP & TRS*
Joyce Deasy *DIR-Education Services*
Dan Tarchick *DIR-SAL & MKT*
Kevin Weaver *DIR-Client/Server Consulting*
Scott Windisch *DIR-Network Services*
Frank Tallarico *MGR-Network OPR*

Human Resources: Renee Greijack

Purchasing: Donna Pardiny

Total Employees............................45	**Regional Employees** 45
Year Established 1984	**SIC Code**....................................7371

Linett Co., Inc.

6815 Hamilton Ave.
P.O. Box 5370, Pittsburgh, PA 15206
Pittsburgh, PA 15208
County: Allegheny

Phone: (412) 363-3856
Fax: (412) 363-4076

Manufacturer of strapping dispensers. The Company also provides contract metal fabricating services, including metal forming, stamping, tube bending, MIG welding, robotics welding and paint coating. Its clients include the nationwide packaging industry.

Officers: Fred I. Schwartz *P*
Melvin E. Solomon *VP*
Nick Valore *VP-OPR*
Paula Pascarella *CON*

Human Resources: Barbara Santella

Purchasing: Ray Mikita

Total Employees..............................30	**Regional Employees** 30	
Year Established 1946	**SIC Code**......................................3499	
Annual Revenues ($000) 2,500		

Littell Steel Co., Inc.

Rte. 51
P.O. Box 298
New Brighton, PA 15066
County: Beaver

Phone: (412) 843-5212
Fax: (412) 843-5211

Fabricator of structural steel and carbon steel plate used in the construction of buildings, bridges, monuments, machinery and equipment, and a provider of steel erection services. The Company serves industrial and general contractors. Its recent projects include Washington Redskin Stadium in Landover, MD; Ocean City Convention Center in Ocean City, MD; Union Electric Steel addition in Burgettstown, PA; and the Jewish Community Center in Pittsburgh, PA.

Officers: Murray C. Thaw *CH & CEO*
Roland Heil *P & COO*
Robert M. Thaw *VP-SAL*

Human Resources: Gene A. Barbato *SEC & TRS*

Purchasing: Gordon Holmes

Total Employees..............................49	**Regional Employees** 49	
Year Established 1946	**SIC Code**......................................3441	
Annual Revenues ($000)..10,000+		

Little Earth Productions, Inc.

2211 Fifth Ave.
Pittsburgh, PA 15219
County: Allegheny

Phone: (412) 471-0909
Fax: (412) 471-0910
Internet Address: www.littlearth.com

Manufacturer of gifts, fashion accessories and furniture from recycled materials, including truck tire inner tubes, street signs, billboards, bottle caps and license plates. The Company's product line includes belts, handbags, wallets, planners, checkbook covers, address books, journals, photo albums, CD holders, T-shirts and caps. Its newly introduced furniture line includes bar stools, chairs, tables, benches and mirrors. The Company markets its products through approximately 1,100 retail outlets in 20 countries.

Officers: Robert Brandegee *C-OWN & P*
Ava Demarco *C-OWN & VP*
Michael Betz *CON*
John Galbraith *DIR-MFG*

Human Resources: James Murray-Coleman *VP-OPR & SAL*

Purchasing: Kevin McCabe

Total Employees............................48	**Regional Employees** 48
Year Established 1993	**SIC Code**......................................3171
Annual Revenues ($000) 3,100	

Lockhart Co.

River Rd.
P.O. Box 1165, Pittsburgh, PA 15230
McKees Rocks, PA 15136
County: Allegheny

Phone: (412) 771-2600
Fax: (412) 771-2737
Internet Address: www.lockhart.com

Vertically integrated holding company engaged in the wholesaling of aluminum products and the manufacturing of chemicals. Through the Company's Lockhart Aluminum, Inc. (LAI), which is also located at the above address, it processes and distributes aluminum, including sheet, plate and extrusions, primarily to the heavy transportation industry. LAI operates branch warehouse and sales offices in Lansdale, PA; Knoxville, TN; and Dallas, TX. Its products are marketed by salespeople to customers in New York, Ohio, Pennsylvania, West Virginia and Canada. Lockhart Chemical Co., a subsidiary of the Company located in Gibsonia, PA, manufactures a range of corrosion inhibitors and emulsifying additives for paint coatings and lubricants.

Officers: Tony Gosse *P*
Brian Benjamin *VP-FIN*
Nancy Pudelsky *VP-SAL & MKT*
Scott Carothers *OPR MGR*

Human Resources: Amy Lewis

Purchasing: Hector Desimone *Materials MGR*

Total Employees...........................100
Year Established 1890   **SIC Code**.....................................5051

Long Manufacturing Co., Inc., Walter

86 Walter Long Rd.
P.O. Box 310, Library, PA 15129
Finleyville, PA 15332
County: Washington

Phone: (412) 348-6631
Fax: (412) 348-8411

   Provider of metal fabrication services to manufacturing industries. The Company specializes in bending, rolling, burning, shearing and welding of carbon steel, stainless steel and aluminum from 10" diameter to 10' diameter and in material from 1/8" to 4" thick. It operates an additional facility located at 1315 Bingham St. in Pittsburgh, PA.

Officers: Robert I. Long *C-OWN & P*
David S. Long *C-OWN, VP & SEC*
Robert G. Long *C-OWN, VP & TRS*

Total Employees.............................43   **Regional Employees** 43
Year Established 1898   **SIC Code**.....................................3443

Longwood at Oakmont, Inc.

500 Rte. 909
Verona, PA 15147
County: Allegheny

Phone: (412) 826-5700
Fax: (412) 826-5706

   Nonprofit, full-service continuing care retirement community. The Facility is comprised of 187 independent living units and a 59-bed skilled nursing complex located on a 51-acre campus.

Officers: Thomas F. Rockenbach, Jr. *EDIR*
Pamela B. Leibensperger *Associate EDIR*
Joseph A. Wenger *Associate EDIR*

Human Resources: Joanne Campagna

Total Employees............................180	**Regional Employees** 180	
Year Established 1991	**SIC Code**.....................................8361	
Annual Revenues ($000) 5,600		

Lorenzi, Dodds & Gunnill, Inc.

100 Wood St., 8th Fl
Pittsburgh, PA 15222
County: Allegheny

Phone: (412) 261-6062
Fax: (412) 261-1922

Provider of architectural and civil engineering services specializing in site engineering. The Company also offers design and planning services. It serves clients throughout Maryland, Pennsylvania and West Virginia, and part of Virginia. A branch office is located in Waldorf, MD.

Officers: James C. Lorenzi *P*
William P. Durkee *VP*
William H. Lorenzi *AST-SEC & AST-TRS*

Human Resources: Julius J. Lorenzi *VP, SEC & TRS (Purchasing)*

Total Employees............................40	**Regional Employees** 16	
Year Established 1953	**SIC Code**.....................................8711	
Annual Revenues ($000) 3,400		

Louise Child Care, Inc.

366 S. Aiken Ave.
Pittsburgh, PA 15232
County: Allegheny

Phone: (412) 661-7340
Fax: (412) 661-0146

Nonprofit provider of child care and professional development services to the child care community. The Company's operations consist of five child care centers located throughout Pittsburgh serving children up to six years of age; three respite care centers in Homestead, McKeesport and Pittsburgh, PA, providing care for children while parents are attending drug and/or alcohol rehabilitation sessions; and child care home services in approximately 35 private residences throughout Allegheny County for children up to age 12. The Company also provides professional training, mentoring, consultation and management services to meet the needs of organizations and individuals who care for children through its Pittsburgh Child Care Institute at Five Station Square Dr. E. in Pittsburgh, PA.

Officers: Carol Barone-Martin *EDIR*
Cheryl Edmonds *DIR-Child Care*
Jane Fulton *DIR-Public Relations & DEV*
Cindy Popovich *DIR-Mentoring*
Annette Santella *DIR-Training*
Jack Yoedt *CON*

Purchasing: Dawn Groskopf

Total Employees	125	**Regional Employees**	125
Year Established	1904	**SIC Code**	8351
Annual Revenues ($000)	3,100		

LSC Acquisition Co., Inc.

100 Herrmann Rd.
Pittsburgh, PA 15239
County: Allegheny

Phone: (412) 795-6400
Fax: (412) 795-6442

Contract manufacturer of precision machined parts using screw machines, computer and numerically controlled lathes, and rotary transfer machines. The Company does business as LSC Co.

Officers: Robert L. Baiz *CEO*
Barnaby Myhrum *P*

Human Resources: Carole Graham

Total Employees	45	**Regional Employees**	45
Year Established	1927	**SIC Code**	3451
Annual Revenues ($000)	5,000		

LTV Steel Co.-Pittsburgh Coke Plant

4650 Second Ave.
Pittsburgh, PA 15207
County: Allegheny

Phone: (412) 227-4000
Fax: (412) 227-6543

Coke plant operating five coke oven batteries with a total of 315 ovens. The Plant processes 4,300 tons of coke per day, with an annual production capacity of 1.6 million tons of metallurgical coke. The processed coke is shipped to LTV Steel blast furnaces in East Chicago, IN, and Cleveland, OH, by a fleet of railroad hopper cars. The Plant is a unit of LTV Steel Co. (LSC), which is headquartered in Cleveland, OH. LSC is a subsidiary of The LTV Corp., which is also headquartered in Cleveland, OH, and listed on the NYSE.

Officers: David Griener   *Plant MGR*
Edward De Iuliis   *Area MGR-Maintenance*
Jeffrey Drummond   *Area MGR-OPR*

Human Resources: Ken Magness   *Human Resource MGR*

Total Employees......................15,000	**Regional Employees** 735
Year Established 1984	**SIC Code**....................................3312

LTV Steel Co.-Tin Mill Division, Aliquippa Plant

Franklin Ave.
P.O. Box 490
Aliquippa, PA 15001
County: Beaver

Phone: (412) 378-5309
Fax: (412) 378-5307

Producer of black plate, tin plate, tin-free steel and tin-coated sheet used by customers to manufacture food and beverage cans, aerosol cans, bottle crowns and closures, paint cans, pails, and other types of containers. The Mill's products are also used in making oil filters, fasteners, trays, utility sheds, swimming pool panels, film magazines, commercial ceiling grid systems, tubing, battery cases, curtain rods, toys, shelving, air cleaners, book binding and other products. The Mill is a unit of LTV Steel Co. (LSC), which is headquartered in Cleveland, OH. LSC is a subsidiary of The LTV Corp., which is also headquartered in Cleveland, OH, and listed on the NYSE.

Officers: Bill Stephans   *MGR-OPR*

Human Resources: Jim Lawrence   *MGR-Industrial Relations*

Total Employees......................15,000	**Regional Employees** 545
Year Established 1984	**SIC Code**....................................3471

Lucent Technologies, Inc.

2200 Liberty Ave., Ste. 100
Pittsburgh, PA 15222
County: Allegheny

Phone: (412) 338-8220
Fax: (412) 338-8222
Internet Address: www.lucent.com

Designer, builder and deliverer of a wide range of public and private networks, communications systems and software, consumer and business telephone systems and microelectronics components. The Company is headquartered in Murray Hill, NJ, and is listed on the NYSE. The facility located at the above address is a branch office of its Business Communications Systems unit, which develops, manufactures, markets and services advanced communications products and systems for business customers worldwide. These include telephone, wireless and voice processing systems, call centers, data networking and multimedia networks and structured cabling systems. The Company also operates a Business Communications Systems unit office in Robinson Township, PA, serving small business clients, and a Network Systems unit office in Murrysville, PA. The local employees provide sales and service for business customers throughout Western Pennsylvania.

Officers: Emily Lampich *Large Business SAL MGR*
Kevin Phelan *Field Services GMGR*
Peter Roedersheimer *Large Business SAL MGR*

Total Employees....................121,000	**Regional Employees** 285
Year Established 1869	**SIC Code**.....................................5963
Annual Revenues ($000) 23,000,000		

Lukens, Inc.—Washington/Houston Operations

Woodland & Griffith Aves.
Washington, PA 15301
County: Washington

Phone: (412) 222-8000
Fax: (412) 222-2790

Manufacturer and marketer of stainless steel sheet, strip, plate, hot bands and slabs. The Plant is a unit of Lukens Inc., which is headquartered in Coatesville, PA, and listed on the NYSE. The Plant sells its products to domestic and foreign stainless steel service centers, fabricators and OEMs.

Officers: Joseph K. Kusic *VP & GMGR*

Human Resources: John Bechdel *DIR-Human Resources*
Jack Greene

Total Employees............................800	**Regional Employees** 800
Year Established 1945	**SIC Code**.....................................3312

Lutheran Affiliated Services, Inc.

1323 Freedom Rd.
Cranberry Township, PA 16066
County: Butler

Phone: (412) 776-1100
Fax: (412) 776-0811

Nonprofit provider of geriatric health care services claiming to be one of the largest such providers in Western Pennsylvania. The Organization offers programs in assisted living, Alzheimer's treatment, skilled nursing, subacute care, primary physician care, aging research and education, and full-service continuing care retirement communities. In addition, its expertise has been utilized in consulting contracts with other area health care providers. The Organization's senior communities consist of: LAS/Passavant Retirement Community in Zelienople, PA, which provides housing and services for more than 650 older adults from residential and assisted living to total skilled nursing care; LAS/Samaritan HealthCare, Inc. in Cranberry Township, PA, which has developed LAS/Crown Pointe Retirement Communities in Butler, PA, with 101 condominiums and 103 assisted living apartments, and in Greensburg, PA, with 103 condominiums and 98 assisted living apartments; LAS/St. John Specialty Care Center in Mars, PA, a 334-bed specialty care facility that offers Alzheimer's care, subacute care and long-term care; and The Village at Spring Crest in Latrobe, PA, a senior condominium community that offers 40 condominium units. The Organization's other operations include: Geriatric Care Services, Inc. in Butler, Greensburg, Mars and Zelienople, PA, which is a primary care practice staffed by general practitioners and specialists trained in geriatrics; LAS Foundation in Cranberry Township, PA, which provides professional management and oversight of capital funding for the Organization; LAS/Aging Research & Education Center in Mars, PA, which provides research, education, program development and training for geriatric care issues; and Salem Service Corp. in Cranberry Township, PA, which provides project management consulting services.

Officers: Michael C. Hendrickson, Ph.D. *P*
William J. Grego *COO*
Thomas G. Chase *CFO*
Robert E. Johnson *SVP-MKT*
William T. Pratt *P-Samaritan HealthCare & Salem Services*

Human Resources: Jody L. Reid *DIR-Human Resources*

Purchasing: Bonnie Harmon

Total Employees	1,100	**Regional Employees**	1,100
Year Established	1986	**SIC Code**	8051
Annual Revenues ($000)			50,000

Lutheran Services for Families

Beaver Rd.
P.O. Box 70
Zelienople, PA 16063
County: Butler

Phone: (412) 452-4453
Fax: (412) 452-6576

Nonprofit provider of social services operating through two segments: Lutheran Youth & Family Services provides comprehensive care in response to the individual needs of troubled youth and their families in close cooperation with other service providers; and Lutheran Youth & Family Services Foundation supports the Organization's charitable activities. The Organization's main campus, located at the above address, comprises 325 acres and is home to five residential cottages, an emergency shelter, group home, chapel, St. Stephen's Lutheran Academy, a partial hospitalization program, and offices serving both its Family Foster Care and WrapAround service programs. The five residential cottages can house up to 50 children and adolescents between the ages of six and 18 who participate in a psychiatric residential treatment program. The group home has a capacity of 9 girls and is for girls ages six to 18. St. Stephen's Lutheran Academy is a small private school with an enrollment of approximately 125 day and resident students. The partial hospitalization program provides services to youth who require less than inpatient psychiatric hospital care, but more intense services than those offered in outpatient treatment programs. The Organization's other facilities include a supervised apartment independent living complex at 6338 Aurelia St. in Pittsburgh; and Family Foster Care and WrapAround branch offices at 3936 Perrysville Rd. in Pittsburgh and in Shelocta, PA. The Organization is operated and maintained by the Evangelical Lutheran Church of America which is headquartered in Washington, D.C.

Officers: Charles T. Lockwood, Ed.D. *EDIR*
Demetrios Marousis *DIR-Programs*
Barbara Senatore *DIR-MGT Services*
Sherri L. Williams *DIR-FIN*

Human Resources: Roxanne Edwards *Deputy DIR-Human Resources*

Purchasing: Thomas Woodring *DIR-Facilities MGT*

Total Employees	281	**Regional Employees**	250
Year Established	1854	**SIC Code**	8322
Annual Revenues ($000)			7,702

M. J. B. Co., Inc.

704 Second Ave.
Pittsburgh, PA 15219
County: Allegheny

Phone: (412) 471-2867
Fax: (412) 471-2865

Holding company for two subsidiaries, Duquesne Litho, Inc. (DLI) and Laser Images, Inc. (LII), and an affiliate, Duquesne Quick Copy, Inc. (DQCI), all located at the above address. DLI, a commercial printing company, offers four-to-six color printing, short or long runs, an art department and complete bindery services. LII offers color separating and extensive electronic prepress services. DQCI offers duplicating and short run printing.

Officers: James P. Condio *P*
Steven M. Condio *SEC*

Human Resources: William T. Collins, Jr.

Purchasing: Gregory J. Condio *TRS*

Total Employees	37	**Regional Employees**	37
Year Established	1946	**SIC Code**	2752
Annual Revenues ($000)	4,889		

Mac Plastics, Inc.

250 W. Wylie Ave.
Washington, PA 15301
County: Washington

Phone: (412) 222-2600
Fax: (412) 222-4585

Provider of custom blow molding, decorating (including painting, pad printing and silk screening), assembly and contract manufacturing services. The Company states that it is one of the fourteen largest industrial blow molders in the U.S. The Company operates more than thirty molding machines, covering a wide range of capabilities, with products ranging from less than one pound to twenty pounds. It can manage an entire project from technical design and engineering through final assembly and shipping. The Company serves the housewares, juvenile furniture, automotive, recreation, toy, lawn and garden, industrial, medical, seasonal and components markets.

Officers: Rudolph DiNardo *P*
James DiNardo, Sr. *VP-Facilities & Equipment*
Norman C. DiNardo *VP-SAL & MKT*

Human Resources: Karen Hess
Purchasing: Nancy Beatty

Total Employees 300-400	**Regional Employees** 300-400
Year Established 1963	**SIC Code**....................................3089
Annual Revenues ($000) 37,000	

Mackin Engineering Co.

M

R.I.D.C. Park W., 117 Industry Dr.
Pittsburgh, PA 15275
County: Allegheny

Phone: (412) 788-0472
Fax: (412) 787-3588

Provider of civil engineering services. The Firm offers planning and design services for roadways, bridges and development projects; addresses environmental and traffic issues; and provides construction management and inspection services during the actual construction. Its services have included land surveying; site development; hydrologic and hydraulic analysis and design; storm water detention design; storm and sanitary sewer design; coordination with utility and railroad companies; roadway location studies and design; roadway drainage design; preparation of soil erosion and sedimentation control plans and narrative; environmental impact statements; wetland delineation and mitigation plans; categorical exclusion evaluations; riverfront planning and design; preparation of right-of-way plans; highway lighting design; preparation of traffic control plans; highway interchange design; intersection design; performance of traffic counts and traffic studies; traffic signalization design; bridge inspections, bridge rehabilitation design; final bridge design; preparation of construction plans, specifications and estimates; shop drawing review and construction consultation; and construction management and construction inspection and testing. The Firm has provided these services to all eleven Engineering Districts of the Pennsylvania Department of Transportation, the Pennsylvania Turnpike Commission and an array of counties, municipalities, industries, railroads, and public, semi-public and private clients throughout the Commonwealth of Pennsylvania. The Firm maintains a branch office in Mechanicsburg, PA.

Officers: Italo V. Mackin *P*
Richard G. Jones *EVP*
Jerome J. Schwertz *SVP*

Human Resources: Barbara D. Burtyk *(Purchasing)*

Total Employees..........................100	**Regional Employees** 88
Year Established 1960	**SIC Code** 8711
Annual Revenues ($000) 7,100	

Magee Plastics Co.

303 Brush Creek Rd.
Warrendale, PA 15086
County: Allegheny

Phone: (412) 776-2220
Fax: (412) 776-9696

Designer and manufacturer of thermoplastic composites for aircraft interior applications. The Company's product list includes over 15,000 items, ranging from sidewall panels to window shades. It has sold thousands of complete retro-fit kits to the major domestic and international airlines for use in many different types of commercial aircraft. It also sells to OEMs on a limited basis (i.e., Airbus, Boeing, Douglas and Fokker). In addition, the Company designs thermoplastic composites for railroads, including AMTRAK coaches, and General Electric and General Motors locomotives. Most of the Company's parts are vacuum formed or compression molded.

Officers: Ted N. Magee *CH & CEO*
Mary Lou Magee *P & COO*
Sean P. Magee *SEVP*
Glen H. Maus *VP*
Kelly S. Magee *SEC & TRS*

Purchasing: William Lytle

Total Employees...............................63
Year Established 1968

Regional Employees 63
SIC Code.....................................3089

Magee-Womens Health Corp.

300 Halket St.
Pittsburgh, PA 15213
County: Allegheny

Phone: (412) 641-1000
Fax: (412) 641-4343
Internet Address: www.magee.edu

Nonprofit operator of the Magee-Womens Hospital, a specialty hospital for women and infants located at the above address. With nearly 9,000 deliveries each year, the hospital claims to be one of the largest private providers of obstetrical services in the United States and one of the top 10 hospitals in the United States in treatment volumes for gynecologic cancers. It offers a wide range of services including high-risk pregnancy programs, neonatal intensive care facilities, oncology research and treatment, plastic surgery, a menopause education and consultation center, an osteoporosis prevention and treatment center, a health center for women age 45 and over, gynecological/urological programs, infertility programs, genetic services, educational programs and services, and ancillary services. The hospital has 290 adult beds, 96 bassinets and 63 neonatal intensive care unit beds. It also runs outreach clinics and programs, conferences and volunteer programs involving women-related issues. The outreach clinics are located in Pittsburgh at the Letsche School, Hill House Center, Mathilda Theiss Center and Bethlehem Haven, as well as in the South Side and in Wilkinsburg, and in Aliquippa and Clairton, PA. In addition, Womancare Centers are located in Bethel Park, Monroeville, Moon Township, Oakland, Pleasant Hills and Wexford, PA. The hospital is affiliated with the University of Pittsburgh School of Medicine. It trains in excess of 650 interns, residents and paraprofessionals annually. The Company's other subsidiaries include The Children's Center of Pittsburgh, Magee-Womens Health Foundation and Magee-Womens Health Service Corp.

M

Officers: David A. Smith *CH*
Raymond LeBoeuf *VCH*
Irma E. Goertzen *P & CEO*
Mary Sue Embertson *CFO*
Peter W. Eisenbrandt *TRS*
Frances Todd Steward *SEC*
Gina Baker *AST-SEC*

Human Resources: Linda McAbee *DIR-Human Resources*

Purchasing: John Deighan *DIR-Purchasing*

Total Employees..........................1,890	**Regional Employees** 1,890
Year Established 1911	**SIC Code**.....................................8069
Annual Revenues ($000) 128,705	

Mallet & Co., Inc.

Arch St. Ext.
P.O. Box 474
Carnegie, PA 15106
County: Allegheny

Phone: (412) 276-9000
Fax: (412) 276-9002

Manufacturer of a variety of cooking oils and custom food processing equipment for the wholesale baking and food service industry. The Company operates a subsidiary, Nippon Mallet Ltd., which is located in Tokyo, Japan.

Officers: Robert I. Mallet *P*
Aaron E. Margolis *EVP*

Regional Employees.....................100	
Year Established 1939	**SIC Code**.....................................2079

Mallet's Gateway Terminal, Inc.

Chartiers Industrial Park, 2150 Roswell Dr.
Pittsburgh, PA 15205
County: Allegheny

Phone: (412) 922-2700
Fax: (412) 922-2905

Provider of third-party warehousing, trucking and logistics services on a public or contract basis. The Company has expertise to receive, store, inventory and distribute goods on the behalf of clients. It also provides value-added services, such as consolidated transportation, inventory tracking, repackaging, customized computer needs, real estate analysis and more. In addition, it offers full service food grade warehousing and distribution, and just-in-time delivery. The Company operates an additional facility at 1600 W. Carson St. in Pittsburgh, PA, offering a combined total of 300,000 square feet of warehouse space with 50 truck doors and 30 car rail sidings.

Officers: Mervin Mallet *OWN*
Christoph M. Harlan *P*
Mark Connors *GMGR*

Total Employees.............................40
Year Established........................1960
Annual Revenues ($000)...4,000

Regional Employees....................40
SIC Code....................................4200

Managed Care of America, Inc.

820 Parish St.
Pittsburgh, PA 15220
County: Allegheny

Phone: (412) 922-2803
Fax: (412) 922-3071

Holding company for 16 related health care administration companies providing both private label and direct contract third-party claims administration, pharmacy benefit management, managed care consulting, PPO plans and utilization review. The Company also provides wellness programs, prescription care and mail service, stop loss insurance and Section 125 plan administration. Additional offices are located in Alpharetta, GA; and Cleveland, Columbus and Dayton, OH. The Company's subsidiaries consist of American SelectCare Corp.; Bayou Acquisition Corp.; BP Agency, Inc.; BP Agency of Georgia, Inc.; Benefit Planners & Assoc., Inc.; Buckeye Benefit Concepts, Inc.; Continental Printing Services, Inc.; EBCares, Inc. d/b/a CARE Network; EBRx, Inc.; Employee Benefit Claims, Inc.; Enterprise Underwriting Services, Inc.; Managed Care of America Consulting, Inc.; Penn Reinsurance Ltd.; SelectCare Access Corp.; and Texas Benefits Administrators, Inc. In addition, the Company is the owner of a software business, Managed Care Software, which is currently licensed to 24 HMO, PPO and PHOs serving over 2.5 million covered lives.

Officers: Dennis Casey *Senior Executive*
Charles E. Davidson *Senior Executive & GC*
Tim Horn *Senior Executive*
Phyllis L. Hughes *Senior Executive, SEC & TRS*
Jay Ver Hulst *Senior Executive*

M

Total Employees............................165	**Regional Employees** 90
Year Established 1974	**SIC Code** 6411
Annual Revenues ($000) 24,000	

Management Science Assoc., Inc.

6565 Penn Ave.
Pittsburgh, PA 15206
County: Allegheny

Phone: (412) 362-2000
Fax: (412) 363-5598
Internet Address: www.msa.com

Provider of analytical software and information-based systems. The Company specializes in data management and data warehousing, business analysis, media services, and custom workflow integration and software. Its data management services include designing, editing, cleaning and integrating databases with expertise in marketing, distributor sales and inventory; customer information; direct marketing and fulfillment data; sales force intelligence; media and advertising research; internal sales; and financial analysis. Its data analysis and business consulting services include gathering and interpreting data on customer loyalty, retention and switching; advertising and marketing mix analysis; segmentation, targeting and list scoring; and promotion and price elasticity analysis. The Company also develops custom software applications in areas such as personnel and time management, project tracking and management, executive information systems, sales force automation and enterprise integration applications. The Company operates two local divisions: Computer/Communications Management integrates and maintains systems for more than 200 firms in the Pittsburgh area; and Pyromet Automation Services develops fully integrated process automation, dynamic scheduling and reporting systems for the steel and process industries. The Company maintains branch offices in Chicago, IL; Boston, MA; New York, NY; Winston-Salem, NC; Toronto, Ontario, Canada; Kuala Lumpur, Malaysia; and Cardiff, Wales.

Officers: Alfred Kuehn, Ph.D. *OWN & CH*
Viv Penninti *P & CEO*
Bernie Ryan *SVP*
William Tarlo *VP-FIN*

Human Resources: Mary Ann Victor *VP*

Total Employees............................505	**Regional Employees** 463
Year Established 1963	**SIC Code** 8742

Mannesmann Demag Corp.

Airport Office Park, Bldg. 5, 345 Rouser Rd.
Coraopolis, PA 15108
County: Allegheny

Phone: (412) 269-5600
Fax: (412) 269-5619

Supplier of complete metallurgical equipment and plants to the iron, steel and nonferrous metals industry. The Company offers engineered products, services and technology from the worldwide Mannesmann network for both new and revamped facilities. Its products and services include EBT furnaces, ladle furnaces, complete vacuum metallurgy systems and know-how package; MRP converters for refining and stainless steel purposes; BOF steelmaking shops; continuous casting plants for slabs, blooms, rounds and billets; and complete rolling mill systems for ferrous and nonferrous including slab, plate and hot strip mills, cold mills, pickling lines, galvanizing lines and annealing and pickling lines for stainless steel. Its tubular and hydraulic group products include welded pipe/tube mills, seamless pipe/tube mills, cold pilger mills for copper, steel, nickel and alloys, cold drawing benches, extrusion presses, forging presses, metal powder presses, tube finishing equipment and complete plants. The Company is a subsidiary of Mannesmann Capital Corp. (MCC), which has headquarters in New York, NY. MCC is a subsidiary of Mannesmann AG, which is headquartered in Duisburg, Germany, and listed on the Frankfurt Stock Exchange.

Officers: Ingo Boettcher *P*
　　　　　　　Rolf Brandenburg *EVP & CFO*
　　　　　　　Bruce Allison *VP-Contracts*
　　　　　　　Ronald Ashburn *VP-Continuous Casting & Hot Mills*
　　　　　　　Wilhelm Bungert *VP-Pipe & Tube Mills*
　　　　　　　Michael Corso *VP-Technical Services*
　　　　　　　Kevin Deliman *VP-SAL & MKT*
　　　　　　　Bernfried Stache *VP-Steel Making*
　　　　　　　Rich Sweitzer *VP-Cold Mills & Processing Lines*

Human Resources: Thomas Trumble *Human Resources MGR*

Purchasing: John Kubasiak *MGR-Purchasing*

Total Employees 200	**Regional Employees** 200
Year Established 1965	**SIC Code** 3542
Annual Revenues ($000) 120,000	

MARC & Co., Inc.

Four Station Sq., Ste. 500
Pittsburgh, PA 15219
County: Allegheny

Phone: (412) 562-2000
Fax: (412) 562-2022

Full-service provider of advertising services including consumer, retail and general advertising. The Firm's other services include sales promotion, public relations, direct marketing and market research. It also does business under the name MARC Advertising. The Firm's subsidiaries include Electronic Images in Pittsburgh, PA; Evans & Fitzgerald in Coral Gables, FL; and Marketing/Promotion/Strategies in Indianapolis, IN.

M

Officers: Anthony L. Bucci *P & CEO*
Norbert J. Sieber, Jr. *EVP & GMGR*
Michele S. Fabrizi *SVP & DIR-Client Services*
Edward L. Fine *SVP & Executive Creative DIR*
John H. Harpur *SVP & Media DIR*
Stuart M. Zolot *SVP-FIN & ADM*

Human Resources: Fran Gargotta

Total Employees	154	**Regional Employees**	139
Year Established	1955	**SIC Code**	7311
Annual Revenues ($000)	18,600		

Marco Contractors, Inc.

377 Northgate Dr.
P.O. Box 515
Warrendale, PA 15086
County: Allegheny

Phone: (412) 935-8160
Fax: (412) 935-8159

General contractor specializing in retail construction. The Company serves clients nationwide.

Officers: Martin R. Smith *P (Human Resources)*

Total Employees	50	**Regional Employees**	20
Year Established	1987	**SIC Code**	1542
Annual Revenues ($000)	15,000		

Marian Manor Corp.

2695 Winchester Dr.
Pittsburgh, PA 15220
County: Allegheny

Phone: (412) 563-6866
Fax: (412) 563-1250

Nonprofit owner and operator of Marian Manor, a nursing home providing personal, intermediate and skilled nursing care for the frail elderly. The facility consists of three buildings containing 48 personal care beds and 174 intermediate and skilled nursing beds. It also offers child care and adult day care services as well as a senior citizen center and an intergenerational program. The Company is owned by the Sisters of the Holy Spirit.

Officers: Sister Eileen Chlebowski *Administrator (Purchasing)*

Total Employees............................300	**Regional Employees** 300
Year Established 1956	**SIC Code**.......................................8059

Markovitz Enterprises, Inc.

1101 Muriel St.
Pittsburgh, PA 15203
County: Allegheny

Phone: (412) 431-8250
Fax: (412) 431-1177

Manufacturer of steel-related products through three operating divisions. The Badger Industry Division in Zelienople, PA, manufactures bellow type expansion joints. The Flowline Division in Whiteville, NC, and New Castle, PA, manufactures stainless steel butt-welled fittings. The Quality Rolls Division in New Castle and Zelienople, PA, manufactures forged hardened steel rolls.

Officers: James C. Markovitz *CEO*
James S. Markovitz *P*
R. Matthew Fleig *VP-SAL*
Frank T. Roberts *VP-Technical Services & DEV*
James B. Walter *VP-OPR*
Paul R. Heckman *MGR-Quality Assurance*

Total Employees............................410	**Regional Employees** 123
Year Established 1981	**SIC Code**.......................................3325

Marmon/Keystone Corp.

225 E. Cunningham St.
P.O. Box 992, Butler, PA 16003
Butler, PA 16001
County: Butler

Phone: (412) 283-3000
Fax: (412) 283-0558
Internet Address: www.marmonkeystone.com

Wholesaler and distributor of tubular and bar products that claims to be the largest stocking distributor of specialty tubing and chrome-plated bar in the world. The Company offers over 10,000 sizes and grades of standard and line pipe; pressure, mechanical and structural tubing; structural steel; aluminum pipe and tubing; nickel alloy pipe and tubing; chrome and stainless bar; alloy tubing, large OD heavy wall seamless; and hone and suitable-to-hone fluid power tubing.

Its services include threading, beveling and cutting to customer specifications. The Company's customers are primarily those in transportation, construction, agriculture, food processing, aerospace and capital goods industries. M/K Express, a subsidiary trucking company headquartered in East Butler, PA, is a common/contract carrier serving customers throughout the continental United States. The Company operates at more than 40 locations in the U.S., Belgium, Canada, England, France and Mexico. Its affiliates include Future Metals, Inc. in Ft. Lauderdale, FL; Marmon/Keystone Anbuma in Belgium; Marmon/Keystone Canada Inc. and Specialty Steels in Canada; and the Wheeler Group in England. In addition, Marmon/Keystone de Mexico S.A. de C.V. operates a sales office in Monterrey, Mexico and Marmon/Keystone S.A. operates a sales office in Paris, France. The Company is a member of The Marmon Group, Inc., which is head-quartered in Chicago, IL.

M

Officers: Norman E. Gottschalk, Jr. *P*
Robert M. Kaniecki *VP-ADM*
Rick Matalone *VP-MER*
Andrew Seka *VP & CON*
William J. Bittner *GVP*
Dan Devlin *GVP*
Tim Spatafore *GVP*
John F. Porfidio *P-Future Metals, Inc.*
Graham Wheeler *P-Wheeler Group*
Douglas Williams *P & GMGR-Canadian OPR*
Jean-Francois Lievin *GMGR-Belgium & France*

Human Resources: Linda McCue *DIR-Human Resources*

Purchasing: Dave Ehlers *DIR-Purchasing*

Total Employees ....1,300+	**Regional Employees** 245
Year Established 1907	**SIC Code**......................................5051
Annual Revenues ($000)...500,000+	

Mars National Bank, The

145 Grand Ave.
P.O. Box 927
Mars, PA 16046
County: Butler

Phone: (412) 625-1555

National commercial bank offering a wide range of deposit and loan products. In addition to the Bank's main office which is located at the above address, it operates branch offices in Butler, Cranberry Township, Gibsonia and Mars, PA.

Officers: Charles A. Norton *CH*
Derek O. Van Buskirk *VCH*
Dallas C. Hipple *P*
Keith B. Hughes *VP*

R. Bruce Mensch *SEC*
Annamary McMullen *Cashier & OPR Officer*

Total Employees	102	**Regional Employees**	102
Year Established	1900	**SIC Code**	6021
Annual Revenues ($000)	200,000 (Assets)		

Marsh & McLennan, Inc.

USX Tower, 600 Grant St., Ste. 5500
Pittsburgh, PA 15219
County: Allegheny

Phone: (412) 288-8800
Fax: (412) 288-8884

Provider of insurance brokering activities and professional counseling services on risk management issues, including risk analysis, coverage requirements, self-insurance, and alternative insurance and risk financing methods, as well as claims collection, injury management, loss prevention and other insurance related issues. The Company, which is headquartered in New York, NY, is a subsidiary of Marsh & McLennan Cos., Inc., which is also headquartered in New York, NY, and listed on the NYSE.

Officers: Norbert Forrester *MDIR*

Total Employees	25,000	**Regional Employees**	95
Year Established	1891	**SIC Code**	6411
Annual Revenues ($000)	3,000,000+		

Marshall, Dennehey, Warner, Coleman & Goggin

USX Tower, 600 Grant St., Ste. 2900
Pittsburgh, PA 15219
County: Allegheny

Phone: (412) 394-4090
Fax: (412) 394-4095

Provider of legal services with approximately 260 attorneys. Exclusively a defense litigation firm, it represents insurers and self-insureds in the areas of product liability; professional liability; malpractice; workers' compensation; employment law; bad faith; toxic tort; motor carrier; fire; admirality; and coverage and premise liability. The Firm, which is headquartered in Philadelphia, PA, operates additional branch offices in Wilmington, DE; Livingston and Marlton, NJ; Allentown, Doylestown, Erie, Harrisburg, Lancaster, Newtown Square, Norristown, Scranton and Williamsport, PA. The Pittsburgh office serves clients in western Pennsylvania and West Virginia and has approximately 25 attorneys.

Officers: Robert J. Coleman *CH, P & TRS*
Robert S. Goggin *EVP*
John P. Penders *EVP & SEC*
P. Brennan Hart *Managing Shareholder-Pittsburgh, PA*
Scott G. Dunlop *Managing Attorney-Pittsburgh, PA*

M

Human Resources: Dorothy Keenan *(Philadelphia, PA)*

Purchasing: Angelina McGarry *(Philadelphia, PA)*

Total Employees............................550	**Regional Employees** 45	
Year Established 1963	**SIC Code** 8111	

Marshall Elevator Co.

2015 Mary St.
Pittsburgh, PA 15203
County: Allegheny

Phone: (412) 431-1340
Fax: (412) 431-5775

Manufacturer and servicer of elevator products. The Company's products include hydraulic, traction, passenger, residential and freight elevators as well as dumbwaiters, handicapped lifts, stage lifts and custom-designed systems for signal towers. Its Marshall Electronics division designs and builds control and communication systems for industry. The Company is a franchised distributor of Dover Elevator Systems, Inc. Some of its recent installations have included elevators at American Video Glass Co., Bayer Corp., Magee-Womens Hospital, McKeesport Little Theatre, NASA Robotics, Point Park College, Quaker Valley Middle School and the Zone 1 Police Station.

Officers: Robert S. Jamison, Jr. *P & CEO*
Eric E. Stefanko, Sr. *EVP & COO*
David A. Heiner *VP & AST-SEC*
Ronald A. Mehringer *VP-Electronics Division*

Human Resources: Gary R. Wolf *CON*

Total Employees............................75	**Regional Employees** 75
Year Established 1818	**SIC Code** 3534
Annual Revenues ($000)..7,000+	

Martin & Macfarlane, Inc.

2610 Fifth Ave.
Pittsburgh, PA 15213
County: Allegheny

Phone: (412) 681-8311
Fax: (412) 687-6037

Provider of outdoor advertising displays such as billboards and posters. The Company, doing business as Martin Media, meets the needs of advertisers with 2,321 poster displays and 318 giant 14′ x 48′ bulletins located throughout Southwestern Pennsylvania in Allegheny, Armstrong, Beaver, Butler, Fayette, Indiana, Lawrence, Mercer, Washington and Westmoreland Counties. It also offers marketing support and research. The Company, which is headquartered in Paso Robles, CA, operates approximately 20 branch offices in Arizona, California, Connecticut, Kansas, Nevada, Ohio, Pennsylvania, Texas and Washington, D.C. It is a subsidiary of Martin N. McFarland Corp., which is also headquartered in Paso Robles, CA.

Officers: Barry Heffner *VP & GMGR*

Purchasing: Dave Lamberger

Regional Employees......................66
Year Established........................1982   **SIC Code**....................................3993

Masterplan, Inc.

308 Seventh Ave.
Pittsburgh, PA 15222
County: Allegheny

Phone: (412) 434-0990
Fax: (412) 261-4348
Internet Address: www.hefren.com

Holding company for financially related businesses engaged in providing investment, financial planning and public finance underwriting services, all of which are located at the above address. Hefren-Tillotson, Inc. (HTI) claims to be one of the oldest and largest full-service investment firms headquartered in Western Pennsylvania. Its services are offered to both individual and corporate clients. HTI's Corporate Planning Services Group provides business owners with an array of services, including helping to establish and manage their pension, profit-sharing and 401(k) plans. A fully integrated division of HTI, Shelby Kern Frederick & Shelby, is a public finance underwriter offering comprehensive solutions to municipalities and non-profit institutions seeking access to the capital markets. Masterplan Consulting, Inc. offers a variety of insurance products and financial planning services. HTI operates branch offices in Beaver, Butler and Indiana, PA.

Officers: Willard Tillotson, Jr. *CEO-Hefren-Tillotson, Inc.*

R. Drew Kistler *VCH-Hefren-Tillotson, Inc.*
Kim Tillotson Fleming *P-Hefren-Tillotson, Inc.*
Richard L. Bryant *EVP & TRS-Hefren-Tillotson, Inc.*
James G. Meredith *EVP-Hefren-Tillotson, Inc.*
Craig Tillotson *EVP-Investments-Hefren-Tillotson, Inc.*
Dave Watters *EVP-Hefren-Tillotson, Inc.*
Edward J. Wetzel *EVP-SAL-Hefren-Tillotson, Inc.*

Total Employees..............................80   **Regional Employees** 80
Year Established 1948   **SIC Code** 6211

Mathias & Co., Inc., A. H.

950 Penn Ave.
Pittsburgh, PA 15222
County: Allegheny

Phone: (412) 281-1800
Fax: (412) 281-8243

Provider of traditional reprographic services including blueprinting, large document xerographic copying, photo reproduction, color copying and printing; and advanced digital technology for scanning, plotting and printing from hard copy, file and modem. The Company also provides color reprographics like the trademarked Color Direct process for color photographic prints up to 4' x 8' and offers mounting, laminating and framing for presentations, exhibit and display pieces. In addition, it is a VAR of Hewlett-Packard, Oce and Xerox large format copiers, plotters and printers backed up by service and repair technicians. The Company inventories specialty and bond papers, vellum, mylar, inks, toners and developers for all plain paper and diazo printers.

Officers: Herbert A. Mathias, Jr. *P*
Todd Mathias *VP*
Chris Mathias *MGR-Graphics*
Mark Mathias *MGR-SAL & MKT*

Human Resources: Patty Gallagher *Office MGR*

Total Employees..............................40   **Regional Employees** 40
Year Established 1892   **SIC Code** 2752
Annual Revenues ($000)..2,000+

Mauro Co., The A. G.

RIDC Industrial Park, 310 Alpha Dr.
Pittsburgh, PA 15238
County: Allegheny

Phone: (412) 782-6600
Fax: (412) 963-6913

Wholesaler, retailer and distributor of door and cabinet hardware and bathroom accessories. The Company supplies doors, frames, locks, butt hinges, exit panic devices, door closers, decorative and cabinet hardware, thresholds, security door hardware, bathroom cabinets and accessories, and specialty items for commercial, residential and institutional buildings. It can also provide fabricating capabilities for special door and frame modifications. Branch offices are located in Orlando, FL; Baltimore, MD; and Harrisburg, PA.

Officers: Raymond J. Mauro *CEO*
Richard C. Miles *P*

Total Employees............................150	**Regional Employees** 70
Year Established 1927	**SIC Code**......................................5072
Annual Revenues ($000)...20,000+	

MAX Environmental Technologies, Inc.

1815 Washington Rd.
Pittsburgh, PA 15241
County: Allegheny

Phone: (412) 343-4900
Fax: (412) 854-5536

Representative of an integrated group of companies that offers a broad base of environmental solutions for industrial waste generators and agencies of state and federal government. Through affiliate companies—Allegheny Liquid Systems Inc. (ALSI) and Mill Service Inc. (MSI)—the Company provides a full line of hazardous and nonhazardous waste management services for customers across a 12-state region and Canada. ALSI operates a nonhazardous waste pretreatment facility on Pittsburgh's Northside. The facility, with a capacity of 300,000 gallons per day, processes industrial wastewaters and sludges. MSI operates RCRA- and CERCLA-approved hazardous treatment, storage and disposal facilities in Bulger and Yukon, PA. The Company serves a variety of industries, including steel, oil and gas production, pharmaceutical, chemical, petrochemical and cosmetics manufacturing. Other customers include the Department of the Army,

Department of Energy, Department of the Navy, Environmental Protection Agency and the Pennsylvania Department of Environmental Protection. Additional turnkey services offered through the Company include remediation, alternative waste management options such as beneficial reuse, reclamation and recycling, mobile filter press services and drummed waste services.

M

Officers: L. William Spencer *P & CEO*
Philip Costantini *EVP & CFO*

Total Employees..............................80
Year Established 1958

Regional Employees 75
SIC Code....................................4953

Maynard & Co., Inc., H. B.

Eight Parkway Center
Pittsburgh, PA 15220
County: Allegheny

Phone: (412) 921-2400
Fax: (412) 921-4575
Internet Address: www.hbmaynard.com

Provider of international management consulting services. The Firm has worked with over 3,000 clients to improve operational effectiveness, quality, employee involvement and cost efficiency. Its customized project solutions are formed by integrating consulting, computer and training expertise.

Officers: Roger M. Weiss *P*
Edward J. Gill *VP-SAL & MKT*
Denis J. Meinert *VP-FIN*
Kenneth E. Smith *VP-OPR*

Human Resources: Jacki Francis

Total Employees..............................60
Year Established 1934

Regional Employees 50
SIC Code....................................8742

McCabe & Scarlata, Inc.

Riverside Commons, 700 River Ave., Ste. 400
Pittsburgh, PA 15212
County: Allegheny

Phone: (412) 323-8500
Fax: (412) 323-8502

Provider of disability management services specializing in cost containment issues, doing business as Options. The Company's services include physician panel development, managed care, medical bill repricing and auditing, independent medical exams, peer reviews, medical case management, vocational rehabilitation and expert testimony. It operates branch offices located in Charlotte, NC; Altoona, Lebanon and Philadelphia, PA; and Dallas, Houston and San Antonio, TX; and Charleston, WV.

Officers: Joseph McCabe *CH*
Antonia Scarlata *CEO*
Michael Lindberg *P*

Human Resources: Judith Lightner

Total Employees............................170	**Regional Employees** 65
Year Established 1981	**SIC Code** 6411

McConway & Torley Corp.

109 48th St.
Pittsburgh, PA 15201
County: Allegheny

Phone: (412) 682-4700
Fax: (412) 682-4725

Manufacturer and remanufacturer of steel castings for the railroad industry. The Company's products include railroad couplers, yokes, knuckles and related parts. It exports its products overseas in addition to distributing them within the United States. The Company operates distribution centers in Olathe, KS, and Woodlawn, TX, and plants in Kutztown and Pittsburgh, PA. Its subsidiaries include MCT Properties, Inc. and MCT Trading, Inc. The Company is an ESOP and is a subsidiary of MCT Holdings, Inc., which is headquartered in Baltimore, MD.

Officers: Buddy F. E. Bell *P & CEO*
Bryan G. Deschamps *VP-ADM & TRS*
MaryAnn Glover *VP-ENG & Quality Assurance*
Joseph F. Kahl *VP-SAL & MKT*
Frank J. Klein *VP-MFG*

Human Resources: Rose L. Andricik *VP-Human Resources*

Total Employees............................550	**Regional Employees** 225
Year Established 1869	**SIC Code** 3325

McCormick Co., J. S.

Center City Tower, 650 Smithfield St., Ste. 1050
Pittsburgh, PA 15222
County: Allegheny

Phone: (412) 471-7246
Fax: (412) 471-7247

M

Manufacturer of carbon and graphite products. The Company also produces dry mixes for foundry applications. It operates a plant located in Boyers, PA.

Officers: J. Brandon Snyder *P*
Lance Spernak *CFO*
Joseph L. Stein *VP & GMGR*

Total Employees..............................50
Year Established 1870   **SIC Code**....................................3624
Annual Revenues ($000)...5,000+

McCrackin Ford, Inc.

7209 McKnight Rd.
Pittsburgh, PA 15237
County: Allegheny

Phone: (412) 931-6960
Fax: (412) 367-0199

Automobile dealership selling new Ford vehicles and used vehicles. The Company also provides automobile rentals, parts and service. In addition, it operates an auto body shop.

Officers: Robert W. McCrackin *P*
Timothy G. McCrackin *VP*

Human Resources: Carolyn J. Zola *SEC, TRS & CON*

Total Employees..............................95   **Regional Employees** 95
Year Established 1968   **SIC Code**....................................5511
Annual Revenues ($000)...42,000+

McCrory & McDowell

312 Blvd. of the Allies
Pittsburgh, PA 15219
County: Allegheny

Phone: (412) 281-9690
Fax: (412) 281-5925

Provider of a range of financial and consulting services, including audits of financial statements, tax planning and preparation, estate planning, business consulting, valuation services, litigation services and investment planning. The Firm serves a variety of clients, including construction companies, law firms, nonprofit orgranizations, retailers, manufacturers and the medical sector, as well as individuals. Its divisions, both of which are located at the above address, consist of Computer Resources, which provides computer consulting and training, and Diversified Medical Management, which provides medical consulting. The Firm is affiliated with Jeffreys Henry International, an international association of accounting firms with offices in over 100 cities worldwide.

Officers: Kenneth C. McCrory *MDIR*
Gregory Hardy *DIR*
D. Michael McDowell *DIR*
Timothy Reed *DIR*
Michael Rollage *DIR*

Human Resources: Gilbert Davis *DIR*

Total Employees............................49   **Regional Employees** 49
Year Established 1951   **SIC Code**....................................8721

McCutcheon Enterprises, Inc.

250 Park Rd.
Apollo, PA 15613
County: Armstrong

Phone: (412) 568-3623
Fax: (412) 568-2571

Provider of waste management services, including emergency spill response and site remediation, environmental consulting and laboratory services, transportation and specialized equipment, water and wastewater treatment services, sludge management and land reclamation, dredging and lagoon cleaning, and spill and plant maintenance sorbents and products. The Company has the capabilities to handle, transport and dispose of hazardous, nonhazardous, industrial and municipal waste materials. It is equipped with tank trailers, sealed dump trailers, rolloff trailers, pan van trailers, emergency response trailers and specialized rolloff containers.

Officers: Calvin S. McCutcheon *P*
Timothy R. Dobrosky *Lab & Plant OPR Supervisor*
Robert A. Carter *Senior Consultant*

Total Employees............................65   **Regional Employees** 65
Year Established 1947   **SIC Code**....................................4953

McGinley Maintenance, Inc.

130 Lincoln Ave.
Charleroi, PA 15022
County: Washington

Phone: (800) 624-6826
Fax: (412) 483-5569

Provider of contract janitorial services to commercial and industrial clients in Florida, Maryland, North Carolina, Ohio, Pennsylvania, Virginia and West Virginia.

Officers: John M. McGinley *P (Purchasing)*
Elizabeth McGinley *SEC & TRS*

Total Employees............................400	**Regional Employees** 200
Year Established 1961	**SIC Code**......................................7349

McGuire Memorial

2119 Mercer Rd.
New Brighton, PA 15066
County: Beaver

Phone: (412) 843-3400
Fax: (412) 847-2004

Nonprofit intermediate care facility for the mentally retarded. With five physicians and a nursing staff, the Facility provides speech, occupational and physical therapy and educational programs to 91 individuals.

Officers: Sister Mary T. Markelewicz *Administrator*

Total Employees............................250	**Regional Employees** 250
Year Established 1963	**SIC Code**......................................8361

McMurray Hills Manor

249 W. McMurray Rd.
Canonsburg, PA 15317
County: Washington

Phone: (412) 941-7150
Fax: (412) 941-6554

Nonprofit, 123-bed nursing and rehabilitation center for the elderly. The Center offers subacute, skilled and intermediate care. It also provides assisted living facilities. The Center's rehabilitation services include physical, occupational and speech therapy. It is owned and managed by American Health Foundation, which is headquartered in Dublin, OH.

Officers: John Hammerle *P*

Total Employees............................145	**Regional Employees** 145
Year Established 1965	**SIC Code**......................................8052

Medaphis Physician Services Corp.

Seven Parkway Center, Ste. 375
Pittsburgh, PA 15220
County: Allegheny

Phone: (412) 937-5700
Fax: (412) 937-5701
Internet Address: www.medaphis.com

   Provider of business management services to the health care industry. These services enable health care providers to outsource to the Company business management functions associated with the delivery of health care, thereby allowing physicians and hospitals to focus on delivering quality medical services to their patients. The services provided by the Company include both revenue and cost management services. Revenue management services encompass billing and accounts receivable management services consisting of medical coding, automated patient billing, claims submission, capitation analysis, past due and delinquent accounts receivable collection and contract negotiations with payors, including managed care organizations and other services associated with the revenue cycle of a health care provider. Cost management services include comprehensive practice management services consisting of front office administration, benefit plan design and administration, cash flow forecasting and budgeting, general consulting services and other services associated with the management of the costs of running a practice for a health care provider. The Company is headquartered in Atlanta, GA. It is a subsidiary of Medaphis Corp., which is also headquartered in Atlanta, GA, and listed on the NASDAQ. The Company operates additional regional faciltes in Greensburg and Johnstown, PA.

Officers: Deb Zimkus *Regional SVP-North Central*

Human Resources: Eric Conti

Total Employees......................10,000	**Regional Employees** 243
Year Established 1985	**SIC Code**......................................8741
Annual Revenues ($000) 608,313	

Medic Computer Systems, Inc.

Foster Plaza VI, 681 Anderson Dr.
Pittsburgh, PA 15220
County: Allegheny

Phone: (412) 937-0690
Fax: (412) 937-0113
Internet Address: www.medcmp.com

Developer and marketer of integrated computer systems to the health care industry. The Company's products consist of several practice management systems, clinical information and patient records systems and electronic data interchange (EDI) services designed to reduce cost and facilitate patient care in the physician practice. Its systems consist of hardware, software, installation and training. The Company contracts with customers for transaction-based EDI services which include electronic patient billing, insurance claims and payment posting. It also provides software and hardware maintenance, and sells forms, supplies and other services to its customers. The Company, which is headquartered in Raleigh, NC, is listed on the NASDAQ.

Officers: Richard Goldberg *VP-Customer SAL*

Total Employees........................1,200	**Regional Employees**....................100
Year Established........................1978	**SIC Code**.......................................7373
Annual Revenues ($000)...191,787	

Medrad, Inc.

One Medrad Dr.
Indianola, PA 15051
County: Allegheny

Phone: (412) 767-2400
Fax: (412) 767-4295

Developer, manufacturer and marketer of equipment and disposable products that enhance the clarity of medical images of the human body. The Company's principal products are vascular injection systems, including injectors, compatible syringes and other disposable products, and a line of magnetic resonance (MR) products, including MR surface coils, disposable endorectal coils and related products. Its vascular injection systems are used in angiography and computed tomography procedures for the delivery of contrast media to patients. These injectors control the flow rate, volume and pressure of contrast media injection and synchronize such injection with the imaging equipment. The Company also markets a number of image enhancement products that are used as part of, or in conjunction with, medical imaging systems. In addition, it designs and markets an x-ray film transport and exposure device for angiography and distributes a real-time image enhancer for fluoroscopy systems, a roadmapping system for fluoroscopy images in interventional angiography procedures and a combination roadmapping and enhancement system. The Company's service organization, with offices in 45 cities, provides customers with equipment installation, repair services and preventive maintenance programs for its vascular injection systems, and MR and image enhancement products. Its primary customers include hospitals, medical centers, outpatient imaging centers and OEMs of imaging scanners. The Company maintains sales offices in Europe as well as Brazil, Japan and Singapore, serving clients in more than 55 countries. In fiscal 1996, international sales accounted for approximately 29% of its sales. As of October 2, 1995, the Company became a subsidiary of Schering Berlin Inc., based in Cedar Knolls, NJ, which is the U.S. holding company of Schering AG (SA). SA is headquartered in Berlin, Germany, and listed on the Frankfurt Stock Exchange. Prior to the acquisition, the Company was listed on the NASDAQ.

Officers: Thomas H. Witmer *P & CEO*
John P. Friel *SVP & GMGR*
A. Kenneth Grob, Ph.D. *SVP-OPR, Quality & Productivity*
Michael T. Howard *SVP-FIN & ADM, & CFO*
Russell M. Evans III *VP-SAL & Service*
Joseph B. Havrilla *VP New Products, Vascular Injection*
Philip B. Jarvi *VP-Corporate Quality Assurance & Regulatory Affairs*
Clifford E. Kress *VP-MKT, Vascular Injection*
John R. Tedeschi *VP-INTL*
Joshua J. Ziff *VP-Business DEV*
Steve F. Oertel *AST SEC*

Human Resources: Gary W. Bucciarelli *VP-Human Resources & TRS*
Martin J. Resick

Total Employees	780	**Regional Employees**	615
Year Established	1964	**SIC Code**	3845
Annual Revenues ($000)	111,000		

Mele Management Corp.

840 Jefferson Ave.
Washington, PA 15301
County: Washington

Phone: (412) 222-0924
Fax: (412) 222-0835

Owner and operator of supermarkets. Jefferson Foods Inc. does business as Jefferson Avenue Foodland in Washington, PA. Plaza Foods Inc. does business as Canonsburg Shop 'N Save in Canonsburg, PA. The two supermarkets offer grocery items, bakeries, deli departments, seafood, floral sections and video rentals.

Officers: John Mele, Jr. *P*
Frank Mele *VP*

Total Employees	500	**Regional Employees**	500
Year Established	1977	**SIC Code**	5411

Mennonite Publishing House, Inc.

616 Walnut Ave.
Scottdale, PA 15683
County: Westmoreland

Phone: (412) 887-8500
Fax: (412) 887-3111
Internet Address: www.mph.lm.com

Nonprofit publisher, doing business as Herald Press, operating through four divisions. Congregational Publishing provides print, visual and people resources for congregational, family and personal use for Sunday school, worship, family life education, leadership training, evangelism and personal reading. Trade Publishing produces titles in the areas of current issues, peace and justice, missions and evangelism, family life, personal experience, juvenile fiction, adult fiction, Bible study, inspiration, devotional, church history, and Christian ethics and theology. Printing Services offers outside printing as well as in-house printing and support services to the Company's publishing and retailing functions. Its support services include manufacturing, mailing, distribution, personnel, maintenance, accounting, finance and computer services. Provident Bookstores support the Company in its purpose and ministry by being its retailing facility. The stores serve all ages with educational, inspirational, informational and entertaining literature. They are located in Bloomington, IL; Goshen, IN; and Doylestown, Ephrata, Lancaster, New Holland, Scottdale and Souderton, PA.

M

Officers: J. Robert Ramer *P*
Levi Miller *VP-Congregational Publishing*
Reuben Savanick *VP-Printing Services*
Paul Schrock *VP-Trade Publishing*
Jack Scott *VP-Provident Bookstores*

Human Resources: Awanda Pritts *Human Resources DIR*

Purchasing: Kent Hartzler *Trade Publishing*

Total Employees............................254	**Regional Employees** 100
Year Established 1908	**SIC Code**.....................................2731
Annual Revenues ($000) 15,000	

Mercer, Inc., William M.

One Mellon Bank Center, 500 Grant St., Ste. 4200
Pittsburgh, PA 15219
County: Allegheny

Phone: (412) 355-8800
Fax: (412) 355-8877

Provider of actuarial and human resource consulting services. The Firm's services include employee benefits, compensation, human resource planning, pension, and communications capabilities. Headquartered in New York, NY, the Firm is a subsidiary of Marsh & McLennan Cos., Inc., which is also headquartered in New York, NY, and listed on the NYSE.

Officers: Alan Balla *Office Head*

Human Resources: Denise Horvath

Total Employees........................7,700	**Regional Employees** 85
Year Established 1937	**SIC Code**.....................................8748

Merchants Bancorp of Pennsylvania, Inc.

222 Market St.
Kittanning, PA 16201
County: Armstrong

Phone: (412) 543-1125
Fax: (412) 545-8336

Bank holding company for the Merchants National Bank of Kittanning (Bank). On November 19, 1994, the Board of Directors of the Bank approved the reorganization of the Bank into a one bank holding company structure. After approval by regulatory authorities and the Bank's shareholders, the reorganization was completed on January 12, 1995. The Bank provides a wide array of deposit and loan services. It operates three branch offices located in Kittanning, West Kittanning and Worthington, PA.

Officers: Paul E. Dunmire *CH & CEO*
James W. White *VCH*
James R. Drenning *P & COO*

Human Resources: Joan Tatsak *VP*

Purchasing: Gary Hornberger *VP*

Total Employees..............................49	**Regional Employees** 49
Year Established 1897	**SIC Code**......................................6712
Annual Revenues ($000) ....115,490 (Assets)	

Merck-Medco Rx Services of Pennsylvania No. 2, L.L.C.

1810 Lincoln Hwy.
North Versailles, PA 15137
County: Allegheny

Phone: (412) 829-3200
Fax: (412) 829-3286

Provider of mail order prescription services to individuals and to corporations, such as insurance companies and governmental agencies. The Company is a subsidiary of Merck-Medco Managed Care, L.L.C. (MMMC), which is headquartered in Montvale, NJ. MMMC is a subsidiary of Merck & Co., Inc., which is headquartered in Whitehouse Station, NJ, and listed on the NYSE.

Officers: Christopher J. Iversen *VP & GMGR*

Human Resources: Leanne Grafton *Human Resources MGR*

Regional Employees....................250	
Year Established 1986	**SIC Code**......................................5912

Mercury Printing, Inc.

801 Wood St.
Pittsburgh, PA 15221
County: Allegheny

Phone: (412) 241-1189
Fax: (412) 241-7411

Provider of single and multicolor commercial printing, high resolution image-setting and complete desktop publishing services.

Officers: David R. Gilbreath *P*
Kevin Cardillo *Production MGR*
Charlotte B. Temple *SEC & TRS*

Total Employees............................39	**Regional Employees**....................39
Year Established........................1959	**SIC Code**......................................2752
Annual Revenues ($000)...3,600	

Merrill Lynch, Pierce, Fenner & Smith, Inc.

Liberty Center, 1001 Liberty Ave.
Pittsburgh, PA 15222
County: Allegheny

Phone: (412) 566-6500
Fax: (412) 566-6553

Full-service broker-dealer specializing in financial planning and investment banking. Other Pittsburgh area offices are located in Beaver, Greensburg, New Kensington, Sewickley and in the South Hills. The Company, which is headquartered in New York, NY, operates approximately 500 branch offices throughout the United States. It is a subsidiary of Merrill Lynch & Co., Inc., which is also headquartered in New York, NY, and is listed on the NYSE.

Officers: Robert Herman *Resident VP*
James Brady *Resident MGR-Greensburg Office*
John Bridge *Resident MGR-New Kensington Office*
Lee Rowland *Resident MGR-South Hills Office*
Sam Spanos *Resident MGR-Beaver Office*

Regional Employees....................175	
Year Established........................1820	**SIC Code**......................................6211

MetalTech

2400 Second Ave.
Pittsburgh, PA 15219
County: Allegheny

Phone: (412) 391-0483
Fax: (412) 391-4223

Manufacturer of hot dip galvanized (zinc-coated) steel coils and sheets for applications in agriculture, residential/commercial construction, appliances, highway construction, automotive products and service centers.

Officers: G. Watts Humphrey, Jr. *CH*
Peter A. Stringi *P*
Wilson J. Farmerie *GPTR*
Edwin H. Gott, Jr. *GPTR*
Thomas Grudovich *AST to CH*

Human Resources: Robert W. Riordan *GPTR*

Total Employees............................90	**Regional Employees** 90
Year Established 1984	**SIC Code**....................................3479

Metplas, Inc.

Highlands Industrial Park, Three Acee Dr.
Natrona Heights, PA 15065
County: Allegheny

Phone: (412) 295-1900
Fax: (412) 295-3055

Provider of contract precision machining, laser cutting and manufacturing services. Approximately 70% of the Company's work is in non-metallic material, including thermoplastics, thermoset sheet, angle and rod, as well as protruded shapes. Metal machining and laser cutting make up the balance of its production. The Company serves a variety of industries, including electronics, medical equipment, pollution control, power distribution and transportation. Its clients have included ABB, ADtranz, Cutler-Hammer, FMC, General Electric and Respironics.

Officers: Russell E. Finsness *P*
Karen Conroy *Customer Service MGR*
Kevin Siverd *OPR MGR*

Human Resources: James Carroll *Accounting MGR*

Purchasing: Jean Heller-Hendrick *Materials Coordinator*

Total Employees............................48	**Regional Employees** 48
Year Established 1981	**SIC Code**....................................3599
Annual Revenues ($000) 4,500	

Meyer, Darragh, Buckler, Bebenek & Eck

Frick Bldg., 437 Grant St., Ste. 2000
Pittsburgh, PA 15219
County: Allegheny

M

Phone: (412) 261-6600
Fax: (412) 471-2754

Provider of legal services with 75 attorneys. The Firm's practice areas include litigation and appellate practice in all federal and state courts, complex commercial and construction litigation, product liability, insurance and reinsurance, general negligence, professional liability, toxic substances, workers' compensation, civil rights, arbitration and mediation, property loss litigation, collection and foreclosure, insurance coverage disputes, investment and tax planning, international, finance and banking, bankruptcy, pension matters, estate planning and estate administration, labor and employee relations, municipal, environmental, real estate, land use planning and administrative law. The Firm serves a broad spectrum of corporate, business, professional and individual clients on a local, regional and international basis. It operates branch offices in Altoona and Greensburg, PA; and Charleston and Morgantown, WV.

Officers: John L. MacCorkle *MPTR & MEM-Executive Comm.*
Eric N. Anderson *MEM-Executive Comm.*
Carl A. Eck *MEM-Executive Comm.*
John M. Noble *MEM-Executive Comm.*

Human Resources: Carol C. Cottom

Purchasing: Brenda F. Mehagan

Total Employees............................200	**Regional Employees** 143
Year Established 1913	**SIC Code** 8111
Annual Revenues ($000) 16,000	

Meyer, Unkovic & Scott LLP

Oliver Bldg., 535 Smithfield St., Ste. 1300
Pittsburgh, PA 15222
County: Allegheny

Phone: (412) 456-2800
Fax: (412) 456-2864

General practice law firm with 52 attorneys. The Firm's areas of practice include business, real estate, litigation, employment and employee benefits, international trade, licensing and distribution, intellectual property, construction and development, bankruptcy and commercial claims, tax, business succession, immigration and estate planning. Its clients range from large corporations and financial institutions to emerging businesses and individuals.

Officers: Robert Mauro *MPTR*
Frederick J. Francis *MEM-MGT Comm.*
Kenneth G. Judson *MEM-MGT Comm.*
James R. Mall *MEM-MGT Comm.*
Dennis Unkovic *MEM-MGT Comm.*

Human Resources: Patricia L. Hess

Total Employees...........................110   **Regional Employees**...................110
Year Established 1943   **SIC Code** 8111

MHF, Inc.

300 W. Grandview Blvd.
Zelienople, PA 16063
County: Butler

Phone: (412) 452-3900
Fax: (412) 452-3907

Provider of local and long haul trucking, warehousing, consolidation and distribution services. The Company offers full truckload dry van freight transportation throughout the continental U.S. It operates a fleet of 101 tractors and 251 trailers, with a satellite terminal in Macon, GA. The Company's other businesses, all located at the above address, include MHF Logistical Solutions, a provider of hazardous waste disposal services; MHF Signs, a manufacturer of signage; and MHF Truck Service, a provider of truck maintenance and repair services. In addition, MHF Aviation, which is located at the Zelienople Airport, provides aircraft repair services; and MHF Warehouse, with facilities at the above address, and in Butler, PA, and Parsippany, NJ, provides general warehousing with rail service at each site.

Officers: Dan Wylie *P*
Gary Gill *VP-OPR*
Jeff Wylie *VP*
Tom Wylie *VP-Warehouse OPR*

Human Resources: Randy Kester *VP-Maintenance & Personnel (Purchasing)*

Total Employees...........................180
Year Established 1983   **SIC Code**.....................................4213
Annual Revenues ($000) 12,000

Microbac Laboratories, Inc.

100 Marshall Dr.
Warrendale, PA 15086
County: Allegheny

M

Phone: (412) 772-2424
Fax: (412) 772-7877
Internet Address: www.ncinter.net/~lab

Provider of analytical testing services for water, air, wastewater, hazardous wastes and solid wastes in order to comply with environmental requirements. The Company also offers quality and nutritional testing of foods and dairy products, domestic household testing of well waters and in-house contaminants such as lead in paint and radon, and has the capability to test for Legionella and other pathogens. Its environmental testing capabilities include microbiological testing, chemistry analysis, field services, industrial hygiene, and ores and mineral assays; food testing capabilities include bacteriological testing, food chemistry, sanitation programs and field services. The Company operates additional laboratories in Corona, CA; Venice, FL; Atlanta, GA; Hammond, IN; Louisville, KY; Clinton, MA; Charlotte and Fayetteville, NC; Cincinnati, OH; Bradford, Erie, Hanover, Ingomar, Johnstown, New Castle and Pittsburgh (2), PA; Brownsville, TX; and Newport News, VA. The Company typically performs more than 10,000 tests a day for thousands of clients coast to coast. It provides environmental analyses to private individuals, government agencies, environmental engineering firms, commercial and industrial clients; food chemistry and microbiological analyses to private individuals and public municipalities, small manufacturers and Fortune 500 food companies, fruit and produce growers, packing and processing plants, retail and wholesale food retailers, national fast food restaurants, and worldwide food service and hospitality companies. The Company is affiliated with Orbeco Analytical Systems, Inc., which is headquartered in Farmingdale, NY.

Officers: A. Warne Boyce *CH & CEO*
J. Trevor Boyce *P*
David J. Danis *VP*
Steven M. Johnson *VP & CFO*
Mark A. Matrozza *VP*

Human Resources: Lynette A. Bauer

Purchasing: Robert W. Morgan *SVP*

Total Employees............................220	**Regional Employees** 100
Year Established 1969	**SIC Code**......................................8734
Annual Revenues ($000) 16,000	

Millennia Technology, Inc.

1105 Pittsburgh St.
Cheswick, PA 15024
County: Allegheny

Phone: (412) 274-7741
Fax: (412) 274-2235

Provider of turnkey custom manufacturing of electronic and electromechanical products. The Company was formerly known as the Triangle Circuits Contract Assembly Division. Its service offerings include engineering and CAD designs, component procurement, surface mount technology and through-hole component placement, test development, and automatic test equipment and functional test performance. The Company's local clients include Medrad, Respironics and Westinghouse, for whom it produces printed circuit board assemblies.

Officers: Michael D'Ambrosio, Sr. *P & CEO*
Alan Caponi *CON*
Ron Kautz *MFG MGR*
Bernadine Paga *SAL MGR*
Henry Totzke *Quality Assurance MGR*

Human Resources: Dennis Pricer

Purchasing: Michael D'Ambrosio, Jr.

Total Employees	135	**Regional Employees**	135
Year Established	1984	**SIC Code**	3672
Annual Revenues ($000)	10,000		

Miller Spring & Manufacturing Co., Henry

Ali St.
P.O. Box 7826
Pittsburgh, PA 15215
County: Allegheny

Phone: (412) 782-0700
Fax: (412) 782-1646

Manufacturer of hot wound coil springs for heavy industry and railroads. The Company is a subsidiary of Standard Car Truck Co., which is headquartered in Park Ridge, IL.

Officers: David J. Jablonowski *VP*

Purchasing: Joe Bowman

Total Employees	94	**Regional Employees**	94
Year Established	1947	**SIC Code**	3493

Miller-Thomas-Gyekis, Inc.

3341 Stafford St.
P.O. Box 43029
Pittsburgh, PA 15204
County: Allegheny

Phone: (412) 331-4610
Fax: (412) 331-8871

Roofing and sheet metal contractor serving architects, engineers, owners and general contractors in the Tri-State area. The Company provides slate, tile, shingle and metal slope roofing and all types of architectural sheet metal work for commercial, industrial and institutional projects.

Officers: Mathew E. Miller, Jr. *P*
    Edward A. Boozel *SEC & TRS*

Human Resources: Raymond R. Heberle *EVP*

Purchasing: Daniel M. Mester

Total Employees	75	**Regional Employees**	75
Year Established	1957	**SIC Code**	1761
Annual Revenues ($000)	5,000		

Minuteman Lubricants

539 Marwood Rd.
Cabot, PA 16023
County: Butler

Phone: (412) 352-4451
Fax: (412) 352-9543

Manufacturer and marketer of a complete line of industrial and commercial private label lubricants, including engine oils, hydraulic oils, transmission fluids, gear lubricants, greases, metalworking lubricants, antifreeze and specialty products. The Company serves customers in New York, Ohio, Pennsylvania, Virginia and West Virginia. It operates two additional packaging and distribution facilities located in Medina, OH, and Jane Lew, WV. The Company is a division of American AGIP Co., Inc. (AACI), which is headquartered in New York, NY. AACI is a subsidiary of AGIP Petroli (AP), which is headquartered in Rome, Italy. AP is a part of ENI S.p.A., which is listed on the New York and Milan Stock Exchanges.

Officers: Joseph W. Krisky *Business Unit MGR*
    Ty Giesler *MGR-MFG & Blending*

Human Resources: Pam Rape *Senior Accountant*

Purchasing: Joe Schmidlin *MGR-OPR & Customer Service*

Total Employees	45	**Regional Employees**	33
Year Established	1975	**SIC Code**	2992

Mistick PBT

1300 Brighton Rd.
Pittsburgh, PA 15233
County: Allegheny

Phone: (412) 322-1121
Fax: (412) 322-9336

Provider of general contracting, construction management and design/build services for commercial and multifamily residential properties. The Company's projects include office buildings, schools, banks, churches, townhouses and retirement facilities. In addition to new construction, it has expertise in historic rehabilitation. Insurance Restoration Services (IRS), a division of the Company located at the above address, provides disaster recovery and emergency preparedness planning for commercial and residential property owners. IRS's contracting and consulting services include building reconstruction and restoration, building and contents cleaning, water extraction, dehumidification and disinfection, emergency board-up, decontamination, duct cleaning and emergency planning. Mistick Management, another division of the Company also located at the above address, provides property management services.

Officers: D. Thomas Mistick *P*
David J. Mistick *VP-Asst MGT*
Robert Mistick *VP & COO*

Human Resources: Marianne Majewski

Total Employees	125	**Regional Employees**	125
Year Established	1953	**SIC Code**	1542
Annual Revenues ($000)	25,000		

Mitsubishi Electric Power Products, Inc.

Thorn Hill Industrial Park, 512 Keystone Dr.
Warrendale, PA 15086
County: Allegheny

Phone: (412) 772-2555
Fax: (412) 772-2146
Internet Address: www.mitsubishi.com

Manufacturer of high voltage and extra high voltage "puffer" circuit breakers and gas insulated substations rated from 38 to 550 kV. These state-of-the-art products are used by North American electric utility companies to increase the reliability, efficiency and safety of electrical transmission, while at the same time reducing the risk of environmental damage and visual pollution associated with older equipment. The Company supplies customers in Central and South America, Asia, the Middle East and Europe, as well as North America. The Company operates regional offices in Los Angeles, CA, St. Louis, MO, and

Charlotte, NC, to assist in serving customers and backing-up its network of independent sales representatives who call on U.S. customers. Another office, for generator design liaison, is located in Orlando, FL, and a project office is located in San Juan, Puerto Rico. The Company is a subsidiary of Mitsubishi Electric America, Inc. (MEAI), which is headquartered in Cypress, CA. MEAI is a subsidiary of Mitsubishi Electric Corp., which is headquartered in Tokyo, Japan, and listed on the Tokyo Stock Exchange.

M

Officers: Roger L. Barna *P*
John Yamamaru *EVP*
Jack Greaf *VP-MKT*
Bruce Hampton *VP, TRS & AST-SEC*
Katsuya Takamiya *SEC*
Alan Olschwang *AST-SEC*

Human Resources: Jill Hixson

Purchasing: Ray Madia

Total Employees 75-100	**Regional Employees** 75-100
Year Established 1985	**SIC Code** 3613

MK Consulting Services, Inc.

Penn Center W. One, Ste. 300
Pittsburgh, PA 15276
County: Allegheny

Phone: (412) 787-5622
Fax: (412) 787-5652

Provider of a wide range of employment services, including the placement of contract personnel and permanent employees within the MIS, telecommunications and engineering sectors. The Company also completes turnkey projects, including feasibility studies, functional specifications through detail design, programming, system implementation and user training. In 1996, it established MK Executive Search, Inc., which is engaged in the permanent placement of executive, management, financial, accounting and purchasing professionals nationwide. The Company serves a diverse client base spanning the steel, manufacturing, chemical, environmental, pharmaceutical, computer, finance, banking, health and transportation industries, including enterprises ranging from Fortune 500 international firms to start-up emerging businesses. The Company operates a branch office in Steubenville, OH.

Officers: Chrystalla Mercouri *P*

Human Resources: Regina Bykowski *DIR-MKT & Recruiting*

Total Employees.............................55	**Regional Employees** 50
Year Established 1992	**SIC Code** 8742
Annual Revenues ($000) 2,300

MMC&P Retirement Benefit Services, Inc.

One Gateway Center, 11th Fl.
Pittsburgh, PA 15222
County: Allegheny

Phone: (412) 394-9300
Fax: (412) 261-1207
Internet Address: www.rctirementbenefils.com

Provider of qualified retirement plan design and consulting, actuarial services, administration and recordkeeping for defined benefit and defined contribution retirement plans for over 400 corporate, nonprofit, private and professional clients. The Firm also provides benefit payments and daily valuation recordkeeping and administration of 401(k) plans. Approximately 80% of its clients are located in the Tri-State area.

Officers: John P. Parks *P & CEO*
         James M. Thomas *VP & Senior Consultant*

Human Resources: Barbara S. Jordon *(Purchasing)*

Total Employees............................30	**Regional Employees** 30
Year Established 1940	**SIC Code**....................................8748

Modern Transportation Services, Inc.

1612 Perry Hwy.
P.O. Box 390
Portersville, PA 16051
County: Butler

Phone: (412) 368-8000
Fax: (412) 368-3102

Transportation company specializing in dedicated hauling, carrying all types of freight for clients throughout the continental U.S. and Canada. The Company also provides expedited freight services. Its fleet consists of 175 tractors and 230 trailers (including vans and flat beds), with various facilities located in Atlanta, GA; Chicago, IL; Massillon, OH; Philadelphia, PA; and Dallas, TX. The Company's affiliate, ModernTrans, Inc., also located at the above address, offers freight brokerage services.

Officers: Neil E. Strosnider *P*
         Tim Kuhlman *MGR-OPR*

Human Resources: Jim Kosior

Purchasing: William J. Doyle *VP*

Total Employees	200	**Regional Employees**	56
Year Established	1987	**SIC Code**	4213
Annual Revenues ($000)	18,000		

M

Mon Valley Travel, Inc.

100 Smithfield St.
Pittsburgh, PA 15222
County: Allegheny

Phone: (412) 255-8747
Fax: (412) 765-2614
Internet Address: www.monvalley.com

Retail travel agency specializing in business, group and recreational travel. The Company's services include air and ground transportation, hotel accommodations, meeting services and travel consultation. Its clients are primarily located in the Pittsburgh metropolitan area, however, approximately 20% of its business is derived from clients outside the Western Pennsylvania area. Additional branch offices are located in Kansas City, MO, and Morgantown, WV. The Company is affiliated with BTI Americas, Inc., which is headquartered in Northbrook, IL.

Officers: Alex Zelenski *P*
Marc Zelenski *COO*

Human Resources: Bonnie Viverito *EVP*

Purchasing: Robert Septak

Total Employees	104	**Regional Employees**	94
Year Established	1959	**SIC Code**	4724
Annual Revenues ($000)	44,000		

Mon Yough Community Services, Inc.

500 Walnut St.
McKeesport, PA 15132
County: Allegheny

Phone: (412) 675-8526
Fax: (412) 675-8888

Nonprofit provider of mental health, mental retardation, drug and alcohol, forensic and vocational rehabilitation services through various programs, outpatient services, and support and treatment centers. The Organization's goal is to help people stay in their home communities, reach their full potential and become productive members of society by providing professional, caring treatment and working to eliminate discrimination toward people who are mentally, emotionally and/or physically challenged. Its services are available to residents of Clairton, Coal Valley, Dravosburg, Elizabeth Borough, Elizabeth Township, Forward Township, Glassport, Jefferson Borough, Large, Liberty Borough, Lincoln Borough, McKeesport, Pleasant Hills, Port Vue, South Versailles, Versailles, West Elizabeth and White Oak, PA. The Organization is affiliated with Allegheny County Mental Health/Mental Retardation/Drug and Alcohol/Homeless and Hunger Program.

Officers: Frank Pillitteri *EDIR*

Human Resources: Lacy Richardson, Ph.D.

Purchasing: Sharon Biega

Total Employees	328	**Regional Employees**	328
Year Established	1969	**SIC Code**	8093
Annual Revenues ($000)	9,973		

Mon-Vale Health Resources, Inc.

Country Club Rd.
Monongahela, PA 15063
County: Washington
Phone: (412) 258-1000
Fax: (412) 258-1365

Nonprofit operator of the Monongahela Valley Hospital, a full-service 292-bed hospital with a 180-member medical staff representing over 40 medical specialties. The hospital, located at the above address, provides medical and surgical, obstetrics/gynecology, psychiatric, critical and cardiac care, rehabilitation, emergency medicine, and drug and addictive disease treatment and services. It also offers comprehensive oncology services, including the Charles L. and Rose Sweeney Melenyzer Regional Cancer Center for radiation therapy and chemotherapy, and an Inpatient Unit for the treatment of cancer; a subacute care unit; a Same Day Surgery Center; and an Education Conference Center. In addition to Monongahela Valley Hospital, Inc., the Company's other subsidiaries include Monongahela Medical Supply Co., located at the above address; Pennsylvania Health Choice Plan/Southwestern Pennsylvania (PHCP/SP), located in Belle Vernon, PA; and The Residence At Hilltop, an assisted living facility located in Carroll Township, PA.

Officers: Anthony M. Lombardi *P & CEO*
Louis J. Panza, Jr. *SVP & TRS*
Patrick J. Alberts *VP-ADM & Support Services*
Thomas J. Cullen *VP-Professional Services & MGT*
David M. Mastovich *VP-MKT*
Sharon A. Munson *VP-Nursing*
Robert J. Pecarchik, Ph.D. *VP-Education & Planning*
Donna Ramusivich *VP-Professional Services & Quality*
Victoria Levitske *COO-PHCP/SP*

Human Resources: Charles Nicholls *VP-Human Resources*

Purchasing: Vickie Harkins *DIR-Materials MGT*

Total Employees............................989	**Regional Employees** 989
Year Established 1972	**SIC Code**.....................................8062
Annual Revenues ($000) 177,000	

M

Monongahela Connecting Railroad Co., The

4166 Second Ave.
Pittsburgh, PA 15207
County: Allegheny

Phone: (412) 227-4903
Fax: (412) 227-4034

Railroad servicing LTV Steel Co.'s Pittsburgh Coke Plant and Metaltech, both of which are located in Pittsburgh, PA. The Company is a subsidiary of LTV Steel Co. (LSC), which is headquartered in Cleveland, OH. LSC is a subsidiary of The LTV Corp., which is also headquartered in Cleveland, OH, and listed on the NYSE.

Officers: Dan P. Hennessy *P-LTV Railroads*
Dale R. Innocenti *Superintendent*

Human Resources: Jay D. Heath *GMGR-Human Resources*

Total Employees..............................31	**Regional Employees** 30
Year Established 1885	**SIC Code** 4011

Moon Airport Motel, Inc.

1160 Thorn Run Rd.
Coraopolis, PA 15108
County: Allegheny

Phone: (412) 262-2400
Fax: (412) 264-9373
Internet Address: www.traveler.net/htio/custom/servico/3805.html

Owner and operator of the Clarion-Royce Hotel, featuring 193 guest rooms and four suites. The hotel also contains 6,200 square feet of banquet/meeting space with banquet seating for 500. Its dining/entertainment facilities consist of Pastels restaurant and Remingtons lounge. The Company is owned by Servico, Inc., which is headquartered in West Palm Beach, FL, and listed on the ASE. The hotel was formerly known as the Royce Hotel.

Officers: Bruno Bragazzi *GMGR*

Total Employees............................115	**Regional Employees**...................115
Year Established 1976	**SIC Code** 7011
Annual Revenues ($000) 5,000	

Mosites Construction Co.

4839 Campbells Run Rd.
Pittsburgh, PA 15205
County: Allegheny

Phone: (412) 923-2255
Fax: (412) 788-1169

Provider of construction and development services through two divisions. The Building Division performs commercial, light industrial and institutional construction and renovation. The Heavy Division performs bridge construction and refurbishment, tunnel renovation, river lock and dam renovations. The Company's clients include the University of Pittsburgh, Carnegie Mellon University, H. J. Heinz, The May Co., J. C. Penney's, Westinghouse, the Pennsylvania Department of Transportation, the Port Authority Transit and the Pennsylvania Turnpike Commission. The Company generally operates in Ohio, Pennsylvania and West Virginia.

Officers: Donald A. Mosites *P-Building Division*
Steven T. Mosites *P-Heavy Division*
M. Dean Mosites *VP*
David N. Rubis *VP*

Total Employees............................500	**Regional Employees** 500
Year Established 1961	**SIC Code**......................................1622
Annual Revenues ($000) 50,000	

Mountain View Hotel, Inc.

1001 Village Dr.
Greensburg, PA 15601
County: Westmoreland

Phone: (412) 834-5300
Fax: (412) 834-5304

Full-service hotel, doing business as the Mountain View Inn, located in the Laurel Highlands. The Hotel serves the leisure and corporate market with 93 guest rooms, executive suites, four corporate apartments, 12,000 square feet of meeting and banquet space, a dining room, tavern and gift shop. Its outside grounds feature lush gardens, Victorian gazebos, a swimming pool and a corporate party pavilion.

Officers: Vance E. Booher III *C-OWN & Innkeeper*
Victoria Booher *C-OWN & Innkeeper*
Mark Conte *GMGR*
Donna Kleman *DIR-SAL*
Ann Nemanic *DIR-MKT*

Human Resources: Cheryl Yuhouse

Purchasing: Don Ghion

Total Employees............................150	**Regional Employees** 150
Year Established 1924	**SIC Code** 7011
Annual Revenues ($000) 4,000			

Mt. Lebanon Office Equipment Co., Inc.

1817 Banksville Rd.
Pittsburgh, PA 15216
County: Allegheny

Phone: (412) 344-4300
Fax: (412) 344-4880

   Provider of consultation services and layout, design, sales and installation of business furniture to clients throughout Western Pennsylvania. The Company furnishes boardrooms, executive offices, reception areas, managerial offices, clerical and computer areas, training rooms and lunchrooms. It also offers buying programs for office supplies and business machines.

Officers: James M. Droney, Sr. *CH*
   James M. Droney, Jr. *P*
   John M. Silvestre *VP*

Human Resources: Kevin McNamara

Total Employees............................30	**Regional Employees** 30
Year Established 1960	**SIC Code** 5044
Annual Revenues ($000) 7,000			

Mt. Macrina Manor

520 W. Main St.
Uniontown, PA 15401
County: Fayette

Phone: (412) 437-1400
Fax: (412) 430-1095

   Nonprofit, 120-bed long-term care facility, which offers intensive rehabilitation services, wound care and compassionate care through a holistic approach. The Facility also cares for residents with Alzheimer's and other forms of dementias.

Officers: Sister Ruth Plante *P*

Human Resources: Celeste L. Golonski *EDIR*

Purchasing: Dorothy Madore

Total Employees............................165	**Regional Employees** 165
Year Established 1971	**SIC Code** 8051

Mt. Pleasant Publishing Corp.

229 Pittsburgh St.
P.O. Box 222
Scottdale, PA 15683
County: Westmoreland

Phone: (412) 887-7400
Fax: (412) 887-5115

Publisher of six weekly newspapers serving local communities in Westmoreland County, PA, through its Laurel Group Newspapers division. The Company's publications, with a combined total circulation (as of August 1996) of 22,831, consist of The Advisor, serving the Youngwood-New Stanton area with a circulation of 3,418; The Independent-Observer, serving Scottdale with a circulation of 3,316; The Jeannette Spirit, serving Jeannette with a circulation of 2,172; The Ligonier Echo, serving the Ligonier Valley with a circulation of 4,692; The Times-Sun, serving the West Newton area with a circulation of 3,342; and The Mount Pleasant Journal, serving the greater Mount Pleasant area with a circulation of 5,891. Through its Laurel Group Press division, the Company provides commercial printing, specializing in web and sheet fed printing, offering everything from business cards to catalogs. It also offers photography services, specializing in dance school photography as well as the design and printing of dance books and programs.

Officers: Joseph F. Soforic *P*
Richard L. Zahrobsky *VP*
Joseph T. Soforic, Jr. *SEC & TRS*

Purchasing: Jim Sprinkle

Total Employees	60	**Regional Employees**	60
Year Established	1873	**SIC Code**	2711

Mulach Parking Structures Corp.

100 Leetsdale Industrial Dr.
Leetsdale, PA 15056
County: Allegheny

Phone: (412) 266-2500
Fax: (412) 266-2561

Full-service designer and builder of parking structures throughout the United States. The company provides architectural and engineering services, construction management, general contracting, financing and operations management of parking structures. It operates a branch office in Denton, TX.

Officers: Steven C. Thomas *CH & CEO*
Ray Horsmon *EVP*

Human Resources: Judith Thomas *VCH & Human Resources DIR*

Total Employees	42	**Regional Employees**	39
Year Established	1974	**SIC Code**	1771
Annual Revenues ($000)	25,000		

M

Mulach Steel Corp.

100 Leetsdale Industrial Dr.
Leetsdale, PA 15056
County: Allegheny

Phone: (412) 266-1400
Fax: (412) 266-0131

Provider of structural steel service warehousing and sales to customers throughout the eastern United States. The Company is also active in real estate development and is currently renovating and building offices, warehousing and an intermodal cargo handling facility at Leetsdale Industrial Park. The Company's warehousing and distribution facility is also located in Leetsdale, PA.

Officers: Steven C. Thomas *CH & CEO*
Ray Horsmon *EVP*
Jim Safranek *VP*

Human Resources: Judith Thomas *VCH & Human Resources DIR*

Total Employees	40	**Regional Employees**	40
Year Established	1951	**SIC Code**	5051
Annual Revenues ($000)	15-20,000		

Municipal Authority of Westmoreland County

Rte. 30 W. & S. Greengate Rd.
P.O. Box 730
Greensburg, PA 15601
County: Westmoreland

Phone: (412) 834-6500
Fax: (412) 834-3794

Nonprofit municipal authority organized to provide municipal services, primarily consisting of water collection, treatment and distribution, and the operation of a solid waste landfill in Westmoreland County. The Authority operates division offices in McKeesport, Scottdale and Vandergrift, PA. Its water treatment plants are located in Bell Township, McKeesport and South Connellsville, PA.

Officers: Christopher Kerr *Resident MGR*
Michael Kenney *Distribution Superintendent*
Tom Peto *Production Superintendent*
Jacob Skezas *Business MGR*

Total Employees..............................260	**Regional Employees** 260
Year Established 1942	**SIC Code**......................................4941
Annual Revenues ($000) 38,000	

Munroe, Inc.

1820 N. Franklin St.
Pittsburgh, PA 15233
County: Allegheny

Phone: (412) 231-0600
Fax: (412) 231-0647

Designer and manufacturer of basic oxygen furnace water-cooled hoods, American Society of Mechanical Engineers code pressure vessels, heat exchangers, fractionating columns, jacketed pipe and tubular boiler components. The Company's services include complete boiler house installation; field construction services, including boiler repair, heat exchanger retubing, code welding and pressure vessel alterations; and control room, operator cab and pulpit, electric furnace roof and industrial mechanical construction. Its plants are located in Ringgold, GA; Youngstown, OH; and Oakmont, PA.

Officers: Philip F. Muck *P & CEO*
Donald W. Capone *VP-SAL*
John Lekse *MGR-Construction*
Peter C. Isager *Chief Engineer*

Human Resources: Stephen E. Zemba *CON*

Purchasing: Daniel S. Travaglini *MGR-Purchasing*

Total Employees..............................200	**Regional Employees** 75
Year Established 1835	**SIC Code**......................................3443

Mutual Aid Ambulance Service, Inc.

561-563 W. Otterman St.
P.O. Box 350
Greensburg, PA 15601
County: Westmoreland

Phone: (412) 834-4311
Fax: (412) 834-2810

Nonprofit provider of advanced life support services as the primary, municipally designated provider to two-thirds of Westmoreland County as well as portions of Fayette County. The Company handles approximately 43,000 requests for emergency medical services annually. This does not include the requests for its specialty response teams. These teams provide for emergency medical response to hazardous material situations. The response provides specially trained personnel for decontamination, medical surveillance and medical rehabilitation. This same team provides rescue services, disaster response, special event coverage and out-of-the-ordinary responses. The Company has 24 Pennsylvania Department of Health-licensed advanced life support units. In addition, it operates three wheelchair vans and six specialty vehicles. These units are strategically located throughout the Company's service area at nine stations in Delmont, Greensburg, Latrobe, New Alexandria, New Stanton, Pleasant Unity, Scottdale, Stahlstown and Tarrs, PA.

Officers: Joseph G. Yencha *CEO*
William E. Groft *DIR-OPR*
Dennis Todaro *CON*

Human Resources: Paul Colligan *Advanced Life Support DIR*

Purchasing: Richard Ponko *DIR-Special OPR*

Total Employees............................197	**Regional Employees** 197
Year Established 1968	**SIC Code** 4119

Nabisco Biscuit Co.

6425 Penn Ave.
Pittsburgh, PA 15206
County: Allegheny

Phone: (412) 365-9300
Fax: (412) 365-9356

Producer of cookies and crackers. The Company's product line includes Better Cheddars, Chick'N Biskit, Chips Ahoy!, Ritz, Ritz Bits Sandwiches, Swiss Cheese, Twigs and Wheat Thins. Its annual production is 60,000 pounds. The Company is headquartered in East Hanover, NJ. It is a subsidiary of Nabisco, Inc., which is headquartered in Parsippany, NJ, and listed on the NYSE.

Officers: Jack Crossey *Plant MGR*

Regional Employees.....................408	
Year Established 1918	**SIC Code** 2052

National Carbide Die Corp.

Two Juniper St.
P.O. Box 96
McKeesport, PA 15135
County: Allegheny
Phone: (412) 751-8000
Fax: (412) 751-4244

Manufacturer of custom compacting tools and dies for the powder metal and ceramic industries. The Company serves clients nationwide, with a major concentration of customers in the St. Mary's, PA, area.

Officers: Thomas E. Friday *P*
Regis Bazylak *MFG MGR*
Mark Booth *ENG MGR*
Donald Ruffing *SAL MGR*

Human Resources: Douglas Risher

Total Employees.............................95	**Regional Employees** 95
Year Established 1946	**SIC Code**....................................3544
Annual Revenues ($000) 6,800	

National City Bank of Pennsylvania

National City Center, 20 Stanwix St.
Pittsburgh, PA 15222
County: Allegheny
Phone: (412) 644-8111
Fax: (412) 644-7723
Internet Address: www.national-city.com

Diversified financial services company whose principal activity consists of providing general retail and commercial banking services through 268 banking offices in 23 western Pennsylvania counties. The Bank is one of ten banks, and the largest, within National City Corp. (NCC), which is headquartered in Cleveland, OH, and listed on the NYSE. In June 1996, NCC acquired Integra Financial Corp., which was headquartered in Pittsburgh, PA, and listed on the NYSE. The Bank's subsidiary, Altegra Credit Co. (ACC), which is headquartered in the Allegheny Center Mall in Pittsburgh, PA, is a nonconforming mortgage portfolio-based lender and wholesale lender. It operates 16 branch offices located throughout the Eastern U.S. primarily serving individuals, with one of its branch offices in Moon Township, PA. ACC's subsidiary, The Loan Zone, which is headquartered in Columbus, OH, is a nonconforming lender dealing primarily with unsecured loans through 38 branch offices in Indiana, Kentucky and Ohio.

Officers: Thomas W. Golonski *P*
Paul Clark *EVP-Retail Banking*
Stephen G. Hartle *EVP-Trust & Private Client Group*

David L. Tiemann *EVP-Credit ADM*
John C. Williams, Jr. *EVP-Corporate Banking*
Robert Mercer, Jr. *P-Altegra Credit Co.*

Human Resources: Holly Merriman

Total Employees..........................4,700	**Regional Employees** 2,300
Year Established 1989	**SIC Code**......................................6021

National Consulting Group, Inc.

The Hartley-Rose Bldg., 425 First Ave.
Pittsburgh, PA 15219
County: Allegheny

Phone: (412) 261-3848
Fax: (412) 261-4456
Internet Address: www.psgweb.com

Provider of a broad range of integrated end user and technical support services to major corporate clients with locations throughout the United States. The Company, doing business as PSG, offers customized solutions in four primary areas of expertise: Technology Migration Services—planning, installation, conversion and support for the implementation of desktop technologies in networked environments; Internet and Intranet Projects—designing, developing and deploying solutions that utilize the latest Web technologies to reduce costs, enhance communications and deliver immediate business value; Education and Training Programs—curriculum design, a flexible approach and trainers are combined with administration and program management in a training package for both standard and custom applications; and Technical Support and Customer Service Solutions—helping organizations support the users of technology with integrated Help Desk/Solution Center services, deskside assistance, hardware/software support and network administration solutions. The Company also provides application developers, technical writers and staffing for other critical technology initiatives. Its clients include Alcoa, Armco, City of Pittsburgh, General Electric, PPG Industries, SmithKline Beecham, TRW, U.S. Steel, Union Carbide and Westinghouse. The Company operates a branch office in Heathrow, FL.

Officers: Jacqueline R. Zanardelli *C-OWN & CEO*
Cyndee Miller *VP*
Luke Sossi *VP*
Chris Sweeney *VP*

Human Resources: Wayne R. Zanardelli *C-OWN & EVP*

Purchasing: Pat Bronder

Total Employees..........................160	**Regional Employees** 158
Year Established 1984	**SIC Code**......................................8742
Annual Revenues ($000) 9,000	

National Hydraulics, Inc.

1000 Water St.
P.O. Box 20
Scottdale, PA 15683
County: Westmoreland

Phone: (412) 887-0420
Fax: (412) 887-0438

Manufacturer of hydraulic equipment including cylinders, valves, pumps and motors. The Company also offers hydraulics repair. It serves the steel mill, coal mining, construction and truck rebuild markets in Maryland, Ohio, Pennsylvania and West Virginia.

Officers: Frank Brush *P*
　　　　　　 David Hower *SEC & TRS*

Total Employees............................50
Year Established 1981

Regional Employees 50
SIC Code....................................3593

National Institute for Occupational Safety & Health—Pittsburgh Research Center

Cochrans Mill Rd.
P.O. Box 18070
Pittsburgh, PA 15236
County: Allegheny

Phone: (412) 892-6601
Fax: (412) 892-6614
Internet Address: www.usbm.gov

Nonprofit government laboratory which originated in 1910 when the U.S. Bureau of Mines was established by Congress. The Pittsburgh Research Center (Center) has since evolved into one of the world's foremost mining research facilities, pursuing an aggressive, innovative program to promote the safety and health of the nation's miners. The Center's staff is composed of specialists in many disciplines, including engineering, geology, physics, chemistry, industrial hygiene, psychology and computer science. Its major areas of research are dust and toxic substances; hearing loss prevention; mining injury prevention; and disaster prevention and response. Over the years, the Center has gained prominence in a number of areas of expertise where advances continue to be made. It works to improve the safety of explosives and blasting materials approved by the Federal Government for use in coal mines, and researches effective devices and techniques to prevent, detect and suppress underground mine fires and explosions. Major areas of strata control research include preventing mine roof falls and improving layout of longwall coal mines. The Center is a part of the National Institute for Occupational Safety and Health, which is a division of the Centers for Disease Control and Prevention, which is under the auspices of the U.S. Department of Health and Human Services.

Officers: Richard W. Metzler *Acting RES DIR*
Jacqueline H. Jansky *Staff Scientist/Technology Transfer Officer*

Human Resources: Idelle Bailen

Purchasing: Joseph Gilchrist

Total Employees............................275	**Regional Employees** 275
Year Established 1910	**SIC Code**.....................................8733

National Roll Co.

Railroad Ave.
Avonmore, PA 15618
County: Westmoreland

Phone: (412) 697-4533
Fax: (412) 697-4319

Manufacturer of centrifugally cast and static-cast alloy rolls for the ferrous and nonferrous rolling industry. Through Vertical Seal Co., a division of the Company located in Titusville, PA, it manufactures babbited bearings for steel, power and paper-related industries. The Company is a subsidiary of Rolls Technology, Inc. (RTI), a Delaware corporation. RTI is a subsidiary of Akers International AB, which is headquartered in Stockholm, Sweden.

Officers: Andrew L. Blaskovich *P*
Sherwood B. Stephens *CFO*
David B. Collins *SVP*
Thomas P. Adams *VP-Metallurgy*
Paul F. Fleiner *VP-SAL & MKT*
David F. Joller *VP-MFG*

Human Resources: Christopher R. Schiano *DIR-Industrial Relations*

Purchasing: Gerald F. Curran

Total Employees............................315	**Regional Employees** 260
Year Established 1893	**SIC Code**.....................................1041
Annual Revenues ($000)..40-45,000	

National Torch Tip Co., Inc.

50 Freeport Rd.
Pittsburgh, PA 15215
County: Allegheny

Phone: (412) 781-4200
Fax: (412) 781-1075

Manufacturer of welding equipment and accessories. The Company's products include oxy-fuel consumables for flame cutting, welding, heating, steel mill applications and special purposes; gas welding and cutting equipment; all types of brazing and welding rod, wire and electrodes; maintenance welding products, including specialty electrodes, filler metals and surfacing powders; pressure gauges for industrial gas pressure regulators; eye and face safety protection products; contact tips, nozzles, liners and related consumables for all MIG welding torches; plasma-cutting consumables and front-end replacement parts; compressed gas connections, fittings, repair parts, hose fittings and related supplies; and welding accessories and supplies. The Company operates two plants, the Winona plant in Hanoverton, OH, and the Weldit plant in Sharpsburg, PA. In addition, the Company has two divisions, Hi-Alloy Weld Specialties in Houston, TX, and National Welding Alloys in Sharpsburg, PA, in addition to a subsidiary, National Torch Tip Ltd., located in Canada.

Officers: David S. Werner *P*
Terry Cumiskey *VP-SAL & MKT*
Francis Dadowski, Jr. *SEC & TRS*
Scott Hopkin *GMGR-Weldit*
Richard Oliveri *P-National Welding Alloys*

Total Employees............................200		**Regional Employees** 150
Year Established 1931		**SIC Code**......................................3548

Nature's Blend Wood Products, Inc.

202 First Ave.
Ford City, PA 16226
County: Armstrong

Phone: (412) 763-7057
Fax: (412) 763-3753

Manufacturer of oak cabinet doors.

Officers: Carl Auer *P*

Total Employees..............................60		**Regional Employees** 60
Year Established 1985		**SIC Code**......................................2431

Nello Construction Co., a Division of G.I.T.O., Inc.

Three Glass St.
Carnegie, PA 15106
County: Allegheny

Phone: (412) 276-0010
Fax: (412) 276-8123

Provider of a full range of engineering and construction services. The Company is comprised of two divisions. Nello Construction Co. is the general construction division and provides engineering and design, demolition, excavation, concrete, masonry, carpentry and millwork. Nello Construction Management of Pennsylvania provides full project management and construction management services. The Company's projects include production plants, schools and public works, primarily within a 100-mile radius of Pittsburgh.

Officers: Janet Torriero *P*
George D. Leasure *VP*

Total Employees................................60	**Regional Employees** 60
Year Established 1952	**SIC Code**......................................1500
Annual Revenues ($000) 15,000	

Nemacolin Woodland Resort and Spa

Rte. 40
P.O. Box 188
Farmington, PA 15437
County: Fayette

Phone: (412) 329-8555
Fax: (412) 329-6198

Owner and operator of an English Tudor Inn-style resort with 98 guest rooms and 40 two-bedroom condominiums located on a golf course. In June 1997, the Resort opened the La Fayette wing, a 124-room addition modeled after the Ritz in Paris. The Resort features nine restaurants and lounges, conference facilities totaling 40,000 square feet of space, golf courses, an adventure center, a spa with a complete fitness center, a pool, an equestrian center, a downhill ski area, an activities center and a 20,000-square-foot shopping arcade. It also has a miniature golf course, tennis courts and a croquet court, and offers fishing, nature walks, canoeing, badminton, shuffleboard, volleyball, horseshoes, surrey rides, paddleboats and trails for jogging, biking and hiking. In addition, the Resort features the Joseph A. Hardy, Sr. art collection of American and foreign paintings, Tiffany lamps and windows, drawings, sculptures, prints and antiques. The Resort is located 65 miles southeast of Pittsburgh, situated on nearly 1,000 acres in the Laurel Mountains.

Officers: Joseph A. Hardy, Sr. *OWN*
Maggie Hardy Magerko *P*
Michael King *VP-OPR*
Pattie Cantu-Leithead *DIR-MKT & SAL*
Jim Oliver *DIR-Food & Beverage*

Human Resources: Wanda Anker

Total Employees............................500		**Regional Employees** 500	
Year Established 1987		**SIC Code**......................................7011	

NeuralWare, Inc.

202 Park West Dr.
Pittsburgh, PA 15275
County: Allegheny

Phone: (412) 787-8222
Fax: (412) 787-8220
Internet Address: www.neuralware.com

Supplier and developer of neural network software for the development and deployment of on-line solutions for commercial, industrial, government and scientific applications. The NeuralWorks product line forms a high-performance technical computing environment providing nonlinear mathematics through neural networks to produce state-of-the-art software solutions. The Company's customer support engineers provide technical support for its software products as well as technical application support for enduser applications. Its engineers also provide neural network modeling services and application trouble shooting capabilities in addition to resource information for the entry-level neural network user. The Company offers five training courses on how to apply advanced technologies in a variety of industries. Its software is utilized by diverse industries, including chemicals, petrochemicals, pharmaceuticals, utilities, food and beverage, pulp and paper, glass and metal, insurance, medical, portfolio management and database management.

Officers: Jane Klimasauskas *P & CEO*
Casey Klimasauskas *CTO*
Bernie Cerasaro *DIR-Strategic Partnering*
Tony Rathburn *GMGR-Tools Division*

Human Resources: Mary Lopus

Total Employees............................40		**Regional Employees** 40	
Year Established 1987		**SIC Code**......................................7372	

Neville Chemical Co.

2800 Neville Rd.
Pittsburgh, PA 15225
County: Allegheny

Phone: (412) 331-4200
Fax: (412) 771-0226

Manufacturer of hydrocarbon resins. The Company's products include petroleum-based hydrocarbon resins, coumarone-indene resins, modified hydrocarbon resins, petroleum hydrocarbon resins, nonstaining antioxidants and plasticizers used principally in the manufacture of adhesives, coatings, inks and rubber. The Company operates an additional manufacturing and sales facility in Anaheim, CA, and a sales office in Chicago, IL. The Company is affiliated with Nevcin Polymers B.V. located in Uithoorn, The Netherlands, and Alliance Technical Products, Ltd. located in Stonehouse, England. The Company serves customers in 36 countries throughout North and South America, Europe, Africa and the Middle and Far East.

Officers: L. Van V. Dauler, Jr. *CH & P*

Total Employees	450	**Regional Employees**	400
Year Established	1925	**SIC Code**	2821

New Elliott Corp.

901 N. Fourth St.
Jeannette, PA 15644
County: Westmoreland

Phone: (412) 527-2811
Fax: (412) 527-8442
Internet Address: www.elliott-turbo.com

Designer, manufacturer and supplier of a broad range of turbomachinery. The Company, doing business through its subsidiary, Elliott Turbomachinery Co., Inc., produces air and gas compressors, steam turbines, power recovery turbines, power generation equipment, tube tool products and burnishing products. It also provides project management, research and development, design engineering, fabrication and fieldservice expertise. The Company markets its products to refineries, chemical facilities and ethylene plants as well as power generation, automotive, pharmaceutical and other industrial applications. Sales offices are located in City of Industry, CA; Miami, FL; East Brunswick, NJ; and in Canada, The People's Republic of China, Saudi Arabia, Singapore and Switzerland. Service offices are located in Benicia, CA; East Chicago, IN; Plaquemine, LA; Donora, PA; and in Taiwan. Sales and services offices are located in Jacksonville, FL; Harahan, LA; Houston, TX; and in Canada, England, Italy and Mexico. Additional subsidiary operations are located in Stuart, FL; Salina, KS; Harvey, LA; and Yorktown, VA. The Company's headquarters facility is comprised of 40 buildings on 108 acres. Manufacturing space is approximately 800,000 square feet under one roof; another 200,000 square feet houses engineering and various administrative functions. Its Donora, PA, facility is a 90,000 square foot service shop specializing in repairs, vibration analysis, rotor storage, dynamic rotor balancing up to 75,000 pounds capacity at-speed rotor balancing, and shop machining lathes. Ebara Corp. in Japan and MAN GHH in Germany own 45% of the Company.

Officers: Paul R. Smiy *CH & CEO*
Ronald D. V. Turner *P & COO*
Eugene J. Dickert *SVP*
Klaus P. Fischer *VP, GC & SEC*
John J. Lapina *VP-FIN & CFO*
John N. Brenzia *TRS*

Human Resources: Janice O. Garlock *VP-Human Resources*

Purchasing: Allan Johnson

Total Employees.........................1,875	**Regional Employees** 1,280
Year Established 1910	**SIC Code** 3511
Annual Revenues ($000) 289,000	

New Heritage, Inc.

314 E. Eighth Ave.
Homestead, PA 15120
County: Allegheny

Phone: (412) 464-1300
Fax: (412) 461-7118

Nonprofit, community-based agency providing social services to the homebound elderly. The Agency operates four senior activity centers and provides a variety of other services to meet the needs of older adults age 60 and over and their families in southeastern Allegheny County communities. Its services include offering information and referrals for anyone with questions about services and benefits for older adults; providing older adults with assistance in applying for public benefits programs sponsored by the Commonwealth of Pennsylvania; providing comprehensive care management to frail, homebound elderly for services needed to maintain their physical, social and financial well-being; and home support services, including personal assistance services, senior companions, home-delivered meals and telephone reassurance. In addition, the Agency provides referrals to support services offered by other organizations, including adult day care, respite care, homemaking/personal care, chore service, long-term care assessment and personal care home placement. The Agency's senior activity centers consist of Heritage House Center located at the above address; Homestead Park Center in Munhall, PA; Lafferty Center in Baldwin, PA; and Leland Center in Baldwin, PA. All of the facilities serve lunch to seniors.

Officers: Gary Gushard *P*
Janet A. Carr *EDIR*
Easter Baker *VP*
Marygrace Koziel *SEC*
Steven Zacks *TRS*

Human Resources: Hyman Richman *Personnel Officer*

Total Employees............................67 **Regional Employees** 67
Year Established ....1972 **SIC Code**......................................8082
Annual Revenues ($000) 800

New Image Press, Inc.

4433 Howley St.
Pittsburgh, PA 15224
County: Allegheny

Phone: (412) 683-1300
Fax: (412) 683-1390
Internet Address: nipress@aol.com

Provider of printing services offering prepress, commercial printing and bindery production. The Company's prepress operations feature a Macintosh-based digital system supporting high-resolution input and output, in addition to traditional graphic arts photography and stripping. Its printing capabilities range from five-color production to simple black on white. It finishes jobs with hot foil stamping and embossing, die cutting, and a full range of bindery services. The Company's finished products may include direct mail packages, stitched or perfect bound books, pocket folders, stationery, newsletters and other business literature. It primarily serves clients in Western Pennsylvania.

Officers: David W. Brown *OWN & P*

Human Resources: David W. Brown, Jr. *CON & Business MGR*

Total Employees............................30 **Regional Employees** 30
Year Established ....1980 **SIC Code**......................................2752
Annual Revenues ($000) 2,500

Newcomer Products, Inc.

Rte. 982 N.
P.O. Box 272
Latrobe, PA 15650
County: Westmoreland

Phone: (412) 694-8100
Fax: (412) 694-8620
Internet Address: www.industry.net/newcomer

Manufacturer and finisher of tungsten carbide products for solving metal removal needs on numerous applications in many industries. The Company's inserts and tools are widely used in conjunction with indexable tooling on all types and sizes of machine tools. Typical applications include turning large rolls and shafts and machining huge forgings in the heavy capital goods industries as well as the high production machining of countless steel and alloy parts on automatic machine tools in the automotive and similar high production industries. Other applications include turning, milling and boring the super-tough alloys used in jet engines and aerospace equipment, general purpose machining of numerous metallic materials in all types of industries, high velocity machining of regular and special analysis metals and many other industrial machining applications. The Company operates a second manufacturing plant in Wilmington, NC. It also maintains a distribution center in Walled Lake, MI. The Company is a subsidiary of the Daniels Group, Inc., which is headquartered at 609 Penn Ave. in Pittsburgh, PA.

Officers: Robert S. Jacobs *P*
Dennis Andrison *DIR-OPR*
John Kvall *Technical DIR*
Ronald Peters, Ph.D. *DIR-SAL & MKT*
Theodore Smith *TRS*

Human Resources: Ed Brinker *Human Resource DIR*

Purchasing: Jim Renz *Purchasing Agent*

Total Employees 222	**Regional Employees** 198
Year Established 1945	**SIC Code** 3545

NexTech

300 Braddock Ave.
Turtle Creek, PA 15145
County: Allegheny

Phone: (412) 825-4300
Fax: (412) 825-4309

Manufacturer of hot dip galvanized (zinc-coated) steel coils for applications in metal building components, mobile and modular homes, HVAC, construction products, agricultural products, residential and commercial construction, and service centers.

Officers: G. Watts Humphrey, Jr. *CH*
James Anderson *P*
Wilson J. Farmerie *GPTR*
Edwin H. Gott, Jr. *GPTR*
Thomas Grudovich *AST to CH*

N

Human Resources: Robert W. Riordan *GPTR*

Total Employees..............................65 **Regional Employees** 65
Year Established ....1990 **SIC Code**.....................................3479

Nicholson Construction Co.

12 McClane St.
P.O. Box 98, Bridgeville, PA 15017
Cuddy, PA 15031
County: Allegheny

Phone: (412) 221-4500
Fax: (412) 221-3127
Internet Address: www.nicholson-rodio.com

Full-service geotechnical contractor, providing services in ground treatment, ground improvement, and structural support and underpinning. The Company develops solutions for applications such as tunneling, bridge foundations, slope stabilization, retaining walls, building support, dam remediation, hydraulic cutoffs and site improvement. It serves clients throughout the United States in a variety of industries, including general building, industrial/manufacturing, power, transportation and water/sewer. The Company operates a regional office in Boston, MA, and has a sister company, Denver Grouting Services, in Broomfield, CO. The Company is a subsidiary of Stirling Ltd., which is headquartered in London, England.

Officers: Jean F. Kissenpfennig *P & CEO*
Daniel D. Uranowski *COO*
Seth L. Pearlman *DIR-Business DEV*
Andrew D. Walker *Regional MGR*

Human Resources: John S. Oliverio

Total Employees..............................96 **Regional Employees** 68
Year Established ....1955 **SIC Code**.....................................1629
Annual Revenues ($000) 50,000

NOMOS Corp.

2591 Wexford Bayne Rd., Ste. 400
Sewickley, PA 15143
County: Allegheny

Phone: (412) 934-8200
Fax: (412) 934-5488
Internet Address: www.nomos.com

Developer and manufacturer of radiation therapy (RT) solutions and equipment. The Company develops and manufactures products and technologies aimed at maximizing the potential of intensity modulated radiation therapy (IMRT) as a therapeutic tool in the fight against cancer. IMRT is delivered through PEACOCK®, a system that shapes or conforms radiation beams produced by linear accelerators to the size, shape and location of a tumor. IMRT matches the radiation dose to the tumor contour, minimizing the impact on surrounding healthy tissue or organs to reduce the side effects normally associated with RT. IMRT has been used to treat cancers of the brain, head and neck, spinal cord, esophagus, kidney, lung, lower extremities and prostrate, and is expected to be used to treat breast in the near future. Because of its precision, PEACOCK has also been used to deliver therapy to infants and to patients who were no longer candidates for conventional RT. Over 30 medical and research sites worldwide currently offer or perform research on IMRT using PEACOCK as a treatment option for cancer patients.

Officers: John A. Friede *CH*
Mark P. Carol, M.D. *P & CEO*
Robert L. Graham *VP & CFO*
Gilbert V. Peterson *VP & COO*
Edward S. Sternick, Ph.D. *VP-Clinical Affairs*
Marvin L. Sussman, Ph.D. *VP-Product Assurance & Support*

Human Resources: Mark D. De Bruyn

Purchasing: Eileen Stamps

Total Employees............................82	**Regional Employees** 82	
Year Established 1979	**SIC Code**......................................3845	
Annual Revenues ($000) 5,000		

Normandy Industries, Inc.

200 Jones St.
P.O. Box 40
Verona, PA 15147
County: Allegheny

Phone: (412) 826-1825
Fax: (412) 826-1731

Manufacturer of plastic pipe fittings, plastic valve and meter boxes, and drainage specialty products, all through the Company's Normandy Products Co. division, also located at the above address. The Company operates a factory located in Middlefield, OH.

Officers: Robert L. Americus *P*
Lanny Seed *VP*

Total Employees............................60	**Regional Employees** 10
Year Established 1947	**SIC Code**....................................3089

North Hills News Record

137 Commonwealth Dr.
Warrendale, PA 15086
County: Allegheny

Phone: (412) 772-3900
Fax: (412) 772-3915
Internet Address: www.newsrecord.com/www/nhnr

Publisher of the North Hills News Record, a newspaper with a daily circulation of 19,969 and a Sunday circulation of 19,723, covering the municipalities and neighborhoods that make up the North Hills area of Pittsburgh. The Company also offers commercial printing (web press, offset and sheet feed), web page online design, creative print advertising design and database marketing services. It is a subsidiary of Gannett Co., Inc., which is headquartered in Arlington, VA, and listed on the NYSE.

Officers: S. Mark Adkins *P, CEO & Publisher*
Richard Leonard *Executive Editor*
David C. Fritz *Managing Editor*
Suzette Cook *MKT DIR*
Fred Foutz *Circulation DIR*
Jack Robb *Advertising DIR*
Darrell Sandlin *Production DIR*

Human Resources: Debbie Alexander *Human Resources DIR*

Purchasing: Linda Feltman *FIN DIR*

Total Employees............................115	**Regional Employees**....................115
Year Established 1962	**SIC Code** 2711

North Side Foods Corp.

2200 Rivers Edge Dr.
New Kensington, PA 15068
County: Westmoreland

Phone: (412) 335-5800
Fax: (412) 335-2249

Processor of pork products serving clients in the food service industry. The Company operates through its two packing plant divisions, North Side Packing Co. of Pennsylvania (NSPC) which is also located at the above address, and North Side Packing Co. of Georgia (NSPC) in Cumming, GA. Through NSPC, the Company is a major supplier of products such as sausage patties, diced sausage, pizza topping and bacon bits to the McDonald's Corp., accounting for 70% of its annual sales. The remaining 30% of the Company's annual sales are generated through its Ember Farms product line which includes sausage patties and links, bacon products and pizza toppings. The Ember Farms product line serves a variety of national accounts, including Bennigan's Restaurants, H. J. Heinz Co., Kings Family Restaurants, Little Caesars Pizza, Marriott Hotels, Perkins Family Restaurants, Steak and Ale Corp., Sysco Restaurants and the United States Armed Forces. The Company is also engaged in a joint venture with the Martin-Brower Co. of Chicago, IL. The joint venture business, known as Hub One Logistics, Ltd., operates distribution facilities in City of Industry, CA; Atlanta, GA; Chicago, IL; and Cheswick, PA.

Officers: Robert G. Hofmann II *CH & P*
Mark Hofmann *SVP*
Joseph Brado *VP-MIS*
Gina M. Turoscy *VP-MFG*
Susan Wellinger *VP-SAL*
Robert G. Muhl *CFO*
Joseph Rockey *Strategic Planning DIR*

Human Resources: Renee A. Simoncelli *Human Resources MGR*

Purchasing: Timothy Cunningham

Total Employees	300	**Regional Employees**	200
Year Established	1909	**SIC Code**	2013
Annual Revenues ($000)	100,000+		

Northern Area Multi-Service Center of Allegheny County

209 13th St.
Pittsburgh, PA 15215
County: Allegheny

Phone: (412) 781-1175
Fax: (412) 781-5597

Nonprofit provider of social services to individuals and families as well as the elderly and the mentally retarded. The Organization offers a wide variety of programs and services including counseling, transportation, in-home services, adult day care, protective services, a senior companion program and part-time employment for the elderly. It also operates nine senior citizen centers located in Etna, Glenshaw, the Highlands area in Tarentum, Millvale, Ross, Sharpsburg, Springdale, West Deer and the 27th Ward, which serve 130,000 meals a year. In addition, it provides residential services to 20 mentally retarded adults in its six houses and apartments. Through The Landmark Assn., which is managed by Pennsylvania Residential Developers, Inc., the Organization operates personal care residences for the elderly at three locations: Landmark East, in Verona, PA; Landmark Manor, in Allison Park, PA; and Landmark North, in Pittsburgh, PA. The homes provide a total of 229 beds, 24-hour staff care, three meals a day, and medical, recreational and religious services.

Officers: Jerry Donatelli *CEO*
Betty Apitsch *Resident DIR-The Landmark Assn.*

Human Resources: Diane Lucente

Total Employees............................300	**Regional Employees** 300
Year Established 1950	**SIC Code**.....................................8322
Annual Revenues ($000) 8,000	

Northwest Airlines, Inc.

Pittsburgh International Airport
P.O. Box 12327
Pittsburgh, PA 15231
County: Allegheny

Phone: (412) 472-3440
Fax: (412) 472-3442

Commercial airline operating 10 daily nonstop flights: seven from Pittsburgh to Detroit, MI, and three from Pittsburgh to Minneapolis, MN. The Company also handles various ground charters including UPS passenger flights from Pittsburgh to Aruba. The Company is headquartered in Eagan, MN. It is a subsidiary of Northwest Airlines Corp., which is also headquartered in Eagan, MN, and listed on the NASDAQ. The Company's reservations/information number is (800) 225-2525.

Officers: Christine Craig *MGR-Customer Service & Ground OPR*

Regional Employees.......................60	
Year Established 1926	**SIC Code** 4512

Norton Pakco Industrial Ceramics

55 Hillview Ave.
Latrobe, PA 15650
County: Westmoreland

Phone: (412) 539-6000
Fax: (412) 539-6070

Engineer, manufacturer and installer of customized protective systems made of ceramic wear-resistant materials for power plants, mineral processing plants, chemical processing plants, steelmaking factories and other manufacturing facilities. The Company and its affiliate, Norton Co., based in Worcester, MA, are divisions of Saint-Gobain Norton Industrial Ceramic Corp., headquartered in King of Prussia, PA, which is a subsidiary of Saint-Gobain Corp., headquartered in Paris, France, and listed on the Paris Stock Exchange.

Officers: James C. McHugh *P*
Tim Marth *OPR MGR*

Human Resources: Mary Lou Hamacher

Regional Employees....................130
Year Established 1985   **SIC Code**....................................3498
Annual Revenues ($000)..20,000+

NOVA Chemicals, Inc.

400 Frankfort Rd.
Monaca, PA 15061
County: Beaver

Phone: (412) 774-1000
Fax: (412) 773-2423
Internet Address: www.nova.ca.com

Manufacturer and marketer of polystyrene, expandable polystyrene resin and styrenic co-polymers. These resins go into the production of foam packaging, cups and insulation as well as engineering resins in automobile instrument panels, high heat food containers, cutlery and plastic toys. The Company is headquartered in Calgary, Alberta, Canada. It is a subsidiary of NOVA Corp., which is also headquartered in Calgary, Alberta, Canada, and listed on the New York and Toronto Stock Exchanges. The facility located at the above address houses one of the Company's five plastics manufacturing plants. An office in Coraopolis, PA, houses the headquarters of the Company's Plastics Business Unit, and its Development and Technical Services support group.

Officers: Dan Boivin *P*
Dave Clarke *VP-Polymer SAL & MKT*
Bill Greene *VP-Styrenics*
John T. Bressler *MFG MGR-Dylite*
George Elliott *MFG Support MGR*

Lou Fontana *MFG MGR-Dylark*
Phil Gramatges *Site MGR*
James T. Sampson *MGR-Safety, Health, Environment &*
Risk/Community Affairs
Mark Lesky *Public Affairs*

N

Human Resources: Janet Kelly
Arnie Wensky

Purchasing: Alan Osan

Regional Employees....................550
Year Established........................1981   **SIC Code**....................................2821
Annual Revenues ($000)..250,000

Novum, Inc.

5900 Penn Ave.
Pittsburgh, PA 15206
County: Allegheny

Phone: (412) 363-3300
Fax: (412) 362-5783

Provider of research testing and development services to the pharmaceutical industry. The Company operates additional facilities in Washington, D.C. and Seattle, WA.

Officers: Randall Smith *P*

Human Resources: Paul Vanderweil *DIR-Human Resources*

Total Employees..........................100   **Regional Employees** 85
Year Established........................1972   **SIC Code**....................................8734

Nu-Metrics, Inc.

University Dr.
P.O. Box 518
Uniontown, PA 15401
County: Fayette

Phone: (412) 438-8750
Fax: (412) 438-8769
Internet Address: www.nu-metrics.com

Manufacturer of traffic data monitoring equipment. The Company's products include vehicle distance measuring instruments, portable traffic counters and classifiers, spread spectrum wireless data collection and control, and specialized transportation software for the transportation industry, utility companies and governmental departments. Over 10,000 of its traffic counters, which feature vehicle magnetic imaging technology, are in use throughout the United States and approximately 60 countries worldwide.

Officers: Harry R. Sampey, Ph.D. *P & CEO*
Lester Auer *VP-MFG*
Barbara A. Kovell *VP-MKT*

Human Resources: Gregory L. Friend *VP-OPR*

Purchasing: Ron Lex

Total Employees............................52	**Regional Employees** 52
Year Established 1970	**SIC Code**....................................3829

Nuclear Components, Inc.

200 Monkey Wrench Rd.
Greensburg, PA 15601
County: Westmoreland

Phone: (412) 527-3000
Fax: (412) 523-2116

Manufacturer of major components for nuclear applications and miscellaneous commercial machining. The Company specializes in complicated fabrications. It offers precision machining, including milling, lathe and welding.

Officers: Robert F. Czarnecki *P*
Dean W. Czarnecki *VP-MFG*
Donald J. Czarnecki *VP, SEC & TRS*
Robert R. Czarnecki *VP-ENG & Quality Control*
Donald N. Deutsch *Contracts MGR*
Michael Scalzo *Quality Control MGR*
Ronald E. Johnston *CON*
Eugene W. Cindric *MFG ENG*

Purchasing: John Skoretz *Purchasing MGR*

Total Employees............................95	**Regional Employees** 95
Year Established 1956	**SIC Code**....................................3559
Annual Revenues ($000) 7,000	

Oberg Industries, Inc.

Silverville Rd.
P.O. Box 368
Freeport, PA 16229
County: Armstrong

Phone: (412) 295-2121
Fax: (412) 295-2588
Internet Address: www.oberg.com

Manufacturer of precision carbide stamping and lamination dies used to produce a variety of metal components for the automotive, electronics, semiconductor, health care and container industries. The Company also supplies a wide range of precision-stamped metal components as well as precision plastic injection mold tooling and plastic component parts. In addition, it offers a number of support services, such as precision machining and parts manufacturing, and reel-to-reel plating. The Company's operations include Oberg Manufacturing Co. (carbide and steel stamping dies), which is located at the above address; Independent Tool & Die (container tooling and carbide wear parts), Oberg Carbide Punch & Die (carbide bushings and punches) and Oberg Precision Components (plastic injection molds, die cast dies and compact tooling), all located on Oberg Dr. in Freeport, PA; Oberg Stamping & Technology Center (precision stampings) at 275 N. Pike Rd. in Sarver, PA; Special Oberg Services (die replacement components) at 273 N. Pike Rd. in Sarver, PA; and Oberg Arizona (stamping plating, molding and micro-machining) in Chandler, AZ. It also maintains international sales and technical support offices in Taufkirchen, Germany; Beijing, People's Republic of China; and Singapore.

Officers: D. Eric Oberg *CH*
Ralph E. Hardt *P & CEO*
Lawrence L. Bloom *SVP-OPR-Tooling & Metal Components*
William V. Nolf *SVP-OPR-Plastics Tooling & Plastic Components*
Ronald M. Norris *SVP-SAL & Market DEV*
Wes E. Elliott *VP-Business & Technical DEV*
John J. Maholtz *VP-MKT*
John L. Rozic *VP-INTL SAL*
John P. McCann *CFO*
Lou DiNunzio *DIR-Corporate Quality*
Karen S. Oberg *DIR-Corporate Planning*
Harry Walters *Corporate DEV & Legal Affairs*

Human Resources: Melissa S. Croll

Purchasing: Thomas A. Polzcynski

Total Employees	579	**Regional Employees**	482
Year Established	1948	**SIC Code**	3544
Annual Revenues ($000)	70,000		

Observer Publishing Co.

122 S. Main St.
Washington, PA 15301
County: Washington

Phone: (412) 222-2200
Fax: (412) 229-2754

Publisher, printer and provider of information services. The Company owns and publishes one daily newspaper and three weekly publications reaching approximately 110,000 households in the southwestern corner of Pennsylvania. It also provides full-color, offset printing services for various other publications and supplements, and offers on-line, audio text information services. The Observer-Reporter, with offices in Washington and Waynesburg, PA, has a daily circulation of 37,592 and a Sunday circulation of 39,696. Its coverage area consists of Washington and Greene Counties and parts of Allegheny County. The Record-Enterprise, with offices in Burgettstown and McDonald, PA, has a weekly circulation of 5,000. Its coverage area consists of Avella, Burgettstown, Cecil Township, Cross Creek Township, Findlay Township, Hanover Township, Independence Township, Jefferson Township, McDonald, Midway, Mt. Pleasant Township, North Fayette Township, Oakdale, Robinson Township, Smith Township and South Fayette Township, PA. The Company's subsidiary, Cornerstone Publications, located in McMurray, PA, publishes two weekly publications. The Advertiser, with a circulation of 32,269, covers Bethel Park, Canonsburg, Cecil Township, Peters Township and Upper St. Clair, PA. The Almanac, with a circulation of 32,349, covers Bridgeville, Castle Shannon, Greentree, Mt. Lebanon, Scott Township, South Fayette Township and Upper St. Clair, PA.

Officers: John L. S. Northrop *P & Co-Publisher*
William B. Northrop *VP & Co-Publisher*
Edward R. DeVoge *VP & GMGR*
Thomas P. Northrop *AST-Publisher*
William B. Northrop, Jr. *AST-Publisher*

Human Resources: Patti J. Lacock *VP & SEC*

Purchasing: R. Allen Schatz *CFO*

Total Employees............................235 **Regional Employees** 235
Year Established ....1902 **SIC Code** 2711
Annual Revenues ($000) 18,000

Ohiopyle Prints

410 Dinnerbell Rd.
P.O. Box 9
Ohiopyle, PA 15470
County: Fayette

Phone: (412) 329-4652
Fax: (412) 329-1001
Internet Address: www.ohiopyleprints.com

Textile screen printer of caps, T-shirts, sweatpants and sweatshirts for men, women and children. The Company offers two lines of preprinted sportswear as well as custom and contract screenprinting services to clients nationwide. Its "My Town Originals™" line is marketed through grocery stores; the "Ohiopyle" line is marketed through outdoor recreation/outfitters.

Officers: Scott H. Bortree *PTR*
Fred E. Wright *PTR*

Human Resources: Nancy Watts

Total Employees...........................100	Regional Employees 100	
Year Established 1981	SIC Code.....................................2262	
Annual Revenues ($000)..10,000+		

O

OHM Remediation Services Corp.

1000 RIDC Plaza, Ste. 600
Pittsburgh, PA 15238
County: Allegheny

Phone: (412) 963-2300
Fax: (412) 963-2327
Internet Address: www.ohm.com

Provider of a wide range of environmental services, primarily to government agencies and large chemical, petroleum, transportation and industrial enterprises. In addition to its technology-based, on-site remediation services, the Company also offers a broad range of other services, including site assessment, engineering and remedial design. The Company, which is headquartered in East Findlay, OH, operates regional offices nationwide. It is a subsidiary of OHM Corp., which is also headquartered in East Findlay, OH, and listed on the NASDAQ. The Company's other local facility is an equipment shop at 2130 William Pitt Way in Pittsburgh.

Officers: Robert Weber *Division MGR*

Human Resources: Robert E. McGregor *(Findlay, OH)*

Purchasing: Winston F. McColl *(Findlay, OH)*

Total Employees........................3,100	Regional Employees 80	
Year Established 1969	SIC Code....................................4953	
Annual Revenues ($000) 551,000		

Olsen O'Leary Assoc., Inc.

565 Epsilon Dr.
Pittsburgh, PA 15238
County: Allegheny

Phone: (412) 963-7272
Fax: (412) 963-9773

Provider of marketing incentive programs, including the design, implementation and fulfillment of merchandise and travel award programs. The Company also handles sales and productivity programs. It recently developed a debit card promotion which rewards participants with a customized Master Card that may be redeemed anywhere. The Company serves clients nationwide.

Officers: Mickey Horowitz *CEO*

Ira Horowitz *P*
Harold S. Dunn *EVP*

Human Resources: Kathleen Tomina *Human Relations*

Total Employees............................43	**Regional Employees** 43
Year Established 1962	**SIC Code**....................................4724

Olsten Staffing Services

Four Gateway Center, 2nd Fl.
Pittsburgh, PA 15222
County: Allegheny

Phone: (412) 261-7200
Fax: (412) 261-5647
Internet Address: www.olsten.com

Provider of temporary and permanent human resource staffing services, serving a broad array of clients in business, industry and government. Olsten Corp., which is headquartered in Melville, NY, and listed on the NYSE, operates hundreds of branch offices throughout North America, South America and Europe. The Company operates additional local branch offices in Cranberry Township, Greensburg, Monroeville and Pittsburgh (2), PA. It also operates an Olsten Financial Services office at the above address and an Olsten Health Services office in Greensburg, PA.

Officers: Milana Milosh *VP*
Brenda Avery *Regional DIR*

Human Resources: Cindy Cheran
Donna Marie Miskoleze

Purchasing: Chris Purcell

Total Employees......................11,000	**Regional Employees** 48
Year Established 1950	**SIC Code**....................................7363
Annual Revenues ($000) 3,377,729		

Omega Systems, Inc.

Omega Bldg., 160 N. Craig St.
Pittsburgh, PA 15213
County: Allegheny

Phone: (412) 681-7575
Fax: (412) 681-8128

Provider of information systems consulting services specializing in project development and the management of mainframe, mid-range, client-server and PC environments. The Company has expertise in strategic and applications consulting, software integration, EDI, millennium compliance and Internet/Intranet services.

Officers: William D. Mariotti *P*
             Kathy Gennuso *VP*
             Richard Smith *CFO*

Human Resources: Jay Murray *DIR-Human Resources*

Purchasing: Dick Smith

Total Employees............................100	**Regional Employees** 100
Year Established 1976	**SIC Code**......................................7379
Annual Revenues ($000) 6,000	

Oncology Nursing Society

501 Holiday Dr.
Pittsburgh, PA 15220
County: Allegheny

Phone: (412) 921-7373
Fax: (412) 921-6565

Nonprofit national organization of more than 25,000 registered nurses dedicated to patient care, teaching, research and education in the field of oncology. The Organization's mission is to provide optimal care to persons with an actual and/or potential diagnosis of cancer. Since the society was established, 197 chapters have been formed to provide a network for education and peer support at the community level. In addition, another level of membership, consisting of 30 Special Interest Groups, facilitates national networking of members in an identified subspecialty area. The Organization's subsidiary, Oncology Nursing Press, Inc., located at the above address, has produced numerous books and publications designed to assist the professional nurse to develop a foundation of knowledge about oncology nursing or to remain up-to-date on developments in the field. The Organization's affiliates, also located at the above address, include the Oncology Nursing Foundation, which was established to enhance the quality of cancer nursing throughout the disease process and the Oncology Nursing Certification Corp., whose purpose is to develop, administer and evaluate a program for the certification of oncology nurses. The Organization maintains a research department in Seattle, WA.

Officers: Pearl Moore *EDIR*
             Bridget Culhane *Deputy EDIR*
             Len Mafrica *Deputy EDIR-Oncology Nursing Press, Inc.*
             Cyndi Miller Murphy *Deputy EDIR-Oncology Nursing Certification Corp.*

Total Employees.............................70	**Regional Employees** 67
Year Established 1975	**SIC Code**......................................8621
Annual Revenues ($000) 6,404	

One Call Systems, Inc.

115 Evergreen Heights Dr.
Pittsburgh, PA 15229
County: Allegheny

Phone: (412) 415-5000
Fax: (412) 415-5023

Provider of inbound (800 and 888) and outbound call center services 24 hours per day every day of the year. The Company offers lead processing, inbound survey, customer service, seminar registration and order entry for a variety of clients. It specializes in service to the utility industry by providing underground damage prevention information ("Call Before You Dig"). The Company operates a branch facility in Dallas, TX.

Officers: Michael T. McNamara *OWN & P*

Human Resources: Deborah L. DeFazio *VP-FIN (Purchasing)*

Total Employees............................107	**Regional Employees** 80
Year Established 1984	**SIC Code**.....................................7389

Orbital Engineering, Inc.

1344 Fifth Ave.
Pittsburgh, PA 15219
County: Allegheny

Phone: (412) 261-9100
Fax: (412) 261-2308

Provider of design, engineering and project control services. The Company's engineering capabilities encompass a variety of disciplines, including structural, mechanical, electrical, instrumentation, piping, chemical process, environmental and process control. Its services include investigations and assessments; plant inspections and surveys; feasibility studies; conceptual designs and planning; engineering design, detailed drawing and specifications; permitting assistance; construction management; and commissioning and start-up. The Company serves clients in the petroleum, chemical, metals, pulp and paper, automotive, pharmaceutical and utility industries. It operates branch offices in Birmingham, AL; Oak Brook, IL; Whiting, IN; Cleveland and Toledo, OH; Philadelphia, PA; and Charleston, WV.

Special Designations: ENR_{500}

Officers: Robert J. Lewis *CEO*
                     Patrick S. Dolan *P*

Human Resources: Mike Khoury

Purchasing: Roni Walters

Total Employees..........................305	**Regional Employees** 105	
Year Established........................1969	**SIC Code**......................................8711	
Annual Revenues ($000) 24,000		

Owens & Minor, Inc.

One Stuart Plaza
P.O. Box 339
Greensburg, PA 15601
County: Westmoreland

Phone: (412) 837-5700
Fax: (412) 830-7425

Distributor of medical and surgical supplies to hospitals, primary care facilities, integrated health care systems, health care networks and group purchasing organizations. The Company, which is headquartered in Glen Allen, VA, is listed on the NYSE. From its 49 distribution centers nationwide, the Company distributes approximately 300,000 finished medical and surgical products produced by approximately 3,000 supplier partners to more than 4,000 health care customers nationwide. The majority of its sales consist of dressings, endoscopic products, intravenous products, needles and syringes, sterile procedure trays, surgical products and gowns, sutures and urological products. The Greensburg Division, operating out of the facility located at the above address, serves clients in portions of New York, Ohio, Pennsylvania and West Virginia.

Officers: Connie Stimmel *Division VP*

Total Employees........................3,425	**Regional Employees** 200	
Year Established........................1882	**SIC Code**......................................5047	
Annual Revenues ($000) 3,000,000		

Oxford Development Co.

One Oxford Centre, 301 Grant St., Ste. 4500
Pittsburgh, PA 15219
County: Allegheny

Phone: (412) 261-1500
Fax: (412) 642-7543

Full-service, commercial real estate developer with expertise in the areas of real estate development, building operations and management, construction management, and leasing and brokerage services. The Company has developed, owned, managed, leased and/or sold over 40 million square feet of commercial space, including retail centers, office buildings, hotels, distribution operations, recreational facilities, apartments and convention centers. It also has the oversight responsibility for more than 12.5 million square feet of commercial real estate. The Company has three affiliates located in downtown Pittsburgh, Bakewell Corp., a professional parking management company; Central Property Services, Inc., a commercial cleaning and maintenance company; and Oxford Real Estate Advisors, Inc., an institutional investment management advisory firm. Its other holdings, all located in Monroeville, PA, include the ExpoMart of Pittsburgh, an exhibition center; Racquet Club Apartments, a residential apartment development; Racquet Club of Pittsburgh, a health and fitness facility; and the Radisson Hotel-Pittsburgh.

Officers: Edward J. Lewis *CH & CEO*
David M. Matter *P & COO*
Mark E. Mason *GPTR*
Frank A. Molinero *SVP*
Scott Bergstein *VP-Office & Industrial Leasing & Brokering*
Eric Cartwright *VP-DEV*
Steven J. Guy *VP-FIN & CFO*
Richard I. Miller *VP & GC*
George E. Whalen *VP-Property MGT*
Brian M. Albert *AST-GC & SEC*

Human Resources: Kathleen A. LaMarca

Total Employees	1,365	**Regional Employees**	1,365
Year Established	1962	**SIC Code**	6512
Annual Revenues ($000)	86,000		

P&B Transportation, Inc.

601 Marco Rd.
Apollo, PA 15613
County: Armstrong

Phone: (412) 727-3477
Fax: (412) 727-2306

Contract carrier for Allegheny Teledyne Corp. The Company operates approximately 85 trucks and travels throughout the Continental U.S.

Officers: Bonnie Riggle *P*
Carol Williams *SEC & TRS*

Human Resources: Daniel Reed

Total Employees	150	**Year Established**	1980
SIC Code	4213		
Annual Revenues ($000)	8,000		

PAGE Imaging, Inc.

642 Ft. Duquesne Blvd.
Pittsburgh, PA 15222
County: Allegheny

P

Phone: (412) 281-7233
Fax: (412) 281-5107
Internet Address: www.page2000.com

Employee-owned full-service visual communications company specializing in the design, electronic prepress and print production of all types of marketing communications materials, packaging, labels, display and exhibit graphics. The Company is comprised of three divisions. Electronic Imaging/Prepress provides extensive capabilities in high quality scanning, retouching, film output and proofing, as well as data management and archiving. The Photo Lab offers a full range of commercial photographic printing services and products, including exhibit graphics and the latest technology in large format digital color imaging. The Graphic Design Group is a full-service design studio, well versed in the creative development and production of all forms of marketing materials, including brochures, annual reports, packaging, displays and direct mail. The Company's clients include corporations, advertising agencies and printers primarily in the Tri-State area.

Officers: Thomas J. Naughton *P, CEO, SEC & TRS*
Robert C. Manuel *EVP & COO*
Leslie A. Moss *VP*

Human Resources: Edward Lackman

Total Employees	70	**Regional Employees**	70
Year Established	1890	**SIC Code**	7336

Paladin Packaging & Display, Inc.

1728 Rte. 30 W.
P.O. Box B
Clinton, PA 15026
County: Allegheny

Phone: (412) 899-3291
Fax: (412) 899-3298
Internet Address: www.boxes1.com

Provider of corrugated design and manufacturing services. The Company produces point-of-purchase displays, specialty and interior packaging, and shipping containers, and provides fulfillment services. Its customers include Bayer, BMG, Capital Records, General Nutrition Center, Heinz, Pittsburgh Brewery, Poly Gram Records, Revco and Time-Life. The Company's subsidiaries include Keystone Die, Inc. in Oakdale, PA, and Packaging Specialists, Inc. in Carnegie, PA.

Officers: Tom Flickinger *CEO*
Christopher Donohue *P*
Fred Broad *SEC & TRS*
John Millspaugh *GMGR*

Human Resources: Mary Holub

Purchasing: Cherie Carroll

Total Employees.............................50	Regional Employees 50	
Year Established 1982	SIC Code.....................................2653	
Annual Revenues ($000)...15-20,000		

Palket Co., Inc., R. A.

1181 Airport Rd.
P.O. Box 629
Aliquippa, PA 15001
County: Beaver

Phone: (412) 375-6611
Fax: (412) 375-1011
Internet Address: www.tristate.pgh.netnews.com

Publisher of The News, a weekly community newspaper with a circulation of 66,656 covering Beaver County and Northwestern Allegheny County, including Coraopolis and Sewickley, PA.

Officers: Raymond A. Palket *Publisher*
Kathy Palket *P*

Total Employees ....50+	Regional Employees...................50+
Year Established 1961	SIC Code 2711

Panhandle Food Sales, Inc.

1980 Smith Township State Rd.
Burgettstown, PA 15021
County: Washington

Phone: (412) 947-2216
Fax: (412) 947-4940

Manufacturer of pizza products and hot food items. The Company produces Billy Boy's Pizza and many private label pizzas. Its hot food line includes Haluski hot sausage entrees, stuffed cabbage rolls and numerous other entrees. The Company markets its products to grocery stores primarily in the eastern U.S.

Officers: William S. Dugas, Jr. *P (Human Resources)*
David V. Dugas, Sr. *VP*

Purchasing: Mike Devereaux

Total Employees.............................30	Regional Employees 30
Year Established 1964	SIC Code.....................................2099

Pannier Corp.

207 Sandusky St.
Pittsburgh, PA 15212
County: Allegheny

Phone: (412) 323-4900
Fax: (412) 323-4962
Internet Address: www.pannier.com

Manufacturer of industrial marking devices and identification equipment. The Company also operates a graphics division in Gibsonia, PA, which manufactures directional signs and other related products and a precision machining division in Sarasota, FL, which serves the automotive industry and steel mills.

Officers: Albert J. Carvelli *CEO*

Human Resources: Beverly Turczyn

Purchasing: Howard Langston

Total Employees	200	**Regional Employees**	180
Year Established	1899	**SIC Code**	3953

Paper Products Co., Inc.

36 Terminal Way
Pittsburgh, PA 15219
County: Allegheny

Phone: (412) 481-6200
Fax: (412) 481-4787

Wholesale distributor of industrial packaging, disposable food service products and sanitary maintenance supplies and equipment. The Company offers a complete line of packaging products and equipment consisting of films, tapes, labels, cartons, machinery, bags, strapping, cushioning and dunnage, specialties and sanitary maintenance, as well as a variety of services. Its food service products consist of aluminum foil, aprons, bags, bowls, boxes, can liners, caps/hats, charcoal, cleaning supplies, containers, cups/glasses, cutlery (plastic), diet kits, doilies/coasters, dispensers, domes, facial tissue, feminine hygiene, food service film, garnishettes, gloves, guest checks, hair nets, ice and snow melters, lids, napkins, pans, paper, placemats, plates, platters, reusable mugs/bowls, scouring pads, straws, tablecovers, tape, toilet paper, paper towels, towelettes, tray covers, trays, tubs, twine, twist ties, wipers and wraps. Its sanitary maintenance products include janitorial supplies, restroom care products, floor care products, carpet care products, equipment (i.e. air vacuums, buffers, burnishers, insecticide foggers and parking lot sweepers) and specialty products (i.e. glass cleaners, graffiti removers, herbicides, metal polishes and wall cleaners). The Company primarily serves clients in the Tri-State area.

Officers: Dan R. Lackner *CEO*
Paul F. Lackner *P*
J. Joseph Lackner *VP*
Joseph F. Lackner *SEC*
Gary Devlin *SAL MGR*
John Lohman *SAL MGR Institutional*

Purchasing: Douglas Townshend *VP*

Total Employees............................55	**Regional Employees** 55
Year Established 1913	**SIC Code**...................................5113

Papernick & Gefsky, P.C.

One Oxford Centre, 301 Grant St., 34th Fl.
Pittsburgh, PA 15219
County: Allegheny

Phone: (412) 765-2212
Fax: (412) 765-3319

Multifaceted law firm with 10 attorneys. The Firm's practice areas include commercial and real estate financing, banking law and business planning, corporations and partnerships, and estate planning and civil litigation. It litigates in all areas of its practice in both state and federal courts, and before state and federal administrative agencies. The Firm's clients include business concerns of all sizes; individuals; partnerships; trusts and estates; real estate developers; charitable organizations; manufacturing concerns; lending institutions including commercial banks and savings institutions, high-tech companies, title insurance companies, major commercial and residential lenders, and retailers. It operates three branch offices located in Bethel Park, Monroeville and the North Hills area of Pittsburgh, PA.

Officers: Alan Papernick *P*
Martin I. Gefsky *VP*

Human Resources: Toby S. Rood *Administrator*

Total Employees............................40	**Regional Employees** 40
Year Established 1971	**SIC Code**...................................8111

Parent & Child Guidance Center

2644 Banksville Rd.
Pittsburgh, PA 15216
County: Allegheny

Phone: (412) 343-7166
Fax: (412) 343-8249

Nonprofit provider of mental health and mental retardation services to residents of Allegheny County. The Agency offers opportunities for healthy growth and development with the help of mental health services, including outpatient treatment, consultation and education for parents, professionals, schools and community groups. It also offers seminars and educational programs for those dealing with separation, divorce, remarriage or family alcoholism. The Therapeutic Pre-School helps young children with long-term and complex needs; the Independent Supports Coordination Unit provides support services to individuals diagnosed with mental retardation. The facility located at the above address houses the Therapeutic Pre-School, outpatient services, community services and the Independent Supports Coordination Unit. A satellite office in McKeesport, PA, provides mental retardation services for individuals in the Mon-Yough area of Allegheny County.

Officers: Thomas Gregory *EDIR*
Jeffrey Felton *Associate DIR*
Diane Len *Associate DIR*

Human Resources: Audrey Bett

Total Employees	100	**Regional Employees**	100
Year Established	1954	**SIC Code**	8322
Annual Revenues ($000)		4,300	

Paris Contracting Co., Inc., Alex E.

Rte. 18
P.O. Box 369
Atlasburg, PA 15004
County: Washington

Phone: (412) 947-2235
Fax: (412) 947-3820

Provider of construction services, including mass earth excavation and site development, water and sewer line installation, coal reclamation, pump station and plant construction, mechanical piping, demolition, formed concrete construction, earthen dam construction, air rotary drilling, mine stabilization, heavy construction, haul and dispose of flyash, and landfill construction. The Company serves clients throughout the Tri-State area.

Officers: Emanuel A. Paris III *P*
Eric A. Paris *VP*
Carrie L. Paris *SEC*

Human Resources: Timothy A. Paris *VP*

Total Employees	108	**Regional Employees**	108
Year Established	1928	**SIC Code**	1623
Annual Revenues ($000)		14,000	

Parker/Hunter, Inc.

USX Tower, 600 Grant St., Ste. 3100
Pittsburgh, PA 15219
County: Allegheny

Phone: (412) 562-8000
Fax: (412) 562-7843

Investment banking and investment firm with 21 offices located throughout Ohio, Pennsylvania and West Virginia. The Firm engages in most aspects of the investment business, including the underwriting of corporate and municipal securities, corporate and municipal finance, venture capital, equity research, mutual funds and insurance, taxable and tax-exempt fixed income securities, asset management, portfolio management and evaluation, market making, and the handling of stock and bond transactions on most stock exchanges and in over-the-counter markets. The Firm's 125 investment executives handle the financial needs of its clients, most of whom are individuals. The primary function of the Firm's Investment Banking Department (IBD) is to serve as financial advisor and consultant to a select number of corporations and to assist them in raising capital to meet their financing requirements, usually through the public underwriting or the private placement of common stock or long-term debt. The IBD also provides merger, acquisition and financial advisory services. The Firm's branch offices are located in Cleveland (2), Marietta, Painesville, Salem and St. Clairsville, OH; Clarion, DuBois, Johnstown, Meadville, Monessen, New Castle, Oil City, Philadelphia, Pittsburgh (2) (Monroeville and South Hills), Sewickley, Uniontown and Washington, PA; and Wheeling, WV.

Officers: Robert W. Kampmeinert *CH & CEO*
John D. Frankola *SVP*
Boyd S. Murray *SVP*
Craig A. Wolfanger *SVP*

Human Resources: James A. Yard

Total Employees...........................300   **Regional Employees** 220
Year Established 1902   **SIC Code** 6211

Parks Moving and Storage, Inc.

740 Commonwealth Dr.
Warrendale, PA 15086
County: Allegheny

Phone: (412) 776-3224
Fax: (412) 776-0049

Provider of moving and storage services. The Company, an agent for United Van Lines, offers household goods moving and storage, corporate relocations, records storage, special commodity transfer and special display transport throughout the United States. Its subsidiaries consist of Parks Moving and

Storage-South, Inc. in Uniontown, PA; Parks Moving Systems, Inc. in Philadelphia, PA; Parks Van and Storage, Inc. in Harrisburg, PA; and Parks-Centre Carriers, Inc. in State College, PA.

Officers: Barton B. Williams *P*

Human Resources: Judy Goehring

Total Employees............................156	**Regional Employees** 99
Year Established 1910	**SIC Code**....................................4213
Annual Revenues ($000) 13,000	

Passavant Hospital

9100 Babcock Blvd.
Pittsburgh, PA 15237
County: Allegheny

Phone: (412) 367-6700
Fax: (412) 367-4776

Nonprofit hospital that claims to be the nation's oldest Protestant hospital and the largest provider of health care services in northern Allegheny and southern Butler counties. A nonteaching hospital, the Hospital has a total of 296 beds—272 acute care beds, four of which are Level II neonatal beds, and 24 long-term beds. The Hospital's centers of emphasis—emergency medicine, cancer treatment, orthopedics, obstetrics, gynecology and cardiac care—form a core of clinical services designed to meet the most prevalent health care needs of the community. Its subsidiaries include Sherwood Oaks Lifetime Care Community at 100 Norman Dr. in Cranberry Township, PA; and North Care Realty, Passavant Hospital Foundation and Passavant Professional Assoc., Inc., all located at the above address. North Hills Suburban MRI at 1140 Perry Hwy. in Pittsburgh, PA, is a joint venture with Suburban General Hospital. In January 1997, the Hospital announced its intent to merge with the University of Pittsburgh Medical Center (UPMC). Under the terms of the proposed merger, the Hospital was to remain an independent entity within the UPMC system. The merger was expected to be completed by mid- to late-summer 1997.

Officers:
Norman G. Heard *CH*
Joseph F. Long *VCH*
Ralph T. DeStefano *P & CEO*
Raymond J. Beck *EVP & CFO*
Thomas K. Charles *VP-Ambulatory Services & Planning*
Dan R. Kraft *VP-OPR*
Margaret A. Shaffer *VP-Patient Services*
Frank Van Atta *VP-FIN*

Human Resources:
Marilyn L. Slagel *VP-Education, Human Resources & MKT Communications*
Karen Habenstein *DIR-Human Resources*

Purchasing: Paul Wheeler *DIR-Materials MGT*

Total Employees.........................1,408 **Regional Employees** 1,408
Year Established ....1849 **SIC Code**.....................................8062
Annual Revenues ($000) 78,766

Patrinos Painting & Contracting Co., T. D.

3191 Industrial Blvd.
Bethel Park, PA 15102
County: Allegheny

Phone: (412) 854-2700
Fax: (412) 854-8108

Provider of contract painting services primarily for commercial and industrial facilities throughout the United States.

Officers: Demetrios T. Patrinos *P*
Donald E. Mahramas *VP*

Human Resources: Evelyn Grueso

Purchasing: Dale Arnold

Total Employees...........................200 **Regional Employees** 100
Year Established ....1972 **SIC Code**.....................................1721

Patterson Co., Inc., R. T.

230 Third Ave.
Pittsburgh, PA 15222
County: Allegheny

Phone: (412) 227-6600
Fax: (412) 227-6672

Provider of installation engineering and construction management services to the iron, steel, aluminum, glass and chemical industries. The Company's engineers and technical personnel have extensive process and engineering experience in providing services from the appropriation phase through installation, start-up and commissioning. Its consulting engineering and design capabilities include project management and planning, civil, structural, architectural, piping, HVAC, mechanical, electrical, instrumentation and control, environmental, specifications, crane surveys and inspection, structural inspection, expediting, plant inspection, surveying, construction management, PLC software, and estimating, scheduling and simulation. The Company's clients include Acme Steel, Alcoa, Bethlehem Steel, General Electric, J&L Specialty Steel, Lone Star Steel, LTV Steel, Lukens, Mellon Bank, PPG Industries, Sony, U.S. Steel and Weirton Steel. It operates additional offices in Evansville and Highland, IN; and Brooklyn Heights, OH.

Officers: James J. Jagus *CH*
Roy L. Patterson *P*
Thomas G. Cohelnik *VP*
Trevor N. Farrand *GMGR & MKT MGR*
Michael J. Donohue *MGR-Brooklyn Heights, OH*
Ronald E. Evans *MGR-Highland, IN*
Fred R. Tomino *MGR-Evansville, IN*

Human Resources: Robert Goulding

Purchasing: Joe Veltre

Total Employees	200	**Regional Employees**	110
Year Established	1959	**SIC Code**	8711
Annual Revenues ($000)	15,000		

Paychex, Inc.

Foster Plaza Nine, 750 Holiday Dr.
Pittsburgh, PA 15220
County: Allegheny

Phone: (412) 921-5090
Fax: (412) 921-5165
Internet Address: www.paychex.com

   Provider of payroll processing, human resource and benefits outsourcing solutions for small to medium-sized businesses. The Company, which is headquartered in Rochester, NY, and listed on the NASDAQ, has over 100 locations and serves more than 250,000 clients nationwide. The Company claims to be a leading U.S. payroll processor with a comprehensive product offering, including payroll tax returns, direct deposit and other payroll services. Its human resource and benefits outsourcing services include a professional employer organization, 401(k) record keeping, section 125 cafeteria plans and employee handbooks. The local office serves clients in Western Pennsylvania and parts of West Virginia.

Officers: Tom Belprez *District SAL MGR*

Total Employees	4,200	**Regional Employees**	40
Year Established	1971	**SIC Code**	8721
Annual Revenues ($000)	566,000		

PBM, Inc.

Sandy Hill Rd., R.D. 6
Box 387-A
Irwin, PA 15642
County: Westmoreland

Phone: (412) 863-0550
Fax: (412) 864-9255

Designer, manufacturer and marketer of ball valves, other related valves, and automation products and services for use in solving fluid control problems and applications. The Company's product lines are available in sizes from 3/8" to 8", in 13 basic metals and alloys, and several soft seat and seal materials. These include 2-way ball valves; flush tank ball valves; diverter port ball valves; 3, 4 or 5-way multiport ball valves; sanitary ball valves; blast furnace valves and fittings; marine valves; special application valves, including aseptic, angle drain, fire-test, cryogenic or other customer-specified configuration; pneumatic and electric automation packages; and direct mount actuation. The Company supplies its products and services to process industries, including the pharmaceutical, biotechnical, chemical, paints and varnishes, food and beverage, cosmetics, pulp and paper, marine, resins and plastics, microelectronics, adhesives and sealants, nuclear and wastewater treatment sectors.

Officers: James Brennan *OWN*
Stuart J. Zarembo *P & CEO*
Roberta A. Breene *MKT MGR*
Phil Estep *DIR-MFG*
John Martin *CON*

Human Resources: Betty Thompson

Purchasing: Geralyn Defelice

Total Employees............................100
Year Established 1899

Regional Employees 100
SIC Code....................................3494

PDS Acquisitions, Inc.

One Quality Way
Irwin, PA 15642
County: Westmoreland

Phone: (412) 863-1100
Fax: (412) 863-3308

Holding company for its subsidiary, Precision Defense Services, Inc. (PDSI), a machine shop which is also located at the above address. PDSI specializes in precision machining, inspection, testing, special processing and assembly operations utilizing computer and numerically controlled, NC, conventional and customer-designed equipment. It has vast experience working with exotic materials including inconel, stainless steel, titanium, copper nickel, monel, hastalloy, zirconium, nitralloy, stellite, aluminum and steel. PDSI's machined products include omega and canopy seals, radar housings, hydraulic rotary actuators, jet engine shafts, nuclear core structural components and instrumentation assemblies, valves, compressor housings, antenna bases, piston rings, studs, nuts, bushings, steam generator plates and heat exchanger hardware, and commercial and military aircraft components.

Officers: Robert J. Perkins *P*
Robert L. Demangone *VP-FIN*
Eric J. Loadman *VP*
Thomas L. Swiers *SEC & TRS*
Peter Barclay *ENG MGR*
Rich Dubinsky *Shop Supervisor*
Frank Osikowicz *Contracts/Estimating MGR*
Robert Warren *DIR-Quality*

Human Resources: Joan Gruber

Purchasing: Jeff Adams *Purchasing & Production MGR*

Total Employees	79	**Regional Employees** 79
Year Established	1945	**SIC Code** 3499
Annual Revenues ($000)		5,900

Peacock Keller Ecker & Crothers, LLP

70 E. Beau St.
Washington, PA 15301
County: Washington

Phone: (412) 222-4520
Fax: (412) 222-3318

Provider of legal services with 14 attorneys. The Firm maintains a full-service general law practice serving individual and business clients. It operates a branch office in Waynesburg, and four convenience offices used only for appointments in Bridgeville, California, Claysville and McMurray, all located in Pennsylvania.

Officers: Douglas R. Nolin *MPTR*
Charles C. Keller *Senior PTR*

Human Resources: Carol A. Andrews *Personnel & MKT DIR*

Total Employees	39	**Regional Employees** 39
Year Established	1925	**SIC Code** 8111

PEAK Technical Services, Inc.

Penn Center, Bldg. Two, William Penn Hwy.
Pittsburgh, PA 15235
County: Allegheny

Phone: (412) 824-7325
Fax: (412) 825-3339
Internet Address: www.peaktechnical.com

Provider of temporary technical personnel services offering a staff of engineers, designers, draftsmen and programmers. The Company operates branch offices in Santa Ana, CA, and Troy, MI, serving clients nationwide.

Officers: Joseph V. Salvucci *P & CEO*
Thomas Hand *CFO*
Michael Sylvester *Branch MGR-Pittsburgh, PA*

Human Resources: Jarvis D. Cotton

Total Employees..........................600	**Regional Employees**...................150
Year Established.........................1967	**SIC Code**......................................7363

Penn Champ Inc.

Railroad & Lincoln Ave.
P.O. Box 55
East Butler, PA 16029
County: Butler

Phone: (412) 287-8771
Fax: (412) 287-6404

Manufacturer of private label aerosol and liquid household, health and beauty, and automotive products. The Company's aerosol household products include air fresheners, all-purpose cleaner, bathroom cleaner, carpet cleaner, fabric finish, furniture polish, laundry stain remover, oven cleaner and spray disinfectant; liquid household products include all-purpose cleaner, bathroom cleaner, concentrated fabric softener, laundry detergent, liquid cleanser, oil soap, ammonia glass cleaner and wool wash; health and beauty care products include shave creams, hair sprays, deodorants and skin care products; automotive aerosol products include battery cleaner, battery protector, carburetor and choke cleaner, engine degreaser and upholstery cleaner; and automotive liquid products include carburetor cleaner, gas stabilizer and injector cleaner. The Company provides private label programs for a broad range of organizations, including A&P, CVS, Hills Department Stores, Kmart, Kroger, Osco Drug, Pathmark, Shoprite, Schnuck's, Shopko, Stop & Shop, Target, Thrift Drug, Venture and Woolworth. The Company is a subsidiary of Bissell, Inc., which is headquartered in Grand Rapids, MI.

Officers: Roger Roelofs *GMGR*
Mike Slomkoski *Plant MGR*
Mike Drolet *Technical DIR*

Human Resources: Patti Bauer

Purchasing: Tony Campbell

Total Employees............................135
Year Established 1932

Regional Employees 135
SIC Code.....................................2899

P

Penn Detroit Diesel-Allison, Inc.

11 Progress Ave.
Cranberry Township, PA 16066
County: Butler

Phone: (412) 776-3237
Fax: (412) 776-0980

Distributor of Detroit Diesel Engines, Hercules Engines, Carrier Transicold and Allison Transmissions. The Company also provides parts and service, and operates a machine shop. It serves the truck, marine, construction, industrial and power generation industries. Headquartered in Philadelphia, PA, the Company operates additional branch offices located in Buffalo and Syracuse, NY, and Bedford, Harrisburg and Reading, PA, which serve customers throughout Pennsylvania and most of New York. The branch office located at the above address serves clients in Western Pennsylvania.

Officers: C. Christopher Cannon *CEO*
Gerald Tiffan *P*
John M. Stephenson *Branch MGR*

Human Resources: Gary Clemente

Purchasing: Peter Garvey

Total Employees............................400
Year Established 1982
Annual Revenues ($000) ....11,500 (Cranberry Township, PA branch)

Regional Employees 50
SIC Code.....................................3714

Penn Line Service, Inc.

300 Scottdale Ave.
P.O. Box 462
Scottdale, PA 15683
County: Westmoreland

Phone: (412) 887-9110
Fax: (412) 887-0545

Multidivisional specialty contractor active in the industrial, electrical, communication, coal and highway industries. The Company's capabilities include line construction and maintenance; commercial and industrial wiring; tree trimming, utility line clearance, right-of-way clearing and maintenance; and reclamation, landscaping and installation of fence, guard rail and road signs. Its fleet of equipment includes over 800 road and off-road units. The Company's subsidiaries include Forest Construction Co., which is headquartered at the above address with an operations office in Clarksburg, WV, providing electrical expertise for the mining industry; Olde Towne Electric Co. in Manassas, VA, an electrical contractor specializing in new construction and renovation projects for major commercial customers as well as installation and service for residential accounts; and Tri-County Electric Co., Inc. in Elkins, WV, engaged in commercial and industrial electrical installation projects. The Company serves over 300 customers throughout Delaware, District of Columbia, Indiana, Kentucky, Maryland, Michigan, New Jersey, New York, North Carolina, Ohio, Pennsylvania, South Carolina, Tennessee, Virginia and West Virginia.

Officers: Hendrick I. Penn III *P & CEO*
Paul Mongell *VP-FIN*
Larry Roberts *VP*
Lawrence W. Quigley *SEC*
James Wishart *TRS*

Human Resources: Thomas C. Respet *MGR-Corporate Services*

Total Employees	830	**Regional Employees**	175
Year Established	1940	**SIC Code**	1629
Annual Revenues ($000)	54,000		

Penn Mutual Group, The

Four Gateway Center, Ste. 1337
Pittsburgh, PA 15222
County: Allegheny

Phone: (412) 497-1800
Fax: (412) 338-0240

Provider of planning services and products to business owners and professionals in the areas of succession planning, retirement planning and estate planning. The Company also provides insurance reviews and products in the areas of life insurance, health insurance, employee benefits and executive benefits for small to medium-size closely-held companies. It operates branch offices in Erie and New Castle, PA, and Elkins, WV, and serves clients throughout the Tri-State area. The Company is an affiliate of The Penn Mutual Life Insurance Co., which is headquartered in Philadelphia, PA.

Officers: Richard C. Snebold, Jr. *MPTR*
John Cardwell *Associate MGR*
Michael D. Ulizio *Investment Coordinator*

Human Resources: Louis R. Satryan *DIR-Recruiting*

Total Employees	45	**Regional Employees**	30
Year Established	1864	**SIC Code**	6400
Annual Revenues ($000)	12,000		

Penn Needle Art Co., Inc.

6945 Lynn Way
P.O. Box 5693
Pittsburgh, PA 15208
County: Allegheny

Phone: (412) 441-7551
Fax: (412) 441-6505

Manufacturer and distributor of window coverings, including curtains and draperies, sold to a niche market of national chain stores and independent retailers. The Company's manufacturing plant is located in Spring Church, PA.

Officers: Paul Berger *P*
    Steven Berger *VP*

Total Employees............................50	**Regional Employees** 50
Year Established 1955	**SIC Code**......................................2391

Penn Perry, Inc.

109 Shenot Rd.
Wexford, PA 15090
County: Allegheny

Phone: (412) 934-7700
Fax: (412) 935-9488

Contractor providing roofing, sheet metal and related construction services. The Company offers tile, slate and metal roofing as well as metal siding products. Its sheet metal capabilities include gutter fabrication, metal copings, gravel stops, flashing fabrication, specialty sheet metal fabrication, architectural domes/spires, metal fascias, mansard systems and custom metal roofing. Its roofing department capabilities include single-ply membranes, built-up roofing, roof coatings, maintenance projects, roof deck installation and replacement, metal roofing, new construction projects, and inspection and roof surveys. The Company also provides in-plant insulation and fabricating services. It serves institutional (schools, churches and government facilities), commercial (office buildings and other commercial structures), architectural (roofing and siding on architectural buildings) and industrial (steel mills, power plants, chemical and coal plants) clients primarily in the Northeastern U.S. The Company also operates a warehouse and sales facility in Colonial Heights, VA.

Officers: Arthur F. White *P*
    Thomas A. Day *VP-OPR*
    Warren R. Schorr *VP*
    Glenda L. Martin *CON*

Total Employees............................52	**Regional Employees** 35
Year Established 1957	**SIC Code**......................................1761
Annual Revenues ($000)..5-6,000	

Penn State Beaver Campus

Brodhead Rd.
Monaca, PA 15061
County: Beaver

Phone: (412) 773-3500
Fax: (412) 773-3557
Internet Address: www.br.psu.edu

Nonprofit, public educational institution situated on a 98-acre campus located 30 miles north of Pittsburgh. The School is one of 23 Penn State campuses located throughout the Commonwealth of Pennsylvania. It offers the first two years of instruction in most of the more than 180 baccalaureate degree majors that are offered at the Pennsylvania State University, which is located in University Park, PA. It also offers five two-year associate degree programs in Hotel, Restaurant and Institutional Management; Letters, Arts and Sciences; Electrical Engineering Technology; Mechanical Engineering Technology; and Science (general option). The School reported an enrollment of 785 students for Fall 1996 with an average class size of 22. The on-campus residence halls house 314 students. Other Penn State locations include Allentown, Altoona, Berks, Delaware County, DuBois, Fayette, Hazleton, McKeesport, Mont Alto, New Kensington, Ogontz, Erie-The Behrend College, Harrisburg, Schuylkill, Shenango, Wilkes-Barre, Worthington-Scranton, York and the Milton S. Hershey Medical Center in Hershey, PA.

Officers: Dennis M. Travis, Ph.D. *Campus Executive Officer*
Robert C. Dewitt, Ph.D. *DIR-Student Affairs*
Gary B. Keefer, Ph.D. *DIR-Academic Admissions*
Amy M. Krebs *DIR-University Relations & Brodhead Cultural Center*
Regina S. Miller *Interim DIR-Enrollment MGT*
Richard T. Sosnowski *Financial Officer*

Human Resources: W. Luke Taiclet *DIR-Business Services (Purchasing)*

Total Employees	154	**Regional Employees**	154
Year Established	1965	**SIC Code**	8221

Penn State McKeesport Campus

University Dr.
McKeesport, PA 15132
County: Allegheny

Phone: (412) 675-9000
Fax: (412) 675-9185
Internet Address: www.mk.psu.edu

Nonprofit, public educational institution situated on a 52-acre campus. The School is one of 23 Penn State campuses located throughout the Commonwealth of Pennsylvania. It offers the first two years of instruction in more than 180 baccalaureate degree majors that are offered at the Pennsylvania State University, which is located in University Park, PA. It also offers five two-year associate degree programs in Business Administration; Electrical Engineering Technology; Letters, Arts and Sciences; Mechanical Engineering Technology; and Science (general option). In addition, the School offers a number of nondegree and professional development certificate programs, both on campus and at other locations throughout the Pittsburgh metropolitan area. The School reported an enrollment of 892 students for Fall 1996. Other Penn State locations include Allentown, Altoona, Beaver, Berks, Delaware County, DuBois, Fayette, Hazleton, Mont Alto, New Kensington, Ogontz, Erie-The Behrend College, Harrisburg, Schuylkill, Shenango, Wilkes-Barre, Worthington-Scranton, York and the Milton S. Hershey Medical Center in Hershey, PA.

Officers: JoAnne E. Burley, Ph.D. *Campus Executive Officer*
Nancy Herron, Ph.D. *DIR-Academic Affairs*

Human Resources: J. Kirk Urey *(Purchasing)*

Total Employees............................109	**Regional Employees** 109
Year Established 1947	**SIC Code**.....................................8221
Annual Revenues ($000) 3,900	

Penn State New Kensington Campus

3550 Seventh Street Rd.
New Kensington, PA 15068
County: Westmoreland

Phone: (412) 339-5466
Fax: (412) 339-5434
Internet Address: www.nk.psu.edu

Nonprofit, public educational institution. The School is one of 23 Penn State campuses located throughout the Commonwealth of Pennsylvania. It offers the first two years of instruction in more than 180 baccalaureate degree majors that are offered at the Pennsylvania State University, which is located in University Park, PA. It also offers two baccalaureate degree and eight associate degree programs in the fields of business, allied health, arts and sciences, and engineering technology. The School enrolls approximately 1,000 students with an average class size of 20. Other Penn State locations include Allentown, Altoona, Beaver, Berks, Delaware County, DuBois, Fayette, Hazleton, McKeesport, Mont Alto, Ogontz, Erie-The Behrend College, Harrisburg, Schuylkill, Shenango, Wilkes-Barre, Worthington-Scranton, York and the Milton S. Hershey Medical Center in Hershey, PA.

Officers: Catherine Gannon, Ph.D. *CEO*
Steven C. Hoops, Ph.D. *DIR-Academic Affairs*
Larry Pollock, Ph.D. *DIR-Student Affairs*
Patricia Quinn Winter *DIR-DEV & University Relations*

Human Resources: Lolita Sharp *DIR-Business & FIN (Purchasing)*

Total Employees............................110
Year Established........................1958

Regional Employees...................110
SIC Code......................................8221

Penna-Flame Industries, Inc.

R.R. 3, Rte. 588 W.
Box 14B
Zelienople, PA 16063
County: Butler

Phone: (412) 452-8750
Fax: (412) 452-0484

Provider of metal heat treating, stress relieving, cryogenics and flame hardening services to the steel industry. The Company also supplies bar stock material 3" to 9.5", and offers saw cutting, rough turning, grinding and polishing.

Officers: James P. Orr *P*
David E. Carnahan *VP*

Total Employees............................30
Year Established........................1968
Annual Revenues ($000)...2,000

Regional Employees....................30
SIC Code......................................3398

Pennsylvania Brewing Co.

800 Vinial St.
Pittsburgh, PA 15212
County: Allegheny

Phone: (412) 237-9400
Fax: (412) 237-9406
Internet Address: www.pennbrew.com

Owner and operator of a German brewery and the Penn Brewery restaurant. The Company's line of beers include All Star Lager, Altbier, Kaiser Pils, Maerzen, Maibock, Oktoberfest, Pastorator, Penn Dark, Penn Gold, Penn Pilsner, St. Nikolaus, Weizen and Weizen Bock. The restaurant offers German beers and cuisine as well as wine and spirits in a German "beer hall" setting.

Officers: Thomas V. Pastorius *P*
Mary Beth Pastorius *DIR & Restaurant MGR*

Total Employees............................45
Year Established........................1986
Annual Revenues ($000)...3,500

Regional Employees....................45
SIC Code......................................2082

Pennsylvania Drilling Co.

500 Thompson Ave.
McKees Rocks, PA 15136
County: Allegheny

Phone: (412) 771-2110
Fax: (412) 771-3167

Provider of contract drilling services and manufacturer of drilling equipment. The Company's contracting business does drilling for foundation test borings, mineral exploration, monitoring wells, hazardous waste, geotechnical instrumentation, grouting and construction. Its equipment has high-capacity auger and coring capabilities. It also operates a fleet of off-road all-terrain vehicles and truck-mounted equipment. The Company's work is centered around the Tri-State area with projects in the surrounding states and as far away as 500 miles or more. The Company's Pendrill manufacturing division produces tools for the drilling industry and performs job shop work. It is equipped with computer and numerically controlled (CNC) lathes and CNC milling equipment. It also stocks a substantial inventory of raw material and finished tools. The Company is both a distributor and retail supplier selling products throughout Canada, Mexico and the United States.

Officers: Thomas B. Sturges *P*
James R. Dravenstott *VP*
Robert Kennedy *SEC & AST-TRS*

Human Resources: Ralph R. Sands *TRS & CON*

Purchasing: Frank Jones

Total Employees	50	**Regional Employees**	50
Year Established	1900	**SIC Code**	3532
Annual Revenues ($000)	4-6,000		

Pennsylvania Fashions, Inc.

155 Thornhill Rd.
Warrendale, PA 15086
County: Allegheny

Phone: (412) 776-9780
Fax: (412) 776-4111

Owner and operator of a chain of more than 200 retail apparel stores located in 36 states offering men's and women's apparel. The Company's line of clothing sells at a starting price of $9.99, not exceeding $12.99. The stores operate under the name Rue 21 or as the 9.99 Stockroom. The Company's distribution center is located in Brilliant, OH.

Officers: Cary Klein *OWN, P & CEO*
David Mizzoni *SVP-MER*
Mark Drobka *VP-MIS*
Irv Neger *VP-MER*
Mary Jed Olson *VP-PDEV*
Rob Spokane *VP-FIN*
Kim Wiesmann *VP-Real Estate*

Human Resources: Gloria Roberts *VP-OPR*

Total Employees..........................1,600	**Regional Employees**.................200+
Year Established.........................1974	**SIC Code**......................................5621
Annual Revenues ($000)..150,000		

Pennsylvania Hospitality Assoc. L.P.

1406 Beers School Rd.
Coraopolis, PA 15108
County: Allegheny

Phone: (412) 262-3600
Fax: (412) 262-6221

Owner of the Holiday Inn-Pittsburgh Airport, which features 257 guest rooms. The Hotel also contains eight meeting rooms and three window rooms containing a combined total of 8,000 square feet of function space and an aquacade with an additional 3,600 square feet of space. Its amenities include a gift shop, indoor pool, sun deck and Funny Bone comedy club. The Company is owned by Evergreen Capital Corp., which is headquartered in Milford, CT. The Hotel is managed by Servico, Inc., which is headquartered in West Palm Beach, FL, and listed on the ASE.

Officers: Ivan Malik *GMGR*

Total Employees...........................175	**Regional Employees**..................175
Year Established.........................1973	**SIC Code**......................................7011
Annual Revenues ($000)..7,000		

Pennsylvania State Education Assn.

333 Blvd. of the Allies
Pittsburgh, PA 15222
County: Allegheny

Phone: (412) 471-7752
Fax: (412) 471-8729

Nonprofit association providing services in support of public education and its members who are employed throughout the educational community. The

Association's services include collective bargaining, contract administration, instructional and professional development, political action, intergroup relations and in-service programs to public schools. It has a membership of 140,000 teachers, support personnel, students, retired educators and administrative personnel from throughout Pennsylvania. The Association operates 22 offices in Pennsylvania, including its headquarters in Harrisburg. It is affiliated with the National Education Assn., headquartered in Washington, D.C., which has more than 2.3 million members nationwide.

Officers: David Gondak *P*
Carolyn C. Dumaresq, Ed.D. *EDIR*

Total Employees	250	**Regional Employees**	47
Year Established	1852	**SIC Code**	8621

Peoples Home Savings Bank

1427 Seventh Ave.
Beaver Falls, PA 15010
County: Beaver
Phone: (412) 846-7300
Fax: (412) 846-0718

Community-oriented state-chartered mutual savings bank offering traditional deposit, and mortgage and consumer, particularly automobile, loan products. The Bank provides a full range of retail banking services, with emphasis on one- to four-family residential mortgages and consumer lending. Currently, all mortgage loans are originated for portfolio. The Bank's deposits are insured under the Savings Assn. Insurance Fund as administered by the Federal Deposit Insurance Corp. In addition to its corporate headquarters and main office located at the above address, the Bank operates eight branch offices in Beaver and Lawrence Counties, PA, in Aliquippa, Baden, Beaver, Beaver Falls, Darlington, Ellwood City, New Brighton and Rochester, PA. PHS Bancorp, M. H. C., which is also located at the above address, owns approximately 51% of the Bank's common stock.

Officers: James P. Wetzel, Jr. *P & CEO*
David E. Ault *VP-Community Banking & AST-SEC*
Richard E. Canonge *VP-FIN, TRS & CFO*
John M. Rowse *SEC*

Human Resources: Paul W. Jewell *VP-Human Resources & Business DEV*

Total Employees	81		
Year Established	1888	**SIC Code**	6036
Annual Revenues ($000)	202,216 (Assets)		

Perma-Cote Industries, Inc.

29 Industrial Dr.
P.O. Box 1103, Uniontown, PA 15401
Lemont Furnace, PA 15456
County: Fayette

Phone: (412) 628-9700
Fax: (412) 628-9653
Internet Address: www.permacote.com

Manufacturer of PVC-coated rigid/steel conduit and related products serving the electrical construction industry. The Company distributes its corrosion-protected products through agents, warehouses and distributors nationwide. These products can be found worldwide in chemical plants, oil refineries, offshore drilling platforms, airports, and wastewater treatment and desalination plants. The Company operates two manufacturing facilities in Uniontown, PA, located at 42 Feathers Ave. and on Rte. 119 N. in the Uniontown Industrial Park.

Officers: Joseph P. Gearing *P*
Shirley Gearing *SEC & TRS*

Human Resources: Harry M. Sages *CON*

Purchasing: Daniel Gearing *VP-OPR*

Total Employees	131	**Regional Employees**	130
Year Established	1968	**SIC Code**	3479
Annual Revenues ($000)			17,000

Peters Holding Co.

9800 McKnight Rd.
Pittsburgh, PA 15237
County: Allegheny

Phone: (412) 366-1666
Fax: (412) 369-9223

Holding company providing construction services for commercial and nonprofit corporations through its two businesses, CMI General Contractors, Inc., and Peters Building and Construction Co., both of which are also located at the above address. The Company's clients include Family House, La Roche College, Lowes, Redevelopment Authority of Washington County, Sears Roebuck Co. and Shady Side Academy.

Officers: Bruce C. Peters *CH*
M. Raymond Hildreth *P & COO*

Total Employees	45	**Regional Employees**	45
Year Established	1987	**SIC Code**	1541
Annual Revenues ($000)			24,000

Petroclean, Inc.

2 Dorrington Rd.
P.O. Box 92
Carnegie, PA 15106
County: Allegheny

Phone: (412) 279-9556
Fax: (412) 279-7082
Internet Address: www.petroclean.com

Provider of environmental contracting and consulting services, including Phase I, II and III site assessments, hydrogeological investigations, engineering design, remedial investigation/feasibility studies, environmental audits, comprehensive above ground and underground tank management, waste management and 24-hour emergency spill response. The Company has served clients in industry and government in more than twenty states. It is affiliated with EGC, Inc., which is located in Waterford, PA.

Officers: Terry McAuliffe *P*
Drew McCarty *VP-SAL & MKT*
Robert Adams *SEC & TRS*

Human Resources: William Ferroli

Purchasing: Harry Kramer *CON*

Total Employees................................80	**Regional Employees** 70
Year Established 1978	**SIC Code**......................................4959
Annual Revenues ($000) 7,000	

Pevarnik Bros., Inc.

1302 Memorial Dr.
P.O. Box 389
Latrobe, PA 15650
County: Westmoreland

Phone: (412) 539-3516
Fax: (412) 539-2289

General building contractor of industrial, institutional and commercial buildings. The Company's projects include schools, churches and water treatment plants. It serves clients in Maryland, West Virginia and Western Pennsylvania.

Officers: Gervase J. Pevarnik *CEO & VP*
James Pevarnik *VP-OPR*
Donald Pennesi *CON*
Ruth M. Tantlinger *SEC*

Total Employees.............................135	**Regional Employees** 95
Year Established 1947	**SIC Code**......................................1542
Annual Revenues ($000) 25,000	

PG Publishing Co.

34 Blvd. of the Allies
Pittsburgh, PA 15222
County: Allegheny

Phone: (412) 263-1100
Fax: (412) 263-1486

Publisher of the Pittsburgh Post-Gazette. The newspaper has a daily circulation of 241,389, a Saturday circulation of 237,038 and a Sunday circulation of 441,488 (1996 figures). The Company maintains a sales office in Houston, PA, located at 2453 W. Pike St. It also operates 19 distribution centers located in Allison Park, Bethel Park, Bridgeville, Coraopolis, Corliss, Cranberry, Donora, East Hills, East Liberty, Hope Hollow, McKeesport, Meadowlands, Monaca, Monroeville, North Hills, Overbrook, Sharpsburg, Tarentum and West Mifflin, PA. Through its PG Link service, the Company provides telephone information such as updates of the news, sports, stocks and weather by calling 261-1234. The Company is a subsidiary of Blade Communications, Inc., which is headquartered in Toledo, OH.

Officers: William Block, Sr. *CH*
John Robinson Block *Co-Publisher & Editor-in-Chief*
William Block, Jr. *Co-Publisher & P*
John G. Craig, Jr. *Editor & VP*
Robert B. Higdon *VP & GMGR*
Madelyn Ross *Managing Editor*
Michael McGough *Editorial Page Editor*

Human Resources: Wayne Bierregaard *Human Resources DIR*

Total Employees......................1,300	**Regional Employees** 1,300
Year Established 1786	**SIC Code** 2711

PGT Trucking, Inc.

One PGT Way
Monaca, PA 15061
County: Beaver

Phone: (412) 728-3500
Fax: (412) 728-1852

Provider of flat-bed transportation of steel and nonferrous metals, building materials and heavy machinery. The Company's fleet consists of approximately 600 tractors and 700 trailers (including owner-operators' equipment). It maintains major terminals in Birmingham, AL; Atlanta, GA; Gary, IN; Detroit, MI; Asheville, NC; Monaca, PA; and Proctor, WV. In addition, the Company is represented by agencies in 30 states primarily east of the Mississippi River and in the southwestern U.S.

Officers: Patrick A. Gallagher *P & CEO*
Joseph M. Vargo *EVP*

Joseph P. Edmiston *EDIR-OPR*
Tim O'Hara *EDIR-Agency DEV*
Kevin McGavick *Community Relations Liaison*

Total Employees............................630	**Regional Employees** 105
Year Established 1981	**SIC Code**.....................................4213

PIAD Precision Casting Corp.

R.D. 12
Box 38
Greensburg, PA 15601
County: Westmoreland

Phone: (412) 838-5500
Fax: (412) 838-5520

Operator of a job shop providing full-service casting, machining and plating. The Company manufactures functional components for machinery, switchgear, transformers and hardware used in the electrical, valve and pump, lock hardware, marine hardware and firefighting equipment industries. It operates a subsidiary, Latrobe Machining Corp., located in Latrobe, PA. The Company is jointly owned by Choptank Holdings, Inc., based in Pittsburgh, PA, and Piel & Adey GmbH & Co., based in Solingen, Germany.

Officers: Karl Schweisthal *P & CEO*
Karl Krieger *OWN-Choptank Holdings, Inc.*
Holger Schweisthal *Production MGR*
Tony Poploskie *CON*
Larry Harnish *SAL & MKT*

Human Resources: Audra Hier

Purchasing: Nicholas Kostelac

Total Employees............................120	**Regional Employees** 120
Year Established 1968	**SIC Code**.....................................3366
Annual Revenues ($000) 15,000	

Pietragallo, Bosick & Gordon

One Oxford Centre, 301 Grant St., 38th Fl.
Pittsburgh, PA 15219
County: Allegheny

Phone: (412) 263-2000
Fax: (412) 261-5295

Provider of legal services with approximately 50 attorneys. The Firm's practice areas include litigation, business, corporate and real estate.

Officers: William Pietragallo *MPTR*

Total Employees............................116	**Regional Employees**...................116
Year Established 1987	**SIC Code** 8111

Pilkington Technical Mirrors

851 Third Ave.
Brackenridge, PA 15014
County: Allegheny

Phone: (412) 224-1800
Fax: (412) 224-8754

Manufacturer of automotive side mirrors and optical thin film coatings. The Company also performs glass fabrication. It is a division of Pilkington Plc, which is headquartered in St. Helens, England, and listed on the London Stock Exchange.

Officers: James Masterman *P*
Jay B. Ericsson *GMGR*
Frank Mauro *FIN MGR*

HumPurchasing: Josephine Guy

Total Employees............................130	**Regional Employees** 130
SIC Code 3231	
Annual Revenues ($000)..10,000+	

Pitney Bowes Inc.

645 Alpha Dr.
Pittsburgh, PA 15238
County: Allegheny

Phone: (412) 963-6782
Fax: (412) 963-6864

Manufacturer, marketer and lessor of an array of business equipment and provider of services. The Company's products include mailing systems—postage meters, mailing machines, address hygiene software, manifest systems, letter and parcel scales, mail openers, mail room furniture, folders, and paper handling and shipping equipment; facsimile systems—including a wide range of facsimile systems and supplies; and copying systems—including a wide range of copying systems and supplies. The Company, which is headquartered in Stamford, CT, is listed on the NYSE. The Pittsburgh district office, located at the above address, serves clients in Eastern Ohio, Western Pennsylvania and part of West Virginia.

Officers: Denny G. Durst *DIR*

Total Employees......................25,000	**Regional Employees** 95
Year Established 1920	**SIC Code**....................................5044
Annual Revenues ($000) 3,900,000	

Pitt Ohio Express, Inc.

45 26th St.
Pittsburgh, PA 15229
County: Allegheny

Phone: (412) 232-3015
Fax: (412) 232-3392

Regional less-than-truckload freight carrier specializing in the short haul transport of general commodities. The Company offers direct service to approximately 14,000 points throughout Delaware, the District of Columbia, Northern Kentucky, Maryland, New Jersey, Ohio, Pennsylvania, Northern Virginia and West Virginia. While it handles over 5,000 shipments daily, the Company's service profile reveals that greater than 97% of its deliveries are made overnight and 99% within two days. The Company's fleet consists of approximately 370 tractors, 800 trailers and 280 straight trucks. It operates additional terminals in Baltimore and Cumberland, MD; Cincinnati, Cleveland and Columbus, OH; Allentown, Harrisburg, Norristown and West Middlesex, PA; and Charleston, WV.

Officers: Charles L. Hammel III *P*
Robert F. Hammel *EVP*
Ronald Ciotti *VP-OPR*
Geoffrey Muessig *VP-SAL*
Robert E. Taylor *VP-FIN*
Ronald Uriah *VP-Safety*

Human Resources: Beth Bolin

Purchasing: Bernadette Vita

Total Employees..........................1,700	**Regional Employees** 300
Year Established 1979	**SIC Code**.......................................4212
Annual Revenues ($000) 128,000	

Pittsburgh Annealing Box Co.

801 Kroll Dr.
Pittsburgh, PA 15233
County: Allegheny

Phone: (412) 231-5877
Fax: (412) 231-4843

Manufacturer of heat-resistant alloy fabrications, annealing inner covers, retorts, muffles, breeching, furnace fixtures, pickle hooks and galvanizing kettles. The Company's subsidiaries include ALL Clad and Clad Metals, both located in Canonsburg, PA; and Capital Resource Group and NABCO located near the above address.

Officers: Sam Michaels *P & CEO*
                John A. Kenna *VP*

Total Employees...........................350
Year Established 1893   **SIC Code** 3443

Pittsburgh Ballet Theatre, Inc.

2900 Liberty Ave.
Pittsburgh, PA 15201
County: Allegheny

Phone: (412) 281-0360
Fax: (412) 281-9901

Nonprofit organization whose primary function is to provide cultural enrichment through the art of dance. The Organization's public performances are held
at the Benedum Center for the Performing Arts in downtown Pittsburgh. In addition to providing public performances, the Organization offers art education programs and lectures on various topics. It also operates a nationally acclaimed pre-
professional school, the Pittsburgh Ballet Theatre School, located at the above
address. The school has an enrollment of 400 and offers 12 levels of instruction for
a fully integrated education in dance and academics that draws students from
around the world.

Officers: Steven B. Libman *MDIR*
                David Holladay *School DIR*
                Mary Ellen Miller *DIR DEV*
                Gail Murphy *DIR MKT*
                Terrence S. Orr *Artistic DIR*
                Jay Romano *FIN DIR*
                Robert Neu *Production MGR*

Total Employees............................80   **Regional Employees** 80
Year Established 1969   **SIC Code**....................................7922
Annual Revenues ($000) 6,600

Pittsburgh Business Times

2313 E. Carson St., Ste. 200
Pittsburgh, PA 15203
County: Allegheny

Phone: (412) 481-6397
Fax: (412) 481-9956

Publisher of the Pittsburgh Business Times, a weekly business-oriented newspaper with a paid circulation of 13,600 and a total readership of 46,000. The
Company also publishes The Employment Paper (TEP), a weekly paper providing job-related information and listings with a circulation of 31,000. TEP is dis-

tributed free and is available at more than 600 sites throughout Pittsburgh. The Company is a subsidiary of American City Business Journals, which is headquartered in Charlotte, NC.

Officers: Alan Robertson *Publisher*
Paul Furiga *Editor*
Rick Lindner *Advertising DIR*
Dena Trusiak *Circulation DIR*
Richard Cerilli *Production MGR*

Human Resources: Tom Gagliardi *CON*

Total Employees............................40	**Regional Employees** 40
Year Established 1981	**SIC Code** 2711
Annual Revenues ($000) 3,500	

Pittsburgh Catholic Educational Programs

109 Washington Place
Pittsburgh, PA 15219
County: Allegheny

Phone: (412) 281-2376
Fax: (412) 281-4675

Nonprofit organization working with and assisting economically disadvantaged individuals. The Organization currently operates four programs for individuals living in Allegheny County: Operation Rainbow–Out-of-School Program for youth age 16 to 21 years; Older Adult Employment Program for adults age 45 and older; Single Point of Contact for AFDC clients; and Knowledge Connections–In-School Library Corps Program operated within certain housing developments. Over the years, the Organization has operated programs for clients of Allegheny County, the City of Pittsburgh, and Greene and Washington Counties.

Officers: Rev. Kris Stubna *P*
Dolores Davis *EDIR*

Total Employees............................30	**Regional Employees** 30
Year Established 1965	**SIC Code** 8322

Pittsburgh City Paper, Inc.

911 Penn Ave., 6th Fl.
Pittsburgh, PA 15222
County: Allegheny

Phone: (412) 560-2489
Fax: (412) 281-1962
Internet Address: www.pghcitypaper.com

Publisher of the Pittsburgh City Paper, a news and entertainment weekly, providing extensive arts and entertainment coverage, as well local news coverage and comprehensive events listings. The newspaper has a circulation of approximately 50,000 with an estimated readership of 435,000 throughout the Greater Pittsburgh metropolitan area. It is available for free at 1,100 locations.

Officers: Brad Witherell *P*

Human Resources: Scott Watson

Purchasing: Greg Brozovich

Total Employees	33	**Regional Employees**	33
Year Established	1991	**SIC Code**	2711
Annual Revenues ($000)			1,500

Pittsburgh Corning Corp.

800 Presque Isle Dr.
Pittsburgh, PA 15239
County: Allegheny

Phone: (412) 327-6100
Fax: (412) 325-9701

Manufacturer and marketer of PC GlassBlock, a glass block product, and FOAMGLAS, a cellular glass insulating product. PC GlassBlock is available worldwide in a wide range of patterns and sizes for use in commercial, industrial and residential applications. Primary applications of FOAMGLAS, also available worldwide, are in roof insulation of nonresidential buildings; in walls, floors and roofs of buildings for storage of frozen food; and in the piping and equipment found in industrial processes. The Company operates plants in Sedalia, MO, and Port Allegany, PA, and a subsidiary, Nippon Pittsburgh Corning, in Tokyo, Japan. The Company is jointly owned by PPG Industries, Inc., headquartered in Pittsburgh, PA, and Corning Inc., headquartered in Corning, NY, both of which are listed on the NYSE.

Officers: Donald E. Schlegel *P & CEO*
Wayne D. Carroll *VP-Technology & DEV*
David M. Ellis *VP & Counsel*
John C. Rusnak *VP-FIN*

Human Resources: Richard C. McPherson *VP-Human Resources*

Total Employees............................725		**Regional Employees** 100	
Year Established 1937		**SIC Code**.....................................3299	
Annual Revenues ($000) 100,000			

Pittsburgh Crankshaft Service, Inc.

6515 Hamilton Ave.
P.O. Box 5256
Pittsburgh, PA 15206
County: Allegheny

Phone: (412) 361-3496
Fax: (412) 361-3360

Distributor of engine and chassis parts, remanufacturer of crankshafts, and provider of shop supplies and machine shop services. These services include short blocks assembly; magnaflux inspection; crankshaft, camshaft and internal grinding; flywheel resurfacing; dynamic balancing; head and block work; rebabbiting services; connecting rods, key way and diesel block reconditioning; pressure testing; sand blasting; and hard chroming. The Company operates branch facilities in Cleveland, OH, and Harrisburg, PA.

Officers: Jutta Prizio *P & CEO*
Anita Prizio *VP*

Total Employees..............................54		**Regional Employees** 50	
Year Established 1950		**SIC Code**.....................................3599	
Annual Revenues ($000) 10,000			

Pittsburgh Cut Flower Co.

1901 Liberty Ave.
Pittsburgh, PA 15222
County: Allegheny

Phone: (412) 355-7000
Fax: (412) 391-0649

Wholesale provider of flowers and floral supplies. The Company serves clients in Maryland, Ohio, Pennsylvania and West Virginia.

Officers: Donald Hook *CH*
Robert Luthultz *P*
Jeffrey Hook *VP*

Total Employees..............................50
SIC Code 5193

Pittsburgh Design Services, Inc.

Hammond & Gregg Sts.
P.O. Box 469
Carnegie, PA 15106
County: Allegheny

Phone: (412) 276-3000
Fax: (412) 276-1216

Provider of structural and mechanical engineering and drafting services. The Company is also a manufacturer of fabricated structural steel; overhead material handling equipment, such as cranes and hoists; industrial reheat furnaces; and industrial process equipment. In addition, it provides installation, service and repair parts for its equipment.

Officers: Warren W. Fitzpatrick *P*
         Beth A. Noonan *SEC & TRS*

Human Resources: Keith C. Fitzpatrick *VP*

Purchasing: Amy Losego

Total Employees............................50	**Regional Employees** 50
Year Established 1970	**SIC Code**......................................5084
Annual Revenues ($000) 8,000	

Pittsburgh Flatroll Co.

31st St. & Allegheny Valley Railroad
Pittsburgh, PA 15201
County: Allegheny

Phone: (412) 765-3322
Fax: (412) 765-3430

Owner and operator of a rolling mill manufacturing custom-rolled sheets, plates and rectangular bar using specialty alloy. These products are used for defense, aerospace and nuclear applications. The Company has in-house capabilities for conditioning slabs, hot rolling, cold rolling, annealing, batch pickling, shot blasting, roller flattening, stretch leveling, shearing and sawing. It also provides conversion mill processing on both a volume basis for major mill customers and on a small quantity basis for developmental processing.

Officers: Lawrence A. McKee *P*
         Jack Gilmore *VP & COO*

Total Employees............................47	**Regional Employees** 47
Year Established 1991	**SIC Code**......................................3312
Annual Revenues ($000) 8,000	

Pittsburgh Hilton and Towers

Gateway Center, 600 Commonwealth Place
Pittsburgh, PA 15222
County: Allegheny

P

Phone: (412) 391-4600
Fax: (412) 594-5161
Internet Address: www.hilton.com

Hotel featuring 711 guest rooms and 31 suites. It specializes in banquets and conventions and claims to offer the city's largest ballroom—in excess of 17,000 square feet of function space that can accommodate up to 2,000 people. The Hotel's facilities include two restaurants, two lounges, health club and hair salon. It is owned and operated by Hilton Hotels Corp., which is headquartered in Beverly Hills, CA, and listed on the NYSE.

Officers: Conrad Wangeman *GMGR*
Tim Zugger *Resident MGR*
Patrick Cook *DIR-SAL*
Scott Lovejoy *DIR-Catering*
Wayne Spence *DIR-Front Office*

Human Resources: Leslie Ferrier

Purchasing: Jim O'Quinn

Total Employees............................400	**Regional Employees** 400
Year Established 1959	**SIC Code** 7011
Annual Revenues ($000) 30,000		

Pittsburgh Institute of Aeronautics

Five Allegheny County Airport
P.O. Box 10897, Pittsburgh, PA 15236
West Mifflin, PA 15122
County: Allegheny

Phone: (412) 462-9011
Fax: (412) 466-0513
Internet Address: www.piainfo.org

Nonprofit post-secondary school providing aviation maintenance training, truck driver training and contract training. The School offers Associate degrees in Avionics Technology and Aeronautical Maintenance Technology. It enrolls approximately 200 students.

Officers: John Graham *P & CEO*
Donald Newton *EVP*
James Mader *Dean*
Robert F. Leonard *DIR-Admissions*

Total Employees..............................50	**Regional Employees** 40
Year Established 1929	**SIC Code** 8249
Annual Revenues ($000) 3,000		

Pittsburgh Logistics Systems, Inc.

2060 Pennsylvania Ave.
Monaca, PA 15061
County: Beaver

Phone: (412) 709-9000
Fax: (412) 709-9010
Internet Address: www.pghlogistics.com

Provider of third party transportation/logistics management services to the metals, heavy manufacturing, health care and retail industries. The Company's core offering is a program called Total Transportation Management. Under this program, the Company becomes the client's in-house traffic/transportation department, managing any and all aspects of inbound, outbound and interplant shipments. The Company maintains no ties to any one carrier but has relationships with many and the ability to provide dedicated carriage service when it is needed. The Company has developed a proprietary software package—PLS2000™—to assist professionally trained personnel in managing the movement of products throughout the globe. It also offers consulting, less-than-truckload management, asset management, and freight bill audit and payment services. The Company maintains employees at a number of client sites, including Chicago, IL; Oak Park, MI; Cleveland, Middletown and Youngstown, OH; and Ellwood City and Pittsburgh, PA.

Officers: Gregg A. Troian *P & CEO*
Jack W. Goisse *SVP-OPR*
Charles A. Friend *VP-Regional OPR*
Timothy G. Sheedy *VP-FIN*
Peter P. Scolieri *DIR-SAL & MKT*

Human Resources: Karen M. Wynn *MGR*

Total Employees............................85	**Regional Employees** 50
Year Established 1991	**SIC Code**....................................4731
Annual Revenues ($000) 100,000	

Pittsburgh Mailing Systems, Inc.

170 Bilmar Dr.
Pittsburgh, PA 15205
County: Allegheny

Phone: (412) 922-8744
Fax: (412) 937-1730

Provider of direct marketing services consisting of market segmentation, computer imaging, fulfillment and mail distribution. The Company's services include file conversion; list enhancement; duplicate elimination and merge/purge capability; laser, impact and direct impression printing; bindery and insertion; and presort and mailing provided to advertising agencies, banks and financial institutions, retailers, membership organizations, fund-raisers, telemarketing companies, publishers and Fortune 500 companies.

Officers: Fred F. Smallhoover, Sr. *P*
               Fred M. Smallhoover, Jr. *VP-SAL*
               Bernard T. Henciak *SEC & TRS*

Total Employees............................75	**Regional Employees** 75	
Year Established 1983	**SIC Code**....................................7371	
Annual Revenues ($000) 3,000		

Pittsburgh Marriott City Center

112 Washington Place
Pittsburgh, PA 15219
County: Allegheny

Phone: (412) 471-4000
Fax: (412) 394-1017

Hotel featuring 400 guest rooms, including five parlor suites with connecting guest rooms and a Presidential Suite. The Hotel also contains 24 meeting rooms totaling 24,000 square feet of banquet and conference space, and three foyers useful for meeting registrations, receptions, breaks and exhibits. Its facilities include the Steelhead Grill, serving breakfest, lunch and dinner; the Lounge; and an indoor swimming pool, health club and sauna. The Hotel is owned by Host Marriott Corp. in Bethesda, MD, and managed by Interstate Hotels Corp. in Pittsburgh, PA, both of which are listed on the NYSE. It was formerly known as the Hyatt Regency Pittsburgh.

Officers: Barbara McMahon *GMGR*
               Thomas Martini *DIR-Hotel SAL*
               Bill Paviol *DIR-Group SAL*
               Jean Stefan *DIR-Catering*

Human Resources: Mary Varone

Purchasing: Joe Communale

Total Employees...........................200	**Regional Employees** 200
Year Established 1996	**SIC Code** 7011

Pittsburgh Mercy Health System, Inc.

1400 Locust St.
Pittsburgh, PA 15219
County: Allegheny

Phone: (412) 232-8111
Fax: (412) 232-7380
Internet Address: www.mercylink.org

Nonprofit, comprehensive, integrated Catholic system of health care designed to meet the holistic health needs of the individual and the community. The System operates several major entities. The Mercy Hospital of Pittsburgh, which is located at the above address, is a 506-licensed bed teaching and general referral hospital. It offers a full spectrum of medical and surgical services as well as pediatrics, obstetrics, rehabilitation, psychiatry and emergency services. Also located at the hospital is the Mercy Heart Institute, Mercy Cancer Institute, a 37-licensed bed Skilled Nursing Facility and a Level I Regional Resource trauma center. In addition, it sponsors six residency programs, operates a diploma school of nursing and offers fellowships in pediatrics, critical care medicine, cardiovascular anesthesia, and head and neck and microvascular surgery. Mercy Life Center Corp. works in collaboration with Mercy Hospital's Skilled Nursing Facility and Center for Aging to provide a continuum of senior care services to patients of St. Joseph Nursing and Health Care Center, a 158-licensed bed skilled nursing facility located in Bloomfield-Garfield and residents of St. Pius X Residence, a 26-licensed bed personal care home in Brookline. In addition, it holds a management contract for Southwestern Nursing and Rehabilitation Center, a 120-licensed bed skilled nursing facility located in Pleasant Hills. Mercy Primary Care, Inc. operates a primary care network offering family practice, pediatrics, obstetrics/gynecology and internal medicine services through medical practices in Arlington Heights, Brentwood, Dormont, Greentree, Hill District, Library, McMurray, Monroeville, North Side, Pleasant Hills, Plum, Ross Township, Scott Township, South Side, St. Clair Village, Uptown, West View, Wexford and Wilkins Township, PA. Mercy Providence Hospital, which is located at 1004 Arch St. in Pittsburgh, PA, is a 146-licensed bed community hospital providing 24-hour treatment of medical, surgical and psychiatric emergencies, geriatric medicine, oncology, cardiac telemetry, behavioral health and rehabilitation. Northern Southwest Community Mental Health/Mental Retardation/Drug and Alcohol Services is a community-based continuum of more than 50 specialized programs and services for individuals and families experiencing mental illness, mental retardation or addiction to alcohol or other drugs, with treatment and support services offered in the North Side, North Hills, South Side and South Hills sections of Pittsburgh. Pittsburgh Mercy Foundation, which is located at the above address, is engaged in fund development and other charitable activities on behalf of the System and its subsidiaries. South Hills Outpatient Rehabilitation Enterprises, which is located at 2000 Oxford Dr. in Bethel Park, PA, is a joint partnership between the System and St. Clair Management Resources, Inc., offering comprehensive outpatient physical, occupational and speech therapy; psychology; work hardening and work capacity evaluation; and injury prevention programs. The System is sponsored by the Eastern Mercy Health System, which is headquartered in Radnor, PA.

P

Officers: Sister Joanne Marie Andiorio, Dr.P.H. *P & CEO*
Stephen D. Adams *EVP-Corporate Affairs & CIO*
Robert W. Kocent *EVP-Continuum of Care Services*
JoAnn V. Narduzzi, M.D. *EVP-Medical MGT*
Mark R. Scott *EVP & CFO*
Howard A. Zaren, M.D. *EVP-Hospital Services*
Michele R. Cooper *VP-Healthy Communities Institute, Network DEV & Planning, & MKT*
Bernard H. Crowley *VP-Managed Care; EDIR-Mercy Physician Hospitals Organization*
Susan N. Heck *VP-Institute Services*
Judy Herstine *VP-Primary Care; COO-Mercy Primary Care, Inc.*
Sister Patricia Mary Hespelein *VP-Mission Services*
Thomas J. Mattei, Pharm.D. *VP-OPR*
Barbara J. Schneck *VP-Senior Care Continuum*
Sister Kathi Sweeney *VP-Ambulatory Care*
Sandra P. Twyon *VP-Patient Services*
Charles R. Vargo *VP-Ancillary Services*
Douglas G. Smith *P-Pittsburgh Mercy Foundation*

Human Resources: Rosalie E. Barsotti *VP-Human Resources*

Purchasing: Terrence Parker *DIR-Materials MGT*

Total Employees	4,084	**Regional Employees**	4,084
Year Established	1847	**SIC Code**	8062
Annual Revenues ($000)			260,000

Pittsburgh Opera, Inc.

711 Penn Ave., 8th Fl.
Pittsburgh, PA 15222
County: Allegheny

Phone: (412) 281-0912
Fax: (412) 281-4324

Nonprofit opera company presenting internationally acclaimed artists. For the past 16 years, the Opera has presented a minimum of four operas on the mainstage. In concert with the Opera's mainstage productions, it produces several smaller works, that are less often performed, at its Pittsburgh Opera Center at Duquesne (POCD). All POCD performances in the community are presented free of charge. The Opera emphasizes free educational and outreach programs to develop the audience of tomorrow by introducing adults and children to the rich cultural heritage of the opera. The ticket-buying public has demonstrated its support of the Opera through more than 90% audience attendance for many years. The Opera's mainstage performances are held at the Benedum Center for the Performing Arts, at Seventh St. and Penn Ave. in downtown Pittsburgh.

Officers: Mark J. Weinstein *EDIR*
Tito Capobianco *Artistic DIR*
Michelle Kruggel *DIR-Public Relations*
Maria Levy *DIR-Artistic OPR*
Sally Moxom *DIR-Communications*
Ken Tarasi *DIR-FIN*
Janet White *DIR-DEV*

Human Resources: Carol Brinjak *Office MGR*

Total Employees 21-300	**Regional Employees** 21-300
Year Established 1940	**SIC Code** 7922
Annual Revenues ($000) 4,044	

Pittsburgh Plastics Manufacturing, Inc.

129 McCarrell Lane
Zelienople, PA 16063
County: Butler

Phone: (412) 452-6100
Fax: (412) 452-9125

Manufacturer of liquid-filled and polymer gel-filled plastic products, including insoles and medical products. The Company serves clients worldwide.

Officers: James E. Zona *P & CEO*
Mark Vernallis *COO*
Thomas P. Davis *VP-SAL & MKT*
Charlene Finau *DIR-FIN*

Purchasing: Lisa Keller

Total Employees 110	**Regional Employees** 110
Year Established 1985	**SIC Code** 3081
Annual Revenues ($000) 9,000	

Pittsburgh Plaza Hotel Corp., Inc.

1500 Beers School Rd.
Coraopolis, PA 15108
County: Allegheny

Phone: (412) 264-7900
Fax: (412) 262-3229

Owner and operator of the Pittsburgh Plaza Hotel. The Hotel features 200 guest rooms, an exercise room with sauna, meeting rooms, an Eat 'N Park restaurant and courtesy transportation to and from the Pittsburgh International Airport.

Officers: Margaret DiCorpo *P*
Thomas P. Sheehan *SEC*

Total Employees..............................50	**Regional Employees** 50
Year Established 1990	**SIC Code** 7011

Pittsburgh Public Theater Corp.

Allegheny Sq.
Pittsburgh, PA 15212
County: Allegheny

Phone: (412) 321-9800
Fax: (412) 323-8550
Internet Address: www.pghpublictheater.org

Nonprofit professional theater company bringing together gifted actors, directors and designers from across the country and around the world for its performances. Well over 100,000 theatergoers in the Pittsburgh region attend presentations at the Theater each year and thousands more are served through educational and outreach programs, including student matinees, trainee employment, discussion sessions, and special services for individuals with disabilities and senior citizens. The Theater produces six plays per season from a variety of genres. The Pittsburgh Public Theater, located at the above address, seats 457 people. Its production shop is located at 437 Bingham St. in Pittsburgh, PA.

Officers: William D. Hunt *P*
Carolyn M. Byham *SEC*
John D. Houston II *TRS*
Stephen Klein *MDIR*
Edward Gilbert *Artistic DIR*
Alan Harrison *Audience DEV DIR*
Leslie J. Wild *Senior DEV Officer*

Human Resources: Mary M. Sabol

Purchasing: Cynthia J. Tutera *GMGR-ADM & FIN*

Total Employees 110-300	**Regional Employees** 110-300
Year Established 1974	**SIC Code** 7929
Annual Revenues ($000) 4,000	

Pittsburgh Sports Assoc. Holding Co.

Civic Arena, 300 Auditorium Place, Gate 9
Pittsburgh, PA 15219
County: Allegheny

Phone: (412) 642-1300
Fax: (412) 642-1859
Internet Address: www.pittsburghpenguins.com

Holding company controlling the Pittsburgh Hockey Assoc. (PHA), the owner of the Pittsburgh Penguins National Hockey League franchise. The Penguins play their home games at the Pittsburgh Civic Arena, which is located at the above address. Southpointe Rink Assoc., L.P., a subsidiary of PHA, owns and operates Iceoplex at Southpointe in Canonsburg, PA. The indoor ice skating, roller skating and soccer facility also serves as the training site for the Penguins. In addition, the Company operates Igloo Development Assoc., which was formed to evaluate development opportunities at and around the Pittsburgh Civic Arena.

Officers: Howard Baldwin *C-OWN & CH*
Roger Marino *C-OWN*
Thomas Ruta *C-OWN*
Charles Greenberg *P-Igloo Development Associates*
Donn Patton *P-Pittsburgh Hockey Associates*
John H. Kelley *EVP*
Gregory D. Cribbs *VP & GC*

Total Employees............................112	**Regional Employees**....................112
Year Established 1967	**SIC Code**......................................7941

Pittsburgh Symphony Society

Heinz Hall, 600 Penn Ave.
Pittsburgh, PA 15222
County: Allegheny

Phone: (412) 392-4800
Fax: (412) 392-4909

Nonprofit organization operating the Pittsburgh Symphony, which annually presents 24 weeks of classical subscription concerts, a seven-week pops subscription series, special holiday concerts, a Fiddlesticks family concert series plus a series of educational concerts and other special events in the orchestra's home, Heinz Hall. The Organization also offers free-admission summertime concerts in area parks along with a series of community outreach concerts throughout Southwestern Pennsylvania. In addition, the orchestra records and engages in extensive domestic and international touring.

Officers: Donald I. Moritz *P & CEO*
Gideon Toeplitz *EVP & MDIR*
Mariss Jansons *Music DIR*

Human Resources: Elizabeth Helbling

Total Employees............................170	**Regional Employees** 170
Year Established 1896	**SIC Code**......................................7929
Annual Revenues ($000) 23,000	

Pittsburgh Tank Corp.

135-C Meadow Lane
Canonsburg, PA 15317
County: Washington

Phone: (412) 746-9422
Fax: (412) 745-8644

Designer, manufacturer and erector of dry-bulk storage silos, liquid storage tanks, American Society of Mechanical Engineers code designed pressure vessels and vibratory bin discharges. The Company's products serve the dry-bulk storage needs of the chemical, petrochemical, food processing, plastics and agricultural industries.

Officers: James M. Bollman *C-OWN & P*

Human Resources: Philip M. Duvall *C-OWN & VP*

Purchasing: Rod Temple

Total Employees..............................37	**Regional Employees** 37
Year Established 1988	**SIC Code**......................................3443
Annual Revenues ($000) 3,500	

Pittsburgh Technical Institute

635 Smithfield St.
Pittsburgh, PA 15222
County: Allegheny

Phone: (412) 471-1011
Fax: (412) 471-9014

Two-year, coeducational, nonsectarian, independent institution of higher education providing career education in selected business and technical areas enrolling approximately 830 students. The School offers the Associate in Specialized Technology degree in Computer-Aided Drafting, Graphic Design, Computer Programming, Computer Systems Specialist and Electronics Technology; the Associate in Specialized Business degree in Business Administration; and diploma programs in Electronic Pre-Press Technology and Electronics Technology with options in Microcomputer Technology or Telecommunications. The School operates an additional facility at 110 Ninth St. in Pittsburgh, PA.

Officers: J. R. McCartan *P*
Connie Friedberg *VP-Financial Services*
Cynthia Reynolds *VP-Admissions*
Johanna Schaffner *VP-Faculty DEV*
Mark Scott *VP-Career DEV*

Human Resources: Nancy Sheppard

Purchasing: George Topich

Total Employees..........................148	**Regional Employees** 148
Year Established 1946	**SIC Code**....................................8249
Annual Revenues ($000) 7,765		

Pittsburgh Theological Seminary

616 N. Highland Ave.
Pittsburgh, PA 15206
County: Allegheny

Phone: (412) 362-5610
Fax: (412) 363-3260

Nonprofit graduate-level theological educational institution. The Seminary's programs prepare students for ordained ministry or lay church leadership. Approximately 40% of its student body is Presbyterian, 23% United Methodist and the rest is a diverse mixture of denominations. The Seminary is particularly known for its Metro-Urban Institute, which provides specialized coursework for persons practicing ministry in an urban setting, and the Center for Business, Religion and Professions, which conducts an average of six programs a year geared toward the integration of the worlds of business and faith and covers diverse topics of particular interest to the business community. The Seminary also offers a range of continuing education programs for interested clergy and laypeople. It has an enrollment of 283 students.

Officers: Carnegie Samuel Calian *P*
Richard Barnhart *VP-DEV*
Richard Oman *VP-Academics*
Lisa Foster *DIR-Seminary Relations*

Human Resources: Douglas Clasper *VP-Business*

Total Employees............................75	**Regional Employees** 75
Year Established 1794	**SIC Code**....................................8221

Pittsburgh Tool Steel, Inc.

1535 Beaver Ave.
Monaca, PA 15061
County: Beaver

Phone: (412) 773-7000
Fax: (412) 774-4069

Manufacturer of cold-drawn precision metal shapes in bar and coil form. The Company serves a variety of manufacturing industries.

Officers: Lawrence M. Megan *P*
R. Frank Cremeens *VP*
Brian L. Greaves *CON*

Human Resources: Shirley A. Caratelli *Personnel DIR*

Total Employees..............................55	**Regional Employees** 55
Year Established 1902	**SIC Code**.......................................3316
Annual Revenues ($000) 6,000		

Pittsburgh Transportation Co.

5931 Ellsworth Ave.
Pittsburgh, PA 15206
County: Allegheny

Phone: (412) 665-8123
Fax: (412) 363-8954

Provider of transportation services, with a fleet of more than 600 vehicles including taxis, limousines, buses, shuttles, school buses, vans, V.I.P. coaches and wheelchair vans. The Company also provides ground transportation management services and parking services. While it primarily serves clients in Allegheny County, it provides limousine services throughout the Commonwealth of Pennsylvania. Yellow Cab Co. of Pittsburgh is an affiliate.

Officers: Herbert B. Conner *OWN*
James D. Campolongo *P & CEO*
Edward Boll *TRS*

Human Resources: Arch MacLennan

Total Employees............................300	**Regional Employees** 300
Year Established 1913	**SIC Code**.......................................4011

Pittsburgh Tube Co.

Cherrington Corporate Center, 600 Clubhouse Dr., Ste. 200
Coraopolis, PA 15108
County: Allegheny

Phone: (412) 299-7900
Fax: (412) 299-2619

Producer and global marketer of welded and cold-drawn mechanical steel tubing. The Company's tubular products are distributed through service centers or sold directly to OEMs of automobiles and truck components, construction and farm equipment, appliances and general industrial equipment. Typical applications include hydraulic cylinders, axles, transmission shafts, steering and suspension components; drill rod casings; electrical conduit; automobile components; tie rods; and motor housings. The Company's divisions consist of the Darlington Division in Darlington, PA; Fairbury Division in Fairbury, IL; General Tube Division in Dixmoor, IL; Jane Lew Division in Jane Lew, WV; Monaca Division in Monaca, PA; Monroe Tube Division in Monroe, NY; and TecFAB Division in Richmond, IN.

Officers: Richard C. Huemme *CH, P & CEO*
Warren R. MacKenzie *VP-SAL & MKT*
John R. Meneely *VP-FIN*
Robert C. Schnatterly *VP & DIR-INTL DEV*

Human Resources: Patricia Tuleibitz *VP-Human Resources*

Total Employees	610	**Regional Employees**	260
Year Established	1924	**SIC Code**	3317
Annual Revenues ($000)	118,300		

Pittsburgh Vision Services

300 S. Craig St.
Pittsburgh, PA 15213
County: Allegheny

Phone: (412) 682-5600
Fax: (412) 682-8104

Nonprofit community-based agency formed by the consolidation of the Greater Pittsburgh Guild for the Blind with the Pittsburgh Blind Assn. in May 1997. The Agency's mission is to provide programs and services for people in Allegheny and surrounding counties who are blind, visually impaired or have other physical or mental handicaps. Its Rehabilitation Services consist of Personal Adjustment to Blindness Training, a residential rehabilitation program designed to meet the needs of people who have lost or are losing their sight; Low Vision Services, including a clinic staffed by a licensed optometrist for those who are experiencing difficulty with loss of vision; and Access Technology, which provides evaluation and training utilizing state-of-the-art computer equipment that is adapted for low vision and unsighted people. Its Vocational Services consist of Employment, offering job training and work preparation; Employment and Community Transition Programs, which teach vocational and independent living skills to the disabled; and the Business Enterprise Venture, which provides business guidance to those wishing to become self-employed. Its Senior Services offer a variety of services aimed at the elderly population, including home assistance, escort service, daytime programs for the developmentally disabled and outreach to seniors in the communities. The Agency also offers a variety of outreach services, including intake and evaluation, supportive assistance in the home setting, public education, prevention of blindness and preschool vision testing, and recreational opportunities for the vision impaired. In addition, it provides employment for people who are visually impaired in manufacturing of products for retail sale and government contract work, and operates a retail shop, Visions (located at the above address), that specializes in products for people with low vision and products made by the blind. A branch office is maintained in Bridgeville, PA.

Officers: Dennis J. Huber *P*
Richard Welsh, Ph.D. *VP*

Human Resources: Robert McKee

Purchasing: Leroy Bettwy

Total Employees	175	**Regional Employees**	175
Year Established	1910	**SIC Code**	8331
Annual Revenues ($000)			6,500

Pittsburgh's Ohio Valley General Hospital

Heckel Rd.
McKees Rocks, PA 15136
County: Allegheny
Phone: (412) 777-6161
Fax: (412) 777-6363

Nonprofit 148-bed hospital with a medical staff of more than 225 physicians representing 36 medical and surgical specialties. The Hospital's services include emergency and primary care, specialty medicine, cancer care, cardiology, cardiac rehabilitation, critical care, general and specialty surgery, respiratory therapy, rehabilitation, obstetrics and gynecology, home care, occupational medicine and social services. Its special programs include HealthSource physician and information referral service; Seniority health and wellness membership program for people 50 years and older; BusinessFit occupational medicine program; Healthtalk community education programs and speakers network; Bioscreening lab tests; Lifeline emergency response system; and Care a Lot For Tots field trip for young children. The Hospital operates several satellites and joint ventures including the Blue Cross Primary Care Center in Robinson Township, PA, a joint venture with Blue Cross of Western Pennsylvania that provides primary care, diagnostic testing and health resources through the HealthPLACE education center and library; the Ohio Valley General Hospital-Harmarville Outpatient Rehabilitation Center in Moon Township, PA; approximately 22,000 square feet of space in the Twin Towers Building Physician Center on Route 60 in Robinson Township, PA, that houses physician offices and a Diagnostic Suite; and a Wound Care Center located in Twin Towers that offers specialized treatment for chronic, nonhealing wounds.

Officers: Frank J. Clements *CH*
William F. Provenzano *P*
David W. Scott *SVP*
Karen Bray *VP-Nursing*
Mark Bondi *AST to P-Community Outreach & Physician Relations*
Jocelyn Miller *AST to P-Strategic Planning*

Human Resources: Beth G. Conte *DIR-Human Resources*

Purchasing: Lisa J. Hare *DIR-Material MGT*

Total Employees............................560
Year Established 1901   **SIC Code**.....................................8062
Annual Revenues ($000) 45,581

Pittsburgh-Fayette Express, Inc.

400 Main St.
P.O. Box 141, Charleroi, PA 15022
Belle Vernon, PA 15012
County: Fayette
Phone: (412) 929-2220
Fax: (412) 929-9702

Trucking company transporting general commodities between points in Pennsylvania and throughout the continental United States. The Company specializes in handling less-than-truckload shipments between all points in Ohio, Pennsylvania and West Virginia. It operates a fleet of approximately 30 tractors and 50 trailers.

Officers: Francis M. Prezioso *P (Human Resources)*
John T. Prezioso *VP (Purchasing)*

Total Employees............................45   **Regional Employees** 45
Year Established 1978   **SIC Code**.....................................4212
Annual Revenues ($000) 4,800

Plantscape, Inc.

3101 Liberty Ave.
Pittsburgh, PA 15201
County: Allegheny

Phone: (412) 281-6352
Fax: (412) 281-4775

P

   Provider of horticultural products and services. The Company designs, installs and services interior plantscaping and provides exterior landscaping and maintenance for commercial clients primarily in the Tri-State area but also in other East Coast and Midwest states. The Company also manufactures artificial plants and trees under the Mall Silks® brand name and ships its products throughout the United States, Europe and South America. In addition, it wholesales a line of Christmas products that are sold to holiday decorators nationwide and provides Christmas decorating services for more than 200 corporations and malls. The Company's retail operations include two Plant & Flower Warehouse stores, located at 3043 Washington Rd. in McMurray, PA, and 3801 Liberty Ave. in Pittsburgh, plus seasonal "The Christmas Store" sites in shopping malls in the Washington, D.C., Cleveland, OH, and Pittsburgh, PA, metropolitan areas. The Christmas Store division is located at 3116 Penn Ave. in Pittsburgh, PA.

Officers: Carole Horowitz *P*
Don R. Horowitz *EVP*
Thomas Horowitz *VP*
Cindy Urbach *VP*
Fred Heiser *CON*
Judy Erno *MGR-Customer Services*

Human Resources: Kathy Johnson *Human Resources MGR*

Purchasing: Janet Massick *Purchasing MGR*

Total Employees............................225	**Regional Employees** 205	
Year Established 1973	**SIC Code**..781	
Annual Revenues ($000) 6,000		

Pleasant Trucking, Inc.

2250 Industrial Dr.
P.O. Box 778
Connellsville, PA 15425
County: Fayette

Phone: (412) 628-5347
Fax: (412) 628-5868

   Regional truckload carrier primarily serving the Northeast. The Company spots trailers for loading and/or unloading, provides multiple pickups and deliveries, performs scheduled service and otherwise trys to meet all of the specific transportation needs of its customers. The Company also provides dedicated equipment to several of its customers. The Company's less-than-truckload service is basically call and demand that includes expedited service using automobiles, vans, pickup trucks and tractor trailers throughout the U.S. The Company has signed agreements with all major East Coast Steamship Lines for the handling of break-bulk and containerized import and export shipments at Baltimore, MD; New York/New Jersey Piers; Philadelphia, PA; and Norfolk, VA. In addition, it is licensed to transport malt beverages. The Company's fleet consists of 79 Company-owned and owner operator tractors, 147 Company-owned and owner operator trailers, two mini-vans and two pickup trucks. The Company's agents are A&B Transportation Services in Pasadena, CA; Four Daughters Delivery in Baltimore, MD; and Robert Cahill in Front Royal, VA.

Officers: John R. Morrow, Sr. *P*
Gerald Kinneer, Jr. *VP-OPR*
Richard D. Morrow *SEC & TRS*
Michael J. Bosilovich *Traffic & SAL MGR*

Human Resources: Bruce Cameron

Purchasing: George E. Miles III *CON*

Total Employees...........................105	Regional Employees 90	
Year Established 1985	SIC Code....................................4200	
Annual Revenues ($000) 9,822		

Plotkin Bros. Supply, Inc.

1050 Ohio Ave.
Glassport, PA 15045
County: Allegheny

Phone: (412) 678-5140
Fax: (412) 678-1379

Distributor of pipe, valves, fittings, plumbing, tools and industrial supplies to contractors, engineering firms and industrial markets. The Company's PCI Controls and Instrumentation division, which is also located at the above address, provides automated vales, controls and instrumentation. The Company maintains in-house machining capabilities.

Officers: Harvey Feldman *C-OWN & P*
Stewart Metosky *C-OWN & TRS*
Ginnie Furio *CON*
Paul Schreck *Information Systems MGR*

Purchasing: Barry Weiser

Total Employees...........................54	Regional Employees 54	
Year Established 1959	SIC Code....................................5085	
Annual Revenues ($000) 20,000		

Plum Machine & Welding Co.

555 Davidson Rd.
Pittsburgh, PA 15239
County: Allegheny

Phone: (412) 793-6390
Fax: (412) 793-8961

Job shop providing machining, fabrication and assembly primarily for billet casting steel mills. The Company serves clients worldwide.

Officers: Rich Kastelic *PTR*
Justine Leczkowski *PTR*

Human Resources: Patricia Kastelic

Purchasing: Kevin Leczkowski *Plant MGR*

Total Employees............................30	**Regional Employees** 30
Year Established 1967	**SIC Code**....................................3599
Annual Revenues ($000) 1,800	

Plung & Co., Louis

Four Gateway Center, 9th Fl.
Pittsburgh, PA 15222
County: Allegheny

Phone: (412) 281-8771
Fax: (412) 281-7001

Certified public accounting firm providing accounting and related services to individuals and commercial clients primarily in the Tri-State area. The Firm's specialty areas include real estate, manufacturing, closely held businesses, distribution, and retail accounting and tax.

Officers: Louis Plung *MPTR*
Donald Plung *Senior PTR*
Howard Plung *Senior PTR*
Richard Gross *PTR*
Earl Kaiserman *PTR*
Bill Swope *PTR*

Human Resources: Barbara Garlock *PTR*

Total Employees............................34	**Regional Employees** 34
Year Established 1921	**SIC Code**....................................8721

Point Park College

201 Wood St.
Pittsburgh, PA 15222
County: Allegheny

Phone: (412) 391-4100
Fax: (412) 391-1980
Internet Address: www.ppc.com

Nonprofit, independent four-year liberal arts educational institution. The College offers more than 50 majors and concentrations through its seven academic departments to approximately 2,400 full- and part-time students. It offers Bachelor's and Associate's degrees in a number of majors including accounting, applied history, arts management, behavioral sciences, biological sciences, business management, children's theatre, computer science, dance, education, engineering technology, English, environmental protection science, film and video production, human resources management, journalism and communications, political science, psychology, public administration, respiratory therapy and theatre arts. The College also awards the Master of Arts degree in journalism and communications and the International Master of Business Administration degree.

Officers: Katherine Henderson, Ph.D. *P*

Human Resources: Mary Ann Wilkeson *Human Resources Officer*

Purchasing: Ruth Rauluk

Total Employees	420	**Regional Employees**	420
Year Established	1960	**SIC Code**	8221
Annual Revenues ($000)	23,500		

Point Spring & Driveshaft Co.

7307 Grand Ave.
Pittsburgh, PA 15225
County: Allegheny

Phone: (412) 264-3152
Fax: (412) 264-4325

Distributor of parts and provider of services to the transportation industry, primarily for heavy-duty trucks Class 6-8. The Company specializes in suspension, drivetrains, brakes and hydraulics. It operates four parts and service shops that market its products: Island Spring & Driveshaft in Pittsburgh (Neville Island), PA; Point Spring & Driveshaft, with facilities in Greensburg, PA, and Fairmont, WV; and Valley Spring & Driveshaft in New Castle, PA.

Officers: William F. Ryan *P*

Human Resources: John Reder *SAL DIR*

Purchasing: Mark Scherer

Total Employees.............................70
Year Established........................1926
Annual Revenues ($000) 10,000

Regional Employees 35
SIC Code....................................3493

Polar Water Co.

45 W. Noblestown Rd.
Carnegie, PA 15106
County: Allegheny

Phone: (412) 429-5550
Fax: (412) 429-8491

Bottler of drinking, spring and distilled water in three- and five-gallon return-able bottles and nonreturnable 16-ounce, 1.5-liter, one-gallon and 2.5-gallon pack-ages. The Company also distributes a range of bottled water dispensers, office refreshment systems and drinking water systems. The Company markets its products to residential and commercial accounts directly and through retail gro-cery stores throughout Western Pennsylvania. The Company operates additional facilities in Washington, D.C.; Cincinnati and Columbus, OH; Beaver Falls, PA; Alexandria, Norfolk and Richmond, VA; and Wheeling, WV. The Company is a subsidiary of Suntory Water Group, Inc., which is headquartered in Atlanta, GA.

Officers: Harry Hersh *P*
David Hill *VP & Division MGR*

Human Resources: Frank Budzik *Human Resources MGR*

Regional Employees ....100+
Year Established........................1903

SIC Code....................................2086

Polycom Huntsman, Inc.

90 W. Chestnut St.
Washington, PA 15301
County: Washington

Phone: (412) 225-2220
Fax: (412) 225-7170
Internet Address: www.polycom-huntsman.com

Compounder of thermoplastics and producer of color and additive concen-trates and filled polymers. The Company operates two plants in Donora, PA, with additional plants in Oxnard, CA; Lake Charles, LA; St. Clair, MI; Lockport, NY; Conneaut, OH; Charleston, SC; and Donchery, France. It distributes its products to domestic and international markets, including the food service, packaging and automobile industries.

Officers: Ralph Andy *P & CEO*
Lawrence Welsh *EVP*
George Abd *VP*
Keith James *VP*

Total Employees............................300
Year Established 1977   **SIC Code**......................................2821

Poppe Tyson, Inc.

The Crane Bldg., 40 24th St.
Pittsburgh, PA 15222
County: Allegheny

Phone: (412) 402-0200
Fax: (412) 402-0150
Internet Address: www.poppe.com

Full-service traditional and interactive advertising agency. The Firm uses the latest interactive technologies and strategic marketing techniques not only to represent companies online, but to enable them to transact business online. Its service offerings include database marketing, response handling, secure transaction processing and relationship marketing solutions. The Company is headquartered in New York, NY. It is a subsidiary of Bozell Jacobs Kenyon and Eckhardt, Inc., which is also headquartered in New York, NY.

Officers: Fergus O'Daly *CEO*
Ray Werner *SVP & GMGR*
Bob Bernardini *Senior PTR & DIR-Client Service*
John Chepelsky *Senior PTR & Creative DIR*
Pat Wockley *PTR & Media DIR*

Human Resources: John Penezic *PTR-FIN & ADM*

Total Employees............................400   **Regional Employees** 44
Year Established 1917   **SIC Code**......................................7311
Annual Revenues ($000) ....240,000 (Billings)

Port Authority of Allegheny County

2235 Beaver Ave.
Pittsburgh, PA 15233
County: Allegheny

Phone: (412) 237-7000
Fax: (412) 237-7101

Nonprofit provider of public transportation, also known as the Port Authority Transit, or PAT. PAT provides a network of public transportation services to persons traveling within a 730 square mile area, which includes the City of Pittsburgh and all of Allegheny County, PA. It operates a fleet of 900 buses, 55 light rail vehicles, 6 rehabilitated trolleys and the Monongahela Incline and sponsors ACCESS, a paratransit program for senior citizens and persons with disabilities. PAT provides public transportation services to 260,000 riders daily and more than 75 million riders annually. It is funded through a combination of fare revenues as well as local, state and federal funds. Among its facilities, PAT provides service via two exclusive busways—the 4.3-mile South Busway and the 6.8-mile Martin Luther King, Jr. East Busway—and the "T," a 25-mile light rail system, of which 12 miles were recently rehabilitated. Included in the project was construction of PAT's downtown subway and the reopening of its historic Allentown rail route. On October 27, 1994, PAT began construction on the 8.1-mile Airport Busway/Wabash HOV Facility. In addition, plans are underway for a 2.3-mile extension of the Martin Luther King, Jr. East Busway and to rehabilitate the remaining 13 miles of the "T" Light Rail Transit System. Operating locations include the Collier Division, East Liberty Division, Harmar Division, Ross Division, South Hills Village Rail Center and West Mifflin Division.

Officers: Paul P. Skoutelas *EDIR*
Janice Blahut *DIR-MKT & Business DEV*
Jason Fincke *DIR-Corporate Services*
Claudia Hussein *DIR-FIN*
Thomas Letky *DIR-OPR*
John Prizner *DIR-Planning, ENG & Construction*
M. Susan Ruffner *DIR-Legal Services*

Human Resources: Ronald Clark *DIR-Human Resources*

Total Employees.........................2,972
Year Established.........................1964   **SIC Code**.....................................4111

Portec, Inc.-Railway Maintenance Products Division

900 Freeport Rd.
P.O. Box 38250
Pittsburgh, PA 15238
County: Allegheny

Phone: (412) 782-6000
Fax: (412) 782-1037

Engineer, manufacturer and marketer of joint bar products for joining rail, and insulated joints used in railroad signaling track circuits. The Division also supplies track lubrication systems as well as jacking systems for freight car and locomotive maintenance. It maintains a 100,000-square foot manufacturing plant in Huntington, WV. The Division is a part of the Railroad Products segment of Portec, Inc., which is headquartered in Lake Forest, IL, and listed on the NYSE.

Officers: John S. Cooper *GMGR & SVP-Portec, Inc.*

Total Employees	68	**Regional Employees**	23
Year Established	1905	**SIC Code**	3743
Annual Revenues ($000)	19,000		

Power Piping Co.

Four Allegheny Center, Ste. 401
Pittsburgh, PA 15212
County: Allegheny

Phone: (412) 323-6200
Fax: (412) 323-6334

   Prime contractor providing project management of total project responsibility for contracts containing significant self-performing scopes of work. The Company has the capability to engineer, procure, install, operate and maintain piping systems. It also provides comprehensive maintenance and overhaul services supporting industrial facility clients through both project specific and annual services agreements; mechanical installation and overhaul services for piping, instrumentation and process equipment, including constructability reviews, equipment procurement and project construction; and repair or replacement services of boiler components, fuel and combustion systems, feedwater equipment, flue gas and air pollution systems and piping systems. The Company is a subsidiary of the MYR Group Inc., which is headquartered in Rolling Meadows, IL, and listed on the NYSE.

Officers: Stephen J. Janaszek *P*
Louis F. Kesselman *VP*
O. Nicholas Kratsas *DIR-Business DEV*

Total Employees	200	**Regional Employees**	200
Year Established	1963	**SIC Code**	3498

Power Systems Technology, Inc.

1121 Boyce Rd., Ste. 2400
Pittsburgh, PA 15241
County: Allegheny

Phone: (412) 941-3140
Fax: (412) 941-3172

   Manufacturer and remanufacturer of motors, generators, coils, switchgear and various power protection devices. The Company's products serve both OEMs and the aftermarket. It operates additional facilities in Baton Rouge, LA; and Cincinnati and Dayton, OH. The Company does business as SYTEK.

Officers: Jaykar Krishnamurthy *P*
Dave Albright *VP*

Human Resources: Denise Wacker

Total Employees ....100+	**Regional Employees** 3
Year Established 1990	**SIC Code** 3677
Annual Revenues ($000)..10,000+	

Powerex, Inc.

200 Hillis St.
Youngwood, PA 15697
County: Westmoreland
Phone: (412) 925-7272
Fax: (412) 925-4393

Developer, manufacturer and marketer of power semiconductors, claiming to be the largest supplier of high-power semiconductors in North America. The Company's product line includes Discrete Rectifiers, Thyristors and Mosfets, as well as assemblies and custom-built modules for individual application requirements. The module line also includes Darlington Transistor Modules, IGBT Modules, Intelligent Power Modules, Fast-Recovery Diode Modules, Thyristor Modules and Rectifier Diode Modules. The Company exports to Europe, South America and the Pacific Rim. It is a joint venture corporation between General Electric Co. and Mitsubishi Electric Corp.

Officers: Stanley R. Hunt *P*
　　　　　Joseph A. Sibenac *CFO*

Human Resources: Don Stahl

Purchasing Director: Ed Hunt

Total Employees............................300	**Regional Employees** 290
Year Established 1986	**SIC Code** 3674
Annual Revenues ($000) 84,000	

Powers & Garrison, Inc.

Warner Centre, 332 Fifth Ave., Ste. 600
Pittsburgh, PA 15222
County: Allegheny
Phone: (412) 263-2088
Fax: (412) 263-0517

Provider of court reporting and video services, including the stenographic transcription of meetings and hearings and the videotaping of depositions, weddings and other functions. The Company serves clients in the Tri-State area.

Officers: Joseph C. Garrison *CH*
　　　　　Linda D. Hughes *P & CEO*
　　　　　Bernadette Higgins *SEC & TRS*

Human Resources: Suzanne Waugaman

Purchasing: Kimberly Yester

Total Employees............................39	**Regional Employees** 39
Year Established 1975	**SIC Code**....................................7338
Annual Revenues ($000) 1,500

PPR Realty, Inc.

9401 McKnight Rd., Ste. 106
Pittsburgh, PA 15237
County: Allegheny

Phone: (412) 367-8028
Fax: (412) 367-2718
Internet Address: www.prudentialpreferred.com

Real estate brokerage firm doing business as The Prudential Preferred Realty. The Company operates 18 branch offices with more than 500 independent sales associates throughout the Pittsburgh metropolitan area. Its facilities are located in Aliquippa, Allison Park, Beaver, Beaver Falls, Bethel Park, Butler, Cranberry Township, Greensburg, Hidden Valley, McMurray, Monroeville, Moon Township, Murrysville, Pittsburgh (4) and Sewickley, PA.

Officers: Ronald F. Croushore *C-OWN & P*
Helen V. Sosso *C-OWN & EVP*

Purchasing: James G. Saxon *CFO*

Total Employees............................80	**Regional Employees** 80
Year Established 1990	**SIC Code**....................................6531
Annual Revenues ($000) 19,000

Precise Technology, Inc.

501 Mosside Blvd.
North Versailles, PA 15137
County: Allegheny

Phone: (412) 823-2100
Fax: (412) 823-4110

Manufacturer of custom injection molded plastic parts for the health care, medical and thin-wall packaging industries. The Company's plants are located in Newark, DE; St. Petersburg, FL; Des Plaines, IL; West Lafayette, IN; South Grafton, MA; Excelsior Springs, MO; Rochester, NY; and Pittsburgh and State College, PA. It is a subsidiary of Mentmore Industrial Holdings, which is headquartered in New York, NY.

Officers: John R. Weeks *P*
Michael Farrell *SVP*

Human Resources: Leslie Quealy *Human Resources*

Total Employees	1,000	**Regional Employees**	130
Year Established	1965	**SIC Code**	3089
Annual Revenues ($000)	130,000		

Preschool Development Programs, Inc.

116 Federal St., Ste. 360
Pittsburgh, PA 15212
County: Allegheny

Phone: (412) 231-3700
Fax: (412) 231-0402

Nonprofit provider of comprehensive child development services to preschool children. The Company also provides outreach and training services to parents so that they may further develop the skills and abilities that they need to build a better life for their children and for themselves. It provides three specific programs consisting of consultant services to preschool and child care programs throughout Pennsylvania; a day care center serving families from the North Side community of Pittsburgh; and a Head Start program for children and families on the north side and west side of Pittsburgh. The Company operates 11 centers located throughout the north side and west side of Pittsburgh.

Officers: Eugenia Boggus *P*
C. Ellis Perkins *EDIR*
Nedra L. Bartko *Administrative Service MGR*
James Jordan *Accountant*

Human Resources: Margaret Sides

Total Employees	105	**Regional Employees**	105
Year Established	1980	**SIC Code**	8351
Annual Revenues ($000)	2,900		

Pressley Ridge Schools, The

530 Marshall Ave.
Pittsburgh, PA 15217
County: Allegheny

Phone: (412) 321-6995
Fax: (412) 321-5313
Internet Address: www.pressleyridge.org

Nonprofit agency that provides an array of social and mental health services and special education programs for troubled children and their families in Maryland, Ohio, Pennsylvania and West Virginia, serving more than 1,400 clients each day. The Agency's direct care services include treatment foster care, emergency shelter foster homes, day school/partial hospitalization, therapeutic residential care, intensive family preservation, as well as research, training and advocacy on a national level. These services are staffed by professionals in the fields of special education, mental health, social work, counseling, psychology and psychiatry. The Agency's other Pennsylvania facilities are located in Greensburg, Ohiopyle, Sewickley and Uniontown, PA. It also operates four sites in Maryland, one in Ohio and eight in West Virginia.

Officers: William Clark Luster *EDIR*

Human Resources: Jeff Jamison

Purchasing: John Mikash

Total Employees	700	Regional Employees	350
Year Established	1832	SIC Code	8361
Annual Revenues ($000)			35,000

Pressure Chemical Co.

3419 Smallman St.
Pittsburgh, PA 15201
County: Allegheny

Phone: (412) 682-5882
Fax: (412) 682-5864
Internet Address: www.presschem.com

Provider of technical expertise for the manufacture of specialty chemicals, and the development of chemical processes, utilized in virtually all of the major industrial and consumer segments. The Company performs development and scale-up research on a contract basis and provides toll manufacturing of semi-commercial quantities of products employing its unusual high-pressure pilot plant facility. The Company continues to serve its original market for small quantities of novel materials and for services designed specifically for the basic researcher through its Specialty Products division. The pilot plant is equipped with high-pressure reactors with rated pressures to 10,000 PSIG, glass and glass-lined equipment sized to 1,000 gallons, and a research-scale supercritical fluid extraction system. The Company manufactures large quantities of fine organic chemicals, pharmaceutical intermediates, organometallic catalysts and specialty polymer products.

Officers: Lawrence J. Rosen *CH*
Alan C. Stout *P*
David A. Bird *TRS*

Human Resources: Holly Bauer

Purchasing: Joni Tajc

Total Employees	40	Regional Employees	40
Year Established	1969	SIC Code	2869
Annual Revenues ($000)			7,500

Price Waterhouse LLP

USX Tower, 600 Grant St., Ste. 2800
Pittsburgh, PA 15219
County: Allegheny

Phone: (412) 355-6000
Fax: (412) 391-0609
Internet Address: www.pw.com

Provider of services to assist clients in implementing strategies to improve business performance, effecting organizational and strategic change, using information technology for competitive advantage, and meeting audit and tax requirements. The Firm's U.S. operations are headquartered in New York, NY, with more than 15,000 employees in over 100 offices in major cities throughout the nation. The Firm's world headquarters, also located in New York, NY, oversees a global network of more than 400 offices practicing in 119 countries and territories. The Pittsburgh office provides industry-specific auditing, tax and consulting services for industrial and consumer product manufacturers, emerging technology companies, financial institutions, public utilities and energy companies. The Firm also provides services in the areas of employee benefits, personal finance, dispute analysis and corporate recovery, international tax, multistate tax, and mergers and acquisitions.

Officers: James C. Stalder *MPTR*

Human Resources: David E. Smiddle

Total Employees......................53,000	**Regional Employees** 180
Year Established...1902 (Pittsburgh)	**SIC Code**....................................8721
Annual Revenues ($000) 5,020,000	

Print Tech of Western Pennsylvania

3405 Babcock Blvd.
Pittsburgh, PA 15237
County: Allegheny

Phone: (412) 364-0114
Fax: (412) 364-9247

Commercial quick printer offering a variety of prepress, printing, bindery, mailing and copying services. The Company operates three additional facilities located in Aspinwall, Monroeville and in downtown Pittsburgh, PA.

Officers: Robert F. Weingard, Jr. *P*

Human Resources: Linda Liberto

Total Employees..............................32	**Regional Employees** 32
Year Established 1970	**SIC Code**....................................2759
Annual Revenues ($000) 3,900	

Pro River, Inc.

7500 Brooktree Rd., Ste. 303
Wexford, PA 15090
County: Allegheny
Phone: (412) 933-5550
Fax: (412) 933-5555

Owner and operator of a regional restaurant chain, doing business as the Red River Barbeque & Grille. The Company's restaurants specialize in southwestern-style barbeque. The restaurants are located at 9805 McKnight Rd. in Pittsburgh, PA (160 seats); Columbia (240 seats), Frederick (175 seats) and Waldorf (200 seats), MD; and Woodbridge (200 seats), VA. The Company also distributes Red River Barbeque & Grille-brand barbecue sauce to supermarkets in Western Pennsylvania, including Food Gallery, Foodland, Giant Eagle, Kuhn's and Stop-N-Shop.

Officers: Ronald A. Sofranko *P & CEO*
Andrew Batch *VP & COO*
Frank Napoli *VP & CFO*

Human Resources: Marcy Dickson *DIR-Training & Human Resources*

Total Employees............................250	**Regional Employees** 70	
Year Established 1987	**SIC Code**......................................5812	
Annual Revenues ($000) 10,000		

Process Development & Control, Inc.

1075 Montour W. Industrial Park
P.O. Box 51, Imperial, PA 15126
Coraopolis, PA 15108
County: Allegheny
Phone: (412) 695-3440
Fax: (412) 695-8635

Manufacturer of butterfly valves and dampers to control the flow of air, water or gas. The Company's engineered butterfly valves and dampers are produced in cast iron, stainless or carbon steels, and are available in a size range of 2" through 60". Its products are utilized for industrial, utility and wastewater applications, as well as compressors, furnaces, natural gas recovery, process equipment and HVAC installations throughout the world market. The Company's services include the mounting of pneumatic, electric, hydraulic and manual actuation to provide a ready-to-install control component.

Officers: William T. Keegan *P & CEO*
Larry Boustead *MKT & Customer Service MGR*
Gary Lee *SAL MGR*

Fran Mirage *Plant MGR*
Ron Koch *Chief ENG*

Human Resources: Kimberli S. Ramsey *Accounting & ADM MGR*

Purchasing: Edward Larson *Purchasing MGR*

Total Employees............................30	**Regional Employees** 30
Year Established 1970	**SIC Code**....................................3494

Professional Service Industries, Inc.

850 Poplar St.
Pittsburgh, PA 15220
County: Allegheny

Phone: (412) 922-4000
Fax: (412) 922-4013

Provider of environmental consulting, engineering and testing services. The Company offers construction testing and quality control, materials testing and certification, nondestructive examination and testing, roof and pavement consulting, geotechnical engineering and drilling services, environmental and asbestos consulting, analytical services and training programs. The Company, also known as PSI, is headquartered in Lombard, IL, and operates more than 150 branch offices nationwide. The local facility serves clients throughout Eastern Ohio, Western Pennsylvania and a portion of West Virginia.

Officers: Stephen C. Fitzer *P & CEO*
Murray Savage *CFO*
Howell Branum *COO-Geotechnical & Construction Materials ENG*
Richard Sanfilippo *COO-Environmental & Analytical*

Human Resources: Mary Grider

Total Employees........................3,250	**Regional Employees** 170
Year Established 1881	**SIC Code**....................................8748
Annual Revenues ($000) 176,530	

Professional Staffing, Inc.

Campbells Run Business Center, 300 Business Center Dr.
Pittsburgh, PA 15205
County: Allegheny

Phone: (412) 788-1490
Fax: (412) 788-0879

Professional employer organization (PEO), sometimes referred to as an employee leasing or staffing company. PEOs deliver their services by establishing and maintaining an employer relationship with the workers assigned to its clients and by contractually assuming substantial employer rights, responsibilities and risks for its clients. The Company serves small to mid-size businesses located primarily in Western Pennsylvania, which seek the Company's services because they lower payroll costs; reduce the burden of employer-related, nonproductive paperwork; reduce liabilities resulting from regulatory noncompliance; and improve employee benefits and morale.

Officers: James R. Wanner *P*
Stanley A. Rososinski *EVP*
Patrice M. D'Amico *CON*

Human Resources: Frances K. Horn *DIR-Human Resources*

Total Employees................1,000	**Regional Employees** 1,000
Year Established 1985	**SIC Code**....................................7363
Annual Revenues ($000) 17,000		

ProMinent Fluid Controls, Inc.

R.I.D.C. Park W., 136 Industry Dr.
Pittsburgh, PA 15275
County: Allegheny

Phone: (412) 787-2484
Fax: (412) 787-0704

Producer of measurement, control and metering equipment and systems for water treatment and disinfection applications. The Company's major activity is the manufacturing and marketing of liquid chemical feed and control equipment and systems. It began with the development and manufacture of electronic, solenoid diaphragm metering pumps for domestic and wastewater treatment applications. It now manufactures a complete line of solenoid and motor-driven metering pumps, dry polymer feeders, analyzer/control instrumentation and sensors, chlorine-free chlorine dioxide and ozone generators, filtration products and pre-engineered packaged systems. The Company is one of approximately 30 worldwide subsidiaries of ProMinent Dosiertechnik GmbH, which is headquartered in Heidelberg, Germany.

Officers: Viktor Dulger *P*
M. C. Sandy Chu *VP & GMGR*
Ken Gibson *Industrial MKT MGR*
John Hall *Product/Training MGR*
Bob Jump *ENG & MFG MGR*

Human Resources: Fran Perfett *Financial/Human Resources MGR (Purchasing)*

Total Employees.............50	**Regional Employees** 50
Year Established 1979	**SIC Code**....................................3825
Annual Revenues ($000) 7,000		

Prudential Securities, Inc.

USX Tower, 600 Grant St., Ste. 2700
Pittsburgh, PA 15219
County: Allegheny

Phone: (412) 562-3800
Fax: (412) 562-5515

Full-service broker-dealer and investment banking firm. The Company, which is headquartered in New York, NY, operates approximately 280 branch offices throughout the United States. It is a subsidiary of The Prudential Insurance Co. of America, which is headquartered in Newark, NJ.

Officers: Michael McClain *FVP & Resident MGR*

Regional Employees......................60
SIC Code 6211

QSi Technologies, Inc.

51 QSi Lane
Allison Park, PA 15101
County: Allegheny

Phone: (412) 443-5500
Fax: (412) 443-4420

Manufacturer of bellows that function as heat exchangers for the medical industry. The Company's bellows are incorporated into disposable membrane oxygenators and are responsible for cooling and then warming blood during open heart surgery or other critical operations such as organ transplantations. It also manufactures bellows and flexible connectors for the automotive industry that are used in steering column devices, as flexible exhaust connectors and for exhaust gas recirculation. In addition, the Company's patent-pending technology is being used in crossover connectors designed for certain V-Engines.

Officers: Bruce A. Wright *CH, VP & GMGR*
Ronald W. Wallace *P*
David B. Docherty, Sr. *VP & DIR*
B. Douglas Wright *SEC & DIR*

Human Resources: Stewart F. Kretz *CON & TRS*

Purchasing: David B. Docherty, Jr. *DIR*

Total Employees..............................60	**Regional Employees** 60
Year Established 1987	**SIC Code**....................................3499
Annual Revenues ($000) 4,000	

Quality Building Services, Inc.

R.D. 6
Box 508
Greensburg, PA 15601
County: Westmoreland

Phone: (412) 836-5169
Fax: (412) 836-4305

Provider of janitorial services to commercial and industrial clients throughout Western and Central Pennsylvania, Eastern Ohio and West Virginia. The Company also distributes and repairs janitorial equipment.

Officers: Charles Strobel *CEO*
Tom Byerly *OPR DIR*
Lyn Strobel *CFO*

Human Resources: Terry McKnight

Purchasing: John Guzik

Total Employees............................420	**Regional Employees** 390
Year Established 1973	**SIC Code**....................................7349
Annual Revenues ($000) 4,800	

Quality Fabricating, Inc.

509 Hahntown-Wendel Rd.
P.O. Box 628
Irwin, PA 15642
County: Westmoreland

Phone: (412) 864-2887
Fax: (412) 864-9684

Fabricator of high-precision custom components for a variety of industries, including electronics, environmental, communications, health care and transportation. The Company's products include computer chassis and electrical enclosures. It serves clients in the eastern U.S.

Officers: Betty M. Bozich *P*
George Bozich *VP-OPR*
Cathy Varsamis *VP-FIN*

Total Employees............................75	**Regional Employees** 75
Year Established 1983	**SIC Code**....................................3499

Quality Services, Inc.

559 Rodi Rd.
P.O. Box 17090
Pittsburgh, PA 15235
County: Allegheny

Phone: (412) 371-9110
Fax: (412) 371-0261

Provider of a variety of cleaning services tailored to the specific needs of each account, including daily janitorial service, hard surface floor maintenance, carpet cleaning, window cleaning, fluorescent light fixture cleaning, marble and brass restoration, building security and emergency service. The Company serves government, industry, business and nonprofit organizations throughout the Western Pennsylvania area. It currently services 8 million square feet of commercial space each night in over 200 locations. Employees are hired from the local area of the account they service.

Officers: Charles R. Cole *P*

Human Resources: Von Snyir

Purchasing: Nanci R. Fisher

Total Employees	700	**Regional Employees**	675
Year Established	1976	**SIC Code**	7349
Annual Revenues ($000)	8,500		

R&M Electronics, Inc.

Rte. 910 & McIntyre Rd.
P.O. Box 1107
Gibsonia, PA 15044
County: Allegheny

Phone: (412) 443-8222
Fax: (412) 444-6833

Provider of contract manufacturing services ranging from design through volume production of printed circuit boards, electronic and electromechanical devices. The Company's manufacturing services include material procurement, fabrication, printed circuit board assembly and finished product assembly. It also offers automated in-circuit testing, burn-in and functional testing together with documentation, packaging and distribution. In addition, it has extensive surface mount technology capabilities, automated axial and DIP insertion equipment. The Company operates two divisions, Donotech Electronic Manufacturing in Owingsville, KY, and QMD in Raleigh, NC.

Officers: Herb P. Beers *P*

Total Employees	325	**Regional Employees**	65
Year Established	1979	**SIC Code**	3672

Raff Printing and Bindery Co.

2201 Mary St.
P.O. Box 42365
Pittsburgh, PA 15203
County: Allegheny

Phone: (412) 431-4044
Fax: (412) 488-0770

Commercial printer offering a variety of products and graphic services, including envelopes, books, booklets, brochures, posters, snap and continuous forms, and annual reports. The Company also offers fulfillment services for kits and folders. It serves all types of clients primarily located in the Tri-State area. The Company's affiliate, Adform Co. in Monessen, PA, is a rotary printer.

Officers: Frederick C. Aheimer, Sr. *P*
Frederick Aheimer, Jr. *VP*
Kym Yeckel *SEC & TRS*
Joseph Kubicek *MGR-MKT Communication*
Ron Veckel *Production MGR*

Human Resources: Denise Lucas *MGR-ADM*

Purchasing: Norma Keener

Total Employees............................70	**Regional Employees** 70
Year Established 1936	**SIC Code**....................................2752
Annual Revenues ($000) 9,000

Ranbar Electrical Materials, Inc.

Rte. 993
P.O. Box 607
Manor, PA 15665
County: Westmoreland

Phone: (412) 864-8200
Fax: (412) 864-8232

Manufacturer of wire enamel coatings and electrical insulation varnishes, coatings and compounds for industrial users. The Company is affiliated with Ranbar Technology Inc., which is headquartered in Glenshaw, PA.

Officers: Randall L. C. Russell, Ph.D. *P & CEO*
Raymond G. Smith *VP & GMGR*
Rodney J. Francis *CFO*
Randall L. Russell *SEC*

Human Resources: Arlene M. Abbott *Human Resources MGR*

Total Employees............................60	**Regional Employees** 60
Year Established 1995	**SIC Code**....................................2851

Ranbar Technology, Inc.

1114 William Flinn Hwy.
Glenshaw, PA 15116
County: Allegheny

Phone: (412) 486-1111
Fax: (412) 487-3313

Manufacturer of alkyd and polyester resins, insulating varnishes, industrial coatings and specialty products. The Company serves clients in the paint, tubular steel and the electrical repair industries. It is affiliated with Ranbar Electrical Materials, Inc., which is headquartered in Manor, PA.

Officers: Randall L. C. Russell, Ph.D. *P & CEO*
Raymond D. Kushner *VP & GMGR*
Rodney J. Francis *CFO*
Randall L. Russell *SEC*

Human Resources: Arlene M. Abbott *Human Resources MGR*

Total Employees..............................49	**Regional Employees** 49
Year Established 1984	**SIC Code** 2851

RAS Industries

12 Eighty Four Dr.
Eighty Four, PA 15330
County: Washington

Phone: (412) 228-1395
Fax: (412) 229-9389

Manufacturer of preformed architectural millwork items under its Life-Time® Pre-Formed Millwork™ brand name. The Company offers more than 2,000 decorative items for the building industry, including accents, arches, brackets, decorative moldings, classic entryways, louvers, pediments and window treatments. Its products are made from space-age polymers, poured into molds, cured, formed into exact rigid replicas then prime painted, with a density similar to white pine. The product line brings the realism of wood millwork and plaster accents to new construction, remodeling projects, historic renovation, custom designs or commercial installations. The Company's products are marketed internationally to builders and contractors, and through lumber yards and building supply centers.

Officers: Mohammed P. Khan *P*
Janine Franc *DIR-FIN*
Don Stitch *DIR-Advertising & MKT*
David Warholak *DIR-SAL*

Human Resources: Linda Crow

Purchasing: Richard Knob *DIR-MFG*

Total Employees............................130	Regional Employees 130
Year Established 1984	SIC Code......................................3089
Annual Revenues ($000)...10,000+	

RB&W Corp.

Narrows Run Rd.
P.O. Box 347
Coraopolis, PA 15108
County: Allegheny

Phone: (412) 264-1260
Fax: (412) 262-2637

Engineer and manufacturer of cold-formed products and related hardware, primarily internally threaded parts and miscellaneous formed metal components and assemblies that are produced in high volume by cold-forming, cold-extrusion and specialized secondary operations. The Company manufactures certain trade-marked items that are used in volume in the automobile and truck industry and segments of the farm and machinery businesses. These include lock nuts which find principal use in applications where vibration is a problem and controlled tightening is desired. The Company, which is headquartered in Cleveland, OH, operates additional plants in Kent, OH, and Toronto, Ontario, Canada. It is a subsidiary of Park-Ohio Industries, Inc., which is also headquartered in Cleveland, OH, and listed on the NASDAQ.

Officers: Craig Cowan *GMGR*
Stan Tarorick *Plant MGR*

Total Employees............................300	Regional Employees 85
Year Established 1939	SIC Code......................................3452
Annual Revenues ($000)...10,000+	

Rearick Tooling, Inc.

2025 Shady Plain Rd.
Apollo, PA 15613
County: Armstrong

Phone: (412) 478-1135
Fax: (412) 478-1137

Manufacturer of carbide dies and components for a variety of industrial customers throughout the United States.

Officers: Samuel H. Rearick *P*

Purchasing: Joyce Rearick

Total Employees..............................60
Year Established 1982

Regional Employees 60
SIC Code......................................3544

R

Recra Environmental, Inc.

3000 Tech Center Dr.
Monroeville, PA 15146
County: Allegheny

Phone: (412) 825-9833
Fax: (412) 825-9727

Environmental testing laboratory, doing business as Recra LabNet. The Company, which is headquartered in Amherst, NY, operates additional laboratories in Detroit, MI; Cleveland, OH; and Houston, TX. The Company claims that its local facility is Western Pennsylvania's largest environmental testing laboratory. It provides legally defensible data to major industrial corporations, including PPG, U.S. Steel and Westinghouse, as well as federal, state and local governments.

Officers: Robert Stadelmaier *P*
Joseph F. Sawyer *VP*

Human Resources: Joanne Simanic

Purchasing: Linda Bordone

Total Employees............................185
Year Established 1977
Annual Revenues ($000) 15,000

Regional Employees 35
SIC Code......................................8731

Red Valve Co., Inc.

700 N. Bell Ave.
P.O. Box 548
Carnegie, PA 15106
County: Allegheny

Phone: (412) 279-0044
Fax: (412) 279-7878

Manufacturer of six major product lines: pinch valves, control pinch valves, Tideflex in-line check valves, pressure sensors, Redflex expansion joints and knife gate valves. The Company markets its products worldwide primarily to the wastewater treatment, chemical, power and mining industries. In addition to its corporate headquarters, a research and development center and manufacturing facility are also located at the above address. The Company maintains two other manufacturing sites in Gastonia, NC, and in the United Kingdom.

Officers: Spiros G. Raftis *CH*
George Raftis II *P*
Chris Raftis *VP-SAL*

Human Resources: Joseph P. Myers

Total Employees............................180
Year Established 1953

Regional Employees 80
SIC Code......................................3491

Redstone Presbyterian SeniorCare

6 Garden Center Dr.
Greensburg, PA 15601
County: Westmoreland

Phone: (412) 832-8400
Fax: (412) 836-3710

Nonprofit owner and operator of the Redstone Highlands, a retirement community providing long-term care to more than 215 older adults of Westmoreland County and the six surrounding counties. The center offers several levels of care for its residents in a campus setting. These levels consist of independent living care for those living at the center's senior apartment housing and residential congregate housing; personal care; health care including intermediate nursing care and skilled care; and Alzheimer's care. The center provides a variety of services for its residents, including social services, activity and fitness programs, a medical clinic, a chapel and a staff chaplain, housekeeping, security, an emergency response system, scheduled transportation, basic cable television and all utilities. The center is managed by Presbyterian SeniorCare, which is located in Oakmont, PA.

Officers: Robert Schweikert *P*
Ronald G. Barrett *EVP-Redstone Highlands*
Judie Wohnsiedler *AST-Administrator*

Human Resources: Wally Perkins *Personnel Consultant*

Total Employees............................100
Year Established 1980

Regional Employees 100
SIC Code......................................8059

RedZone Robotics, Inc.

2425 Liberty Ave.
Pittsburgh, PA 15222
County: Allegheny

Phone: (412) 765-3064
Fax: (412) 765-3069
Internet Address: www.redzone.com

Developer, manufacturer and integrator of specialized robotic systems, inspection and control systems, and intelligent vehicle technologies for work in hazardous environments. With capabilities in mechanical design, electronics, controls, software development, sensing and system integration, the Company implements solutions and develops products for use in government and commercial sectors. It has provided systems and services for the following application areas: (1) The Company designs and builds systems that perform remote decontamination, demolition, emergency response, materials transport, ordnance retrieval and other work tasks in hazardous environments. While most of these systems are for work at commercial and government nuclear sites, they are also useful in hazardous waste, space, military and industrial operations. (2) The Company provides robotic and sensing systems to perform inspection tasks in hazardous environments. Its robotic inspection systems deploy visual, ultrasonic and other nondestructive evaluation sensors to remotely or automatically accomplish a variety of inspection tasks. (3) The Company's control systems are used in hazardous environments and range from specialized, one-of-a-kind controllers for robotic systems to industrial process controllers that are produced in quantities. (4) The Company conducts comprehensive research, development and deployment of intelligent vehicle technologies, including specialized vehicle configuration and design, control hardware and software, and autonomous driving systems.

Officers: J. Todd Simonds *CH & CEO*

Human Resources: Nancy Rost

Purchasing: Scott Perry

Total Employees..............................40
Year Established 1987

Regional Employees 40
SIC Code....................................3569

Reed Smith Shaw & McClay

435 Sixth Ave.
Pittsburgh, PA 15219
County: Allegheny

Phone: (412) 288-3131
Fax: (412) 288-3063
Internet Address: www.slpetrak@rssm.com

Provider of legal services with more than 370 attorneys. The Firm claims to be one of the largest law firms in the nation serving businesses and individuals. It represents clients in a broad spectrum of legal concerns, including antitrust, asbestos, bank regulatory, bankruptcy, China/Asia, communications, construction, consumer financial services, corporate and securities, education, employee benefits, environmental, family business, financial institutions, first amendment, franchise, government contracts and export compliance, government relations, health care, immigration, insurance coverage, intellectual property, international, labor, matrimonial/family law, non-profit organizations, product liability, project finance, real estate, satellite transactions, tax, technology, trade secrets, trusts and estates, utilities and white collar crime. The Firm operates branch offices throughout the nation's Mid-Atlantic region in Washington, D.C.; Newark and Princeton, NJ; New York, NY; Harrisburg and Philadelphia, PA; and McLean, VA.

Officers: Daniel I. Booker *Firm MPTR*
Michael L. Browne *MPTR-Philadelphia, PA*
David C. Evans *MPTR-Washington, D.C.*
Robert W. Hartland *MPTR-Pittsburgh, PA*
Gregory B. Jordan *DIR-Practice DEV*
John M. Wood *DIR Legal Personnel*
Gary A. Sokulski *EDIR*

Human Resources: Aaron A. Herbick

Total Employees............................868	**Regional Employees** 416
Year Established 1877	**SIC Code** 8111

Reed & Witting Co.

5000 Baum Blvd.
Pittsburgh, PA 15213
County: Allegheny

Phone: (412) 682-1000
Fax: (412) 682-1043

Commercial printer providing complete electronic prepress services, including scanning and binding. The Company also performs in-house multicolor process work as well as point-of-purchase and fulfillment services. It primarily serves retail clients in the Tri-State area.

Officers: Edward J. Cyphers *P*

Total Employees............................37	**Regional Employees** 37
Year Established 1900	**SIC Code**....................................2759
Annual Revenues ($000) 6,000	

Reese Bros., Inc.

925 Penn Ave., Ste. 600
Pittsburgh, PA 15222
County: Allegheny

Phone: (412) 355-0800
Fax: (412) 261-9730

Fully integrated outbound/inbound teleservices firm with experience in the fields of telecommunications, insurance, financial services, business-to-business and nonprofit fund-raising. The Company operates 12 call centers containing over 1,200 PC-based workstations with a calling capacity of more than 300,000 hours per month. These centers are located in Cedar Rapids and Clinton, IA;

Altoona, Charleroi, Greensburg, Johnstown, Monroeville, New Castle, Oil City and Pleasant Hills, PA; Toronto, Ontario, Canada; and at the above address. The Company's creative services department offers creative copywriting, digital design and production to develop fulfillment and corporate materials. In addition, its printing and distribution center provides a wide range of printing, mailing and lettershop services for an annual capacity of 15 million pieces.

Officers: Barry Reese *P & CEO*
Jim Epstein *EVP & COO*
Ralph Reese *VP*
Linda Manfredi *Chief Teleservices Officer*
Jim Wander *Chief SAL & MKT Officer*

Human Resources: Susan Burgess

Purchasing: Karen Zovko

Total Employees	1,800	**Regional Employees**	1,100
Year Established	1974	**SIC Code**	7389

Reflex Services, Inc.

Manor Oak Two, 1910 Cochran Rd., Ste. 344
Pittsburgh, PA 15220
County: Allegheny

Phone: (412) 341-8842
Fax: (412) 341-3650

Provider of managers, executives and professionals for interim assignments, special projects and permanent placements. The Company serves a wide variety of industries, with clients primarily in the Tri-State area.

Officers: Thomas C. Kohn *P*
F. Murray LaDuke *CON*

Total Employees	160	**Regional Employees**	140
Year Established	1985	**SIC Code**	7363
Annual Revenues ($000)	5,000		

Regency Hall Nursing Home, Inc.

9399 Babcock Blvd.
Allison Park, PA 15101
County: Allegheny

Phone: (412) 366-8540
Fax: (412) 369-9789

Nonprofit long-term skilled and intermediate nursing facility, providing professional nursing, recuperative and geriatric care. The 143-bed Facility also provides occupational, physical and speech therapies. Attached to the Facility is an adult day care center which conducts a day program for senior adults who require structured and supervised care. It is owned and operated by Vincentian Sisters of Charity, which is based in Pittsburgh, PA.

Officers: Sister Dorothy Dolak *Administrator*

Human Resources: Michael Grubisha

Total Employees............................180	**Regional Employees** 180
Year Established 1966	**SIC Code**.....................................8051
Annual Revenues ($000) 6,000	

Rehabilitation Center & Workshop, Inc.

Woodward Rd. Extension, R.D. 6, Box 524
Greensburg, PA 15601
County: Westmoreland

Phone: (412) 838-9101
Fax: (412) 837-3508

Nonprofit sheltered workshop providing contract packaging, assembly and manufacturing. The Company's services include shrink wrapping, packing, repacking, labeling, removing labeling, and the manufacturing of masonry lime blocks.

Officers: Charles Copeland *P*
Albert Elias *VP*
Donald Shirer *GMGR*

Total Employees..............................55	**Regional Employees** 55
SIC Code 8331	

Rehabilitation Institute of Pittsburgh, The

6301 Northumberland St.
Pittsburgh, PA 15217
County: Allegheny

Phone: (412) 521-9000
Fax: (412) 521-0570

Nonprofit provider of comprehensive medical rehabilitation services to children and adults on an inpatient, outpatient, subacute, day program and home care basis. The Institute is licensed for 129 inpatient beds. Coordinated care provided under the direction of a case manager and physician is available for persons with injuries from accidents, brain damage, stroke, amputation, cerebral palsy, Prader-Willi Syndrome, emotional disorders, learning disabilities, spina bifida, speech defects, orthopedic and pain problems and cancer. The Institute's services include physical, occupational and speech therapy; rehabilitation nursing; nutritional; psychological; vocational; behavioral; rehabilitation technology; rehabilitation engineering; orthotics; and social services. In addition, it provides educational services for persons ages two through 21 years with cerebral palsy and neurological disorders. While the Institute's primary service area is Eastern Ohio, Western Pennsylvania and West Virginia, patients come from throughout the United States for its nationally renowned Prader-Willi Program.

Officers: John A. Wilson *P & CEO*
Thomas J. Hemming *EVP*
Charles G. Schuessler *VP-FIN & TRS*

Human Resources: Robert Brown

Total Employees............................530	**Regional Employees** 530
Year Established 1902	**SIC Code**......................................8093
Annual Revenues ($000) 26,000	

Reichhold Chemicals, Inc.

262 Millers Run Rd.
P.O. Box 219
Bridgeville, PA 15017
County: Allegheny

Phone: (412) 257-5700
Fax: (412) 257-5743

Manufacturer of polyester resins including unsaturated polyester resins, emulsion polymers and formulated adhesives. The Company, which is headquartered in Durham, NC, operates more than 60 plants throughout the United States, Canada, Mexico and the United Kingdom and distributes its products internationally. The plant located at the above address is a production facility.

Officers: Tony Cantor *Plant MGR*

Total Employees........................5,000	**Regional Employees** 99
Year Established 1944	**SIC Code**......................................2821

Reinhold Ice Cream Co.

800 Fulton St.
Pittsburgh, PA 15233
County: Allegheny

Phone: (412) 321-7600
Fax: (412) 321-8456

Manufacturer and wholesaler of bulk ice cream and ice cream novelties. The Company produces over 120 flavors of ice cream, frozen yogurt, sorbet and sherbet. It also offers a line of novelties ranging from ice cream sandwiches to frozen milkshakes. The Company markets its line of ice cream and frozen yogurt under the Reinhold brand name and its ice cream novelties under Nancy Grey. The Company distributes its products to retail stores, schools, nursing homes, correctional facilities and hospitals in Western Pennsylvania and parts of Ohio and West Virginia. The Company operates a second manufacturing facility that is located on the North Side of Pittsburgh.

Officers: Robert Mandell *P*

Human Resources: Michael Mandell *VP*

Total Employees	40	**Regional Employees**	35
Year Established	1890	**SIC Code**	2024
Annual Revenues ($000)		6,000	

Reliable Financial Corp.

428 Station St.
Bridgeville, PA 15017
County: Allegheny

Phone: (412) 221-7700
Fax: (412) 257-1216

Savings and loan holding company for its subsidiary, Reliable Savings Bank, PaSA (Bank), a state-chartered savings bank. The Bank's principal business historically has consisted of attracting savings and applying these funds primarily to the origination of one-to-four family residential real estate loans to local borrowers. It also engages, to a much lesser extent, in commercial business, commercial real estate, lease finance, developed lot and land development lending. The Bank's principal sources of income are mortgage loans, investment securities and interest-earning deposits. Its primary market areas are in Allegheny and Washington Counties, PA. In addition to the Bank's main office and corporate headquarters located at the above address, it operates two branch facilities in Bethel Park and McDonald, PA. On September 29, 1994, the Company, which was formerly listed on the NASDAQ, became a wholly owned subsidiary of First Commonwealth Financial Corp. (FCFC). FCFC is headquartered in Indiana, PA, and listed on the NYSE.

Officers: Edward H. Eiter, Jr. *VP & COO*
  Kelvin L. Pier *VP-Credit Services*
  Gregory B. Swango *VP & CFO*

Total Employees	38	**Regional Employees**	38
Year Established	1925	**SIC Code**	6712
Annual Revenues ($000)		163,000 (Assets)	

Renaissance Center, Inc.

910 Penn Ave.
Pittsburgh, PA 15222
County: Allegheny
Phone: (412) 261-0875
Fax: (412) 471-6645

R

Nonprofit provider of social and vocational rehabilitation services to people with serious mental illness. The Organization's services are tailored to individual needs and are delivered in a variety of settings throughout Allegheny County. It also operates two businesses to train and employ people with mental illness: a bulk mailing facility and a remanufacturer of cartridges for laser printers. Both businesses operate out of the above address. In addition, the Organization operates a second downtown site, as well as satellite centers in Bellevue, East Liberty and McKees Rocks, and mobile psychiatric rehabilitation units in various community settings.

Officers: Harold Hartger *EDIR*
                Patrick Haver *P*

Human Resources: R. Douglas Clewett

Total Employees 115	**Regional Employees** 115
Year Established 1957	**SIC Code** 8361
Annual Revenues ($000) 3,200

Renda Broadcasting Corp.

900 Parish St.
Pittsburgh, PA 15220
County: Allegheny
Phone: (412) 875-9500
Fax: (412) 875-9504
Internet Address: www.@wshh.com

Owner and operator of 10 radio stations located in four states. The Company's local stations, both of which are located at the above address, are WJAS-AM 1320, offering a nostalgia format, and WSHH-FM 99.7, offering a soft adult contemporary format. Its other stations, all FM broadcasters, include KBEZ in Tulsa, OK; KHTT in Muskogee, OK; KMGL in Oklahoma City, OK; WEJZ in Jacksonville, FL; WFKS in Palatka, FL; WGUF in Marco, FL; WWGR in Ft. Myers, FL; and WWRR in Brunswick, GA. An affiliate, Renda Radio, Inc., is the licensee of WECZ-AM and WPXZ-FM in Punxsutawney, PA.

Officers: Anthony F. Renda *OWN & P*

Human Resources: Maryann Kelly

Purchasing: Karen Sobek

Total Employees 300	**Regional Employees** 60
Year Established 1974	**SIC Code** 4832

Renewal, Inc.

339 Blvd. of the Allies
Pittsburgh, PA 15222
County: Allegheny

Phone: (412) 456-1441
Fax: (412) 456-1448
Internet Address: www.insdir.com/renewalinc

Nonprofit organization dedicated to the renewal of individuals in the criminal justice system and to their return to society as responsible citizens. The Organization provides residents with beds in dormitory settings, with common recreation facilities offering television, board games, reading and visiting areas in a closely monitored and structured environment. In addition to a five-step renewal process program, it offers counseling, employment and education services. The Organization serves the community of Allegheny County and the Pennsylvania Department of Corrections.

Officers: Joseph Belechak *P*
Robert R. Perry, Ph.D. *EDIR*

Human Resources: Vijay Kumar *Associate DIR*

Purchasing: Dwarkesh Vakharia *MGR-Business & Technology*

Total Employees	38	**Regional Employees**	38
Year Established	1976	**SIC Code**	8322
Annual Revenues ($000)	2,500		

Republic Engineered Steels, Inc.

220 Seventh Ave.
Beaver Falls, PA 15010
County: Beaver

Phone: (412) 846-5500
Fax: (412) 847-5171

Producer of cold-drawn steel bars straightened and cut to specified lengths and shapes. The 176,000 square foot plant has an annual shipping capacity of approximately 54,000 tons. The Company, which is headquartered in Massillon, OH, is listed on the NASDAQ. It operates nine additional plants located in Connecticut, Illinois, Indiana, Maryland and Ohio.

Officers: Jerry Richie *Plant MGR*

Total Employees	4,372	**Regional Employees**	125
Year Established	1989	**SIC Code**	3316

ResourceNet International

1201 Freedom Rd.
P.O. Box 5000
Cranberry Township, PA 16066
County: Butler

Phone: (412) 772-2500
Fax: (412) 772-2820
Internet Address: www.resourcenet.com

Distributor of paper and industrial supplies, including printing papers, industrial paper products, foodservice disposables, and washroom maintenance and janitorial supplies and equipment. The Company is headquartered in Covington, KY. It is a subsidiary of International Paper Co., which is headquartered in Purchase, NY, and listed on the NYSE. The Pittsburgh division services clients in the Tri-State area.

Officers: Kevin R. Lethers, Sr. *VP & GMGR*
Timothy E. McCarty *SAL MGR*
James W. O'Donnell *SAL MGR*
Susan L. Brook *Administrative MGR*

Regional Employees........................60
Year Established..........................1833

SIC Code......................................5113

Rickmart, Inc.

1317 E. Carson St.
Pittsburgh, PA 15203
County: Allegheny

Phone: (412) 431-0915

Owner and operator of two grocery stores doing business as Schwartz Market. In addition to the store located at the above address, a second Pittsburgh store is located at 800 E. Warrington Ave.

Officers: Martin J. Dorfner *P*
Richard R. Stanton *VP*

Total Employees..............................34
Year Established..........................1985

Regional Employees 34
SIC Code......................................5411

Ritter Engineering Co.

Williams Dr., Bldg. 100
Zelienople, PA 16063
County: Butler

Phone: (412) 452-6000
Fax: (412) 452-0766

Provider of fluid power and motion control products. The Company specializes in the sale of a variety of components for fluid handling systems to diversified end users and OEMs. It also designs, fabricates and installs customer-engineered fluid handling systems and manufactures a line of hydraulic flanges, special high pressure regulators-filters, manifolds and a patented six-way transfer valve. The Company operates warehouse, shop and office facilities located in Bloomington and Chicago, IL; Detroit, MI; Erie, Philadelphia, State College and West Mifflin, PA; and Madison and Milwaukee, WI. The Hydraulic Co. of America (HCOA), also located at the above address, is a subsidiary of the Company. HCOA is a franchised, industrial distributor organization. It develops lubrication and fluid power systems from components manufactured by the principal firms it represents. HCOA also designs and manufactures a variety of specialized products and control components related to fluid handling and lubrication applications. In addition, it provides installation and start-up contracts for the systems it develops. HCOA's capabilities and engineered systems are sold worldwide.

Officers: H. Jay Williams *P & CEO*
Ed Biagetti *GVP*
Gary Williams *GVP*
Rick Williams *GVP*

Human Resources: Andrew J. Chomos *CFO*

Purchasing: Pat Bogacki

Total Employees	200	**Regional Employees**	120
Year Established	1951	**SIC Code**	3569
Annual Revenues ($000)		54,000	

Riverside Builders Supply, Inc.

Main St. & Pennsylvania Ave.
Coraopolis, PA 15108
County: Allegheny

Phone: (412) 264-8835
Fax: (412) 264-2011

Producer of ready-mixed concrete and distributor of various construction materials. The Company's products include aggregates, Portland cement, mortar, reinforcement for concrete and specialty products for residential, major highway and airport projects. It also produces PennDOT-certified concrete, including special fast-set concrete used for emergency patch projects.

Officers: Joseph P. Homitsky, Sr. *P*
Joseph P. Homitsky, Jr. *SVP*
Jean Homitsky *VP*
Melissa K. Wisen *SEC & TRS*

Total Employees............................34	**Regional Employees** 34
Year Established 1966	**SIC Code**......................................3273
Annual Revenues ($000) 8,500	

Rizzo Assoc., Inc., Paul C.

105 Mall Blvd., Ste. 270-E
Monroeville, PA 15146
County: Allegheny

Phone: (412) 856-9700
Fax: (412) 856-9749
Internet Address: pcra@pgh.net

Provider of environmental consulting engineering services to domestic and international clients in five main areas: environmental compliance for industry; hazardous waste management services; solid waste management services; dam safety and rehabilitation; and site hazard evaluation. This multidisciplinary structure enables the Firm to address the various issues its clients face, whether they are evaluating development of solid waste management facilities, identifying and evaluating remedial alternatives at Superfund sites or designing hydroelectric power plants. The Firm specializes in projects with substantial levels of regulatory involvement and comprehensive reporting requirements. Because of this specialization, it represents clients in negotiations with regulators and participates in public hearings. The Firm operates branch offices in Newark, DE; Columbus, OH; Mt. Pleasant, SC; and Buenos Aires, Argentina. In addition, it works throughout Europe with an affiliate in Genoa, Italy.

Officers: Paul C. Rizzo, Ph.D. *CEO*
Carl M. Rizzo *Principal*
Nishikant R. Vaidya, Ph.D. *Principal*
Robert R. Bennett *VP-OPR*
Deborah A. Lange *VP-Environmental Practice*

Human Resources: Mary F. Smith

Total Employees............................35	**Regional Employees** 28
Year Established 1984	**SIC Code** 8711

Robert Morris College

881 Narrows Run Rd.
Coraopolis, PA 15108
County: Allegheny

Phone: (800) 762-0097
Fax: (412) 299-2425
Internet Address: www.robert-morris.edu

Nonprofit, four-year, private, coeducational institution enrolling approximately 4,000 undergraduate and 990 graduate students at the College's two locations. Undergraduate degrees consist of the Bachelor of Science in business administration with 19 different concentrations, including accounting, aviation management, business teacher education, communications management, economics, finance, finance/economics, health services management, hospitality management, human resource management, logistics management, long-term health care management, management, MIS, marketing, nursing and managed care administration, operations management/decision sciences, sport management and tourism management; the Bachelor of Arts degree is awarded with concentrations in communications, economics, communications education, English, English education, applied mathematics and social science; the Bachelor of Science degree is awarded in economics, information systems, applied mathematics, applied mathematics education and social sciences; and the Associate's degree is awarded in business administration, computer and office information systems, liberal arts and radiologic technology. The College awards the Master's degree in business administration and the Master of Science with concentrations in accounting, computer information systems, finance, health services management, marketing and sport management. The Master of Science is also awarded in business education, communications and information systems, instructional leadership and taxation. The Moon Township Campus, located at the above address, is situated in a residential area 15 miles from downtown Pittsburgh and five miles from the Pittsburgh International Airport. This 230-acre campus enrolls nearly 1,000 resident students and more than 1,500 commuters. The downtown Pittsburgh Center is located at 600 Fifth Ave. It is comprised of an eight-level classroom and a library facility.

Officers: Edward A. Nicholson, Ph.D. *P*
Frank Burdine *VP-Institutional Advancement*
Richard Ritchic *VP-Business Affairs*
Jo-Ann Sipple *VP-Academic & Student Affairs*

Human Resources: Lou Goodman

Total Employees 590	**Regional Employees** 590
Year Established 1921	**SIC Code** 8221

Robicon

500 Hunt Valley Dr.
New Kensington, PA 15068
County: Westmoreland

R

Phone: (412) 339-9500
Fax: (412) 339-8100

Manufacturer of power conversion equipment including power controllers and variable speed drives. The Company provides silicon-controlled rectifiers, power systems and AC motor drives to industrial, scientific and municipal markets worldwide, and has installed its products in 57 countries. It is a subsidiary of High Voltage Engineering Corp., which is based in Wakefield, MA.

Officers: Jody Kurtzhalts *P*

Human Resources: Bob Bell *VP-Human Resources*

Purchasing: Cole Kurtz *Supplier Relations DIR*

Total Employees	420	**Regional Employees**	420
Year Established	1964	**SIC Code**	3625
Annual Revenues ($000)	80,000		

Robinson Industries, Inc.

400 Robinson Dr.
P.O. Box 100
Zelienople, PA 16063
County: Butler

Phone: (412) 452-6121
Fax: (412) 452-0388
Internet Address: www.robinsonfans.com

Precision engineer, designer and manufacturer of fans, blowers and exhausters for a variety of industrial applications. The Company develops equipment to meet specific customer requirements and provides a line of pre-engineered fans for standard industrial applications. The Company's products include airfoil, radial blade, radial tip, backward incline, backward curve and axial flow fans, as well as pressure blowers, surgeless blowers, industrial exhausters and high-temperature fans. It also offers a fan repair and rebuilding service to pinpoint and correct causes of equipment failure and provides maintenance and inspection services to help prevent breakdowns and production delays. The Company serves customers throughout the U.S. and is building an international market presence in a broad range of industries, including chemical, petrochemical, cement, mining, steel, aluminum, pulp and paper, incineration, power generation, marine, ceramic, glass and pollution control. The Company's subsidiaries are Robinson Fans Florida, Inc. in Lakeland, FL; Robinson Fans Service and Equipment Co., Inc. in Trussville, AL; and Robinson Fans West, Inc. in Salt Lake City, UT.

Officers: William H. Henderson *CH*
Ronald C. Myers *P*
H. Les Gutzwiller *VP-ENG*
Carl Staible *VP-SAL*
Dom Codispot *NATL SAL MGR*
Jay Henderson *INTL SAL MGR*
Doug Bollinger *CON*

Human Resources: Cathy Powell *Personnel MGR*

Purchasing: Wilbur Boots *Purchasing MGR*

Total Employees..........................234	**Regional Employees** 184
Year Established 1892	**SIC Code**....................................3564

Robinson Travel Systems, Inc.

6507 Wilkins Ave.
Pittsburgh, PA 15217
County: Allegheny

Phone: (412) 661-2600
Fax: (412) 661-8225

Travel management company, doing business as Gateway Travel, specializing in the management of small- to medium-size corporate accounts. The Company's management program is tailored to the specific needs of its customers and offers educational seminars, written travel policies, travel trend analysis and travel vendor negotiation. Approximately 75% of its business is with corporate clients; the remaining 25% is leisure travel. In addition to the Company's corporate headquarters located at the above address which handles both corporate and leisure travel, it operates five on-site corporate travel offices in Pittsburgh, one in Warrendale, PA, and one in San Jose, CA; and leisure travel offices in Bethel Park, Murrysville and Sewickley, PA.

Officers: Donald M. Robinson *CH*
James M. Pekins *P*
James A. Harris *VP-FIN*

Total Employees.............................65	**Regional Employees** 65
Year Established 1978	**SIC Code**....................................4724
Annual Revenues ($000) 45,000	

Rochester Machine Corp.

1300 Allegheny St.
P.O. Box 94
New Brighton, PA 15066
County: Beaver

Phone: (412) 843-7820
Fax: (412) 846-9805

Manufacturer of custom-built equipment and components for a variety of industries. The Company's 145,000 square foot shop offers complete precision machining, fabricating and assembly facilities. It can repair or build to specifications and has a lifting capacity of 50 tons.

Officers: Jeffrey Bruce *P*
Charles Bruce *VP*
Mark Lewarchik *GMGR*

Total Employees............................31	**Regional Employees** 31
Year Established 1917	**SIC Code**.....................................3599

Rodgers Agency, Inc., The

Foster Plaza V, 651 Holiday Dr.
Pittsburgh, PA 15220
County: Allegheny

Phone: (412) 922-1651
Fax: (412) 922-5117

Full-service independent insurance agency representing a number of insurance companies. The Agency offers all forms of commercial and personal insurance which includes life and benefits for local, national and international exposures.

Officers: Andrew F. Rodgers *P*
Peter L. Kostorick *SVP*
Kenneth J. O'Brien *SVP*
James M. Wehar *SVP & CFO*
Susan R. Wehar *SEC & TRS*

Human Resources: Maureen Voight

Total Employees............................34	**Regional Employees** 34
Year Established 1957	**SIC Code**.....................................6411
Annual Revenues ($000) 30,000	

Roediger-Pittsburgh, Inc.

3812 Rte. 8
Allison Park, PA 15101
County: Allegheny

Phone: (412) 487-6010
Fax: (412) 487-6005

Manufacturer of biosolids management process systems for municipal and industrial water and wastewater residuals. The Company's sludge and slurry handling equipment includes tower belt filter presses, lime post treatment modules, polymer systems (liquid and dry), sieve drum concentrators, gravity belt thickeners, fine bubble diffusers, mobile dewatering units, thermal sludge dryers and wastewater treatment systems. The Company claims that its facility is the largest dewatering equipment production site in the Western Hemisphere. The Company is a subsidiary of Roediger Anlagenbau GmbH, which is headquartered in Hanau, Germany.

Officers: David E. Gibson *P*

Human Resources: A. James Rubino *CFO*

Purchasing: Paul R. Borland

Total Employees	50	Regional Employees	50
Year Established	1978	SIC Code	3589
Annual Revenues ($000)	6-10,000		

Rose, Schmidt, Hasley & DiSalle, P.C.

Oliver Bldg., 535 Smithfield St., Ste. 900
Pittsburgh, PA 15222
County: Allegheny

Phone: (412) 434-8600
Fax: (412) 263-2829

Provider of legal services with 30 attorneys. The Firm's practice areas include corporate and commercial, real estate, estate planning and domestic relations. The Firm operates a branch office in Washington, PA.

Officers: Richard DiSalle *CH*
Edmund M. Carney *P*

Human Resources: Joan M. Mitsch *DIR-ADM (Purchasing)*

Total Employees	57	Regional Employees	57
Year Established	1903	SIC Code	8111

Rosenbluth International

One Gateway Center
Pittsburgh, PA 15222
County: Allegheny

Phone: (412) 263-6180
Fax: (412) 263-6200

Provider of travel management services offering comprehensive corporate, leisure and meeting travel programs. The Company, which is headquartered in Philadelphia, PA, claims to be the second-largest travel management company in the world. It operates over 1,200 locations throughout the United States and in more than 50 countries around the world.

Officers: Hal Rosenbluth *P & CEO*
Sharon Ruzzi *GMGR*

Human Resources: Cecily Carel *DIR (Philadelphia, PA)*

Total Employees........................3,600	**Regional Employees** 79
Year Established 1892	**SIC Code**....................................4724
Annual Revenues ($000) 2,700,000	

R

Roth Computer Register Co., Inc.

1600 Saw Mill Run Blvd.
Pittsburgh, PA 15236
County: Allegheny

Phone: (412) 884-5700
Fax: (412) 885-4904

Marketer of business-related support systems and supplies for the hospitality, retail, and food and drug industries, serving customers throughout the Tri-State area. The Company's products include fast food and fine dining systems, hotel and motel front desk systems, point-of-sale systems, inventory control systems, cash registers, electronic scales and labelers, touchscreen systems, accounting software, ingredient printers and related supplies, including paper rolls, ribbons, rollers and labels. It sells and supports products from a variety of manufacturers, including Compaq, CRS, Esper, Micros, Pony Computers, Samsung and TEC. The Company also offers reconditioned and used equipment. In addition, it provides in-house and in-store repair services.

Officers: Paul W. Roth, Sr. *P*

Human Resources: John E. Roth *VP*

Total Employees............................30	**Regional Employees** 30
Year Established 1951	**SIC Code**....................................3579
Annual Revenues ($000)..3-5,000	

Rothman Gordon Foreman & Groudine, P.C.

Grant Bldg., 310 Grant St., 3rd Fl.
Pittsburgh, PA 15219
County: Allegheny

Phone: (412) 338-1100
Fax: (412) 281-7304

Provider of diversified legal services to individuals and corporations. The Firm is staffed with 30 attorneys. Its primary practice areas include business and corporate law, civil litigation, estate planning and administration, insurance matters, banking and finance law, workers' compensation and social security, real property law, and employment and labor law.

Officers: Emil W. Herman *P*
Louis B. Kushner *VP & MGT Comm.*
Thomas R. Solomich *SEC & MGT Comm.*
Mark L. Unatin *TRS & MGT Comm.*

Human Resources: David A. Charnock *Administrator (Purchasing)*

Total Employees............................80	**Regional Employees** 80
Year Established 1954	**SIC Code** 8111

Royston Laboratories

128 First St.
Pittsburgh, PA 15238
County: Allegheny

Phone: (412) 828-1500
Fax: (412) 828-4826

Manufacturer of waterproofing membranes; pipeline corrosion prevention tapes, mastics, handy caps and accessories; and molding components. The Company markets its products to gas utilities and contractors, and to the Department of Transportation for bridge maintenance purposes. The Company is a division of Chase Corp., which is headquartered in Braintree, MA, and listed on the ASE.

Officers: Gregory A. Pelagio *GMGR*

Human Resources: Kenneth Howells *CON*

Total Employees............................43	**Regional Employees** 43
Year Established 1971	**SIC Code**....................................2899

RPS, Inc.

1000 RPS Dr.
P.O. Box 108, Pittsburgh, PA 15230
Coraopolis, PA 15108
County: Allegheny

Phone: (412) 269-1000
Fax: (412) 269-3109
Internet Address: www.shiprps.com

Provider of delivery services, claiming to be the second-largest ground small package carrier in the United States. The Company serves customers in the small package market in North America and between North America and Europe focusing primarily on the business-to-business delivery of packages weighing up to 150 pounds. The Company provides ground service to 100% of the United States population and overnight service to 45% of the United States population. Through its subsidiary, RPS, Ltd., service is provided to 100% of the Canadian population. The Company also provides service to Mexico through an arrangement with another transportation provider. Its service extends to 27 European countries through an alliance with General Parcel Logistics, GmbH. In addition, the Company provides service offshore to Puerto Rico, Alaska and Hawaii via a ground/air network operation in cooperation with other transportation providers. The Company offers other specialized transportation services to meet specific customer requirements in the small package market. The Company conducts its operations primarily with 8,300 owner-operated vehicles and, in addition, owns more than 8,100 trailers. As of December 31, 1996, the Company operated 370 facilities, including 25 hubs. The Company is a subsidiary of Caliber System, Inc., which is headquartered in Akron, OH, and listed on the NYSE. Additional Pittsburgh area sites are located in Crafton and Youngwood, PA.

Officers: Ivan T. Hofmann *P*
Mary Coulter *VP-Customer Service*
Eric Damon *VP-FIN*
Ed DiSalvo *VP-SAL*
Bram Johnson *VP-MKT*
Tom Warren *VP-OPR*

Human Resources: Lee Holly *VP-Human Resources*

Purchasing: Steve Lynch *MGR-Purchasing*

Total Employees ....15,000+	**Regional Employees** 1,300
Year Established 1985	**SIC Code** 4215
Annual Revenues ($000) 1,300,000	

RTR Business Products, Inc.

5110 Old William Penn Hwy.
P.O. Box 67
Murrysville, PA 15668
County: Westmoreland

Phone: (412) 733-7373
Fax: (412) 733-7005

Wholesaler and retailer of Jetfax, Konica and Minolta office equipment and supplies. The Company's equipment includes copiers, color copiers, printers, high speed and network printers, facsimile machines, document imaging systems and multi-functional equipment. It also offers training, service and supplies for the equipment. The Company serves a wide variety of customers in Western Pennsylvania.

Officers: Richard L. McCormick *OWN & P*
Mark Korbar *Service MGR*
Mark Power *SAL MGR*

Human Resources: Alan Latta *CON (Purchasing)*

Total Employees..............................45	**Regional Employees** 45
Year Established 1966	**SIC Code**....................................5044
Annual Revenues ($000)...4-5,000	

Russell, Rea, Zappala & Gomulka Holdings, Inc.

CNG Tower, 625 Liberty Ave., Ste. 3100
Pittsburgh, PA 15222
County: Allegheny

Phone: (412) 562-1000
Fax: (412) 562-0222

Provider of financial services through its three subsidiaries. RRZ Capital Markets, Inc. is a full-service corporate finance company that manages a fund to provide mezzanine and equity capital for management buyouts and acquisitions. It also provides corporate finance advisory service to small- and middle-market companies. RRZ Investment Management, Inc. is a registered investment advisor providing custom-designed investment management plans to public and private pension funds, endowments and foundations. RRZ Public Markets, Inc. is an underwriter and trader of municipal bonds serving the capital needs of state, local and municipal government entities. All three companies are based at the above address with branch offices in Erie and Philadelphia, PA. They serve clients in New Jersey, Ohio and Pennsylvania.

Officers: Charles R. Zappala *CH*
Charles A. Gomulka *P*

Regional Employees.......................39	
Year Established 1978	**SIC Code** 6211

Ruthrauff, Inc.

400 Locust St.
McKees Rocks, PA 15136
County: Allegheny

Phone: (412) 771-6800
Fax: (412) 771-4222

Provider of mechanical contracting and engineering services to clients in Western Pennsylvania. The Company's capabilities include complete heating, ventilating and air conditioning; sheet metal fabrication and installation; heating, ventilating, air conditioning and fire protection service; plumbing; industrial process piping; building automation and energy management systems; and in-house engineering and design services.

Officers: Ignatius C. Laux *CH*
David G. Faller *P & CEO*

Human Resources: Nora L. Faller *EVP*

Purchasing: Glenn E. Lynn

R

Total Employees...........................200	Regional Employees 200
Year Established 1934	SIC Code 1711
Annual Revenues ($000) 27,000	

Ryan Enterprise, Inc., J. R.

3333 California Ave.
Pittsburgh, PA 15212
County: Allegheny

Phone: (412) 761-3333
Fax: (412) 761-3660
Internet Address: www.pghlimo.com

Holding company engaged in the transportation business through its subsidiary, Pittsburgh Limousine, Inc. (PLI), which is also located at the above address. PLI operates a fleet of approximately 35 vehicles, featuring a complete line of stretch, super-stretch and ultra-stretch limousines as well as executive sedans, Lincoln town cars, passenger vans and mini-buses. PLI services both corporate and personal accounts throughout the Pittsburgh metropolitan area and is accustomed to handling all types of special requests.

Officers: John J. Ryan *P & CEO*
James R. Shento *VP-OPR*

Total Employees.............................72	Regional Employees 72
Year Established 1987	SIC Code 4119

Ryan Moving & Storage, Inc.

185 Colonial Manor Rd.
P.O. Box U
Irwin, PA 15642
County: Westmoreland

Phone: (412) 864-6800
Fax: (412) 864-4062

Provider of moving and storage services. The Company offers local and long distance moving of household goods and high-value products; commercial office moving; warehousing and distribution of commercial and household goods; and international household goods relocation. It also provides interstate transportation of general commodities through an affiliate, Ryan Xpress, Inc., which is also located at the above address. The Company operates additional office and warehouse facilities located in Baltimore, MD; Erie, PA; and at 286 Corliss St. in Pittsburgh, which total 80,000 square feet of space. It is an agent for Allied Van Lines, Inc., which is headquartered in Naperville, IL.

Officers: Richard L. Ryan *P & CEO*
Erik T. Ryan *EVP*

Human Resources: Cathy Lutton *Administrative AST (Purchasing)*

Total Employees............................75	**Regional Employees** 75
Year Established 1930	**SIC Code**....................................4213
Annual Revenues ($000) 4,000

Rycon Construction, Inc.

1900 Andrew St.
Munhall, PA 15120
County: Allegheny

Phone: (412) 462-1900
Fax: (412) 462-1901

Provider of general contracting services including new construction and renovations. The Company works with commercial, industrial and institutional buildings, specializing in health care facilities, office renovations and retail construction. Its clients include Carnegie Mellon University, Duquesne Light, HealthAmerica, JC Penney, The May Co., National City Bank, The Roxy Cafe, University of Pittsburgh Medical Center, Westinghouse and Woodson's All-Star Grille. The Company also operates a division that works with smaller projects.

Officers: Todd Dominick *P (Purchasing)*
William Taylor *VP & SEC (Human Resources)*
Michele Dominick *TRS*

Total Employees............................85	**Regional Employees** 85
Year Established 1989	**SIC Code**....................................1542
Annual Revenues ($000) 31,000

Sable, Makoroff & Gusky, P.C.

Frick Bldg., 437 Grant St., 7th Fl.
Pittsburgh, PA 15219
County: Allegheny

Phone: (412) 471-4996
Fax: (412) 281-2859

Commercial law firm with 25 attorneys, providing legal services in the areas of business reorganization, commercial loans and financing, construction and surety, corporate, creditors' rights, general and commercial litigation, environmental, insurance defense, labor and employment, real estate, wills and estate planning.

Officers: Robert G. Sable *MPTR*

Human Resources: Karen Brown

Total Employees	52	**Regional Employees**	52
Year Established	1975	**SIC Code**	8111

R

SAI Consulting Engineers, Inc.

300 Sixth Ave.
Pittsburgh, PA 15222
County: Allegheny

Phone: (412) 392-8750
Fax: (412) 392-8785
Internet Address: www.saiengr.com

Employee-owned provider of consulting engineering services for civil engineering projects. The Firm's services include site design, structural design, highway design, streetscaping, structural inspection, underwater inspection, construction management and architectural support services. The Firm can provide specific technical expertise to supplement the in-house capabilities of its clients or can integrate its civil, structural and electrical engineering services to assist clients from preliminary studies and initial planning through detailed design, construction management and construction inspection. The Firm has completed hundreds of projects for a variety of industries, businesses and government agencies, such as public utilities, developers, industrial facilities, colleges and universities, school districts, contractors, architects, engineers, hospitals, and local, state and federal government. The Firm serves clients throughout the Commonwealth of Pennsylvania and other surrounding states.

Special Designations: ENR_{500}

Officers: Donald V. Gennuso *P*
Robert T. Balkovec *VP-Project DEV*
Victor E. Bertolina *VP-ENG*
James J. Lombardi *VP-Construction*

Human Resources: Mary Lynn Kiefer

Purchasing: Walter S. Krasneski, Jr. *MKT/SAL MGR*

Total Employees	120	**Regional Employees**	120
Year Established	1975	**SIC Code**	8711
Annual Revenues ($000)	11,500		

Saint Vincent College Corp.

300 Fraser Purchase Rd.
Latrobe, PA 15650
County: Westmoreland

Phone: (412) 532-6600
Fax: (412) 537-4554

Nonprofit operator of a private educational institution rooted in the tradition of the Catholic faith and the heritage of Benedictine monasticism. Saint Vincent College, located 35 miles east of Pittsburgh, is a four-year school offering a curricula designed around a basic liberal arts core. This core includes the study of literature, philosophy, social sciences, laboratory sciences, mathematics, theology and language. The college awards the Bachelor's degree in a wide range of majors. It also offers preprofessional programs in chiropractic, dentistry, law, medical, optometry, podiatry, theology and veterinary studies. The college enrolls approximately 1,200 men and women. The Corporation also operates the Saint Vincent Seminary, a four-year graduate school sharing the same campus that trains students for the priesthood and offers graduate courses in theology leading to a Master's degree.

Officers: James L. Murdy *CH*
Rt. Rev. Douglas R. Nowicki, O.S.B *Archabbot & Chancellor*
Rev. Martin R. Bartel, O.S.B. *P-Saint Vincent College*
Very Rev. Thomas Acklin, O.S.B. *Rector-Saint Vincent Seminary*
Brother Norman Hipps, O.S.B. *Provost-Saint Vincent College*
Brent Cejda, Ph.D. *Academic Dean-Saint Vincent College*
Rev. Frank Ziemkiewicz, O.S.B. *Dean of Students-Saint Vincent College*
Alice Kaylor *Associate Academic Dean-Saint Vincent College*
Rev. Reginald Bender, O.S.B. *TRS-Saint Vincent College*

Human Resources: Jill Clements

Total Employees............................312		**Regional Employees** 312
Year Established 1846		**SIC Code**.....................................8221
Annual Revenues ($000) 23,000			

Saks Fifth Avenue

513 Smithfield St.
Pittsburgh, PA 15222
County: Allegheny

Phone: (412) 263-4800
Fax: (412) 263-4880

Specialty retailer featuring designer apparel for men and women. The Store also retails fine jewelry, women's designer handbags, accessories, shoes and furs, and operates a full-service beauty salon. Its major brand names include Chanel, Donna Karan, Escada, Giorgio Armani, Gucci, Hugo Boss, St. John, Valentino and

Zegna. The Store is a unit of Saks & Co. (S&C), which is headquartered in New York, NY. S&C comprises 40 full line stores, eight resort stores and three main street stores. In addition, it operates 34 Off 5th outlet stores and Folio, a separate direct mail business. S&C is a subsidiary of Saks Holdings, Inc., which is also headquartered in New York, NY, and listed on the NYSE.

Officers: Valerie Swayzee *GMGR*

Human Resources: Donald Heron *AST GMGR-ADM*

Regional Employees....................190
Year Established 1944   **SIC Code** 5632

Salem Group, Inc.

Arch St. Extension
P.O. Box 2222, Pittsburgh, PA 15230
Carnegie, PA 15106
County: Allegheny

Phone: (412) 276-5700
Fax: (412) 923-2206

Holding company for the Salem Corp. (SC) which was formerly listed on the American Stock Exchange prior to its acquisition in September 1996. SC, which is also located at the above address, is a designer, engineer and installer of heavy industrial equipment primarily for the metals, coal and other minerals industries. SC operates in three business segments: industrial furnaces, metal processing equipment and minerals processing equipment. The industrial furnaces segment, through Salem Furnace Co. (SFC) which is also located at the above address, designs, engineers and constructs thermal processing equipment, ovens and furnaces in a wide range of sizes and for various end uses. SFC's reheat furnaces are designed for the ferrous and nonferrous metals industries to reheat ingots, slabs, blooms, billets and other materials preparatory to forging, rolling and other shaping. The metal processing equipment segment, through Herr-Voss Corp. (HVC) in Callery, PA, designs, engineers and manufactures strip, plate and coil processing systems and equipment for the continuous processing of ferrous and nonferrous metals. Such equipment includes a wide range of precision machinery and auxiliary equipment which is designed to cut, join, slit, level, clean and coat metals in coil or sheet form. The primary markets for HVC's equipment are metal service centers, steel mills, metals producers and large manufacturers of metal products. The minerals processing equipment segment, through Industrial Resources, Inc. which has facilities at the above address and in Fairmont, WV, designs, manufactures and installs material handling, processing and related equipment and systems for the coal, rock, cement, utility and oil industries. Through West Virginia Electric Corp. in Fairmont, WV, this segment designs and installs complete electrical systems for processing and material handling systems used by the coal, rock, cement, utility and oil industries. Through A. L. Lee Corp. in Lester, WV, this segment designs, manufactures and rebuilds equipment for the mining industry, consisting of rockdusters, face fans, conveyors and personnel carriers, and distributes related mining equipment and spare parts.

Officers: A. A. Fornataro *P & CEO*
              Donald L. Hoylman *GVP*
              J. William Uhrig *VP*
              George A. Douglas *CON & TRS*
              David D. Struth   *SEC*
              W. Robert Wright *AST-SEC*

Human Resources: Richard L. Watterson *Corporate Administrator-Employee Benefits*

Total Employees............................816   **Regional Employees** 438
Year Established 1903   **SIC Code**....................................3549
Annual Revenues ($000) 150,000

Salvucci Engineers, Inc.

355 Fifth Ave., Ste. 1200
Pittsburgh, PA 15222
County: Allegheny

Phone: (412) 392-8600
Fax: (412) 392-8623

Multidisciplinary engineering and consulting firm providing services in all areas of engineering, including architectural, chemical, civil, electrical, HVAC, material handling, mechanical, piping, process control and scheduling. The Firm offers a complete line of construction engineering services, from feasibility studies and preliminary engineering through the final phases of construction and start-up. Its projects include a wide range of commercial, industrial and government facilities, serving clients worldwide.

Officers: Joseph Salvucci *CH & CEO*
              Alfred K. Hodil *P & GMGR*
              John L. Caldart *MGR-Piping Department*

Human Resources: Pat A. Patrizio *DIR-OPR (Purchasing)*

Total Employees............................40   **Regional Employees** 40
Year Established 1953   **SIC Code**....................................8711

Sarris Candies, Inc.

511 Adams Ave.
Canonsburg, PA 15317
County: Washington

Phone: (412) 745-4042
Fax: (412) 745-5642
Internet Address: www.sarriscandies.com

Manufacturer of a complete line of chocolate products. The Company is a wholesale distributor of chocolate products marketed in 180 retail stores through-out the Tri-State area, including Giant Eagles, Hallmark stores and Thrift Drugs. It also produces a complete line of fund-raising products. In addition, the Company operates a retail store at the above address, which displays many gift and novelty items and contains an ice cream parlor featuring homemade ice cream.

S

Officers: Frank H. Sarris *P*
William F. Sarris *VP*
Athena Sarris *SEC & TRS*

Human Resources: Irene M. Pihiou

Total Employees	175	**Regional Employees**	175
Year Established	1963	**SIC Code**	2066

Sauer, Inc.

30 51st St.
Pittsburgh, PA 15201
County: Allegheny

Phone: (412) 687-4100
Fax: (412) 687-3486

Provider of mechanical and industrial contracting services performing process piping, HVAC and plumbing for both new construction and renovation/retrofit work. The Company has extensive experience with commercial, institutional and industrial projects nationwide. It operates branch offices in Jacksonville, FL, and Columbus, OH.

Officers: William N. Steitz, Jr. *C-OWN & P*
Charles D. Steitz *C-OWN & EVP*
Russell L. Boczkowski *VP*
Emily J. Landerman *VP-Business DEV*
Timothy M. Steitz *VP & C-OWN*
Neil J. Wickersty *VP*

Human Resources: Terence R. Kiliany

Purchasing: Benjamin Hart

Total Employees	450	**Regional Employees**	125
Year Established	1876	**SIC Code**	1711
Annual Revenues ($000)			136,100

Sauereisen Cements Co.

RIDC Industrial Park, 160 Gamma Dr.
Pittsburgh, PA 15238
County: Allegheny

Phone: (412) 963-0303
Fax: (412) 963-7620
Internet Address: www.sauereisen.com

Manufacturer of corrosion-resistant materials for industrial construction and specialty cements. The Company's corrosion-resistant materials product line includes coatings, linings and flooring; chemical-resistant refractories; mortars; membranes and expansion joints; substrate repair materials; and grouts. These products are used in a wide range of applications by the pulp and paper, waste-water treatment, power, chemical, petrochemical, refining, food and beverage, pharmaceutical, and steel industries, and for substrate repair. The Company's technical cement line consists of more than 20 different chemical, hydraulic and air-setting inorganic materials. These products are used for bonding, potting, encapsulating and sealing, serving the automotive, appliance and lighting indus-tries. Its original product, Insulute Adhesive Cement, is still used in most auto-mobiles produced in the U.S. The Company's products are distributed worldwide through a network of domestic representatives and international licensees. The Company operates an additional manufacturing and research facility on Freeport Rd. in Harmar Township, PA.

Officers: Ferd J. Sauereisen *CH*
Patrick E. Connell *P*
David J. Leonard *CFO*

Human Resources: William P. Sauereisen *VP*

Purchasing: Susan Smolic

Total Employees................................48	**Regional Employees** 47
Year Established 1899	**SIC Code**......................................2891

Saunier-Wilhem Co.

3216 Fifth Ave.
Pittsburgh, PA 15213
County: Allegheny

Phone: (412) 931-1660
Fax: (412) 621-6219

Distributor of bowling and billiards products as well as trophies, table games and related supplies and services. The Company also operates a warehouse and retail outlet in Birmingham, AL, and a game board manufacturing facility for pool tables in Greensboro, NC. It serves customers throughout the continental United States and in Canada.

Officers: James F. Wilhem *P*

Human Resources: Thomas Boyle *SEC*

Total Employees............................52	**Regional Employees** 23
Year Established 1920	**SIC Code**.....................................5091
Annual Revenues ($000) 3,500	

S

Saxonburg Ceramics, Inc.

100 Isabella St.
P.O. Box 688
Saxonburg, PA 16056
County: Butler

Phone: (412) 352-1561
Fax: (412) 352-3580

   Manufacturer of technical ceramics including a complete line of alumina, steatite, cordierite, magnesia and refractory ceramics. The Company's ceramic elements are used to produce a variety of products including immersion heaters for molding plastics, heating elements, thermocouples, nuts and bolts, stereo and amplifier components, and lighting. A second manufacturing facility is located in Monroe, NC, that is devoted predominantly to alumina substrates and to manufacturing MgO products.

Officers: Furman South IV *P*
R. Terrence Gaab *VP-MFG & CFO*
Conan McManus *DIR-SAL & MKT*

Human Resources: Vince Castrucci

Total Employees...........................175	**Regional Employees** 90
Year Established 1924	**SIC Code**.....................................3264
Annual Revenues ($000) 10,000	

Scalise Industries Corp.

381 Colonial Manor Rd.
Irwin, PA 15642
County: Westmoreland

Phone: (412) 863-6300
Fax: (412) 863-6600

   Mechanical and sheet metal contractor providing planning and specification services, design/build engineering services, fabricated HVAC ductwork and piping, installation, maintenance services and indoor air quality solutions. The Company serves commercial clients primarily in the Tri-State area.

Officers: Mark R. Scalise *P & CEO (Purchasing)*

Human Resources: Anna M. Pier

Total Employees............................150	**Regional Employees** 150
Year Established 1946	**SIC Code** 1711
Annual Revenues ($000) 18,000	

Schaffner Manufacturing Co., Inc.

Schaffner Center, 21 Herron Ave.
Pittsburgh, PA 15202
County: Allegheny

Phone: (412) 761-9902
Fax: (412) 761-8998

Manufacturer of buffing wheels, buffing compounds and coated abrasive products for the metal finishing industry. The Company offers a complete line of nearly 5,000 different compound formulations to finish all kinds of metals and most plastics. It operates an additional manufacturing site in Jackson, MS.

Officers: James R. Schaffner *CH & CEO*
G. Jay Schaffner III *P (Purchasing)*
J. Allen Schaffner *VP-Production*
Paul E. Schaffner II *VP-SAL*
William M. Schaffner *VP-FIN*

Total Employees..............................86	**Regional Employees** 81
SIC Code 3291	
Annual Revenues ($000)..8,000+	

Schaller's Bakery, Inc.

826 Highland Ave.
Greensburg, PA 15601
County: Westmoreland

Phone: (412) 837-3660
Fax: (412) 837-6764

Commercial bakery producing breads, cakes and pastry products. The Company serves customers, including schools, institutions and retail facilities, throughout Western Pennsylvania.

Officers: Warren E. Schaller *P*
Weddell B. Schaller *SVP*
R. Scott Schaller *Night Shift Foreman*

Human Resources: Toni L. Oien

Purchasing: Wayne E. Schaller *SEC & TRS*

Total Employees............................48	**Regional Employees** 48
Year Established 1902	**SIC Code**....................................2051
Annual Revenues ($000) 2,000	

Scheirer Machine Co., Inc.

S

3200 Industrial Blvd.
P.O. Box 670
Bethel Park, PA 15102
County: Allegheny

Phone: (412) 833-6500
Fax: (412) 833-8110

Machine shop, with more than 15 computer and numerically controlled machine tools and a full compliment of manual machines. The Company provides OEM and replacement parts for steel mills, power plants, packaging machinery, engineering firms, maintenance companies, machinery fabricators, foundries, construction companies, municipalities, plastics companies, glass manufacturers, food companies, mining industries, heavy machinery, pumps, paper manufacture, welding, waste management, electric products, the tool and die industry and the government. It can efficiently produce quantities from one to 5,000 pieces.

Officers: Marlene B. Scheirer *OWN & P*
Eric Scheirer *VP*
Michael W. Branchen *SAL MGR*

Purchasing: Audrey Walbert

Total Employees............................52	**Regional Employees** 52
Year Established 1969	**SIC Code**....................................3599
Annual Revenues ($000) 4,500	

Schiff, Inc.

1107 Washington Blvd.
Pittsburgh, PA 15206
County: Allegheny

Phone: (412) 441-5760
Fax: (412) 441-0133
Internet Address: www.schiffprinting.com

Commercial sheet fed printer with expertise in computer graphics and image-setting. The Company also provides in-house bindery services and offers foil stamping, die cutting, embossing, pocket folder assembly and perfect binding.

Officers: Samuel Schiff *OWN & P*
William H. Schiff *VP*
Belva J. Schiff *CON*

Purchasing: Renee Nesbitt

Total Employees............................32	**Regional Employees** 32
Year Established 1954	**SIC Code**....................................2759

Schneider Downs & Co., Inc.

1133 Penn Ave.
Pittsburgh, PA 15222
County: Allegheny

Phone: (412) 261-3644
Fax: (412) 261-4876
Internet Address: www.sdcpa.com

Certified public accounting and business advisory firm that claims to be the largest regional accounting firm in Western Pennsylvania. The Firm's services range from traditional accounting, auditing, tax compliance, tax planning, estate planning, succession planning, retirement planning and employee benefits consulting to management advisory services that encompass litigation support, business valuations, due diligence, turnaround, financial analysis, forensic accounting, productivity improvement, reengineering and business systems consulting. Servicing principally small- to middle-market closely held companies, the Firm's practice is focused on a variety of industries, including high technology, manufacturing, construction, automobile dealerships, professional service firms, natural resources, not-for-profits, transportation and women-owned businesses. The Firm operates a branch office in Columbus, OH. It is a member of the International Group of Accounting Firms, an association of independent, autonomous accounting firms, with approximately 140 member firms maintaining offices in 60 countries.

Officers: Raymond W. Buehler, Jr. *P & Co-Managing Shareholder*
Kenneth A. Rowles *Co-Managing Shareholder*
Don Alan Linzer *Principal*
Thomas G. Claassen *Shareholder*
Thomas J. Conroy *Shareholder*
David E. Kolan *Shareholder*
F. Jeffrey Kovacs *Shareholder*
Ronald A. Kramer *Shareholder*
Paul M. Matvey *Shareholder*
Brian C. O'Brien *Shareholder*
Jeffrey A. Wlahofsky *Shareholder*
Eric M. Wright *Shareholder*

Human Resources: Jean M. Callahan

Total Employees..........................144	**Regional Employees** 125
Year Established 1956	**SIC Code**....................................8721

Schneider's Dairy, Inc.

726 Frank St.
Pittsburgh, PA 15227
County: Allegheny

Phone: (412) 881-3525
Fax: (412) 881-7722

S

Processor and distributor of dairy products including milk, ice cream, sour cream and dips; juice drinks; and teas. The Company operates branch distribution facilities in State College and Washington, PA. A subsidiary, Valley Farms Dairy, operates a processing plant in Williamsport, PA. The Company markets its products under the brand name Schneider's Dairy and distributes throughout most of Pennsylvania and Eastern New York.

Officers: William J. Schneider *P*
William F. Jones, Jr. *COO*
Edward W. Schneider *VP*
Paul L. Schneider *VP*
Kenneth J. Schneider *SEC*
Edward W. Schneider, Jr. *SAL MGR*
William D. Schneider *Plant MGR*

Human Resources: David W. Schneider *CON*

Total Employees............................275	**Regional Employees** 150
Year Established 1935	**SIC Code**.....................................2026

Schultheis Bros. Co., Inc.

1001 Millers Lane
P.O. Box 14098
Pittsburgh, PA 15239
County: Allegheny

Phone: (412) 793-8000
Fax: (412) 793-3627

Contractor providing heating, ventilating, air conditioning and roofing services primarily to commercial and residential clients in Southwestern Pennsylvania. The Company's capabilities range from residential repair to commercial design/build.

Officers: Richard J. Schultheis *P*
Edward E. Golembiesky *VP*
Elizabeth S. Foster *SEC & TRS*

Total Employees..............................88	**Regional Employees** 88
Year Established 1947	**SIC Code** 1711
Annual Revenues ($000) 7,000	

Science Applications International Corp.

P.O. Box 18288
Pittsburgh, PA 15236
County: Allegheny

Phone: (412) 892-4704
Fax: (412) 892-4736
Intornot Addrocc: www.saic.com

Provider of technical and management support services to the U.S. Department of Energy's Federal Energy Technology Center, a facility that conducts and manages research projects to develop advanced technologies applicable to fossil energy and the environment. The Company can also provide broadbased expertise to clients in the areas of energy, the environment, computer systems and communications. The Company, which is headquartered in San Diego, CA, has employees in 350 locations, including all 50 states and at least 12 countries. It states that it is the world's largest employee-owned high technology company providing services and products to government and private sector clients in a multitude of disciplines, including space, information technology, systems integration, national security, transportation, health care, energy, telecommunications and the environment.

Officers: Kenneth A. Hartenbach *AVP & Division MGR-Pittsburgh Office*

Human Resources: Maureen Henry-Labella *(Purchasing)*

Total Employees	22,000	**Regional Employees**	32
Year Established	1969	**SIC Code**	8711
Annual Revenues ($000)	2,200,000 (2,000 in Southwestern PA)		

Scottdale Bank & Trust Co., The

150 Pittsburgh St.
Scottdale, PA 15683
County: Westmoreland

Phone: (412) 887-8330
Fax: (412) 887-3836

Commercial bank providing a variety of deposit, loan and trust-related products and services. In addition to the Bank's corporate office and a banking facility located at the above address, it operates branch offices in Connellsville, Mt. Pleasant and Vanderbilt, PA.

S

Officers: Maryland Kiefer *CH*
Donald Kiefer *P*
David Powell *EVP*
Charles King *VP*
Robert Ferguson *SEC*
Lawrence Kiefer *TRS*

Total Employees............................63
Year Established.......................1901   **SIC Code**...................................6022
Annual Revenues ($000)...........................130,000 (Assets)

Sebastian Enterprises, Inc.

308 Leopard Lane
Beaver, PA 15009
County: Beaver

Phone: (412) 774-7880
Fax: (412) 774-7994
Internet Address: www.novaord.com/sebastian

Owner and operator of restaurants, provider of catering services and developer of real estate. The Company operates Bert's Wooden Indian, the Casual Cafe and the Wooden Angel restaurants, all of which are located at the above address, with a combined seating capacity of approximately 450. Its real estate holdings include residential, commercial, retail and multi-family properties in Beaver, PA. In addition, the Company offers wine consulting and education.

Officers: Alex E. Sebastian *P*
David E. Sebastian *VP*
Julia M. Sebastian *SEC & TRS*
Art Mangie *Kitchen MGR*
Deborah Rickard *Special Events MGR*

Total Employees............................70   **Regional Employees**...................70
Year Established.......................1948   **SIC Code**...................................5812
Annual Revenues ($000)...3,000+

Second National Bank of Masontown, The

110 S. Main St.
Masontown, PA 15461
County: Fayette

Phone: (412) 583-7701
Fax: (412) 583-2012

Independent community bank providing a variety of deposit and loan services to individuals and businesses in Fayette County, PA. The Bank operates three branch offices located at 2951 National Pike in Chalk Hill, PA; Rte. 40 E. in Grindstone, PA; and 173 Morgantown St. in Uniontown, PA.

Officers: Edward E. Vignali *CH*
Harry D. Reagan *VCH & CEO*
Scott M. Allen *VP & Senior Loan Officer*
David B. Martin *VP & Cashier*
Pauline J. Bakewell *CON*

Human Resources: J. Patrick Hall *P (Purchasing)*

Total Employees	58	**Regional Employees**	58
Year Established	1935	**SIC Code**	6021
Annual Revenues ($000)	152,191		

Sedgwick James of Pennsylvania, Inc.

USX Tower, 600 Grant St., 12th Fl.
Pittsburgh, PA 15219
County: Allegheny

Phone: (412) 566-5750
Fax: (412) 566-7359

Provider of risk services offering insurance brokerage, risk management, employee benefits and related consulting services to companies of all sizes and in all industries. The Company claims to be one of the largest of its kind in the world. It operates a network of more than 260 offices located in 63 countries. The Company is a subsidiary of Sedgwick James, Inc., located in New York, NY, which is a subsidiary of the Sedgwick Group Plc. The parent company is headquartered in London, England, and listed on the London Stock Exchange.

Officers: John P. Moskal *Managing Executive*
R. George Voinchet *VCH*
Paul J. Trageser *VP*
James G. Undereiner *VP*
Rosemarie Rodden *Communications Coordinator*

Human Resources: Nancy E. Rodriguez

Total Employees	400	**Regional Employees**	70
Year Established	1858	**SIC Code**	6411
Annual Revenues ($000)	1,000,000+		

Sell Corp., Wayne W.

236 Winfield Rd.
Sarver, PA 16055
County: Butler

Phone: (412) 352-9441
Fax: (412) 352-2688

Trucking company operating flat bed, dump and tank trailer trucks used to haul materials such as cement, limestone, pig iron, dirt and gypsum. The Company is licensed to haul bulk commodities throughout the continental United States.

Officers: Wayne W. Sell *P*
James Beechey *VP*
John Sell *SEC*

Total Employees..............................85
Year Established 1965   **SIC Code** 4213

Semtek Systems, Inc.

One Parks Bend, Ste. 73826
P.O. Box 210
Vandergrift, PA 15690
County: Westmoreland

Phone: (412) 845-5470
Fax: (412) 845-5472

Provider of system solutions, electronic design, printed circuit boards, electronic assembly and custom-designed cables. The Company's service capabilities include electronic contract design and development, mechanical contract design and development, printed circuit board assembly and testing (through-hole and SMT), cable and harness assembly, and chassis assembly. It can offer contract only engineering services, design/build services or turnkey projects from concept through production. The Company serves clients nationwide.

Officers: Raymond P. Pugliese *P & CEO (Human Resources)*

Purchasing: Michael Krummey *VP*

Total Employees..............................42   **Regional Employees** 42
Year Established 1989   **SIC Code** 3679

Sentient Systems Technology, Inc.

2100 Wharton St.
Pittsburgh, PA 15203
County: Allegheny

Phone: (412) 381-4883
Fax: (412) 381-5241
Internet Address: www.sentient-sys.com

Supplier of advanced augmentative communication products for those with speech, learning and physical disabilities. The Company's dynamic display synthesized speech devices can be customized to accommodate the users' respective disabilities allowing them to communicate. It also offers digitized speech devices. The Company has provided communication solutions for thousands of non-speaking individuals around the world.

Officers: Tilden Bennett *P*
Gary Kiliany *VP*

Total Employees............................61
Year Established 1983
Regional Employees 50
SIC Code....................................3669

ServiceWare, Inc.

333 Allegheny Ave.
Oakmont, PA 15139
County: Allegheny

Phone: (412) 826-1158
Fax: (412) 826-0577
Internet Address: www.serviceware.com

Developer and marketer of the Knowledge-Paks® line of knowledge bases for corporate help desks, small businesses and home users. The Company's complete, ready-to-use knowlege bases are used worldwide by thousands of customer support analysts, LAN administrators and end users to solve problems. These knowledge bases embed into virtually all leading help desk and problem resolution software products and offer consistently correct answers, resulting in fewer escalations to second-level experts, higher productivity, increased user satisfaction and reduced costs. In addition, the Company's software tools and services enable organizations to author and deploy custom knowledge bases quickly and easily. It operates branch offices in Lake Forest and Santa Clara, CA; Chicago, IL; and Tokyo, Japan.

Officers: Jeffrey Pepper *P & CEO*
Rajiv Enand *SVP-Business DEV*
Suzanne Nicastro *VP-MKT*
Ted Teele *VP-Worldwide SAL*

Human Resources: Lee Marzka

Purchasing: Paul McDermott *CFO*

Total Employees............................110	**Regional Employees** 99		
Year Established 1991	**SIC Code**......................................7372		
Annual Revenues ($000)..5,000+			

Seton Hill Child Services, Inc.

1011 Old Salem Rd., Ste. 109
Greensburg, PA 15601
County: Westmoreland

Phone: (412) 836-0099
Fax: (412) 836-1346

Nonprofit provider of child care services to clients in Westmoreland County, PA. The Organization serves more than 400 children from six weeks through 12 years of age. Its centers offer Head Start, Early Head Start, Pre-School, Infant-Toddler, School Age, Evening Care, Saturday Care and Family Day Care Services. The Organization is funded through private client fees, federal funds for Head Start and Pennsylvania Title XX through the Child Care Assistance Program. Its facilities are located in Greensburg (2), Irwin, Jeannette (2), Latrobe, Mt. Pleasant and New Kensington, PA.

Officers: Sarah G. Dye *EDIR*
Toni Hajek *Program Coordinator*

Total Employees............................100	
Year Established 1966	**SIC Code**......................................8351

Seton Hill College

Seton Hill Dr.
Greensburg, PA 15601
County: Westmoreland

Phone: (412) 834-2200
Fax: (412) 830-4611
Internet Address: www.setonhill.edu

Nonprofit, Catholic liberal arts college for women. The College's 18 departments offers 42 majors, with the opportunity to self design a major. It awards the Bachelor of Arts, Bachelor of Fine Arts, Bachelor of Science, Bachelor of Music and Bachelor of Social Work degrees. It also offers preprofessional preparation for dentistry, law, medicine, occupational therapy, optometry, physical therapy, podiatry and veterinary medicine. At the graduate level, the College awards the Master of Arts degree in elementary education. It enrolls approximately 900 undergraduate students and 50 graduate students and has a student-faculty ratio of 13 to 1. The College's 200-acre campus, which contains 16 buildings, is located 35 miles east of Pittsburgh.

Officers: JoAnne W. Boyle, Ph.D. *P*
Mary Ann Gawelek, Ph.D. *VP-Academic Affairs*
Barbara C. Hinkle *VP-Enrollment Services*
Harold Gene Moss, Ph.D. *VP-Institutional Advancement*
Paul Roman *VP-FIN*
Sister Lois Sculco *VP-ADM & Student Services*

Human Resources: Connie Schober

Purchasing: Karen Sarneso

Total Employees............................277	**Regional Employees** 277
Year Established 1883	**SIC Code**....................................8221
Annual Revenues ($000) 15,000	

Seven Springs Farm, Inc.

R.R. 1
Champion, PA 15622
County: Westmoreland

Phone: (814) 352-7777
Fax: (814) 352-7911
Internet Address: www.7springs.com

Owner and operator of the Seven Springs Mountain Resort, a ski resort and convention center. The Resort offers accommodations in its hotel, lodge, cabins, chalets and mountain-top condominiums. It has more than ten shops, including a full-service hair salon, massage therapy and floral shop on the premises. Its dining facilities include a coffee shop, dining room, slopeside grill, pizza shop and several lounges with nightly entertainment. As for recreational facilities, the Resort offers an 18-hole championship golf course, horseback riding, indoor miniature golf, hiking, mountain biking, swimming, bowling, outdoor tennis courts and an Alpine slide. From December through March, it operates 30 slopes and trails for skiing, more than half of which are available for night skiing, and a half-pipe and snowboard park for snow boarders. The slopes are serviced by 10 chairlifts. The Resort is able to provide convention facilities for groups from 10 to 1,000 people. It has 18 meeting rooms located on three floors of the convention center wing and in the main lodge.

Officers: James N. McClure *P*
Scott L. Bender *VP-Resort OPR*
Frank S. Sujansky *SEC*
Frank J. Kovak *TRS*

Human Resources: Jean Pelliccione

Purchasing: Arnie Pritts

Total Employees...1,300 (W)/800 (S)	**Regional Employees** 684
Year Established 1932	**SIC Code** 7011

Shackelford's & Maxwell's, Inc.

827 Penn Ave.
Pittsburgh, PA 15221
County: Allegheny

S

Phone: (412) 247-1476
Fax: (412) 244-8633
Internet Address: www.ftd.com/shackmax

Full-service retail florist, garden center and interior landscaper. The Company specializes in commercial and residential floral products which include fresh flower arrangements, blooming plants, green plants, silk flowers and plants, fruit baskets, gourmet baskets, gift baskets, weddings and other related items. Its garden center provides new lawn mowers, repair for used mowers, snow blowers, annuals, shrubs, fertilizers and insecticides. Its interior landscape division specializes in business plantings and maintenance, and holiday decorating, removal and storage, serving office buildings, restaurants and malls. Through Wilkinsburg Wholesale Florist, the Company wholesales flowers. The Company operates 16 locations throughout the Pittsburgh metropolitan area.

Officers: Basil M. Vergato *P*
Michael A. Vergato *VP*
John Moores *SEC & TRS*

Human Resources: Bruce Vergato *VP (Purchasing)*

Total Employees...........................180
Year Established 1901
Annual Revenues ($000) 6,000
Regional Employees 180
SIC Code.......................................5992

Shandon, Inc.

171 Industry Dr.
Pittsburgh, PA 15275
County: Allegheny

Phone: (412) 788-1133
Fax: (412) 788-1138

Manufacturer and distributor of laboratory-related equipment and supplies. The Company's products include histology, cytology and pathology laboratory equipment and supplies; autopsy/mortuary tables, sinks, refrigerators and dissecting stations; blood gas and electrolyte analyzer supplies; plastic, injection-molded laboratory consumables; and laboratory stains and reagents. It operates additional facilities in England, Finland, France and Germany, with two subsidiaries, ALKO Diagnostics Corp. located in Holliston, MA, and Whale Scientific, Inc. located in Denver, CO. The Company is a subsidiary of Thermo Instrument Systems Inc., which is headquartered in Sunnyvale, CA, and listed on the ASE. The Company is also known as Shandon Lipshaw.

Officers: Colin Maddix *P & CEO*
Dennis Hall *VP-Quality*
William J. Hayes *VP-MKT*
William E. Moisey *VP-SAL*
Mark J. Zinsky *CFO*
Steven Jamison *OPR MGR*

Human Resources: Claudia Boykin

Total Employees.............................450
Year Established........................1967
Annual Revenues ($000) 75,000

Regional Employees 130
SIC Code......................................3821

Sheraton Inn Pittsburgh North

910 Sheraton Dr.
Mars, PA 16046
County: Butler

Phone: (412) 776-6900
Fax: (412) 776-1115

Hotel featuring 191 guest rooms and 16,726 square feet of function space which can accommodate groups of up to 1,500 people, including what it claims to be is one of the largest ballrooms in Pittsburgh measuring over 14,000 square feet. The Hotel also contains a complete health facility, heated indoor/outdoor swimming pool, jacuzzi, saunas, salon, travel agency, gift shop, florist, the Pavillion Cafe and Tremont House restaurants, and the Expression lounge. The Hotel is owned by Warrendale Hotel Assoc.

Officers: Dale Thomson *GMGR*
John P. Kress *DIR-SAL & MKT*

Human Resources: Ruth Naland

Total Employees............................225
Year Established........................1985

Regional Employees 225
SIC Code......................................7011

Sheridan Broadcasting Corp.

960 Penn Ave., Ste. 200
Pittsburgh, PA 15222
County: Allegheny

Phone: (412) 456-4000
Fax: (412) 391-3559

Broadcaster owning and operating radio stations. The Company's local stations are WAMO AM 860 (adult urban contemporary); WAMO FM 106.7 (urban); and WSSZ FM 107.1 (adult urban contemporary). The Company also has two radio networks, the American Urban Radio Network, with sales offices in

Chicago, IL, Detroit, MI, and New York, NY, and the Sheridan Broadcasting Network, which provide news, sports and entertainment to approximately 340 radio stations across the nation. In addition, the Company owns and operates radio station WUFO in Buffalo, NY.

Officers: Ronald R. Davenport *CH*
Jerry Lopes *P-American Urban Radio Network*
Peter J. Kochis *VP & CFO*
Alan L. Lincoln *VP & GMGR-WAMO & WSSZ*

Human Resources: Kathleen E. Gersna *SEC*

Total Employees...........................100   **Regional Employees** 65
SIC Code 4832

Sherrard, German & Kelly, P.C.

One Oliver Plaza, 35th Fl.
Pittsburgh, PA 15222
County: Allegheny

Phone: (412) 355-0200
Fax: (412) 261-6221

Provider of legal services with 20 attorneys. The Firm's practice areas include banking and consumer compliance, estate planning and administration, commercial litigation and arbitration, business and corporate law, and taxation.

Officers: Alexander C. Sherrard *P*
Robert D. German *MPTR*
Samuel J. Pasquarelli *MPTR*

Human Resources: Pennie A. Deluzio *(Purchasing)*

Total Employees..............................35   **Regional Employees** 35
Year Established 1990   **SIC Code** 8111

Shiloh Industrial Contractors, Inc.

204 Commerce Blvd.
P.O. Box 603
Lawrence, PA 15055
County: Washington

Phone: (412) 745-5460
Fax: (412) 745-8891

Commercial and industrial construction company performing civil, mechanical and electrical construction, maintenance and engineering. The Company's civil group engineers, procures and performs excavation, sewer lines, foundations, steel erection and modification, flatwork, sheeting, elevated steel platforms, pre-engineered metal buildings, equipment relocation and installation, brick and block work, and more. The mechanical group procures and performs the fabrication and installation of process pipe, ductwork, plumbing, underground utilities and more. The electrical group's services include high and low voltage distribution, instrumentation, process control, computers, control panels, maintenance, procurement, lighting, lightning protection, grounding, cathodic protection, emergency generators, high voltage distribution, substation construction and renovation. The Company primarily serves clients in the Tri-State area in a broad range of industries, including chemical, copper, glass, printing, coal, steel, zinc, recycling, utility, paper, plastics, transportation, petroleum, petrochemical, waste treatment and government.

Officers: William J. Janusey *P*
Edward H. Janusey *VP*
Michael A. Janusey *VP*
Robert E. Janusey *VP*
Robert E. Fetcko *VP*
Edward J. Budavich III *CON*

Total Employees	104	**Regional Employees**	104
Year Established	1986	**SIC Code**	1542
Annual Revenues ($000)	8-10,000		

Siemens Business Communications Systems, Inc.

Penn Center West II
Pittsburgh, PA 15276
County: Allegheny

Phone: (412) 788-1180
Fax: (412) 787-4584

Provider of private telecommunications solutions and computer telephony integration (CTI) applications. The Company claims to have pioneered CTI, as well as PBX-to-host and -LAN interfaces. It offers total telecommunications and network solutions for businesses of all sizes. The Company, which is headquartered in Santa Clara, CA, operates 70 branch offices nationwide. The Pittsburgh office provides sales and service to clients throughout Western Pennsylvania and Northern West Virginia. The Company is a subsidiary of Siemens AG, which is headquartered in Munich, Germany, and listed on the Frankfurt Stock Exchange.

Officers: Diane B. Salvatora *Branch General MGR*

Total Employees	5,800	**Regional Employees**	50
Year Established	1969	**SIC Code**	3679

Simmons Co., Inc., R. A.

5390 Progress Blvd.
Bethel Park, PA 15102
County: Allegheny

S

Phone: (412) 831-7400
Fax: (412) 833-6360

Distributor of hardware and software products, doing business as Simmons Business Systems. The Company's product line includes Brandt Inc. currency equipment and retail systems; Konica Business Machines, U.S.A. digital and analog photocopiers and printers; IBM/Lexmark laser printers and typewriters; IBM PC's and accessories; and Panasonic facsimile. It also provides service and support for its products. The Company directly markets its products to corporations, educational institutions, nonprofit organizations, law firms, government agencies and other entities in Western Pennsylvania and parts of West Virginia. Branch offices are located in Johnstown, PA; and Morgantown and Wheeling, WV.

Officers: Ronald A. Simmons *P*
David A. Ross *VP-Brandt*
Joseph M. Solomon *VP-Office*

Human Resources: Edward B. Murphy *VP-FIN (Purchasing)*

Total Employees............................60
Year Established 1975

Regional Employees 45
SIC Code....................................5044

Sisterson & Co. LLP, D. G.

Grant Bldg., 310 Grant St., Ste. 2101
Pittsburgh, PA 15219
County: Allegheny

Phone: (412) 281-2025
Fax: (412) 338-4597

Certified public accounting firm whose primary focus is serving the needs of privately owned companies that are headquartered in the Tri-State region. The Firm's services include accounting, auditing, business/corporate transactions, strategic and business plans, litigation and claims services, wealth accumulation and retention planning, individual and partnership taxation, corporate taxation, business acquisitions-due diligence, financial investigations and corporate finance. It has extensive experience working with manufacturing, wholesaling, venture capital, real estate, oil and gas, and investment companies.

Officers: David W. Simpson *MPTR*
Frank J. Mandell *PTR*
John J. Sieger *PTR*
William E. Troup *PTR*
Grant M. Wirth *PTR*

Human Resources: Harry J. Keefe

Total Employees	72	**Regional Employees**	72
Year Established	1926	**SIC Code**	8721

SKC Inc.

863 Valley View Rd.
Eighty Four, PA 15330
County: Washington

Phone: (412) 941-9701
Fax: (412) 941-1369
Internet Address: www.skcinc.com

Manufacturer of air sampling equipment and sample collection media. The Company's equipment is used to determine the amount and types of chemicals in air for safety and workplace compliance, industrial hygiene and occupational health studies, indoor air quality maintenance, and environmental air sampling applications. Its instruments include air sample pumps for personal and area sampling, calibrators and sampling accessories. The Company claims to be the world's largest producer of sorbent sample tubes, manufacturing over 100 different types of tubes for sampling more than 500 different gases and vapors. Its other sample collection media includes gas sample bags, filters, impingers and passive organic vapor samplers. The Company's products are distributed in the United States through its headquarters office located at the above address, and branch offices in Fullerton, CA; Houston, TX; and Appomattox, VA. Worldwide distribution is handled through a branch office in Blanford Forum, Dorset, England, and distributors in 44 countries.

Officers: Richard L. Guild *P*

Human Resources: Nannie Brown

Purchasing: Deborah Orpen

Total Employees	130-150	**Regional Employees**	85
Year Established	1962	**SIC Code**	3829

Skelly and Loy, Inc.

520 Seco Rd.
Monroeville, PA 15146
County: Allegheny

S

Phone: (412) 856-1676
Fax: (412) 856-5730
Internet Address: www.info-mine.com/skelly.loy

International consulting firm providing professional services in engineering and environmental sciences. The Firm is organized into six service areas. The Cultural Resources Service Group's staff includes archaeologists, soil scientists and historic resource surveyors, and are responsible for meeting state and federal regulatory agency requirements. The Engineering Service Group functions within two primary engineering disciplines, mining and civil engineering. The mining segment can guide mine development from initial exploration and feasibility evaluation through delivery of the mine product to the user. The civil segment concentrates on site development, wastewater treatment and construction stake-out projects. The Harrisburg and Pittsburgh Environmental Service Groups provide their environmental services to the Pennsylvania Department of Transportation, as well as a wide range of private clients and Departments of Transportation in other states. The Waste Management Service Group provides expertise in environmental waste and related fields, including Phase I environmental audits, remediation, groundwater monitoring and remediation, and asbestos and lead-based paint studies. The Technical Services Group's services include CADD, drafting, technical support, graphics and publishing, word processing, filing and other general functions. Since its inception, the Firm has provided consulting services in more than 20 states and in 16 foreign countries. The Firm is headquartered in Harrisburg, PA.

Officers: Sandra Loy Bell *CEO*
John W. Gunnett *P*
Robert E. McClure *EVP*
Mark A. Williams *EVP*

Human Resources: James S. Nevada *SEC & TRS*

Total Employees	130	**Regional Employees**	62
Year Established	1969	**SIC Code**	8744
Annual Revenues ($000)	10,100		

Slippery Rock University

17 Maltby Dr.
Slippery Rock, PA 16057
County: Butler

Phone: (412) 738-0512
Fax: (412) 738-2266

Nonprofit, public, liberal arts educational institution awarding bachelor's and master's degrees. The University's four colleges, the College of Education, the College of Health and Human Services, the College of Information Science and Business Administration, and the College of Arts and Sciences together offer more than 65 majors along with an extensive study-abroad program. A large proportion of its students major in education. The University also operates a graduate school and a program offering Doctoral degrees in physical therapy and nursing. With an approximate enrollment of 7,500, including students from 65 foreign countries, approximately 1,600 students graduate annually. The University offers off-campus programs, including classes in Cranberry, PA. It is a member of the State System of Higher Education and funded by the Commonwealth of Pennsylvania.

Officers: G. Warren Smith II, Ph.D. *P*
Charles T. Curry *VP-Administrative Affairs & FIN*
Charles D. Foust *VP-Academic Affairs & Provost*
Sharon Johnson, Ph.D. *VP-Student Affairs*
Robert Mollenhauer *VP-University Advancement*

Human Resources: Lynne Motyl

Total Employees............................858	**Regional Employees** 858
Year Established 1889	**SIC Code**....................................8221
Annual Revenues ($000) 73,500	

Smith Barney, Inc.

One PPG Place, 13th Fl.
Pittsburgh, PA 15222
County: Allegheny

Phone: (412) 392-5800
Fax: (412) 392-0318

Full-service broker-dealer and investment banking firm. Other Pittsburgh area offices are located in Monroeville and downtown Pittsburgh at One Mellon Bank Center. The Company, which is headquartered in New York, NY, operates approximately 500 branch offices throughout the United States. It is a subsidiary of The Travelers Corp., which is headquartered in Hartford, CT, and listed on the NYSE.

Officers: Samuel Robb, Jr. *SVP & Resident MGR-One PPG Place Branch & Monroeville Branch*

Regional Employees....................130	**SIC Code** 6211

Smith Co., A&B

4250 Old William Penn Hwy.
P.O. Box 1776, Pittsburgh, PA 15230
Monroeville, PA 15146
County: Allegheny

Phone: (412) 858-5400
Fax: (412) 372-3734
Internet Address: www.absmith.com

Retailer, wholesaler and distributor of art, engineering, drafting and surveying products. The Company claims to be the Tri-State area's largest supplier of these items. It represents over 300 different manufacturers and carries in excess of 50,000 different products. The Company markets art supplies, specialized art products, graphic art materials, Hewlett-Packard inkjet plotters and inkjet supplies, Xerographic copiers and supplies, recycled laser toner cartridges for laser printers and copiers, surveying equipment (sells, rents, adjusts and repairs the equipment), furniture and accessories, general supplies, and a variety of engineering, architectural and drafting supplies and equipment, including custom-printed forms. The Company also performs its own converting in-house from jumbo mill rolls of paper. This capability allows it to convert plotter, xerographic and diazo papers as well as vellums, tracing papers and films to fit customer requirements. In addition, the Company operates two retail facilities, Colours-The Art Store, located at Sixth and Wood Sts. in downtown Pittsburgh, and Mini-Art Mart, located at the above address.

Officers: Stuart J. Smith *CEO*

Human Resources: Mark Spirer

Purchasing: Martin H. Smith *P*

Total Employees	30	**Regional Employees**	30
Year Established	1914	**SIC Code**	5049

Smith Ford, Inc., Bob

3200 Library Rd.
Pittsburgh, PA 15234
County: Allegheny

Phone: (412) 881-0001
Fax: (412) 881-0220

Automobile dealership selling Ford vehicles. The Company offers a full-line of new and used cars and provides parts, service and body shop repairs.

Officers: Dolores Smith *OWN*
Anthony Godino *SEC & TRS*

Total Employees	105	**Regional Employees**	105
Year Established	1971	**SIC Code**	5511

Smith, Inc., A. J.

4700 Clairton Blvd.
Pittsburgh, PA 15236
County: Allegheny

Phone: (412) 885-2799
Fax: (412) 885-2279
Internet Address: www.ajsmith.com

Commercial contractor specializing in interiors focusing on the retail, office and hospital markets nationwide.

Officers: Allen J. Smith *P*
Joseph Carozza *Project MGR*
Richard Celani *Estimator*

Human Resources: Robin Sweich

Purchasing: Mike Reinhardt

Total Employees	150	**Regional Employees**	150
Year Established	1985	**SIC Code**	1542
Annual Revenues ($000)	10,000		

SmithKline Beecham Consumer Healthcare

100 Beecham Dr.
P.O. Box 1467, Pittsburgh, PA 15230
Pittsburgh, PA 15205
County: Allegheny

Phone: (412) 928-1000
Fax: (412) 928-1080

Developer, manufacturer and marketer of pharmaceuticals and vaccines, consumer medicines, health-related products and clinical testing services. The Company's offerings include cough and cold remedies, antacids, smoking cessation products, oral hygiene products and other general medicines marketed under such brand names as Aquafresh, Contac, N'ice, Nicoderm, Nicorette, Oxy, Sominex, Sucrets, Tagamet, Tums and Vivarin. The Company is a business sector of SmithKline Beecham Plc, which is headquartered in London, England, and listed on the London Stock Exchange. The local facility oversees the Company's North American Consumer Healthcare operations. Its manufacturing plants are located in St. Louis, MO; Clifton, NJ; and Aiken, SC. A research and development center is located in Parsippany, NJ.

Officers: John B. Ziegler *EVP*
Douglas B. Cox *VP & DIR-MKT Services & Corporate Communications*
Joseph J. McEnroe *VP & DIR-FIN & ADM*
Alan B. Schaefer *VP & DIR-SAL & Oral Care*

Human Resources: William E. Mills *VP & DIR-Human Resources*

Total Employees	1,900	**Regional Employees**	300
Year Established	1830	**SIC Code**	2834
Annual Revenues ($000)	700,000+		

Snavely Forest Products, Inc.

660 Delwar Rd.
P.O. Box 9808, Pittsburgh, PA 15227
Pittsburgh, PA 15236
County: Allegheny

Phone: (412) 885-4000
Fax: (412) 885-6050

Wholesaler of lumber and engineered wood products, provider of millwork and distributor of related products.

Officers: Christian M. Snavely *CH*
Stephen V. Snavely *P & CEO*
Donald L. Steinhart *EVP*
John A. Stockhausen *VP-FIN & CFO*

Human Resources: Susan Fitzsimmons

Purchasing: John Dignazio

Total Employees	170	**Regional Employees**	60
Year Established	1902	**SIC Code**	5031
Annual Revenues ($000)	133,000		

Snodgrass, A.C., S. R.

101 Bradford Rd., Ste. 100
Wexford, PA 15090
County: Allegheny

Phone: (412) 934-0344
Fax: (412) 934-0345
Internet Address: www.srsnodgrass.com

Certified public accounting firm claiming to rank as one of the top 100 accounting firms in the United States and as one of Pittsburgh's largest regional accounting firms. It offers a full range of audit, tax, profit enhancement, outsourcing and management consulting services to middle-market clients throughout the Tri-State area. The Firm services clients in a variety of fields, including banking, auto dealers, health care, nonprofit organizations, construction, manufacturing, government and closely held businesses. It operates branch offices in Ashtabula, Mentor and Steubenville, OH; Beaver Falls, PA (110 Central Sq. Dr.); and Wheeling, WV.

Officers: John V. Kinnunen *P*
Richard A. Rocereto *MPTR-Beaver Falls, PA Office*
John (Jack) R. Salvetti *MPTR-Wexford, PA Office*

Human Resources: Robert C. Padgett

Total Employees...........................115   **Regional Employees** 57
Year Established 1946   **SIC Code**....................................8721
Annual Revenues ($000) 11,500

Snyder Associated Cos., Inc.

409 Butler Rd.
P.O. Box 1022
Kittanning, PA 16201
County: Armstrong

Phone: (412) 548-8101
Fax: (412) 545-2989

Owner and operator of approximately 17 different companies. Two significant subsidiaries are Allegheny Mineral Corp. (AMC), a producer of Type "A" lime-stone and pulverized lime products, and Glacial Sand & Gravel Co. (GS&GC), a producer of Type "A" concrete, and masonry sands and gravel. Both companies are headquartered at the above address. AMC, with a total of 50 employees, oper-ates plants located in Harrisville, PA, and Slippery Rock, PA. GS&GC, with a total of 35 employees, operates two plants located in Bridgeburg, PA.

Officers: Elmer A. Snyder *P*

Total Employees...........................350
Year Established 1941   **SIC Code**....................................1442

Society of Automotive Engineers, Inc.

400 Commonwealth Dr.
Warrendale, PA 15096
County: Allegheny

Phone: (412) 776-4841
Fax: (412) 776-5760

Nonprofit educational and scientific network of engineers, business executives, educators and students from more than 80 countries who come together to share information and exchange ideas for advancing the engineering of mobility sys-tems through meetings, books, technical papers, magazines, reports, continuing education programs and electronic databases. The Organization is a major source of technical information and expertise used in designing, building, maintaining and operating self-propelled vehicles, whether land-, sea-, air- or space-based. It collects, organizes, stores and disseminates information on cars, trucks, aircraft, space vehicles, off-highway vehicles, marine equipment and engines of all types. Some 15,000 individuals comprise the volunteer membership of more than 600 of the organization's technical committees, each dealing in detail with a specific subject vital to a particular mobility-related industry or engineering discipline. The committees write and maintain thousands of mobility engineering standards used every day by industry and government; more than 600 new automotive and aerospace engineering standards are added each year. The Organization's monthly magazines, Automotive Engineering and Aerospace Engineering, are editorially focused to inform over 140,000 engineers, business executives and government officials around the world about the latest mobility engineering developments. Its Global Mobility Database references over 120,000 books, magazine articles, standards, technical papers and news sources from around the world. Other offices are located in Washington, D.C., and Troy, MI. A subsidiary, the Service Technicians Society is also located at the above address, with an additional subsidiary, the Performance Review Institute located in Warrendale, PA at 402 Commonwealth Dr.

Officers: David C. Holloway, Ph.D. *P*
Max E. Rumbaugh, Jr. *EVP & SEC*
Ray Morris *EDIR-Products & Services*
Stanley C. Theobald *DIR-FIN & ADM Group*
Will Willems *DIR-Publications, MKT & Public Relations Group*

Human Resources: Maryann Ihrig *MGR-Human Resources*

Total Employees	350	**Regional Employees**	260
Year Established	1905	**SIC Code**	8699
Annual Revenues ($000)	35,800		

Solid State Measurements, Inc.

110 Technology Dr.
Pittsburgh, PA 15275
County: Allegheny

Phone: (412) 490-0268
Fax: (412) 490-0271

Designer, manufacturer and marketer of advanced test equipment to the global semiconductor industry. The Company claims that it has been the leading supplier of spreading resistance profiling (SRP) since it was founded by the inventor of the technique. The SRP products are complimented by a comprehensive line of capacitance-voltage (CV) systems. The Company claims that it currently enjoys the dominant worldwide market position in both SRP and CV systems. They are used in epitaxial silicon process development laboratories and in process control for microprocessors and memory devices. The Company operates customer support facilities in San Jose, CA; Dresden, Germany; and Tokyo, Japan.

Officers: Robert G. Mazur *CH*
Charles A. Thomas *P & CEO*
Kathleen M. Hassett *VP-FIN*
John R. Rogers *VP-ENG*
Mark Wilson *VP-MKT*
Blake Wotring *VP-OPR*

Total Employees............................70
Year Established........................1970
Annual Revenues ($000)...11,500

Regional Employees....................60
SIC Code....................................3823

Sony Chemicals Corp. of America

1001 Technology Dr.
Mt. Pleasant, PA 15666
County: Westmoreland

Phone: (412) 696-7500
Fax: (412) 696-7555
Internet Address: www.sony.com

Manufacturer of thermal transfer ribbons for bar code label printers serving clients throughout North and South America. The Company is a subsidiary of Sony Chemicals Corp., which is headquartered in Tokyo, Japan. The Company is located at the Sony Technology Center-Pittsburgh (STCP), which is, physically, the largest Sony facility in the world encompassing 800 acres. The STCP also houses operations of American Video Glass Co. and Sony Electronics, Inc. (see separate profiles).

Officers: Joseph P. Morgan, Jr. *P*
Mark Pihl *VP-OPR*
Rick Kelly *DIR-Emerging Markets*
Kevin Young *DIR-Business DEV*

Human Resources: Sally Mueller *Human Resources DIR*

Purchasing: David Corbin

Total Employees..........................140
Year Established........................1962

Regional Employees..................140
SIC Code....................................5065

Sony Electronics, Inc.

1001 Technology Dr.
Mt. Pleasant, PA 15666
County: Westmoreland

Phone: (412) 696-7000
Fax: (412) 696-7211
Internet Address: www.sony.com

Manufacturer of rear projection and 35″ Trinitron® television, 7″ and 35″ cathode ray tubes for large screen and rear projection television and aperture grills for Sony Trinitron televisions. The Company is headquartered in Park Ridge, NJ. It is a subsidiary of the Sony Corp. of America (SCOA), which is headquartered in New York, NY. SCOA is a subsidiary of the Sony Corp., which is headquartered in Tokyo, Japan, and is listed on the New York and Tokyo Stock Exchanges. The Company is located at the Sony Technology Center-Pittsburgh (STCP), which is, physically, the largest Sony facility in the world encompassing 800 acres. The STCP also houses operations of Sony Chemicals Corp. of America and American Video Glass. (see separate profiles).

Officers: Tadakatsu Hasebe *P-ENG & MFG Group*
Jim Bass *VP-Videoscope Business*
Shohei Hasegawa *VP-Display Device Pittsburgh*
Hiroshi Tsuki *VP-ENG*
Michael Koff *Public Relations MGR*

Human Resources: Lou Ann Walters *Human Resources MGR*

Regional Employees ....1,200+
Year Established 1990   **SIC Code** 3671

South Hills Health System

Coal Valley Rd.
P.O. Box 18119
Pittsburgh, PA 15236
County: Allegheny

Phone: (412) 469-5000
Fax: (412) 469-7049
Internet Address: www.shhspgh.org

Nonprofit health care network with a medical staff comprised of more than 400 physicians in over 32 specialties, including more than 80 primary care physicians throughout its service area. The System consists of a variety of facilities offering an array of medical and related services. Located at the above address, Jefferson Hospital provides comprehensive inpatient and outpatient medical services and emergency care with 392 beds; HOME Systems provides medical equipment and supplies for the home; and Jefferson Surgery Center is an outpatient, same-day surgery center connected to Jefferson Hospital. Located at 1800 West St. in

Homestead, PA, Homestead Emergency & Family Medicine Center provides emergency, outpatient and family medical care; Home Health Agency provides nursing and support services in the home; The Foundation provides fund-raising in support of the health system's programs and services for the community; Willis Nursing Center provides skilled nursing care and rehabilitation services with 74 beds; and The Homestead, a personal care residence, provides 24-hour personal care and supervision of the elderly in a family living environment. The Counseling Center provides counseling and support for individuals and families at its 4129 Brownsville Rd. location in the Brentwood section of Pittsburgh. Family Hospice, located at 1910 Cochran Rd. in the South Hills section of Pittsburgh, provides skilled care and support for terminally ill patients and their families. The System's affiliates include Jefferson Radiation Oncology Center in Pleasant Hills, PA, and South Hills Magnetic Imaging Institute in Bethel Park, PA.

Officers: William R. Jennings *P & CEO*
James Nania *EVP & CFO*
Gary Perecko *EVP & COO*

Human Resources: Robert Valasek *VP-Human Resources*

Purchasing: Robert Cunningham *Corporate DIR-Materials MGT*

Total Employees..........2,755	**Regional Employees** 2,755
Year Established 1973	**SIC Code**..........8062
Annual Revenues ($000) 243,653	

Southwest Services, Inc.

2866 Glenmore Ave.
Pittsburgh, PA 15216
County: Allegheny

Phone: (412) 531-4803
Fax: (412) 531-9230

Nonprofit organization serving older adults, providing a continuum of care that fosters general well-being and empowers adults age 60 and over to live independently and with dignity in their own homes for as long as possible. The Organization performs essential, innovative and affordable services on two primary levels. Community Services for healthy, active older adults are rendered through eight Senior Community Centers. Programming includes nutrition management, socialization and recreation, life enrichment education, health promotion, volunteer activities, information and referral, annual flu shot clinics, income tax assistance, energy fund and rent rebate assistance, and transportation assistance. Care Management and In-Home Service Programs support frail elderly persons who are at risk of institutionalization. Services may include home-delivered meals, attendant care, in-home counseling, escort driving, telephone reassurance or a senior companion, or an array of other services available through the Allegheny County Department of Aging's service network and accessed via the Organization. The Organization serves clients in southwestern Allegheny County and reaches over 10,000 individuals annually. The Senior Community Centers are located in Bethel Park, Bridgeville, Carnegie, Coraopolis, Dormont, McKees Rocks, Mt. Lebanon and Oakdale, PA.

Officers: Virginia R. Jurofcik *EDIR*
Ruth Ann Howes *DIR-Social Services*
Laura Karl *DIR-DEV*
Patricia P. Oehm *DIR-Community Services*
Nancy A. Shade *DIR-In-Home Services*
Marlene Virgili *Accountant*

Human Resources: Mary McDermott *Executive Office MGR*

Total Employees.............................55   **Regional Employees** 55
Year Established 1973   **SIC Code**....................................8322

Southwestern Pennsylvania Corp.

The Waterfront Bldg., 200 First Ave.
Pittsburgh, PA 15222
County: Allegheny

Phone: (412) 391-5590
Fax: (412) 391-9160

Nonprofit administrative organization for the Southwestern Pennsylvania Regional Planning Commission (Commission) and the Southwestern Pennsylvania Regional Development Council, Inc. (Council), both of which are located at the above address and facilitate development in Southwestern Pennsylvania. Both agencies serve the City of Pittsburgh and Allegheny, Armstrong, Beaver, Butler, Washington and Westmoreland counties. The Council also serves Fayette, Greene and Indiana counties. The Commission, which was formed in 1962, has always been involved in transportation planning for its member units of government. Since 1972, it has also been the designated Metropolitan Planning Organization for the region, responsible for preparing the Long Range Transportation Plan and the Transportation Improvement Program. The Commission is now involved in a range of activities, including local government assistance, business information services, airport systems planning and technical assistance to transit agencies. The Council was created in 1992 to administer a series of state and federal economic development programs. It serves as the Local Development District in southwestern Pennsylvania for the Appalachian Regional Commission. Through its Enterprise Development Program, strategic planning initiatives and technical assistance to local government, the Council helps small- and medium-size businesses expand and increase their employment opportunities. It provides direct services in the areas of business financing, export development, government procurement and electronic market matching.

Officers: John M. Allen, Jr. *CH*
Larry Dunn *VCH*
Robert Kochanowski *P & CEO; EDIR-Southwestern Pennsylvania*

Regional Planning Commission
Charles M. DiPietro *VP; DIR-Transportation Planning-Southwestern Pennsylvania Regional Planning Commission*

Human Resources: Vincent M. Massaro *SEC & TRS; DIR-ADM & CON-Southwestern Pennsylvania Regional Planning Commission (Purchasing)*

Total Employees............................48	**Regional Employees** 48
Year Established 1962	**SIC Code**....................................9532
Annual Revenues ($000) 4,000			

Southwestern Pennsylvania Human Services, Inc.

Eastgate 8
Monessen, PA 15062
County: Westmoreland

Phone: (412) 684-9000
Fax: (412) 684-6227
Internet Address: www.dp.net/~sphs/index.html

Nonprofit provider of a variety of human services through its subsidiaries. Connect, Inc. offers services for the homeless; Diversified Human Services, Inc. operates mental health clinics and a children's day care center, and offers a variety of programs for people with mental retardation, as well as community-based programs for older adults such as senior citizen centers and assistance to homebound seniors; Mon Valley Community Health Services, Inc. operates a primary care clinic and a family planning clinic, and offers the WIC program and a GED program; and the Southwestern Pennsylvania Area Agency on Aging, Inc. manages programs for older adults in Fayette, Greene and Washington Counties, PA. All of these subsidiaries are located at the above address. Additional subsidiaries include Comprehensive Substance Abuse Services of Southwestern PA., Inc., located in Greensburg, PA, which provides substance abuse, DUI and underage drinking rehabilitation services; and Health Plus, Inc., located in Donora, PA, which is a home health agency that provides visiting nurses for those who are homebound, among other services. The Organization's programs and services are available at 50 locations throughout Fayette, Greene, Washington and Westmoreland Counties, PA. The Organization and its subsidiaries are members of the Mon Valley United Way, which is also located at the above address.

Officers: Donald H. Goughler *CEO & EVP*

Human Resources: Jeff B. Mascara *Executive-Corporate ADM*

Purchasing: Lawrence J. Bender *Executive-Corporate FIN*

Total Employees..........................478	**Regional Employees** 474
Year Established 1964	**SIC Code**....................................8322
Annual Revenues ($000) 32,000			

Spang & Co.

100 Brugh Ave.
P.O. Box 751, Butler, PA 16003
Butler, PA 16001
County: Butler

Phone: (412) 287-8781
Fax: (412) 285-4721

Manufacturer of electronic components, toys and electric panelboards through three divisions and a subsidiary. The Magnetics Division, with facilities in Booneville, AR, and at 795 E. Butler Rd. in East Butler, PA, produces magnetic cores and ferrites for the electronics industry. The Spang Power Control Division, located at 5241 Lake St. in Sandy Lake, PA, manufactures transformers, transducers, control panels and power control systems for the automotive, glass and construction sectors. The Spang Specialty Metals Division, located at 154 E. Brook Lane in Butler, PA, manufactures specialty alloys primarily for the electronics industry. Today's Kid Inc., with facilities in Booneville, AR, and Dallas, TX, is a subsidiary that manufactures plastic toys sold in retail stores. The Company distributes its products to international markets.

Officers: Frank E. Rath, Sr. *CH & CEO*
Robert A. Rath *VCH*
Frank E. Rath, Jr. *P*
Charles R. Dorsch *VP-FIN*
William T. Marsh *VP & GC*
Robert A. Rath, Jr. *VP*
Fred J. Artz *TRS*

Human Resources: Robert K. Brown *VP-Personnel*
Stacy Riscoe *Corporate Recruiter*

Purchasing: Susan Seksinski

Total Employees	1,400	**Regional Employees**	700
Year Established	1894	**SIC Code**	6719
Annual Revenues ($000)	120,000		

Specialty Consultants, Inc.

Gateway Towers, Ste. 2710
Pittsburgh, PA 15222
County: Allegheny

Phone: (412) 355-8200
Fax: (412) 355-0465

Internet Address: www.specon.com

Executive search recruiting firm specializing in the real estate, construction and pharmaceutical/biotech research industries. The Firm provides its services to companies nationwide.

Officers: Charles J. Abbott *P*
Joseph R. DiSanti *EVP*
Charles C. Groom *VP*
Paul J. Lewis *MDIR-Real Estate*

Human Resources: Alan R. Clark *DIR-MGT Services*

Purchasing: Frances A. Lipinski

Total Employees............................40	**Regional Employees** 40
Year Established 1970	**SIC Code**......................................7361

Specialty Printing, Inc.

Third St. & Pennsylvania Railroad
P.O. Box 104
Charleroi, PA 15022
County: Washington

Phone: (412) 489-9583
Fax: (412) 489-8219

Web offset commercial printer with cold- and heat-set capabilities. The Company specializes in a number of different products geared for direct mail and newspaper inserts.

Officers: Joseph W. DeStefon *P*

Human Resources: Arlene A. DeStefon *SEC & TRS*

Purchasing: Tim King *Plant MGR*

Total Employees............................40	**Regional Employees** 40
Year Established 1979	**SIC Code**......................................2752
Annual Revenues ($000)..5-6,000	

Springer, Bush & Perry, P.C.

Two Gateway Center, 15th Fl.
Pittsburgh, PA 15222
County: Allegheny

Phone: (412) 281-4900
Fax: (412) 261-1645

Law firm with 24 attorneys providing a broad range of professional services to businesses and individuals. The Firm's business and institutional practice areas include general corporate and business law, commercial litigation, real estate acquisition, development and financing, health and insurance law, employee relations, bankruptcy, creditors' rights and collections, antitrust and trade practices, franchising, trademarks, municipal and school law, corporate tax law, nonprofit corporations, and public and private finance. Its personal practice areas include personal injury and property damage claims, general litigation, residential real estate, divorce and family law, custody and support, adoption, private contract claims, individual tax law, wills, trusts and estate planning, and estate administration. A branch office is located in Moon Township, PA.

Officers: Edward L. Springer *P & CEO*
Joseph Friedman *VP-Litigation*
Robert E. Harper *VP-Personal Services*
Thomas P. Peterson *VP-Business & Financial*
W. Ronald Stout *VP & COO*
Michael J. Hennessy *AVP-MIS*
Henry R. Johnston *AVP-Personal Services*
John F. Perry *AVP-Litigation*
James H. Webster *AVP-Business & Financial*
Stephen F. Ban *SEC*
James C. Kletter *AST-SEC & TRS*

Human Resources: Donald A. Toth *Administrator (Purchaser)*

Total Employees............................43	**Regional Employees** 43
Year Established 1971	**SIC Code** 8111

Sprint Business Services Group

Seven Parkway Center, Ste. 810
Pittsburgh, PA 15220
County: Allegheny

Phone: (412) 937-0310
Fax: (412) 937-0390
Internet Address: www.sprint.com

Provider of business communications, both voice and data, to all business users, including small businesses to global corporations. The local office is a part of Sprint's Business Services Group, which is headquartered in Dallas, TX. It is a segment of Sprint's Long Distance Division, which is headquartered in Kansas City, MO. Sprint Corp. is headquartered in Westwood, KS, and is listed on the NYSE. The local office serves clients in Western Pennsylvania and Northern West Virginia.

Officers: Joe Conlon *Branch MGR-General Business*
William Seneca *Branch MGR-Mid & Majors*

Total Employees......................53,000	**Regional Employees** 45
Year Established 1986	**SIC Code**....................................4813
Annual Revenues ($000) 15,000,000	

St. Anne Home, Inc.

685 Angela Dr.
Greensburg, PA 15601
County: Westmoreland

Phone: (412) 837-6070
Fax: (412) 837-6099

Nonprofit provider of skilled and intermediate nursing care to residents of Southwestern Pennsylvania. In addition to skilled and intermediate nursing care, the 125-bed facility offers individualized Alzheimer's care, geriatric rehabilitation therapies (occupational, physical and speech), restorative nursing care to promote independence, IV therapy, short-term respite care, social and recreational activities, daily religious services, pastoral care, personal savings and checking account management, nutrition counseling and special diet consultation, pharmacy services, dental and podiatry services, and physician services five days per week and on call. Located on the same 10-acre campus is the Villa Angela at St. Anne Home, a 44-unit assisted living apartment building offering residents a wide variety of wellness services, including health assessments, rehabilitation and exercise programs, and medication management, as well as assistance with daily routines, such as cooking, laundry and cleaning. St. Anne Home is a ministry of the Felician Sisters of Pennsylvania.

Officers: Sister Bernice Marie Fiedor *Administrator*
Jeffrey Long *Associate Administrator*

Human Resources: John Alwine *DIR*

Total Employees............................200	**Regional Employees** 200
Year Established 1964	**SIC Code**......................................8051

St. Barnabas Health System

5850 Meridian Rd.
Gibsonia, PA 15044
County: Allegheny

Phone: (412) 443-0700
Fax: (412) 443-4210

Nonprofit organization providing a continuum of medical care including general medicine, general dentistry, specialty outpatient rehabilitative care, home care, retirement living and skilled nursing care through five subsidiaries. The Organization operates on two campuses with more than 330 acres. Valencia Woods Nursing Center is located on the campus at 85 Charity Place in Valencia, PA, while the other facilities are located at the above address. Its two skilled nursing facilities, St. Barnabas Nursing Home and Valencia Woods, provide short- and long-term care to patients with financial need. Together, the facilities have 339 beds. St. Barnabas Medical Center provides managed care through a team of more than 25 doctors, dentists, specialists and medical professionals who together treat more than 23,000 outpatients each year. Through its Home Care Department, a professional staff provides a variety of services for its clients in order to allow them to continue living at home. St. Barnabas Retirement Village offers worry-free living for persons age 65 and over. It operates 252 one-, two- and three-bedroom apartments. St. Barnabas Charitable Foundation is the fund-raising arm of the Organization. The foundation engages in a year-long drive to raise funds for poor and needy nursing home patients. Through the foundation, more than $3.2 million in free medical care and rehabilitation are provided each year.

Officers: William V. Day *P & CEO*
Joseph Hlinka *SVP*
Judith Wagner *VP*
Nancy Brem *AST-VP*

Human Resources: Margaret Horton

Total Employees............................474	**Regional Employees** 474
Year Established 1900	**SIC Code**.....................................8051

St. Clair Health Corp.

1000 Bower Hill Rd.
Pittsburgh, PA 15243
County: Allegheny

Phone: (412) 561-4900
Fax: (412) 572-6752

Nonprofit organization operating the St. Clair Hospital (also located at the above address), a 308-bed facility with a staff of more than 490 physicians representing 10 departments and 31 sub-specialties. In addition to a complete range of medical services, the hospital offers a variety of community-based educational and support groups. It serves residents in the South Hills communities of Baldwin, Bethel Park, Bridgeville, Carnegie, Castle Shannon, Collier, Dormont, Greentree, Heidelberg, Scott Township, South Fayette and Upper St. Clair, PA. Other subsidiaries of the Company include St. Clair Health Ventures, Inc., St. Clair Management Resources, Inc. and St. Clair Memorial Hospital Foundation.

Officers: Gary J. Zentner *CH-St. Clair Memorial Hospital*
Benjamin E. Snead *P & CEO-St. Clair Memorial Hospital*

Total Employees........................1,102	**Regional Employees** 1,102
Year Established 1954	**SIC Code**.....................................8062

St. Francis Health System

4401 Penn Ave.
Pittsburgh, PA 15224
County: Allegheny

Phone: (412) 622-4343
Fax: (412) 622-4858
Internet Address: www.sfhs.edu

Nonprofit health system, with 1,434 licensed beds and 1,217 physicians, comprised of the St. Francis Medical Center, St. Francis Central Hospital, St. Francis Hospital of New Castle, St. Francis Health Care Services, St. Francis Diversified Corp., St. Francis Health Foundation, St. Francis Financial Corp., Bellaire Health Center (Bellaire, OH), Harrisville Health Center (Harrisville, OH) and Powhatan Health Center (Powhatan Point, OH). The 630-bed St. Francis Medical Center at 400 45th St. in the Lawrenceville area of Pittsburgh is the System's regional referral and flagship hospital and claims to be one of Western Pennsylvania's largest tertiary care facilities. It operates St. Francis Cranberry in Cranberry Township, PA, which includes the 150-bed St. Francis Nursing Center-North; an ambulatory care center offering 24-hour emergency, radiology and laboratory services; and a surgery center providing outpatient surgery in a variety of medical specialties. It also operates the 150-bed St. Francis Nursing Center in the Highland Park section of Pittsburgh. Other major facilities of the System include the 202-bed St. Francis Central Hospital at 1200 Centre Ave. in Pittsburgh, which is an acute care hospital specializing in cardiology and cardiovascular surgery; and the 193-bed St. Francis Hospital of New Castle in New Castle, PA, which is a community hospital. St. Francis Medical Center has been contracted as the tertiary service provider for the hospitals comprising the Quorum Health Resources network. They include the Brownsville General Hospital, Clarion Hospital, Fairmont General Hospital, Memorial Hospital of Geneva, Metro Health Center, Miners Hospital, Ohio Valley General Hospital and Tyrone Hospital.

Officers: Sister M. Rosita Wellinger *P & CEO*
Sister Florence Brandt *CEO-St. Francis Medical Center*
Robin Mohr *CEO-St. Francis Central Hospital*
Sister Donna Zwigart *CEO-St. Francis Hospital of New Castle*

Human Resources: David Clark *VP-Human Resources-St. Francis Central Hospital & St. Francis Medical Center*

Purchasing: Bob Clark *DIR-Materials MGT*

Total Employees................3,897	**Regional Employees** 3,228
Year Established 1865	**SIC Code**....................................8062
Annual Revenues ($000) 541,592	

St. George Crystal Ltd.

Brown Ave.
P.O. Box 709
Jeannette, PA 15644
County: Westmoreland

Phone: (412) 523-6501
Fax: (412) 523-0707

Machine manufacturer of 24% full-lead crystal stemware, barware, giftware, lamp and lighting products. The Company sells its products primarily to third-party marketers, and under the Toscany Classic and St. George Crystal Ltd. brand names. The Company also makes glass angels for Treasures Inc., the exclusive North American distributor of authentic Vatican Art reproductions.

Officers: Robert Gonze *P*
Arnold Bowling *VP-MFG*
Thomas Kuehl *VP-FIN*
Melvin Parsons *VP-OPR*

Human Resources: Heidi Henckle

Total Employees	265	Regional Employees	265
Year Established	1985	SIC Code	3231
Annual Revenues ($000)	20,000		

St. George Group, The

CNG Tower, 625 Liberty Ave., Ste. 1600
Pittsburgh, PA 15222
County: Allegheny

Phone: (412) 471-1090
Fax: (412) 471-0526

Provider of integrated marketing communications, including marketing, advertising, public relations and database, direct to an array of local, national and international companies.

Officers: George Garber *P*
Craig Butzine
Bruce Downing *VP*
Marty Giglio *VP*
Dave Kosick *VP*
David Marrangoni *VP*
Timothy White *VP*

Purchasing: Ralph Tester *CON*

Total Employees	48	Regional Employees	48
Year Established	1982	SIC Code	7311
Annual Revenues ($000)	52,000		

St. Moritz Building Services, Inc.

4616 Clairton Blvd.
Pittsburgh, PA 15236
County: Allegheny

Phone: (412) 885-2100
Fax: (412) 885-3953

Provider of janitorial and related services, including office maintenance, floor maintenance, carpet maintenance, furniture cleaning, window cleaning, acoustical ceiling cleaning, construction site cleanup, engineering and disposable supplies. The Company, doing business as Building Services, Inc., serves building tenants, owners and operators, including high-rise office buildings, malls, corporate headquarters, technical and research centers, food courts, universities, department stores, manufacturing facilities, industrial distributors and recreational complexes. The Company cleans in excess of 6 million square feet of property located in Pittsburgh, Western Pennsylvania and neighboring regions.

Officers: Philip L. St. Moritz *P*
James P. Martin *VP-FIN*
Mark D. Moninger *VP-MKT & OPR*

Total Employees............................500   **Regional Employees** 500
Year Established 1968   **SIC Code**....................................7349

Stadtlanders Drug Distribution Co.

600 Penn Center Blvd.
Pittsburgh, PA 15235
County: Allegheny

Phone: (412) 824-2487
Fax: (412) 825-0589

Specialized nationwide pharmacy providing mail-order pharmaceutical services to over 70,000 patients with high-risk/high-cost disease states such as HIV/AIDS and transplant. The Company provides necessary prescription and non-prescription medications, patient information and other comprehensive services to enhance medication compliance. It also operates several retail satellite locations, including Castro Village Pharmacy in Los Angeles and San Francisco, CA; Hutcherson's Pharmacy in Franklin, TN; and Stadtlanders Pharmacy Wellness Center in New York, NY. The Company is a 99%-owned subsidiary of Counsel Corp., which is headquartered in Toronto, Ontario, Canada, and listed on the NASDAQ.

Officers: Morris Perlis *CH & CEO*
Tom Halstead *P & COO*

Human Resources: Dianna Long *Human Resources DIR*

Total Employees............................700
Year Established 1932   **SIC Code**....................................5961
Annual Revenues ($000) 225,000

Standard Bank, PaSB

3875 Old William Penn Hwy.
Murrysville, PA 15668
County: Westmoreland

Phone: (412) 856-0350
Fax: (412) 856-0359

S

State-chartered community savings bank primarily serving individuals in Allegheny and Westmoreland counties. The Bank's business is focused on offering a wide variety of financial products, including mortgage, consumer and personal loans; checking and savings products; and mutual funds and annuities. In addition to its corporate headquarters and a banking office which are located at the above address, the Bank operates branch offices in Ligonier, Mt. Pleasant, Monroeville, Scottdale and Wilkinsburg, PA, with supermarket branch offices in Greensburg and Latrobe, PA

Officers: Timothy K. Zimmerman *P*
John R. Henderson, Jr. *COO*
Colleen M. Brown *CFO*
D. Jay Brown *Chief Lending Officer*

Human Resources: Dana L. LaVerde

Purchasing: Barbara D. Marsalek

Total Employees	70	**Regional Employees**	70
Year Established	1913	**SIC Code**	6036
Annual Revenues ($000)	210,632 (Assets)		

Standard Forged Products, Inc.

75 Nichol Ave.
McKees Rocks, PA 15136
County: Allegheny

Phone: (412) 778-2020
Fax: (412) 778-2025

Manufacturer of carbon and alloy steel circular forgings, including industrial wheels, rollers, sheave wheels and crane wheels, for railroad axles. The Company operates three plants: Allegheny Axle at 528 Negley Ave. in Butler, PA, which finishes and mounts axles; Johnstown Axle in Johnstown, PA, which forges, finishes and mounts axles; and McKees Rocks Forgings, which is located at the above address and produces circular forgings. The Company is a subsidiary of Trinity Industries, Inc., which is headquartered in Dallas, TX, and listed on the NYSE.

Officers: Justin S. Modic *General Plant MGR*
Mark McGinley *General SAL MGR*

Human Resources: Vince Cappuzzi

Purchasing: Joe Nichols

Total Employees............................350	**Regional Employees** 230	
Year Established 1986	**SIC Code**......................................3312	

Standard Steel

107 Gertrude St.
P.O. Box 71
Latrobe, PA 15650
County: Westmoreland

Phone: (412) 537-7731
Fax: (412) 539-0645
Internet Address: www.standardsteel.com

Integrated manufacturer of steel forgings, including railway wheels, axles, springs and mounted wheel sets for the locomotive, freight and transit markets and cast steel ingots, billets and seamless rolled rings for construction, oil field, aerospace, power generation, bearings, defense, food machinery, mining, gears, other forgers and general industrial markets. The Company is a division of Freedom Forge Corp., which is headquartered in Burnam, PA. It operates field sales offices in Glastonbury, CT; Naperville, IL; and Cranberry Township, PA.

Officers: James A. Spendiff *P & COO*
John O. Parke *VP-OPR*
Dan L. Patterson *VP & CON*
John Cummings *Latrobe Plant MGR*

Human Resources: Thomas J. McGuigan *VP-Human Resources*
Gary Heimbach

Purchasing: James McCarter

Total Employees.......................1,050	**Regional Employees**...................115	
Year Established 1795	**SIC Code**......................................3312	
Annual Revenues ($000) 155,500		

Stanford Lumber Co., Inc.

2001 Rte. 286
Pittsburgh, PA 15239
County: Allegheny

Phone: (412) 327-6800
Fax: (412) 327-9302
Internet Address: www.cyberyard.com/stanford

Owner and operator of lumber yard/home center stores, doing business as Stanford Home Centers, providing do-it-yourselfers and contractors with over 25,000 products. The Company also offers a variety of services, including custom millwork of mantels, bookcases, shelves, lumber planing, moldings, intricate architectural millwork and countertops; installation of doors, windows, garage doors/openers, roofing, gutters, Armstrong floor tile, water heaters, vanities, toilets, water filters, faucets, garbage disposals, laundry tubs, kitchen sinks and Bronco Barn kits; repair of storm windows, window screens, small engines, lawnmowers, snowblowers and weed trimmers; assembly of mowers, wheelbarrows, clipper/shredders, patio furniture, gas and charcoal grills, kitchen cabinets and dog houses; cutting of sheet acrylic, screens, lumber, plywood, copper and plastic pipe, rope, chain, cable, carpet runners, indoor and outdoor carpeting, closet maid shelving, and keys and re-key locksets; rental of Rug Doctor Carpet Cleaning machines; sharpening of scissors, knives, mower blades, hand/miter saws, chain saw chains and circular saw blades; and delivery. In addition to a store located at the above address, the Company operates a site at 5550 Rte. 356 in Leechburg, PA.

Officers: Robert H. Piekarski *P & CEO*
Carl Piekarski *VP*
Lorraine Piekarski *SEC & TRS*

Human Resources: Carol Miller *Personnel MGR*

Purchasing: Susan Piekarski *MKT MGR*

Total Employees............................125	**Regional Employees** 125	
Year Established 1953	**SIC Code** 5211	
Annual Revenues ($000) 13,000		

Stanko Products, Inc.

Donahue Rd., R.D. 12
Box 210
Greensburg, PA 15601
County: Westmoreland

Phone: (412) 834-8080
Fax: (412) 834-8907

Designer, manufacturer and assembler of densifiers, conveyors, glass crushers and handling systems for worldwide markets under its DENS-A-CAN International and Stanko Products trade names. The Company also offers contract machining and fabricating services, with approximately half of its production time devoted to these clients.

Officers: Gregory A. Stanko *P & GMGR*
Frances M. Stanko *SEC*
Jeffrey T. Stanko *TRS*

Human Resources: Kelly R. Stanko

Purchasing: Jeffrey Lloyd

Total Employees.............................30	**Regional Employees** 30	
Year Established 1964	**SIC Code** 3535	
Annual Revenues ($000)......................................1,500-2,000		

Star Bedding Co. of Pittsburgh, Inc.

1441 Metropolitan St.
Pittsburgh, PA 15233
County: Allegheny

Phone: (412) 231-2800
Fax: (412) 231-0766

Manufacturer of bedding products under the Serta and Star Bedding brand names, doing business as the Serta Mattress Co. The Company's market area encompasses portions of New York and Pennsylvania. The Company is a subsidiary of S-N Bedding Co., Inc. (SBCI), which is headquartered in Holbrook, MA. SBCI is a subsidiary of Silentnight Holdings Plc, which is headquartered in Salterforth Colne, Lancashire, England.

Officers: Teresa Powell *MGR*

Total Employees............................90	**Regional Employees** 90
Year Established 1918	**SIC Code**....................................2515

Star Cable Assoc.

381 Mansfield Ave., Ste. 100
Pittsburgh, PA 15220
County: Allegheny

Phone: (412) 937-0099
Fax: (412) 937-0145

Cable television provider serving 42,000 customers in approximately 300 communities in rural Louisiana, Ohio and Texas. The Company offers on average 35 to 40 channels, including local television stations, a full line of popular cable networks, community message channels and pay-per-view (limited areas). The Company claims that it is the 73rd-largest cable provider in the nation. The Company's facilities are located in Ville Platte, LA; Youngstown, OH; and Brazoria and Daingerfield, TX.

Officers: James C. Roddey *CEO*
Michael R. Haislip *P*
Dan Skantar *DIR-Communications*

Human Resources: Steve Hogle

Purchasing: Bill Elliott

Total Employees............................75	**Regional Employees** 6
Year Established 1986	**SIC Code**....................................4841
Annual Revenues ($000) 15,600	

Station Square Hotel Assoc.

7 Station Square Dr.
Pittsburgh, PA 15219
County: Allegheny

Phone: (412) 261-2000
Fax: (412) 261-2932

Owner and operator of the Sheraton Hotel Station Square, which is also located at the above address. The Hotel has 292 rooms and is situated across the Monongahela River from downtown Pittsburgh. The 15-story facility contains two restaurants, cocktail lounge, ballroom and meeting and banquet rooms that can accommodate up to 2,000 guests. Its additional amenities include a fitness center, indoor pool, whirlpool, sauna and business center. The Hotel is a franchise of ITT Sheraton Corp.

Officers: Eugene F. Connelly *CEO & EVP*
James Stanton *GMGR*
Theresa Thomas *AST-GMGR*
Sara Buzzannco *DIR-MKT*

Human Resources: Carol Dunbar *DIR-Human Resources*

Total Employees..........................350	**Regional Employees** 350
Year Established 1981	**SIC Code** 7011

Steel City Products, Inc.

630 Alpha Dr.
Pittsburgh, PA 15238
County: Allegheny

Phone: (412) 963-7271
Fax: (412) 963-7503

Distributor of automotive accessories, including functional and decorative car and truck accessories such as floor mats, seat covers, mirrors, running boards and lights; car care products, including waxes and paints; chemicals such as antifreeze, windshield washer fluid and motor oil; and car repair and maintenance items, including spark plugs, windshield wipers, and air and oil filters. The Company's product selection has recently been expanded to include selected "hard parts" such as brake rotors and non-food pet supplies. Its customers include general merchandise retail chains, automotive specialty stores, grocery chains, drug stores, hardware stores and other automotive accessory distributors. Most of its customers are based in the northeastern United States, although some stores are located as far west as Iowa and as far south as Florida. The Company acquires its merchandise from a large number of suppliers and carries many nationally advertised brand names. Oakhurst Co., Inc. (OCI), which is listed on the NASDAQ Small Cap market, was formed as part of a merger transaction in July 1991. As a result, the Company became a majority-owned subsidiary of OCI, and most of its value was vested in OCI. This occurrence caused the Company's stock price to fall below the NASDAQ minimum bid price of $1 per share, causing its removal from the NASDAQ listing. Although the Company's corporate headquarters are located at the above address, its Form 10-K registration lists Grand Prairie, TX, as the address of its principal executive offices, which is actually OCI's corporate headquarters.

Officers: Bernard H. Frank *CH & CEO*
Terrance W. Allan *P & COO*
Marten D. Hemsley *CFO*

Total Employees...........................70   **Regional Employees** 70
Year Established 1947   **SIC Code**....................................5013
Annual Revenues ($000) 21,000

Stern and Assoc., Inc., Daniel

211 N. Whitfield St., Ste. 240
Pittsburgh, PA 15206
County: Allegheny

Phone: (412) 363-9700
Fax: (412) 363-6032
Internet Address: www.sgi.net/ds&a

Provider of physician recruitment, and medical staff development and planning services. The Company's physician recruitment business segment serves clients such as university and community hospitals, multispecialty groups, health maintenance organizations and private practitioners, and offers contract development and negotiation services. The Company also builds medical staff development plans that enable client hospitals to calculate the growth of their medical staffs and to maximize their market shares. The Company's strategic approach includes both quantitative statistical analyses of physicians, the hospital and the community, and qualitative analyses of physicians' needs, preferences, allegiance and referral patterns. The Company primarily serves clients in the Northeastern region of the U.S.

Officers: Daniel Stern *P*
Gregory Porter *SVP*
Mark DeRubeis *VP*
Philomena G. Thomas *VP*

Human Resources: Patricia Russ

Total Employees...........................30   **Regional Employees** 30
Year Established 1970   **SIC Code**....................................8742
Annual Revenues ($000) 1,800

Stevens Painton Corp.

650 Ridge Rd.
Pittsburgh, PA 15205
County: Allegheny

Phone: (412) 787-1995
Fax: (412) 787-0554

S

Contractor providing full-service design/build capabilities to industry. The Company, with headquarters in Middleburg Heights, OH, maintains its Eastern Division operations out of the above address. Other local operations include two subsidiaries, Chemsteel and Continental Design & Management Group, both based in Canonsburg, PA. (Refer to the Continental Design & Management Group profile for additional information.)

Officers: Vince P. Gravelle *CH*
Robert G. Navarro *VCH & COO*
Gary Knopf *P-Midwestern OPR*
Alex J. Pociask *P-Eastern OPR*

Total Employees............................200	**Regional Employees** 100	
Year Established 1970	**SIC Code**......................................1500	
Annual Revenues ($000) 77,000		

Stimple & Ward Co.

3400 Babcock Blvd.
Pittsburgh, PA 15237
County: Allegheny

Phone: (412) 364-5200
Fax: (412) 364-5299

Manufacturer of electrical coils for motors. The Company also produces magnet wire through its S&W Wire division, located in Cranberry Township, PA. The Company's products are primarily used by OEMs and the motor repair industry.

Officers: Raymond M. Love *P*
Tom F. Hibbs *VP*
Thomas J. Love *TRS*

Total Employees..............................49	**Regional Employees** 49	
Year Established 1898	**SIC Code**......................................3621	
Annual Revenues ($000) 6,000		

Stout Group Ltd.

Rte. 136 & Mitchell Rd.
P.O. Box 789, Washington, PA 15301
Eighty Four, PA 15330
County: Washington

Phone: (412) 225-1000
Fax: (412) 228-2579

Excavation/site development contractor and provider of railroad and transit construction. The Company's services include heavy and civil construction, site development, infrastructure, demolition, equipment rental, railroad construction and rehabilitation. It serves the public and private sectors, providing civil services throughout the Tri-State area and railroad and transit construction work throughout the nation and abroad.

Officers: Thomas P. Stout *P*
Steven P. Stout *VP*
Joseph M. Mihalic *VP*
John W. Golding *CFO & TRS*

Purchasing: Ray J. Burow

Total Employees 50-100	**Regional Employees** 50-100
Year Established 1984	**SIC Code** 1629
Annual Revenues ($000) 40,000	

Stroehmann Bakeries, Inc.

Buncher Industrial District, Bldg. 20-B
Leetsdale, PA 15056
County: Allegheny

Phone: (412) 741-0971
Fax: (412) 741-0975

Bakery producing breads and rolls under the brand names of D'Italiano, Dutch Country and Stroehmann. The Company, which is headquartered in Horsham, PA, operates six bakeries located in Olean, NY, and in Harrisburg, Hazelton, Norristown, Sayre and Williamsport, PA. The local facility is engaged in the wholesale distribution of the Company's baked goods to grocery stores, schools and institutions throughout the Tri-State area.

Officers: Gary Stom *MGR*
Tom Orlando *DIR SAL-Western Pennsylvania*

Total Employees........................3,500	**Regional Employees** 78
Year Established 1924	**SIC Code** 2051
Annual Revenues ($000)...320,000+	

Sugar Creek Rest L.P.

R.D. 2
P.O. Box 80
Worthington, PA 16262
County: Armstrong

Phone: (412) 445-3146
Fax: (412) 445-7354

Owner and operator of Sugar Creek Rest, a 44-bed personal care and 114-bed nursing home facility. The Company also provides clerical and administrative support to its affiliated businesses: 268 Center (doing business as the Mechling/Shakely Veterans Center) in Cowansville, PA, a psychiatric and addiction rehabilitation center for veterans; Armstrong Retirement Village in Worthington, PA, a retirement community comprised of 10 independent living units; Countryside Convalescent Home in Mercer, PA, a 48-bed nursing home and 36-bed personal care facility; Emlenton Laurel Manor in Emlenton, PA, a 40-bed personal care facility and operator of 10 assisted living apartments; and Sugar Creek Health Management in Worthington, PA, a provider of consulting and management services for other nursing homes. In total, these facilities offer long-term and rehabilitative care to more than 360 adults, and employ approximately 300.

Officers: Phillip E. Tack *P*
Kenneth R. Tack, Jr. *VP*
Matthew P. Tack *TRS*
Steven Tack *SEC & DIR-OPR*

Total Employees............................145   **Regional Employees**..................145
Year Established........................1972   **SIC Code**....................................8051
Annual Revenues ($000)...6,000+

Super Valu Northeast Region

Finley Rd.
P.O. Box 29
Belle Vernon, PA 15012
County: Fayette

Phone: (412) 929-7800
Fax: (412) 925-5727

Wholesale distributor of groceries and frozen food products to supermarkets. The regional office, located at the above address, oversees the Company's Mid-Atlantic, Milton and Pittsburgh Divisions. Also located at the above address is a warehouse facility. The Pittsburgh Division's administrative headquarters and distribution facility are located in New Stanton, PA. The division is responsible for serving customers in Maryland, Ohio, Pennsylvania and West Virginia, including the Country Market, Foodland and Shop N' Save supermarkets as well as independent grocers. Super Valu Stores, Inc. is headquartered in Eden Prairie, MN, and listed on the NYSE.

Officers: Nick Connavino *P-Super Valu Northeast Region*
Tom D. Miller *P-Super Valu Pittsburgh Division*
Ted Terek *P-Super Valu Milton Division*

Human Resources: Fran Lynch

Regional Employees.................1,000   **SIC Code**....................................5141

Superbolt, Inc.

500 Superior St.
P.O. Box 683
Carnegie, PA 15106
County: Allegheny
Phone: (412) 279-1149
Fax: (412) 279-1185

Manufacturer of Superbolt® Tensioners designed as direct replacements for hex nuts. These devices can be threaded onto a new or existing bolt, stud, threaded rod or shaft. The main thread serves to position the tensioner on the bolt or stud against the hardened washer and the load bearing surface. Once it is positioned, actual tensing of the bolt or stud is accomplished with simple hand tools by torquing the jackbolts which encircle the main thread. The Company's products are used to solve bolting problems in virtually all heavy industries.

Officers: Rolf Steinbock *CEO*
Robert Steinbock *P*
Allan Steinbock *VP*

Total Employees.............................60   **Regional Employees** 60
Year Established 1984   **SIC Code**....................................3452
Annual Revenues ($000) 6,000

Superior Litho, Inc.

939 W. North Ave.
Pittsburgh, PA 15233
County: Allegheny
Phone: (412) 321-0920
Fax: (412) 321-6061

Provider of commercial printing, electronic prepress, foil stamping, embossing, die cutting, folding and glueing services. The Company also operates a full electronic prepress department which can take any medium of data, convert to film and color proof. In addition, it has full bindery capabilities, which include stitching, die cutting, embossing and foil stamping.

Officers: Andrew J. Horn *P*

Human Resources: Alfred T. Russo, Jr. *GMGR*

Purchasing: Stephen Rattay

Total Employees............................30		**Regional Employees** 30	
Year Established 1965		**SIC Code**....................................2752	
Annual Revenues ($000) 3,800			

Superior Valve Co.

2200 N. Main St.
Washington, PA 15301
County: Washington

Phone: (412) 225-8000
Fax: (412) 225-6188

Manufacturer of valves and accessories used in air conditioning and refrigeration systems, and compressed gas cylinder valves for the welding, carbonic and medical gas industries. The Company also provides specialty gas valves to the semiconductor industry and to the automotive industry for alternative fuel vehicles. It is a division of Amcast Industrial Corp., which is headquarterted in Dayton, OH, and listed on the NYSE.

Officers: Gerald Leary *VP & GMGR*
Scott W. Boyd *Compressed Gas Business Unit MGR*
Dwight Nafziger *Automotive Business Unit MGR*
Paul L. Wellener III *Refrigeration Business Unit MGR*

Human Resources: Doug Patterson

Regional Employees....................300		
Year Established 1938	**SIC Code**....................................3492	

Svedala Bulk Materials Handling

4800 Grand Ave.
Pittsburgh, PA 15225
County: Allegheny

Phone: (412) 269-5000
Fax: (412) 269-5030

Manufacturer of large-scale equipment and systems for the bulk materials handling, coal preparation and heavy industrial machinery markets. The Company's products include stacker/reclaimers; railcar dumpers/wagon tipplers; grab unloaders; barge/ship loaders and unloaders; barge, ship and train positioning systems; self-unloading bulk carrier systems; ash handling systems; coal preparation equipment; and belt conveyor components. Along with its products, the Company provides field service and replacement parts. Its products are marketed under the brand names FACO, McNally Wellman and Stephens-Adamson. The Company also operates facilities located in Belledille, Ontario, Canada, and Sorocaba, Brazil. It is one of 34 international subsidiaries of Svedala Industri AB, a company with headquarters in Malmo, Sweden, and listed on the Stockholm Stock Exchange.

Officers: Ray Koper *VP & GMGR*
Roy Behling *VP-SAL & MKT*
James W. Schuster *VP-OPR*
R. Keith Ference *MKT MGR*

Human Resources: Sandi Marx *Personnel MGR*

Purchasing: Robert Zappie *Purchasing MGR*

Total Employees............................600	**Regional Employees** 225	
Year Established .... 1890's	**SIC Code**......................................3532	
Annual Revenues ($000) 100,000		

Swindell Dressler International Co.

5100 Casteel Dr.
P.O. Box 15541, Pittsburgh, PA 15244
Coraopolis, PA 15108
County: Allegheny

Phone: (412) 788-7100
Fax: (412) 788-7110

Designer, manufacturer and installer of kilns and complete plants for the worldwide ceramic industry. The Company's products include bell kilns, shuttle kilns, tunnel kilns, dryers and kiln car moving systems, as well as the design and construction of complete plants. Because different types of kilns are used in different parts of the ceramic industry, the Company has three industrial groups, each specializing in their segment of the industry. The Structural Clay Products group includes face brick, paving brick, quarry tile, roof tile, sewer pipe, flower pots and structural tile. The Whitewares group includes sanitaryware, dinnerware, floor and wall tile, electrical porcelain and nucleated glass products. The Technical Ceramics group includes refractories, abrasives, spark plugs, ferrites, carbon products, ceramic colors, electronic ceramics, automotive catalytic converter substrates and advanced ceramics. The Company has built more than 1,000 production kilns and 50 ceramic plants in 35 countries. It operates sales offices in Melbourne, Australia; Montery, Mexico; and Tangshen, People's Republic of China.

Officers: David F. Gaylord *CH*
Richard J. Wright *P*
John D. Houston II *SEC*

Human Resources: Marybeth Hudak

Purchasing: Russ Dean

Total Employees............................100	**Regional Employees** 80	
Year Established 1915	**SIC Code**......................................3567	
Annual Revenues ($000) 25,000		

Systems Modeling Corp.

504 Beaver St.
Sewickley, PA 15143
County: Allegheny

S

Phone: (412) 741-3727
Fax: (412) 741-5635

Developer and supporter of innovative computer software dedicated to simulation, which is the modeling of a real or proposed system to describe observed behavior and/or predict future behavior before time or money is invested. The Company's products, Arena, Cinema and SIMAN, are currently in use in more than 5,000 organizations worldwide. In 1996, the simulation software technology of Arena was applied to vertical markets such as call centers (Call$im), manufacturing (MP$im) and business processing (BP$im). In 1997, it released TEMPO, a finite capacity scheduling tool. In addition to a branch office located in Dallas, TX, the Company maintains a network of representatives in 20 countries around the world.

Officers: C. Dennis Pegden, Ph.D. *P*
John Hammann *COO*
Mary Kirsch *CFO*

Total Employees...........................50	**Regional Employees** 46
Year Established 1982	**SIC Code** 7371

Tajon Warehousing Corp.

601 Broad St.
Sewickley, PA 15143
County: Allegheny

Phone: (412) 749-4800
Fax: (412) 749-4820

Full-service materials handling and public warehousing enterprise. The Company, doing business as Arrow Terminals Co., loads and unloads barges, rail cars and trucks, and provides value-added services such as crushing, screening and packaging. It has three primary river terminals in Chicago, IL; Industry, PA; and Houston, TX. The Company also operates an automated packaging line for Golden Cat in Philadelphia, PA, where it bags through a high speed computerized bagging line, over 75,000 tons of absorbent clay annually. In addition, it operates 40 facilities for BIDS Inc., an affiliate of CSX Transportation. At these facilities, the Company loads and unloads bulk commodities such as sand, soda ash and lime; liquid commodities such as asphalt and ethanol; and other commodities, including plastic pellets. The Company operates similar facilities for Union Pacific Railroad in Triumph, IL, and Dallas, TX. The Company's other activities include the operation of a floating crane that is dedicated to Wheeling Pittsburgh Steel Corp., which has the capacity to unload approximately 350,000 tons of iron ore and 400,000 tons of steel slabs annually; the operation of a barge-to-rail car pneumatic unloading system for pebble lime for Chemical Lime Co. in New Martinsville, WV; a partnership with American Commercial Barge Line Co. in the barging of approximately 4 million tons of bauxite annually on the Orinoco River in Venezuela; and a vessel terminal and warehousing facility in Vlissingen, The Netherlands, serving the European steel and foundry industry.

Officers: Ron Chutz *P*
Michael J. Chutz *VP-MKT & Corporate Services*
Tim Chutz *VP*
Joe Pontoli *VP*

Human Resources: Ernest Becker

Purchasing: Rebecca Ridge

Total Employees	410	**Regional Employees**	50
Year Established	1981	**SIC Code**	4491

Taylor Milk Co., Inc.

348 Merchant St.
Ambridge, PA 15003
County: Beaver

Phone: (412) 266-8001
Fax: (412) 266-9285

Producer of dairy products and fruit juices distributed to customers throughout the Tri-State area, including retail stores, restaurants, schools and other institutions.

Officers: Joseph S. Taylor, Jr. *CH*
Joseph S. Taylor III *P*
David Taylor *VP*
Gregory Taylor *VP*
Richard Schmitt *GMGR*

Total Employees	70		
Year Established	1929	**SIC Code**	2026

TCG - Pittsburgh

2500 Allegheny Center Mall
Pittsburgh, PA 15212
County: Allegheny

Phone: (412) 338-9090
Fax: (412) 316-9999
Internet Address: www.tcg.com

Competitive local exchange carrier operating a fiber-optic network spanning more than 350 route miles making entrance into approximately 250 buildings throughout Allegheny County, PA. The Company provides access to long distance carriers and corporate end users. The Pittsburgh office is a unit of Teleport Communications Group, Inc., which is headquartered in Staten Island, NY, and listed on the NASDAQ.

Officers: Bob Annunziata *P & CEO*
Trudy Van Kirk *VP & GMGR*
Paul Zanotto *DIR-OPR & ENG*
Joe Ruffing *SAL MGR*
James O'Connor *CON*

Human Resources: Linda Marx *Administrative MGR*

Total Employees......................2,050	**Regional Employees**....................48	
Year Established.......................1988	**SIC Code**....................................4813	
Annual Revenues ($000)...283,400		

TCI of Pennsylvania, Inc.

300 Corliss St.
Pittsburgh, PA 15220
County: Allegheny

Phone: (412) 875-1100
Fax: (412) 331-7452

Provider of telecommunications services to 400,000 residential and business customers throughout Southwestern Pennsylvania. The Company's services include basic and premium cable TV, Pay Per View, The Sega Channel, Digital Music Express and private communications networks for businesses and institutions. It operates service centers at 655 Rodi Rd. and 5211 Brownsville Rd. in Pittsburgh and at 814 E. Pittsburgh St. in Greensburg, PA. The Company is a subsidiary of Tele-Communications, Inc., which is headquartered in Denver, CO, and listed on the NASDAQ.

Officers: Jeff Harshman *OPR DIR*
Sharon McCarthy *OPR DIR*

Total Employees...........................550	**Regional Employees**..................550
Year Established.......................1984	**SIC Code**....................................4841

Technical Communications, Inc.

100 Bettis Rd.
Dravosburg, PA 15034
County: Allegheny

Phone: (412) 469-2260
Fax: (412) 469-1631

Provider of graphic art and documentation preparation services, including word processing, phototypesetting, data conversion, computer graphics, illustrations and posters; 35-mm slides, flipcharts and vugraphs; catalogs, text and workbooks; flyers and brochures; awards and certificates; user, operator and maintenance manuals to commercial and military specs; training and human resources materials; reports, specifications and forms; commercial and technical editing and writing; and projections, renderings and schematics. The Company serves clients in the government, industry and business sectors. Its headquarters are located in Stuart, FL.

Officers: Cordon Hale *P*
Jessie D. Shoaf *VP*

Purchasing: Mary Ann Shumber

Total Employees............................32	**Regional Employees** 30
Year Established 1964	**SIC Code**....................................2791

Technical Solutions, Inc.

3907 Old William Penn Hwy., Ste. 402
Murrysville, PA 15668
County: Westmoreland

Phone: (412) 733-2100
Fax: (412) 733-2099

Supplier of contract technical services, specializing in providing technical employees at all levels in all disciplines. These include engineers, designers, drafters, technicians, project managers and software engineers. The Company's employees are available for short-term, long-term or permanent placement. It charges a fixed hourly billing rate that includes payroll taxes, insurance, fringe benefits, recruiting, training, labor costs and administration. The Company serves clients in Eastern Ohio and Western Pennsylvania.

Officers: Janice G. McMaster *P*

Total Employees...........................116	**Regional Employees**...................116
Year Established 1991	**SIC Code**....................................7363
Annual Revenues ($000) 5,000	

Technosystems Consolidated Corp.

217 Ninth St.
Pittsburgh, PA 15222
County: Allegheny

Phone: (412) 288-1300
Fax: (412) 288-1354

Provider of inventor assistance services through its subsidiaries, Intromark Inc., Invention Submission Corp. and Technosystems Service Corp., all of which are located at the above address. The Company assists clients worldwide with all types of new products, ideas and/or innovations.

Officers: Martin S. Berger *P*

Total Employees...........................150
Year Established 1984   **SIC Code**....................................8742

TECTYL Industrial Products

491 Railroad St.
Rochester, PA 15074
County: Beaver

Phone: (412) 774-2025
Fax: (412) 728-6825
Internet Address: www.thomasregister/valvoline.com

Manufacturer of solvent-borne and waterborne waxes, rust preventive oils, waterborne paints (alkyds, acrylics and epoxy esters), solvent-borne and water-borne asphalt, and hot melts. The Company focuses on serving the automotive, automotive components, truck, trailer, intermodal container, general industrial, marine and military markets throughout North America. The plant located at the above address is owned by the Valvoline Co. (VC), which is headquartered in Lexington, KY. VC is a division of Ashland, Inc., which is headquartered in Ashland, KY, and listed on the NYSE.

Officers: Pat Nelson *Plant MGR*

Regional Employees.......................50
Year Established 1939   **SIC Code**....................................2851
Annual Revenues ($000) 20,000

TEDCO Construction Corp.

TEDCO Place
Carnegie, PA 15106
County: Allegheny

Phone: (412) 276-8080
Fax: (412) 276-6804

General contractor engaged in both new construction and renovation projects for a variety of commercial, institutional and industrial clients. The Firm serves clients in Southwestern Pennsylvania with selected projects in neighboring states. Its current new construction projects include a cogeneration facility and residence hall at Duquesne University; a student center at Robert Morris College in Moon Township, PA; and a standing work order with the University of Pittsburgh Medical Center/WPIC. Its renovation projects include the Patrick Henry Library at Robert Morris College in Moon Township, PA; the Palace Theater in Greensburg, PA; and work at the Graphic Arts Technical Foundation. Approximately 60% to 80% of the Firm's work is negotiated.

Officers: Theodore H. Frantz *P*
Barbara J. Frantz *VP*

Total Employees............................50	**Regional Employees** 50
Year Established 1977	**SIC Code**....................................1542
Annual Revenues ($000) 26,000		

TEI Analytical Services, Inc.

35 W. Point Rd.
P.O. Box 534
Washington, PA 15301
County: Washington

Phone: (412) 228-2155
Fax: (412) 228-9874

Provider of nondestructive testing and inspection services to a broad range of commercial customers. The Company utilizes radiographic, ultrasonic, magnetic particle, liquid penetrant and visual inspection methods to determine qualities such as the efficacy of manufacturing methods and soundness of structure of bridges, aircraft, fossil and nuclear power plants, highways, buildings, cast and forged iron and steel goods, gas and oil pipelines, and related facilities. It serves clients nationwide and abroad.

Officers: Gary E. Weiss *P*
Joyce A. Rockwell *TRS*
Scott E. Weiss *GMGR*

Total Employees............................40	**Regional Employees** 30
Year Established 1987	**SIC Code**....................................8734

Teichmann, Inc., Henry F.

3009 Washington Rd.
McMurray, PA 15317
County: Washington

Phone: (412) 941-9550
Fax: (412) 941-3479
Internet Address: www.hft.com

Provider of engineering and contracting services to the domestic and international glass industry. The Company is engaged in the design, procurement, construction and startup of the glass making process, having provided such services in over 40 countries worldwide. It designs and installs all types of batch plants, cullet systems and batch handling systems; designs, builds and commissions complete process facilities for high quality container glass operations; updates furnaces, supplies complete decorating lines, and modernizes annealing and quality control operations; and reengineers existing furnaces. The Company claims to have engineered and constructed virtually every type of glass furnace, with expertise ranging from small day tanks to large tonnage tableware melters, and from lead crystal to the increasingly more important environmental waste recycling furnaces. It also provides fossil-fuel melters, electric melters, mix-melters and oxy-fuel technologies to the fiberglass industry.

Officers: Newton N. Teichmann *CH*
Archie L. McIntyre *P*
Dave E. Defibaugh *MGR-SAL*
Kenneth E. Lemasters, Jr. *CON*

Human Resources: Kathy Andrews

Purchasing: Tim J. Farley *DIR-Purchasing*

Total Employees	35	**Regional Employees**	35
Year Established	1947	**SIC Code**	8711
Annual Revenues ($000)	15,000+		

Telesis Computer Corp.

207 Sigma Dr.
Pittsburgh, PA 15238
County: Allegheny

Phone: (412) 963-8844
Fax: (412) 963-1373
Internet Address: www.telesismfg.com

Owner and developer of TelesisMFG, a fourth generation relational database that operates in a Windows environment. TelesisMFG is a multi-company, multi-location software solution that meets the needs of a variety of manufacturers in the repetitive, assemble to order and the make to order environments. TelesisMFG targets the automotive, medical, electronic and general purpose manufacturing industries. The TelesisMFG core business system comprises 12 modules that address the financial, distribution and manufacturing side of the business as well as many "extended" modules to fit the varied needs of the individual manufacturer. The Company also provides hardware, networking, implementation and training in addition to its application software. The Company primarily serves clients in the Northeastern United States.

Officers: Joseph P. Juliano *P*
Nancy Hrynkiw *EVP*
Joseph D. Juliano, Jr. *VP*
Cindy Sulecki *CFO*

Human Resources: Rose Berardelli

Purchasing: Paul Pusateri

Total Employees	100	**Regional Employees**	100
Year Established	1983	**SIC Code**	7372
Annual Revenues ($000)	15,000		

Tenneco Packaging

One 28th St.
Pittsburgh, PA 15222
County: Allegheny

Phone: (412) 471-5325
Fax: (412) 471-7568
Internet Address: www.tenneco-packaging.com

Manufacturer of corrugated boxes distributed to customers throughout the Tri-State area. The Company, which is headquartered in Evanston, IL, is an industry segment of Tenneco Inc. (TI). TI is headquartered in Greenwich, CT, and is listed on the NYSE.

Officers: Robert Palermo *GMGR*
Scott Miller *Plant MGR*

Regional Employees......................85
Year Established 1991   **SIC Code**....................................2653

Tenser Phipps & Leeper, Inc.

419 Friday Rd.
Pittsburgh, PA 15209
County: Allegheny

Phone: (412) 821-8960
Fax: (412) 821-7425

Food broker serving grocery stores throughout the Tri-State area.

Officers: Louis F. Leeper *CEO*
James Leeper *P*

Total Employees..........................350   **SIC Code**....................................5141

Testa Machine Co., Inc.

28 Baird Ave
P.O. Box 416
Slovan, PA 15078
County: Washington

Phone: (412) 947-9397
Fax: (412) 947-9998

Machining job shop rebuilding and manufacturing steel/aluminum mill and coal mining equipment. The Company primarily serves industrial customers throughout the New York, Ohio, and Pennsylvania region.

Officers: Richard Lounder *OWN & P*
Judy Lounder *SEC*

Human Resources: Chuck Cunningham

Purchasing: Richard M. Lounder, Jr.

Total Employees.............................48	Regional Employees 45
Year Established 1943	SIC Code.....................................3599
Annual Revenues ($000) 4,000	

TETRA Technologies, Inc.

Park West One, Cliff Mine Rd., Ste. 600
Pittsburgh, PA 15275
County: Allegheny

Phone: (412) 788-8300
Fax: (412) 788-8303

Specialty inorganic chemical company marketing products, services and process technologies to a variety of markets, including oil and gas, agriculture and environmental services. The Company, which is headquartered in The Woodlands, TX, is listed on the NASDAQ. The local facility is a process technologies engineering and sales office and a part of the Company's Process Technologies Group Division. This division provides engineered systems and services that treat industrial and municipal wastewater and in some cases, solid waste streams, to ensure compliance with environmental effluent requirements, to achieve on-site waste minimization and/or to recover reusable constituents. These systems employ the Company's proprietary biological filtration, metals removal and resource recovery technologies.

Officers: David G. Scruppi *Office MGR (Purchasing)*

Total Employees..........................940	Regional Employees 40
Year Established 1981	SIC Code.....................................2819
Annual Revenues ($000) 161,000	

Texas Instruments Inc.

300 Oxford Dr.
Monroeville, PA 15146
County: Allegheny

Phone: (412) 856-3600
Fax: (412) 856-3636
Internet Address: www.ti.com

Headquartered in Dallas, TX, and listed on the NYSE, the Company's Software Development Systems (SDS) unit operates facilities in Dallas and Houston, TX; Bangalore, India; and at the above address. At the local facility, engineers develop state-of-the-art compilation systems for embedded digital signal processing (DSP) development in the C, C++ and Ada programming languages as well as debuggers, profilers, runtime systems, simulators and emulators. SDS is a unit of the worldwide DSP organization within Texas Instrument's Semiconductor Group. SDS develops software development tools for TMS320 DSPs and for microcontrollers. These tools produce highly efficient code to provide the maximum throughput for these devices.

Officers: Michael Hames *VP-Semiconductor Group & Worldwide MGR-Digital Signal Processing*
Gregory Golian *MGR-Software DEV Systems*

Human Resources: Michelle Seibert

Total Employees......................59,927	**Regional Employees** 65	
Year Established 1938	**SIC Code**......................................3674	
Annual Revenues ($000) 9,940,000		

Thermal Industries, Inc.

301 Brushton Ave.
Pittsburgh, PA 15221
County: Allegheny

Phone: (412) 244-6400
Fax: (412) 244-6496

Manufacturer and distributor of vinyl-framed, made-to-order windows. The Company's windows include double and triple-paned replacement windows in a variety of styles, bow or bay window units and garden units. In addition, it has developed a line of replacement sliding doors and patio enclosure systems. Vinylium Corp. (VC), a subsidiary, extrudes rigid and dual-durometer PVC profile extrusions which are used solely in the Company's window manufacturing operations. VC also markets a line of vinyl planking and railing extrusions for use in porch decks and boat docks. The Company's windows are primarily sold to remodeling or home improvement contractors for use in residential retrofit remodeling. These contractors are contacted by sales employees working out of the Company's corporate headquarters and 19 warehouse-sales offices located primarily within the northeast quarter of the United States. Deck and dock products are sold across the continental United States. It also has several distributors in the north-central states and a commercial sales department for direct sales to rental or commercial property owners. All manufacturing is done at the Company's Murrysville, PA, factory. The finished windows are shipped to its warehouses and to distributors in Company-owned or leased trucks and by commercial carrier.

Recent Events: On January 7, 1997, the Company and H. I. G. Investment Group, L.P. (HIG) in Miami, FL, announced that the Company and affiliates of HIG had entered into a definitive merger agreement which provided for a wholly owned subsidiary of HIG to acquire the Company. On May 30, 1997, the Company announced that its merger with Heat Acquisition, Inc. had been approved by its shareholders. As a result, the Company is no longer listed on the NASDAQ Small Cap.

Officers: David H. Weis *CH & CEO*
David Rascoe *P*
Todd Rascoe *EVP*
Thomas Andres *VP-MFG*
Jay Deems *VP-Midwest*
Arthur Poland *VP*
Eric Rascoe *SEC & TRS*

Total Employees...........................540	Regional Employees 390
Year Established 1960	SIC Code.....................................3442
Annual Revenues ($000) 41,357	

Thermal Transfer Corp.

1100 Rico Rd.
Monroeville, PA 15146
County: Allegheny

Phone: (412) 351-3013
Fax: (412) 856-0256

Designer, engineer and manufacturer of heat transfer equipment. The Company's products include recuperators, heat exchangers, fired heaters and gas coolers. The majority of its products are sold to industrial customers operating in the primary metals industry. The Company is a subsidiary of Air & Water Technologies Corp., which is headquartered in Branchburg, NJ, and listed on the ASE.

Officers: Timothy W. Ottie *VP & GMGR*

Human Resources: Benjamin B. Jones

Total Employees.............................50	Regional Employees 50
Year Established 1938	SIC Code.....................................3443
Annual Revenues ($000) 12,000	

Thermo-Twin Industries, Inc.

1155 Allegheny Ave.
Oakmont, PA 15139
County: Allegheny

Phone: (412) 826-1000
Fax: (412) 826-0455

Manufacturer, marketer, distributor and installer of custom-made thermalized aluminum, vinyl and wood clad windows along with doors, specialty millwork and other related products for retailers, wholesalers, distributors and commercial job sites. The Company's subsidiaries include Thermo-Twin of Ohio, Inc., which operates retail outlets in Stow and Toledo, OH; and Thermo-Twin of Pennsylvania, Inc., a lessor of manufacturing equipment which is also located at the above address.

Officers: James F. Dalton *P*
Joseph A. Palermo *VP*
James A. Bunting *SEC & TRS*

Human Resources: James P. Shields *GC*

Purchasing: Barry Holland *Plant OPR*

Total Employees	147	Regional Employees	140
Year Established	1972	SIC Code	3442
Annual Revenues ($000)			16,000

Thorp Reed & Armstrong

One Riverfront Center
Pittsburgh, PA 15222
County: Allegheny

Phone: (412) 394-7711
Fax: (412) 394-2555
Internet Address: www.thorpreed.com

Provider of legal services with 82 attorneys. The Firm's practice areas include litigation, labor and employment relations, corporate and business law, employee benefits, environmental law, construction law, health care law, intellectual property, and tax and estate issues. It serves a broad client base, including Fortune 500 corporations, start-up ventures, charitable organizations and individuals. The Firm operates a branch office in Wheeling, WV.

Officers: Douglas E. Gilbert *MPTR*
John A. Rosicky *EDIR*

Human Resources: Kathleen M. Sullivan *Human Resources DIR*

Total Employees	185	Regional Employees	180
Year Established	1895	SIC Code	8111

Three Rivers Aluminum Co., Inc.

71 Progress Ave.
Cranberry Township, PA 16066
County: Butler

Phone: (412) 776-7000
Fax: (412) 776-7088

Manufacturer of a complete line of custom-designed residential and commercial windows and doors, primarily for retrofit and historical renovation projects. The Company's manufacturing capabilities include tempering, finishing, glass insulating and extrusions for windows and doors for commercial, institutional, high-rise and low-rise buildings. Its custom windows have been installed in the Statue of Liberty and the Empire State Building. In addition to the Company's corporate headquarters and a manufacturing plant which occupy a 950,000 square foot facility located at the above address, it operates plants in Red Oak, IA, and Shanghai, People's Republic of China. The Company also maintains branch operations in Denver, CO; Washington, D.C.; Chicago, IL; Baltimore, MD; Detroit, MI; Minneapolis, MN; St. Louis, MO; New York, NY; and Pittsburgh, PA. A subsidiary, Skytech Systems, which is located in Bloomsburg, PA, manufactures sky lights, folding glass walls and sun rooms. The Company is most often referred to by its tradename, TRACO.

Officers: Robert Randall *P & CEO*
John Kalakos *VP & GMGR-Commercial*
Bart Mosser *VP & GMGR-Commercial*
Bill Stevens *CFO*

Human Resources: Eric Dean

Purchasing: Ernie Groover

Total Employees........................1,100	**Regional Employees** 875	
Year Established 1943	**SIC Code**....................................3442	
Annual Revenues ($000) 130,000		

Three Rivers Bank and Trust Co.

500 Fifth Ave.
McKeesport, PA 15132
County: Allegheny

Phone: (412) 664-8700
Fax: (412) 664-8980

Commercial, Pennsylvania-chartered bank with 24 branch locations throughout Allegheny, Washington and Westmoreland Counties, PA. The Bank conducts a general retail banking business, including granting commercial, consumer, construction, mortgage and student loans, and offering checking, interest-bearing demand, savings and time deposit accounts as well as comprehensive trust services. It also offers wholesale banking services to other banks, merchants, government units and other large commercial accounts. The Bank is a subsidiary of USBANCORP, Inc., which is headquartered in Johnstown, PA, and listed on the NASDAQ.

Officers: W. Harrison Vail *P & CEO*
Louis S. Klippa *EVP*
Thomas J. Chunchick *SVP-ADM*
Harry King *SVP-Community Banking*
Vincent Locher *SVP-Commercial Lending*
James F. Ackman *VP-Consumer Loans*
Fred Geisler *VP-Construction Lending*

Human Resources: Richard Barron *VP-Human Resources*

Regional Employees.....................422
Year Established 1964   SIC Code.....................................6022
Annual Revenues ($000) 839,234

Three Rivers Optical Co.

Seven Crawford St.
McKees Rocks, PA 15136
County: Allegheny

Phone: (800) 756-2020
Fax: (800) 756-0034

Operator of a wholesale optical laboratory supplying eyeglass lenses and frames to retail optical stores, opticians, optometrists and ophthalmologists throughout the United States.

Officers: William C. Seibert *P*
              Madeline T. Seibert *VP, SEC & TRS*

Human Resources: Edward Schiefer *GMGR*

Purchasing: Joseph Seibert

Total Employees..............................75   Regional Employees 74
Year Established 1969   SIC Code.....................................3827

Three Rivers Youth

2039 Termon Ave.
Pittsburgh, PA 15212
County: Allegheny

Phone: (412) 766-2215
Fax: (412) 766-2212
Internet Address: www.trfn.clpgh.org/try

Nonprofit agency serving abused, neglected, runaway and homeless youth and their families—youths whose lives have been damaged by physical and sexual abuse, abandonment, school failure, early pregnancy, and drug and alcohol abuse. The Agency specializes in youth 12 through 21 years of age providing a comprehensive and integrated spectrum of educational, vocational, residential, day treatment and in-home services. These include six therapeutic group homes, including two for females and one for males, two teen parenting group homes and an intensive treatment unit for females, in Allegheny and Washington counties; Pathways, offering its Youth Employment Training Program and Pregnant and Parenting Youth Program, both in Wilkinsburg, PA; runaway and homeless youth programs, consisting of The Loft in Wilkinsburg, PA, The Hub in Pittsburgh, PA, and the Transitional Living Program in Wilkinsburg, PA; therapeutic services, including the Day Treatment/Partial Hospitalization Program in Pittsburgh, PA, and the Wraparound Program in Pittsburgh, PA, offering individualized mental health services; and Try Safety Zone, operating an emergency shelter offering assessment, crisis intervention and counseling for youth who are in violation of the City of Pittsburgh curfew ordinance, located in the Public Safety Building in downtown Pittsburgh.

Officers: David C. Droppa, Ph.D. *CEO (Human Resources)*
Harold C. Shields *P*
Fred Brodbeck *CFO*
Grace McClelland *DIR-Programs*
Judith S. Michael, Ph.D. *DIR-Evaluation & Quality Improvement*
Carmelle R. Nickens *DIR-MKT & DEV*

Purchasing: Debbie Lazan

Total Employees	150	**Regional Employees**	150
Year Established	1880	**SIC Code**	8322
Annual Revenues ($000)	3,724		

Tile City of Pennsylvania, Inc.

728 Rebecca Ave.
Pittsburgh, PA 15221
County: Allegheny

Phone: (412) 241-3700
Fax: (412) 241-6926

Owner and operator of 17 retail stores selling flooring, carpeting, wall coverings and window blinds. The stores, known as Tile City & Carpet, carry a variety of national brands. The stores are located in Steubenville, OH; and Ambridge, Bridgeville, Charleroi, Greensburg, Johnstown, Murrysville, New Castle, New Kensington, North Versailles, Pittsburgh (2), Pleasant Hills and Uniontown, PA. The Company also operates outlet stores in Butler and McKeesport, PA, and a retail store at its corporate facility at the above address.

Officers: Lawrence A. Hamburg *OWN & P*
Duane Johnson *District MGR & MGR-Ceramic*
Frank Rodzwicz *MGR-Vinyl*
Kate Young *MGR-Wall Paper*

Purchasing: Mark Verdun *MGR-Carpet*

Total Employees	100	**Regional Employees**	90
Year Established	1954	**SIC Code**	5713
Annual Revenues ($000)	15,000		

Tippins, Inc.

435 Butler St.
P.O. Box 9547
Pittsburgh, PA 15223
County: Allegheny

Phone: (412) 781-7600
Fax: (412) 781-7612
Internet Address: www.tippins.com

Designer, engineer, installer and commissioner of rolling mill equipment for the metals industry, including the steel and non-ferrous markets. The Company's operations include two divisions, Tippins Process Automation and Tippins Used Equipment, both of which are located at the above address, and Tippins Asia Ltd., in Bangkok, Thailand.

Officers: George W. Tippins *CH*
John E. Thomas *C-OWN, P & CEO*
John H. Tippins *C-OWN*
William H. Tippins *C-OWN*
Robert Bixby *VP-OPR & ENG*
Eduardo Carballal *VP-Electrical*
William H. Scherle *VP & General SAL MGR*
Simon X. Weng *P-Tippins Asia Ltd.*

Human Resources: Larry Scott

Purchasing: Bob Simmers

Total Employees............................350	**Regional Employees** 350	
Year Established 1932	**SIC Code**......................................3547	
Annual Revenues ($000) 105,000		

Titus & McConomy LLP

Four Gateway Center, 20th Fl.
Pittsburgh, PA 15222
County: Allegheny

Phone: (412) 642-2000
Fax: (412) 642-2950
Internet Address: www.titusmcconomy.com

Provider of legal services with 20 attorneys. The Firm's practice areas comprise general and complex business and commercial litigation, including antitrust, construction, corporate, employment, discrimination, environmental, ERISA, high technology, insurance coverage, lender liability, maritime, personal injury, product liability, professional liability, RICO, securities, shareholder and derivative and toxic tort; banking/finance; business compensation and tax advice and planning; estate planning and administration; health care and intellectual property, including patents, trademarks and copyrights; mergers, acquisitions and reorganizations; private placements and syndications; and real estate transactions.

Officers: James McConomy *MPTR*

Total Employees............................52	**Regional Employees** 52
Year Established 1981	**SIC Code** 8111

Tomanetti Food Products, Inc.

625 Allegheny Ave.
Oakmont, PA 15139
County: Allegheny

Phone: (412) 828-3040
Fax: (412) 828-2282

Manufacturer and distributor of pizza crusts and specialty items such as focaccia crusts and whole wheat crusts, as well as breadsticks and flat breads. The Company also produces frozen pizza under its Graindance and Soydance brand names that are distributed to health food stores nationwide.

Officers: Thomas P. Mulvey *P*

Human Resources: Chris Presutti

Purchasing: Bob Finlay

Total Employees............................45	**Regional Employees** 45
Year Established 1960	**SIC Code**...................................2045
Annual Revenues ($000) 2,200

Towers Perrin

USX Tower, 600 Grant St., Ste. 3800
Pittsburgh, PA 15219
County: Allegheny

Phone: (412) 497-3000
Fax: (412) 497-3099
Internet Address: www.towers.com

Provider of a comprehensive array of management consulting services to help organizations manage their investment in people. The Firm advises its clients on human resource management, employee benefits, risk management, compensation and communications, as well as on overall strategy and organizational effectiveness. The Firm, which is headquartered in New York, NY, operates approximately 70 offices throughout North and South America, Europe, Australia and Asia. It advises large and small organizations in both the public and private sectors.

Officers: John T. Lynch *CEO*
                Kenneth L. Keffer *Pittsburgh Office MGR*

Human Resources: Ken Ranftle *DIR-Human Resources (Valhalla, NY)*

Purchasing: Karen Brown

Total Employees..........................6,500	**Regional Employees** 50
Year Established 1871	**SIC Code**......................................8742

Trans World Airlines, Inc.

Pittsburgh International Airport
Pittsburgh, PA 15231
County: Allegheny

Phone: (412) 472-3101

Commercial airline operating six daily nonstop flights from Pittsburgh to St. Louis, MO. The Company, which is headquartered in St. Louis, MO, is listed on the ASE. Trans World Express, a subsidiary of the Company, operates six daily nonstop flights from Pittsburgh to JFK Airport in New York, NY. The Company's reservations/information number is (800) 221-2000.

Officers: John Stack *Station MGR*

Regional Employees......................49	**SIC Code**......................................4512

Transarc Corp.

The Gulf Tower, 707 Grant St.
Pittsburgh, PA 15219
County: Allegheny

Phone: (412) 338-4400
Fax: (412) 338-6977
Internet Address: www.transarc.com

Developer of enterprise-scale distributed systems. The Company's distributed computing tools are DCE, Distributed CICS and Encina; its file systems products are AFS and DFS. The Company is a subsidiary of International Business Machines Corp., which is headquartered in Armonk, NY, and listed on the NYSE. The Company distributes its products direct to end users through the worldwide IBM Transarc Software sales force and through a network of international resellers and OEMs.

Officers: Alfred Z. Spector *CH*
Jeffrey L. Eppinger *CTO & Acting COO*
Elizabeth Hines *VP-Product Support*
Katie Kean *VP-PDEV*
Dione Kennedy *VP-North American SAL*
Philip L. Lehman *VP-Services*
Mark Sherman *VP-Product MGT*
Gary Voight *VP-Worldwide Transaction Systems SAL*

Human Resources: Debra Burk

Total Employees ....375+	**Regional Employees** ....250+
Year Established 1989	**SIC Code** 7373

Transtar, Inc.

135 Jamison Lane
P.O. Box 68
Monroeville, PA 15146
County: Allegheny

Phone: (412) 829-3460
Fax: (412) 829-3395

Holding company operating a variety of transportation-related businesses that are engaged in railroad and water shipping. The Company's water activities include inland waterway barges, Great Lakes shipping and dock facilities in Conneaut, OH. Its operating companies include Bessemer and Lake Erie Railroad Co. in Monroeville, PA; Birmingham Southern Railroad Co. in Birmingham, AL; Duluth Missabe and Iron Range Railway Co. in Duluth, MN; Elgin, Joliet and Eastern Railway Co. in Joliet, IL; The Lake Terminal Railroad Co. in Lorain, OH; McKeesport Connecting Railroad Co. in Monroeville, PA; The Pittsburgh & Conneaut Dock Co. in Conneaut, OH; Union Railroad Co. in Monroeville, PA; USS Great Lakes Fleet, Inc. in Duluth, MN; and Warrior & Gulf Navigation Co. in Mobile, AL.

Officers: Robert S. Rosati *P & CEO*
Robert N. Gentile *VP-Law*
Frank J. Habic *VP-OPR*
Joseph W. Schulte *VP-FIN*
George E. Steins *VP-ADM*
Rudy Vignovic *VP-MKT*

Human Resources: Richard Kashurba *DIR-Human Resources*

Total Employees 3,400	**Regional Employees** 600
Year Established 1988	**SIC Code** 6719
Annual Revenues ($000) 500,000	

Trau & Loevner, Inc.

5817 Centre Ave.
Pittsburgh, PA 15206
County: Allegheny

Phone: (412) 361-7700
Fax: (412) 361-8221

Manufacturer of imprinted sportswear for men, women and youth. The Company's merchandise is available in many different body styles and an array of vivid colors. It produces two different lines of clothing with two different price points. TNT is a competitively priced sportswear line comprised of 50% cotton/50% poly blend fabrics. Saavy is a line of heavyweight fleece and 100% cotton jersey clothing. The Company has licensing agreements with major universities, Warner Bros., Minor League Baseball and the National Hockey League. Its products are distributed to retailers nationwide.

Officers: Howard Loevner *C-P*
Steven Loevner *C-P*

Human Resources: Caroline Hellwig

Purchasing: Roger Stivers

Total Employees............................90	**Regional Employees** 90
Year Established 1897	**SIC Code**....................................2389
Annual Revenues ($000)..20,000+	

Tri-Arc Manufacturing Co.

6815 Hamilton Ave.
Pittsburgh, PA 15208
County: Allegheny

Phone: (412) 363-9055
Fax: (412) 363-4076

Manufacturer of steel, aluminum and stainless steel rolling ladders and work platforms. The Company supplies its products to many of the national retail chains, and to material handling distributors and major national catalogs. The Company also designs and manufactures custom products for the airline, pharmaceutical and automotive industries.

Officers: Fred I. Schwartz *P*
Ron Schwartz *VP-SAL & MKT*
Melvin E. Solomon *VP*
Nick Valore *VP-OPR*
Paula Pascarella *CON*

Human Resources: Barbara Santella

Purchasing: Ray Mikita

Total Employees............................50	**Regional Employees** 50
Year Established 1959	**SIC Code**....................................3499
Annual Revenues ($000) 5,500	

Tri-State Hydraulics, Inc.

1250 McKean Ave.
Charleroi, PA 15022
County: Washington

Phone: (412) 483-1790
Fax: (412) 489-0911

Distributor of fluid power products and provider of full-fluid power products repair and service. The Company's Glassport Cylinder Works division, which is also located at the above address, manufactures hydraulic and pneumatic mill-type cylinders. The Company primarily serves clients in the worldwide steel industry.

Officers: Janice M. Kramer *P*
James D. Palmer II *VP-OPR*
Bob Yonko *Plant MGR*

Human Resources: Cheryl P. Wall *SEC & TRS*

Purchasing: James D. Palmer, Sr. *GMGR*

Total Employees............................52	**Regional Employees** 52	
Year Established 1958	**SIC Code**......................................3593	

Tri-State Truck Service, Inc.

62 Steubenville Pike
Burgettstown, PA 15021
County: Washington

Phone: (412) 729-3900
Fax: (412) 729-3510

Wholesale distributor of gasoline, diesel fuel, home heating oil, motor oil and lubricants to customers throughout the Tri-State area doing business as Tri-State Wholesale Oil Co. Products offered by the Company include Sunoco gasoline and Castrol, Kendall, Quaker State, Sunoco, TSO Premium, Valvoline and WolfsHead motor oils. It also is engaged in the collection of used oil, antifreeze and wastewater for recycling applications. The Company maintains bulk plants and warehouses in East Butler and Uniontown, PA, as well as at its corporate headquarters located at the above address.

Officers: Anthony J. Guiffre, Sr. *P*
Jeannie Galownia *CON*
JoAnn Stanley *SAL MGR*

Human Resources: Anthony W. Guiffre, Jr. *VP & TRS (Purchasing)*

Total Employees............................35	**Regional Employees** 35	
Year Established 1961	**SIC Code**......................................5171	
Annual Revenues ($000) 12,000		

Tri-Tech Services, Inc.

55 Old Clairton Rd.
Pittsburgh, PA 15236
County: Allegheny

Phone: (412) 655-8970
Fax: (412) 655-8973

Provider of international consulting, engineering, marketing and training services, with expertise in quality assurance and quality control. While the Company's original product was providing quality system auditing services, it has diversified into both training and consulting in Total Quality Management, Statistical Techniques, ISO 9000 and QS-9000 Quality System Development, ISO 14001 Environmental System Development and a variety of related, specialized services. The Company's Marketing Services Division offers customer and employee satisfaction surveys, market research, lead generation and customer management services. The Company has the capability to support the activities of any type of organization, including those located abroad. It has developed quality systems and performed audits for enterprises in Brazil, Canada, France, Germany, Italy, Japan, Mexico and Puerto Rico. The Company's corporate headquarters and Eastern Regional offices are located at the above address. It also operates a Midwest Regional office in Mishawaka, IN, and a Southern Regional office in Greensboro, NC.

Officers: Robert E. Marino *P*
David J. Kudlock *VP*
Barry Bare *Acting Midwestern Region OPR MGR*
Arnie Jeremics *Southern Region OPR MGR*
John Martin *Eastern Region OPR MGR*
Carolyn Church *Southern Region SAL MGR*
Ross Marino *Eastern Region SAL MGR*
Paul Rothwell *Midwestern Region SAL MGR*
Robert Balint *MKT Services MGR*

Human Resources: Peggy Skalican

Purchasing: Jill Urso

Total Employees............................70	**Regional Employees** 45
Year Established 1987	**SIC Code** 8711

Triangle Circuits of Pittsburgh, Inc.

931 Third St.
Oakmont, PA 15139
County: Allegheny

Phone: (412) 828-5322
Fax: (412) 828-5803

Provider of CAD design services and manufacturer of bare printed circuit boards. The Company produces an average of 500 different PC board orders per month, with run sizes ranging from small lots in a few days to lot sizes of thousands of parts at industry standard leadtimes. Its technical capabilities cover the vast majority of rigid board requirements, including single-sided, double-sided through ten-layer boards. The Company's services incude CAD design layout of printed circuits and laser photoplotting, with complete electrical testing facilities. It primarily serves clients in Maryland, New York, Ohio, Pennsylvania, Virginia and West Virginia.

Officers: Michael D'Ambrosio, Sr. *P & CEO*
Alan Caponi *DIR*

Human Resources: Dennis Pricer

Purchasing: Nick Calabrese

Total Employees............................110	**Regional Employees**...................110
Year Established 1979	**SIC Code**.....................................3672
Annual Revenues ($000) 10,000	

Triangle Tech, Inc.

1940 Perrysville Ave.
Pittsburgh, PA 15214
County: Allegheny

Phone: (412) 359-1000
Fax: (412) 359-1012

Owner and operator of educational institutions and a travel agency. Known as The Triangle Tech Group, the Company operates technical schools located in Dubois, Erie and Greensburg, PA, as well as at the above address. The schools offer two-year Associate in Specialized Technology degree programs in Mechanical Computer-Aided Drafting and Design; Architectural Computer-Aided Drafting and Construction; Maintenance Electricity and Construction; Refrigeration, Heating, Ventilation and Air Conditioning; and Carpentry and Construction Technology. The Company also operates the Business Careers Institute located in Greensburg, PA, which is a decentralized facility of Triangle Tech Greensburg. The business school offers two-year Associate in Specialized Business degree programs in Executive Secretarial; Medical Secretarial; Computerized Accounting; and Business Computer Applications. The Company's schools enroll approximately 1,340 students. In addition, the Company operates Electra Travel, Inc., located in McMurray, PA, which provides business and leisure travel services.

Officers: James R. Agras *CH & CEO*
Timothy J. McMahon *P & COO*
Rudy J. Agras *EVP*
Electra P. Agras *SEC*

Human Resources: Sofia A. Janis

Purchasing: Kathy Borkowski

Total Employees...........................191 **Regional Employees** 127
Year Established ....1944 **SIC Code**....................................8249

Tribune-Review Publishing Co., The

Cabin Hill Dr.
Greensburg, PA 15601
County: Westmoreland

Phone: (412) 834-1151
Fax: (412) 838-5171
Internet Address: www.tribune-review.com

Publisher of the Tribune-Review, a newspaper with a daily circulation of 81,695 and a Sunday circulation of 142,235 (9/30/96 figures), primarily serving residents of Allegheny and Westmoreland Counties, PA. The Company operates branch offices in Charleroi, Connellsville, Indiana, Latrobe and Monroeville, as well as at Station Square and in the North and South Hills of Pittsburgh. In addition to a printing and distribution facility located at the above address, the Company anticipated the late 1997 opening of a second "Newsworks" facility in Marshall Township, PA. The Company's subsidiaries include the Blairsville Publishing Co., located in Blairsville, PA, which publishes The Dispatch, a weekly newspaper with a circulation of 20,100; and T-R Printing and Publishing Co., located on Rte. 136 in Irwin, PA, which publishes the Standard Observer, a daily (Monday through Saturday) newspaper with a circulation of 10,100 serving the Irwin and North Huntingdon area, and the Community News, a weekly newspaper with a circulation of 20,575 serving the McKeesport, North Versailles and Penn Hills area. In May 1997, the Company acquired three additional daily newspapers, the Daily Courier, at 127 W. Apple St. in Connellsville, PA, with a circulation of 10,628; the Leader-Times, at 112-121 N. Grant Ave. in Kittanning, PA, with a circulation of 11,353; and the Valley Independent, at Eastgate 19 in Monessen, PA, with a circulation of 17,264. The Company estimates a total daily readership of 478,000 in eight counties in Pennsylvania—Allegheny, Armstrong, Cambria, Fayette, Indiana, Somerset, Washington and Westmoreland. The Sunday Tribune-Review reaches readers as far south as West Virginia, west to Youngstown, OH, north to Erie, PA, and east to Harrisburg, PA.

Officers: Edward H. Harrell *P*
Richard M. Scaife *Publisher-Tribune-Review*
George A. Beidler *VP & Executive Editor-Tribune-Review*
Lee B. Templeton *GMGR-Pittsburgh Tribune-Review Edition*
Kraig Cawley *MKT DIR-Tribune-Review*
Carroll Quinn *Circulation DIR-Tribune-Review*
Jeff Simmons *Circulation MGR-Pittsburgh Tribune-Review*
David A. House *Editor-Pittsburgh Tribune-Review*
Paul J. Koloski *Editorial Editor-Tribune-Review*

Jeffrey Domenick *City Editor-Pittsburgh Tribune-Review*
John Jennings *Business MGR-Blairsville Publishing Co. & Editor-The Dispatch*
Kristy Green *GMGR-Leader Times*
Barb Retaino *GMGR-Daily Courier & Valley Independent*
Craig Smith *GMGR-T-R Printing and Publishing Co.*

Human Resources: Art McMullen *Tribune-Review*

Total Employees	872	**Regional Employees**	872
Year Established	1889	**SIC Code**	2711

Trigon Inc.

124 Hidden Valley Rd.
Canonsburg, PA 15317
County: Washington

Phone: (412) 941-5540
Fax: (412) 941-8322

Holding company for two operating businesses. FPD Co., also located at the above address, manufactures titanium and other specialty metal closed die forged and machined components for the aerospace and orthopedic implant markets. StelKast Co., at 800 Vinial St. in Pittsburgh, PA, designs, develops, markets and distributes orthopedic implants to doctors and hospitals across the U.S.

Officers: Peter N. Stephans *CH & CEO*
Donald A. Stevens *P-StelKast Co.*
David B. Tenison *VP & GMGR-FPD Co.*

Total Employees	60	**Regional Employees**	60
SIC Code	3399		

TriLogic Corp.

35 Morganza Rd.
Canonsburg, PA 15317
County: Washington

Phone: (412) 745-0200
Fax: (412) 745-5950
Internet Address: www.tri-logic.com

Provider of computer network design, configuration and implementation services for clients primarily in the Tri-State area. The Company also distributes hardware and peripheral equipment for a variety of vendors, including Acer, Bay Networks, Chipcom, Cisco, Compaq, Dataram, Digital, Hewlett-Packard, IBM, Novell, SGI and Zenith. A branch office is located in Warrensville Heights, OH.

Officers: J. Eric Bruce *P*
Darryl Robinson *VP*

Human Resources: Karen Sowers

Purchasing: Rory Robinson

Total Employees............................41	Regional Employees 26	
Year Established 1981	SIC Code.....................................5045	
Annual Revenues ($000) 13,346		

Trimark Engineers/Constructors, Inc.

USX Tower, 600 Grant St., 22nd Fl.
Pittsburgh, PA 15219
County: Allegheny

Phone: (412) 471-5900
Fax: (412) 471-2988
Internet Address: www.trimrk.com

Full-service project implementation organization staffed by professionals and support personnel experienced in all facets of engineering. The Company's areas of expertise include control systems, mechanical/piping, process engineering, civil/structural, electrical/power, architectural/HVAC, purchasing/expediting, scheduling/estimating, project management, construction management and software systems. The Company provides value-added services in retrofitting existing plants and facilities for technological change, efficiency, product quality improvement and productivity gain. It also provides in-house staging facilities for the programming and testing of process control systems. The Company serves the chemical, food, glass, metals and light manufacturing industries. It is a subsidiary of Midrex Corp., which is headquartered in Charlotte, NC.

Officers: Vincent S. Dimsa *P*
Marvin M. Rosenfeld *CON*
John R. Welding *GMGR-Business DEV*
David R. McCulloch *DIR-ENG*

Human Resources: Dolores J. Kosko

Purchasing: Betty A. Colaizzi

Total Employees...........................160	Regional Employees 160	
Year Established 1969	SIC Code 8711	
Annual Revenues ($000) 12,000		

Trinity Holdings, Inc.

610 Beatty Rd.
Monroeville, PA 15146
County: Allegheny
Phone: (412) 856-1739
Fax: (412) 856-1932

Owner and operator of five publishing-related subsidiaries. Gateway Press, Inc. (GPI), located at the above address, claims to be Pittsburgh's largest publisher of weekly suburban newspapers. GPI produces 15 publications circulated to more than 80,000 homes throughout suburban Pittsburgh. Its web press printing facility has full-color capability and complete typesetting, layout and design abilities. GPI operates branch offices in Carnegie, Cranberry, Coraopolis, Sewickley and the South Hills area of Pittsburgh. PennySaver Publications of Pennsylvania, Inc. (PPPI), located at 511 Rodi Rd. in Pittsburgh, publishes 76 zoned shopper publications distributed weekly to over 700,000 homes throughout the Pittsburgh metropolitan area by U.S. mail. PPPI claims to be Pittsburgh's only complete direct mail advertising system, with offices in McKees Rocks and in the North and South Hills areas of Pittsburgh. Buckeye Publishing Co., Inc. (BPCI), located in Lisbon, OH, publishes The Morning Journal, a daily morning newspaper with a circulation of 14,100 serving Columbiana County, OH. BPCI also produces a total market shopper publication and has web offset printing and typesetting facilities. East Central Communications, Inc. (ECCI), located in Rantoul, IL, publishes four weekly newspapers in southern Illinois, the Gibson City Courier, Piatt County Journal-Republican, Rantoul Press and the Target Shopper. ECCI has web offset printing, sheet feed printing and typesetting facilities. Midland Communications, Inc., located in Lansing, IL, serves the Chicago metropolitan area with full-service web offset printing, composition, typesetting and inserting facilities. The Company is a subsidiary of Trinity International Holdings Plc, which is headquartered in Chester, England, and listed on the London Stock Exchange.

Officers: Kevin T. Aylmer *CEO*
Robert P. Penvose *CFO*
Gene M. Carr *VP-SAL & MKT*
Ed Dewitt *VP & GMGR-Midland Communications, Inc.*
John Blanchflower *Publisher-Buckeye Publishing, Inc.*
Dennis C. Kaster *Publisher-East Central Communications, Inc.*
Mark Laskowski *Publisher-Gateway Press, Inc.*

Total Employees	600	**Regional Employees**	350
Year Established	1980	**SIC Code**	2711

Trombino Music Centers, Inc.

1049 Broad Ave.
Belle Vernon, PA 15012
County: Fayette

Phone: (412) 929-6707
Fax: (412) 929-2049

Owner and operator of retail stores selling pianos and organs throughout the Pittsburgh metropolitan area. Brands of pianos offered by the stores include Baldwin, Bosendorfer, Boston by Steinway, Kohler & Campbell, Samick, Steinway, Wurlitzer and Yamaha; brands of organs include Lowrey and Yamaha Clavinovas. The Company operates its stores under the names Trombino Piano Gallerie in downtown Pittsburgh; Piano Piano in Mt. Lebanon; Trombino Music Center in Belle Vernon (located at the above address), Greensburg and Monaca; and Trombino Piano and Organ in Monroeville and Pittsburgh.

Officers: Robert A. Trombino *P (Purchasing)*
Norma J. Trombino *SEC & TRS*

Total Employees	50	**Regional Employees**	50
Year Established	1963	**SIC Code**	5736
Annual Revenues ($000)			6,500

Troyer Potato Products, Inc.

42 Swihart Rd.
Canonsburg, PA 15317
County: Washington

Phone: (412) 746-1162
Fax: (412) 796-1167
Internet Address: www.troyerfarms.com

Manufacturer and distributor of snack foods, including pretzels, potato chips, popcorn, tortilla chips and extruded snacks. The Company's products are marketed regionally under its Dan Dee and Troyer Farms brand names. The Company is headquartered in Waterford, PA. Its local site is a distribution and pretzel manufacturing facility.

Officers: Clifford Troyer *P*
Craig Troyer *VP*
Daniel Troyer *VP-SAL*
Mark Troyer *VP*
Steven Troyer *VP*
Dick Sorensn *Plant MGR*
Mitchell Willis *CON*

Total Employees	390	**Regional Employees**	40
Year Established	1967	**SIC Code**	2052
Annual Revenues ($000)			40,000

Tru-Weld Grating, Inc.

2000 Corporate Dr.
P.O. Box 1238
Wexford, PA 15090
County: Allegheny

Phone: (412) 934-5320
Fax: (412) 934-5348

Manufacturer and fabricator of carbon steel, corten and stainless steel grating and stair treads. The Company's products are used in many commercial, industrial and infrastructure flooring applications for catwalks, platforms, mezzanines, etc. The Company serves its clients in the U.S. and Canada from manufacturing/fabricating facilities located in Litchfield, IL; Saegertown, PA; and Wetaskiwin, Alberta, Canada.

Officers: Martin M. Shaffer *P*

Human Resources: Michele Paulos

Purchasing: Todd Shaffer *MGR-Production Services*

Total Employees	150	**Regional Employees**	30
Year Established	1983	**SIC Code**	3441
Annual Revenues ($000)	20,000		

TruServ Corp.

One Servistar Way
P.O. Box 1510, Butler, PA 16003
East Butler, PA 16029
County: Butler

Phone: (412) 283-4567
Fax: (412) 284-6320

Member-owned wholesaler representing more than 10,300 retailers. The Company operates as a marketing and purchasing cooperative for retail hardware, lumber, home center, rental, garden, automotive and commercial/industrial stores located throughout all 50 states and 44 countries. It also engages in manufacturing and provides functional services that support its core operations. The Company is comprised of a family of retail businesses, including Coast to Coast, Coast to Coast Home & Auto, Grand Rental Station, Home & Garden Showplace, InduServ Supply, ServiStar Hardware, Taylor Rental Center and True Value. The Company was formed on July 1, 1997, by a merger between Cotter & Co. in Chicago, IL, and Servistar Coast to Coast Corp., located at the above address. The combined company is now headquartered in Chicago, IL. Its local operations oversee the Company's lumber, rental, commercial and industrial business segments.

Officers: Bernie Day *SVP-Lumber*

Human Resources: Russ Thomas *SVP-Human Resources*

Purchasing: Gene O'Donnell *EVP-MER, Advertising & Inventory Control (Chicago, IL)*

Total Employees	1,500	Regional Employees	500
Year Established	1910	SIC Code	5072
Annual Revenues ($000)	4,500,000		

Try-Again Homes, Inc.

365 Jefferson Ave.
P.O. Box 1228
Washington, PA 15301
County: Washington

Phone: (412) 225-0510
Fax: (412) 225-7210

Nonprofit social service agency providing a wide variety of supportive services to the disadvantaged, abused and neglected children and families of Southwestern Pennsylvania and West Virginia. The Agency's programs include foster care, counseling, family preservation, independent/transitional living, entrepreneurial training, and drug and alcohol treatment services. It operates branch offices in Uniontown, PA; and Charleston, Fairmont and Parkersburg, WV.

Officers: Mary Warman Terry *EDIR*
Karen Barkley *DIR-Social Services*
Sara Geis *AST DIR-Social Services*
Pamela Hall *CON*
Patricia A. Lewis *DEV Coordinator*
Alison Leon *West Virginia State DIR*

Human Resources: Patrice Penvose *Executive SEC*

Total Employees	85	Regional Employees	40
Year Established	1976	SIC Code	8322
Annual Revenues ($000)	3,700		

Tube City, Inc.

12 Monongahela Ave.
P.O. Box 2000
Glassport, PA 15045
County: Allegheny

Phone: (412) 678-6141
Fax: (412) 678-2210

Processor of scrap and waste metals both for its own account and on a tolling basis for steel mills. The Company also brokers scrap metals from other scrap dealers for direct shipment to mills. Effective August 1, 1995, the Company entered the slag processing and metal recovery business through its Olympic Mill Services division and has secured eight contracts to date. The Company's processing facilities are located in Birmingham, AL; Gary, IN; and Fairless Hills and West Mifflin, PA. It operates sales offices in Birmingham, AL; Gary, IN; Sparrows Point, MD; Charlotte, NC; Cleveland, OH; and Philadelphia, PA. The Company's slag processing and metal recovery operations are on the sites of contracted steel mills.

Special Designations: FB-P$_{500}$

Officers: I. Michael Coslov *CH & CEO*
Joseph Curtin *P*
Thomas E. Lippard *SVP-FIN & ADM, & GC*

Human Resources: Linda Musacchio

Total Employees 300	**Regional Employees** 150	
SIC Code 5093		
Annual Revenues ($000) 524,000		

Tucker Arensberg, P.C.

One PPG Place, Ste. 1500
Pittsburgh, PA 15219
County: Allegheny

Phone: (412) 566-1212
Fax: (412) 594-5619
Internet Address: www.tuckerlaw.com

Provider of legal services with 50 attorneys. The Firm's practice areas include commercial loans and financing, banking, commercial recoveries, bankruptcy, litigation, corporate, employee relations, estate planning and probate, securities, tax, ERISA, environmental, administrative, health care, school and municipal law, and government relations. It operates branch offices in Greensburg, Harrisburg and Moon Township, PA.

Officers: Charles J. Vater *Managing Shareholder*
Henry S. Pool *P*
Gary P. Hunt *Board MEM*
Jeffrey J. Leech *Board MEM*
Beverly Weiss Manne *Board MEM*
Ralph F. Manning *Board MEM*
Gary E. Wieczorek *Board MEM*

Human Resources: Pamela J. Maxson

Total Employees 100	**Regional Employees** 98	
Year Established 1900	**SIC Code** 8111	

Turner Construction Co.

Koppers Bldg., 436 Seventh Ave., Ste. 1400
Pittsburgh, PA 15219
County: Allegheny

Phone: (412) 255-5400
Fax: (412) 255-0249

General contractor and construction management firm engaged in many types of construction projects, including office buildings, apartment houses, hospitals and health-care, educational and cultural buildings, hotels, department stores, shopping centers, airline terminals, stadiums and other sports facilities, industrial buildings and parking structures. The Company, which is headquartered in New York, NY, operates 34 offices worldwide. It is a subsidiary of The Turner Corp., which is also headquartered in New York, NY, and listed on the ASE. The local office is responsible for the western portion of New York and Pennsylvania as well as West Virginia and Canada. It is currently engaged in construction projects for the Alcoa Corporate Center, Lazarus downtown Pittsburgh department store, Magee-Womens Hospital and the Greater Buffalo International Airport.

Officers: James I. Mitnick *VP*

Human Resources: Dick Esau

Purchasing: Neil L. Platz

Total Employees	2,500	**Regional Employees**	75
Year Established	1902	**SIC Code**	1542
Annual Revenues ($000)	85,000 (Locally)		

Turtle Creek Valley Mental Health/Mental Retardation, Inc.

723 Braddock Ave.
Braddock, PA 15104
County: Allegheny

Phone: (412) 351-0222
Fax: (412) 351-0180

Nonprofit agency designed to meet the needs of the community by providing mental health counseling and treatment; mental retardation therapy and activities; and drug and alcohol programs for families, individuals, adolescents and schools. The Agency provides a wide variety of services to residents of Allegheny County, PA, including a 24-hour emergency help/crisis intervention hotline for anyone who needs help (461-1004); confidential therapeutic counseling for adults, children, adolescents and families with mental health, drug or alcohol problems; rehabilitation programs for adults with mental retardation; training and social rehabilitation for mentally ill adults; partial hospitalization programs offering day and evening programs for mentally ill adults; residential programs for adults with mental retardation and mental illness; family support services, including recreational programs, family aid and respite care for children and adults with mental retardation; preventive services, including mental health, mental retardation, drug and alcohol programs; drug and alcohol programs for schools and businesses; a DUI education and intervention program; an information and referral program that connects people with other agencies, groups or individuals; case management activities that coordinate services for consumers with mental illness and mental retardation; and an intensive case management unit that provides close coordination of services and aspects of daily living for those experiencing chronic mental illness. The Agency's facilities are located in Braddock, Bridgeville, Homestead, Munhall, the South Side of Pittsburgh and Turtle Creek.

Officers: Melvin W. Haber *EDIR*
Josephine Ulrich *Clinical DIR*
John A. Eddy *CON*

Human Resources: Paul C. McGaughey

Total Employees	300	**Regional Employees**	300
Year Established	1970	**SIC Code**	8093
Annual Revenues ($000)	10,000		

Typecraft Press, Inc.

45 S. 23rd St.
P.O. Box 4295
Pittsburgh, PA 15203
County: Allegheny

Phone: (412) 488-1600
Fax: (412) 488-7546
Internet Address: www.typecraftpress.com

Provider of commercial printing services offering nonheatset web printing with auxiliary capabilities to provide complete in-house work. The Company's primary products are newspapers, newspaper inserts, catalogs, magazines and newsletters. It also provides general printing services including traditional typesetting, desktop publishing and imaging, sheet press capabilities with one-, two- and five-color presses, bindery and mailing services.

Officers: John A. Major *P*
Richard G. Major *VP*
Bernard A. Klein *SEC*
Edward J. Major *TRS*
Victor Borrelli *SAL MGR*

Total Employees	90	**Regional Employees**	90
Year Established	1938	**SIC Code**	2752
Annual Revenues ($000)	11,400		

U.S. Tool & Die, Inc.

Keystone Commons, 200 Braddock Ave.
Turtle Creek, PA 15145
County: Allegheny
Phone: (412) 823-3773
Fax: (412) 823-6669

Specialty engineering and fabrication company serving the nuclear power industry with safety-related handling equipment, containers and racks for spent nuclear fuel and high-level radioactive waste. The Company's products and services include spent fuel storage racks; cask internals; storage and shipping containers; special tools and handling equipment; fuel consolidation systems; close tolerance weldments; and build-to-print fabrication. Its engineering design and analysis services include seismic, structural, thermal-hydraulic, finite element, criticality and licensing support. In addition to the Company's machine shop capabilities, it provides precision forming and welding capability for a variety of metals, including carbon steel, stainless steel and aluminum. The Company serves government and industry in the United States, Europe and Pacific Rim countries.

Officers: Robert L. Moscardini *P (Human Resources)*
James Baird *Production MGR*
Robert Heusey *Quality Assurance MGR*
Christopher Srock *ENG MGR*
Jennifer McDade *CON*

Total Employees..............................62   **Regional Employees** 62
Year Established 1950   **SIC Code**....................................3444
Annual Revenues ($000) 5,000

U-S Safety Trolley Corp.

3089 Washington Pike
Bridgeville, PA 15017
County: Allegheny
Phone: (412) 221-4400
Fax: (412) 221-6828
Internet Address: www.universalstandard.com

Manufacturer of electrical equipment, doing business as Universal Standard Safety Trolley Corp. The Company's products include SPAN-GUARD insulated conductor bar systems for overhead cranes; SmartRail electronic control communication systems that superimpose control signals over the main power conductors; STARLINE BUSWAY systems for stationary power distribution to machines, lights, equipment and other electrical loads; and TRI-BAR and FOUR-BAR conductor bar systems for cranes, hoists, monorails, electrified conveyors and other moving machinery. The Company's subsidiary, Electric Busway Corp., is a distributor of the busway and power distribution equipment; and Star Products, a division of the Company, represents the busway product group. Both operations are also located at the above address.

Officers: Joel C. Ross *P*
                Steven L. Ross *VP*

Human Resources: Jon D. Dixon *VP*

Purchasing: John Quayle

Total Employees..............................35
Year Established 1960

Regional Employees 35
SIC Code....................................3643

Ultra Precision, Inc.

2220 Silverville Rd.
P.O. Drawer E
Freeport, PA 16229
County: Armstrong

Phone: (412) 295-5161
Fax: (412) 295-3200

Manufacturer of tool and die equipment for industrial customers throughout the United States. The Company can design and build new dies and repair, alter or rebuild existing dies. It produces spare parts in tungsten carbide or tool steel to customer prints or can design tooling to customer requests.

Officers: Robert W. Grafton *P*
                Frank P. Paz *SEC*
                Robert L. Stevenson *TRS*

Human Resources: Catherine I. Yates *Administrative AST*

Purchasing: Timothy R. Kurn

Total Employees..............................46
Year Established 1969
Annual Revenues ($000) 3,700

Regional Employees 46
SIC Code....................................3544

Union Apparel, Inc.

Mt. Pleasant Rd.
P.O. Box 384
Norvelt, PA 15674
County: Westmoreland

Phone: (412) 423-4900
Fax: (412) 423-4760

Manufacturer of men's and women's sport coats and blazers. The Company also operates a manufacturing facility located in Costa Rica.

Officers: Leo Borg *P*
John Kardos *VP*

Total Employees..........................780
Year Established 1976

Regional Employees 180
SIC Code....................................2337

Union Camp Corp.

72 Wilson Rd.
Eighty Four, PA 15330
County: Washington

Phone: (412) 746-2700
Fax: (412) 746-9519

Manufacturer of corrugated cartons and display-related products. The Company, which is headquartered in Wayne, NJ, is listed on the NYSE. It operates a total of 26 container manufacturing plants.

Officers: Raymond O. Gravely *GMGR*
Richard G. Knause *SAL MGR*

Regional Employees....................160
Year Established 1960

SIC Code....................................2653

Union Switch & Signal Inc.

1000 Technology Dr.
Pittsburgh, PA 15219
County: Allegheny

Phone: (412) 688-2400
Fax: (412) 688-2399

Designer, engineer, manufacturer and distributor of integrated railway signaling, control and automation systems, and on-board and wayside control components. The Company's domestic customers include the Class 1 freight railroads, regional and short line railroads, and mass transit authorities in North America. It also supplies rail and mass transit authorities in Australia, India, Pakistan, the People's Republic of China, South Korea and other countries in Asia and South America. Its other facilities include a manufacturing plant in Batesburg, SC, and a service center in Kingston, Ontario, Canada. The Company is a subsidiary of Ansaldo Signal N.V. (ASN), which is headquartered in Amsterdam, The Netherlands, and listed on the NASDAQ. ASN is a majority-owned subsidiary of Ansaldo Trasporti S.p.A. (ATS), which is headquartered in Naples, Italy, and listed on the Milan Stock Exchange. ATS is a majority-owned subsidiary of Finmeccanica S.p.A., a major Italian industrial company headquartered in Rome, Italy, and listed on the Italian Stock Exchange.

Officers: James N. Sanders *Acting P & CEO*
Anthony A. Florence *VP-Corporate & Investor Relations*

Michael Grossman *VP-Systems OPR*
Brian McCurrie *VP & CFO*
Chinnarad Mokkapati *VP-Customer Quality*

Human Resources: Raymond Stetz *DIR-Human Resources*

Purchasing: Tom Pidgeon *VP-Purchasing & Business Re-engineering*

Total Employees............................900	**Regional Employees** 450
Year Established 1881	**SIC Code** 3743

Uniontown Health Resources, Inc.

500 W. Berkeley St.
Uniontown, PA 15401
County: Fayette

Phone: (412) 430-5000
Fax: (412) 430-3342

Nonprofit holding company operating the Uniontown Hospital, which is also located at the above address. The general medical and surgical hospital has a total of 200 beds and is staffed with 165 physicians representing all specialties and disciplines of medicine. The hospital's services include a 24-Hour Emergency Department, Cardiac Rehabilitation Program, Comprehensive Rehabilitation Service, CT Scanner, Digestive Health Center, Family Care Network Center, Hemodialysis & Peritoneal Dialysis, Laparoscopic Cholecystectomy Procedures, Lithotripsy, MRI, Progressive Care Center for transitional care, SameDay Surgery, SameDay Overnight Surgery and Sophisticated Ophthalmology Services. It also offers a variety of self-help groups, assistance and support groups, and educational programs. The Company's other subsidiary, Fayette Home Care, is located on Woodlawn Ave. in Uniontown, PA. It provides visiting nurse services and hospice care.

Officers: Alvin S. Mundel *CH*
Paul Bacharach *P*
Richard DeHaas *CH-Board of Trustees-Uniontown Hospital*
Firooz Taghizadeh, M.D. *P-Medical Staff-Uniontown Hospital*

Total Employees............................860	**Regional Employees** 860
Year Established 1902	**SIC Code** 8062

Uniontown Newspapers, Inc.

8-18 E. Church St.
P.O. Box 848
Uniontown, PA 15401
County: Fayette

Phone: (412) 439-7500
Fax: (412) 439-7528

Publisher of the Herald-Standard, a daily newspaper with a daily circulation of 30,943 and a Sunday circulation of 32,934, distributed to Fayette County and parts of Greene and Washington Counties, PA. The Company is a subsidiary of Calkins Newspapers, Inc., which is headquartered in Levittown, PA.

Officers: Grover J. Friend *P*
Edward J. Birch *SVP & TRS*
Val J. Laub *Publisher*

Total Employees ....200+
Year Established 1888   **SIC Code** 2711

Unisource Worldwide, Inc.

55 38th St.
Pittsburgh, PA 15201
County: Allegheny

Phone: (412) 621-2121
Fax: (412) 621-2069

Distributor of papers, supplies and packaging systems for commercial printing, business imaging, general manufacturing and food processing. The Company, which is headquartered in Valley Forge, PA, is listed on the NYSE. It operates more than 140 distribution facilities throughout North America offering over 75,000 products.

Officers: Ronald H. Moyer *Division MGR*
Jim Hall *Segment MGR-Supply Systems*
Ken Winterhalter *Segment MGR-Commercial Printing & Business Imaging*
Robert C. Janke *OPR MGR*

Human Resources: Karen Pikovsky *Human Resources Coordinator*

Regional Employees 41
Year Established 1907   **SIC Code** 5111

Unisys Corp.

Park West One, Cliff Mine Rd.
Pittsburgh, PA 15275
County: Allegheny

Phone: (412) 788-6960
Fax: (412) 788-7773
Internet Address: www.unisys.com

Provider of information management services through three businesses: information services (consulting, outsourcing, solutions and systems integration); computer systems (solutions and technologies including systems, software and enterprise, departmental, desktop and mobile computer platforms); and customer services (services and products supporting distributed computing environments). The Company, which is headquartered in Blue Bell, PA, is listed on the NYSE.

Officers: Gary Holler *Global Customer Services*
Jeff Jones *Information Systems Group*
G. Ronald Monaco *Computer Systems Group*

Total Employees ....32,000+   **Regional Employees** 35
Year Established 1986   **SIC Code**.....................................5045
Annual Revenues ($000) 6,400,000

United Air Lines, Inc.

Pittsburgh International Airport
Pittsburgh, PA 15231
County: Allegheny

Phone: (412) 472-3400
Fax: (412) 472-5148
Internet Address: www.ual.com

Commercial airline operating five daily nonstop flights from Pittsburgh to Chicago, IL. The Company is headquartered in Elk Grove Township, IL. It is a subsidiary of UAL Corp., which is also headquartered in Elk Grove Township, IL, and listed on the NYSE. United Express, another subsidiary of the Company, operates five daily nonstop flights from Pittsburgh to Washington, D.C. The Company's reservations/information number is (800) 241-6522.

Officers: Helen Smalich *GMGR*

Regional Employees......................60
Year Established 1926   **SIC Code**.....................................4512

United Cerebral Palsy of the Pittsburgh District

4638 Centre Ave.
Pittsburgh, PA 15213
County: Allegheny

Phone: (412) 683-7100
Fax: (412) 683-4160
Internet Address: www.trfn.clpgh.org/ucp/

Nonprofit agency serving people with physical and/or cognitive disabilities who reside in Allegheny County. Most of the Agency's participants are affected by cerebral palsy, brain injury and other neurological conditions. The Agency's operations include residential support services in 15 different communities; independent living education; vocational support; information and referral; advocacy; home visiting to individuals and families; and three innovative projects that focus on mentoring or employment. The Agency is funded by the United Way, Office of Vocational Rehabilitation, Allegheny County Department of Federal Programs, Mental Health/Mental Retardation Office, Office of Long-Term Care, contracts with private organizations and private insurance. The Pittsburgh District office is an affiliate of United Cerebral Palsy Assn.'s national organization, which is headquartered in Washington, D.C. All of the national organization's 185 affiliates, located throughout the United States, operate independently.

Officers: E. Paul Dick *P*
                 Al Condeluci, Ph.D. *EDIR*
                 Joyce Redmerski *CON*
                 Susan Benn *DIR DEV*

Human Resources: Paulette Gulakowski

Purchasing: Dan Rossi *DIR*

Total Employees	200	**Regional Employees**	200
Year Established	1951	**SIC Code**	8322
Annual Revenues ($000)			3,600

United Methodist Services for the Aging

700 Bower Hill Rd.
Pittsburgh, PA 15243
County: Allegheny

Phone: (412) 341-1030
Fax: (412) 571-5111

Nonprofit organization providing services and housing for the elderly through its four subsidiaries at its complex known as Asbury Heights. The complex is comprised of seven buildings situated on 30 acres of property located in the Mt.

Lebanon suburb of the City of Pittsburgh. Asbury Foundation raises, manages and distributes funds; Asbury Health Center operates the Organization's 145 intermediate and skilled care beds, 30 residential rooms, 40 assisted living beds and 102 apartments; Asbury Place operates a 40-bed Alzheimer's/dementia facility; and Wesley Hills, Inc. owns and operates 19 townhomes.

Officers: John J. Zanardelli *EDIR*
Sally J. Gange *Associate DIR & CFO*
Helen T. Davis *Administrator*
Karen Petrucelli *Senior DIR-DEV*

Human Resources: Eric Larson *Senior DIR-Human Resources*

Purchasing: Mark Tkach *DIR-Materials MGT*

Total Employees.............................250	Regional Employees 250
Year Established 1908	SIC Code......................................8059
Annual Revenues ($000) 13,800	

United Parcel Service

521 N. Center Ave.
New Stanton, PA 15672
County: Westmoreland

Phone: (412) 925-4876

Provider of extensive ground and air shipping services to approximately 200 countries and territories worldwide, including a full array of guaranteed services such as Sonic Air same day delivery, Early A.M. delivery, Next Day Air, Second Day Air and Three Day Select. The facility at the above address is the headquarters of the Laurel Mountain District, which encompasses Western Pennsylvania, West Virginia and Cumberland, MD. Additional facilities located within the seven-county Pittsburgh metropolitan area include the Company's airport and North Side operations, as well as locations in Aliquippa, Butler, Crafton, New Kensington, Uniontown and Washington, PA. The Company's headquarters are located in Atlanta, GA.

Officers: John Warrick *Laurel Mountain District MGR*

Regional Employees..................2,901	
Year Established 1907	SIC Code......................................4212

United Sciences, Inc.

5310 N. Pioneer Rd.
Gibsonia, PA 15044
County: Allegheny

Phone: (412) 443-8610
Fax: (412) 443-7180
Internet Address: www.nauticom.net/www/usi

Manufacturer and servicer of Continuous Emission Monitors (CEMs). The CEM market originated from the Clean Air Act of 1970 and subsequent legislation that requires certain industries, including but not limited to electric utilities, to purchase and install instrumentation to continuously monitor the emission of "smokestack" pollutants. Typical pollutants include sulfur dioxide, nitric oxides, carbon monoxide and particulate smoke. The Company is a majority owned subsidiary of Bowthorpe, Plc, which is headquartered in Crawley, West Sussex, England.

Officers: John E. Traina *P*
Richard L. Myers *VP*

Total Employees..............70	**Regional Employees** 70
Year Established.......... 1978	**SIC Code**.......................3826

United States Filter Corp.

181 Thorn Hill Rd.
Warrendale, PA 15086
County: Allegheny

Phone: (412) 772-0044
Fax: (412) 772-1360
Internet Address: www.usfilter.com

Manufacturer of wastewater treatment equipment. The Company, which is headquartered in Palm Desert, CA, is listed on the NYSE. The local facility also contains a sales office.

Officers: Rob Joyce *VP & GMGR*

Human Resources: Dan Daugherty

Purchasing: Dan Miller

Regional Employees...................125	
Year Established 1953	**SIC Code**.......................3589

United Way of Allegheny County

One Smithfield St.
P.O. Box 735
Pittsburgh, PA 15230
County: Allegheny

Phone: (412) 261-6010
Fax: (412) 394-5376

Nonprofit organization whose mission is to mobilize diverse human and financial resources to respond to the health and human service needs of people and foster their self-sufficiency. To achieve this mission, the Organization listens and responds to the community; involves the community in helping others through its fund-raising and volunteer mobilization efforts; educates the community about critical needs and effective services; convenes and develops community leadership; collects and distributes financial contributions throughout the year; invests contributions in a network of health and human services that make a positive impact on community needs; links people in need with people who can help; and organizes the human service network to reduce fragmentation.

Officers: William J. Meyer *P & Chief Professional Officer*
Robert J. Krasman *EVP*

Human Resources: Jim Morrisey

Purchasing: Darlene Habblett

Total Employees............................100	**Regional Employees** 100
Year Established 1927	**SIC Code**......................................8399
Annual Revenues ($000) 36,400	

Universal Auto Radiator Manufacturing Co.

1000 Saw Mill Run Blvd.
Pittsburgh, PA 15220
County: Allegheny

Phone: (412) 481-9440
Fax: (412) 481-5074

Manufacturer of vehicular radiator and heater cores primarily for OEMs.

Officers: H. G. Gerrick *CH*
Pete Rossin, Jr. *P*
Sean M. Deneen *VP*

Total Employees............................100	**Regional Employees** 100
Year Established 1948	**SIC Code**......................................3714

Universal Welding, Inc.

5578 Old William Penn Hwy.
P.O. Box N
Export, PA 15632
County: Westmoreland

Phone: (412) 327-5550
Fax: (412) 325-1335

Provider of welding, machining and fabricating services. The Company has reconditioned, manufactured or fabricated heavy industrial components for most major industries in the United States. From restoring crane wheels or sophisticated roll rebuilding to complete rehabilitation of a 5,000-ton forging press, the Company claims that it has the expertise to solve any component repair problem.

Officers: Thomas J. Woods *P*

Total Employees	30	**Regional Employees**	30
Year Established	1952	**SIC Code**	3599

University of Pittsburgh

4200 Fifth Ave.
Pittsburgh, PA 15260
County: Allegheny

Phone: (412) 624-4141
Internet Address: www.pitt.edu

Nonprofit, state-related, public research university offering certificate, baccalaureate, master's and doctoral programs to a student body of approximately 32,000. The University operates regional campuses in Johnstown (Cambria County) and Bradford (McKean County) which offer certificate, associate and baccalaureate programs, in Greensburg (Westmoreland County) which offers certificate and baccalaureate programs, and in Titusville (Crawford County) which offers certificate and associate programs and other lower-division curricula. In total, the University offers more than 400 distinct degree programs and numerous dual, joint and cooperative degree programs. Certificate programs are available through many of the schools and through the University Center for International Studies (UCIS). The UCIS coordinates the international research and interdisciplinary instructional programs at the University. During fiscal year 1996, the University conferred 6,754 degrees. The campus, located in the Oakland area of Pittsburgh, is situated on 132 acres, with more than 90 academic, research and administrative buildings, and residence halls.

Officers: J. W. Connolly *CH*
Mark A. Nordenberg *Chancellor & CEO*
James V. Maher *Senior Vice Chancellor & Provost*
Thomas P. Detre *Senior Vice Chancellor-Health Sciences*
Jeffrey A. Romoff *Senior Vice Chancellor-Health ADM; P & CEO-*

University of Pittsburgh Medical Center
Jerome Cochran *AST Chancellor-Business*
Robert Gallagher *Interim Vice Chancellor-Student Affairs*
Lewis M. Popper *GC*

Human Resources: Ronald Frisch

Total Employees........................9,621
Year Established 1787
Annual Revenues ($000) 805,463

Regional Employees 9,004
SIC Code....................................8221

University of Pittsburgh Medical Center System

200 Lothrop St.
Pittsburgh, PA 15213
County: Allegheny

Phone: (412) 647-2345

Nonprofit, comprehensive, academic health care system dedicated to providing patient care, educating the next generation of health care professionals and advancing biomedical knowledge through basic and clinical research. The System manages the activities of its core hospitals and programs. The System consists of four divisions: Hospital Services, Diversified Services, Insurance Services and Physician Services. The Hospital Services division currently is comprised of UPMC Beaver Valley; UPMC Braddock; UPMC Presbyterian, which includes the Eye and Ear Institute, Montefiore University Hospital and Western Psychiatric Institute and Clinic; UPMC Shadyside; UPMC South Side; and UPMC St. Margaret's. A number of other hospitals in western Pennsylvania are affiliated. Overall, the core hospitals (not those affiliated with the System) have approximately 2,700 beds. The System's six schools of the health sciences—Dental Medicine, Health and Rehabilitation Sciences, Medicine, Nursing, Pharmacy and the Graduate School of Public Health—provide for the education of health care professionals, conduct basic and clinical research, and enhance knowledge of diagnosis, treatment and prevention of a broad range of diseases and health-related problems. Satellite clinics are located in Oakland, Greenfield, Hazelwood, downtown Pittsburgh, Squirrel Hill and Greensburg as well as at the Pittsburgh International Airport. Other satellites include the Blue Cross/Blue Shield Health Center at the University of Pittsburgh Medical Center in Oakland, and the University of Pittsburgh Medical Center Matilda Theiss Medical Center in the Hill District of Pittsburgh.

Officers: Jeffrey A. Romoff *P & CEO*
John W. Paul *EVP & COO*
Dean Eckenrode *SVP-Insurance Services Division*
James M. Herndon, M.D. *SVP-Physician Services Division & Chief Medical Officer*
Michele M. McKenney *SVP-Diversified Services Division*

Scott Becker *VP-Network DEV*
George Board, Ph.D. *VP-Government Relations*
Louise Brown *VP-DEV*
Ronald J. Forsythe *VP-Facilities & Construction*
George A. Huber *VP-Legal Services*
Loren H. Roth, M.D. *VP-Managed Care*
Dan Drawbaugh *CIO*
Gail Wolf *Chief Nursing Officer*
Richard Benfer *P-UPMC Braddock*
Stanley Kevish *P-UPMC St. Margaret*
George Korbakes *P-UPMC Beaver Valley & UPMC South Side*
Henry Mordoh *P-UPMC Presbyterian & UPMC Shadyside*
Diane P. Holder *VP-Psychiatric Services, Western Psychiatric Institute & Clinic*

Human Resources: Sid Seligman *VP-Human Relations*

Total Employees......................16,000
Year Established........................1893 **SIC Code**....................................8062
Annual Revenues ($000)..800,000

University Orthopaedics, Inc.

Kaufmann Bldg., 3471 Fifth Ave., Ste. 1010
Pittsburgh, PA 15213
County: Allegheny

Phone: (412) 687-3900
Fax: (412) 687-0802

Provider of medical services specializing in all phases of orthopaedic surgery. The Center's divisions/areas of focus include joint replacements, primary care sports medicine, orthopaedic sports medicine, pediatric orthopaedics, spinal surgery, foot and ankle injuries, musculoskeletal oncology, hand and upper extremity injuries, and orthopaedic trauma. Its facilities include the Center for Adult Orthopaedics, also located at the above address; the Center for Children's Orthopaedics, located on the third floor of the Children's Hospital of Pittsburgh; and the Center for Sports Medicine, located at Craig St. and Baum Blvd. in Pittsburgh. The Center operates satellite offices in Aliquippa, Bethel Park and Murrysville, PA. It is an affiliate of the University of Pittsburgh Medical Center.

Officers: James H. Herndon, M.D. *CH-Department of Orthopaedic Surgery*

Total Employees...........................112 **Regional Employees**....................112
Year Established........................1976 **SIC Code**....................................8011

Uptegraff Manufacturing Co., R. E.

Uptegraff Dr.
P.O. Box 182
Scottdale, PA 15683
County: Westmoreland

Phone: (412) 887-7700
Fax: (412) 887-4748

Manufacturer of single- and three- phase small power transformers and three-phase submersible transformers; three-phase padmount transformers 1,000 through 10,000 kVA; secondary and primary substation transformers; current limiting (air core) reactors up to 80 kVAR per phase; shunt (iron core) reactors up to 1,200 kVAR (three-phase); and single-phase and three-phase station service transformers up to 69,000 volt class. All of the Company's products are custom built and engineered to customer specifications. It serves clients in the utility and industrial sectors.

Officers: Susan U. Endersbe *P (Human Resources)*
Robert P. Endersbe *VP-MFG*
Joseph Schwemmer *TRS*

Purchasing: William Mlinarcik

Total Employees	60	**Regional Employees**	60
Year Established	1926	**SIC Code**	3612
Annual Revenues ($000)	5,000		

Urban League of Pittsburgh, Inc.

One Smithfield St., Ste. 300
Pittsburgh, PA 15222
County: Allegheny

Phone: (412) 227-4802
Fax: (412) 227-4870

Nonprofit membership organization dedicated to the achievement of social and economic equality for African Americans. The Organization specifically provides programs and services in the areas of education, employment, economic development, health and quality of life, youth development and housing. The Organization is an affiliate of the National Urban League, Inc., which is headquartered in New York, NY.

Officers: Esther L. Bush *P & CEO*
William Thompkins *VP*

Human Resources: Vincent Lepera *CFO (Purchasing)*

Total Employees	70	**Regional Employees**	70
Year Established	1918	**SIC Code**	8399
Annual Revenues ($000)	4,000		

Urish Popeck & Co., LLC

Three Gateway Center, 24th Fl.
Pittsburgh, PA 15222
County: Allegheny
Phone: (412) 391-1994
Fax: (412) 391-0724

Certified public accounting firm providing a variety of professional services for manufacturing, health care, retail, professional and nonprofit organizations. The Firm also offers business and computer consulting. It maintains a branch office in Washington, PA, and anticipates the opening of a second branch sometime in 1998 in State College, PA. The Firm is a regional representative of BDO Seidman LLP (BSL), which is headquartered in New York, NY. BSL is a part of the BDO worldwide organization, which is headquartered in Brussels, Belgium.

Officers: Kenneth Urish *MPTR*

Total Employees	53	**Regional Employees**	53
Year Established	1976	**SIC Code**	8721

US Airways Federal Credit Union

1453 Beers School Rd.
P.O. Box 1289
Coraopolis, PA 15108
County: Allegheny
Phone: (412) 269-3011
Fax: (412) 269-3058

Nonprofit, member-owned, full-service financial cooperative. The Institution's products and services include savings accounts, certificates, Christmas club accounts, full-service accounts, debit cards, national access ATM cards, VISA cards, personal loans, new and used vehicle loans, mortgage loans, money market-type accounts and financial planning services, in addition to value-added services. While the Institution's membership was formerly composed primarily of USAir and USAir-affiliated employees, it has amended its charter to include additional select employee groups. Branch offices are located in San Diego, CA; Washington, D.C.; Indianapolis, IN; Baltimore, MD; Boston, MA; Syracuse, NY; Charlotte and Winston-Salem, NC; and Philadelphia, PA.

Officers: Ralph B. Canterbury *P & CEO*
Joseph C. Cirelli *EVP*
Ralph W. Canterbury *VP-Technology & Communications*
Dennis F. Colo *VP-FIN*
Molly L. Hevia *VP-MKT*

Human Resources: Mark S. Brennan *VP-Human Resources*

Total Employees............................216 **Regional Employees** 182
Year Established ....1953 **SIC Code**.....................................6061
Annual Revenues ($000) ....401,000 (Assets)

US Airways Group, Inc.

Pittsburgh International Airport
P.O. Box 12346
Pittsburgh, PA 15231
County: Allegheny

Phone: (412) 472-7000
Internet Address: www.usairways.com

Commercial airline, known as USAirways, operating approximately 525 daily flights out of the Pittsburgh International Airport. The Company flies to destinations throughout the continental United States, Canada, Europe, the Bahamas, Bermuda, the Caribbean and Puerto Rico. Pittsburgh is a regional hub along with Baltimore, MD; Charlotte, NC; and Philadelphia, PA. Both the Company and its operating subsidiary, US Airways, Inc., are headquartered in Arlington, VA. The Company is listed on the NYSE. Its reservations/information number is (800) 428-4322.

Officers: Chris Doan *SVP-Maintenance*
Robert Oaks *SVP-OPR*
Malcolm Armstrong *VP-Safety & Compliance*
William Barr *VP-Flight OPR*
Alan Crellin *VP-Ground Services*

Total Employees.......................42,402 **Regional Employees**..............11,800
Year Established ....1939 **SIC Code**.....................................4512
Annual Revenues ($000) 8,140,000

USA Gourmet Inc.

1016 N. Lincoln Ave.
Pittsburgh, PA 15233
County: Allegheny

Phone: (412) 231-8222
Fax: (412) 231-7002

Wholesale and retail bakery concentrating on croissants, Danish, cakes, pies and cookies. The Company supplies approximately 150 regular accounts, including food purveyors, hotels and restaurants. One of its larger accounts is Las Vegas-based Harrahs' Hotels. The Company also has a catering department that supplies breakfasts and lunches, primarily for downtown businesses. The Company's retail bakeries are located at 441 Smithfield St., 2115 Penn Ave. and at the above address.

Officers: Jim Simakas *P*
              Cathy Simakas *VP*

Total Employees............................100	**Regional Employees** 100
Year Established 1986	**SIC Code**....................................5461

USA Waste Services, Inc.

Park West Two, 2000 Cliff Mine Rd., Ste. 420
Pittsburgh, PA 15275
County: Allegheny

Phone: (412) 494-4966
Fax: (412) 490-0168

   Provider of non-hazardous solid waste management services, consisting of collection, transfer, disposal, recycling and other miscellaneous services to municipal, commercial, industrial and residential customers. The Company, which is headquartered in Houston, TX, and listed on the NYSE, maintains its Central Region headquarters at the above address, overseeing the Company's operations in Illinois, Indiana, Iowa, Maryland, Michigan, Minnesota, North Dakota, Ohio, Pennsylvania, West Virginia and Wisconsin. Its local businesses and facilities include Arden Landfill in Washington; M. C. Arnoni Landfill in Library; Martin's Washington Hauling in Washington; Monroeville Landfill in Monroeville; North Huntingdon Hauling in North Huntingdon; Tri-Valley Transfer in Kittanning; Tri-Valley Waste Systems in New Kensington; and Valley Landfill in Irwin.

Officers: Charles A. Wilcox *Regional VP*
              Vahé Gabriel *Regional CON*

Total Employees........................9,800	**Regional Employees** 450
Year Established 1971	**SIC Code**....................................4953
Annual Revenues ($000) 1,313,388	

USX Corp.

USX Tower, 600 Grant St.
Pittsburgh, PA 15219
County: Allegheny

Phone: (412) 433-1121
Fax: (412) 433-5733
Internet Address: www.usx.com

   Diversified company engaged in the energy business through the USX-Marathon Group, in the steel business through the USX-U.S. Steel Group and in the gas gathering and processing business through the USX-Delhi Group. The Company has three classes of common stock, all of which are listed on the NYSE: USX-Marathon Group, USX-U.S. Steel Group and USX-Delhi Group. The Marathon Group, based in Houston,TX, is engaged in worldwide exploration, production, transportation and marketing of crude oil and natural gas, and domestic refining, marketing and transportation of petroleum products. The U.S. Steel Group, based in Pittsburgh, PA, is primarily engaged in the production and sale of steel mill products, coke and taconite pellets through its U.S. Steel operations. U.S. Steel claims to be the largest integrated steel producer in the United States. The U.S. Steel Group is also engaged in the management of mineral resources, domestic coal mining, engineering and consulting services, and technology licensing. Other businesses that are part of U.S. Steel Group include real estate development and management, and leasing and financing activities. The Delhi Group, based in Dallas, TX, is engaged in the purchasing, gathering, processing, transporting and marketing of natural gas. The financial information of the Marathon Group, the U.S. Steel Group and the Delhi Group, taken together includes all accounts that comprise the consolidated financial information of the company. The total number of active employees of USX headquarters not assigned to a specific group is 248. (Refer to the USX-U.S. Steel Group profile for additional information.)

Officers: Thomas J. Usher *CH & CEO*
Robert M. Hernandez *VCH & CFO*
Gretchen R. Haggerty *VP & TRS*
Kenneth L. Matheny *VP & CON*
Victor G. Beghini *VCH-Marathon Group & P-Marathon Oil Co.*
David M. Kihneman *P-Delhi Group*
Paul J. Wilhelm *P-U.S. Steel Group*

Human Resources: Dan D. Sandman *SVP-Human Resources, GC & SEC*

Total Employees......................42,195	**Regional Employees** 6,176
Year Established 1901	**SIC Code** 2911
Annual Revenues ($000) 23,800,000	

VA Pittsburgh Healthcare System

Delafield Rd.
Pittsburgh, PA 15240
County: Allegheny

Phone: (412) 784-3900
Fax: (412) 784-3743

Nonprofit major medical, surgical, psychiatric, tertiary and community care health-care system consisting of three campuses operating under one management, which is located at the above address. The University Drive division is located in the Oakland District of Pittsburgh adjacent to the University of Pittsburgh. This campus serves as the acute care division and has approximately 200 operating beds distributed among medicine, surgery, neurology, critical care and rehabilitation medicine. It also operates a primary care outpatient clinic in St. Clairsville, OH. The Aspinwall Progressive Care Center, located at the above address, is a geriatric center with 400 operating beds of which 160 are intermediate and 240 are nursing home care beds. Programs supporting the geriatric center include primary care, adult day health care and hospice care. The Highland Drive division at 7180 Highland Dr. in Pittsburgh, provides comprehensive acute and long-term care psychiatric treatment, including comprehensive substance abuse, post-traumatic stress disorder, schizophrenia and a comprehensive homeless program. In addition to its 270 acute and extended psychiatry beds, it contains a 60-bed Transitional Care Center and a 74-bed Homeless Domiciliary. The System is also a regional center for the treatment of ex-prisoners of war and supports three Veterans Outreach Centers in McKeesport and Pittsburgh, PA, and Wheeling, WV. The System is affiliated with the University of Pittsburgh School of Medicine and with the University's other schools of health sciences. The mission of the System is fourfold: patient care, education, research and primary backup to the Department of Defense health care system in time of national emergency as Western Pennsylvania's Coordination Center for the National Disaster Medical System. To maintain these diversified and highly specialized functions, it has been designated as a National Liver Transplant Center, Regional Cardiac Surgery Center, Oncology Network Center and Dialysis Center. The System is owned and operated by the Department of Veterans Affairs in Washington, D.C.

Officers: Thomas A. Cappello *DIR*
Janet S. Stout *Associate DIR*
Joseph A. Williams, Jr. *Associate DIR-Patient Care Services*
Ernest Urban, M.D. *Interim Chief of Staff*

Human Resources: Andrew Pinchak

Purchasing: Bill Leuthold

Total Employees........................2,600   **Regional Employees** 2,600
SIC Code 8062

Valley Health System

1000 Dutch Ridge Rd.
Beaver, PA 15009
County: Beaver

Phone: (412) 728-7000
Fax: (412) 728-5322

Nonprofit health care delivery system providing comprehensive care for residents of northwest Allegheny County, Beaver County and surrounding areas, including parts of Ohio and West Virginia. The System is comprised of two hospitals, The Medical Center, Beaver, located at the above address, and Sewickley Valley Hospital, at 720 Blackburn Rd. in Sewickley, PA; as well as Seniors' Health Connection, Women's Health Connection and the Rheumatology Center in Center Township, PA; imaging and laboratory services in Hopewell Township, PA; Family Practice Center in Beaver Falls, PA; home care and a satellite laboratory in Chippewa Township, PA; Sewickley Surgical Center in Edgeworth, PA; Moon Township Family Health Center in Moon Township, PA; Marshall Township Family Health Center in Marshall Township, PA; and Staunton Clinic in Bellevue, PA. The System has a total of 689 acute, skilled and short procedure beds and 57 bassinets, with a staff of 574 physicians. Its services include cancer treatment, cardiology, emergency, home care, major surgery/outpatient, maternity and child care, occupational medicine, plastic and reconstructive surgery, psychiatric/mental health, pulmonary medicine, rehabilitation, rheumatology, services for seniors, skilled nursing, education and community outreach. In October 1996, the respective boards of Sewickley Valley Hospital and The Medical Center, Beaver, voted final approval for a merger of both hospitals.

Officers: Larry Crowell *P & CEO*
Norman Mitry *CFO*
Donald Spalding *EVP; P-Valley Medical Facilities*
Dorothy Bellhouse *VP-Corporate Planning*
Jim Cooper *COO-Sewickley Valley Hospital*
Walt Van Dyke *COO-The Medical Center, Beaver*

Human Resources: Rosanne Saunders *VP*

Total Employees..........................3,483	**Regional Employees** 3,483
Year Established 1894	**SIC Code**....................................8062

Valley National Gases, Inc.

9189 Marshall Rd.
Cranberry Township, PA 16066
County: Butler

Phone: (412) 452-8904
Fax: (412) 452-8837

Distributor of industrial, medical and specialty gas, and welding supplies. The Company's major brands include All-State, Alloy Rods, BOC Gases, ESAB, L-Tec, Lincoln, Tweco and Western Enterprises. The Company, which is headquartered in Wheeling, WV, operates facilities in Delaware, Kentucky, Maryland, New Jersey, North Carolina, Ohio, Pennsylvania, Tennessee, Virginia and West Virginia. In addition to its site at the above address, other Pennsylvania offices are located in Altoona, Chaleroi, Greensburg, Indiana, Johnstown, New Castle, Philipsburg, Pittsburgh, Punxsutawney, Uniontown, Washington and West Mifflin.

Officers: Gary West *CH*
Larry Bandi *P & CEO*
John Bushwack *COO*
Bill Kennedy *VP-MKT*
Fred Semenik *VP-OPR*
Keith Woodruff *VP-Safety & Compliance*
Jerry Girod *GMGR-Cranberry Township*

Human Resources: Jerry McGlumphy *VP-Human Resources*

Total Employees...........................420	**Regional Employees** 90
Year Established 1958	**SIC Code**....................................2813
Annual Revenues ($000) 65,000	

Valley News Dispatch

210 Fourth Ave.
Tarentum, PA 15084
County: Allegheny

Phone: (412) 224-4321
Fax: (412) 226-7787

Publisher of the Valley News Dispatch, a newspaper with a daily circulation of 34,212 and a Sunday circulation of 33,707. The newspaper is distributed to readers in parts of Allegheny, Armstrong, Butler and Westmoreland Counties, PA, from as far north as Kittanning and as far south as Fox Chapel. The Company also provides contract printing services for a number of other publications including two affiliates, The Herald, a weekly newspaper based in Sharpsburg, PA, and the North Hills News Record, a daily newspaper based in Warrendale, PA. The Company is a subsidiary of Gannett Co., Inc., which is headquartered in Arlington,VA, and listed on the NYSE.

Officers: Lawrence Jock *Publisher*

Total Employees............................300
Year Established 1892   **SIC Code** 2711

Valspar Corp., The

1501 Reedsdale St., Ste. 400
Pittsburgh, PA 15233
County: Allegheny

Phone: (412) 231-6100
Fax: (412) 231-6446
Internet Address: www.valspar.com

Manufacturer of high-performance coatings for the interior and exterior surfaces of food and beverage cans. The Company also produces coatings for nonfood cans, such as aerosol, paint and oil, plus coatings for closures and crowns, and coatings for flexible packaging—paper, film and foil. Its technologies include waterborne, high solids, electrodeposition, UV/EB, solvent-borne and powder. The facility located at the above address is the administrative headquarters of the Packaging Coatings Group (PCG) division of the Company, which is headquartered in Minneapolis, MN, and listed on the NYSE. In fiscal year 1996, the PCG division accounted for 27%, or $235 million, of the Company's total revenue. The PCG's other local sites include a plant at 372 Cleveland St. in Rochester, PA, and a facility at 2000 Westhall St. in Pittsburgh, PA, which houses a plant and the central technical laboratory. Additional plants are located in Azusa, CA; Covington, GA; Carol Stream, IL; Toronto, Ontario, Canada; and in Europe and the People's Republic of China.

Officers: William L. Mansfield *VP-Packaging Coatings Group*

Total Employees........................2,800	**Regional Employees** 300
Year Established 1806	**SIC Code**......................................2899
Annual Revenues ($000) 859,799	

Valvoline Co.

501 Railroad St.
Rochester, PA 15074
County: Beaver

Phone: (412) 774-2020
Fax: (412) 728-7327

Manufacturer and packager of oil products primarily for the automotive indus-try. The plant located at the above address is owned by the Valvoline Co. (VC), which is headquartered in Lexington, KY. VC is a division of Ashland, Inc., which is headquartered in Ashland, KY, and listed on the NYSE.

Officers: Donald W. Zahn *OPR MGR*

Regional Employees......................70   **SIC Code** 2911

Van Dyk Business Systems, Inc.

800 Trumbull Dr.
Pittsburgh, PA 15205
County: Allegheny

Phone: (412) 279-1400
Fax: (412) 279-9394

Dealer of Sharp Electronics products, offering sales, service and supplies. The Company's office equipment product line includes copiers, facsimile machines, electronic filing, LCD and printers. It operates a branch facility in Youngwood, PA. The Company serves clients in Allegheny, Beaver, Butler, Greensburg, Washington and Westmoreland Counties, PA.

Officers: Ronald G. Linaburg *CH*
                Leonard A. Lutes *P & CEO*
                David P. Kadyk *VP-Service*
                Donald Costa *CON*
                Ronald L. Bathurst *OPR MGR*

Purchasing: Bob Kelly

Total Employees..............................76	**Regional Employees** 75
Year Established 1984	**SIC Code**......................................5999
Annual Revenues ($000) 11,333	

Vanadium Enterprises Corp.

98 Vanadium Rd.
Bridgeville, PA 15017
County: Allegheny

Phone: (412) 221-1100
Fax: (412) 220-3003
Internet Address: www.vanadium.com

Holding company, doing business as the Vanadium Group, comprised of four operating subsidiaries that offer a broad range of engineering, consulting, environmental, management and construction-related services primarily to utility, industrial and government clients. The Company's services include facilities operations and maintenance, engineering and design, environmental engineering, land engineering and geographic information systems, risk and crisis management services, telecommunication and software services, construction services and bulk industrial supplies. Construction Rental & Supply, Inc. in Pittsburgh, PA, provides rental equipment and consumable supplies to contractors, fabricators, steel erectors, electric utilities, institutional clients and manufacturers in the Tri-State market. Jones Krall, Inc. provides construction and maintenance services through its offices in El Segundo, CA, and Bridgeville, PA. SE Technologies, Inc. is an engineering, consulting and management services firm with offices in Bridgeville, PA; Chattanooga, TN; and South Melbourne, Australia. SSI Services, Inc. is a highly specialized organization providing services necessary to operate and maintain government facilities, risk and crisis management services, and telecommunication and software services with offices in Granite City, IL; West Point, NY; Bridgeville, Harrisburg and Pittsburgh, PA; Houston, TX; and McLean, VA.

Officers: Matthew D. Schneider *P & CEO*
Bal K. Gupta *EDIR & SEC*
Paul W. Fallert *TRS*
Ray M. Kathiresan *CIO*

Human Resources: Andra M. Tokarsky

Total Employees	1,000	**Regional Employees**	250
Year Established	1989	**SIC Code**	8711
Annual Revenues ($000)			73,000

Vangura Surfacing Products, Inc.

14431 Rte. 30
Irwin, PA 15642
County: Westmoreland

Phone: (412) 824-0772
Fax: (412) 824-0709

Manufacturer of solid surface tops including wooden and laminated counter tops and casement.

Officers: Edward Vangura *P*
Don Hornynk *VP*

Total Employees..............................65
Year Established 1971

Regional Employees 65
SIC Code....................................2541

Vanstar Corp.

Liberty Center, 1001 Liberty Ave., 9th Fl.
Pittsburgh, PA 15222
County: Allegheny

Phone: (412) 355-0499
Fax: (412) 355-0477
Internet Address: www.vanstar.com

Provider of integrated technology services and products to design, build and manage computer network infrastructures of Fortune 1000 companies and other large enterprises. The Company focuses on reducing the total cost of ownership for computing technology; gaining control and management of distributed networks; increasing enduser productivity and satisfaction; reducing the risk involved with adopting new technology; keeping pace with new technologies to plan for future network strategies; and providing technology-based solutions to meet overall business strategy. The Company, which is headquartered in Pleasanton, CA, is listed on the NYSE. It operates more than 100 offices in all major U.S. markets. The local office works with clients in Western Pennsylvania and in West Virginia, including ALCOA and Heinz.

Officers: Glenn P. Wallace *District MGR*

Human Resources: Ginger Devereaux *Human Resources MGR (Pleasanton, CA)*

Purchasing: Ahmad Manshouri *SVP-Procurement OPR (Pleasanton, CA)*

Total Employees ....6,500+
Year Established 1976
Annual Revenues ($000) 2,500,000

Regional Employees 90
SIC Code....................................5045

Vector Security, Inc.

5700 Corporate Dr.
Pittsburgh, PA 15237
County: Allegheny

Phone: (412) 364-2600
Fax: (412) 364-2712

Retailer, installer, servicer and monitor of fire and burglary alarm security systems for residential and commercial applications. The Company also offers temperature control systems, intercom systems and vacuum control systems. It operates a local branch office at 3400 McKnight E. Dr. in Pittsburgh, PA; with other branch sites in Landover, MD; Haddonfield and Pennington, NJ; Youngstown, OH; Erie, Lancaster and Philadelphia, PA; and Leesburg, Manassas and Richmond, VA. The Company is a subsidiary of the Philadelphia Contributionship for the Insurance of Houses from Loss by Fire, which is head-quartered in Philadelphia, PA.

Officers: John A. Murphy *P*
Ron Lipari *SVP-Western Region*
Pam Petrow *SVP-Central Stations*

Human Resources: Louise Urbanek

Purchasing: Gordon Zeiler *VP & GMGR*

Total Employees	325	**Regional Employees**	87
Year Established	1988	**SIC Code**	7382

Vectran Corp.

2170 William Pitt Way
Pittsburgh, PA 15238
County: Allegheny

Phone: (412) 963-1221
Fax: (412) 963-7205

Manufacturer of industrial radio remote control systems used to control cranes, locomotives, loaders, doors, balers, soaking pits and other related equipment. The Company also manufactures radio modems and custom applications using radio links. It claims to be the largest supplier of digital radio control systems. The Company's customers include steel producers, specialty steel producers, utilities, mining installations, basic aluminum facilities and industry in general. It designs, engineers and manufactures all its electronic equipment, including the radio and system interfacing equipment.

Officers: Robert R. O'Farrell *P*
Jeffrey A. McCann *VP*

Human Resources: Jacinta Dvorak

Total Employees	50	**Regional Employees**	50
Year Established	1976	**SIC Code**	3669
Annual Revenues ($000)			5,000

Veka, Inc.

100 Veka Dr.
Fombell, PA 16123
County: Beaver

Phone: (412) 452-1000
Fax: (412) 452-1019
Internet Address: www.veka.com

Manufacturer of vinyl PVC lineal extrusions for window and door suppliers in North America. The Company and its affiliate, Veka West, Inc. in Reno, NV, are subsidiaries of Veka Holdings Inc. (VHI), which is based in Wilmington, DE. VHI is a subsidiary of Veka AG, which has its headquarters in Sendenhorst, Germany.

Officers: C. Lawrence Irwin *P*
Walter W. Stucky *EVP*
James H. Druschel *SEC & TRS*

Human Resources: Brian J. Shearer

Purchasing: Laura Thoma

Total Employees	350	**Regional Employees**	350
Year Established	1983	**SIC Code**	3089
Annual Revenues ($000)			80,000

Ventana Plastics Co.

6001 Enterprise Dr.
Export, PA 15632
County: Westmoreland

Phone: (412) 325-3400
Fax: (412) 327-4540

Fabricator of custom vinyl window shapes for the window manufacturing industry. The Company also manufactures and markets its Series 2000 Garden Window to window fabricators and dealers. Its products are used in residential construction for both new and remodeling applications throughout the U.S.

Officers: Guenther Pennekamp *P*
Tony Pauly *VP & GMGR*
Kim Fondrk *SAL MGR*
Ann Pauly *ADM MGR*
John Seba *Production MGR*

Human Resources: Denise Yocum

Purchasing: Mike Smith

Total Employees	120	**Regional Employees**	120
Year Established	1987	**SIC Code**	3089
Annual Revenues ($000)			5,000

Verland

212 Iris Rd.
Sewickley, PA 15143
County: Allegheny

Phone: (412) 741-2375
Fax: (412) 741-3299

Nonprofit provider of services for individuals who are mentally and developmentally disabled. Through two divisions, The Verland Foundation Inc. (TVFI) and Verland CLA (VCLA), the Organization provides choices, supports and options for 190 individuals. TVFI, located at the above address, offers intermediate care for individuals with mental retardation within 10 homes, an activities center and a stable at its campus. It also operates similar facilities in Allegheny, Fayette and Mercer Counties. TVFI's Intermediate Care Facility/Other Related Conditions project offers supports and services to individuals with physical disabilities who formerly lived in nursing homes, preparing them for the transition to gainful employment and independent living. VCLA, located in Coraopolis, PA, provides supports and options to individuals who are mentally disabled in 17 private homes throughout Allegheny County.

Officers: Carol B. Mitchell *P & CEO*
John J. Roth *CON*
George J. Geisler *Executive Program DIR*
Barbara Dudeck *DIR-Nursing*

Human Resources: Sandy Diegelmann
Kelly Lollobrigida

Total Employees 525		**Regional Employees** 505	
Year Established 1978		**SIC Code** 8361	
Annual Revenues ($000) 16,000			

Versatech, Inc.

6012 Enterprise Dr.
P.O. Box 608
Export, PA 15632
County: Westmoreland

Phone: (412) 327-8324
Fax: (412) 327-9190

Machine shop engaged in the manufacture of precision-machined parts. Through Versa-Fab, Inc., located in Monroeville, PA, the Company provides computer and numerically controlled (CNC) machining, CNC punching and bending, electrostatic painting, welding and assemblies.

Officers: Richard L. Versaw *P*
Raymond J. Szwedko *VP*
Joyce M. Versaw *TRS*

Total Employees.............................90	**Regional Employees** 90
Year Established 1974	**SIC Code**.......................................3599
Annual Revenues ($000) 10,000	

Vesuvius McDanel Co.

510 Ninth Ave.
Beaver Falls, PA 15010
County: Beaver

Phone: (412) 843-8300
Fax: (412) 843-5644

Manufacturer of industrial and technical ceramics for the glass industry. The Company is a division of Vesuvius USA (VU), which is headquartered in Champaign, IL, with international headquarters in Brussels, Belgium. It is a subsidiary of Cookson Group Plc, which is headquartered in London, England, and listed on the London Stock Exchange.

Officers: Les Crittenden *GMGR*

Human Resources: Art Penebaker *Human Relations DIR*

Regional Employees....................130	**SIC Code**.......................................3255

Vesuvius USA

50 N. Green Lane
Zelienople, PA 16063
County: Butler

Phone: (412) 452-6050
Fax: (412) 452-7317

Manufacturer, marketer and servicer of fully integrated mechanical and refractory systems for flow control and stream protection of molten metal. The Company's systems include furnace, ladle and tundish slide gates, process control and automation equipment as well as a wide range of refractory components and qualities for all steel grades. It also provides project management engineering and on-site assistance. The facility located at the above address, which encompasses a manufacturing plant and sales office, serves the ferrous industry. The Company's North and South American operations are headquartered in Champaign, IL, with international headquarters in Brussels, Belgium. It is a subsidiary of Cookson Group Plc, which is headquartered in London, England, and listed on the London Stock Exchange. The Company also operates a research and development center located at 4604 Campbells Run Rd. in Pittsburgh, PA, which employees approximately 45.

Officers: Louis Sebastian *GMGR-East Region*

Regional Employees....................125	**SIC Code**.......................................3297

Vista Metals, Inc.

1024 E. Smithfield St.
P.O. Box 94
McKeesport, PA 15135
County: Allegheny

Phone: (412) 751-4600
Fax: (412) 751-1850

Manufacturer of sintered tungsten carbide for tooling-related applications.

Officers: William F. Riley *P*
Gregg W. Riley *EVP*
Brian S. Riley *Corporate VP*
Jeffrey M. Scales *VP-OPR*
John W. Torgent *VP-SAL*
Mark A. Shelleby *SEC & TRS*

Total Employees...........................150   **Regional Employees** 150
Year Established 1969   **SIC Code**....................................3544

VITAC

Southpointe, 101 Hillpointe Dr.
Canonsburg, PA 15317
County: Washington

Phone: (412) 514-4000
Fax: (412) 514-4111
Internet Address: www.vitac.com

Provider of complete captioning services to broadcast, video, industrial, government and educational program suppliers. The Company specializes in real-time captioning of live television programs and events and claims to be a leader in providing off-line captioning of prerecorded programs, including entertainment programs, home videos, and informational and instructional videos. The Company captions more than 290 hours of programming each week, including news, daytime drama, talk and entertainment programs, sports and prime time programs. Its clients include ABC, CBS, CNN, FOX, NBC, PBS, Columbia TriStar, Discovery Communications, Lifetime Television, MCA-TV, Paramount Domestic Television, Saban Entertainment and Warner Bros. The Company's headquarters, which are located at the above address, is equipped with 10 caption control rooms for live captioning, eight off-line captioning stations and a satellite dish farm that can downlink 12 different satellites. Its other facilities include a sales/production office in Burbank, CA; a production office in Washington, D.C.; and a sales office in Tampa, FL.

Officers: Ed Fulesday *CH*
Joseph R. Karlovits *P*
Martin H. Block *EVP-FIN & ADM*

Dave Crane *EVP-OPR & ENG*
Jeff Hutchins *EVP-Planning & DEV*
Deborah Popkin Schuster *VP-SAL & GMGR*
Chuck Karlovits *DIR-FIN & ADM*
Tracey Taylor Perles *DIR-Corporate DEV*

Human Resources: Marcia Rymarchyk

Purchasing: Doug Karlovits

Total Employees..........................107   **Regional Employees** 84
Year Established 1986   **SIC Code**....................................4899
Annual Revenues ($000) 4,800

VNA Services and Foundation, Western Pennsylvania

154 Hindman Rd.
Butler, PA 16001
County: Butler

Phone: (412) 282-6806
Fax: (412) 282-7517
Internet Address: www.vna.com

   Nonprofit parent corporation for five subsidiaries, all of which are headquartered at the above address, providing home health care services to residents of Armstrong, Butler and Northwestern Westmoreland Counties, PA, and surrounding areas. Visiting Nurses Assn., Western Pennsylvania, provides professional nursing, physical and occupational therapy, rehabilitation therapy, speech therapy, enterostomal therapy, medical social service, home health aide service, nutritional counseling, in-home IV therapy, care of mothers and newborns, laboratory services, care of the terminally ill and diabetic counseling, with additional branch offices in Butler, Ford City, Saxonburg, Vandergrift, West Sunbury and Zelienople, PA. VNA Complete Care, Western Pennsylvania, provides a full range of home health care services and promotes wellness to the general public. VNA Hospice, Western Pennsylvania, provides physical, emotional and spiritual care for patients and their families during the final phase of life. VNA Medical Equipment and Supplies, Western Pennsylvania, provides home medical equipment and supplies, ranging from hospital beds, wheelchairs, and trapeze and patient lift equipment to oxygen and respiratory equipment, ostomy supplies and breast prostheses. VNA Pharmacy, Western Pennsylvania, is a full-service pharmacy.

Officers: Nancy L. Bohnet *P & CEO*
Chris Hengler *VP*
John Ilcyn *VP*
Penny Milanovich *VP*
Liz Powell *VP*
Kristy Wright *VP*

Human Resources: Jessica Eichner

Purchasing: Doug Bollman

Total Employees	380	Regional Employees	380
Year Established	1969	SIC Code	8082
Annual Revenues ($000)	15,000		

Vocational Rehabilitation Center of Allegheny County, Inc.

1323 Forbes Ave.
Pittsburgh, PA 15219
County: Allegheny

Phone: (412) 471-2600
Fax: (412) 471-3894

Nonprofit provider of vocational services whose mission is to help people with disabilities enter the workforce and find dignity as wage-earning independent citizens. The Agency's services include vocational counseling, psychological evaluation and counseling, work evaluation, work adjustment, job coaching, skills training, job placement, transitional employment and sheltered employment. While its services are open to individuals nationwide, the majority of its clients reside in Western Pennsylvania. The Agency's clients include those with developmental and physical disabilities, chronic mental health problems, and clients with hearing and visual impairments. It also serves clients with problems arising from heart disease, arthritis and head trauma as well as alcohol and drug abuse. The Agency's training programs help participants acquire skills to meet the needs of many local companies. Individuals are trained to handle direct mail, microfilming-microfiche, printing, sorting, collating, packaging, shrink wrapping, metal fabrication, mechanical and electrical assembly and subassembly, and corrugated partition assembly. The Agency's Mon Valley Rehabilitation division is located in Rostraver Township, PA.

Officers: Robert J. Mather *P & CEO*
Thomas A. Bach *VP-Human Services*

Human Resources: Judith A. Romah *Corporate SEC*

Purchasing: David C. Scapes *VP & TRS*

Total Employees	139	Regional Employees	139
Year Established	1927	SIC Code	8331
Annual Revenues ($000)	6,986		

Voegele Co., Inc.

200 Bridge St.
P.O. Box 9543
Pittsburgh, PA 15223
County: Allegheny

Phone: (412) 781-0940
Fax: (412) 781-7876

Contractor specializing in commercial and industrial roofing, sheeting, insulating, window/skylight replacement and complete retrofit work. With in-house design and engineering capabilities, the Company is a single source responsibility contractor. Its subsidiary, EXTECH/Exterior Technologies, Inc. (ETI), also located at the above address, is a manufacturer of windows, skylights, curtainwalls and storefronts, specializing in commercial and industrial work. ETI also manufactures hurricane glazing and security glazing products and operates a branch office in Ft. Lauderdale, FL.

Officers: William P. Voegele, Jr. *P*
Francis E. Coholich *VP*

Total Employees	65	**Regional Employees**	61
Year Established	1943	**SIC Code**	3442
Annual Revenues ($000)	8,000		

Voest-Alpine Industries, Inc.

Penn Center W., Bldg. IV, Ste. 400
Pittsburgh, PA 15276
County: Allegheny

Phone: (412) 747-4600
Fax: (412) 747-4646
Internet Address: www.steelnet.org/vaii

Supplier of single source technology, hardware and automation processes for both the construction of new steelmaking plants and the upgrading of existing plant facilities. The Company currently maintains six technical divisions, including Automation, Casting, Environmental, Rolling Mills, Steelmaking and COREX®, and an After Sales division. These divisions offer total design, engineering, manufacturing, installation, maintenance and servicing for the complete spectrum of ironmaking, steelmaking, continuous casting, rolling mills, strip processing, automation and environmental technologies for the steel industry. The Company is a subsidiary of Voest-Alpine Industrieanlagenbau, GmbH (VAIG), which is headquartered in Linz, Austria. VAIG is a subsidiary of VA Technologie AG, which is also headquartered in Linz, Austria, and listed on the Austrian Stock Exchange.

Officers: Klaus Nettlebeck *P*
Hal Dietrick *EVP-Technical DIR*
Otto L. Hiris *EVP-COREX® Technology*
E. Paul Fredo *VP-ADM & FIN*
Michael T. McGuire *VP-SAL & MKT*
R. Bruce Genter *Division MGR-Steelmaking*
Manfred Lixi *Division MGR-Environmental*
Wayne Pottmeyer *Division MGR-Rolling Mills & Processing Lines*
Andrew Procopio *Division MGR-Continuous Casting*
Virginia Gorrell *MGR-After SAL*

Purchasing: Kurt Wolf *MGR-Purchasing*

Total Employees............................120	**Regional Employees** 120
Year Established 1992	**SIC Code**......................................5084
Annual Revenues ($000) 90,000	

Voest-Alpine Services & Technologies Corp.

Penn Center W., Bldg. IV, Ste. 404
Pittsburgh, PA 15276
County: Allegheny

Phone: (412) 747-4680
Fax: (412) 747-4699

Provider of specialized maintenance services to the steel industry. The Company, also known as VAST, offers two main lines of products and services: off-site maintenance for all styles and designs of casting machines; and standard and custom automatic, electromechanical and hydraulic lifting equipment for handling virtually any size or shape of product, from small forgings to 200-ton slabs. In addition to keeping clients informed of technical developments in these two fields, the Company also offers parts tracking, field inspections, equipment analysis, operational advice, upgrades, modifications and machine alignments. Its caster maintenance facilities are located in Baltimore, MD; Detroit, MI; and Provo, UT. These plants serve metal producers throughout North America. The Company also offers technical consulting services to its customers. The Company is a subsidiary of Voest-Alpine International Corp. (VAIC), which is headquartered in New York, NY. VAIC is a subsidiary of VA Tech International GmbH, which is headquartered in Linz, Austria, and listed on the Austrian Stock Exchange.

Officers: Thomas J. Nugent *P*
George Born *VP-SAL & MKT*
Leland Chandler *VP-OPR*
Kevin Cotter *CON*

Total Employees............................225	**Regional Employees** 20
Year Established 1990	**SIC Code**......................................7699

Wahl Refractories, Inc.

1330 Market St.
McKeesport, PA 15132
County: Allegheny

Phone: (412) 673-6888
Fax: (412) 673-6889
Internet Address: www.wahl@nwohio.com

Provider of installation, repair and maintenance of refractories for a variety of industries, including ferrous and nonferrous metals, heat treating and forging, hospitals, petrochemical, power distribution, industrial ceramics, cement and limestone, waste incineration, pharmaceutical and process. The Company's services include brickwork, gunnite, ramming, pre-cast shapes, ceramic fiber, fiberkote, fireproofing, cast-in-place refractories, field forming, refractory pumping, insulating fire brick, pre-cast shapes, mixer rental, engineering and project management. The Company, which is headquartered in Fremont, OH, maintains its Construction Division at the above address.

Officers: Daniel H. Lease *CH*
Daniel W. Lease *P*
Dave Glasser *VP-SAL*
Dave McKeefrey *VP-MKT*
Howard Roenigk *DIR-ENG*

Human Resources: Sally Fleming

Purchasing: Joseph Bragg *DIR-Construction Services*

Total Employees..............................70
Year Established 1921
Annual Revenues ($000) 12,000
Regional Employees 35
SIC Code......................................3255

Wakefield Electronics Group, Inc.

760 Beechnut Dr.
Pittsburgh, PA 15205
County: Allegheny

Phone: (412) 921-9000
Fax: (412) 821-2254
Internet Address: www.shillsdata.com

Direct marketer of network connectivity and data communications products for LAN, WAN, AS/400 and mainframe computer networks, doing business as South Hills Datacomm. The Company's business consists of four major selling channels—catalog, VAR, direct and international. Its "Solutions"catalog features more than 200 pages of network diagrams, product specifications and technical references with a product line consisting of hubs, routers, switches, cables, bridges, adapters, connectors, converters, data cabinets, operating systems and wireless LANs. Its VAR program customers include nonstocking resellers, systems integrators, online service providers, contractors and installers throughout the U.S., ranging in size from one person to worldwide operations. Its direct sales program targets large corporations, hospitals and universities who need a high volume of data communications and network connectivity products, often including custom-built items. Its international business is based primarily on long-term, high-volume relationships with systems integrators throughout Mexico, Central America, South America, the Caribbean, Asia and the Pacific Rim. In addition to its headquarters and warehouse in Pittsburgh, the Company maintains sales offices in Oakland, CA; Schaumburg, IL; and Taichung, Taiwan; as well as sales and stocking facilities in Miami, FL; Sao Paulo, Brazil; Santiago, Chile; Bogota, Columbia; and Hato Ray, Puerto Rico. The Company is a subsidiary of Diploma Plc, which is headquartered in London, England, and listed on the London Stock Exchange.

Officers: Robert Karabinos *COO*
David V. Schmidt *CFO*
Gregory J. Lonsway *VP-INTL SAL*
Paul Carosi *DIR-MIS & MKT*
Daniel M. Marchitello *DIR-Field SAL*
Gus S. Vasilakis *DIR-SAL*

Human Resources: Lisa Lindow

Purchasing: Jim Machak

Total Employees	125	**Regional Employees**	78
Year Established	1935	**SIC Code**	3669
Annual Revenues ($000)	40,000		

Washington and Jefferson College

60 S. Lincoln St.
Washington, PA 15301
County: Washington

Phone: (412) 222-4400
Fax: (412) 223-6108
Internet Address: www.washjeff.edu

Nonprofit, private, coeducational liberal arts college with an enrollment of approximately 1,125 undergraduate students and a student-to-faculty ratio of 12-1. The College offers 19 majors and 18 special programs, as well as cooperative international education programs with institutions in Colombia, England and Russia. It awards the Bachelor of Arts degree for major fields of study in accounting, art, art education, biology, business administration, chemistry, economics, English, French, German, history, industrial chemistry and management, mathematics, philosophy, physics, political science, psychology, sociology and Spanish. The departments with the largest enrollments are accounting, biology, business administration, English and psychology. The College is located at the intersection of two major interstate highways, I-79 and I-70, and is comprised of 44 buildings.

Officers: Howard J. Burnett, Ph.D. *P*
Duane L. Lantz *VP-Business*
Thomas P. O'Connor *VP-Enrollment MGT*
G. Andrew Rembert, Ph.D. *VP-Academic Affairs*

Human Resources: Albert Brown

Purchasing: Paul Nagy

Total Employees............................233	**Regional Employees**...................233
Year Established........................1781	**SIC Code**....................................8221
Annual Revenues ($000)...31,000

Washington Federal Savings Bank

77 S. Main St.
P.O. Box 511
Washington, PA 15301
County: Washington

Phone: (412) 222-3120
Fax: (412) 225-2085

   Provider of a full range of financial services for both personal and business banking needs, including retail checking and savings products, mortgage and consumer loans, and commercial services. The Bank claims to be the largest locally owned and managed financial institution headquartered in Washington County, PA. It operates six branch offices located in Canonsburg, Hickory, McMurray and Washington (Franklin Mall, Tylerdale and Washington Mall), PA.

Officers: Richard L. White *P & CEO*
Kenneth E. Arthur *VP-Delivery Services*
John T. Gregor, Sr. *VP & COO*
Michael P. Pirih *VP-Retail Banking Services*
Raymond W. Steinmetz, Jr. *VP-Financial Services & TRS*
Suzanne L. Taylor *VP-Administrative Services & SEC*
Pamela B. Toth *VP-Retail Lending Services*
John C. Wishart *VP-Commercial Lending Services*

Human Resources: Maryann Franco *Human Resources MGR*

Purchasing: Richard A. Beck *Office Services MGR*

Total Employees............................158	**Regional Employees**...................158
Year Established........................1899	**SIC Code**....................................6035
Annual Revenues ($000)...........................393,000 (Assets)

Washington Hospital, The

155 Wilson Ave.
Washington, PA 15301
County: Washington

Phone: (412) 225-7000
Fax: (412) 222-7316

Nonprofit hospital serving residents in Greene, Washington and adjacent counties in Pennsylvania. The Hospital's areas of expertise include complete cardiac care, including diagnostics, catheterizations, surgery and rehabilitation; critical care; diagnostic medicine and imaging; emergency care; family practice centers; free-standing outpatient surgery and diagnostic care; full-service cancer center; and occupational medicine and rehabilitation. Its primary care specialties include family practice, obstetrics and gynecology, women's health care, pediatrics, internal medicine and psychiatry. The Hospital's surgical specialties include arthroscopic, cardiovascular surgery, dental and oral surgery, general surgery, head/neck surgery, laparoscopic surgery, laser surgery, lithotripsy, ophthalmology, orthopedics, plastic surgery, thoracic surgery and vascular surgery. The Hospital offers its health care services at additional facilities throughout Washington, PA, including the Family Outreach Center, Family Practice Center, Greenbriar Treatment Center, Home Health Service, Neighbor Health Center and Occupational Medicine Center. Other operations include the Children's Therapy Center in McMurray, PA; Family Practice Centers in Avella, Canonsburg and Cecil, PA; Greene County Medical Plaza in Waynesburg, PA; Occupational Rehabilitation Center in Meadow Lands, PA; and Waterdam Medical Plaza in McMurray, PA.

Officers: Telford W. Thomas *P & CEO*
Gary B. Weinstein *EVP*
Colleen C. Allison *VP-Support Services & Risk MGT*
Rodney D. Louk *VP-Information Services*
Helen R. Romano, Ed.D. *VP-Patient Care*
Michael Roney *VP-FIN*
Anthony P. Zelenka *VP-Clinical Support Services & Plant OPR*
Kevin D. Brown *DIR-Planning & MKT*
Richard J. Mahoney *DIR-The Washington Hospital Foundation*

Human Resources: William H. Cline *VP-Human Resources*

Total Employees........................1,539
Year Established 1897   **SIC Code**....................................8062
Annual Revenues ($000) 242,550

Washington Motel Assoc.

340 Racetrack Rd.
Washington, PA 15301
County: Washington

Phone: (412) 222-6200
Fax: (412) 228-0709

Owner and operator of the Holiday Inn Meadowlands, which features 138 guest rooms and 10,000 square feet of function space. The hotel also contains Maxwell's restaurant, Whispers Lobby Bar and Nitelite, a dance club. Its recreational facilities include a complete spa with sauna, jacuzzi, steam room, exercise equipment and outdoor pool. The Company is owned by Servico, Inc., which is headquartered in West Palm Beach, FL, and listed on the ASE.

Officers: Chuck DeSantis *GMGR*

Total Employees	150	**Regional Employees**	150
Year Established	1973	**SIC Code**	7011
Annual Revenues ($000)			6,000

Washington Mould Co.

Greene & Madison Aves.
P.O. Box 518
Washington, PA 15301
County: Washington

Phone: (412) 225-7700
Fax: (412) 225-0273

Gray and ductile iron foundry and contract machine shop. The Company manufactures custom component and maintenance parts for OEMs of highway construction and coal pulverizing equipment. B. P. Tracy Co., also located at the above address, is a division of the Company that markets replacement parts for underground mining machinery.

Officers: Norman A. Greig *P*
          Joan Baldwin *CFO*

Human Resources: Alan Lessig

Purchasing: Janice Swart

Total Employees	35	**Regional Employees**	35
Year Established	1917	**SIC Code**	3321
Annual Revenues ($000)			2,900

Washington Tool & Machine Co., Inc.

Baird Ave.
P.O. Box 873
Washington, PA 15301
County: Washington

Phone: (412) 225-7470
Fax: (412) 225-7484

Machine job shop primarily engaged in providing machining services for steel and related industries. The Company serves clients within an approximate 400 mile radius of Washington, PA.

Officers: Howard A. Patterson *P*
David R. Andrews *VP*

Total Employees............................80	**Regional Employees** 80
Year Established 1957	**SIC Code**......................................3599
Annual Revenues ($000) 7,000	

Watson Industries, Inc.

616 Hite Rd.
P.O. Box 11250, Pittsburgh, PA 15238
Harwick, PA 15049
County: Allegheny

Phone: (412) 362-8300
Fax: (412) 274-5770

Manufacturer of coatings for the rigid and flexible packaging industry, with the Company's Watson-Standard Co. focusing on outside coatings and Waston-Rhenania Co. focusing on inside coatings. A plant is located on Neville Island in Pittsburgh.

Officers: H. Knox Watson III *P*
Michael A. Caruso, Jr. *EVP*
James E. Lore *VP*
Gary E. Silke *VP*

Human Resources: Pete Duffy *Human Resources MGR*

Total Employees............................200	
Year Established 1902	**SIC Code**......................................2851

Watson Rehabilitation Services, D. T.

301 Camp Meeting Rd.
Sewickley, PA 15143
County: Allegheny

Phone: (412) 741-9500
Fax: (412) 749-2323

Nonprofit operator of the 44-bed D. T. Watson Rehabilitation Hospital, which is also located at the above address, and situated on a 97-acre campus. The hospital is a comprehensive rehabilitation facility offering inpatient and outpatient services for adults and children recovering from strokes, amputations, brain injuries, spinal cord injuries, and other impairments and conditions. Its specialized services include lymphedema treatment, vision therapy, hydrotherapy, pediatric rehabilitation, equestrian therapy, and back care and rehabilitation. The hospital offers outpatient rehabilitation services at the Sewickley YMCA-Watson Rehabilitation Physical Therapy Center, which is located just a few miles from the hospital's main campus. In addition, its Watson Back Center operates a satellite location in Wexford, PA. The Organization's other operations include D. T. Watson Educational Services, which provides individualized educational programming for approximately 140 children, from 3 to 12 years of age, diagnosed with autism/pervasive developmental disorder, neurological impairment, cerebral palsy and muscular dystrophy in a variety of specialized and inclusive environments; and the Margaret H. W. Watson Foundation, the fund-raising arm which promotes philanthropic support for the Organization.

Officers: Robert N. Gibson *P & CEO*
K. Jean Ahwesh *VP-External Affairs; P-Margaret H. W. Watson Foundation*
William Somerset, D.O. *VP-Medical Affairs & Medical DIR*
Linda Wetsell *CFO*
Jean L. Becker, Ph.D. *P-D. T. Watson Educational Services*

Human Resources: Amy Bennett

Purchasing: Jack Skosnik

Total Employees............................260	**Regional Employees** 260
Year Established 1917	**SIC Code**......................................8069

Weinman Pump & Supply Co.

110 Delta Dr.
Pittsburgh, PA 15238
County: Allegheny

Phone: (412) 963-6633
Fax: (412) 963-7040

Engineer, fabricator and distributor of industrial hydraulic components and systems. The Company operates a branch office in Amherst, NY.

Officers: C. Dana Chalfant *CH*
Dana D. Chalfant *P & CEO*
John M. Muempfer *EVP*
Joe F. Zsolcsak *SEC & TRS*

Total Employees............................73	**Regional Employees** 61
Year Established 1919	**SIC Code**.....................................5085

Weld Tooling Corp.

3001 W. Carson St.
Pittsburgh, PA 15204
County: Allegheny

Phone: (412) 331-1776
Fax: (412) 331-0383
Internet Address: www.bugo.com

Manufacturer of BUG-O SYSTEMS and Cypress welding equipment and electrical assembly for customers throughout the world. The Company also operates a service center for the repair of welding equipment. It maintains three divisions, Cypress Welding Equipment in Houston, TX, which manufactures welding equipment, and WTC Electronics in Erie, PA, and WTC Micro in Boston, MA, both of which manufacture electronics.

Officers: Herbert E. Cable, Sr. *CH*
Herbert E. Cable, Jr. *P*

Total Employees...........................118	**Regional Employees** 80
Year Established 1948	**SIC Code**.....................................3549
Annual Revenues ($000) 10,000	

Weleski Transfer, Inc.

140 W. Fourth Ave.
Tarentum, PA 15084
County: Allegheny

Phone: (412) 224-3330
Fax: (412) 224-1182

Provider of relocation services, including interstate movement of household goods, acting as an agent of Atlas Van Lines. The Company's subsidiaries include Modern Travel Agency in Natrona Heights, PA, a full-service corporate and leisure travel agency; Weleski Self Storage, Inc. in Creighton, PA, an operator of commercial and residential storage facilities; Weleski Terminals in Tarentum, PA, an operator of a barge loading/unloading facility specializing in the handling of coarse aggregates and coal; Weleski Truck Service in Tarentum, PA, an operator of a full-service light/heavy truck repair facility; and WelMart, Inc. in Freeport, PA, an operator of a full-service gasoline station, convenience and food store.

Officers: Gary L. Weleski *P*
F. Lynn Thompson *VP*

Human Resources: Michael J. Chick *GMGR*

Total Employees	110	**Regional Employees**	110
Year Established	1909	**SIC Code**	4213
Annual Revenues ($000)	12,000		

Welland Chemical, Inc.

899 Third St.
P.O. Box 26
Newell, PA 15466
County: Fayette

Phone: (412) 938-2237
Fax: (412) 938-2239

Manufacturer of nitric acid (67% and 60%), as well as specialty blends and 98% strong nitric acid. The Company also produces mixed acid to various specifications. Its customers include manufacturers of stainless steel, electronics, medicines and propulsion fuels. The Company is a subsidiary of Welland Chemical Ltd., which is headquartered in Mississauga, Ontario, Canada.

Officers: Ron Lerario *Plant MGR*

Human Resources: Lori Campbell

Purchasing: Marvin Miller

Total Employees	41	**Regional Employees**	41
SIC Code	2819		

WESCO Distribution, Inc.

Commerce Ct., Four Station Sq., Ste. 700
Pittsburgh, PA 15219
County: Allegheny

Phone: (412) 454-2200
Fax: (412) 454-2505

Wholesale electrical and industrial distribution company carrying more than 100,000 products from over 5,000 manufacturers. The Company operates three U.S. and two Canadian warehouse distribution centers and maintains over 325 stocking distributors located throughout the United States, Canada, Puerto Rico and other international markets. It has the ability to serve large, multilocation industrial firms and contractors. Major markets served by the Company include commercial and industrial construction, industrial OEMs, industrial processors and producers, and electric utilities. Other local facilities include a 200,000 square foot distribution center in Cranberry Township, and sales offices in Lawrenceville and Murrysville, PA. The Company is a holding of Clayton, Dubilier & Rice, which is headquartered in New York, NY.

Officers: B. Charles Ames *CH*
Roy W. Haley *P & CEO*
John R. Burke *VP-EESCO*
William M. Goodwin *VP-INTL*
Mark E. Keough *VP-Product MGT & Supply*
James H. Mehta *VP-Business DEV*
James V. Piraino *VP-MKT*
Patrick M. Swed *VP-Industrial & Construction*
Donald H. Thimjon *VP-Utility*
Robert E. Vanderhoff *VP-Manufactured Structures*
Stanley Weiss *VP-Industry Relations*

Human Resources: Michael S. Dziewisz

Total Employees ....4,500+		**Regional Employees** 180
Year Established 1922		**SIC Code** 5063
Annual Revenues ($000) 2,600,000			

West Homestead Engineering and Machine

W. Seventh Ave.
Homestead, PA 15120
County: Allegheny

Phone: (412) 464-4400
Fax: (412) 464-1950

Designer and engineer of rolling mill equipment; retrofitter of existing mills; producer of iron and steel work rolls and back-up rolls, slag pots and commercial castings; and supplier of spare parts and machinery primarily to the heavy metal industries. The Company's corporate offices and engineering division are located at the above address, which is also the location of its machine shop and heat treating facility. The Company's steel foundry is in Midland, PA, and its iron foundry in Lima, OH. The Company's other division, Wheeling Machine & Foundry, is located in Wheeling, WV. Also known as WHEMCO, the Company is a division of Park Corp., which is headquartered in Cleveland, OH.

Officers: William G. Cook, Jr. *P & CEO*
Frank De Vito *VP-Mechanical SA*
Samuel Hague *VP-Roll SA*
F. Ronald Vidil *VP-ENG Division*
Robert Zabelsky *VP-Quality*

Total Employees ....500+
Year Established 1982

Regional Employees 400
SIC Code....................................3325

West Penn Laco, Inc.

331 Ohio St.
Pittsburgh, PA 15209
County: Allegheny

Phone: (412) 821-3608
Fax: (412) 821-8187

Distributor of industrial gases, welding supplies and body shop supplies. In addition to the Company's main office and store located at the above address, it operates a fill plant and store at 1830 Liverpool St. in Pittsburgh, as well as distribution outlets located in the East Liberty and South Hills areas of Pittsburgh and in Coraopolis, PA. The Company markets to manufacturers, repair service centers and medical communities in Allegheny and the surrounding counties.

Officers: William E. Richards *P*
Howard S. MacKay *VP & SAL MGR*

Human Resources: Neil A. MacKay *VP & GMGR*

Total Employees............................42
Year Established 1928
Annual Revenues ($000) 7,000

Regional Employees 42
SIC Code....................................5084

Western Pennsylvania Healthcare System, Inc., The

4800 Friendship Ave.
Pittsburgh, PA 15224
County: Allegheny

Phone: (412) 578-5000
Fax: (412) 578-1296
Internet Address: www.westpennhospital.com

Nonprofit corporation with three subsidiaries—The Western Pennsylvania Hospital (located at the above address), The Western Pennsylvania Hospital Foundation (located at 4818 Liberty Ave. in Pittsburgh) and West Penn Corporate Medical Services, Inc. (located at the above address)—and one affiliate—Suburban General Hospital (located at 100 S. Jackson in Bellevue, PA). The Western Pennsylvania Hospital (TWPH) is a 542-bed tertiary care medical center which offers technologically advanced, comprehensive, medical care, education to health care professionals and research in such areas as cancer and heart disease. TWPH's specialty programs include the Western Pennsylvania Cardiovascular Institute, Western Pennsylvania Cancer Institute, Burn Trauma Center, high-risk obstetrical services, a Level III Neonatal Intensive Care Unit, Joslin Center for Diabetes, TWPH-Vintage Care for Seniors and Breast Diagnostic Imaging Center. The Western Pennsylvania Hospital Foundation conducts fund-raising to support the mission of TWPH. West Penn Corporate Medical Services, Inc. is a management services organization that provides a broad spectrum of services to physician practices throughout the Pittsburgh metropolitan area. The Suburban General Hospital is a 195-bed community hospital which offers general medical and surgical services, as well as outpatient, emergency, cardiac and intensive care services.

Officers: Charles M. O'Brien, Jr. *P & CEO*
Alan Cecala *SVP; CEO-West Penn Corporate Medical Services, Inc.*
James M. Collins *SVP-Managed Care & Network DEV*
Jerry J. Fedele *SVP & GC*
Thomas H. Prickett *SVP; P & CEO-Suburban General Hospital*
James L. Rosenberg *SVP & COO*
David A. Samuel *SVP & CFO*
Arlene A. Snyder *SVP; P-The Western Pennsylvania Hospital Foundation*

Human Resources: Carlo A. Oliverio *DIR-Human Resources*

Purchasing: Roger E. Graziano *DIR-Materials MGT*

Total Employees 3,376	**Regional Employees** 3,376
Year Established 1848	**SIC Code** 8062
Annual Revenues ($000) 262,536	

Western School of Health and Business Careers, Inc.

William Penn Place, 421 Seventh Ave.
Pittsburgh, PA 15219
County: Allegheny

Phone: (412) 281-2600
Fax: (412) 281-0319

Owner and operator of a trade and technical school offering programs leading to specialized Associate degrees. The Company operates two campuses, one at the above address enrolling approximately 425 students and one at One Monroeville Center in Monroeville, PA, enrolling approximately 200 students. Both campuses offer Dental Assistant, Medical Assistant, Medical Assistant Specialist, Medical Office Administration, Medical Records Technician, Microcomputer Specialist, Paralegal Specialist and Pharmacy Technician programs. The downtown campus also offers Anesthesia Technologist, Child Care Supervisor, Diagnostic Medical Sonographer, Histologic Technician, Optician, Respiratory Therapy and X-ray Technician programs.

Officers: Ross M. Perilman *P (Human Resources & Purchasing)*

Total Employees	55	**Regional Employees**	55
Year Established	1980	**SIC Code**	8249
Annual Revenues ($000)	5,000		

Westin William Penn Hotel

530 William Penn Place
Pittsburgh, PA 15219
County: Allegheny

Phone: (412) 281-7100
Fax: (412) 553-5252

Hotel with 595 guest rooms and 39 meeting and banquet rooms for groups from 10 to 1,200 people. The Hotel offers a variety of guest services including personal voice-mail, a business center, fitness center, AT&T Language Line, two restaurants, various shops and a bank on the property. It is listed as a National Historic Landmark. The Hotel is owned by Servico, Inc., which is headquartered in West Palm Beach, FL, and listed on the ASE. It is operated by Westin Hotels & Resorts, which is headquartered in Seattle, WA.

Officers: Joe Berger *GMGR*
　　　　　Craig Davis *DIR-MKT*

Human Resources: Jim McKenna *Human Resource MGR*

Total Employees	380	**Regional Employees**	380
Year Established	1916	**SIC Code**	7011

Westmoreland County Chapter of the Pennsylvania Assn. for Retarded Citizens

R.D. 12, Donohoe Rd.
Box 179
Greensburg, PA 15601
County: Westmoreland

Phone: (412) 837-8159
Fax: (412) 837-7453

Nonprofit, private organization claiming to be the largest provider of mental retardation services in Westmoreland County as well as the county's only provider of educational advocacy services to children with mental retardation. The Organization, also known as The Arc Westmoreland, annually serves in excess of 1,500 people—children and adults with developmental disabilities and their families—through a wide range of programs and services. The Organization's offerings include community residential services; programs designed to teach job and daily living skills to foster independence and integration of clients; work activity centers which provide employment; advocacy to provide support and technical assistance in obtaining appropriate services in the areas of education and mental health; emotional and informational support to parents; home-based early intervention services; and day care for children six weeks to six years of age. The Westmoreland Arc Foundation, Inc. (WAFI) was formed in 1994 to provide financial support to the Organization. WAFI seeks grants to finance new programs and conducts other fund-raising activities.

Officers: Karen A. Hecker *EDIR*
Donald F. Kauffman *P*
J. Robert Stemler *P-The Westmoreland Arc Foundation, Inc.*
James Gray *Business MGR*

Human Resources: Chuck Quiggle

Purchasing: Gary Schickel

Total Employees............................181
Year Established.........................1954

Regional Employees...................181
SIC Code.....................................8331

Westmoreland County Community College

400 Armbrust Rd.
Youngwood, PA 15697
County: Westmoreland

Phone: (412) 925-4000
Fax: (412) 925-1150
Internet Address: www.westmoreland.cc.pa.us

Nonprofit, comprehensive two-year college offering associate, diploma and certificate programs in more than 40 majors. Students pursue studies in the career areas of accounting, allied health, business, computer information systems, engineering science and industrial technology, horticulture, hospitality management, human services, media technology and office administration. The College also offers extensive noncredit programming which includes classes to improve job and computer skills and to update knowledge in various health care fields. A Business and Industry Center provides customized training and educational programs for business, industry and nonprofit agencies. In addition to the main campus in Youngwood, located 35 miles southeast of Pittsburgh, the College operates four education centers: Alle-Kiski Center in New Kensington; Bushy Run Center in Export; Laurel Center in Latrobe; and Mon Valley Center in Belle Vernon, PA. It enrolls approximately 6,200 students.

Officers: Daniel C. Krezenski, D.Ed. *P*
Ronald E. Eberhardt *VP-Administrative Services*
Daniel J. Obara, Ph.D. *VP-Academic Affairs & Student Services*
Gregory L. Hricenak *Associate VP-Business & Community Relations*

Human Resources: Lauren Farrell

Purchasing: Kimberly Himler

Total Employees............................645	**Regional Employees** 645
Year Established 1970	**SIC Code**....................................8222
Annual Revenues ($000) 19,482	

Westmoreland Health System

532 W. Pittsburgh St.
Greensburg, PA 15601
County: Westmoreland

Phone: (412) 832-5050
Fax: (412) 832-4313
Internet Address: www.westmoreland.org

Nonprofit operator of Westmoreland Regional Hospital, located at the above address, which serves residents throughout Westmoreland County, PA. The 402-bed hospital (includes 46 skilled care beds) offers a full array of general medical and surgical services, including a Comprehensive Cancer Care Center offering surgery, chemotherapy and radiation therapy, as well as access to national clinical trials and extensive psycho-social support services; cardiac care including the Chest Pain Emergency Center; Westmoreland for Women offering a wide range of services for those planning/considering pregnancy or for gynecological care; and the Barclay Rehabilitation Center featuring a hospital-based medical rehabilitation inpatient unit and four community-based outpatient facilities. Other subsidiaries include CareGivers of Southwestern PA at 501 W. Otterman St. in Greensburg, PA, operating a private duty registry that provides homemaker, live-in and home health aide services, and professional care management; Convenient Care Products at 501 W. Otterman St. in Greensburg, PA, carrying a full line of brand name medical equipment and supplies for purchase and/or rent; the SurgiCenter at Ligonier at 221 W. Main St. in Ligonier, PA, specializing in outpatient ophthalmic procedures and plastic surgery using laser technology; Westmoreland Primary Health Center at 446 W. Pittsburgh St. in Greensburg, PA, offering access to health care services through a network of primary care physicians with 11 sites throughout Westmoreland County, PA; and Westmoreland Regional Hospital Foundation, located at the above address, collecting gifts/contributions in support of hospital programs and services. With the exception of Convenient Care Products, all of its subsidiaries are nonprofit.

Officers: Joseph J. Peluso *P & CEO*
Jeffrey T. Curry *SVP & CFO*
Carol A. Bucci *VP-Legal Affairs*
Joseph L. Burkley, Jr. *VP & EDIR-Westmoreland Regional Hospital Foundation*
Richard W. Caruso *VP-FIN*
Francine Hovanec *VP-Patient Care Services*
Larry V. Sedlemeyer *VP-Planning & MKT*
John Sphon *VP-Convenient Care Products & Westmoreland Primary Health Center*

Human Resources: Joseph Herbert *VP-Human Resources*

Purchasing: Gary Metcalfe *Division MGR-Support Services*

Total Employees	1,921	**Regional Employees**	1,921
Year Established	1895	**SIC Code**	8062

Westmoreland Mechanical Testing and Research, Inc.

Old Rte. 30, Westmoreland Dr.
P.O. Box 388
Youngstown, PA 15696
County: Westmoreland

Phone: (412) 537-3131
Fax: (412) 537-3151
Internet Address: www.wmtr.com

Independent laboratory serving the materials testing needs of the aerospace, nuclear, medical and oil industries. Complete with full-machining capabilities and state-of-the-art equipment, the Company has the expertise to conduct a wide range of testing programs dealing with all types of alloys and materials, as well as composites. In addition to standard tests, it specializes in custom-designed tests for finished parts, odd shapes and difficult materials. The Company is organized into seven areas: Chemical Analysis, Creep/Stress Rupture Division, Fatigue Division, Fracture Mechanics Division, Mechanical Division, Physical Metallurgy Division and the Machine Shop. Each division is fully supported by complete computer data capabilities and operates under strict quality control procedures to ensure precise, accurate testing and documentation. The Company has developed a bulletin board system that enables it to download test results directly into a client's computer even as the test program is proceeding.

Officers: Donald J. Rossi *P*
               James D. Rossi *VP*

Purchasing: Michael J. Rossi *VP*

Total Employees............................100	**Regional Employees** 100
Year Established 1967	**SIC Code**......................................8734

Whale's Tale, The

250 Shady Ave.
Pittsburgh, PA 15206
County: Allegheny

Phone: (412) 661-1800
Fax: (412) 661-6525
Internet Address: www.trfn.clpgh.org/orgs/wt

Nonprofit operator of youth and family counseling centers. The Organization's programs work with individuals who are dealing with alcohol and drug problems, runaways, homelessness, behavioral problems, abused and neglected youth, and many other family crises. It also provides a range of outclient, emergency shelter, residential and independent living services for the counseling, prevention, education, intervention and treatment of these situations. The Organization's facilities are located in Allentown, Lawrenceville, McKeesport, Millvale, Penn Hills, Pittsburgh, Plum, Shadyside (2), Shaler, Washington and Wilkinsburg (2), PA.

Officers: Dianna L. Green *P*
               Christopher P. Smith *EDIR*

Human Resources: Cathy Bartolomucci *Personnel MGR*

Purchasing: Deborah Murphy *Purchasing Agent*

Total Employees............................200	**Regional Employees** 200
Year Established 1970	**SIC Code**......................................8322
Annual Revenues ($000) 8,000	

Wheat First Butcher Singer

One PPG Place, Ste. 2200
Pittsburgh, PA 15222
County: Allegheny

Phone: (412) 394-3100
Fax: (412) 394-3166
Internet Address: www.wheatfirst.com

Provider of a comprehensive range of financial services, including securities brokerage, investment banking and asset management, to individual and institutional investors worldwide. The local facility is one of 125 branch offices of Wheat, First Securities, Inc., which is headquartered in Richmond, VA. Another branch office is located in Monroeville, PA. The Company is a subsidiary of Wheat First Butcher Singer, Inc., which is also headquartered in Richmond, VA.

Officers: Roger A. Hannigan *MDIR & Branch MGR-Pittsburgh Office*
Joseph O'Donnell *Branch MGR-Monroeville Office*

Total Employees...............2,770	Regional Employees 60	
Year Established 1934	SIC Code.......................6211	
Annual Revenues ($000) 405,000		

Wheelabrator Air Pollution Control, Inc.

441 Smithfield St.
Pittsburgh, PA 15222
County: Allegheny

Phone: (412) 562-7300
Fax: (412) 562-7254
Internet Address: www.wapc.com

Provider of pre-engineered and custom-engineered air pollution control systems and services for a wide variety of industrial and utility applications. The Company designs and supplies equipment and systems to control particulate emissions and acid gas emissions. These include fabric filters, electrostatic precipitators and flue gas conditioning systems for particulate control; wet or dry scrubbers for SO_2 and other gas control; systems for NO_x emission control; and comprehensive aftermarket services. The Company also operates Wheelabrator Canada, Inc., a division in Milton, Ontario, Canada, which provides similar services to clients in Canada, and branch sales offices in Chicago, IL, and Kansas City, MO. The Company is a subsidiary of Wheelabrator Technologies Inc., which is headquartered in Hampton, NH, and listed on the NYSE.

Officers: Paul Feira *P*
Antonio DoVale, Jr. *VP & GMGR*
Patricia Evans *CON*

Human Resources: Mary Jane Romanovich *Human Resources Coordinator*
Purchasing: William Blank

Total Employees...........145	Regional Employees...........114	
Year Established 1913	SIC Code.......................8711	
Annual Revenues ($000) 70,000		

Wheeling-Pittsburgh Steel Corp.

Four Gateway Center
P.O. Box 230, Pittsburgh, PA 15230
Pittsburgh, PA 15222
County: Allegheny

Phone: (412) 288-3511
Fax: (412) 288-3555
Internet Address: www.wpsc.com

Manufacturer of steel products, including hot-rolled and cold-rolled sheet, coated products such as galvanized, prepainted and tin mill sheet. The Company also manufactures a variety of fabricated steel products, including roll formed corrugated roofing, roof deck, form deck, floor deck, culvert, bridge form and other products used primarily by the construction, highway and agricultural markets. The Company is headquartered in Wheeling, WV. It is a subsidiary of WHX Corp., which is headquartered in New York, NY, and listed on the NYSE. The Company's Pittsburgh area operations consist of the facility located at the above address, containing marketing and customer service offices, and a plant in Allenport, PA, producing cold-rolled steel, with an annual capacity of approximately 950,000 tons.

Officers: John R. Scheessele *CH, P & CEO*
Fred G. Chbosky *EVP & CFO*
Charlotte Palmer *MGR-Advertising & Market Planning*

Human Resources: Daniel C. Keaton *VP-Human Resources (Wheeling, WV)*

Purchasing: John Ratti *DIR (Wheeling, WV)*

Total Employees 5,200	**Regional Employees** 300
Year Established 1920	**SIC Code** 3312
Annual Revenues ($000) 1,200,000		

White Consolidated Industries, Inc.

Three Parkway Center
Pittsburgh, PA 15220
County: Allegheny

Phone: (412) 928-3321
Fax: (412) 928-9407

Provider of international export and licensing services for the North American major appliance and floor care factories owned by AB Electrolux, a company headquartered in Stockholm, Sweden. The Company, which is headquartered in Cleveland, OH, is a subsidiary of AB Electrolux, which is listed on the NASDAQ. The Company's local operation does business as WCI International Co. (WCIIC). WCIIC markets Eureka, Frigidaire, Gibson, Kelvinator, Leonard, Philco, Tappan and White-Westinghouse brand appliances to customers outside the United States. It provides sales and after-sales service to a global distributor network operating in 135 countries. In addition, the Company licenses its trademarks and relevant technology internationally.

Officers: James L. Rushworth *P*
Joseph D. Standeven *SVP-Technical Services; & P-Kelvinator & Philco INTL*
Rob A. Golensky *VP & CON*
Don Rossetter *DIR-Distribution*

Human Resources: Karen Gourdie *MGR-Human Resources*

Total Employees............................120	**Regional Employees**...................117
Year Established 1985	**SIC Code**......................................5064

Wholey & Co., Inc., Robert

1501 Penn Ave.
Pittsburgh, PA 15222
County: Allegheny

Phone: (412) 261-7292
Fax: (412) 261-7298
Internet Address: www.wholey.com

Wholesale distributor of seafood, meat, poultry and produce to supermarkets, restaurants and food service operations throughout the Pittsburgh metropolitan area. The Company's seafood products are also distributed nationally. In addition, it owns and operates Wholey's, located at 1711 Penn Ave. in the Strip District area of Pittsburgh, which is a specialty seafood store that sells meat, poultry, produce and other food items, and cookware. The Company's other operations include Federal Logistics, New Federal Cold Storage and Wholey International.

Officers: Robert L. Wholey III *P*
Richard Reynolds *CFO*

Human Resources: Theresa Lippert

Total Employees............................200	**Regional Employees** 200
Year Established 1912	**SIC Code**......................................5146

Williamhouse

One Wedding Lane
Scottdale, PA 15683
County: Westmoreland

Phone: (412) 887-5400
Fax: (412) 887-8077

Converter of paper, producing wedding invitations and business envelopes. The Company is a division of American Pad & Paper Co., which is headquartered in Dallas, TX, and listed on the NYSE.

Officers: Terrence J. McNeill *VP & GMGR*
Dick Ahlborn *Plant MGR*

Human Resources: Renee Wrights *DIR-Human Resources*

Regional Employees 900
Year Established 1959   **SIC Code** 2679

Williams and Co., Inc.

901 Pennsylvania Ave.
Pittsburgh, PA 15233
County: Allegheny

Phone: (412) 237-2211
Fax: (412) 237-2468

Distributor of metals including aluminum, brass, copper, nickel and stainless steel, as well as steel tubing, welding and related supplies, fasteners, fittings, and refrigeration and air conditioning equipment and supplies. In addition, the Company owns and operates a store of the same name, also located at the above address, which markets the refrigeration, air conditioning and heating equipment and supplies to commercial customers. The Company, which is headquartered in Exton, PA, is a subsidiary of Cawsl Corp., which is headquartered in Wynnwoode, PA.

Officers: Dennis M. Oates *P & CEO*
Kurt V. Christensen *EVP-FIN*
Jerry Pierman *Regional GMGR*

Human Resources: Frank W. Miller *EVP-Human Resources*

Purchasing: Bill Schmid *EVP-Purchasing & MKT*

Total Employees 515   **Regional Employees** 150
Year Established 1907   **SIC Code** 5051

Williams Trebilcock Whitehead

Timber Ct., 127 Anderson St., Ste. 301
Pittsburgh, PA 15212
County: Allegheny

Phone: (412) 321-0550
Fax: (412) 321-2431

Provider of architectural, planning and interior design services, as well as engineering coordination, graphic design and financial/evaluation services. The Firm, which is also known as WTW Architects, is staffed with approximately 30 registered architects. It specializes in educational, health care, corporate, commercial, religious, residential, retail and high-tech facilities, and historic renovation and adaptive reuse. A regional branch office is located in Cleveland, OH.

Officers: G. Thomas Williams *CH*
Thomas B. Trebilcock *P*
Paul A. Whitehead *CEO*
Richard De Young *COO*
Richard F. Bamburak *Principal*
Martin B. Chetlin *Principal*
Harold Colker *Principal*
Alan B. Klauss *Principal*
Paul F. Knell *Principal*
Bryant H. Robey *Principal*
Douglas L. Shuck *Principal*
Paul E. Zippel *Principal*

Total Employees............................68
Year Established 1959

Regional Employees 58
SIC Code....................................8712

Wilson-McGinley, Inc.

85 36th St. & Allegheny Railroad
Pittsburgh, PA 15201
County: Allegheny

Phone: (412) 621-4420
Fax: (412) 621-8230

Wholesale beer distributor representing Heineken Brewing Co., Miller Brewing Co. and Seagram Beverage Co. The Company distributes Heineken and Miller products in Allegheny County, PA, and distributes Seagram beverages throughout Allegheny, Cambria, Fayette, Greene, Indiana, Somerset, Washington and Westmoreland Counties, PA. The products are sold to beer distributors, bars and restaurants.

Officers: John R. McGinley *P*
Christopher J. Wilson *VP & TRS*

Total Employees............................40
Year Established 1949

Regional Employees 40
SIC Code....................................5181

Wise Business Forms, Inc.

Bonniebrook Industrial Park
P.O. Box 1666, Butler, PA 16003
Butler, PA 16001
County: Butler

Phone: (412) 283-1666
Fax: (412) 283-7253
Internet Address: www.nextwavecolor.com

Manufacturer and printer of custom continuous business forms and checks, letterheads and matching envelopes, snap-apart forms, cut single sheets, software compatible forms and checks (pre-designed). The Company, which is headquartered in Atlanta, GA, markets its products exclusively through independent distributors. The Company operates additional plants in Alpharetta, GA, and Ft. Wayne, IN. The local facility serves clients in the Northeastern U.S.

Officers: William D. Prettyman *P*
Jeffrey L. Prettyman *EVP*

Human Resources: John J. Beneigh *TRS*

Purchasing: Thomas Yancik *GMGR*

Total Employees............400	**Regional Employees**...............190	
Year Established............1969	**SIC Code**............2761	
Annual Revenues ($000)............35,000		

Wise Machine Co., Inc.

244 S. Cliff St.
Butler, PA 16001
County: Butler

Phone: (412) 287-2705
Fax: (412) 287-5018

Manufacturer of machinery for melt shops, casters, hot mills and finishing mills used in steel making. The Company also produces handling equipment and production parts for power companies, glass producers and mushroom growers. In addition to offering its clients machining, fabrication and assembly capabilities, the Company provides repairs and modification of existing equipment and engineering services for small projects.

Officers: Robert H. Garrard *OWN & P*
Eric O. Garrard *EVP*

Total Employees............45	**Regional Employees**...............45	
Year Established............1945	**SIC Code**............3559	
Annual Revenues ($000)............3,500		

Witco Corp.-Petrolia Plant

100 Witco Lane
Petrolia, PA 16050
County: Butler

Phone: (412) 756-2210
Fax: (412) 756-7985

Manufacturer of petroleum products including white oil, petrolatums and a variety of waxes. These materials are used to produce a range of products including pharmaceuticals and cosmetics. The plant located at the above address is part of the Company's Performance Chemicals Group. The Company, which is head-quartered in Greenwich, CT, is listed on the NYSE.

Officers: Carmen P. Romano *Plant MGR*

Regional Employees.....................218   **SIC Code**......................................2911

Woltz & Wind Ford, Inc.

2100 Washington Pike
Carnegie, PA 15106
County: Allegheny

Phone: (412) 279-4551
Fax: (412) 279-8226

Automobile dealership selling Ford vehicles. The Company also offers parts, service and body repairs. In addition, it sells a variety of used vehicles and provides rental and leasing services.

Officers: Lawrence C. Wind *P*
        Jack May *VP*
        Jacqueline Fraed *SEC & TRS*

Total Employees............................95   **Regional Employees** 95
Year Established 1979   **SIC Code**......................................5511
Annual Revenues ($000) 50,000

Woodings Industrial Corp.

218 Clay Ave.
P.O. Box 851
Mars, PA 16046
County: Butler

Phone: (412) 625-3131
Fax: (412) 625-3176

Provider of engineering services and manufacturer of specialty equipment serving customers in the metals, mining and construction industries worldwide. The Company offers design, engineering and installation services for equipment; plant layout services; and process engineering services. Its manufactured products include tap hole drills, clay guns, tuyeres stocks, valves, ladle cars, tilting iron runners, sampling devices, demonstration equipment, and pneumatic and hydraulic drills. The Company also operates a sales and service office in Columbus, OH; and a sales and service office and small plant in Gary, IN.

Officers: Robert T. Woodings *P*
        Donald E. Howell *VP-OPR*

Human Resources: David M. Draskovic

Purchasing: Tammy Baumgarten

Total Employees............................105	**Regional Employees** 100
Year Established 1947	**SIC Code**.......................................3541

W

Woodlawn, Inc.

41 Shannon St.
Aliquippa, PA 15001
County: Beaver

Phone: (412) 375-5594
Fax: (412) 375-5541

Commercial laundry and provider of textile rental services, offering the rental of table linens, bed linens, towels, aprons and uniforms, as well as entrance mats and wet and dry mops. The Company serves a variety of businesses, including health clubs, restaurants, hotels, motels, hospitals and nursing homes.

Officers: Gregory Keriotis *P*
Judith Cocucci *GMGR*

Human Resources: Mary Ann Robertson

Total Employees..............................70	**Regional Employees** 70
Year Established 1919	**SIC Code**.......................................7213

Woods Quality Cabinetry Co., The

42 Eighty-Four Dr.
Eighty Four, PA 15330
County: Washington

Phone: (412) 228-3040
Fax: (412) 228-8930

Manufacturer of wooden cabinets, counter tops and related products. The Company's cabinetry is available in five hardwoods—oak, ash, maple, cherry and hickory—and is also available in a laminate line. It offers over fifty standard finish/wood combinations and provides custom stains or colors upon request. The Company supplies its products to customers throughout the Northeastern and mid-Atlantic states, including contractors, retail building supply centers and independently operated kitchen and bath dealers. In addition, the Company operates a retail factory-direct showroom, also located at the above address.

Officers: Richard Moffat *C-OWN*
Davis Walker *C-OWN*

Human Resources: Vaughn Hixenbaugh *(Purchasing)*

Total Employees..............................75	**Regional Employees** 75
Year Established 1992	**SIC Code**.......................................2434
Annual Revenues ($000) 4,000	

WPGH Licensee, Inc.

750 Ivory Ave.
Pittsburgh, PA 15214
County: Allegheny

Phone: (412) 931-5300

Owner and operator of WPGH-TV Channel 53, a commercial television station broadcasting 24 hours per day, affiliated with the Fox Broadcasting Co. The Company is a subsidiary of Sinclair Communications, Inc. (SCI). SCI is a subsidiary of the Sinclair Broadcast Group, Inc., which is listed on the NASDAQ. Both companies are headquartered in Baltimore, MD.

Officers: Alan Frank *Regional DIR*
Michael Wolff *Station MGR*

Human Resources: Trudy Miller *Regional Station Administrator*

Total Employees...........................130   **Regional Employees** 130
Year Established 1974   **SIC Code**....................................4833

WPXI Corp.

11 Television Hill
P.O. Box 1100, Pittsburgh, PA 15230
Pittsburgh, PA 15214
County: Allegheny

Phone: (412) 237-1100
Fax: (412) 323-8097

Owner and operator of WPXI-TV, a commercial NBC-affiliated television station broadcasting primarily in Western Pennsylvania and in Maryland, West Virginia and parts of Ohio. The Company and TCI of Pennsylvania, Inc., which is also headquartered in Pittsburgh, PA, are joint owners of PCNC, a cable channel providing news programming. The Company is a subsidiary of Cox Enterprises, Inc., which is headquartered in Atlanta, GA.

Officers: John A. Howell III *VP & GMGR*

Total Employees...........................140   **Regional Employees** 140
Year Established 1957   **SIC Code**....................................4833
Annual Revenues ($000)..30,000+

WQED Pittsburgh

4802 Fifth Ave.
Pittsburgh, PA 15213
County: Allegheny

Phone: (412) 622-1300
Fax: (412) 622-6413
Internet Address: www.wqed.org

Nonprofit owner and operator of two television stations, a radio station and a magazine, all located at the above address. WQED TV 13 went on the air in 1954 as the nation's first community-owned television station. It offers children's shows, drama, ballet, opera, classical music, architecture, public affairs and history broadcasts. Its signal reaches counties in Maryland, Ohio, Pennsylvania and West Virginia. WQEX TV 16 offers a mix of locally produced public affairs programs, PBS programs and classic sitcoms, reaching viewers throughout the Pittsburgh metropolitan area. WQED-FM 89.3 is a 24 hour a day classical music radio station. PITTSBURGH magazine is a city magazine with features and information on the metropolitan area. The Organization also produces local programming and national productions, including "Where in Time is Carmen Sandiego?".

Officers: George L. Miles, Jr. *P & CEO*
Neil B. Mahrer *EVP & COO*
Jayne Adair *EDIR-MKT & DEV*
B. J. Leber *EDIR-Communications & Community Relations*
Carolyn Wean *EDIR-Production*

Human Resources: Kathleen McCraw *DIR-Human Resources*

Purchasing: Robert Petrilli *CFO*

Total Employees............................137	**Regional Employees** 137
Year Established 1954	**SIC Code**......................................4833
Annual Revenues ($000) 20,000	

WRS, Inc.

1000 Napor Blvd.
Pittsburgh, PA 15205
County: Allegheny

Phone: (412) 937-7700
Fax: (412) 922-2418

Provider of an array of services to motion picture, film, audio and videotape professionals. The Company is known as WRS Motion Picture and Video Laboratory. Its services include motion picture processing and printing; video duplication; standards conversion; film-to-tape transfer and tape-to-film transfer; all formats of audio services; audio duplication; restoration/preservation of audio, film and video; audio, film and video asset management; all formats of video services; syndication distribution, including satellite services and shipping/returns worldwide; video post production, including editing of all formats; graphics, including animation and special effects; and fulfillment services, including telemarketing, credit card processing, warehousing, product fulfillment and database management. The Company's newest addition is its Lightspeed Links, an Internet and Intranet service provider serving local and national clients. The Company's other facilities include an airline/video duplication site in Los Angeles, CA; a video duplication site in Atlanta, GA; a film storage vault in Kearny, NJ; a duplication site and film storage vault in Houston, TX; and eight regional sales offices in major cities across the U.S.

Officers: F. Jack Napor *P*
Greg Thomas *EVP*
Russ Scheller *VP-OPR*
Dave Simpson *MGR-Customer Service*

Human Resources: Mary Sokol

Purchasing: Dave Oliver

Total Employees............................300	**Regional Employees** 228
Year Established 1953	**SIC Code**......................................7819

WTAE-TV

400 Ardmore Blvd.
Pittsburgh, PA 15221
County: Allegheny

Phone: (412) 242-4300
Fax: (412) 244-4512
Internet Address: www.wtaetv.com

Commercial television station affiliated with the ABC network. Channel 4 serves viewers throughout the Tri-State region. Its broadcast coverage area extends from Steubenville, OH, to Wheeling and Morgantown, WV, and to Altoona and Johnstown, PA. The station is owned by The Hearst Corp., which is headquartered in New York, NY.

Officers: Frank A. Bennack, Jr. *P & CEO*
James R. Hefner *VP & GMGR*
Joseph W. Heston *VP & Station MGR*

Human Resources: Kathryn J. Vitanza *DIR-Human Resources*

Purchasing: Gloria A. Spence *Resident CON*

Total Employees............................150	**Regional Employees** 150
Year Established 1958	**SIC Code**......................................4833

Wulfrath Refractories, Inc.

Sixth & Center Sts.
P.O. Box 28
Tarentum, PA 15084
County: Allegheny

Phone: (412) 224-8800
Fax: (412) 224-3353

Manufacturer of dolomite refractory products, serving clients in the steel and cement industries throughout North America. The Company's brand names include Sindoform and Sindomix. In addition to its manufacturing plant located at the above address, the Company operates sales offices in Bakerfield, CA; Carrollton, KY; Leesport, PA; Lexington, SC; Austin, TX; St. Catherine, Ontario, Canada; and Tracy, Quebec, Canada. The Company is a subsidiary of Dolomitwerke GmbH, which is headquartered in Wulfrath, Germany.

Officers: Dave Robinson *P*
Hans Klein, Ph.D. *VP-MFG*
Dennis McCort *VP-SAL & MKT*
Gary Zajac *CON*

Total Employees...........................85
Year Established 1980   **SIC Code**....................................3297
Annual Revenues ($000)..10,000+

Wyatt Inc.

4545 Campbells Run Rd.
Pittsburgh, PA 15205
County: Allegheny

Phone: (412) 787-5800
Fax: (412) 787-5845

Full-service interior commercial contractor for both new construction and renovation, specializing in office buildings, health care, educational, large retail and industrial projects. The Company also operates an architectural millwork fabrication plant in West Mifflin, PA, and a branch office in Philadelphia, PA.

Officers: Richard B. Wyatt, Jr. *P*
A. Wesley Wyatt *EVP*
Frederick T. Episcopo *VP*

Human Resources: Jim Grosjean

Purchasing: Anthony Donati

Total Employees..........................400   **Regional Employees** 225
Year Established 1967   **SIC Code**....................................1742
Annual Revenues ($000) 40,000

Xerox of Pennsylvania

750 Holiday Dr., 7th Fl.
Pittsburgh, PA 15220
County: Allegheny

Phone: (412) 937-2400
Fax: (412) 937-2631
Internet Address: www.xerox.com

Provider of a complete range of document processing products and services designed to increase productivity in the office. The Company is a business unit of Xerox Corp., which is headquartered in Stamford, CT, and listed on the NYSE. The facility located at the above address serves clients in Western Pennsylvania. It markets and services copiers, duplicators, digital production publishers, electronic printers, facsimile products, scanners, computer software and supplies.

Officers: Rita Ombres *MGR-SAL OPR*

Human Resources: Jim Klingelhoefer

Regional Employees	300	**SIC Code**	3579
Annual Revenues ($000)	300,000		

XLConnect Solutions, Inc.

109 Gamma Dr.
Pittsburgh, PA 15238
County: Allegheny

Phone: (412) 963-0505
Fax: (412) 963-9276
Internet Address: www.xlconnect.com

Provider of enterprise-wide total connectivity solutions to clients with complex computing and communications requirements. As a single source provider, the Company offers comprehensive internetworking services, applications development services, managed services and telecommunications services. Its solutions are custom-designed to integrate computing and communications devices and equipment with software applications and systems to develop LANs and to link LANs through public and private communications networks and the Internet to form WANs. The Company describes the provision of these services on an integrated basis as a total connectivity solution. The Company, which is headquartered in Exton, PA, is listed on the NASDAQ. It operates 27 branch offices nationwide. The local facility primarily serves clients in Western Pennsylvania and West Virginia. The Company is an 80%-owned subsidiary of Intelligent Electronics, Inc. (IEI), which is also headquartered in Exton, PA, and listed on the NASDAQ. The Company works closely with IEI's XLSource, Inc. subsidiary.

Officers: Richard K. Baily *Regional VP*

Human Resources: Cathy Sigmund

Total Employees......................1,200	**Regional Employees**..................108
Year Established......................1982	**SIC Code**....................................8742
Annual Revenues ($000)..115,000	

XLSource, Inc.

109 Gamma Dr.
Pittsburgh, PA 15238
County: Allegheny

Phone: (412) 963-0505
Fax: (412) 963-9276
Internet Address: www.xlsource.com

Provider of customized information technology solutions and services. The Company maintains partnerships with the industry's top services providers, technology vendors and software developers. The Company focuses its sales and marketing efforts towards selling computer-related products and services to medium-sized businesses, Fortune 1000 corporations, professional firms, and governmental and educational institutions. The Company, which is headquartered in Exton, PA, operates 23 branch offices nationwide. The local facility serves clients in Pennsylvania and West Virginia. The Company is a subsidiary of Intelligent Electronics, Inc. (IEI), which is also headquartered in Exton, PA, and listed on the NASDAQ. The Company works closely with IEI's 80%-owned subsidiary, XLConnect Solutions, Inc.

Officers: Tom Costa *EVP-SAL & MKT*

Total Employees..........................450	**Regional Employees**....................30
Year Established........................1982	**SIC Code**....................................5045

Yanni, Bilkey Investment Consulting Co.

Grant Bldg., 310 Grant St., Ste. 2500
Pittsburgh, PA 15219
County: Allegheny

Phone: (412) 232-1000
Fax: (412) 232-1055
Internet Address: www.yanni-bilkey.com

Provider of investment counseling services. The Firm's services include analysis of past investment performance, establishment of investment goals and objectives, development of appropriate investment strategies, selection of investment managers and the monitoring of ongoing investment performance. Its sole business is evaluating institutional portfolios and providing third-party objective consulting services. It does not seek to manage client portfolios. The Firm is retained by more than 150 clients to assist their boards and investment/finance committees in dealing with their complex responsibilities. It has a broad range of client types including health care organizations, endowments/foundations, corporations, manufacturing and retail businesses, cities and municipalities, utilities and others. In addition to pension plans, the Company provides consulting services for 401(k) plans and funded depreciation accounts.

Officers: Terry Bilkey *Principal*
James E. Yanni *Principal*

Human Resources: Theresa A. Scotti *COO (Purchasing)*

Total Employees	35	**Regional Employees**	35
Year Established	1988	**SIC Code**	6282

Yarborough Development, Inc.

1700 Washington Blvd.
McKeesport, PA 15133
County: Allegheny

Phone: (412) 673-7620
Fax: (412) 673-7318

General contractor engaged in a variety of projects, including schools, four-to-five story high-rises for the elderly and work for the City of Pittsburgh's Housing Authority. The Company also provides its own carpentry, cement and excavation work. Approximately 90% of the Company's projects are performed in Allegheny County.

Officers: Ocie J. Yarborough *P*
R. Lee Totty *VP*

Human Resources: Leslie R. Proctor *Accounting Department MGR*

Purchasing: C. Ray Proctor *SEC & TRS*

Total Employees	75	**Regional Employees**	75
Year Established	1975	**SIC Code**	1542
Annual Revenues ($000)	12,000		

Yerecic Label Co., Inc.

Boyd Rd., R.D. 4
P.O. Box H
Export, PA 15632
County: Westmoreland

Phone: (412) 733-5995
Fax: (412) 733-4710

Manufacturer of pressure-sensitive labels primarily for the grocery, cleaning products, and health and beauty industries. The Company's products are produced under contract for corporate clients and for nationwide retail distribution.

The labels can be produced on various substrates printed in up to eight colors, with U.V. capabilities.

Officers: Arthur Yerecic *P*
Sandy Newsom *VP-ADM*
Richard Thoma *VP-SAL*
Bob Shinsky *VP-MFG*

Total Employees.............................60   **Regional Employees** 60
Year Established 1969   **SIC Code**....................................2672

Yoder Pontiac-Oldsmobile-GMC, Inc.

22426 Perry Hwy.
Zelienople, PA 16063
County: Butler

Phone: (412) 452-9450
Fax: (412) 452-9472

Automobile dealership selling Pontiac and Oldsmobile vehicles and GMC trucks. The Company offers a full line of new and used cars and trucks and repair services for all vehicles.

Officers: A. Richard Yoder *P*
Nancy Yoder *SEC & TRS*

Total Employees.............................30   **Regional Employees** 30
Year Established 1972   **SIC Code**....................................5511

Young Men and Women's Hebrew Assn. and Irene Kaufmann Centers

5738 Forbes Ave.
Pittsburgh, PA 15217
County: Allegheny

Phone: (412) 521-8010
Fax: (412) 521-7044

Nonprofit community center, also known as the Jewish Community Center or JCC, providing a variety of educational and cultural programs for all ages including children, teens, adults, families, single parents and their children, new Americans and the elderly. The Center contains a variety of recreational facilities, including two indoor swimming pools, running/walking track, gymnasium, racquetball/squash courts, Nautilus stations and a freeweight room. Its services include infant, early childhood and after school care; senior programs that provide a range of services from hot lunches to language classes; summer and day resident camps; Jewish singles programs; and teen volunteer programs. In addition, it maintains an outdoor recreational center, the Henry Kaufmann Family

Recreation Park in Monroeville, PA, which has an outdoor pool and tennis courts; and a branch facility at 50 Moffett St. in Pittsburgh, PA. The Center has approximately 15,000 members.

Officers: Alan Garfinkel *P*
Barton R. Schachter *EVP*
Jim Reich *DEV DIR*
Arlene Weisman *DIR-Planning & DEV*

Human Resources: Steve Hecht

Total Employees	150+	**Regional Employees**	150+
Year Established	1895	**SIC Code**	7991

Zimmer Kunz, P.C.

USX Tower, 600 Grant St., Ste. 3300
Pittsburgh, PA 15219
County: Allegheny

Phone: (412) 281-8000
Fax: (412) 281-1765

Civil litigation law firm with 28 attorneys. The defense-oriented Firm is licensed to practice in all state and federal courts in Pennsylvania and West Virginia. It represents many insurance carriers, self-insured corporations and individuals in liability, casualty, coverage and workers' compensation disputes. The Firm operates branch offices in Butler, PA, and Morgantown, WV.

Officers: Raymond H. Conaway *P*
Joseph W. Selep *VP*
Alexander P. Bicket *SEC*
Harry J. Zimmer *TRS*

Human Resources: Steven H. Perry *Administrator*

Total Employees	56	**Regional Employees**	56
Year Established	1988	**SIC Code**	8111

Zimmerman Holding Co.

1350 Old Freeport Rd.
P.O. Box 111254
Pittsburgh, PA 15238
County: Allegheny

Phone: (412) 963-0949
Fax: (412) 963-0229

Holding company doing business through its three subsidiary operations. Both E. E. Zimmerman Co., which is also located at the above address with a warehouse at 2020 Knott St. in Pittsburgh, PA, and Elroy Turpentine Co. in

Swainsboro, GA, are packagers of solvents for the painting and auto industry. The Zimmerman Trucking Co. in Swainsboro, GA, is an over-the-road trucking firm operating five tractors serving the Company and other clients east of the Mississippi.

Officers: Elmer E. Zimmerman II *P*
Kurt D. Cooper *VP*
Edward R. Morris *VP-FIN*

Z

Total Employees................................50	**Regional Employees** 30	
Year Established 1922	**SIC Code**....................................6719	
Annual Revenues ($000) 15,000		

Zinc Corp. of America

Rte. 18, 300 Frankfort Rd.
Monaca, PA 15061
County: Beaver

Phone: (412) 774-1020
Fax: (412) 773-2217

Manufacturer of sulfuric acid and refiner and smelter of zinc, zinc oxide and zinc powder for the steel, rubber, pharmaceutical, paper, brass and die casting industries. The Company's products are distributed internationally. Its facilities include the Balmat-Edwards mining area in Upstate New York and a plant in Palmerton, PA. The Company is a division of Horsehead Industries, Inc., which is headquartered in New York, NY.

Officers: William Smelas *EVP*
Tom Johnston *SVP*
James V. Derby *VP-Technical DEV & Quality Services*
Albert C. Hardies *VP-SAL, MKT & Technical Services*

Human Resources: John Brown *VP-Human Resources*

Purchasing: John W. Collins *VP-Purchasing*

Total Employees........................1,100	**Regional Employees** 700
Year Established 1987	**SIC Code**....................................3339

Zoological Society of Pittsburgh

One Hill Rd.
Pittsburgh, PA 15206
County: Allegheny

Phone: (412) 665-3639
Fax: (412) 665-3661
Internet Address: www.zoo.pgh.pa.us

Nonprofit operator of the Pittsburgh Zoo, located ten minutes from downtown Pittsburgh in the Highland Park section of the city. The 77-acre zoo is home to more than 4,000 animals, including numerous threatened and endangered species. Previously operated by the City of Pittsburgh, it became a private institution in January 1995. With 562,000 visitors in 1994, the zoo estimated that 750,000 people would be visiting in 1997. It is open every day of the year except for Christmas day.

Officers: Barbara Baker, D.V.M. *P & CEO*
Saul Markowitz *MKT DIR*
Margie Marks *Education DIR*
Phil Petraglia *FIN DIR*

Human Resources: Donna Anderson

Total Employees............................180	**Regional Employees** 180
Year Established 1898	**SIC Code**......................................8422
Annual Revenues ($000) 8,500		

Zoresco Equipment Co.

1241 Rodi Rd.
Turtle Creek, PA 15145
County: Allegheny

Phone: (412) 829-2120
Fax: (412) 829-7286

Designer of transportation solutions offering car and truck rentals, sales, service and parts, as well as equipment fabrication. The Company's sales services include new vehicle sales, used vehicle sales, an employee purchase program, nationwide auction services, consignment sales and vehicle appraisal. Its product line includes John Deere residential and commercial lawn and garden products. The Company's leasing services include commercial open-end leases, commercial closed-end leases, commercial used vehicle leases, commercial equipment leases and municipal leases. Its fleet services include a preventive maintenance program, maintenance management program, fleet safety program, emergency road service and vehicle rental. The Company also provides a variety of general services, body and collision services, mechanical services and custom services. In addition, it retails truck accessories at the above address and in Wexford, PA.

Officers: Vic Tedesco *P*
                Ellen Tedesco *VP-FIN*

Human Resources: Lance Alexander *VP & GMGR*

Purchasing: Al Donnelly

Total Employees..............................45
Year Established 1981

Regional Employees 45
SIC Code......................................3713

Z

Indexes

Alphabetical Index of all Companies

B

County Index

Allegheny County

Armstrong County

Beaver County

Butler County

A

B

C

D

E

F

G

H

I

J

K

L

M

P

Westmoreland County

Executive Biography Index

Officer Index

A

B

M

N

O

W

Z

Standard Industrial Classification (SIC) Code Index

5000

9000

Zip Code Index

15217–Squirrel Hill

15218–Swissvale

15219–Pittsburgh (Uptown)

15220–Green Tree

15221–Wilkinsburg

15223–Etna

15224–Bloomfield

15225–Neville Island

15226–Brookline

15227–Brentwood

15228–Mt. Lebanon

15238–Blawnox

15239–Plum

15240–Fox Chapel

15241–Upper St. Clair

15242–P.O. Box Listing

15243–Cedarhurst

15244–Montour

15258–Pittsburgh (Downtown)

15260–Oakland

15272–Pittsburgh (Downtown)